HISTORY OF MENTAL ILLNESS IN INDIA

INDIAN MEDICAL TRADITION

General Editors
DOMINIK WUJASTYK
KENNETH G. ZYSK

Vol. X

HISTORY OF MENTAL ILLNESS IN INDIA

A Cultural Psychiatry Retrospective

HORACIO FABREGA JR.

MOTILAL BANARSIDASS PUBLISHERS
PRIVATE LIMITED • DELHI

First Edition: Delhi, 2009

ISBN : 978-81-208-3370-8

MOTILAL BANARSIDASS
41 U.A. Bungalow Road, Jawahar Nagar, Delhi 110 007
8 Mahalaxmi Chamber, 22 Bhulabhai Desai Road, Mumbai 400 026
203 Royapettah High Road, Mylapore, Chennai 600 004
236, 9th Main III Block, Jayanagar, Bangalore 560 011
Sanas Plaza, 1302 Baji Rao Road, Pune 411 002
8 Camac Street, Kolkata 700 017
Ashok Rajpath, Patna 800 004
Chowk, Varanasi 221 001

Printed in India

By Jainendra Prakash Jain at Shri Jainendra Press,
A-45, Naraina, Phase-I, New Delhi 110 028
and Published by Narendra Prakash Jain for
Motilal Banarsidass Publishers Private Limited,
Bungalow Road, Delhi 110 007

In appreciation of the joys provided by

Sean Nicole, Sydney Kate and Winston Isaac

Foreword

This is the first book to take a comprehensive look at mental illness in India. It approaches the subject from the perspectives of history and social science and leaves no stone unturned in its attempt to paint a picture of the way mental disorders have historically been understood and treated in India in the past and also in the present. While focussing on India, Fabrega's book, especially in its historical discussions of the pre-modern period, inevitably includes the whole of South Asia. Crucial to Fabrega's enterprise is the recognition that mental illness is a universal phenomenon that has affected all peoples throughout documented history. What separates one way of understanding and dealing with it from another is the social and cultural environment in which mental illness occurs.

The modern ideas that make up psychiatry and psychology originated principally in the academic and clinical discourses of Europe and America. But, according to Fabrega, their application is not restricted to these regions. In fact, when the social and cultural settings are properly understood, the tools of psychiatry help to elucidate previously misunderstood or ignored aspects of mental illness in South Asia.

An important part of Fabrega's book examines mental illness in South Asia's indigenous medical tradition of Ayurveda. Understood from the Sanskrit word *unmāda*, a mental disorder was a behavioural condition in which a person acted as if he were intoxicated. What may be considered as the mental or psychological problem went almost completely unremarked. Another form of mental illness found in ancient South Asia and mentioned in the early medical treatises of Ayurveda was possession. Recently, Frederick Smith has clarified the idea of possession in South Asia by showing that there was both good and bad possession; the former was associated with religious rites and activities, the latter with morbid conditions and the medical tradition of Ayurveda.* The current work of Fabrega takes us beyond these basic ideas and helps us to understanding mental illness in a much wider context. In other words, his work may be regarded as a psychological reading of South Asian history and culture that will help to deepen and redefine the history and present understanding of psychiatry and psychology in South Asia. It is a most welcome addition to the scholarship in general and to the series *Indian Medical Tradition*.

Kenneth Zysk
Dominik Wujastyk

* F. M. Smith 2006.

Preface and Acknowledgements

The medicine of traditional India represents an early watershed in the worldwide evolution of medicine. In its many compilations Ayurveda explicitly addresses conditions that one may safely construe as of psychiatric interest. Its texts furnish a lens which one can use to discern how such conditions were conceptualized and dealt with as a form of sickness within the scholarly, academic medical community of traditional India.

Viewed broadly, Ayurveda 'psychiatry' involves only the medical component of the many institutions that India evolved to formulate, understand, and cope with human emotional and behavioural problems. However, this is not to minimize the importance of Ayurveda but to emphasize that a civilization as rich as India's in areas of science, philosophy, moral exposition, literature, art, social and political theory, and religion exemplified a host of other 'non-medical' approaches and solutions to the universal problems of psychological distress, disorder, and social comportment posed by conditions of psychiatric interest. A history of mental illness in India, therefore, involves taking into account not only an understanding of its medicine but also an appreciation of its diverse intellectual and cultural traditions and social practices and institutions outside of medicine per se, for these were also necessarily involved in formulating, appropriating, 'domesticating', coping with, and in the final event healing conditions of psychiatric interest.

It should be emphasized that combing the social and cultural fabric of traditional India searching for its understandings and resources for handling conditions of psychiatric interest constitutes an intellectual enterprise that is fraught with intellectual, academic pitfalls. For social scientists and historians to do so is impious: such an enterprise exemplifies the worst of ethnocentrism and anachronism. It reflects not only hubris and arrogance but is also intellectually, philosophically nonsensical. The concepts 'mental illness' and 'psychiatry' and their representation in the discipline and institution which has evolved around them represent inventions of the modern era and especially its science and medicine as determined by distinct cultural, historical and politico-economic circumstances. How can one presume to realistically discuss something as historically and culturally enmeshed in our history and social fabric as 'mental illness' and 'psychiatry' are in a different society? Such constructs and what they prefer to and shape are the product of a distinct culture, and historical period. Western and modernist ideas, beliefs, and values about behaviour and medical phenomena represent one of many slants and conceits that human communities have evolved to make sense and handle a universal problem; namely, conditions of psychiatric interest. Other societies and historical mentalities simply did not share the theoretical conceits let alone the political, economic, sociological, and cultural conditions which in today's modern world have made 'mental illness' and 'psychiatry' understandable, theoretically meaningful, and also socially problematic.

This book takes into consideration these criticisms and addresses them by drawing on ideas and generalizations based on findings of research from several sciences. It reviews and discusses the implications of the proposition that conditions of psychiatric interest are universal, a proposition supported by diverse lines of research in evolutionary biology, genetics, and comparative epidemiological and clinical psychiatric research. Thus, it is reasonable to presume that in ancient India conditions of psychiatric interest were on display, there to be observed in their respective cultural attire, and dealt with via meaningful social practices and institutions. In other words, while psychiatric conditions are universal they are also shaped, given meaning, and dealt with in cultural terms.

The book builds on the insights of social scientists, especially anthropologists and social historians, who have expounded on the hazards and limitations of comparative research, which are imposed by theoretical problems of cultural relativism and historical anachronism. On the basis of generalizations from studies in cultural medical anthropology and social history of medicine, the argument pursued in this book presumes that all societies and cultures past and present necessarily evolve resources of knowledge and practice in order to cope with behavioural disturbances and breakdowns. The task is to use modern psychiatric and social science insights about sickness behaviour and psychiatric phenomena as a frame of reference for providing a reasonable picture of how conditions of psychiatric interest were formulated and dealt with in

a culture and civilization of long ago. This method of procedure is reflected in the subtitle of this book: a cultural psychiatry retrospective means using contemporary generalizations about conditions of psychiatric interest derived from study of contemporary populations of India and elsewhere as a platform on which to examine the past of India as this has come to be understood in diverse disciplines; and bring to light how it formulated and handled psychiatric conditions.

The science and practice of modern clinical neuroscience psychiatry is not just a 'Western' achievement. India's contemporary academic psychiatry is its equal. Indian scientists and psychiatrists are not just found in India's research and academic, clinical centres, but many, following their training there, have migrated worldwide. The psychiatry research establishments of India and their efforts with respect to research, education, and practice exemplify the best of modern psychiatry worldwide.

India's contemporary psychiatric establishment is special in that it is embedded in an alive, vibrant history and culture whose accomplishments in medical and mental health related knowledge, scholarship, and practice exemplify an ancestry of millennia and have become legendary. In the span of but a few generations India has had to weather the onslaught of imperialism and colonization by an alien culture and its science, medicine, and politico-economic dynamism. In a context of imposed Westernization and modernization India has had to accommodate to the modern perspective about phenomena of psychiatric interest, and considerably more, of course. India has served as a willing and gifted student and appropriated and even perfected its patron's wares. But the mixture of intellectual and practical traditions and resources involving sickness and healing, the ancient and the modern, are pulsating realities in the contemporary social, medical scene that do not easily integrate with one another. Thus, one who intends to sort out the history of psychiatric illness in India has to learn what if any residua and realia of its past ideas, beliefs, and accomplishments in this area of knowledge and practice are represented in its contemporary approach to mental illness.

Looked at differently, India presents one with an opportunity to examine, as though it presented a test case, the cultural evolution of psychiatry. A cultural psychiatry retrospective also involves examining the history of mental illness in India from the standpoint of social and cultural evolution, sorting out what has been retained from the past, what represents the new, and how each of these packages of knowledge and practice relate to one another.

There are many individuals who have provided me with direct, generous assistance in what has been an approximately four-year enterprise. I would like to thank Drs. Deborah P. Bhattarcharyya, Mitchell Weiss, Dominik Wujastyk, Kenneth Zysk, G. Jan Meulenbeld, Richard Shweder, Joseph Alter, and Mary Ganguli. They have addressed my many annoying queries for material, references, and information; however, they cannot be held responsible for limitations if not deficiencies of my base of knowledge and reasoning. Members of the library staff of Western Psychiatric Institute and Clinic have been uniformly patient, helpful, and generous, and I want to single out David Killinsky who has shouldered the bulk of requests. Jane Flanders provided editorial help during early stages of the manuscript. Kendall Stanley has helped me in preparing bibliographies and final manuscripts and my mental health has been kept serviceable as a result of her careful, painstaking work. Friends have provided me with support and encouragement in pursuing something that in today's academic psychiatry community is viewed at best as peripheral and at worst as trivial and off the main road of relevant and supportable topics having practical significance for clinical care. Among persons who have been encouraging and supportive I include Drs. John Fong, Thomas Detre, and Paul Soloff. I want to express special appreciation of my wife, Joan Rome Sporkin, for being patient with my intellectual obsessionalism and providing me with consistent support and encouragement in the face of my intellectual self-absorption.

This book is dedicated to my grandchildren.

Contents

Chapter 1

What a Cultural History of Psychiatry Involves

INTRODUCTION

Ways of thinking about mental illness and psychiatry are products of the modern era. These and related ideas took shape in association with changes in the structure of populations resulting from major cultural, sociological, and politico-economic developments that unfolded in Western societies starting roughly during the late eighteenth century.

Mental illness, as we understand it, is not new to the modern era, however. Studies involving intellectual, social, and medical history of Western societies attest that behavioural syndromes of psychiatric interest resembling our mental illness and practices of healing relating to them have a long genealogy. Historians have traced a medical conceptualization of emotional and behavioural problems well back to societies of the Mediterranean basin during the classical era and followed this through the medieval and into the early modern era from where such ideas slowly changed into their present shape.

Developments during the modern era have cast a distinctive intellectual and moral shadow on psychiatric phenomena. It was principally during the transition to the modern era in Western societies, and especially during the nineteenth century, that psychiatric conditions rose to the level which caused public concern and brought with it devaluation and condemnation. Britain and Europe underwent major politico-economic transformations resulting in populations harbouring poverty, unemployment, and sickness in various forms, and the break-up of families. High levels of social dependence and marginality along with related problems of begging and migration led to the view that such problem populations were dangerous to social order. Persons with psychiatric conditions were lodged among such populations and bore its condemnation. They and others with health as well as social and economic problems generated outcries and empowered reform movements and the building of poor houses, hospitals, and asylums aimed at containing and rehabilitating the poor and the mentally ill. A segment of the medical profession (termed at the time medical alienists) acquired a monopoly on efforts designed to manage, control, and properly care for victims of mental illness. This policy stamped a class of emotional and behavioural disaffections resonant with socially condemned and bothersome overtones as medical phenomena.

The fact that our present understanding of psychiatric conditions and modes of treatment are rooted in the culture and history of Western societies does not mean that the phenomena in question should be viewed as confined to one part of the geography of the world and one segment of human history. Generalizations drawn from modern sciences of evolutionary biology and psychology, psychiatric epidemiology and genetics, cultural anthropology, and social history attest to the worldwide distribution of psychiatric phenomena that suggest that the latter are universal to human populations. The potential and/or vulnerability to develop and show syndromes of behaviour of psychiatric interest are inherent in the biology of Homo sapiens and in all human populations.[1]

This book seeks to understand and explain the way in which syndromes of psychiatric interest have been understood and dealt with in a part of the world different from Western Europe and during time periods much earlier than the modern era. A narrative about such syndromes in traditional and modern India is based on the supposition that their usually negatively perceived nature and socially evolved approaches to treatment are universal. Limitations, imperfections, and vulnerabilities of regulatory systems involving general physiology and central nervous system, inherited from a common hominid/pongid primate ancestor, created the conditions for such problems, as even naturalistic studies of non-human primate behaviour and observations using animal models of psychiatric conditions attest.[2]

The view that behavioural syndromes of psychiatric interest are universal and have a phylogenetic lineage is not only consistent with findings in evolutionary psychiatry and psychology and primate studies but also in surveys of mental illness conducted worldwide.[3] In all socie-

[1] Fabrega 2002a.

[2] Fabrega 2002a.

[3] Fabrega 2002a, 2006b.

ties, strains, conflicts, challenges, and outright psychological traumas are ubiquitous and recurring and, in vulnerable individuals, lead to behavioural irregularities. This is borne out by studies of contemporary psychiatric epidemiologists, many of them from India.[4] Such studies rest on strict criteria of diagnosis and involve modern methods of measurement, reliability and validity that take into account the differences in language and social circumstances of the people studied. Results of epidemiological studies conducted in urban and traditional village settings of India support a view about the universality of psychiatric conditions in the subcontinent and set the stage for their search and analysis in social and cultural spaces of contemporary India.

CIVILIZATIONS AS OBJECTS OF STUDY

A civilization by definition usually encompasses the workings of several large societies, with roots in the historic past, sometimes prehistory, from which the civilization emerged and achieved definition as a complex social, cultural structure. The characteristics and influences of a civilization's influence on its people spans a long historical period that can extend into the modern era. It is usually confined to a well-defined geographic region; it may be ecologically varied, but its regions will likely be fairly similar with respect to climate, altitude, soil composition, and access to water facilities; it has a population that is usually large and demographically, and sometimes ethnically, diverse; it has a wide array of mating systems and family structures; its systems encompass one or more societies that are complex and diverse in political economy and organization; it has persisted over time with cultural institutions and traditions that give it a social identity; it is subject to social and cultural transformations across time; and its peoples are relatively homogenous in culture and religion (or at least relatively persistent in their brand of pluralism), although subject to change in relation to any number of internal and external influences. Quite obviously, societies that have persisted for many millennia in the Indian subcontinent fit this definition of a civilization.

There are advantages to studying the cultural history of social, behavioural phenomena of psychiatric interest in a living and vibrant

---

[4] Taken up later in Chapter 5 and reviewed in S. P. Agarwal *et al.* 2004.

civilization. The richness of a civilization's cultural traditions, including religion, philosophy, moral precepts, literature, law, and medicine means that one can draw on a large body of information that describes ancient and subsequent thought worlds and habit patterns and related ways of life. A civilization whose traditions have persisted and that manifest its characteristics in local communities that still preserve of their elements means that contemporary anthropological studies afford an opportunity to evaluate the life blood of the civilization and the impact that modernity is having on those traditions. It also provides an analyst's reasoned imagination with a window into what life was like in previous eras. Many scholars with different objectives have been drawn to the study of most living civilizations. Hence, there is a large body of social and cultural information about themes that have a bearing on psychiatric phenomena.

In summary, a civilization such as India's delimits, concentrates, shapes, and moulds human material across a large expanse of time. For these reasons alone they are good sources for understanding the unfolding and cultural history of social life in India, as well as other complex societies, including problems of emotional and behavioural wellbeing. Moreover, great civilizations usually evolved systems of writing, traditions of textual interpretation and a form of high culture. Because its people seek stability and order, great civilizations have evolved elaborate repositories of esoteric knowledge and institutions that address the nature of society, the individual, and a range of human problems. Civilizations, in short, comprise the requisite human material but also cultural traditions, values, and institutions that interact to affect the social properties of emotional and behavioural breakdowns. One last point: because great civilizations have persisted over millennia, they enable one to analyze changes in the configuration, meaning, and mode of handling behavioural syndromes of psychiatric significance that have been introduced by modern medicine and psychiatry.

ON CHOOSING INDIA FOR A HISTORY OF PSYCHIATRIC PHENOMENA

The generalization that from a neurobiological standpoint psychiatric conditions are universal emboldens a narrator in his or her quest to describe the social and historical fabric of how such conditions were understood, expressed in behaviour and dealt with in India. The immediate problem becomes one of how and where does the researcher look for the phenomena in question? An analogous problem confronts a cultural anthropologist who ventures into the field of a contemporary non-industrial, non-Western society. However, he or she spends time in, observes, and participates interactively in social life with knowledgeable informants of the society or culture, a 'psychiatric ethnography' of which is desired. After learning the latter's language the anthropologist is able to translate preconceived ideas of relevance into language and constructs that are relevant to that of members of the culture or society.

However, the problem of finding and describing psychiatric phenomena in India prior to the modern era is far more challenging and problematic insofar as the researcher cannot easily visit with, observe, or participate in social life, and directly elicit information from real informants. The researcher must integrate three bodies of information: that recorded in relevant texts, that produced by cultural anthropologists as a result of study of comparatively isolated contemporary village communities (more likely to exemplify traditional ideas and practices), and knowledge germane to general psychiatry and especially cultural psychiatry, a branch that stipulates the pervasive influence of cultural ideas and beliefs in grounding psychiatric knowledge in the first place.

To undertake a history of emotional and behavioural syndromes of psychiatric interest in traditional India cuts across two conceptual lines and admonitions inherent in the philosophy of the social, cultural and historical sciences. Such a historical venture transgresses principles of cultural relativism and historical anachronism: the analyst is said to assume and indeed stipulate, before the effort of an inquiry, that the relevant phenomena are there and the researcher merely has to look for, find, and describe it. While the sins of cultural relativism and historical anachronism are real and compelling, they should and need not impede and certainly not close study and analysis of cultural and historical differences.[5] Provided a sufficiently broad frame of reference is adopted that *includes appreciation and respect for cultural differences,* a comparative study of psychiatric phenomena is a reasonable undertaking and one widely accepted in many branches of the human sciences.

---

[5] Spiro 1986; Fabrega 1993.

This book examines phenomena of psychiatric interest in relation to the interplay of history, culture, and medicine in a part of the world with a social and cultural history different from that of Europe. Such an Indian story attempts to chronicle how such phenomena have been realized, understood, and handled as concrete social, cultural problems and puzzles in themselves, shaped by local conventions of meaning and institutions relatively uncontaminated by Western influences, at least prior to the advent to the British colonial period.

In the Indian subcontinent, and since millennia and for many centuries before the Common Era (BCE), one can presume a rich intellectual tradition of enormous scope and power. It addressed, among many other concerns, emotional and behavioural disaffections, human predicaments, moral dilemmas about the self and its spiritual standing, and outright conditions viewed as disturbances of physico-mental health.[6] A distinctive traditional and ethno-historical framework of ideas and practices framed phenomena that one can surmise with hindsight resembled or were analogous to our psychiatric conditions. The latter are found in texts that adumbrate a distinctive philosophy, spirituality, soteriology, and medicine, one preoccupation and goal of which is relief of human suffering. The texts encompass the Vedas, Buddhism, the Upanishads, Yoga, Tantra, alchemy, and ayurvedic and Siddha medicines.

Mental illness and emotional suffering, broadly understood and not necessarily always conceptualized in medical terms, were part of the amalgam of suffering and disequilibria of the self that constituted central preoccupations of India's scholars, moralists, gurus, priests, popular healers, and philosophers as well as physicians.[7] These and related individuals contributed to traditions that formulated causes, understandings, and cultural implications of emotional suffering and behavioural disaffections viewed in social, moral, spiritual, as well as

---

[6] For example, body and mind as integrated and different from the *ātman* or universal spirit.

[7] Much if not all of any civilization's ethos and culture is geared at quelling, smoothing over, providing answers about, healing, etc., the dilemmas of emotional suffering and social inequalities and suffering exemplified in the human condition, dilemmas very much caused by adverse social circumstances including the political use of structures of power, etc. That India's civilization and culture displays an intellectual and philosophical psychology, and spiritual focus in rather graphic, vivid and special ways seems certain, although it is arguable whether it is unique among early civilizations.

physical and medico/organic terms. They evolved knowledge structures, social practices and institutions[8] directed at alleviating mental health problems filtered and fashioned in terms of indigenous thought worlds, attitudes of mind, and habit patterns. A traditional conception of psychiatric phenomena persists in the India of today challenged by contemporary understandings and practices that differ in content, tone, morality, and religious and philosophical implications.

THEORETICAL BACKGROUND AND CONCEPTUAL FRAME OF REFERENCE

Social scientists and historians who study on a comparative basis the culture and social history of medicine including mental illness have established that modern biomedical descriptions and interpretations are not always appropriate or valid for non-Western, non-industrial societies. A tenet of *cultural psychiatry*[9] is that constructs underpinning modern scientific psychiatry, including not only descriptive terms (anxiety, depression) but also essential aspects (or ontologies) of psychopathology, disorder, disease, and the mental as compared to the bodily and physical, are distinctive if not peculiar to Western history and culture compared to other cultures.

In this book a psychiatric *disorder* will usually refer to a class of human medical problems that is defined, classified and handled on the basis of ideas and practices that govern the discipline of contemporary psychiatry. Disorders have the resonance of 'Western' and modern culture that is regnant in clinical neuroscience or biomedical psychiatry. In other words, this construct represents a time bound, specialized, and culturally distinctive interpretation, in brain-based and brain–behaviour relationships, of selected emotional and behavioural disturbances, discomfitures, and/or problems.

To respect injunctions of social scientists regarding the integrity and importance of cultural and symbolic conventions it is desirable to minimize prejudging phenomena beforehand, especially its negative moral implications and also essential (ontological) characteristics. This is so

---

[8] For example, mythic and ritualistic, educative, soteriological, sectarian institutions.

[9] Fabrega 1989a, 1989b, 1989c, 1993.

because one risks carrying into such a study the Western bias: the cultural ontology of psychiatric conditions (its roots in distinctive concepts about person and world-view) and it moral implications (social condemnation or stigma). In the most general sense, one can propose that all people display emotional and behavioural disaffections and disruptions in habit patterns and social conduct.[10] The phenomena in question can be termed a *psychiatric condition* when (1) manifestations are relatively persistent (not purely situational and fleeting); (2) interrupt and impose a change in the flow of an individual's life arc; (3) produce psychological and associated bodily distress (visceral somatic symptoms); and/or (4) are associated with noticeable and significant changes in adjustment and function viewed against the landmarks expected from within their social, cultural space.[11]

'Psychiatric condition', then, signifies a behavioural syndrome meeting these four criteria that a culturally, linguistically informed external (standing outside the society) analyst 'diagnoses' on the basis of his or her general scientific understanding of a society and culture and of clinical psychiatry. This construct is analytic, made before and apart from venturing into a society one wishes to study, and exemplifies a human universal. However, no assumption is made about either the essence or morality of a psychiatric condition beforehand, specifically, about how it might be perceived, configured, and dealt with in a society. The cross-cultural application of such a construct obviously reflects Western, biomedical and clinical conventions, or construction of the problem. Accepting the inevitability of cultural bias and leaving it aside, one can still examine how psychiatric conditions are understood and played out in the respective society or culture one wishes to investigate in a manner that is scientifically productive.

The concept of a *psychiatric condition*, then, has a broader reach than *psychiatric disorder*: it stretches across cultures and histories. It constitutes a conceptual handle in terms of which one pursues an analysis of behavioural syndromes of psychiatric interest across history and culture. It describes disturbances and disaffections of experience and behaviour including bodily symptoms that take place in and are understood by a people in their everyday life in terms of their own social, moral, reli-

---

[10] Fabrega 1993.

[11] However, not necessarily conceptualized negatively or as sickness by the people themselves, this topic is taken up later in this chapter and especially in Chapters 6 and 8.

gious, and/or medical conventions, whatever or however this might be construed. While a psychiatric disorder answers to the logic and code-book of scientific psychiatry, a psychiatric condition stands for how analogous behavioural and experiential phenomena are expressed and fashioned in terms of thought worlds, attitudes of mind, and habit patterns of real people in contexts governed by distinctive cultural meanings (read in Indian communities). In contemporary Western societies psychiatric conditions that one finds enacted in local contexts, when shunted into mental health care systems, are for the most part named and invariably understood in the terminology of disorders.

A complex therapy culture is found in contemporary societies and it consists of clinical psychologists, professional and lay counsellors, social workers, political administrators, and psychiatrists.[12] Representatives of therapy culture generally employ the language (if not always the model) of medicine or disorders, a language given emphasis and impetus by psychiatry which initially developed it and because vicissitudes of reimbursement require a language of documentation. The line dividing psychiatric disorders/conditions from other disaffections of experience and behaviour is not always sharp and clear; for example, the myriad of human problems dealt with by social welfare agents, lawyers, judges, and pastoral counsellors and psychologists do not necessarily answer to the call of medicine (or psychiatry). However, emotional and behavioural problems dealt in non-medical settings may encompass or overlap with psychiatric conditions. However, conceptually, economically, politically, and even on religious grounds a dividing line can and should be drawn to set apart, on the one hand, what a comparative researcher or mental health professional focuses on (psychiatric condition), and on the other, the concerns of administrators, functionaries, and other non-medical personnel who address the social, cultural, and political implications of social and behavioural disquietudes and dis-composures as required by their institutions and roles. Quite obviously, these two ways of understanding emotional and behavioural problems are not mutually exclusive: psychiatric conditions will also be found in non-medical settings, although represented in a different idiom and exemplifying different imperatives. In India, like in any civilization or society, psychiatric conditions can be assumed to have owned up to a similar social spread across institutional sectors of the social fabric.

---

[12] Furedi 2004.

To spot and make sense of psychiatric conditions and their mode of handling in non-modern contemporary and traditional non-Western societies such as those of the Indian subcontinent an analyst cannot but resort to borrowing some of the language of scientific psychiatry. As discussed earlier, he or she presumes the universality of syndromes of psychiatric significance (possible psychiatric conditions) and searches for them among the personal dilemmas and behavioural disarrangements that meet the criteria described earlier. Social and existential crises or disturbances of being and behaviour can compel self-examination and moral inquiry, bring distress, produce confusion, cause maladaptive coping or frank collapse in social function, compel change in a person's life projects, and elicit attempts of restoration, remediation or frank healing (e.g., involvement in religious, moral, or medical pursuits). They can include dilemmas of the self-resonant with religious, philosophical, and soteriological connotations. An analyst's search may be directed to a real, traditional village community of contemporary India, a temple or sanctuary, a religious sect, or a still living and resonant ancient text in any of the many intellectual traditions that exemplify Hindu culture and civilization. However, local interpretations and modes of handling such conditions may not involve an idea of sickness at all. Instead, ideas, social practices and institutions that frequently encase possible psychiatric conditions should be examined, for example, problems involving morale and motivation, spiritual disaffection, morality, and law and their means of redress. This amalgam of social practices, institutions, organizations, establishments, roles, and coping skills for handling diverse human disaffections, traditionally thought of as non-medical, constitutes an important embodiment and formulary that any society (especially non-modern and non-Western) evolves for coping with social disorders and problems that can include psychiatric conditions. Obviously, the indigenous system of medicine may also serve as a locale or social station where psychiatric conditions (understood in terms of culture specific idiom) are seen and handled. However, an analyst's psychiatric conditions will not be concentrated or sharply encompassed by a society's system of medicine. But if an analyst's criteria of psychiatric condition are met, then exactly where in the institutional fabric of the society syndromes of psychiatric interest are placed is of secondary importance.

Psychiatric conditions and disorders have roots in physiology and neurobiology. They manifest in a composite of emotional and behavioural disarrangements marked by emotional distress and need to re-connect, re-establish, or re-direct the self. Viewed in general terms, phenomena of psychiatric import often include symptoms and signs of bodily distress. The latter are crucially important, since one has to contend with and overcome a Western bias that psychiatric phenomena predominantly involve psychological material, or problems of the psyche. What is psyche-atric is ordinarily assessed, not surprisingly, in terms of the language of descriptive psychopathology which addresses aspects of logicality and reasonableness of thought and forms and levels of emotional experience in comparison to the relative neglect of bodily manifestations.

In modern society emotional and behavioural discomfitures glossed as psychiatric are conceptualized as pathological or *dysfunctional.* Hence, they are referred to as *disturbances, disorders,* or *illnesses.* All of these terms have obvious medical connotations. They are appropriately formulated by a clinician who has been consulted for help and treatment has conducted a formal examination. However, the previous discussion pointed out that the term *psychiatric condition* is used in a generic, non-evaluative (humanistic and neutral) way and applies not only to individuals examined in a medical setting, but also to persons residing in communities who may never be seen by a physician or medical practitioner for they may not regard themselves as sick or disturbed. Provided such persons manifest the associated negative changes described earlier (personal distress, behavioural disturbance or disaffection, and associated impairment of bodily function) the term psychiatric condition will be used regardless of how the phenomenon in question is configured in the idiom of the society and culture. The term can also be used to refer to persons whose behaviour within the culture may not necessarily be viewed as abnormal in any way. The individual may even be viewed as supranormal, that is, as representing or embodying special supernatural attributes and may be regarded as a criminal, sinner, saint, prophet, demon, or witch. The orientation followed in this book, then, respects a moderate cultural relativism, namely, psychiatric conditions are found everywhere but dressed in a local cultural attire, but eschews a hard cultural relativism, namely, such conditions are not relevant to non-Western cultures, or if they are they must meet local criteria of medically relevant pathologies.[13]

[13] Fabrega 1993.

It is a truism that an idea of psychiatric condition is culturally relative and its study involves a form of ethnocentrism.[14] However, were one to maintain a strict cultural relativism when studying culture and psychiatric condition, one could not analyze its expressions and social implications in societies other than modern, Western ones. This strict and immoderate cultural relativism is rejected given findings of modern sciences that establish psychiatric conditions constitute human universals, although always conditioned by social and cultural conventions and prone to change in relation to evolutionary factors.[15]

Orientation adopted here is based on an external, observer-imposed, ultimately clinical-medical point of view. Besides failing to adhere to strict injunctions of cultural and social historians, the orientation risks the criticism of medicalization or 'psychiatric imperialism'. This refers to the unwarranted use of medical labels pertinent to disease in order to refer to culturally embedded behaviour patterns that should be examined and interpreted only within the full envelope of logic, standards, traditions, and conventions about behaviour of any society and culture. However, human problems that today are understood as involving mental health and illness are not only real but highly variegated, universal, and, spread across the social, cultural fabric and institutional sectors of any society.[16] One cannot possibly understand in any reasonable way how psychiatric phenomena have been configured and enacted across the expanse of Indian history without a broad appreciation of how they (psychiatric phenomena) were shaped and dealt with in terms of culture specific ideas and practices not limited just to medicine.

HAZARDS OF SEARCHING FOR PSYCHIATRIC PHENOMENA IN PRE-MODERN INDIA

The term psychiatric condition is compatible with general intellectual notions about human emotional and behavioural phenomena associated with psychological distress and social disorder. Different ideas and terminologies may be used by social scientists and historians to signify

---

[14] Fabrega 1989a, 1989b, 1989c, 1992a, 1992b, 1993.

[15] Spiro 1986; Fabrega 1993, 1997, 2002a.

[16] Like sickness and disease, see Fabrega 1997 and 2002a.

related human problems and, while an idea of a psychiatric 'condition' may not be intended by them, an outside analyst/clinician can anticipate finding conditions of psychiatric interest represented in their writings in many instances. A condition may, but need not, involve deviance or abnormality when seen from within the culture and community. However, psychiatric conditions are associated with a discernible change or interference in the conduct of life. Someone manifesting such an exemplar, were he or she to be evaluated by a socially and culturally informed clinician, would show criteria of change or distress or disturbance in areas of emotion, behaviour, and bodily functioning regardless of community or historical setting and conventions of normality and abnormality. Definition of psychiatric condition presumes a hypothetical individual whose behaviour might be played out in a natural environment or community where the idea of illness or pathology may not be raised – a non-clinical or pre-clinical domain of reference.

A further assumption one might entertain is that in some respects and in some instances any of several diagnostic entities taken from contemporary psychiatry, such as depression, schizophrenia, anxiety, or somatoform disorder, might apply to behaviour and adjustment of a hypothetical individual. The latter, for example, might be represented in what one reads in an ancient text or simply presupposes, based on generalizations about vicissitudes of social life, given an understanding of how adversity plays out in human lives. However, to 'diagnose' psychiatric disorders in such a manner, to force hypothetical persons or circumstances or descriptions of social life found in other historical eras into the straight jacket of contemporary diagnostic categories, is not only conceptually hazardous but also unrealistic and inappropriate. It is true that Indian psychiatric epidemiologists, who survey traditional but contemporary populations in their natural settings, experience little difficulty in applying modern diagnostic labels. Many subjects examined and diagnosed by them do not identify themselves, nor do their kin, as having a mental illness. This fact supports the reasonableness of conducting a cultural historical study of conditions of psychiatric interest in India, but with the understanding that local meanings must be allowed to have sway and diagnostic labels not imposed. For it is how such conditions are understood and dealt with that is of paramount interest.

The intellectual, social, and cultural history of India provides suitable material for one to understand how behavioural phenomena of psychiatric interest were conceptualized and handled in a different idiom and system of practice from that of the West. However, earlier discussion makes apparent that in order to accomplish this satisfactorily a broad net has to be cast over diverse spheres of human thought and conduct. The net has to include material on the history of medicine, religion and spirituality, philosophy, morality, political economy, and general culture Examination of this material chronicles a different social and cultural history from that of the West. Contemporary medicine and psychiatry bracket out considerations of moral, religious, and spiritual health, whereas to do so in a traditional Indian context is not only impossible but also nonsensical.

Considered in strict cultural and historical terms, it is a truism that prior to the modern era Western biomedical ideas and practices relating to our conception of 'psychiatric phenomena' had no basis for application or use in communities of the Indian subcontinent. Indian thought worlds and habit patterns shaped the parameters of what we in hindsight can construe as psychiatric conditions. The former framed the individual in a distinctive cultural psychological attire and world-view. What the 'self' involved and how it resonated subjectively, experientially, morally, and energetically or creatively (the cultural ontology or nature of the self) encompassed ideas about, soul, society, time, cosmology and cosmogony, moral obligation and law, religious devotion, and cultivation of spiritual improvement. Constructs such as these would have been used to formulate how psychological distress and problems of behaviour and social order were understood and coped with as existential realities. This amalgam discussed earlier embodied an Indian or Hindu system of understanding and practice for coping with a range of emotional and behavioural problems which one could equate in a loose sense with its indigenous psychiatry covers what an analyst might qualify as religious, moral re-education, and/or legal as well as medical.[17]

It is to be emphasized that, like in the case of 'psychiatric condition', what 'indigenous psychiatry' refers to represents an anachronistic backward re-interpretation of selected phenomena of interest to an analyst. In the present context, it involves a search through the Hindu amalgam of indigenous ideas, beliefs and social practices and institutions whose functions had the effect of coping, relieving, transmuting, and harnessing along culturally meaningful terms aspects of mental and physical

[17] Conceptualized locally as sickness.

suffering, misery, pain, and demoralization. Indian gurus, priests, philosophers, moralists, physicians or popular healers, householders, or simply run-of-the-mill lay people living in a village and locked into the stratification system of caste *did not* construe their ideas and practices (be these Vedic sacrifices or mantras, methods of meditation, Bhakti devotional exercises, yogic practices of liberation, etc.) as delivering mental health, as healing life's emotional ailments, or as transmuting, via exercises geared to shifting energy and fluids in the body, manifestations of impaired bodily and mental wellbeing including mental illness or psychiatric conditions. Viewed within the culture and society of traditional India, such practices, institutions, roles, and personnel constitute *culturally evolved structures* for coping with a range of human problems that encompass psychiatric conditions. Construing such structures as involved in the business of mental health or equating them with indigenous representations of social organization and practice of psychiatric significance involves an intellectual strategy designed to make something that science informs is universal, namely, psychiatric phenomena, amenable to social, cultural, and historical analysis.

The idea that a mental domain stood apart or astride or inside the self, disconnected from social structures, cosmological and cosmogonic influences; and that it could be targeted and its burdens assuaged via 'mental health practices' is not a representation of the way the traditional Indian society and culture worked. Rather, ideas, behaviour, and practices tied to constructs such as psychiatric condition and indigenous psychiatry represent *our conception* of how Indian people managed through their cultural inheritance to make sense of and relieve the manifestations of phenomena that are universal (psychiatric phenomena). An objective in later chapters will involve delineating, as precisely as ancient texts and writings of anthropologists about Indian populations make possible, what this local idiom and frame of reference about emotional and behavioural disaffections, including psychiatric conditions, was like during the prehistory and history of life in the subcontinent up to the present.

THE CIVILIZATION OF INDIA AS A SUBJECT FOR STUDY

India provides a rich opportunity to study the evolution of psychiatric phenomena in a major non-Western civilization. One reason alone involves its indigenous system of medicine, termed Ayurveda. It embodies a rich set of compilations and emendations of a literate, academic, scholarly, and scientific medicine. Literate medical traditions dating from antiquity provide a close-up view of how psychiatric conditions construed as sickness were understood and dealt with in the distant past. Texts have been amended, redacted, and modified, as were descriptions of the sicknesses they refer to; however, much of Ayurveda has persisted and still draws on its ancient tenets and most recently has had to cope with the challenges of biomedicine.

While not medical in the strict sense of the narrow logic of sickness–symptoms–curing found in Ayurveda (and also parts of Siddha medicine), Yoga, alchemy, and Tantra exemplify a much broader conception of health and wellbeing. They represent traditions found in the subcontinent with enormous physical and mental health implications. They are rooted in and build on ideas and practices exemplified in the Vedas (especially *Atharvaveda* and Upanishads although also *Ṛgveda*) but develop them further by bringing into focus ideas of self-concentration and boily/mental transmutation via distinctive spiritual and ritual practices.

All of the preceding traditions merge and are not always easy to untangle from sectarian religious beliefs and practices, a basic function of which is coping with distress, demoralization, and disordered conditions of life. Hindu sects operate under the dominion of Brahmins, priests, local saints and deities, gurus, and other religious healers and spiritual moral advisors. Ideas and beliefs found in the many, diverse sects of Hinduism are put into practice in family households, local village and urban settings, and regionally as per pilgrimage and temples. These advise and guide individuals seeking emotional help and consolation through devotional rituals that promise realization of transcendence and spiritual liberation. Thus, sectarian religions can be seen as components of indigenous psychiatry since their purpose and accomplishment is to relieve, restore, ameliorate, and transmute not only everyday human emotional and behavioural discomfitures but more pronounced, persistent states of demoralization, distress, and suffering.[18] Finally, India also displayed and still preserves a range of popular, folk-based, often demonic, shamanistic, indigenous medical traditions. These are partly repositories of old, probably pre-Aryan, knowledge and partly a reworking or extrapolation of beliefs and practices found in local settings. They exemplify how behavioural problems are sorted out and resolved not only among hunter-gatherers of contemporary India, often termed tribal peoples, but in traditional villages.

While ayurvedic and Siddha medicine represent a largely rational and secular approach to disease and psychiatric conditions, the disciplines of Yoga, Tantra, alchemy, and sectarian/popular religious traditions are far more encompassing. They are not limited to curing in the strict medical sense, but are proactive: they seek to preserve, relieve, transmute, and extend health not just in a physico-mental sense of a time bound state of sickness but morally and spiritually and stretched out into space and time. They consist of ideas and rituals that aim to reconnect and reanimate structures of emotional and behavioural disaffection and stirrings of bodily distress burdened by the allure, distraction, and oppression of everyday, mundane social life experienced by and beclouding the realization of the inner spiritual self which is seen as embodied in ultimate, universal entities and agencies. A doctrine and set of social practices that are liberating and salvific can hardly be said to exclude the myriad of human forms of distress and disorder inherent in psychiatric conditions as previously described.

Thus, the spiritual, medical, and popular traditions of health promotion and betterment provide an informative frame of reference for examination of psychiatric phenomena in the Indian subcontinent. Ancient texts record important historical events and political, religious, and moral traditions that allow one to infer how social life was lived, as well as the values and sentiments that were important during earlier epochs. They add further insights about how deeply felt problems of emotional and behavioural derailment and disaffection that can include psychiatric conditions have been perceived and dealt with.

In secular medical writings one finds representations of how psychiatric conditions were understood, expressed, and dealt with. They allow comparison of how such conditions were perceived in relation to

---

[18] Details of and the relevance of these and other ways of understanding the shape, meaning, and consequences of psychiatric conditions in India are taken up in subsequent chapters.

other medical conditions. Similarly, in religious and philosophical texts, forms of behavioural and emotional disaffection that raise questions about individual identity, social disorder, and human suffering are likely to be addressed and these include psychiatric conditions. The latter will qualify in special ways, leaving aside any strictly bodily, organic problems or rubrics of psychopathology as these are now understood in contemporary psychiatry. All of this material, when examined carefully, includes information about how psychiatric conditions were interpreted and handled in a social, religious, or philosophical sense. Finally, essential features of psychiatric conditions sometimes involve behaviour that is socially divisive, devalued, and subject to condemnation and even punishment. Thus, the manner in which such manifestations of psychiatric conditions were understood and handled may also be represented in general descriptive and literary texts pertaining to social conventions, obligations, rights, entitlements, moral precepts, and legal proscriptions, such as the Dharmaśāstras.

However, to fully comprehend the cultural representation and history of psychiatric phenomena in India more than ancient texts are needed. Ancient writings of revealed truths and inherited observations and interpretation about social reality and tradition have to be examined in relation to contextual studies of social life in local communities conducted by anthropologists. Anthropologists of the Chicago school, although their ideas may today be dated and superseded, have pointed the way to the importance of interrelating different slants on and levels of Indian civilization.[19] They have emphasized the difference between 'text and context' to single out differences between the meanings of sacred writings and their correlates in 'real' local communities. The *social structure of tradition* has been differentiated from the *social organization of tradition*. The former refers to arrangements of roles and status found in various social groupings such as castes, sects and various types of teachers that embody, cultivate and inculcate the tradition. On the other hand, social organization of tradition refers to the way actual behaviour is put together in any particular instance when elements of tradition are transmitted. The idea of *cultural organization of meanings* inherent in Indian civilization brings to mind its content (ideas, values, legends, myths, spiritual tenets) as embodied in cultural performances and cul-

[19] Redfield 1953, 1956; Singer 1959, 1972; Singer and Cohn 1968.

tural media; for example, marriages, pilgrimages, household rituals, and readings and expositions of recorded and oral traditions.[20]

PROTO-HISTORY OF INDIA: HARAPPAN SOCIETIES OF THE NORTHWEST

Vedic peoples, communities deriving from presumed Indo-Aryan migrants from Western Asia, perhaps not true invaders as tradition suggests, were not the first major political and cultural centred of the subcontinent.[21] As suggested earlier, hunter-gatherers and nomadic pastoralists have a long proto-history in the western part of the subcontinent of India, culminating in villages and presumably towns if not small cities of Baluchistan and in Mehrgarh. The ethnicity and racial composition of such peoples is not clear and their relationship to Aryans is contested. Shaffer and Lichtenstein, and also Kennedy argue persuasively that for too long and with little hard data this region of the subcontinent has been preoccupied with ideas of intrusion and discontinuity, giving priority to the influence of external factors in cultural development, mainly attributed to ethnic intrusions or invasions.[22] They emphasize that the Mehrgarh data raise serious questions about diffusion, invasion, and/or replacement ('an all encompassing explanation') for major South Asian cultural developments. Similarly, in their analysis of mature Harappans they point out that such peoples were or had the potential to interact with a number of culturally similar and different peoples that formed part of the South Asian cultural mosaic.

> Their [the Harappans] cartographic isolation by scholars, combined with the use of paradigms of cyclic and progressive/gradual change, completely fails to depict the full, dynamic, social and geographic system of which they were but one part.[23]

This position seems to weaken the assumption that Vedic peoples comprised a separate ethnic or racial group that brought their oral cul-

---

[20] Other ideas that are useful for understanding the continuity and change in Indian civilization are taken up in later sections and in Chapters 2 and 3.

[21] Kochhar 2000.

[22] Shaffer and Lichtenstein 1995; and also Kennedy 2000.

[23] Shaffer and Lichtenstein 1995: 137.

ture with them from the West and are solely responsible for its development. They emphasize that South Asian cultural history should be studied within a context of continuity with emphasis given to cultural tradition and paleo-ethnicity that spread across the region of the northwest.

At any rate, around 2500 BCE, there were large, architecturally advanced urban societies in the Indus region in the northwest. These societies clearly had a close relationship with societies of the Iranian plateau and Mesopotamian civilization, or at least a commercial one, but whether they were actual colonies or outposts of that civilization is debatable. The size, majesty, social complexity, politico-economic scope, and architectural and artistic achievements of these earliest state societies of the Indus Valley are a source of wonderment and mystery. The Harappan complex of societies is said to date from the third millennium BCE and is believed to have developed out of conglomerations of agricultural societies of the type found in association with Mehrgarh. More specifically, societies of the Indus valley are presumed to have roots that stretch back in time in the northwest connecting with a broad cultural tradition and paleo-ethnicity of people displaying pre- and fully agricultural way of life, although not as imposing as those of Harappans. Archeological remains suggest that Indus societies may have constituted a major and independent Harappan state, with its capital at Mohenjo-Daro. However, whether they conform to typical exemplars of ancient state societies is disputed. They may have served mainly as commercial and mercantile centres. These societies are regarded as sharing some, but certainly lacking other, of the characteristics of contemporaneous Egyptian and Mesopotamian societies of the third and second centuries BCE. However, the few samples of an undecipherable script found in settlements of the Indus basin raise doubts as to whether these societies represent a true state and a civilization.[24]

Little is known about their world-view, systems of morality, religion, and law and, in particular, the actual social life and cultural history of the Indus societies. Archeological remains attest to a highly developed city life with many imposing structures, platforms, baths, and granaries; many individual dwellings had wells, bathrooms, and elaborate drainage systems. Harappan peoples had developed a system of

---

[24] They are said to lack monumental architecture, the script seems to have limited conceptual breadth, and burial practices are not elaborated.

writing, had domesticated a large number of plants and animals, worked in a variety of metals, and included an active artisan class.

Tantalizing hints of religious rituals and forms have been found, but how these people lived, what they believed, how they resolved human problems and conflicts, and in particular how they coped with disease and behavioural problems – all this is totally unknown. There are no physical or textual remains pertaining to religion and government, such as law codes, that would provide indirect clues about how the Harappan culture addressed social problems. This means that nothing is known about beliefs and social practices and methods for treating sickness and handling forms of behavioural deviance that no doubt would have included psychiatric conditions. Harappan societies appear to have been situated in river valleys and coastal areas separated by ecologically complex regions. The cities, which housed local chieftains and other elites, were apparently commercial gateways to a large agricultural hinterland. There may have been a high degree of civic control in the larger cities and possibly in the surrounding countryside as well. If this is so, then major societies probably attracted not only agricultural products and functioned as centres of trade and commerce but would have served as places of refuge and centres of medical care and religious influence. This would imply not only markets for products and wares but also of markets that dealt with health and healing when resources of the countryside proved insufficient.

GENERAL CHARACTERISTICS OF EARLY INDIAN SOCIETIES

The prominence of regionalism, ethnic, religious, caste-based factionalism, and violence during the modern period have led academics and politicians to question India's past political history and its destiny as a modern polity. Scholars are divided as to whether traditional social science notions about the structure, composition, and governance of a society can be applied to India during ancient and medieval times. Some argue that concepts of community, civil society, and statehood, derived from Enlightenment political theory and applied to medieval and early modern Europe, may not apply to the subcontinent and when they are applied the result is less than sanguine.[25] Whether ancient societies were

[25] Inden 2000.

truly politically centralized, what the governing principles of social order consisted of, and how the rulers and kings influenced local affairs of villages are all contested. Thapar uses information and generalizations from archeology and anthropology to provide a rich account of the advent of Vedic people and of subsequent emergence of true state societies from tribes, principalities, and kingdoms.[26] The history of India following Harappan civilization, including the Mauryas and even the Gupta dynasties and up until 1300 CE, is analyzed by Thapar with respect to the fate of tribal communities located away from the periphery of major urban groups. The assimilation and appropriation of tribal groups into Indian traditional culture, social organization, religion, and philosophy is a recurring theme of Thapar's history. Rulers of major regional states managed to entice local tribal leaders and heads of smaller kingdoms to enter the fold of major regional states by offering them protection and prestige associated with Indian civilization. An additional strategy was to award grants of land to Brahmins for purposes of colonizing and acculturating tribal peoples.

Stein theorizes that *communalism* was the basic social pattern, especially in southern India during the medieval period.[27] He holds that a community is both a place and a people with shared sentiments and values, including shared rights or entitlements over human and material resources – in particular, shared land worked by pre-modern technology. Stein emphasizes that communities were corporate organizations united by members' solidarity regarding local affinities, sentiments, and entitlements. They were self-contained and often competed with neighbouring groups, with whom there could be violent conflict.

However, communities of ancient and medieval India did not conform to the European model. They were not natural entities, independent structures composed of more or less autonomous individuals and with a more or less secular ethos. They were bound together by ethnicity, sect, and hereditary lines of descent, but were internally structured by occupation and castes, hierarchically arranged. During the medieval era 'civil society' consisted of local and small societies of considerable complexity that pre-existed and later coexisted with larger and more articulated societies and formally constituted polities and principalities over centuries, if not millennia.

---

[26] Thapar 2002.

[27] Stein 1998.

Thapar and Stein elaborate on the idea of the *segmentary state*, derived from the study of Africa, in order to describe developments in premodern India.[28] This is a political order characterized by numerous centres or domains in which power is distributed among many notables, with full royalty enjoyed by an anointed king. Whereas each domain is administratively autonomous and has its own coercive power, lesser political centres recognize the king's dominance. The segmentary state differs from the unitary state, which covers a fixed territory and has a centralized administration that wields coercive power. In southern India during the medieval period, Stein and Thapar describe a segmentary state, comprised of hundreds of local societies with a communitarian structure. It comprised a number of separate communities whose political leaders, termed chiefs, owe some form of allegiance to kings and bask in the latter's power and anointed status.

Archeologists describe the remains of towns that probably functioned as regional capitals, administrative centres for the ruling and priestly classes along with their military forces, and as centres of commerce and the manufacture of handicrafts and art.[29] The vast majority of the population, however, lived in small communities in the agricultural hinterland. The degree of central control over these villages varied widely. Even today, with a new ethos of democracy and equality in India, and with a recognized need for centralized political control for the equitable administration of law and local affairs, villages enjoy considerable autonomy and are dominated by commonly held ancient traditions of social arbitration and conflict resolution.[30]

THE EMERGENCE OF HINDU CIVILIZATION

The term 'Hinduism' stands for essential characteristics of Indian civilization and is often used to describe its religion that, given its scope, encompasses a whole way of life. In a broad sense, as already suggested, this is based on the Vedas that were compiled sometime during the second century BCE.[31] The revealed knowledge at the base of Hinduism

---

[28] Thapar 2002; Stein 1998.

[29] R. S. Sharma 1983, 1991, 1996.

[30] Srinivas 1966; Moore 1985, 1998.

[31] Zaehner 1962; W. N. Brown 1966; Brockington 1996; Quigley 2003; Michaels 2004; Flood 1996; Jamison and Witzel 2003; Witzel 1979, 1997.

(*śruti*), consist of four collections of hymns and sayings (the Vedas as narrowly construed), writings that expound upon and provide guidelines about how each of these are to be performed and understood (Brāhmaṇas), treatises that provide mystical interpretations of rituals and sayings (Āraṇyakas), and a group of later writings that expound on essentials of religious philosophy and psychology (Upanishads). The Vedas construed broadly are the oldest sacred books of Hinduism and comprise the hymns, rituals, and religious precepts that are a repository of ancient wisdom.

Conceptions, beliefs, and values about spiritual realization and moral, ethical, and law-abiding conduct were initially formulated in the Vedas and comprise the ultimate sources of Indian culture and civilization.[32] Beneath the congeries of gods and across its many sects, one finds in Hinduism a conjunction of religion and spirituality, philosophy and psychology, and moral obligations inherent in social relations among social groups and castes. The implications of scriptural documents for the cultural psychology of India, and influence on psychiatric phenomena, are taken up in a later chapter. For now, two generalizations are appropriate: (1) The Vedas and especially the *Atharvaveda*, outline a world-view that blends religion, spirituality, magic, morality, and a general outlook designed to bring order, harmony, fulfilment, and wellbeing in a generic, holistic sense. Conversely, the Vedas describe the social rules and precepts that when contravened can bring about suffering, misfortune, disease, and mental anguish – which would include disturbances of experience and behaviour. (2) The Vedas attempt to delineate theosophical, soteriological, cosmological, and philosophical, quasi-scientific speculations, beliefs, and tenets about the world and its creatures that are picked up later in the great religions of India – not only Hinduism, but also Buddhism and Jainism – and in the various philosophical schools, including the tradition of Ayurveda medicine. How psychiatric condition was understood and handled as a social phenomenon in the subcontinent can be appreciated by considering the intermixture of two sets of particulars: on the one hand, a highly spiritualized set of religious and moral beliefs and directives regarding social conduct and, on the other, a highly elaborated philosophical psychology about duty, obligation, the nature of the self and the person, and the constitution of the mind and body in health as well as disease. These

32 W. N. Brown 1966; Brockington 1996; Witzel 2003.

two influences incorporate social welfare and medicine and are basic to understanding the Hindu approach to sickness and healing, including psychiatric phenomena. The Dharmaśāstras, discussed in Chapters 2 and 3, are canonical documents that illustrate these generalizations: they expound on the requirements and standards of social conduct and exhort on characteristics of moral, ethical, and spiritual behaviour within the structure of a highly stratified society.

Historians report that the Aryans were in continual conflict with indigenous peoples of the region, whom they subjugated and exploited as slaves. During its later period of hegemony, the Aryan society involved settled agriculture. No major urban centres have been linked to the very early Vedic societies.[33] The emergence of states and cities in the mid-Ganges region around the fifth century BCE is held to have followed a westward migration during the later Vedic period. R. S. Sharma provides a succinct summary of archeological and textual information pertaining to the emergence of the state in the mid-Ganges region.[34]

The worship of the gods Shiva and Vishnu goes back to Vedic times.[35] However, they are relatively minor in the pantheon. The main Vedic gods are nature gods; Rudra, the god of thunder, is important in the *Ṛgveda* but gives way to Shiva. Srinivas writes:

> The important Vedic gods Varuna, Mitra, Rudra, Indra, Agni, Prajapati, and Savitar lose their importance gradually – some of them like Varuna and Vishnu change their character completely – and in their place emerges the trinity made up of Brahma, Vishnu, and Shiva. Brahma does not occur in the Vedas, but seems to have developed during the period of the *Brāhmaṇas*. He declined in importance subsequently, and in the twentieth century Vishnu and Shiva were the two most important gods.[36]

The worship of nature gods described in the Vedas gradually gave way towards a philosophical psychology, becoming more introverted as reflected in the Upanishads, which include philosophical speculations about the nature of the universe and the destiny of the soul. In many ways it marks the origins of India's philosophical psychology. While

---

[33] Kulke and Rothemund 1986; Stein 1998.

[34] R. S. Sharma 1995, 1996.

[35] Actually, archeological remains in Harappan sites suggest worship of a form said to be a forerunner of Shiva, but this is contestable.

[36] Srinivas 1962: 156.

theistic and dualistic ideas are found, a pantheistic explanation of the universe is favoured. An important feature of this text is emphasis on a distinctive psychology of the individual's soul. It heralds a concern for the inner essence of the person, its ancestry in previous and future generations, and its relationship to the world beyond as exemplified in the universal soul or *ātman*.[37]

Controversy surrounds the origins of the social organization of Indian communities, in particular their stratification and hierarchy, including divisions by caste. In general, many view Aryan culture of the later Vedic age as influential in shaping the social structure of caste, but others hold that tribal affinities, genealogical linkages and kinship, and sheer occupational exigencies are important. What priority should be given to the various parameters is highly contested.[38] One may assume that family, caste, lineage or tribe, sects of religion, village, and region are the basic foundational blocks that make up an Indian community, since intimations of many of these divisions are represented in the very earliest canonical literatures. The *varṇa*s are hierarchically arranged general divisions of society based on their importance in the maintenance of order. They encompass political, economic, religious and spiritual considerations. Castes or *jāti*s refer to specific and usually endogamous groupings distinguished by profession, commensality, and degrees of impurity that exemplify in a concrete form the intellectual assumptions inherent in the *varṇa*s. The various castes are distinguished by behavioural customs and beliefs regarding social merit, moral standing, diet, dress, religious practices, marriage patterns, rules of social interaction, and ideas of pollution. In the Vedas, divisions in the social order are represented as logically based, constituting the structural basis of Indian civilization, as manifested in creation myths about the origins of different community groups.

References to the importance of social stratification and the duties and regulations of various social groups found in Vedic writings suggest that the caste system has a very early antiquity. The history of Vedism, Brahmanism, and Hinduism proper is assumed to start with the period when the Aryan peoples entered India from the northwest and slowly migrated into the Gangetic plain. A pre-Aryan common, folk religion of

[37] Reat 1990.

[38] Beidelman 1959; Dumont 1970; Kulke and Rothermund 1986; Stein 1998; Inden 2000; Kennedy 2000; Thapar 2002; Quigley 2003.

interdependent gods and goddesses was incorporated into a polytheistic system sponsored by Brahmins who as priests present offerings of the people to the gods and the latter are identified with the officiant. Ideas about moral determinism tied to actions and their consequences across cycles of existence appear before the formation of the caste system.[39] A period of time associated with the first Upanishads and continuing on to the period when the *Bhagavadgītā* was compiled is viewed as a 'golden age of speculation' during which post-Vedic and pre-Hindu society took shape.[40] Dumont indicates that it was a movement in the religious life that began with the shift from Vedic polytheism to the power of sacrifice, with the early Upanishads proclaiming the identity of individual Self and Universal Being. The idea of transmigration as a consequence of retribution had been important in discussions of renouncers, ascetics, and itinerants. This was a first stage of a movement that travelled from monism and immanence to transcendence and dualism involving a discipline of concentration followed by a discipline of discrimination (*yoga*). It led to efforts

> to reach beyond the *ātman*, the tiny man (*puruṣa*) concealed in the inner heart, leading finally to the dualism of the Sāṃkhya system and to the personal God or Lord with whom the individual communicates by love (*bhakti*).[41]

The injunctions and regulations inherent in the caste system constituted the social amalgam of Indian communities, an important influence on politico-economic order, a determining factor in social relations, law making and enforcement, personality development, and an organizing principle of social experience, social identity and behaviour. In many respects, it continues to be influential despite modernization and Westernization. In light of its importance, caste should figure prominently in the psychology of the Indian people.[42]

Social organization through the caste system and its attendant moral responsibilities was observed all levels from Aryan times through the

---

[39] Dumont 1970.

[40] The psychiatric implications of religious/popular writings is taken up in Chapters 3 and 8.

[41] Dumont 1970: 277.

[42] Beidelman 1959; Srinivas 1952, 1962, 1966; Dumont 1970; Mandelbaum 1970; Lingat 1973; Kakar 1981. The influence of caste on society and culture on aspects of cultural psychology and psychiatric conditions is taken up in Chapter 9.

dynasty of the Mauryas and Guptas and later, was governed by a sacred and scripturally authorized view of behaviour. Religious, ethical, and moral conceptions were prevalent among all those wielding power, from kings, princes, provincial governors, district magistrates, down to village headmen, council members, and leaders of the extended family, who were burdened by having to pay tributes. All pronounced and propounded on the naturalness and sanctity of the law of *dharma*, and their subjects were bound by the same body of social and moral precepts. This outlook was not prevalent among isolated tribes and villages (aboriginals), nor did it hold sway to an equal extent in all communities of the subcontinent during various phases of ancient history. But its influence spread and became dominant as polities expanded and coalesced into kingdoms and eventually states.

The great epics and other popular writings not only articulate values and traditions about social order but also address the nature of being, personhood, and ideal human conduct. The rich scriptural literature is salient, not only in a public, shared sense of a collective awareness of conventions and standards – that is, as a social and cultural history of the people of the subcontinent – but also in subjective, private spheres where it influences experience and behaviour. The social organization of Indian traditions and the basis for virtually all human activity, social and personal, is inculcated by means of pedagogy, familiar tales and aphorisms, folklore, stories of exemplary characters and behaviour, and cultural performances such as plays, dance and music all of which exemplify fundamental philosophical, moral, and religious tenets. The special character of Indian personal identity, what one may term its cultural psychology, is steeped in a scriptural, religious, and highly moral set of traditions that can be traced back to the Vedic age.

TOWARDS AN EVOLUTIONARY SLANT ON PSYCHIATRIC PHENOMENA

Since the emergence of plant and animal domestication and in relation to a fully sedentary way of life approximately 10,000 or so years ago, human societies considered as social structures have changed dramatically in different parts of the globe.[43] Given that medical and psychiatric phenomena are human universals as are ideas, social practices and institutions about them, one can propose that comparative study provides an opportunity for viewing such phenomena in terms of change and transformation. Material about how India has understood and dealt with psychiatric conditions thus provides one with an opportunity to obtain a panoramic view of how such phenomena have unfolded across a large expanse of time. More precisely, it allows one to formulate one scenario of how medicine and psychiatry have evolved in a part of the world governed by cultural, politico-economic or general cultural contingencies different from those of Europe.

In general, ideas about social and cultural evolution are controversial in the social sciences for many reasons. Among other points of view, they are tied to crude social Darwinism, betterment of some compared to others, the idea of progress, and justification for colonial expansion and imperial enterprise. Needless to say, none of these is defensible or implied by contemporary formulations of social and cultural evolution. In other words, with qualifications well outlined by contemporary sociologists and anthropologists, ideas about evolution are not only supportable, but judged as necessary in order to understand societies in a broadly comparative and historical way.[44] Social evolution has been associated with changes in such things as size, complexity, mode of food production and redistribution, political centralization, social stratification, and institutional change. Sociological changes have been correlated with changes in intellectual systems involving philosophy, religion, morality, and medicine and in the institutions that are based on them. It is a truism that the societies of the Indian subcontinent have evolved socially and culturally since the origins of food production in seventh millennium BCE in Mehrgarh, near Sibri, Pakistan, and large-scale urbanization as exemplified in the societies, if not civilizations, that covered and where contemporary with Harappans of the Indus valley during the third century BCE.[45] One focus of this book is on how our understanding and ways of handling psychiatric conditions have changed in relation to changes in societal size and complexity in India, starting with

---

[43] Diamond 1997.

[44] Runciman 1987, 1989, 1998, 2001; Richerson and Boyd 2005; for application to sickness and healing, see also Fabrega 1997.

[45] Shaffer and Lichtenstein 1995.

hunter-gatherer societies analogous to those still found in the subcontinent and ending with the contemporary era.

It is reasonable to propose that psychiatric phenomena, construed in terms of sheer biology, epidemiology and demographic structure, have been a constant in societies of different size and complexity of the subcontinent of India. These phenomena answered to the same types of causes and exhibited manifestations analogous to the psychiatric disorders that contemporary Indian psychiatric epidemiologists have described in traditional communities. This proposition is offered in the light of appreciation of the crucial influence of cultural and historical factors in how the phenomena in question were understood and played out in local contexts of meaning. The proposition would, in fact, apply to any human population and is hardly controversial given that, as mentioned earlier, psychiatric phenomena are based on innate evolutionarily based vulnerabilities to social and ecological strains inherent in the dialectical interplay of society, culture, and ecology.

The concepts and understandings used to make sense of and handle psychiatric phenomena have varied and changed in relation to changes in the culture and history of Indian societies. It is the common themes and modifications of how such conditions have been configured and enacted that in their totality constitutes the cultural history of psychiatric phenomena as discussed in this book. An opportunity to formulate one scenario of evolution of psychiatric phenomena is provided, given the temporal expanse of Indian history and myriad of distinctive factors that have influenced it from within and without, factors that underscore continuities and differences in its culture, social and politico-economic processes that retain and also modify thought worlds, habit patterns, and social practices and institutions.

A history and evolution of psychiatric phenomena construed as a chapter in *a biomedical theory of psychiatry* would involve describing changes affecting incidence, prevalence, distribution, morbidity, and treatment efficacy of specific psychiatric disorders, all of this conceptualized in terms of knowledge structures regnant in the psychiatry of today, as pertaining to schizophrenia and depression. It would also require taking into consideration how such disorders have affected and been affected by demographic and life history characteristics of populations, such as their size, mating patterns, reproductive and mortality rates, sex ratios, age structures, and sociological characteristics. This slant on psychiatric phenomena is not attempted in this book, although generalizations about the demography, public health, and psychiatric epidemiology of India are used when appropriate as a means of providing background. On the other hand, the cultural history and evolution of psychiatric phenomena in India, a chapter in *a social, cultural theory of such phenomena*, is what is taken up in later chapters. It constitutes a very different, but complementary, enterprise compared to the preceding biomedical one. It is conceptualized as a story about the way the respective human problems have been understood and handled as social and cultural phenomena in societies of the subcontinent that differed and changed in relation to size and organization from prehistory onwards to the present. As indicated earlier, such a narrative involves providing an account of the local traditions and institutions (medical, moral, spiritual, philosophical) for assigning meaning, assimilating, and coping with the problems in question and how all of this has changed in relation to history and culture. Cultural history of psychiatric phenomena considered in terms of how a society constructs its own varieties of mental health problems and illnesses is obviously not centred exclusively in the discipline of psychiatry. It requires knowledge of biomedical psychiatry and using the results of its application cross-culturally, to be sure. However, the story told in a cultural history adds to the preceding ideas and generalizations from the behavioural, social and cultural sciences.

TRACKING PSYCHIATRIC CONDITIONS ACROSS A TERRAIN OF CULTURAL HISTORY

Psychiatric conditions are rooted in biology and are manifested as disturbances both in social and psychological behaviour and in bodily ailments. Incidents of them acquire identities as meaningful objects in the social and cultural life of a group. Thereafter, in relation to complex social transformations and across the expanse of cultural evolutionary time, such conditions change in relation to structural, sociological factors and changes in local idioms and practices for managing distress. The changes that psychiatric conditions and their mode of handling undergo across time are complex and far-ranging and are influenced by at least three sets of factors: (1) purely biological factors involving genetic structures, public health and demography that affect vulnerability, incidence and prevalence; (2) social and cultural variables, such as political complexity, religious orientation or strife, regnant spiritual and moral dilemmas, pressures devolving from social stratification and organization, legal institutions and injunctions, and systems of meaning and value all of which are subject to change and in doing so come to impact on a people and shape and modulate the level of psychiatric conditions and how they are configured and handled as concrete eventualities; and (3) behavioural norms and conventions that establish categories for normality and social deviance that also are subject to change and that provide a template for interpretation and action.

It might seem relatively simple to map the human material that makes up communities and societies as a prelude to studying the cultural history of psychiatric phenomena. However, this assumption would be mistaken. One must also consider factors and processes affecting how populations change, how they maintain their size and diverse composition, especially how they are structured as biological entities (size, rate of growth, density, age and sex structures, mating systems, mortality rates). In addition to purely demographic characteristics, one must consider general public health and epidemiological factors.[46] General medical diseases cause or predispose genetically vulnerable individuals to psychiatric condition, and even when they are not the cause, medical diseases are found in association with psychiatric conditions, resulting in complex pictures of sickness that span the body's organic and physiological systems. Besides contaminating the manifest clinical picture of a psychiatric condition, a society's mix and understandings of general medical diseases prevalent in the population also affect how psychiatric conditions are conceptualized, interpreted, and handled as social phenomena by the peoples themselves and by its physicians and health practitioners. A hypothetical incident of pure psychiatric condition is likely to be accorded a different meaning if it is found in a relatively healthy community as opposed to one in which public health is poor and where persons suffer from endemic disease. A mixture of strictly medical-organic disturbances with psychiatric conditions per se, which obviously also have medical/organic bases, is the rule in non-industrial contemporary societies, and one can assume that this was true throughout most phases of human cultural history and evolution. The relatively clean presentation and diagnosis of a psychiatric

[46] Cohen and Armelagos 1984; M. N. Cohen 1989; Swedlund and Armelagos 1990.

disorder devoid of general medical conditions is a modern development and conceit since such disorders are found in individuals from which medical diseases are excluded. Of course, not just bona fide medical, organic diseases cause somatic, bodily signs and symptoms in association with a psychiatric condition. Disaffections of emotion, morale, spiritual motivation, social alienation, and politico-economic hardships, when commanding and sustained and not fleeting, all can and usually do cause changes in internal neuro-vegetative and visceral somatic functions, registering as bodily signs and symptoms. Holistic dilemmas of life and body are found amalgamated in an analyst's psychiatric condition, locally attired, of course. Thus, the manner in which an individual's seemingly psychic problems are experienced and formulated will include the meaning given to sensations of bodily distress and dysfunction.

Besides demographic, public health and genetic factors, social and cultural characteristics of the community can create strains and conflicts and give rise to a psychiatric condition in vulnerable individuals. Two societies with similar human biological material and showing more or less the same degree of social complexity may exhibit different amounts and kinds of psychiatric conditions purely because of different cultural institutions.[47] In addition, of course, social and cultural factors will affect in a major way how derailments of a self are understood and dealt with in a community, derailments stemming from tensions, hardships, and compelling provocations originating from the mix of expectations and commands inherent in social life. A cultural history and theory of psychiatric phenomena also encompasses taking into account the changes in the overall sociological constitution of a society that produce and colour behavioural dilemmas and anomalies. This involves a consideration of posited phases of social evolution.[48]

DEALING WITH THE ENCHANTMENT AND FASCINATION OF INDIA'S APPROACH TO MENTAL LIFE

The civilization of India has long commanded the attention of scholars of philosophy, religion and culture. Western scholars discovered there

[47] Edgerton 1992.

[48] Fabrega 1997; Johnson and Earle 2000; Sanderson 1990, 1995a, 1995b.

an alternative conceptualization of being, social reality, morality, and the overall meaning of human existence. It gripped their imagination and empowered their academic lives, and not always in a sanguine but frequently in a frankly Orientalist way. Starting during the eighteenth century and continuing into the modern era this interest and scholarship in Indian studies and anthropology has continued to flourish. It was natural that the psychological and spiritual features of Indian civilization should exert a strong attraction to and academic interest from members of the existential, psychoanalytic, and psychotherapeutic community who, starting perhaps with Carl Jung, evolved to become highly influential in psychiatry, especially in European and American psychiatry during the mid-point of the twentieth century.

An exemplary illustration of this psychological, psychotherapeutic interest in and fascination with the 'wisdom and insight' of Indian civilization and culture is provided by the work of Erna M. Hoch, a Swiss psychiatrist-psychoanalyst who spent many years, starting in 1956, studying and doing clinical work in different locations of India. Her clinical and theoretical papers dealt with practical experiences and interpretive studies of philosophy and religion. These were collected in a manuscript the title of which aptly captures the appeal of Indian civilization to psychodynamic psychiatry of the second half of the twentieth century: *Sources and Resources: A Western psychiatrist's search for meaning in the ancient Indian scriptures.*[49]

In these articles Hoch describes the mental conditions and psychological outlooks of illiterate Indian peasants, townspeople, as well as the educated elite whom she had occasion to interview, treat, and learn from. She also studied the scriptures, epics, mythological writings, and parables and folklore of India. Hoch's writings intuitively and implicitly describe what, to her psychoanalytically resonant point of view, constitutes the mental health striving and psychological *raison d'etre* of Indian civilization and culture. She traces the mental health, mental healing bases of Hindu traditions and institutions, starting with an analysis of the fundamental condition of *bhaya*, a philosophical-psychological interpretation of human anxiety resulting from the separation of the self from the all-knowing One, continuing on to the prevalence of *śoka*, suffering and sorrow as the lot of mankind resulting from this separation, then through *moha*, the ignorance and delusion that comes about as a result of

[49] Hoch 1993.

the recourse to attachment to the seductive pleasures and values of the material world, and culminating in the possibilities of *mokṣa,* liberation through faith, worship, devotion as well as meditation exercises associated with varieties of Yoga.

An emphasis in these writings is on the traditional Indian basis for equating fantasy and dream with world reality, of viewing ordinary human existence as but one individual's participation in the dream experience or literary and fantastic adventures exemplified by omniscient seers and dreamer, as well divine and semi-divine beings, all of whom shared Indian concerns with and bore on questions involving the pursuit of liberation and restoration of the essential relation between Self and Universal Being.

The work of Wendy O'Flaherty involving selected religious and popular writings of Indian culture, such as Buddhist texts, great epics, and Puranas, elaborates on the theme of what is real and meaningful and complements the more clinical emphasis of Hoch.[50] O'Flaherty provides an evocative picture of the shadowy, inchoate, and always shifting sense of reality as expounded by religious and philosophical scholars, and which works its way into the popular local traditional contexts of India. A cultural slant that nurtures and challenges the interpretation of present burdens of everyday life and provides alternative interpretations of what is binding, significant, and consequential for an individual, has obvious mental health implications. Hence, it comes as no surprise that assortment of beliefs and practices that O'Flaherty draws on are associated with traditional orthodox and heterodox sectarian religions and related philosophical psychology. The tapestry she describes provides a rich narrative that needs to be considered in an interpretation of the social and cultural history of psychiatric condition in India.

The writings of individuals like Hoch and O'Flaherty as well as those of the Indian psychoanalyst Sudhir Kakar, which are taken up in detail in later chapters, are paradigmatic of the interest in and relevance of Hindu civilization to a culturally grounded understanding of mental health thought and practice.[51] It includes material with clinical implications for psychiatric theory. The overriding concern and *raison d'etre* applies to psychiatric condition as human anxiety, misery, sorrow, and suffering, its generic existentialist dimension and shifting sometimes

[50] O'Flaherty 1984.

[51] Kakar 1968, 1981, 1982.

inchoate, configuration. A goal can include obtaining a metaphysical understanding of how human psychological suffering are experienced and prompt need for alleviation and this cannot but include problems of mental health as construed in the ethos and ideology of modern Western societies. Such a perspective about Hindu civilization in relation to the study of psychiatric condition is so much a part of Western intellectual history that it cannot be avoided and may be regarded as perhaps an inevitable component of a motivation to examine the subject with respect to how social life was and still is played out in societies of the subcontinent that exemplify different approaches to social reality and the meaning and purpose of life.

I have already indicated why and how interest in ideas and practices beyond the strictly medical and psychiatric idiom are relevant. However, in what follows, I also emphasize different approaches to the study of psychiatric phenomena in India. I do not rely on a psychoanalytically preconceived perspective about human experience, suffering, and healing in order to analyze how India fits the pattern or exemplifies a variation on a universal theme about emotional and behavioural disaffections glossed here as psychiatric condition. I also do not engage in the hermeneutics or exegeses of philosophical or soteriological texts. Instead, I rely on a general anthropological frame of reference leavened with ideas of social and cultural psychiatry. I seek to describe how psychiatric conditions play out and are interpreted in the light of local symbols and their meanings (their cultural rationale). I have already suggested that psychiatric condition is handled as a naturalistic object as well as in philosophical, moral, and religious terms. In other words, such conditions have a more or less unique realization and resolution in Indian communities of the subcontinent, as in other non-Western civilizations and cultures, of course. It is the interplay between history and social circumstances, demography and health, social conditions and cultural interpretations, and between symptoms and signs in relation to traditions of alleviating and healing, which is of concern here. I attempt to trace these and related developments, to the extent that it is possible, across the expanse of ancient, medieval, and modern history of India and to discuss changes that have occurred in the various dialectics that encompass circumstances involving society, culture, medicine, and mental illness. Material slanted from a psychoanalytical standpoint is included when it informs about traditional beliefs and values.[52]

This book takes the civilization of India as a test case for the cultural study of psychiatric phenomena. Its goal is to discover where in the social and meaning-filled spaces of India one would have viewed psychiatric conditions; how they would have been configured and interpreted in light of the culture; what sorts of social institutions were used to handle them; and the effects and consequences of social customs, traditions, and influence on psychiatric phenomena more generally.

Attempting to examine such topics across the long expanse of time that encompasses the social and cultural history of Indian civilization is an enormous undertaking. Obviously, it is well beyond what can be accomplished realistically. One must paint a broad canvas, select essential landmarks, describe relevant categories and themes, and suggest important factors and developments. With a modest agenda that is descriptive, analytical, but not psychoanalytical or literary, and draws on available empirical information, one is able to hypothesize how psychiatric conditions were configured and enacted and how ideas and attitudes about behaviour problems changed across time in populations of the subcontinent.

The aim of a study of this nature is to more comprehensively understand the *dialectical interplay* of society, culture, ecology, psychiatric phenomena, and indigenous systems of meaning pertaining to mental health ideas and practices and institutions of India. Much is known about the social and cultural history of psychiatric phenomena and of indigenous psychiatry of Western societies. This history provides one slant on the amalgam that constitutes a universal dialectic. A history of this amalgam in a contrastive civilization and culture will afford a different slant on that same interplay but in a different geographic region.

---

[52] Kakar 1968, 1981, 1982.

Chapter 2

Historical and Cultural Overview

INTRODUCTION: PSYCHIATRIC PHENOMENA AS SYMBOLIC AND BEHAVIOURAL MATERIAL

Phenomena of psychiatric interest have little clear representation in the texts that are available about India prior to the modern era. For most of the history of India one cannot see psychiatric phenomena described clearly and of course there is no opportunity to observe its victims directly. Its modern attire is recognized and named starting roughly during the nineteenth century, but description and analysis picks up real momentum during the second half of the twentieth century when a cadre of Indian biomedical psychiatrists comes into the picture. Rather than looking from outside as though inspecting a social tapestry or cultural map of India on which phenomena of psychiatric interest would be depicted for the earlier period, one is forced to construct exemplars of it from within, so to speak. In other words, with a clinically realistic model of what a psychiatric condition involves as per emotion, though, bodily manifestations and behaviour, one attempts to formulate it in theoretical terms using prior knowledge about psychiatry and the influence of culture in shaping experience and behaviour and its disaffections. In this effort, the stipulation reviewed earlier that relevant constructs about the ways in which psychiatric phenomena (psychiatric condition, indigenous psychiatry) are culturally constructed is indispensable. Contemporary knowledge of psychiatry and about Indian culture and psychology is used to shape and give meaning to the relevant constructs.

In shaping exemplars of psychiatric phenomena one has to begin with basic generalizations of what psychiatric conditions consist of. Their biological bases reside in hierarchical information handling systems of the brain that integrate and shape behaviour. Any model of how psychiatric conditions are produced has to accord a central place to the role that symbols and meanings play in shaping them. A model of the human information handling apparatus in the brain has to provide a description of the working of the systems involving attention, perception, memory, executive functions, motivation and emotion, general endocrine processes, and supportive physiological functions of the neural axis. However, it has to also describe what information handling in such systems mean in a social and cultural sense, for example, the significance of stimuli and derived images based on memory and understanding, as these relate to contexts and circumstances in which a person is situated and is motivated to respond. The social imperatives of behaviour and its disturbances are replete with meanings that enter, are incorporated into and processed as information in the neural apparatus. As discussed earlier, while a psychiatric condition embraces complex processes and changes in brain function related to adaptive/maladaptive behaviour, it is also to be construed as symbolic and social material. In other words, social and cultural influences considered in relation to changing historical contexts constitute the structure and integument of psychiatric conditions. When viewed in this way, one in effect is constructing exemplars of psychiatric conditions in the light provided by the social and cultural history of India.

PSYCHIATRIC PHENOMENA IN INDIA'S CULTURAL AND SOCIAL HISTORY

A history of a civilization is a narrative of unfolding events that encompass diverse changes. At a minimum, these encompass sociological, political, economic, intellectual, and cultural phenomena. History describes the social circumstances that situated conditions of psychiatric interest, how they were understood and enacted, changed and what was done about them. A shifting historical context, as it were, has contained the phenomena and moulded it into different shapes. Psychiatric conditions and practices of mental health healing are embedded in a changing panorama of any civilization's history. With respect to India one seeks a general story that describes the changes in the organization of populations in the subcontinent in a suitable chronology of periods. Each of the latter embodied phenomena of psychiatric interest in some discernible form. In theory, one can presuppose that the manner in which such phenomena was distributed and played out in India, displayed continuities as well as differences in relation to historical events as they waxed, waned, and were modified.

However, to understand how psychiatric phenomena were understood and dealt with in a civilization requires more than just a chronology of historical periods, events and processes. It also requires an understanding of how populations actually lived. And for this one needs a social and cultural history of a civilization. A description of thought worlds and habit patterns allows one to get closer to the life of the population. As features of a population's understanding and conduct of social life is brought into focus one gains access to some of the psychological, behavioural material out of which phenomena of psychiatric interest were fashioned and dealt with in the population.

In any civilization the flow of life and local, contextual factors and circumstances will naturally influence experience and behaviour and along with it psychiatric phenomena. India is no exception, and in fact, is a paradigmatic exemplar. A general understanding of India's many intellectual traditions such as philosophy, philosophical psychology, religion, law, morality, and medicine, and the social practices and institutions in terms of which such traditions were displayed and played out, provide a framework in terms of which one can understand how local events of strain and tear in the social fabric take shape and are accorded meaning as syndromes of behaviour (as per conditions of possible psychiatric interest). Generalizations about features of Indian society and culture provide the intellectual material that colour and shape its psychiatric phenomena in a distinctively Indian way.

A complete history of India begins well before 2500 BCE, the date ordinarily cited for the mature phase of Harappan culture in northwest India. This phase is said to precede the advent of the Aryans, whose historical and cultural influence still a contested matter, a period during which the Vedas were compiled. Various phases of urbanization and formation of an early state follow, eventuating in the Mauryan period during fourth century BCE. A complex story of political fragmentation then leads to the consolidation and pre-eminence of the Gupta Dynasty during the fourth and fifth century CE. Kenoyer is particularly clear in elucidating these transitions.[53] This is followed by an era during which the subcontinent was comprised of principalities and kingdoms pro-

[53] Kenoyer 1997, 1998.

ceeding on to consolidated regional states and then to the advent of Portuguese, Muslim and eventually British rule.

Orientalist perspectives, the prerogative of empire building, and requirements linked to colonialism all have influenced how the history and culture of ancient and medieval India has been conceptualized and written.[54] Only a broad outline of this long and complex social and cultural history can be covered in a selective and schematic way, sufficient to provide a baseline for understanding psychiatric phenomena. The goal is to provide a frame of reference within which to analyze influences that shaped experience, behaviour, and social life for these phenomena constitute the amalgam in terms of which psychiatric conditions have manifested and changed over the course of time. In presenting a schematic history of the main characteristics of Indian civilization, emphasis is given to salient forces and developments that contributed to the world-view, religious and moral traditions, and cultural psychology of India.

Why and how religion matters

To comprehend psychiatric conditions in context of Indian social life one has to begin with a model of information handling systems of the brain that includes not only cultural material but also that of religion. Constructs, social practices, and institutions pertaining to spirituality, morality, and philosophy are crucial for understanding the way psychiatric phenomena were shaped in the subcontinent. First of all, there are good reasons for construing religious thinking as a natural by-product of the way innate cognitive processes operate.[55] In this sense, one can think of Homo sapiens as inheriting an innate, biological capacity for forming religious constructs and conducting religious thinking as well as for culture.[56]

Secondly, the way in which contemporary simpler peoples construe themselves, their social world, and the physical habitat involves a shared relatedness, a sense of immediacy, and participation in, with, and through animate, inanimate, and non-living beings or spirits. This form

[54] Kulke and Rothermund 1986; Madan 1987; Stein 1998; Inden 2000; Thapar 2002; Marcovitz 2002.

[55] Atran and Norenzayan 2005; Boyer 1994; Fabrega 2005a, 2005b, 2005c, 2007.

[56] Tomasello 1999.

of relatedness, well documented for hunter-gatherer communities of India, involves experience and behaviour that encompass reverence, awe, respect, appreciation, shared participatory relatedness, and sense of immanence about the world termed a 'relational epistemology' that are hallmarks of religious behaviour.[57]

Thirdly, with due appreciation of the limitations of extrapolating what early human behaviour in India was like from existing contemporary societies, the thought worlds and habit patterns of simpler peoples of today nonetheless represent working exemplars of the earliest human communities. Thus, it is reasonable to suppose that existential anxieties inherent in the life of small-scale communities of the subcontinent displayed a sense of awareness and consciousness of themselves in an unpredictable and dangerous world. In association with innate cognitive processes that dispose one to think in terms of actions of wilful, non-human beings with non-intuitive capacities who could control them, this contributed to a religious orientation.[58] Religion, then, like culture more generally, enters and contextualizes all levels of the hierarchical systems of information handling that are responsible for adaptive behaviour.

Recent findings in the area of the effects of meditation on brain physiology and anatomy and hypnotic suggestion on perception of sensory phenomena bears indirectly on the topic of religion, health, and nervous system functions as these pertain to peoples of the subcontinent.[59] In general, this research shows that a mental or psychological influence, namely, meditation/hypnotic but read in quasi-religious or religious-like, alters neurobiological processes at different levels of the nervous system and in different ways. One is allowed to ask: if psychological influences of this type can blunt, for example, perception and interpretation of sensory phenomena, how much more can analogous psychological, religious influences have on perception/awareness of social and mental woes and general condition of the physiological state of the body (interoception)? And, could such influences, when repeated and sustained as a program of social life, produce long-term effects on brain function and even anatomy that influence mental and physical health?

---

[57] Rappaport 1979, 1999; Ingold 1987, 1993, 1999, 2000; Bird-David 1999; Atran and Norenzayan 2005; Fabrega 2005a, 2005b, 2005c, 2007.

[58] See also Fabrega 2000.

[59] Lazar *et al.* 2005; Raz, Jin, and Posner 2005.

Thus, to the extent that religious practices involving meditation, mystical contemplation, religious reverie, and/or prayer induce mental phenomena roughly analogous to hypnotic suggestion, to that extent they may quiet, subdue, modulate, relieve perception, and worry over social environmental and psychological disturbances. The latter and related factors are inherent in stress responses and have pernicious effects on immunology, neuro-endocrine, and physiology systems. There is a large literature in psychiatry and general and behavioural medicine about the topic of psychological influences on health and physical and mental wellbeing. It describes the 'allostatic load' (roughly, the amount of stress mediators) that individuals carry within stemming from diverse environmental influences and which in turn influence their psychobiological resilience to diverse clinical problems.[60] There is also evidence that mindful meditation and related stress-reduction programs can influence the general physiology and chemistry of body in areas related to health.[61] One can look at this problem area involving religious influence purely from standpoint of a placebo-like effect, although this construct is overly narrow and specialized, reflecting a contemporary point of view and an entirely different frame of reference about medical validity.[62] A basic point is that starting with early human communities of the subcontinent, and equally profoundly as Vedic and later Hindu religious practices came into salience, religious experiences were inherent in the social and psychological thought worlds and habit patterns of Indian, influencing in a positive way sense of wellbeing and physical and mental health.[63] For these and related reasons, then, a model of information-processing systems of brain has to make room for such influences.

However, an innate biological capacity for religious experience and behaviour is only part of why religion is important in any evolutionary comprehension of psychiatric phenomena in India. Understanding the social and cultural evolution of psychiatric phenomena requires one to consider religious phenomena because such phenomena are key components of every society's systems of mental health practices (their in-

---

[60] McEwen 1998; Charney 2004.

[61] Hoffman *et al.* 1982; Carlson *et al.* 2003; Davidson *et al.* 2003; Sudsuang, Chentanez, and Veluvan 1991.

[62] Fabrega 2002b.

[63] Rappaport 1979, 1999; Ingold 1987, 1993, 1999, 2000; Bird-David 1999; Atran and Norenzayan 2005; Fabrega 2005a, 2005b, 2005c, 2007.

digenous psychiatry). Put baldly, beliefs, social practices, institutions and organizations that exemplify religion constitute human, cultural universals. All peoples show this prominently. For India, the influence of religion in understanding psychiatric phenomena is incalculable. Given the importance that basic texts on spirituality, morality, soteriology, and philosophy have in the traditional world-view of peoples of India it is nonsensical to handle religion as though merely a component of culture. The appeal of religion is partly based on the resonance it has with a peoples' need for consolation, promise, hope, sense of existential placement, and relief of misery. Such cognitions and influences 'enter' higher levels of information handling systems of brain, are consolidated and stored, and then propagated to systems that profoundly influence overall thoughts and feelings of wellbeing and confidence of individuals as a result of their participation with group mates in some form of institutional religious behaviour. Religion can affect the health of mind, body, and 'soul' because it constitutes a powerful form of psychological influence on human physiological function as exemplified in the so-called the placebo response.[64] Thus, it is hardly surprising that historians of religion have conceptualized its influence in early human states and civilizations as a result of its health implications.[65]

The biological as well as cultural and social evolutionary history of psychiatric phenomena cannot be understood without taking religion into account. It is partly based on the power that religious practices and institutions have had in contributing to improvement of diverse behaviours that encompass sickness in all its varieties including psychiatric condition. A conception of psychiatric material that encompasses diverse disturbances of 'mental' and 'somatic' experience and behaviour helps to visualize why and how religious practices and institutions of Indian peoples constitute an important component of their way of conceptualizing and handling psychiatric conditions.

INDIAN SOCIETIES IN GENERAL CONTEXT

India and South Asia more generally has served as a theatre for virtually all types of societies that span the continuum of social and cultural com-

[64] Fabrega 2002b.

[65] Avalos 1995, 1999.

plexity.[66] Indeed, the subcontinent has been the home of nomadic, pastoral tribal societies and has served as a base for the evolution of settled, autonomous agricultural tribes, principalities, and aggregations of tribes, kingdoms, states, empires, and then civilizations.[67] According to Stein, human communities (presumably of ancient foragers or hunter-gatherers) inhabited India as far back as 500,000 years ago. Kennedy reviews archeological findings of various prehistoric populations and critically analyzes the claims of various theories that have been proposed about the ancestry of the human species in South Asia. For such communities only physical remains exist and they provide scant information about the social fabric and consciousness of prehistoric communities.[68]

Drawing on assumptions from archeology and cultural anthropology about India and about social and cultural evolution more generally, one can presume that the earliest communities consisted of hunter-gatherers that slowly developed a sedentary lifestyle and produced their own food. Following the advent of pastoral and agricultural societies, and superimposed on an agrarian peasant base, there emerged larger groups, kingdoms, principalities, and politico-economic structures that met the criteria for tribes, chiefdoms, and statehood. Populations found in such societies, which varied as to size, social complexity, and regional influence, concentrated into towns and cities, some of them large, complex, and wielding a powerful control over the hinterland.

During the prehistoric period there were probably isolated pockets of nomadic hunter-gatherers who in social organization and culture resembled the foragers of even earlier millennia. In ancient India, and no doubt during the classical and medieval periods as well, there were wild tribes that were not always connected to ancient principalities and kingdoms.[69] In the centuries BCE in the main areas of habitation – for example, the northwest region and the Ganges plain of north-central India and, somewhat later, in the south – large, complex states developed with strong central bureaucracies having a broad influence over the surrounding territory. If one had information about the social characteris-

---

[66] Stein 1998; Fried 1967; Johnson and Earle 2000; Shaffer and Lichtenstein 1995; Meadow 1996; Kennedy 2000.

[67] R. S. Sharma 1983, 1991, 1995; Jha 1998; Thapar 2002.

[68] Kennedy 1995, 2000.

[69] Guha 1999.

tics of ancient and medieval societies of different size and scope, it would be possible to visualize the full sweep of cultural evolution in the subcontinent, since virtually all types of societies have existed there.[70] The period when the Vedas were transcribed is assumed to be around 1500 BCE. The significance and implications of an Aryan invasion is a deeply contested topic.[71] Aryan peoples are alleged to have invaded from the west and settled in North India. Their religion and culture provided the basis of the civilization of India as we know it today.

HINDUISM, THE CASTE SYSTEM, AND GENDER IN INDIAN SOCIETIES

Preliminary considerations

In India, family, village, a hierarchical social order, religious practices, and region are key markers in terms of which individuals construe themselves and define their social circumstances. The ancient Indo-Iranian language is generally referred to as oldest of the so-called Indo-European languages. It comprises two main groups, Indo-Aryan or Indic and the Iranian. It is the former that is of concern for purposes of understanding the civilization that evolved in the Indian subcontinent. However, little is known with certainty about the archeology and much less about the social life and cultural history of the period preceding the advent of the Indo-Aryan speaking people. To a large extent this state of uncertainty also applies to the Indo-Aryans. The set of beliefs, social imperatives and practices exemplified in the literature and texts of Indo-Aryans, generally referred to as the Vedas and constituting the intellectual foundation of Indian culture and civilization, provide a glimpse of the importance of religion in shaping thought worlds and habit patterns. However, locating and dating the locales where this took place is not possible.[72]

With respect to India, Kennedy construes societies comprising the Harappan achievement or grade (whether 'civilization' is an appropriate

---

[70] Fried 1967; Sanderson 1990, 1995a, 1995b; Johnson and Earle 2000; Sahlins 1972; Gellner 1988; Service 1975.

[71] Kochhar 2000; Kennedy 1995, 2000; Thapar 2002.

[72] Kennedy 1995, 2000; Kochhar 2000.

descriptor is disputed) as protohistoric rather than prehistoric.[73] This is the case because:

> It represents the transitional zone between ancient cultures for which no literary record exists or at present remains undeciphered and the beginning of written history ... Proto-historic archeology is the study of peoples who were living after historic records began but who themselves did not have writing.[74]

For all intents and purposes, then, the social life of traditional India and along with this a formulation of its history about mental illness and mental health practices begins with the Vedas.

A brief resume of the history of Hinduism

Michaels provides a useful scheme for visualizing the spread of religious history in India by positing six epochs, each of which exemplifies a more or less distinctive literature.[75] These include: (1) up to 1750 BCE termed pre-Vedic and for which there does not exist a body of texts; (2) Vedic religions, spreading from 1750 to 500 BCE, and including an early Vedic epoch (1750 BCE to 1200 BCE) comprised by the *Ṛgveda* I–IX and framed in Indo-Aryan languages, Vedic dialect; middle Vedic from 1200 BCE onwards associated with *Ṛgveda* X, *Sāmaveda*, mantras of *Yajurveda*, and earliest Brāhmaṇa parts of *Atharvaveda*; and late Vedic from 900 BCE onwards consisting of *Yajurveda* prose and older prose of Upanishads, the Brāhmaṇas, Āraṇyakas, and perhaps the Śrautasūtras; (3) the epoch of ascetic reformism stretching from 500 BCE to 200 BCE and described as post-Buddhist literature such as the Pali canon, metrical Upanishads, Dharmasūtras, and other special *sūtras* including the grammar of Pāṇini; (4) the period of classical Hinduism from 200 BCE to 1100 CE, starting around 200 BCE with the great epics (*Mahābhārata* and *Rāmāyaṇa*), *The Laws of Manu*, and early philosophical and scientific works; starting around 100 CE with the *Carakasaṃhitā* and continuing on with a number of medieval writings involving philosophical systems, narrative literature, Puranas, Tantras, early sectarian literature and collection of fairy

[73] Kennedy 2000.

[74] Kennedy 2000: 290–291.

[75] Michaels 2004.

tales and works of history; (5) the period of sectarian Hinduism from 1100 to 1850 involving sacred poetry and writing of sects (Yoga, *Saṃnyāsa*-Upanishads and religious historiography); and finally (6) the epoch of modern Hinduism from 1850 onwards with vernacular poetry, novels, dramas and Anglo-Indian literature ending with comics, films, and television as media.

The literature produced in these periods, only a small portion of which is listed here, provides an incremental body of ideas and beliefs that gave and still continues to give shape to religious practices and institutions in the subcontinent. It starts with the Vedas, includes philosophical and soteriolgical writings, the epics and related popular writings of the medieval period, and includes the sacred stories and poetry of the sectarian epoch. In totality, Hinduism provides the foundation for what Biardeau describes as the anthropology of Indian civilization.[76] Details of the religious and cultural anthropology, also termed cultural psychology, of Indian peoples and their influence on psychiatric phenomena is taken up later in this and subsequent chapters. The powerful influence and scope of Hindu religion is what needs emphasis presently.

The scope of Hinduism's influence on human psychology

The people of the subcontinent can be conceptualized as having their ideas and beliefs, modes of experiencing the world and their place in it, the organization of society, the life career of an individual, social relationships with family and group mates, values and ethics, sense of worldly and otherworldly placement, and the scheme in the structure and cycles of time formed and fashioned by the religious, spiritual, and moral world-view exemplified by Hinduism. A distinctive cosmology and cosmogony endows social life with a distinctive sense of belonging and ontology, the individual forming a small part of an endless space and limitless time that keeps changing as a sacred order which in turn governs and gives meaning to cosmos, mundane social life, and individual considered as a repository of a sacred inner being that longs for and needs to connect with the Universal Being that orders all. This is how Flood describes the significance of what he terms the cosmical identifications or homologies represented in the hymn of the cosmic man, *Puruṣasūkta*, found in a late text of the *Ṛgveda*:

---

[76] Biardeau 1989.

> This important hymn shows that the hierarchical, hereditary social groups [*varṇas*] were part of the structure of the cosmos. If the cosmos was in some sense sacred, then so was society which manifested its hierarchical order. Moreover, this order is reflected in sacrifice and in the hierarchical structure of the body ... The social and individual bodies were reflections of each other, and both were part of the larger structure of body of the cosmos. This integration of society and cosmos, of body and society, is the sacred order or law (*ṛta*) of the universe, which is eternal and unchanging, brought to life in Vedic ritual, expressed in the songs of the Vedic seers, and elucidated in the Brāhmaṇas.[77]

In the everyday mundane world of life, death, work, obligations, caste restrictions, and sacrifice, sons honour their dead ancestors by means of myriad of rituals performed by Brahmins. These function as a form of identification and substitution between the dead and the living, further articulating the place of the individual in the scheme of worldly and otherworldly life. Rituals honour and pay homage to ancestors, thereby conferring a form of deity on them and at the same time the rituals serve as symbols of the immortality of those who do the honouring. In addition, a strict schedule of successive rituals mark the rites of passage of the twice-born, namely, those who are initiated as traditional Hindus and allowed to study the Vedas and to enter the four life cycle ending with a possibility for renunciation.[78]

Hinduism and the system of social organization in India

Hinduism includes a determination of the way peoples are divided into groups and in their degree of purity, value, and standards of social relations. These groupings are variously classified as the four *varṇas*, as adumbrated in the Vedas, and later as castes and sub-castes as per the popular literatures. Hinduism and the caste system in particular have been described as two sets of yarns that interweave to form the texture of Indian culture and civilization. Just as it is simplistic to conceptualize Indian culture as distinct from its religion, so is it simplistic to discuss religion in isolation from the organization of social relations in real communities of the subcontinent. The Vedas, following the writings on morality and law, and onto the epics and Puranas describe an amalgam

---

[77] Flood 1996: 49.

[78] Fuller 1992.

of religion, spirituality, morality, and social relations as exemplified in the myriad of castes and sub-castes. Central tenets of Hindu religious philosophy, for example, rebirth or *saṃsāra*, the effects of deeds done by an individual determining one's position in the next birth or karma, sin or *pāpa*, merit or *puṇya*, salvation or *mokṣa*, and morality or *dharma*, are incorporated into and made sense of in terms of the caste system which is viewed as a natural correlate of the order inherent in the Aryan way of life.[79] In the Hindu world-view, the construct of *dharma* is of overwhelming importance. It covers not only the propriety of behaviour in a society structured on the basis of caste, but also how such behaviour corresponds to and upholds the order inherent in the cosmos and the importance of ritual actions in all of this, all of which are taken up later.[80] With respect to caste per se, an important consideration involves ideas of pollution and purity, which are central to the Hindu construction of the social world and of the self.[81] Yet, as the epochs proposed by Michaels suggest, it is very difficult to define Hinduism, since there are no common beliefs or institutions – no church, no shared dogma, central organization, or bureaucracy – that distinguishes Hindus from other peoples.[82] Certain basic ideas are widespread and basic to the cultural psychology of India. These include, for example, the authority of the Vedas, a cosmogony and cosmology that places the individual in a scheme that encompasses the universe and cycles of time, everyday social obligations towards family, tribe, caste and king, ancestor worship, the theory of rebirth and debts incurred as karmic burdens, and a possibility for liberation and release afforded inner concentration on philosophical ideas and by Bhakti. devotional practices in relation to beliefs about major deities like Shiva and Vishnu and countless other gods and goddesses. These elements of religion are not found in all periods of Indian social and cultural history. Rather, they are thought to begin during a particular epoch and thereafter extend forward into succeeding ones (ancestor worship and the importance of the sacrificial fire during the Vedic period, ideas of reincarnation and systems for recording kinship

---

[79] Flood 1996; Michaels 2004.

[80] Halbfass 1988.

[81] Ghurye 1952; Srinivas 1962, 1976; Dumont 1970; Brockington 1996; Quigley 2003; Fuller 1992. For additional aspects of personhood, see Marriott 1955a, 1955b, 1990.

[82] Michaels 2004. Aspects of personhood, see Marriott 1955a, 1955b, 1990.

[82] Michaels 2004.

during the epoch of ascetic reformism) when they are elaborated and modified. Yet, it is hardly possible to become a Hindu except through birth into one of the castes. However, even here there are exceptions, for while caste is fundamental to Hindu beliefs and practices, it is in practice moderated and modulated by its interaction with the religious ideologies of Islam, Christianity, Sikhism and other faiths. Some communities and religious groups even disparage or reject social distinctions based on caste.

In its spread across the subcontinent, Hindu orthodoxy incorporated many groups. Hinduism is not only highly complex but also rich in contradictions. While it has a bias towards pantheism, there exist many deities that are worshipped for a variety of reasons and in a seemingly competitive way. A deity who is worshipped in one group takes precedence over others. Stories from one sacred book are sometimes used to prove the superiority over another. Henotheism, the belief in one god without claiming that he is the only god, is found in the two mains sects. For example, Shaivites may regard Shiva as superior to other gods, and especially to Vishnu, his chief rival, and whereas the converse is the case with Vaishnavites. In the final analysis, however, the dominant or most popular gods of Hinduism (Shiva and Vishnu) are really manifestations of the supreme *Brahman* (neuter).

> Hindus do not regard these different beliefs as mutually contradictory, and theologians reconcile them by making each view of God relative to a particular stage of growth and temperament, individual or collective; ... we find here ... the ability of Hinduism to accommodate different views of God, while at the same time no doubt is left as to which is the truer view.[83]

Brahmanic ideas regarding ritual and custom, central to exemplification of caste, form the core of Hinduism. They are integral to how the various social groups govern their lives, define themselves in comparison to those lower or higher in the hierarchy, and try to change their rank. These ideas have spread virtually all around the subcontinent, not only among Hindus but also among outlying tribes as these incorporate into settled villages. Thus, Hindu social order is highly stratified, made up of a high number of small groups (castes and subcastes) that compete

---

[83] Srinivas 1962: 148.

with one another and give rise to disputes in village affairs.[84] Adopting the customs and way of life of a higher group is often the best way to raising ones position in the hierarchy. This social equation applied to all the castes except the highest. Consequently, it meant that the Brahmanic standards of behaviour spread among all Hindus.

While the three axes of power in the caste system are rules of conduct in relation to ritual observances, economic success, and political influence, and while power in one sphere usually carries over into power in the others, a change in a group's relative standing frequently involves the interaction of all three spheres. In this process of change, basic rules of conduct and habitual ways of thinking, feeling, and behaving that are rooted in Hinduism, as formulated ultimately in the Brahmanic way of life as written into moral and legal codes, invariably come into play. Codes of conduct emphasize caste obligations and chart a life cycle consisting of four stages, that of student, householder, forest dweller, and renunciation). While emphasis on the theme of obligation, denial, abnegation, and renunciation is common in theoretical studies of Indian culture, Madan has drawn attention to the importance and dynamism of the householder's fullness of life.[85]

Family, tribe, and sectarian affiliation

Cultural anthropologists and historians emphasize that there are several other influences shaping ideas, belief, world-view, and social behaviour. These included a large extended family based on two means of coordinating descent and social relations – the *sāpiṇḍya* blood kinship system and the genealogical, fictional *gotra* system – the community marked by the village, and less so, one's region, and later, starting during the epoch of classical Hinduism, the influence deriving from sectarian association. While renunciation and retreat are important cultural themes, a great part of the power and influence that caste and religion have on the person is played out within the family. Rituals that articulate such overlapping influences are realized in observances within a family context. It is in relation to other families, caste and non-caste, that social conduct is regulated and validated. Behaviour between the sexes, and gender dif-

---

[84] Beidelman 1959.

[85] W. N. Brown 1966; Madan 1987.

ferences in identity, power, and social roles, afford one way of appreciating family influences.

Caste is typically regarded by social scientists as the most striking feature of Hindu society. However, according to psychoanalysts, it is the patrilineal extended family and the structure of kinship relations within it that orders the context and sets the predominant tone of social relations in Hindu society.[86] Personal, social, and economic status is established and played out in through rigidly specified hierarchical relations taking place in the male and age-dominated extended family. Male-oriented hierarchy is exemplified in the control of family resources, with elder males making the decisions and women playing a deferential and subordinate role. Such patterns are of predominant influence in village settings, but obtain also in urban settings and among educated persons who are more influenced by Western beliefs and attitudes regarding the individual.[87]

In a practical sense, power, influence, and lines of authority that exemplify the corporate structure of the Indian extended family govern how individuals feel towards and speak to one another, how their obligations and entitlements are, how decisions are made by elders, and how resources are to be apportioned. While age and maleness operate as determining factors in formal, practical, economic, and intra-marital relations, in the area of ritual practices, religious behaviour, and participation in festivals and pilgrimages, females are said to be more influential. Women are said to play a more covert role in arranging marriages.

Families constantly strive to enhance their rank and reputation within their caste. Strict rules are maintained about keeping family concerns private so as not to undermine its reputation. Alliances and connections with other families are used to enhance the status and reputation of a family; for example, in arranging for the marriage of sons and daughters. Achieving higher rank within one's caste, at all levels of the hierarchy, is an extremely important motivation. Relations between castes are perceived and enacted in terms of stipulations set forth by *dharma*. However, appropriate behaviour is not dictated by unchanging norms but is greatly influenced by specific contexts involving hierarchical relationships. What a person's *dharma* entails is influenced by family norms and customs that have in some way to mesh with *jāti*. Appropri-

[86] Kakar 1981; Roland 1988.

[87] Roland 1988.

ate, morally acceptable behaviour is modified by special circumstances (the inner nature of participants) and specifics of time and place. Correct behaviour in social contexts determines a family's self-respect and honour. Feelings of shame come to the fore when social observances are not met.

Social relations as gendered phenomena

The Indian subcontinent, Mandelbaum emphasizes, has been and in many respects continues to be the home of highly patriarchal societies.[88] In them men wield enormous social, religious, and economic influence, whereas women are comparatively disadvantaged. Men have had more power and authority than women, and older men more power than younger men. Only men enjoyed formal and property rights. In traditional India, the two sexes had different spheres of social activity within the household. In northern India in particular, women were limited (if not confined) to the home and were restrained, passive, veiled in public places, and their social relations strictly controlled. A woman's conduct directly affected the family honour of the men closest to her. In a narrow sense, the purdah refers to specific traits of physical covering and spatial enclosures affecting women, but in a broader sense the term includes the beliefs and values associated with the correct behaviour of women, restrictions on their movements outside the household and the requirements for their respectful and deferential demeanour within the home.[89] In general, men expected deference from women, and the legendary devotion of the wife was regarded as a central value of family life in India. Women did not eat with men; they prepared the meal and served the men before eating. A wife walked behind her husband on the street and avoided addressing him by his personal name, because this may have seemed disrespectful. Women were enjoined to adhere to the scriptural ideal of *pativratā*, one who conforms to her husband's will and authority in all respects. Mandelbaum points out that, even in contemporary times, villagers may know little of scripture or the meaning of this particular term yet adhere to the ideal of submissive female behaviour as a matter of course.[90]

---

[88] Mandelbaum 1970, 1988.

[89] Mandelbaum 1988.

[90] Mandelbaum 1970.

Mandelbaum is emphatic in underscoring conflicts in the important relationship between a mother and a son's wife that, as later discussion will make clear, often contribute to significant emotional distress and behavioural disaffection in newly married, often relatively young females. A female's transfer to the household of her husband may be associated with much emotional pain and subsequent loneliness, as she is virtually powerless under the command of her new mother-in-law. This can occasion considerable emotional conflict. Imposition of discipline and control and gradual resistance to this is legendary. As she matures and acquires more confidence, and especially if and when she produces a son, she is less likely to give in to her mother-in-law's demands. At this time, but even earlier of course, quarrels and escalating acrimony and tension are common occurrences.

> A young wife, pushed to desperation, may take extreme measures. In Senapur village near Banares she may become possessed by an evil spirit ... Among the Havik Brahmins of Mysore she may similarly fall prey to malevolent intrusion, or she may starve herself or attempt suicide ... Throughout village India, instances are graphically told of women who drowned themselves in wells.[91]

The influence of these relationships on mental and emotional functioning is taken up later.[92] However, it is well to emphasize here that definitions, expectations, and justifications of male–female relationships are elements that feed into and partly order Indian (cultural) psychology. Such tenets are as binding, unyielding, and as punishing as the one reviewed earlier pertaining to sub-caste and caste relationships.

Michaels, on the other hand, when discussing 'the situation of the woman' paints a more sanguine picture.[93] He acknowledges that the beginning of a marriage may seem to represent a 'pure tragedy' for the new wife and that women in India are generally 'often inconspicuous, surrounded by silence' and highlighted for unusual circumstances (a virgin worshipped as a goddess, a widow who allows herself to be immolated following her husband's death).

> But this exotic perspective too easily loses sight of the fact that it is precisely women in India who uphold traditions, not as architects of

---

[91] Mandelbaum 1970: 90, n. 3.

[92] See Chapters 6 and 9.

[93] Michaels 2004.

> the historically significant temples, and seldom as authors or artists, but in their everyday practices, their religious life, their language, their songs, and their life style, which is formative of the cultural habits.[94]

Caste membership influences greatly the social and ritual behaviour of men and women as it does ordinary social relationships. Whether considered in a logical, scriptural, or structural sense (as *varṇa*) or as a reflection of occupational groupings (*jāti*), caste membership influences family life and particularly the relations between the sexes. Mandelbaum reports that emphasis on stipulations of caste is usually a woman's own affair. She is more insistent in maintaining domestic purity than her husband. He indicates:

> Among the Rajputs of Khalapur, men commonly eat meat, but wives will not. The men must cook their own meat on separate hearths because the women will not touch it or have their kitchens defiled by it ... In South India I have known of women of vegetarian sections of the Badaga of the Nilgiri Hills, who were married to men of non-vegetarian sections. Although among the Badagas as among most other Indian villages, a bride is socially assimilated into her husband's household, these brides do not give up their purer diet. And when such a bride becomes first lady of the house, no meat is ever cooked in her kitchen. If her husband and sons want to eat meat, they must cook it themselves, outside.[95]

Historical factors influencing relations between the sexes

Stein discusses the historical background of male–female differences in social position and behaviour. He indicates that in the early Vedic period caste development was weak, so that intermarriage between groups was common. Both boys and girls were educated, and both memorized the hymns and were properly instructed in their meaning. Hymns make reference to female and male seers, and the former were equal to or exceeded the latter in number, influence and/or level of ascetic pursuits. The texts narrate dialogues in which both sexes have speaking roles. Females may have actually composed some hymns. Women were not barred from public speaking.[96]

---

[94] Michaels 2004: 125.

[95] Mandelbaum 1970: 89.

[96] Stein 1998.

Many of the restrictions placed on females that are classically associated with Indian culture, Stein emphasizes, were not present during the early Vedic period. For example, females could inherit property, could marry when sexually mature and could choose a husband, daughters could take the place of sons in some rituals, and some widows could remarry. Nevertheless, it was understood that for women the purpose of marriage was to produce sons who were needed to perform funeral rites and sacrifices for ancestors. Wives were also subordinate to their husband. In popular literature women are often depicted as sexual creatures that divert men from their ascetic and moral duties. Stein makes speaks forcefully about the decline of female status in the late classical era.

> By the later Vedic period, moreover, the rot had set in and the *Brāhmaṇas* displayed both the curse of caste and the misogyny that was to increase, pervading and disfiguring Indian society up to the present.[97]

As Stein points out, women occupied a complex and sometimes anomalous position in the two major heterodoxies of early India, Buddhism and Jainism. According to a legend, the Buddha rebuked his aunt, who had been his wet nurse, on three occasions when she inquired as to whether women could participate in a mendicant order. He had to be persuaded by his chivalrous follower Ananda of the appropriateness of including women among those who could attain release from rebirth and later wearily agreed to women's ordination. However, the status of women, in both Buddhism and Jainism, particularly on the issue of female salvation, was and remains controversial and highly contested.

Like Stein, Sharma also addresses the historical bases of male–female differences in social position. He indicates that in sacred texts women were bracketed with *śūdras*, the lowest *varṇa,* and also with property. They had virtually no share in inheritance. Texts pertaining to social conduct (*The Laws of Manu*) declare women and *śūdra*s not only servile forever, but also that along with slaves they had no rights to property, particularly landed property. However, women could receive and retain gifts and presents (movable property) given by their relations, but, in actuality, only women of favoured classes could take advantage of such a provision. Sharma indicates that in later times women were regarded as items of property, being treated as chattel in ancient texts.

---

[97] Stein 1998: 58.

> Such passages abound in texts belonging to Gupta and post-Gupta times, and their number goes on increasing in early medieval literature. It therefore appears that the subjection of women, particularly those belonging to upper classes or *varṇas*, become complete in early medieval times.[98]

Stein notes that the advent of Islamic influence during the medieval period was a factor contributing to the further devaluation of women in Indian society.

Kakar, on the basis of his experiences as a practicing psychoanalyst, addresses the psychological aspects of female and male identity.[99] He emphasizes the consistent marked preference for sons all over India, as well as the warmth, intimacy, and relaxed affection of the mother-daughter bond. He points out that preference for a son 'is as old as Indian society itself'. It is hoped, and presented in Vedic verse, that sons will be followed by sons, 'never by females'.

> A prayer in the *Atharvaveda* adds a touch of malice: 'the birth of a girl, grant it elsewhere, here grant a son' ... The ancient Pumsavana rite, still performed over pregnant women in traditional Hindu households, is designed to elicit the birth of a male infant and to magically change the sex of the unborn child if it be a female.[100]

Kakar emphasizes that because of religious precepts there are valid ritual and economic reasons for the preference for males in Indian society and these serve to explain and essentially institutionalize the value of males and patriarchy. Sons are crucial in the performance of many sacraments and rituals, particularly after death of parents and the well-being of their souls. Furthermore, a daughter constitutes a significant expense. She will never contribute to the family and her marriage requires giving up part of family resources as per the institution of dowry. Many poor families incur major debts in seeking a good marriage for their daughter.[101]

---

[98] R. S. Sharma 1995: 95.

[99] Kakar 1981.

[100] Kakar 1981: 57–58.

[101] Kakar 1981.

Comment

Unequal status and the relations between the sexes are important to understanding the fault lines in the social structure. Requirements and expectations coming to bear differentially in men and women create strains and tensions. The social conflicts that follow can, in vulnerable individuals, lead to syndromes that represent psychiatric conditions as these have been construed. Moreover, gender differences and tensions will clearly influence how such episodes are played out. Different syndromes and conditions described in the medical classics and actual clinical pictures encountered in local, folk contexts of mental health practice and care can be expected to consist of and play out in distinctive attires coloured by gender differences. For example, women usually show higher prevalence rates in epidemiological surveys, and spirit-caused sicknesses (described in Caraka's medical classic) appear generally to be more common in females as per cases discussed in Opler, general medical anthropological lore, and the findings of Indian psychiatrists studying traditional villages and populations found in temples.[102]

Family relations and gender differences in conventions and standards of behaviour within the family and mirrored in community settings need to be visualized through the windows of the caste system and that of prevailing religious orientation. Mandelbaum, a cultural anthropologist, describes family and community life, while Kakar, a psychoanalyst, not surprisingly analyses aspects of personality functioning and emotional expression with an emphasis on unconscious factors and the role of basic cultural, ultimately religious, traditions. Both (especially Kakar) discuss behaviour in relation to scriptural authority, ideals of conduct found in classic narrative poems and the Puranas, and common sayings derived from fairy tales and folklore. The relationship between India's symbolic heritage and cultural psychology pertain not only to women but obviously also to men. Behavioural differences between the sexes associated with intimacy, sexuality, responsibility to elders, and competition between the sexes in many areas of family and community life are shown to be related to the common stock of inherited sacred traditions of Hinduism. This is the picture painted by countless ethnographers and by those who have analyzed intra-psychic, unconscious processes and found them to be a blend of the influences of caste, relig-

[102] Opler 1958; Fabrega 1974.

ion, family life dynamics, and differences in experience and behaviour between the two sexes.[103]

In summary, Hinduism and the caste system are the two basic, but interrelated, frameworks of community life in India. Together they define the Indian's social consciousness and sense of social reality. Attitudes, values, and prescriptions for social behaviour are dramatically different between males and females, as well as among the castes that make up the social hierarchy of villages, towns, and cities. Through the complementary influences of Hinduism and caste, individuals are virtually indoctrinated into a world-view that fuses social obligation, morality, spirituality, self-appraisal, and a sense of cosmological, existential placement. These factors determine and individual's behaviour within the family and community. The joint operation of these two influences affects whether a person feels contented and socially and morally worthy. Conversely, under adverse circumstances they can also evoke negative emotions and responses, such as envy, guilt, shame, demoralization, hopelessness, competitiveness, and a sense of social isolation from family and community. Much of what constitute manifestations of psychiatric conditions, then, is bound up with and shaped by the implications of world-views and moral, spiritual injunctions woven into the fabric of the caste system and exemplified in religious sects, including Buddhism and Jainism. Understandably, there are differences between the sexes owing to different rearing experiences, personality dynamics, social expectations, and general position in the culture.

ON THE PERIODIZATION OF INDIAN HISTORY

Introduction

The epochs of Hinduism proposed by Michaels discussed earlier serves one well when the focus is on beliefs and documents of Indian religion and their continuity and change across time. I will continue to refer to them when appropriate. However, there is a need for an encompassing framework that covers broader aspects of cultural and evolutionary change.

---

[103] Hoch 1961a, 1961b, 1993.

Many schemas that describe periods of Indian history have been proposed and are in use. These include, as an example, ancient, medieval, and modern, and Hindu, Muslim, and British. Such schemas are not global and highly general but create problems as well. They are inherently chronological, suggesting distinct periods and factors that correspond to transitions and change. While historical periods should ideally point to salient and distinctive characteristics, they should also capture the structure of social and political life during any one period, independent of strict chronology and political developments. There is also the problem that concepts and principles pertaining to historical periods are based on European models and these imperfectly describe developments in India. I will rely on a schema based on the chronology and discussion provided by Kulke and Rothermund, followed by Thapar and the formulation presented by Chattopadhyaya.[104]

Proto-history and the pre-Vedic phase

What one can denominate as a *pre-Hindu phase* includes the Stone Ages and pre- and early Iron Age as well as developments in the northwest of India associated with societies often thought to comprise a civilization (Indus Valley civilization) that reached maturity during the third millennium BCE and produced the urban complexes of Mohenjo-Daro, Harappa. Kennedy terms this period 'proto-history' and Michaels, the first 'pre-Vedic' epoch.[105] Well before Harappan societies reached their maturity, the subcontinent was home to hunter-gatherers and pastoralists that in time settled into villages in the northwest of India. The origins of farming and herding ways of life in the northwest of India are in the Iranian plateau.[106] The region to the east of this plateau, covering areas of western Pakistan and further east into northwest India has yielded numerous archeological finds of agricultural communities displaying distinctive ceramic styles; for example, Baluchistan in western Pakistan approximately 4500 BCE and Mehrgarh, 250 kilometres northwest of Mohenjo-Daro, and area of uninterrupted occupation of approximately 4500 years until about 2300 BCE.[107] At the latter site 'it was

---

[104] Kulke and Rothermund 1986; Thapar 2002; B. Chattopadhyaya 1994.

[105] Kennedy 2000; Michaels 2004.

[106] Kennedy 2000.

[107] Kochhar 2000; Kennedy 2000.

possible for the first time to convincingly define an 'aceramic' Neolithic development in South Asia'.[108] The dating and characteristics of these farming communities, the relationship of their population to that of Harappa and Mohenjo-Daro, and then to the advent of the Aryans, traditionally thought to have invaded or migrated into northwest India during the first centuries of the second millennium BCE is much disputed. The dominant influence of the Aryans in the subcontinent is assumed to have taken place during the period that followed the dissolution of the Harappan Civilization, beginning around 1700 BCE.

Early or ancient India

The period stretching from mid to late second millennium BCE to the second part of the first millennium comprises an *early historical phase* featured by traditional village/farming and nomadic pastoralism. Michaels describes this as the period when the Vedas became predominant.[109] Here, Vedic spiritual and social political beliefs, injunctions, and practice governed everyday life under the hegemony of Brahmins. The relative stability and order of the earlier centuries of ancient India changed during the last half of the first millennium BCE. Thapar and Flood describes this as a phase that involved chiefdoms and kingdoms (Magadha and Kośala).[110] In general, the first millennium BCE is associated with the rise to prominence of the Brahmanic traditions that involved ritual and the doctrine of renunciation and in time became associated with an ideology of sacral kingship developed in the context of the growth of kingdoms.[111]

The tail end of the early historical phase, particularly the latter half of the first millennium BCE, represents a period of much social, political, economic, intellectual, and religious change and conflict, marked by the advent of heterodox sects of Buddhism and Jainism and other groups which elaborated on methods of contemplation and renunciation. Starting around 500 BCE and continuing into the first millennium of the Common Era, there took place an expansion of sectarian spirituality and worship of many deities. While never fading out of the religious picture,

[108] Shaffer and Lichtenstein 1995: 130.
[109] Michaels 2004.
[110] Thapar 2002; Flood 1996.
[111] Flood 1996.

Vedic sacrifice and the orthodox Brahmanic tradition gave way to worshipping of deities (*pūjā*), a way of communicating love or devotion (*bhakti*). This eventually became the dominant practice of Hinduism.

> Bhakti to a personal God (*Bhagavān*) or Goddess (*Bhagavatī*), became a central, all-pervasive movement. This growth of Hindu theism and devotionalism is reflected in the Sanskrit narrative tradition of the Epics (*itihāsa*), in mythological and ritual treatises known as the Purāṇas, and in devotional poetry in vernacular languages, particularly Tamil.[112]

From about 800 to 400 BCE textual material indicates that new ideologies involving spirituality and self-cultivation have emerged. Knowledge is now given precedence over action and detachment from the mundane world is pursued by means of ascetic practices or *tapas*, celibacy, poverty and begging, and methodologies for training the mind or Yoga. This way of life comprises the renouncer or *śramaṇa* traditions that, while having roots in earlier writings of the Vedas (argued by some as even pre-Vedic times), are elaborated more systematically especially in the Upanishads. The characteristics of such traditions involve pursuit of methods of training the mind. This can be conceptualized as an internalization of the external ritual practices as propounded by Brahmans.

> The purpose of such training is the cultivation of altered or higher states of consciousness, which will culminate in the blissful mystical experience of final liberation from the bonds of action and rebirth.[113]

This is also the period when urbanization becomes an important characteristic of Indian social life in which the tradition of renunciation flourished. Towns and cities under protection of royalty promoted and expanded trade and allowed some personal freedom and social mobility. Cities also brought into play, may in fact have been conditioned by, bureaucracies and institutions of social control that eroded and undermined traditional life as exemplified in village communities. While the latter still contained by far the majority of the population, the intellectual and social life of cities exerted a significant acculturative force in the hinterland. Cities attracted migrants and created demands for crafts and skilled labour. While India has traditionally connected persons to fam-

[112] Flood 1996: 103.

[113] Flood 1996: 81.

ily, community, and caste, creating as it were *social* as compared to *individual* selves, trade, opportunities for advancement via work in temples and government bureaucracies, commercialization and specialization of occupations instilled and encouraged a spirit of self-pursuit which, not surprisingly, resonated with individualistic opportunities provided by the methods of liberation of the renouncer traditions which, in turn, appealed to and attracted residents. One can surmise that this erosion of traditional beliefs and social practices associated with urbanization had psychologically destabilizing effects. City life, then, brought with it changes in thought worlds and habit patterns that, while rewarding and beneficial, undermined traditions and also, one can add, produced social disruption.

Cities were centres of economic activity and places of residence for members of the governing classes and elite, political showpieces, as it were, for tribal chiefdoms and kingdoms. Thus, India as a collection of more or less cohesive social, cultural, and political entities started to take a recognizable shape by the middle and especially latter half of the first millennium BCE. This is the period during which the doctrine of *ahiṃsā* (the ban on harming living creatures) began to take shape. The Vedic religion stipulated that life requires force (*hiṃsā*) against others because everything exists and is created for sacrifice. This stipulation was elaborated into a detailed theory proposed by the Brahmans, members of the highest social class or *varṇa*. At the end of the early historical phase, the theory about non-killing was elaborated and resulted in the practice of vegetarianism.

> It is the time when the immigration of the Indo-Aryans into the northern and middle Ganges plain came to an end, thus completing the transition from the previous semi-nomadic life to a settled existence. Instead of big cattle herds, the individual cow was now emphasized as an animal for pulling carts and plowing. Other factors relating to the change include ... year round agriculture, the emergence of the first kingdoms, the right to inherited real estate, the expansion of trade, and the development of a permanent and caste stratified social order.[114]

[114] Michaels 2004: 153.

Social organization and life in early India

Chiefdoms and kingdoms eventually crystallized into highly bureaucratized and centralized states with true cities centred on the Gangetic Plain. This took place between 600 to 300 BCE.[115] The period stretching into the last half of the first millennium BCE corresponds roughly to Michaels' third epoch of ascetic reformism. Historians indicate that during this first urbanization phase of India there did not exist a hierarchy of power based on landholding, a feature of later periods. In the administration of the state, a wide range of officials and heads of government agencies associated with a kingdom compensated economically and with land grants. Economically, this phase was featured by societies in which showed a monetized economy, long-distance foreign trade, urbanization, and the presence of diverse merchants and crafts. Socially, this is the period when the *varṇa* system of social groupings is presumed to have developed and consolidated. This consisted of *brāhmaṇas, kṣatriyas, vaiśyas*, and the *śūdras*. Slavery of various forms was also a feature of this historical period. The early classical period covers the Mauryan and Gupta empires and reached its high watermark in the third to fourth centuries CE. Michaels terms the period from 200 BCE until 1200 CE the epoch of classical Hinduism.

Foundations of India's medieval quest for immortality and perfect health

In any conceptualization of a people's indigenous psychiatry one naturally searches within recorded traditions of medicine and religion since these are available as texts that are open to examination. In later chapters this material will be taken up in detail. What bears emphasis here is that in mapping India's indigenous psychiatry and its understanding of psychiatric conditions onto its social terrain one seeks a full representation of psychiatric phenomena. Orthodox, establishment, the 'great' and Sanskritic intellectual tradition (of medicine, spirituality) is of paramount importance, of course. It suffuses the thought worlds and habit patterns of the elite, Brahmin classes. And to an indeterminate extent it also suffuses the thought worlds of the twice-born castes. But Indian

[115] Some cultural historians of India mark these dates as delineating the beginnings of a subsequent historical period one can call early classical India.

peoples' thought worlds and habits in areas of health and wellbeing – including mental health and related practices – are only partially illuminated through the analysis of the orthodoxy of the privileged few. One seeks to understand concerns and directives about health and wellbeing that cover the entire intellectual and social landscape. Whether beliefs and practices with mental health implications when viewed in social, cultural context are thought to target bodily or spiritual concerns is irrelevant since *from the vantage point of the outside analyst* the cultural psychological effects of such practices, viewed from without the society, importantly cover mental health and can be ameliorative of manifestations of psychiatric conditions in vulnerable individuals.

Beliefs and practices captured by notions of Tantrism, alchemy, Yoga, and Siddha medicine, and related local popular religions as well as more orthodox Hindu sects represent an influential set of doctrines and movements that gained prominence in later medieval India.[116] Even in the India of today, strands of these traditions are not only alive and well, but pulsating with energy and worldwide influence and generally encompassed within Yoga.[117] All of these traditions of thought and practice initially had and still have as their focus, although not all of them equally, control of the human body and transmutation of its material substrates. They involved practices of austerity, meditation, sexual cultivation, chemical/herbal ingestion, and mental exercise that aimed towards perfected states of body, sexual potency and ideally immortality.

This amalgam of sects, philosophies, soteriological programs, and social and bodily practices is not only important in an intellectual and medical sense (including as a component of India's indigenous psychiatry). It is also important because of its eventual *wide popular appeal to the masses*, starting around 600 CE and flowering during the tenth to eleventh centuries.[118] In its social manifestations, yogic/tantric practices related to Siddha functioned not merely as a system of 'alternative medicine' (to Vedic medicine and Ayurveda), but much more broadly, resembling a counterculture and very much a heterodox tradition that competed with and was reviled and condemned by Brahmanic establishment. The influence of these heterodoxies as cults or communities in

[116] White 1996.

[117] Fields 2001; De Michelis 2004; Alter 2004.

[118] White 1996.

themselves and the spill-over of their ideas and practices into other more established sectarian denominations is what renders important component of the indigenous psychiatry of India throughout its history.

The roots of the quest for perfect health and immortality are to be found in the Vedas and an important legacy of these texts involve ideas, beliefs, and practices exemplified in the Tantrism, Yoga, alchemy, and the alchemy of medieval India. Vedic rituals of sacrifice to the gods involving offerings of fire and *soma* and purification through water benefited the sacrificer and were thought to save him from death, or at least to the perfect life span of 100 years. Agni the god of fire and Soma the god of oblation constituted central elements of the ritual. Early on, Soma the god was associated with the moon by a series of symbolic analogies with vital fluids, both animal and vegetal (*rasa*), as well as rain and waters that functioned as revivifying agents having medicinal properties or remedies for ailments of man.

> The potential of the fluid oblation could not be activated or realized without the dynamic of sacrifice, which also brought two other elements into play: these were fire (*agni*), divinized as Agni, the god of fire; and wind (*vāyu*), the active element of exchange, which conveyed the essence of the sacrificial oblation from the world of humans to the divine realm. This trinity of elements (and gods) was complemented by another conceptual triad, which served and continues to serve as the ground for the network of homologies and analogies that are the framework of the entire sweep of Indian symbol systems. This is the triad constituted by the human being (microcosm), the mediating mechanism of the sacrifice (mesocosm), and the universe as a whole (macrocosm) -which is also conceived as the body of the universal man or god.[119]

The mechanism of the sacrifice eventually took precedence over the sacrificer and the god on whose behalf the ritual was enacted. By the tenth through eighth century BCE the Brāhmaṇas, or Priestly Books of revelation, emphasize that the ritual of sacrifice is of dominating importance in the functioning and maintenance of order in the universe. The triad of fluid–fire–wind becomes influential in medical yogic writings involving constructs about digestion, metabolism, bodily regeneration, human conception, and alchemical models of the reactions involving the chemistry of mercury and sulphur. These elements later come to

[119] White 1996: 11–12.

function in an important way to ideas about the laboratory transmutation of metals and transubstantiation of the material body. White points out that early Vedic ideas about the interplay of the human, divine, and the sacrificial included a mineral and fluid dimension. Ideas pertaining to

> fluid, semen, moon, and mercury on the one hand, and fire, blood, sun, and sulphur on the other – always mediated by the active element of air, wind, and breath – have interacted with one another through the 'sacrificial' structure of microcosm-mesocosm-macrocosm, across a dozen interpenetrating ritual and belief systems and some three thousand years of cultural history.[120]

Early medieval India

Some, but by no means all, historians identify the period following what I have termed early ancient India as involving the beginnings of medieval India. They place the early medieval period roughly from 500 to 1200 CE. On the other hand, Michaels terms the centuries between 200 BCE and 1100 CE as classical India and Thapar dispenses with a nominal classification altogether.[121] To her, the expanse of history up to approximately 1300 CE comprises early India. Instead of nominal descriptors of periods, Thapar in her book on early India relies on salient social, cultural and political characteristics and developments as indicators:

States and Cities of the Indo Gangetic plain	600–300 BCE
Emergence of empire: Mauryan India	321–185 BCE
Rise of the mercantile community	200 BCE–300 CE
Threshold times	300–700 CE
The peninsula: establishing regional kingdoms	500–900 CE
The peninsula: establishing authorities and structures	900–1300 CE

During the early centuries of the Common Era and continuing into the early medieval era major developments involving the intellectual, spiritual, religious, and also the frankly medical life of India took place. These changes are construed here as having an important influence on approaches to mental health and mental health practice; in other words, of laying the groundwork of ideas and practices that comprised what

[120] White 1996: 16.

[121] Michaels 2004; Thapar 2002.

earlier was termed the indigenous psychiatry of India. For example, the core writings of Caraka, a major figure and body of work involving Ayurveda, India's science of health promotion and medicine, were compiled sometime during the early centuries of the Common Era. India's epics (*Mahābhārata, Rāmāyaṇa*), foundational popular works of literature that also embody, reinforce, and elaborate on virtually all of Hinduism's beliefs and practices, were also formulated and compiled during the early medieval era, perhaps even earlier, as surmised by Michaels.

The *Bhagavadgītā*, a central narrative contained within the *Mahābhārata* epic, tells about the advice offered the Prince Arjuna by his charioteer friend Krishna (incarnation of god Vishnu) on the eve of a great epic battle. The god counsels on the importance of correct, responsible action, in accordance with moral obligations, in the mists of imperatives that presage a large number of casualties. The *Bhagavadgītā* expounds and elaborates on ideas that had already been presented in the Upanishads, namely, ideas involving how individuals could transmute Vedic rituals of sacrifice into procedures or rituals of inner concentration and effort that had the effect of purification. Essentially, the *Bhagavadgītā* discusses the different practices of Yoga, specifically, how individuals can achieve immortality and liberation. Dialogues between Arjuna and Krishna in the story, with the god taking a commanding tutorial and educational position or role, describe *haṭhayoga* (the forceful Yoga of the physical body), *jñānayoga* (the Yoga of knowledge or wisdom), *bhaktiyoga* (the Yoga of devotion), *karmayoga* (the Yoga of action), and *mantrayoga* (the Yoga of the recitation of sound). Krishna expounds on the qualities of action that can bring liberation and spiritual cleansings:

> The secret to *karma-yoga* lies not in the action itself but rather in the state or quality of the human mind which gives rise to the action. If the mind is pure ... having sacrificed all selfish or inordinate desire ... and attachment ... to the self-centred fruit of deeds, it cannot be defiled by actions even as they are engaged in daily life ... The mind that remains 'ever' yet alert, lucid and free of the stain of attachment born of ignorance (*avidyā*), allows for a mode of selfless non-covetous action (*niṣkāma karma*) through which salvation is attained.[122]

The *Bhagavadgītā* promises the individual a condition of liberation or state of Being, essentially a silencing of woes, worries, emotional disaf-

---

[122] Whicher 1998: 23.

fections, and suffering, through a union with the Lord. Krishna sees Yoga as involving a complete alignment of an individual's everyday mundane and practical life with the divine Being, namely, Krishna himself. In foregoing attachments in the way of personal feelings, desires, and expectations, the practitioner's mind and life are purified and illuminated.

> Since the Lord is everywhere and in everything, the idea of renouncing or extricating the world in order to seek salvation or enlightenment ultimately becomes superfluous. What one needs to do is to cultivate a higher intelligence (*buddhi*), the 'eye of wisdom' (*jñāna-cakṣus*) in order to discern the purity of Being, the knower, and thereby attain liberation.[123]

Ideas foundational to medieval heterodox traditions involving physical and mental health are found in Vedic sacrifices and myths. Early during the medieval era, one of the (perhaps most) significant schools of Yoga took shape, that ordinarily referred to as classical Yoga and propounded by Patañjali (around 200 CE), also termed *yogadarśana*, and classified as one of the six *darśana*s or philosophical traditions of orthodox Brahmanic Hinduism which also included Nyāya, Vaiśeṣika, Sāṃkhya, Pūrva Mīmāṃsā, and Vedānta (Uttara Mīmāṃsā). Well into the medieval period and in conjunction with various schools of Yoga, and arguably inseparable from them, there developed traditions of Tantra, alchemy, and Siddha medicine.[124] As reviewed earlier, these and related traditions were largely concerned with bringing about changes in the body via regimes of physical fitness, meditation, and alchemical medicinals. They involved breathing and postures, techniques involving control of attention and concentration, control of physiological processes, actual transmutation of the material condition of the body via chemical/herbal preparations, and the harnessing of inner 'serpents' of spiritual and sexual energy located deep within the lower abdomen and lifting them upwards through designated channels into the base of the calvarium or brain.

While the body, viewed in analytical terms, may have served as the model or template through and in terms of which the various practices of Yoga realized their effects, the mental health implications of these

---

[123] Whicher 1998: 24.

[124] White 1996.

procedures and devotional practices should not be ignored. The goals sought and the effects achieved had the effect of improving a sense of emotional as well as bodily wellbeing and instilling a sense of empowerment. Specialist adepts and yogin practitioners, no doubt many of them renouncers and ascetics, probably comprised a small proportion of the population. In this sense, those with higher levels of experience with and success in attaining the goals of cleansing, transmutation and perfection of body and associated states of blissful liberation cannot be said to represent a characteristic of all segments of the Indian population. The spread of these ideas to common people of the lower classes and castes and their incorporation into the devotional and sectarian religious groups that comprised popular religion was already discussed. In addition, it is important to realize that expert yogins also functioned as spiritual, moral teachers and preceptors (gurus) to interested members of the general populace, in addition to their role as priests of the various sects of Hinduism. Thus, in this respect, the benefits associated with various practices of Yoga and especially those associated with Bhakti devotionalism, classically articulated in the *Bhagavadgītā* but reinforced and contextualized in all walks of life through all of the epics and the popular Puranas, had a pervasive effect in affecting the morale and wellbeing in all segments of the population.

During the early medieval period, the much contested Indian feudalism is said to have prevailed. The period that followed this, associated with the advent of Muslim invasion and dynasties, continues as the *medieval period* proper. And some historian would include here the period of British influence although one can term the latter the *early modern and modern* periods. In general, medieval India is associated with regional ruling dynasties, the diminution of a money influence and the existence of a natural economy, the growth of regional languages, literature and art; and the proliferation of sects and castes.

Historians have given considerable social and cultural importance to what is described here as the early medieval period of Indian history. It is held to contrast sharply with the previous early and classical period and set the stage for development of many characteristics of Hindu society and culture that extended into the period of foreign invasion and rule by the Muslims and the British. Chattopadhyaya singles out as important the following characteristics of early medieval India: (1) political decentralization coming into play in the post-Gupta period, with many states, the presence of many semi-autonomous rulers each associated with a hierarchically organized set of *rājapuruṣas* employed by royal courts; (2) the emergence of landed intermediaries, hallmark of Indian feudalism that came into play with the disintegration and decentralization of state authority and major changes in the structure of agrarian relations. This development is linked causally to the practice of land grants given to either Brahmins or religious establishments, although there also existed secular 'fief-holders' and 'free-holders'; (3) market and money economies gave way to self-sufficient villages as units of production; extensive rural networks were prominent, occurring in association with the breakdown of urban centres and commercial networks; all of this led to

> the practice of remuneration in land as a substitute for cash, to the migration of different social groups to rural areas, to an agrarian expansion, and to the crystalization in rural society of *jajmānī* relationships (relationships of interdependence between patrons and clients).[125]

An additional feature of the early medieval period was (4) subjection of the peasantry, analogized to serfdom, which entailed their immobility, forced labour, the payment of exorbitantly high revenues, and a high degree of stratification; (5) the proliferation of the *varṇa* system into many occupational castes. Associated with this came the demarcation of many social groups engaging in labour and that were perceived as impure and dealt with as polluted. The latter coalesced into the formation of the degraded rank of untouchables; and 6) the establishment of a feudal ideology and culture, a key characteristic of which is said to be manifested in the structure of religious associations and behaviours linked to the highly influential Bhakti movement (whose roots are in the earlier Vedic period) that included a local, popular, more or less folk development involving mystical states of religious devotion and loyalty. The pattern of religious devotion associated with Bhakti is regarded as paralleling and having been modelled on the feudal relationship of overlordship. In association with these social and cultural developments, urbane cosmopolitan culture is said to have declined, and with this came a degeneration of feudal courtly culture and degenerate forms of religious practices in princely courts associated with tantric rituals.

---

[125] B. Chattopadhyaya 1994: 11.

Chattopadhyaya sees the early medieval period as pivotal in the development of modern India. The scale of 'certain fundamental changes' within the local levels of polity is what he singles out as unique for this period. It is responsible for the creation of India's regional societies and cultures that 'emerge with distinct personalities'. However, while distinctive in virtually all respects, regional societies also managed to resonate with, personify, and contribute to national, pan Indian characteristics. The social and symbolic correspondence yet individualism of different regions involve such things as social stratification, belief and ideology, codes of social conduct, culture, and religion. He indicates that developments that coalesced during the early medieval period were repeated in subsequent eras and implies that even during periods of later foreign domination basic characteristics of medievalism persisted in areas and removed from centres of power and governance.

Chattopadhyaya and other historians of India emphasize the breakdown of the civilizational matrix of the earlier classical period of India and see in this something resembling a social crisis.[126] This is what accounts for the sharp contrast between the early historical and classical compared to the early medieval periods. The breakdown and crisis came about in association with such things as foreign invasions, expansion in the scale of land grants, consequent domination and exploitation of peasants, defeat and appropriation of tribes and their incorporation into peasant communities, the formation of a hierarchical society, and the decline of urban civilization anyone of which leads to, as Chattopadhyaya terms it, 'tears in the fabric of early historical social order'. The formation of state societies during the early medieval period is singled out for special emphasis: in association with social and political changes, important ideological developments are emphasized, such as the worship through Bhakti of god as a Lord situated in a temple and the re-emergence of *śakti* or the goddess on the Indian religious scene. In fact, Chattopadhyaya draws on the writings of cultural historians who claim that during this period, the religion of the goddess becomes as important a part of the written record as the actual religion of god.

One can safely presume that the social tensions and crises that historians tell about – the period of ascetic reformism (500–200 BCE) and that of the early medieval period (500–1200 CE) – affected the morale, out-

---

[126] B. Chattopadhyaya 1994; Kulke and Rothermund 1986; R. S. Sharma 1983, 1991; Thapar 1984, 2002.

look, and pattern of social adjustment of residents of the communities of the corresponding historical periods. This was reflected in major changes in the structure and content of religious, philosophical, and soteriological thought. It suggests periods when the hegemony of Brahmins was threatened and they were forced to encompass competing social and religious claims. Traditional Brahmanic Hinduism proved insufficient and people modified and expanded their search for hope and meaning. Unstable and changing world-views and religious and spiritual beliefs created fluid emotional tonalities and need for stability and one can suggest that this contributed to emotional and behavioural disequilibria that in vulnerable individuals culminated in psychiatric conditions that required different modalities of mental health practices. During the earlier crisis, Vedic medicine was challenged by renunciant healers who roamed the countryside searching for and learning about sickness and medicinal products, a movement in the theory and practice of medicine that culminated in Ayurveda, India's indigenous scientific, academic medicine. By the time of the second crisis, Ayurveda had been compiled and there are suggestions that the branch of medicine addressing the category of *unmāda* (insanity or psychiatric conditions) may have expanded.

Fortunately, the early periods of Indian history are rich in political, literary, philosophical, medical, legal, and moral/religious documents pertaining to social conduct that allow one to obtain a reasonably detailed if abstract and idealized picture of the character of social life in the subcontinent. Sifting through these diverse literatures provides a baseline in terms of which one may appreciate the prevalence of problems of mental health and illness, all of which are covered later. By extrapolating from reported communal distress, social conflict, and shifting patterns of adjustment one can generalize about how populations fared and institutions managed to provide relief of emotional and behavioural disturbances.

The medieval period that followed the classical period and the great dynasties does not seem to have posed special problems regarding political history and general periodization. However, it does create difficulties regarding an understanding of social life, including aspects of sickness and problems of mental health, as affected by major social upheavals. The period is marked by the beginning of Islam and Muslim influence and their eventual rule. It is also the period when Yoga, Tantra, and alchemy differentiated as complex systems of philosophical and spiritual thought and practice. As discussed earlier, along with the advent of Siddha medicine one can for present purposes think of these traditions as involving medical and especially mental health healing practices. In other words, while all of these systems have roots in Vedic tenets and answer to independent social, economic, philosophical, and soteriological needs and imperatives they can also be viewed as systems that may have answered to the spiritual and mental health needs of segments of the population.

During the medieval era, the general influence of Muslim political control, religion, and general culture operate to produce an overriding compositional motif and harmony in historical accounts; and the dynasties presided over by various sultans and Mughal kings provide the variations of melody and rhythm that mark each segment of the medieval period in a more or less distinctive way. General historians of India concentrate on Hindu culture and society and for the period of Muslim rule give principal attention to questions of imperial expansion and wars, political happenings related to the governance of the provinces and regions of the empire, details of the life around the court, artistic and architectural developments, and general aspects of the religious tensions and conflicts.[127]

On the other hand, general accounts of the societies of Indian Muslims provide comparatively few details about the fabric of social life.[128] The overview of the Muslim impact in India of Ahmad is an example.[129] This covers themes that highlights areas of social life and culture replete with implications about experience and behaviour that one assumes could and would have had major impact on the outlook, conduct, and mental health of members of the population where Hindu–Muslim differences came into focus. To a social and cultural psychiatrist, social happenings and circumstances such as the ones analyzed by Ahmad would appear to have had a major impact on the prevalence of social tensions and conflicts, including problems of emotional experience and social behaviour that may have been reflected in the texture of psychiatric conditions. They would have certainly coloured their manifestations: the sharp ideological differences between Hindu and Muslim outlook, the imposition of Muslim political governance and the influence of

[127] Kulke and Rothermund 1986; Stein 1998; Thapar 2002.

[128] Mujeeb 1967; Ahmad 1964a.

[129] Ahmad 1964b.

associated institutions, the process of conversion and apostasy, iconoclasm and the resort to humiliation and violence, the shifting sands of religious and political tolerance and intolerance, and the various devices that articulated Hindu resistance.

However, it is general aspects of social life that are singled out, and how individuals and families may have coped with the tensions and conflicts is not discussed, but left entirely to the reader's imagination. The synthesis of the Indian Muslims provided by Mujeeb provides another frustrating example.[130] He describes the variety and complexity of religious affiliation, indeed, the changing mosaic of syncretism, that illustrate how elements of Hinduism and Islam could be patched together, including the complex patterns and shifts of religious conversion. Not only are elements of one religious outlook mixed or sewn together with that of another, but elements of the culture at large of a community and of its alleged religion also are conjoined in diverse ways such as to create a complex pastiche on the basis of which experience and behaviour is constructed. The picture painted by Mujeeb provides one with tantalizing hints of the potential impact that upheavals and conflicts in the social fabric would have had in the lives of individuals who, on a daily basis, were trapped by and confronted with conflicts of a political, social, and religious character. Yet, virtually no material is presented that bears directly on social life and even less, if anything, on how individuals coped, the costs imposed on social adjustment as a consequence of social tensions and conflicts, and much less on the consequences for health. Information about social life during the various periods of Indian history is taken up in the next chapter.

---

[130] Mujeeb 1967.

Chapter 3

Social Life in Historical Context

VEDIC PEOPLE

Civilization of India originated in the way of life of Indo-Aryan speakers who followed the Harappans. They are presumed to have entered the northwest and northern part of the subcontinent sometime during the second millennium BCE at a time when the grandeur of Harappan civilization had waned.[131] The myth of an Aryan invasion has figured prominently in the history and culture of India and the West. However, exactly what this invasion might have consisted of remains controversial.[132]

What is not controversial is that Vedic people came to command native indigenous populations and they superimposed ideological supremacy over them. Their culture, for example, beliefs, gods, rituals, and social practices, gained pre-eminence in the northwest part of the subcontinent later spreading eastwards. They are termed Vedic because their way of life is portrayed in India's sacred texts, namely, the four Vedas and numerous associated compilations that elaborated upon the significance of the rituals.[133]

The history, language, religion, political economy, and general culture of Vedic people, stretching from approximately 1500 to 500 BCE, is presumed to be represented in sacred compilations (termed *śruti* for revealed writings) about religion, rituals, and spiritual practices generally associated with Brahmanism. It is assumed that the material in this body of literature was passed on orally and centuries later put down in writing, subsequently amended and expanded. It is unclear exactly when Vedic writings were set down in writing and remains controversial. Later, perhaps starting during second half of the first millennium

---

[131] Thapar 2002; Kennedy 2000; Kochhar 2000.

[132] Kennedy 2000.

[133] Discussed later on in this chapter.

BCE, a number of traditional writings (termed *smṛti*, for tradition) were compiled. These included the two great Indian epics (*Mahābhārata* and *Rāmāyaṇa*), a large body of heroic tales and descriptions of social life termed the Puranas, various scientific texts, and codes of morality and law as these applied to various groupings of society termed the Dharmasūtras and Dharmaśāstras. These later compilations harked back to the Vedas, drew on some of their constructs and beliefs, and elaborated basic characteristics of Indian civilization. They evolved a distinctive world-view (perhaps hinted at in the Veda) encompassing religion, philosophy, morality, social organization and psychology. All of these topics are taken up in subsequent chapters.

In formulating aspects of Indian society and culture, it is useful to speak of the Vedic people as showing a culture dominated by Brahmanism and that which followed and grew out of it, embodied in ideas found in the epics and Puranas, as representing post-Vedic people, sometimes equated with the rise of Hindu culture and religions, or Hinduism.

HINDU THOUGHT WORLDS AND HABIT PATTERNS

The history of Vedic peoples is complex and a subject of continuing scholarship. The scriptures and ancillary writings suggest an early Vedic phase ending around 600 BCE. Social hierarchy and status distinctions were hallmarks of traditional India. The origins of the caste system are the subject of much contestation as are the essential features that hold the system together.[134] In the *Ṛgveda*, the earliest of the four Vedas, two social groups are described, namely, the *ārya*s which were dominant and generally equated with Brahmans, and the *dāsa*s. Political power and colour of skin may have constituted a basic classificatory variable. Next, three classes of society are mentioned, *brahman*, *kṣatra*, and *viś*: poet priests, warrior-chiefs, and common people, respectively. In later hymns involving the sacrifice of the Primeval Being, there is mention of four orders of society, given as *brāhmaṇa*, *rājanya*, *vaiśya*, and *śūdra*. These orders are said to emanate from the mouth, arms, and thighs, and the feet of the Creator, the respective anatomical segments symbolizing the relative power of the four hierarchically arranged orders over each

[134] Ghurye 1952; Kane 1990; Dumont 1970; Marriott 1976, 1990; Quigley 2003.

other. Thus the four orders of society are described as resting on myth and religion.

During the last half of the first millennium BCE when traditional literatures were compiled the four groupings of society are referred to as the four *varṇas*. The rationale for and the functions served by the *varṇas*, their role in the maintenance of social order, are further validated on grounds of purity and pollution as well as theological, philosophical, and occupational grounds. During this same period the system of four phases or stages of life, named *āśramas*, was institutionalized as an integral part of Brahmanic social structure. These referred to four alternate modes of religious living following the period of initiation (as born again or twice-born) into Vedic studies, passing from early learning of Vedas, proceeding to the householder phase and eventually to the phase of forest dweller and hermit involving retreat or renunciation of structured social life. The higher social class of Brahmins controlled religious practices and stood over the warrior and kingly class whose secular power they validated. They controlled religious services and access to groupings of gods associated with each of the original three social orders referred to earlier.[135]

Received documents portray the Vedic social life as aristocratic, hierarchical, and ritualistically controlling. The rationales for and characteristics of Indian castes are highly disputed. A common view is that a comparatively small but learned class of Brahmins held ultimate power by means of religious rituals and practices and articulated much of the ground rules of social life. The class of kings, warriors, and their respective administrators and underlings are said to have followed Brahmins in the social hierarchy. There followed a composite third class of farmers, artisans, and merchants. The social structure was anchored by what one may surmise was a large proportion of the population, namely, common folk, slaves, and later the class that was socially excluded or untouchable. *Śūdras* and other excluded and reviled groups had little if any official representation in the late religiously-based society of Vedic people.

It would appear that only the higher classes had access to official Vedic gods, under the auspices of Brahmin conducted rituals. For them, the undoing and healing of misfortune, including disease and problems of behaviour, was a focus of pleadings and prayers found in the

---

[135] Ghurye 1952.

Atharvaveda. Early texts of the latter involve magical poems along with rituals and social practices that were formulated by a priestly group and recorded in the Vedas. The role of these priests and their relevance to the medicine of the Vedic people is discussed later. In general, it is not clear what proportion of the population participated in rituals and what proportion was excluded. Each *varṇa* had its learned figures but it would appear that the top three were dependent of Brahmin priests for performance of important rituals. Essentially, in Vedic society and traditional Brahmanic theory of *dharma* the fourth *varṇa* and the so-called untouchable below it in the social hierarchy were conceptualized as marginal, polluted, and servile – as though dead, some have claimed – having no political or ideological representation in the social order.

During the second half of first millennium BCE there evolved significant modifications in the way of life of early Vedic peoples. This led to a different version of Indian thought world habit pattern,.and culture (cultural psychology). Many conceptualize this later or post-Vedic phase as marking the beginnings of traditional Hindu civilization as suggested in Chapter 1. It is associated with numerous changes in society and culture. Historical and political changes involve growth and evolution of kingdoms and states from earlier clans and tribes. Many tribal and forest peoples were incorporated and brought into the fold of caste society.[136] Economically, the number of occupations (often termed *jāti*s and resembling *varṇa*s in organization) increased and these were sharply differentiated not only as to occupation but also in terms of patterns of marriage, social functions as per each other and the dominant Brahmin group. *Jātis* came to embody castes. Village life continued to as the basic functional unit of life in the subcontinent, although major periods of urbanization have been described.[137] Intellectual changes in society and culture of post-Vedic people include, for example, the advent and rise to prominence of speculative thought (Upanishads) and the doctrine of individual self or soul and universal life principle; the rise of heterodox sects (Jainism and Buddhism), which challenged the hegemony of Brahmins in spiritual, philosophical, and religious matters; formulation of the doctrine of karma and rebirth, initially expounded by world renouncers and elaborated by heterodox religions; and then appropriation of much of this speculative literature by Brahmins, with a re-formulation of their

[136] Thapar 1984, 1997, 2002; R. S. Sharma 1983, 1991.

[137] R. S. Sharma 1983, 1991, 1995, 1996; Thapar 2002.

social power as based on degree of purity as exemplified in vegetarianism and non-violence or *ahiṃsā;* and formulation and promulgation under Brahmin auspices of strict social and moral codes of behaviour (*dharma*) that were applied to sense of identity and permeated vision of social life of members of the higher *varṇa*s and the numerous social castes that were encompassed by them, and possibly subcastes and grew out of them.

Traditional writings indicate that social behaviour among later Vedic and Hindu people was highly influenced by philosophy and religion. One may presume that at least the favoured classes, namely, the top three including especially the Brahmins, placed great store in ideas about the self and its relationship to metaphysical truths and the nature and creation of the universe. Speculative thought involved not only the nature of social reality and being, but also about the afterlife and the purpose and destiny of man, formulated in terms of doctrine of karma and the transmigration of the soul or self through numerous lifetimes in relation to merits and demerits inherited and added to or diminished by actions in any one lifetime.

The theory of obligation, morality and law described as *dharma* gained pre-eminence as early Hindu civilization took shape. In the Vedas the idea of *dharma* had a very broad and foundational meaning: it encompassed human (Aryan) psychology, social relations (in Aryan societies), and the order that originated (cosmogony), sustained, maintained, and protected the (Aryan) cosmos (via Vedic rituals). One can view *dharma* as exemplified in the worldly correspondence between health, wellbeing, social order, and relations between individuals (the micro- and mesocosm) and the relations of all of this with otherworldly phenomena having to do with what gave rise to and governed the way the cosmos worked (the macrocosm).[138] In its plural sense and verbal form *dharma* had agentive connotations: it referred to actions inherent in the cosmogony and maintenance of the universe as well as actions undertaken by individuals in the everyday life of social relations. As a noun, it denoted concrete specific acts (involving social relations, ritual) or abstract concomitants involving order, sustaining workings of things.

It is mainly the resonance of *dharma* in the (cultural) psychology and social relations that is given attention presently. Everyday social life was sanctioned and protected in terms of philosophical ideas about religious

---

[138] Halbfass 1988, 1991; Michaels 2004.

prayer, obligation, social morality, karmic justification of the *varṇas* and *jātis*, and forms of interaction among the various social groupings (rules involving marriage, commensality). This picture of Hindu society and culture took hold during the centuries just preceding the Common Era and is often termed Sanskritic, so as to signal its literate, complex, and intellectually formulated characteristics as captured in the early indigenous language of India; and sometimes it is termed the 'high' or 'great' tradition of India to signal its association with textual authority and in contrast to the 'small' or 'little' tradition of the village were non-Vedic, popular, folk beliefs were found jostling with ideas derived from the high Sanskritic tradition.

Life in each of the four major divisions of society, whether found in large villages, towns, or actual cities, was permeated by beliefs and values tied to the religious and philosophical truths of the culture. Misfortune was explained as an outcome of moral transgression against behavioural conventions that were stipulated in *dharma* and in terms of inherited karmic debts. To this day, such beliefs explain human misfortunes that include sickness and distress, although the primacy or salience of the theory of karma in everyday explanations varies.[139] In addition, there existed a body of less lofty, more practical, popular and folk beliefs about causes of misfortune, involving gods, ghosts, evil machinations involving sorcery for which divination and exorcism was resorted to. This feature of the 'little' tradition was no doubt expounded by pre-Vedic people and also brought forward by them from their own place of origin. The *Atharvaveda*, for example, consists of omens, beliefs involving demons, and related practices and may have been derived at least in part from folk, popular knowledge of indigenous people of the subcontinent. Many such popular, sometimes termed 'magical', beliefs and practices were inherent in the numerous tribes and communities of hunter-gatherers that existed in isolated regions of the subcontinent and that are still found in the subcontinent and termed 'tribal' peoples.

[139] Babb 1983.

TOWARD THE CLASSICAL ERA OF INDIAN CIVILIZATION

The great ancient Empire of the Mauryas (late fourth century BCE) marks the initial flowering of a dominant, morally and religiously governed polity in the subcontinent. The later Gupta Kingdom and Empire marks the high point of what is termed the classical period of Indian history. These dynasties are associated with central systems of politico-economic order and government in which ultimately sacred ideas about religion, morality, and duty were influential in coordinating and integrating social life. It was reflected through the system of social stratification involving castes, its hold over village and city life, and its theory about the conduct of social life and directives pertaining to the proper stages of life, as promoted by the higher castes. Until around 500 CE, the history of India, particularly as realized in the two ancient empires, was primarily that of the north.[140] The Mauryas and the Guptas did not have a direct impact on South India. In the millennium that followed, various kingdoms centred in the north, east, central (Deccan), and south of India competed for supremacy.

Hindu society and culture was a product of complex intellectual, religious, social, and political developments. During the early classical era, many factors consolidated and set the stage for continued growth. The world-view and religious tradition that gained pre-eminence during the classical period was continually reinforced and has retained its hold on the subcontinent. The philosophical religion of the Upanishads, the chief theological documents of ancient Hinduism that originated during the later Vedic period, gained in influence in 'orthodox' Hinduism and in the competing, heterodox religions of Buddhism and Jainism that emerged during the fifth century BCE. At first these were monastic religions that emphasized moderation, tolerance, nonviolence, and purification of thought via meditation on spiritual and moral verities, and eventually liberation from cycles of existence (*saṃsāra*) stemming from effects of actions taken in previous existence (*karma*). Some of the tenets of the heterodox religions were adopted by the many sects of Hinduism. In the latter, strict practices of meditation and bodily control gave way to emphasis and participation in love and devotion of god(s) as a means of obtaining liberations and salvation.

---

[140] Kulke and Rothermund 1986; Stein 1998; Thapar 2002.

The traditions of India (*smṛti*) consist of writings that are derived from the Vedas and exemplify its values in tales and accomplishments of legendary heroes. These include great epic poems, namely, the *Mahābhārata* and the *Rāmāyaṇa*, and the Puranas, ancient historical legends of a political as well as religious nature. These documents function as a repository of Hindu traditions and values. The Dharmaśāstras, a set of documents that propound moral rules of conduct involving castes and life stages, are also part of tradition and came into prominence after the Vedic age. During the medieval period, a literary and intellectual tradition in the Tamil language, especially poetry, emerged in southern India, later spreading throughout the subcontinent. With the passage of time, the early Vedic gods were appropriated and domesticated to concerns of local cults and sects. Rather than being solitary and controlled mainly by sacrificial rituals, they were often equated with one another and with local tutelary gods, and were appealed to for favours and protection. The doctrines that came to form Mahāyāna Buddhism developed a salvation creed that centred on saints or *bodhisattva*s to whom one prayed for assistance. The Bhakti movements of religious devotion and supplication came into prominence, eventually encouraging mystical practices and ecstatic states of consciousness among its devotees. All of these influences affected each other.

The mental health implications of the *Bhagavadgītā*, a narrative placed within one of the major epic poems of India, the *Mahābhārata*, is taken up in Chapters 6 and 8. Here, its cultural importance deserves emphasis. The content of the *Bhagavadgītā* is extremely influential in shaping the national character of India (its 'cultural psychology') and accelerating the development of the Bhakti or devotional aspect of Hinduism that is rooted in the Vedas but gained prominence later in the south, later spreading throughout India.[141] The story line of the Gītā synthesizes the pantheistic, theistic, and dualistic ideas found in the Upanishads by emphasizing faith in a personal god who is intensely concerned with questions of good and evil as well as human welfare. It identifies the three paths to God: that of knowledge (*jñāna*), of works (*karma*), and of love or devotion (*bhakti*). In this view, then, God is not only reached through a tradition of learning but also available to everyone, including those who are marginal and powerless in society, such as women and the lower castes. While the idea of devotional worship (*bhakti*) is found

[141] The psychiatric implications of *Bhagavadgītā* are taken up in Chapters 6 and 8.

in the Vedic hymns to the god Varuṇa and in *sūtras*, in the *Bhagavadgītā* it is given central importance. Since then the idea of Bhakti has come to have a central place in Hinduism for the population at large as well as for the intellectual community.

The social organization of an Indian society during the classical era, its social and religious institutions and its practitioners in charge of regulating behaviour in conformance to moral and spiritual values, can be likened to a cultural tapestry or fabric whose design told the narratives that motivated individuals and coloured their emotional aspirations and disaffections. In this fundamental sense, psychiatric phenomena are constituted of social and cultural material. As a social order, Brahmins evolved a dominant position in Indian communities as reflected in rituals of purification, validation of secular political rulers, promoters if not actual guardians of behaviour as enjoined in the Dharmaśāstras, and more generally in a structural sense through their domination of the caste structure. Their hegemony and power to control and coerce meant stress and strain for the lower orders. On the other hand, their role as intellectual leaders and social arbiters promised relief via rituals of purification and protection, procedures designed to allay suffering and distress and promote religious and medical healing.

The social and political position and influence of the Brahmin group, and principles sustaining Indian society generally, especially through the caste system and its moral justification, was a psychologically repressive and punitive influence on behaviour. At best, Hinduism and Brahmin power moulded and channelled social and psychological life towards spiritualized and highly moral, duty bound ways of being that were order maintaining, meaningful and fulfilling. At worst, it controlled, repressed and stultified behaviour and experience and, in the process of moulding social order in a spiritual ritualistic direction, constituted religion and a philosophical psychology as the appropriate channel and medium for the justification of successes and the expression of failures in the human drama. Individuals who could not match these expectations or who contravened conventions and standards became casualties and victims of the social system. Conditions of behavioural distress and dilapidation that resulted would have manifested signs and symptoms of mental illness, but configured in idioms that bore the stamp of Hindu values and world-views.

Scholars who examine Indian civilization in historical and anthropological context often rely on important symbols and meanings embodied in ancient texts. One of these is Sanskrit, the classical language of ancient texts that symbolizes essential Indian values and traditions. Sanskrit exemplifies much of what is inherently Indian and as a construct and metaphor has also been used to analyze how ancient native traditions and values have played out on the stage of Indian history. When used by anthropologists and historians, the idea of Sanskritization aims to analyze how ancient religious, philosophical, and medical ideas and values, initially framed in Sanskrit, have come to be modified and used in contemporary times.[142]

Srinivas in particular has used this construct and so have anthropologists of the Chicago school.[143] He argues that there was somewhat more mobility and change in caste society than might appear from the record. From his study of modern Indian communities, he suggests that the process of Sanskritization – here used to describe and make sense of attempts by caste groups, often successful, to raise themselves by adopting the behaviour and customs of higher castes and thus by 'passing' – may have also provided a means of social mobility in ancient times. Sanskritization alleviated the social tension posed by strict adherence to the principles of the caste system, the sense of a static, frozen, society that lead an essentially hopeless view of oneself and the world.[144]

ANCIENT INDIA AS A SETTING FOR PSYCHIATRIC PHENOMENA

Prior to the Vedic age, and putting aside Harappan societies, the subcontinent of India was populated by hunter-gatherers, and more or less typical agricultural and pastoral communities. Distinctive physical health profiles characterize hunter-gatherers and health generally worsens with the advent of larger settled societies. Such family-centred village societies were probably fairly egalitarian, with minimal social stratification. Other things being equal – ecological stress, access to adequate water supplies and sources of food – such societies tend to show gener-

[142] Staal 1963.

[143] Srinivas 1952, 1955, 1962, 1966, 1976. For further discussion of the Chicago school, see section on social change later in this chapter.

[144] Srinivas' ideas are taken up later in this chapter.

ally good physical health.[145] It does not appear that low levels of 'public health', if one can stretch this construct for such small communities, play a major role in compromising mental and emotional wellbeing. Political exploitation would have been comparatively weak, and social controls over appropriate, morally acceptable behaviour rested on inherited traditions and informal procedures of adjudication. Furthermore, hunter-gatherers (family-level societies) show comparative less social coercion and interpersonal strain that can contribute to psychiatric conditions in vulnerable individuals.[146]

During the advent of Vedic societies, which were large, agricultural, tribal, and organized as chiefdoms, one found a high degree of social stratification. With this came behavioural, interpersonal control and prevailing strictures regarding acceptable behaviour, which were promoted and enforced by higher castes and priests. The result would have been, one may presume, greater social strains and pressures that brought stress and possible disturbances of experience and disaffections of behaviour among the vulnerable. However, a countervailing influence would have been opportunities for spiritual participation in sacrifices that reinforced values inherent in moral and ethical codes and in religious rituals and practices all of which provided opportunities for psychological relief given exigencies of poverty, exploitation, and inevitable social tensions. The latter included familial, marital, moral, or religious strains and crises that would have included physiological malfunctions. These would figure as syndromes of sickness and would have been referred to and handled by local, popular medical practitioners, of which there were undoubtedly many kinds. Practitioners relied on religious, magical traditions as well as practical lore based on herbal preparations, diet, and the like. Individuals in whom problems of emotion, morale, and behavioural deviance predominated would have sought the help of non-medical healers; for example, wise persons, village headmen, and local priests and functionaries of religious sects, and spokespersons of cultural traditions.

Hallmarks of psychiatric conditions involve symptoms like anxiety, depression, obsessive ruminations and psychosis, as well as manifestations of physiological distress all of which are realized or expressed not

---

[145] Eaton and Eaton 1996.

[146] As one finds in societies featured by social stratifications and politically sanctioned power, discussed in Chapters 4 and 11.

as discrete abnormalities of pathology or malfunction (raw signs and symptoms) but in cultural attires about self and social reality. Besides ailments that referred to the body, local idiom of distress and disability from such conditions involved marital antagonisms, adultery, suspicions among neighbours, rivalries over land, or acts that contravened social, moral, and legal conventions. Disturbances of emotion and problems saturated with loss of morale stemming from such interpersonal tensions constituted an important idiom of distress for psychiatric conditions.[147] This means that such conditions, while obviously initially manifested in local, family settings, would also have been found in whatever establishments or institutions handled religious breeches and social-moral dilemmas as well as medical problems; in gatherings of village elders who were called upon to provide support and dispense care to the needy and to settle disputes; and in more formal settings were empowered to regulate and maintain social control and enforce sanctions.

This discussion implies that many varieties of psychiatric condition involved experiences and activities that may not have been interpreted in the community as illness, as revealing a mental or behavioural problem, or as a form of deviance or eccentricity. Rather, the condition was expressed in deviations or changes in expression of forms of experience and behaviour enjoined by the highly religious, moral, and philosophical psychology of Hinduism.[148] Nevertheless, if a hypothetical Indian psychiatrist, able to bridge the knowledge gulf between modern diagnosis and local language and meanings, were to visit the past, he or she would have no difficulty in spotting (diagnosing) victims of psychiatric conditions in social settings where grievances, distress, and sufferings were reviewed, where attempts were made to resolve social conflicts, and where decisions were made to repair tears or wounds in the social fabric. The literature in medical anthropology supports this generalization and there is no need to defend and support it here.[149]

Thapar and Sharma discuss the transition to the state, especially its evolving hierarchical system and religious traditions, during the most

[147] Case illustrations of such syndromes found in traditional settings of the India of today are presented and discussed in Chapter 5.

[148] Hindu cultural psychology is discussed in Chapter 9.

[149] Fabrega 1974, 1997. See later chapters for discussion.

pivotal period in the emergence of Hindu culture and society.[150] Thapar suggests that even the least favoured classes and castes were hierarchically structured; they may have included their own hereditary occupations and have insisted on close control over expertise. Members of these occupations would likely have included not only local medical healers per se of diverse orientation and level of expertise, but also many persons devoted to solving human problems and misfortunes that involved religious, moral or purely behavioural conflicts or events that produced psychological distress – some of which may have been psychopathology.

Writings of historians like Thapar and Sharma paint a broad picture of social life.[151] However, when examined in the light of cultural anthropological studies about life in contemporary traditional India, such writings provide a window into the possible causes, social emplacement, and mode of handling of psychiatric conditions, as well as other human problems, in ancient India.[152] Economic setbacks, loss of religious morale, tensions in caste relationships, family conflicts, marital breakdowns, and moral disaffections constitute the way problems of experience and behaviour are realized and communicated. This idiom of distress, which includes manifestations and awareness of bodily pain and malfunction, culturally understood, as well as emotional distress, is how psychiatric conditions originate, unfold, and play out in local settings. A socially stratified, hierarchical society exerts greater control, regulation, denigration, and exploitation of the lower echelons of society that can bring individual strains and stresses. Yet it also means additional layers of 'authorities' or knowledgeable others to whom families can turn for medical healing or adjudication of conflicts.[153] Finally, Sharma's description of sociological factors that involve strains in the populace devolving from political exploitation as well as poverty in general, and Thapar's observations about characteristics of local communities, both imply that social institutions were in place where religious authorities and priests along with medical practitioners would know their clients, or at least the kinds of psychological problems that were common in the community.[154]

---

[150] Thapar 1984, 2002; R. S. Sharma 1995, 1996.

[151] Thapar 2002.

[152] Marriott 1955a, 1955b; Srinivas 1966; Singer 1959, 1972; Singer and Cohn 1968; Marriott 1990.

[153] R. S. Sharma 1995.

[154] Thapar 2002.

Writings of Indian mental health specialists that will be reviewed later indicate that a form of social and cultural psychiatry was already being practiced in ancient Indian communities.[155] This 'psychiatry' would have been configured and expressed through local vocabularies of medical distress and personal suffering, framed in the cultural psychology and medical language of the society. Such a social, cultural psychiatry would have been similar in form, structure, and logic – although obviously different with respect to social and religious tenets – to what was found in other communities of antiquity.

The formation of a central state obviously means centralized social and political control and greater regulation of the population. All of this affects ideology, such as the definition of acceptable, correct, moral behaviour, and the medical policies affecting potential causes of sickness including mental illness. In India, this order seems to have been achieved by means of propaganda and outright control, through vigilant administrators and even spies, all of which penetrated into local communities. Policy directives taken in conjunction with social, ethnic, and religious differences all had the effect of creating more complex influences on how behaviour was interpreted and dealt with generally, particularly behavioural problems. Again, in a rough sense, this would have caused and influenced the distribution of psychiatric conditions.

Undoubtedly in India, as in all societies since prehistoric times, social problems and concerns would have been handled locally at the village level. Problems might have involved such infractions as theft, cattle trespass, negligence with fire, causing a public nuisance, or fouling the water supply; there would have been disputes over land, damage claims, and more intimate violations such as adultery. Such problems are endemic to any society and not necessarily in any of psychiatric importance. However some of them probably were accompanied or caused by mental illness. To repeat, villagers' cultural traditions and religious tenets would provide the social behavioural matrix in which conflicts were enacted; and power differentials among disputants arising from family status, lineage, size of landholdings, and access to other resources would all mesh together in the local politics of conflict resolution.

In addition to village settings and local institutions for social control, personnel of centres of political administration and corporate structures

---

[155] Balodhi 1986a, 1986b, 1987, 1991. See Chapters 11 and 12.

served as additional places where victims of psychiatric conditions would have been shunted to. They included, for example, local 'courts' or formal gatherings governed by state officials, or regional bodies composed of representatives of various villages where local agents of the state administration would have adjudicated conflicts. Most of the social problems dealt with by these political bodies, of course, would have simply involved individuals caught up in all sorts of social and economic conflicts in no way related to psychiatric conditions, although some would have been. Along with establishments where local folk, popular practitioners practiced medicine writ large, encompassing all varieties of physical and mental-emotional complaints, and where healers sought to address problems of social and psychological behaviour, these may have been the settings to which victims of psychiatric conditions would have been referred.

SIGNIFICANCE OF URBANIZATION FOR UNDERSTANDING PSYCHIATRIC PHENOMENA

Societies of the Indus Valley, most strikingly associated with the mature Harappans, clearly display the physical arrangement of dwellings, physical layout, and architectural features that are characteristic of cities. Viewed as a whole, one can infer that the population was comprised of a variety of artisans, craft specialists, bureaucrats, and priests/administrators, peasants who manned the land nearby that fed the rest of the population, and most importantly a large segment of impoverished residents and recent migrants from the hinterland who arrived to city in search of work and employed in menial and/or physically demanding work. City residents can be presumed to have been densely packed living in close proximity to each other. The population no doubt comprised Indo-Aryans, Dravidians, and other indigenous ethnic groups of the region. As emphasized by Kennedy, Meadow, and Shaffer and Lichtenstein, even before the advent of mature Harappans, the whole northwest region of India comprised a biologically and culturally related paleo-ethnic complex of peoples who were sedentary, agricultural, and concentrated in cities.[156] Following this proto- or prehistoric phase of

---

[156] Kennedy 2000; Meadow 1996; Shaffer and Lichtenstein 1995.

urbanization there took place growth of cities during the latter half of the first millennium BCE. Indeed as many as five or six major cities, capitals of major kingdoms, punctuated the Gangetic plains: Rājagṛha (Magadha), Vārāṇasī (Kāśī), Kauśāmbī (Vatsa), Śrāvastī (Kośala), and Champā (Aṅga). Another major city was Sāketa, although it was not a capital (Kośala).[157] From this period on, major cities were regular features of the Indian landscape and associated with empires, kingdom, and regional ruling centres of surrounding hinterland.[158] The establishment of cities in India marks a turning point not only in cultural, intellectual, and scientific development but also with respect to physical and psychological wellbeing of the population.

The cost of the Neolithic, the effects on health of population growth and development of agriculture and sedentary way of life have already been alluded to. Indeed, this topic will be discussed in more detail in the next chapter. Suffice it to say here that a hunter-gatherer way of life that in evolutionary context precede agriculture is generally associated with a lifestyle, pattern of nutrition, living arrangement, and epidemiological mix of distinct infectious diseases that add up to comparatively good health. It compares favourably with epidemiological profiles and health conditions of peoples living in settled, agricultural village level societies. Changes in nutrition, lifestyle, physical exercise, and infectious disease account for this. The advent of cities represents an additional physical health burden, not only from standpoint of distinct types of disease, but also with respect to level of morale, energy, and effects of crowded living conditions. All of these changes have major impact on emotional and behavioural dispositions and states of being that have psychiatric implications. In general, then, factors that contribute to interpersonal and social strife and physical disease become more prominent as towns and then cities develop and grow in size, become major centres of population, and eventually the hallmark of civilized life of early states like those of the Indus valley complex of societies and thereafter.[159]

---

[157] Kulke and Rothermund 1986.

[158] Thapar 2002.

[159] In addition to the significant health cost associated with the Neolithic revolution, which involved populations becoming sedentary, concentrated, with members in close contact with each other, and opportunities created for new infectious agents that were easily communicated. Although disputed, on balance disease becomes a more significant finding in skeletal remains of Neolithic peoples. Archeological skeletons more frequently display an increase evidence of infection and anaemia and dental markers point to periods of possible

Poorer general health and public health hazards in general were factors that contributed negatively to physical and psychological wellbeing in association with village and especially city life for the reasons indicated. In addition, purely as a social and political phenomenon, urbanization can safely be regarded as a major event in the history of psychiatric conditions and indigenous approaches to coping with their manifestations. Cities are the point of concentration of a number of demographic, public health, social, political, religious, and related cultural processes and changes that affected the stability, conduct, and wellbeing of peoples in a major way. Urbanization affected the prevalence and visibility of psychiatric conditions, the problems they posed, and how they were understood and dealt with.

The tragedies of disaster and calamity that cities of the Indus valley civilization exhibited to its residents were more numerous and more momentous than those found in the surrounding villages. The stage on which a city displays its problems is larger, multiform, and more abounding and awe-inspiring: it has expanded its capacity to captivate, challenge, entrap, and persistently disturb and worry people by the recurring scenes and plots of misery that it can display. Cities bore witness, visibly during life spans and experientially across them through memories of older persons, verbally transmitted lore, and to some extent reflected in documents, to the devastating effects that complexity of life could bring. The recurring possibility of community-wide devastation involving things like floods, banditry and theft, physical attack from the hinterland and warfare with competing city states, the possibility of forced participation in corvee [unpaid, forced] labour projects, contaminated water sources, high rates of infectious disease, crime, social divisiveness, malnutrition, epidemics, physical disability, fires, effects of agricultural blight and hunger, and regular and renewable regimes of political exploitation from within or without are among the kinds of generic factors that came with city life and that cast a pervasive net of insecurity, uncertainty, and potential social and psychological malaise.

---

poor health during childhood (M. N. Cohen 1989, 1998). Kennedy (1990: 73) has reconstructed the trauma, disease and lifeways of populations of the subcontinent:

> We conclude from study of the prehistoric skeletal record form South Asia that the socioeconomic transition from hunting-foraging to agricultural-herding practices demanded a significant biological cost, namely the introduction of new diseases maintained among individuals living in higher population densities of village and urban settings, and by nutritional stress relating to dietary deficiencies and arrest in the availability of nutrient resources.

Religion, in its orthodox Brahmanic forms involving ritual practices of diverse varieties, popular and sectarian Hinduism, and heterodox religious traditions such as Buddhism and Jainism provided beliefs and world-views that sustained, gave meaning, provided hope, and furnished the means (cults, rituals, and devotional practices) for coping with misfortune and disorder. Fuller provides a rich description of the way popular religious sects and cults surrounding local gods and goddess of village and sanctuaries function in everyday life in contemporary India.[160] While popular Hinduism and devotional practices undoubtedly are phenomena that would have been found among lower castes during the centuries preceding the Common Era, they are generally thought to have achieved prominence during the early medieval era at which time Buddhist influences were prominent, especially with respect to ways of casting spells and coping with ailments attributed to spirit attack and out-right possession.[161]

The existence of comparably large urban centres starting with the Indus valley and moving on from there to cities of the Gangetic plains and thereafter, when viewed from a general standpoint, represent a major transforming event in the social history of psychiatric phenomena in the subcontinent. Although strict archeological data is wanting, one can assume that in cities of pre-modern India there was a more or less elite if not priestly group having medical as well as religious functions. In addition, the cities themselves and villages in the surrounding hinterland included local, folk healers and practitioners that people turned to in times of sickness and that blended ideas about medicine with popular religion. Whether in northwest India BCE or in later cities to the east and thereafter during the Common Era, strictly construed Vedic medicine and mental health practices extended into the lower classes and indigenous people can be contested. However, one can have little doubt that popular, demonic, magical, and shamanistic practices of healing that targeted physical as well as mental health problems were displayed in abundance. Furthermore, the cities appear to have been large enough to concentrate psychiatric phenomena. The size, density, and relatively circumscribed perimeter of the cities means that there would have been enough cases of chronic, dilapidated conditions of mental illness to compel civic attention. Family members would have

[160] Fuller 1992.

[161] Strickmann 2002.

had principal responsibility of caring for the sick, including psychiatric conditions. In addition, there would have existed more formal ways of dealing with and confining chronic cases that posed social problems of order as per progressive behavioural dilapidation, violence and social divisiveness. However, because the system of law and governance in Harappan cities is not known, we have no information suggesting where persons regarded as psychotic, emotionally incapacitated, dangerous or violent were physically set apart, restrained and contained, possibly incarcerated. In general, in a society where practical politically motivated ideas surrounding governance and social control acquire influence on the collective conscience, psychiatric conditions, and other forms of social deviance (prostitution, theft, banditry) that are burdensome are viewed as social and civic problems. The plethora of writings involving duty, obligation, morality, philosophical psychology, cultivation of spiritual-religious way of life, condemnation of violence, emphasis on commensality and sexual norms of behaviour, caste relationships and the various legal texts and responsibility owed to king and his entourage all can be viewed as developments if not necessarily conditioned by life in towns and cities certainly at least influenced by the toxic effects of an urban environment. Religious and moral idioms may retain influence, but together with political considerations they forge practices and institutions for maintaining social order. A question needing clarification is the extent to which ancient Indian civilization, Harappan or pre-Vedic or even pre-Hindu, provided intellectual, politico-economic, and medical resources that served to incorporate and appropriate cases of mental illness in ways that healed victims, supported families and shielded communities burdened by them. Other factors that devolve from urban milieu as per psychiatric phenomena are discussed later.

THE SOCIAL FABRIC OF EARLY MEDIEVAL SOCIETIES

Introduction

Historians usually contend that from the seventh century BCE the subcontinent was seen as one whole complex civilization with a coherent system of political, ideological, economic, and cultural relations and institutions. The Vedic age and the classical period that followed saw the cultural dominance of the north, whereas during the medieval period southern societies began to participate in an important way in the evolution of Indian civilization. Many new religious practices arose and new cultural and literary traditions came into prominence in the south during this time.

Two characteristics of the late classical era that extended into the medieval period can be mentioned. States and smaller communities existed in a fairly balanced relationship, and lesser states were placed under the governance of dominant kingdoms or monarchies. Law enforcement was left in the hands of local groups and guild-like institutions, which implemented the law in conformity with local customs. Smaller, more compact political domains contributed to the definition of regional cultures and economies in India.

The ruler of a particular kingdom closely controlled religious institutions. Temples, set up either by the king or by powerful individuals who donated resources for shrines and buildings for housing the priests, became important destinations for pilgrims. Temples were centres not only for acts of devotion, communion, and prayer but also for healing and the relief of social and psychological problems. As a consequence, the temples served as nuclei for the emergence of urban complexes, and could become regional centres serving economic, administrative, religious and, to an indeterminate extent, healing or medical functions to people of the surrounding hinterland. This undoubtedly involved psychiatric conditions.

The medieval era saw the spread of field agriculture and a dominance of agrarian over pastoral interests. Despite an expansion of agriculture, however, urban complexes continued to be influential as commercial centres, particularly in the production of specialized commodity products and in nurturing town life that contributed to India's reputation as a country of elegance and wealth. Luxury products were marketed by merchants under the supervision of guilds, which also became influential in this age, in the surrounding centres of Southeast Asia and in China during the Tang Dynasty.

Changes during the early medieval period were associated with growth and consolidation of the status of the Brahmins. They were able to consolidate their social and political power as respected authorities in matters involving religion and morality through the performance of rituals. As recipients of large land grants and as administrators of the outlying temples that came in to prominence during this period, members of the Brahmin caste also exercised considerable influence in local affairs. Their allegiance to kings and princes was critical to their hold on political power.

Religious institutions

There were many complex religious developments during the medieval era. In general, they all grew out of and involved emphases and developments inherent in tenets and practices of the previous eras. Brahmin priests presided over sects that can almost be construed as forming a virtually new religion.[162] The establishment of Hindu sects involving the gods Shiva and Vishnu introduced a highly personalized, emotionally heightened kind of religious worship, often taking place in a group setting, referred to as Bhakti, or religious devotionalism. It arose in the south and spread to every part of India. Ever since the *Bhagavadgītā*, religious devotion has been an important force in Hinduism. In the north the Bhakti movement has been associated with Vishnu, especially his manifestation as Krishna, while in the south a deep Bhakti strain has been featured in the worship of both Shiva and Vishnu. Stemming from the schools of worship of these divinities was the idea of love (*anpu* in Tamil) toward god. A devotee oppressed by a sense of sin and unworthiness craved the grace (*kṛpā*) of god. Devotional practices gained in salience as compared to ritual mastery and with this went emphasis on the great epics and Puranas compared to Vedic manuals of sacrifice. The relatively simple and optimistic religion of the *Ṛgveda* had gradually come under the influence of the Brahmins, and with this the ritualism and lofty metaphysical speculations of the Upanishads. The Bhakti movement changed all this and featured a highly personalized yet concrete, prosaic world permeated by spirituality. This deepened and extended the strain of puritanism in Indian culture through its 'insistence on love of God as the most important thing in religion'.[163] The worship of gods and the legends of their influence in social life came to dominate as Hinduism acquired its distinctive shape. The medieval Bhakti literature even challenged the idea of inequality, with some sects said to have even recruited followers from several castes in their early evangelical phase. Stein summarizes the Bhakti movement in this way:

---

[162] Renou 1968; Zaehner 1962; Brockington 1996; Flood 2003.

[163] Srinivas 1966: 25.

> Temples were the palaces of reigning gods under the new worship, and inscriptions recorded the benefactions of kings and lesser lords, who were anxious to make visible their piety, and accordingly built shrines and granted vast lands, often whole villages, to Brahmans in recognition of [their] special role ... Nevertheless, even more important than stories of gods in Sanskrit, what fashioned the new faith was poetry that sang the praise of Shiva and Vishnu in demotic languages, beginning with Tamil and launching others on a trajectory into a rich literary outpouring.[164]

Intellectuals and the higher castes may have concentrated on the Upanishads, the *Bhagavadgītā*, and the writings and speculations of wise philosophers. But, this needs to be viewed in relation to local societies displaying different varieties of Sanskritization. Here is Srinivas' description of popular religion today:

> The ordinary man's religiosity has found expression in the punctilious observance of the rules of pollution and purity, in praying as required by family and caste tradition, in the performance of the elaborate rites of passage, in the celebration of calendrical festival, in undertaking fast and religious austerities, in the elaborate propitiation of dead ancestors and local deities, in listening to public reading of religious stories (*harikathā*), and in going on pilgrimages to sacred rivers and to the shrines of reputed deities. The astrologer is consulted at every crisis, and in the rural areas, and especially among the lower castes, the exorcist and the medium of the local deity are also resorted to. Features of the outer environment, including certain plants and animals, are regarded as sacred.[165]

These observations by a cultural anthropologist underscore the fact that religion permeates a Hindu's life at every point. It may also be taken to describe the existential outlook and tangible behavioural pursuits and rituals that came into prominence in the medieval period in relation to the emphasis on devotion and the emergence of the Bhakti movement.

The invigoration of Hinduism is a distinct feature of the medieval period. The great Brahmin philosopher Shankara (788–820 CE) renewed and systematized Vedānta philosophy, integrating and extending traditional Vedic ideas and incorporating important themes associated with Buddhism. He returned to the ancient Upanishads and provided com-

---

[164] Stein 1998: 98.

[165] Srinivas 1962: 159.

pelling explanations of release and salvation transcending those that had been originally articulated in Buddhism and Jainism. Shankara also mimicked the latter's institutions by establishing monasteries (*maṭhas*) as key institutions in many locations.[166] Shankara's system also provided scope for the more popular religious ideas prevalent during this period, thus combining ideas of orthodox Brahmanism and popular Hinduism. Besides making purely intellectual, ideological reforms, Shankara composed hymns in praise of Shiva in popular song forms that served as a cornerstone of the new emphasis on religious devotion.

Popular religious movements emerged that in many respects directly challenged orthodox Brahmanism. The Bhakti movement emphasized the love of God and lifelong devotion through ritual and prayer. The *bhakta*'s submission to the will of God became as important as right conduct was to Brahmanism. The Bhakti movement started in the sixth century CE in South India (Tamil Nadu), whence it spread to the rest of southern India and to the north. A rich religious literature is associated with a number of sects that spun out of the Bhakti movement in southern India. Devotional love and ritual meditative exercises that featured religious longing and seeking integration with the deity were salient characteristics of these popular sects. We will see later that altered states of consciousness, and indeed forms of religious ecstasy and even madness, were prominent features of Bhakti devotional groups. Many local sects were initially associated with the worship of sacred physical landmarks that were believed to emanate and to elicit powerful religious feelings and inspiration. In time, local village landmarks and settings evolved into local gods that became integrated and coordinated with subregional, regional, and national gods. Temples, as indicated earlier, also became important in this movement.

> Where once Buddhist and Jaina ideologies flourished, in part by providing a moral justification for the pragmatic values of merchants and moneyed men, as well as by providing an institutional framework that linked Buddhist and Jain monasteries with the high commerce of the age, these functions were now readily assumed by Hindu temples.[167]

---

[166] Stein 1998: 122.

[167] Stein 1998: 122.

THE LATE MEDIEVAL PERIOD

Muslim culture affected life in the subcontinent during two major periods that culminated in the establishment of the Sultanate of Delhi in 1192 and the Mughal Empire in 1526. Before this time, the northern part of India had been the target of numerous military invasions and expeditions by Muslim forces. From the time of the earliest Muslim conquests, religious tolerance was extended to Jews and Christians in recognition of the similarity of their traditions to Islam. However, pagans, polytheists, and idolaters, who would have included Hindus, posed a problem to Islamic rulers, but no serious, systematic attempt at mass conversion was ever instituted by any sultan or later Mughal emperor. Because the size and spread of the Hindu population rendered such a program unfeasible, toleration of Hindus and of their religion was an expedient option. They were offered a protected status and accommodated themselves to Muslim rule. This accommodation was acceptable because the caste structure of Indian communities had flexibly adjusted to political vicissitudes in the past: the contained, somewhat autonomous political organization of Hindu communities, which included a preservation of caste and its supporting devotional institutions, facilitated a balanced relationship in relation to distant Muslim hegemony.

Islamic authority and influence was more direct and controlling in the towns and cities of the Ganges plain and in parts of the Punjab and Bengal that were placed under military and civilian rulers, including judges and other wise men, of Muslim descent. Islam enjoyed success in Bengal partly because of its prevailing religious institutions. Merchants and artisans who had previously been adherents of Buddhism converted to Islam. Later in the period, Sufi mystics took to preaching a popular Islam in the eastern Ganges delta.

During the period of Mughal rule, there was a mass conversion to Islam among the peasants. This was not so much a result of state policy but of class differences between Bengali lords and the poor and degraded peasantry. As a general rule, writes Stein:

> Most Muslim converts continued to offer worship to the host of folk deities propitiated in the locality in which they lived, and most followed the rules of the castes into which they had been born. In this way Islamic practice itself was altered; ... converts stubbornly maintained many of the caste practices of their Hindu origins; ... customs associated with neighborhood and region flourished, and the persis-

tence of local and regional languages further defeated the development of an entirely unified Islamic community.[168]

SOCIAL CHANGE IN INDIA DURING THE MODERN PERIOD

General introduction

Cultural anthropology is concerned with whole societies, and social change is a staple theme in the discipline. Studying India from the standpoint of cultural anthropology, with an emphasis on changes associated with the modern period, dates from the early 1950s, when Srinivas' *Religion and Society among the Coorgs of South India* (1952) was published. Around that time, Robert Redfield and Milton Singer organized a seminar at the University of Chicago entitled 'Comparisons of Cultures: the Indian Village', which served as a takeoff for the anthropological study of large social structures. The seminar dealt with case histories of eight representative peasant communities of India. Redfield and Singer wrote the foreword to *Village India: Studies in the Little Community*, the product of the seminar. From an emphasis on local communities, anthropologists have extended their interest to the country as a whole.[169] The interplay between local and national settings reveals the impact of social change in the modern era.

In *Village India*, each of eight villages discussed there were examined as to their degree of isolation and autonomy as a social structure, as compared to structures and events in nearby villages and more distant, urbanized regional centres. All researchers are concerned with the relationship between cultural ideas and values and with social structures and relations involving caste in the alleged cultural isolate or small community.[170] They compare them with attitudes in the cities, where the more elaborate, cosmopolitan, and literate traditions of Indian civilization are found. Marriott, for example, taking up ideas taken up later, observes 'little' and 'great' traditions, comparing the ways of life in more isolated communities where a folk, popular culture prevails, to the more cultivated, cosmopolitan, self-consciously articulate culture of the

[168] Stein 1998: 147.

[169] Marriott 1955a. See also note 143.

[170] Particularly Srinivas 1955; Cohn 1955; Gough 1955; Marriott 1955b; Mandelbaum 1955.

cities.[171] Studies such as Marriott's and those of Srinivas and other researchers illustrate and compare the commingling of ideas, beliefs, values, customs, institutions, and social relationships in village life and how all of this change in relation to modernity.[172] These studies set the stage for a more global approach to the anthropological study of the civilization of India.

Social change in small communities of India

Small communities illustrate poignantly how everyday social life is lived under the caste system and how ordinary Indians were affected by social change. Srinivas' observations that are discussed below were made early on in India's political modernization and many of his conceptions need to be revised in light of the growth in influence of modern political parties and their success in using information media to promote social change. Nonetheless, precisely because they focus on early changes they allow one to appreciate more vividly the ramifications of modernization and their potential toll on human coping.

Srinivas' field work in Mysore led him to advance three main concepts that are inextricably involved in the social changes that have taken place in modern India: Sanskritization, (roughly, emphasis on scriptural tenet), caste relationships, and Westernization (roughly, modernization in terms of Western values).[173] He uses these constructs to analyze social change in village settings with emphasis on the caste system and Hinduism. Srinivas emphasizes that the caste system never was a static, fixed system of beliefs and social practices. Movement from one level to another has always been possible, especially in the middle ranges of the hierarchy. In one or two generations a low caste could have its rank moved higher in the hierarchy simply by changing social practices; for example, vegetarianism and teetotalism and by changing aspects of its religion in different ways. Thus, although theoretically disallowed, Brahmin customs, rites, and beliefs could be adopted by a low caste.

> The tendency of the lower castes to imitate the higher has been a powerful factor in the spread of Sanskritic ritual and customs, and in the achievement of a certain amount of cultural uniformity not only

---

[171] Marriott 1955a.

[172] Srinivas 1955, 1962, 1966.

[173] Srinivas 1962, 1966.

throughout the caste scale, but over the entire length and breadth of India.[174]

Social hierarchy is based not only on castes as social entities but also on the occupations of its members, and even elements of their way of life, such as what they eat, their cooking habits, what they wear, personal comportment, customs, and rituals of sacrifice. The influence of a higher caste's entire way of life seeps down through the hierarchy. Attitudes about social relations, marriage conventions and obligations – codes regarding conjugal relationships, the value attached to male and female children, and how widows are supposed to behave – are all part of social and cultural complexes that move up and down the caste hierarchy. Srinivas' concept of Sanskritization, which entails exposure to and change in ideas, values, and core precepts found in the voluminous Sanskrit literature, both secular and sacred, usually results in upward mobility.

The process of Sanskritization becomes the medium through which social change takes place, particularly in the modern era. It affects elements of dress, habit, custom, belief, and ritual behaviour. While Srinivas focuses on the mechanisms that preserve order and structure in the system as a whole, his account provides a detailed social and psychological picture of conflicts and strivings in village life discussed earlier. Many of the factors that social and cultural psychiatrists equate with stress and strain, factors that are held to can predispose to psychiatric condition in vulnerable individuals – social tensions, role conflicts, envy and social marginalization – are implicit in the social changes and modifications of Sanskritic observance and behaviour.[175]

Srinivas also addresses Westernization, defined as

> the changes brought about in Indian society and culture as a result of over 150 years of British rule, [a term that] subsumes changes occurring at different levels – technology, institutions, ideology, values.[176]

Within Westernization he includes humanitarianism ('an active concern for all human beings') and secularization, a term to which he gives special attention. Some of the examples of Westernization that Srinivas

---

[174] Srinivas 1962: 30.

[175] Srinivas 1962, 1966; see also discussion in Fabrega 1997.

[176] Srinivas 1966: 47.

analyzes point up the broad-ranging changes in society and behaviour that are equated with the advent of the British in India. He discusses (1) new institutions, such as newspapers, political elections, and Christian missions; (2) the importation of Western values, emphasizing an active concern for the welfare of all human beings irrespective of caste, economic position, religion, age, and sex – notably differences in the social position and behaviour of males and females, especially within the caste system; (3) reforms in the legal system, (4) advancements in public health, sanitation, and hygiene, and (5) changes in beliefs and in personal and social behaviour related to the above-mentioned changes.

Most Indians never came face to face with a British person during the colonial period and immediately afterward, but all felt the indirect impact of Westernization. The upper castes, especially Brahmins, who became the 'new elite', initially came into contact with the British and experienced major conflicts as result. Srinivas does not focus on the psychological effects of Westernization but mentions nevertheless the sense of inferiority, competition, self-derogation, embarrassment, and disarray among the upper castes created by witnessing the very different attitudes, behaviour, and lifestyle of the British, whose education, knowledge, technological skills, and social power they came to respect but who nonetheless challenged the natives' traditional self-conceptions in a negative way.[177] Srinivas' allusion to psychological difficulties among the new elite is a useful resume of major social changes produced by the British in India. He discusses dilemmas and conflicts of the new elite. These include mixed feelings if not outright reservations about their own society and that of the ruling British.

> Their extreme self-criticism was expressed in their desire to alter or do away with several features and institutions of contemporary India. There were egregious 'evils' such as suttee [cremation of a widow along with the corpse of her husband], thuggee (criminality, antisociality), human sacrifice, female infanticide, slavery, untouchability, and religious prostitution. And then there were others, less conspicuous: polygyny, 'child marriage', dowry, heavy expenditure at weddings and funerals, the segregation of women (purdah), and the traditional ban on divorce, widow marriage, and sea voyage.[178]

---

[177] However, Srinivas also points to positive aspects of this challenge.

[178] Srinivas 1966: 77–78.

A powerful associated effect of Westernization in India was secularization. This change implies that what was earlier seen as religious was losing its hold on the imagination. A holistic and integrated worldview was broken apart, with various aspects of society, including economic, political, legal, and moral considerations became increasingly differentiated from each other. As discussed earlier, in traditional times religion, morality, law, occupation, and social conduct in general were all welded together in terms of ideas of *dharma*, karma, and liberation via meditation and devotion. The new emphasis drew a distinction between church and state that entailed a new Indian concept of a secular state.

Within the concept of secularization Srinivas includes rationalism, by which he means attempts to explain society, behaviour, and the universe purely in empirical, scientific terms according to principles of logic and reason. Secularization had its main impact on Indian concepts of purity and pollution, and by extension Hinduism and the caste system. To highlight the impact of secularization, for Brahmins in particular, Srinivas describes the life of purity and holiness.

> Just as notions of uncleanliness and even sinfulness lie close to pollution, so do cleanliness, spiritual merit, and holiness lie close to purity. While all baths purify the bather, in a sacred river cleanses him, in addition, of sin (*pāpa*), and earns him *puṇya* or spiritual merit. A daily bath in a sacred river (*puṇya snāna*), worshiping in a temple, listening to the narration of religious stories (*harikathā kalākṣepa*), singing devotional songs in company with other devotees (*bhajan*), keeping the company of religious persons (*satsaṅga*), frequent fasting (*upavāsa*), prayer, and meditation (*prārthanā, dhyāna*) – these constitute the essence of a religious life as distinguished from a life devoted to secular concerns.[179]

A widening split in Mysore state within the Brahmin caste between the priests and the laity provides a vivid example of how secularization has affected social relations and the social standing of the Brahmins. As the educated, urbanized class of Mysore, the Brahmins were able to profit professionally and economically from the changes introduced by the British. The success of this caste was associated with changes in values, beliefs, customs, rituals, and lifestyle that came with Westernization and secularization. However, these developments antagonized the priestly group of Brahmins. Lacking the courage to 'throw their

---

[179] Srinivas 1966: 122.

powerful patrons out of the caste', they had to 'bow to the inevitable'. Weakening of priestly authority and prestige and their secularization had undermined their initiatives in social reform. At the time when the studies took place it had not been possible Mysore Brahmins to reinterpret Hinduism in modernist terms for they lacked confidence in initiating religious or social reform.

> They ... (did not have) have the intellectual equipment nor the social position to undertake a reinterpretation of Hinduism that would suit modern circumstances. Since the beginning of the nineteenth century, such reinterpretation has come from the Westernized Hindu elite. The fact that this elite has been anti-ritualistic, as well as inclined to frown upon popular sacrifices, beliefs, and practices, has stripped Hinduism of a great deal of its content.[180]

Srinivas stresses the connections among Sanskritization, Westernization, and secularization through his picture of life in the small community. While his work centres on the Coorgs of Mysore State, his generalizations can be applied in a tentative way to India as a whole.[181] He addresses the major transformations that were taking place and continued unabated up to the present: villages becoming integrated with wider economic, political, and educational systems of the nation-state, improved rural communication and transportation, universal adult franchise, local self-government, the abolition of untouchability, and the rise of political factionalism. All of these influences run counter to the caste system and religious sectarianism.

In summary, Srinivas' analysis presents a social psychology of the stress entailed by modernization. He brings to light mental health implications of politico-economic changes in the structure of lived and rural communities. These effects are proximate to possible cases of stress and psychiatric phenomena. Village level observations of social change provide a contrast with but are complementary to the more public, intellectual, and also ceremonial staging and producing of science as an idiom and vehicle for 'enlightened' modernization and reform in India.

Prakash describes the characteristics of the new language of science in terms of which traditional views about social life and religious orientation were intellectually re-configured ('syntactically translated') by the

---

[180] Srinivas 1966: 134.

[181] See Mandelbaum 1970; Marriott 1955a, 1955b; Singer 1972.

elite and political leaders under the banner of modernism and eventually the nation.[182] The discourse of science came to appropriate native traditions and affected life in community settings. Eventually, ideas pertaining to sickness and psychopathology, as formulated in traditional compared to modern idioms, came into conflict.

Studying social change in Indian civilization as a whole

As Singer indicates in his *When a Great Tradition Modernizes* (1972), the study of any civilization and particularly that of India is a natural extension of the traditional concerns and methods of cultural anthropology. As illustrated above, anthropological studies are confined to small, relatively isolated, self-contained societies or communities whose cultural patterns and social organization are easily delimited. The typical field study might last a year or so. Singer demonstrates that selected features of a complex civilization like that of India can be analyzed systematically by studying its history, its social, cultural, religious traditions, and its foundational texts. The result can indeed be an anthropological study of a civilization as a whole over an extended period, and particularly a study of changes brought by Westernization and modernization.

Singer documents his approach through a variety of materials drawn from several field visits to India, particularly the city of Madras in southern India. First he drew on established knowledge about Indian history, religion, law, medicine, literature, and art. To this he added the direct, first-hand and self-conscious study of selected representatives of a given tradition who are intimately involved in the workings of those institutions and cultural performances that characteristically embody the values, ideas, and traditions of a civilization. He gathered further information through standard anthropological research methods, such as participant-observation, in-depth interviewing of selected expert informants, and critical analysis. These sources enabled him to put together an overall anthropological study of the culture patterns of Indian civilization. He consulted priests associated with various sects and temples; experts in religion and morality; members of various social castes and occupations; artists and performers – actors and dancers – who work in traditional aesthetic genres and express traditional themes; practitioners of indigenous medicine; and lay experts who provide advice and coun-

[182] Prakash 1999.

selling to those troubled by puzzles and conflicts linked to traditional social practices. Singer concludes that India is comprised of a number of cultural structures, seen as interrelated pools of knowledge and practice, embodied in a variety of individuals.

Indian civilization has been an explicit concern of cultural anthropologists for at least half a century. The focus grew out of two overlapping intellectual currents associated with two giants of the discipline. Robert Redfield, a social anthropologist, initially worked in Central America.[183] He described and analyzed cultural traditions and values, social structures, and community relations in various communities of Mexico's Yucatan Peninsula. In broadening his scope to encompass the study of entire civilizations, Redfield used the concepts of 'little' and 'great' traditions. The former refers to the local, concrete, and contextual ways in which life is ordered among the 'unreflecting' members of local, folk communities. 'Great' traditions, on the other hand, embody more formal, intellectual, and textual expositions of a tradition's 'reflective few', the literati, which include political, religious, and aesthetic leaders, as well as ritual experts regarding the culture and society. The literati are typically found in urban centres. They include religious leaders, administrative officials, and other intellectuals conversant with details of history, traditional morality, law, medicine, and art.

In differentiating between these two traditions, Redfield emphasizes the role of towns and cities. He advances the idea of a folk–urban continuum to describe social life and cultural patterns in four types of settings: tribal villages, peasant villages, towns, and cities. At one pole of the continuum is a 'folk' type of society and culture and, at the other, an 'urban' type. In primitive and peasant villages, which are relatively isolated and homogenous, one finds a local, popular, folk society that embody a 'little' tradition. As these come in contact with urbanized societies where the 'great' tradition is found, they shift toward the urban type, which brings about a number of changes in values, ideas, social practices, and traditions.

In Redfield's formulation, 'little' and 'great' traditions are linked in a contemporary sense, since traditions found in local villages now draw on the ideas, values, and traditions found in the big cities. Conversely, even in cities one can find social relations and cultural patterns that mirror those found in surrounding villages. However, Redfield surmises

[183] Redfield 1941, 1955, 1956.

that a historical process links the 'little' traditions of the villages, which over time have grown into 'great' traditions.

Alfred L. Kroeber was another social anthropologist who was particularly interested in cultural history.[184] He theorized that any one culture is a composite of elements borrowed from other cultures. This view applies to simple, isolated cultures, as well as to grand, complex cultures ordinarily encompassed by the idea of a civilization. Each culture type, although initially made up of separate, borrowed elements, is an amalgamation of those elements that over time have led to the creation of a distinctive overall pattern or style. In Kroeber's definition, civilization stands for:

> An assemblage of the styles followed by the inhabitants of a certain area through a certain duration of time, could then consist of a style or manner of government, added to a style of law, and another of social relations, further, a characteristic manner of production and economy, of religious belief and organization, plus what we ordinarily call its style of literature, art, music, and building.[185]

This definition may be usefully applied to the study of Indian civilization.

As indicated earlier in this chapter, beginning about 1000 CE and accelerating after the twelfth century, foreign influences began to be felt throughout the Indian subcontinent. Muslim invaders who came from Arabia, Persia, and Afghanistan made important inroads in India and established the Sultanate in 1206 and the great Mughal Empire of the sixteenth and seventeenth centuries. The coming of the Europeans marked the second wave of outside influence, culminating in British rule after the eighteenth century. All of these foreign influences, imposed by force, were centred in cities and regional centres of colonial administration that were also the most sophisticated settings for the Indian tradition. Each of these foreign influences also represented a separate 'great' tradition that came into contact with that of India, modifying it and competing with it in different ways. In each instance, the 'great' tradition of the subcontinent prevailed; it expanded and modified the foreign influences and emerged more or less intact and in some respects significantly enriched by the impact of outside forces.

---

[184] Kroeber 1963.

[185] Quoted in Singer 1972: 252.

Throughout Indian history, the diverse but integrated traditions that comprise its civilization have been enacted in communities of different size and different levels of traditional learning and sophistication. Indigenous culture has been repeatedly modified by foreign influences and the social changes brought by conquest and colonization, Islamic and European. Since Indian civilization is very ancient, for over 4000 years it has been embodied in competition and appropriation of 'little' and 'great' communities of varying degrees of mutual impact and influence. If one could compare developments over time to trace how social and cultural patterns have changed, one could plot how traditions and ideas have gone through the so-called orthogenetic transformation of 'little' into 'great' traditions.[186] In a rough way, this means the incorporation into 'little' traditions of learned, textually-based traditions and values, what Srinivas calls Sanskritization, as well as other elements of the 'great' traditions, as local patterns in isolated communities began to be influenced by urban ideas and patterns, a process that Marriott calls parochialization.[187]

As Indian civilization evolved over the millennia, cultural ideas, values, and traditions were parcelled out differently among India's myriad social groupings. Knowledge of the foundational scriptures became incorporated in the life of regional communities in distinctive ways. As groups multiplied and spread, sectors of the population developed unique cultural and social structures. From esoteric and devotional religious pursuits; to moral standards and conventions of proper relations among various persons and groups; to the secular resolution of conflicts in tribes, villages, and castes in both rural and urban settings; to concerns about disease and pathology, Indian civilization has maintained an identity, even in its multiplicity, across the millennia. It now struggles with the consequences of independence and the political and economic modernization that has irretrievably altered ancient ways.

In summary, social and cultural anthropologists describe Indian civilization is an assemblage of basic concepts, beliefs, rituals, values, social practices, and religious, moral and secular traditions of knowledge spread throughout in communities of different size, scope, and historic character. One might visualize it as a richly woven tapestry that maps the cultural geography and history of the subcontinent. Scenes

---

[186] Marriott 1955a; Singer 1972.

[187] Marriott 1955b.

portrayed depict ensembles of social and psychological behaviour that reflect the cultural rationale of the civilization.

Social change and psychiatric phenomena during the modern era

Studying the history of mental health and illness problems in India involves two exercises. The first is to explain how vulnerable individuals have expressed psychological distress. What forms have behavioural breakdowns and deviance taken, given the design of the cultural tapestry just described? If the tapestry depicts the cultural conventions and standards of India's 'great' and 'little' traditions, then psychiatric condition consists of aberrations – departures in form and design from those standards and traditions. From the flaws in the tapestry, as it were, from disruptions of normal behaviour and circumstances and breakdowns in form, one can deduce how Indian culture has defined psychiatric condition and dealt with it.

The second exercise explains how such psychiatric phenomena have changed over time and in different locations. Aberrant behaviour and emotional breakdowns would be seen to take different forms depending on what scenes and settings one focuses on. The content, meaning, interpretation and mode of handling of a psychiatric condition would differ, depending on whether one looked at events and circumstances in a small village or in a large urban centre; and if the event occurred in a city, one would focus on the social group and economic standing of the family. Just as one may assume an interpenetration and overlap between tenets of 'great' and 'little' communities, one may suppose that how psychiatric conditions were constructed and played out in those communities would be related to the assumptions, conventions and local emphases prevailing in the culture of the community in question.

Similarly, the configuration and enactment of psychiatric condition would differ, depending on what point over the span of several millennia one chooses to examine, and what type of community. For example, the social material of psychiatric phenomena must have been expressed differently following the period of alleged Aryan expansion, during the major indigenous empires, when Islamic power was consolidated, during the period of European colonial rule, and especially after Independence, when modern psychiatry was incorporated into Indian society and medicine. While the social order and culture that shape experience and behaviour may retain essential features and create recurring stresses and fault lines that predisposed to disturbances, the principal agents and precipitants of a syndrome would obviously vary depending on historical setting. The social history of psychiatric phenomena involves explaining the connectedness and discontinuity between how forms of psychological distress and behavioural breakdown were constructed, played out, and dealt with in the different segments of the fabric of Indian culture.

The advent of the modern era and Westernization marked a major transition in the social and cultural evolution of Indian society. As discussed earlier, a secular world-view, individualist orientation, and fixation on present maladies and their political solutions contrast sharply with traditional views. The spread and growth of new ideas and values challenged established assumptions and practices and created instabilities and contradictions in thought, behaviour and experience.[188] Changes such as these are of theoretical concern to epidemiologists and clinicians since they affect development of personality and undermine established routines and practices, thereby creating vulnerabilities. They are also of importance to political scientists and politically influenced psychologists interested in the consequences of colonialism and modernization. The repercussions of Westernization are a never-ending drama. Through secularization and associated reforms regarding the franchise and the abolition of untouchability, for example, Indian leaders have attempted to create a secular and civic society. Initially there was an attempt to define individuals as contracting civic agents rather than as representatives of family, caste, religion, village, tribe, lineage, and region – the fundamental structural pillars of society. Each religion embodies a system of values that binds its adherents together, as do family, caste, village, and region. However, the elimination of religion in particular, as well as other roots of common identity from the public, civic sphere has in many respects meant the disintegration of individual and social life and has brought chaos and crisis to India since Independence.

As in all traditional societies, the social transformation wrought by Westernization and its various '-isms' has had a destructive impact on community values and traditions, and thus social and psychological stability. In this sense, it has contributed to the production of psychiatric phenomena in vulnerable individuals. Westernization has also brought the importation and imposition of international, biomedical psychiatry,

[188] M. N. Cohen 1998.

a central feature of modern life in the West, in competition with indigenous ways of addressing emotional disorders and disaffections of experience and behaviour.

Obviously, a comprehensive study of the social and cultural history of psychiatric phenomena in Indian civilization that meets only some of these guidelines would be extremely complex and far beyond what one could accomplish in one volume. A complete account is also literally impossible for sheer lack of historical and cultural evidence. All one can do is to use selected information from different disciplines to provide a descriptive and theoretical picture of the range of factors that may have affected how psychiatric condition has manifested in the Indian subcontinent across the expanse of history. A modest, realistic goal is to illustrate how the interplay of beliefs, values, interpretations, religio-moral traditions, and psychological traditions of India have influenced how such conditions were constructed and played out. Special attention is given to indigenous medical traditions and cultural-psychological influences. However, in formulating how these pertain to psychiatric phenomena one has to also address such factors as social history, cultural psychology and ideology that are presented later.

From the standpoint of the present narrative, the modern period in India is associated with major emphases and transformations of society in general that had important ramifications with respect to understanding and handling of psychiatric conditions. These involved activities aimed at improving public health and sanitation, the importation and incursion of biomedicine (the medical tradition that was coming into view in England and the Continent), and eventually the imposition of Western attitudes towards mental/emotional illnesses as features of the distinct medical specialty of psychiatry. The dominant motif of the transformation of society during the modern period involved the penetration and spread of science in Indian communities. Gyan Prakash provides a spirited and penetrating analysis of these social, cultural, and political developments involving the initial staging and then actual internalization and enactment of science in India.[189]

The groundwork for this eventual transformation in matters related to physical and mental health can be traced to developments starting in the late eighteenth century. However, this really took root in earnest during the first half of the nineteenth century. It was during the second

---

[189] Prakash 1999.

half of the nineteenth century that the emergence and functioning of science as a form of cultural authority in most colonial parts of India became evident. Educated elite, mostly of Brahmin background, played a very influential role initially. An enthusiasm for science as a form of social reform and re-vitalization was eventually manifested in major urban metropolitan centres, in particular. Genuine intellectual curiosity was part of this revolution, to be sure, but so was a spirit of reform of society and religion through an inculcation of natural laws over native superstitions.

The city of Calcutta occupied the initial strategic centre of this movement involving the general distribution of the discourse of science. It played a major role as an instrument of social and cultural renewal manifested in an enthusiasm for science as a language of reform. Many reform organizations were established:

> The[ir] objectives varied ... the diffusion of new forms of knowledge, religious and social reform, female education, the promotion of vernacular literature, the improvement of agriculture ... But all of them [the organizations] were formed by and functioned with a sense of the rediscovery of reason. As science was part of this rediscovery, the popularization of its authority emerged as one of the key aims of such organizations.[190]

The distribution of science's authority in the discourse of native elite was first manifest in Bengal but after the mid-nineteenth century was also observable in other provinces, especially in North India. By the late nineteenth century the 'pervasive deployment of science's persuasive power' in North India was evident in the cultural milieu that developed around Hindi language and literature and a Hindu revivalism, more generally. Much thought and effort went into the making of Hindi a language for the production of scientific knowledge.

An intellectual attraction for science has culminated in a passion and a more general, associated social and cultural intoxication that has influenced attitudes and approaches to native medical traditions. It was and is manifest in the way Western-trained Indian physicians and then psychiatrists took to conceptualizing aspects of sickness and psychiatric conditions. These are the two major effects of social change and Westernization in India that bear most directly on my subject. A Hindu medi-

---

[190] Prakash 1999: 54.

cine and psychiatry was manifest in the subcontinent stretching back to the classical and medieval period, as described earlier. This native tradition, a balanced integration or amalgam of spirituality, religion, and naturalism, came into juxtaposition with the increasingly totalistic and reductionist medicine and psychiatry of the modern, contemporary period. A key question in a study of the social and cultural history of psychiatric phenomena is how native, indigenous modes of thinking about and dealing with psychopathology were affected by this invasion of a foreign and modern, and hence highly seductive brand of medical psychology. While the Indian traditions were holistic, personalized, and concerned with all facets of human biological and psychological experience and function, biomedicine and its child neurobiological psychiatry was reductionist and impersonal. A prominent clash of medical traditions can be surmised. All of these developments are taken up in detail in later chapters.

Chapter 4

Demography and Public Health

INTRODUCTION

In seeking to visualize the influence of psychiatric conditions in societies of the subcontinent of India one seeks a picture of where such conditions were located in the population, what they looked like, any associated health problems, and what the effects of all of this may have been on characteristics of the society considered as a corporate structure and, ideally, on the lifeways of persons who displayed such conditions and their families.

One slant on this fuller picture is through incidence and prevalence measures of psychiatric conditions obtained as a result of epidemiological surveys of communities. These provide a numerical estimate of the amount of psychiatric conditions in a population. In Chapter 5, data from contemporary studies in psychiatric epidemiology in Indian populations will be used as rough guidelines to infer distribution and manifestations of psychiatric conditions in earlier eras. Epidemiological figures of psychiatry disorders allow one an estimate and a more or less direct if dry and detached view of morbidity. The real-life effects of such disorders on emotional, cognitive, behavioural, and psycho-physiological functions are abstracted out of the picture. Characteristics of the demography of the population are often excluded, for example, the size, concentration, dispersion, and age/sex distribution. Moreover, epidemiological findings focus on psychiatric phenomena at the exclusion of the myriad of health conditions that aggravate them or merely co-occur with them. A result of such a selected snapshot of a society's load of mental illness is that it is difficult to appreciate the impact that psychiatric disorders have on families, neighbourhoods, and the group.

It needs to be recalled that concentrating on psychiatric phenomena as a problem *sui generis* constitutes a modern conceit. In modern developed nations the nutrition, sanitation facilities, overall level of public health, and prevalence of infectious and systemic diseases contributes to a background of relatively good overall health and wellbeing. This allows one to more clearly estimate how psychiatric disorders impede human flourishing considered in relation to a 'clean slate' of non-psychiatric health problems. In developing nations of today, and especially in societies before the advent of modern scientific knowledge of disease (biomedicine, environmental sciences of public health, and related technological resources and services), adverse conditions of life and the negative impact of the ecology and social environment on the demography and health of populations was pronounced. Poor living conditions and poor general health aggravated and represented important causes of psychiatric conditions. Thus, as a way of placing psychiatric phenomena in real life terms and social and historical context it is appropriate to consider demography and public health conditions of Indian societies.

WHY DEMOGRAPHY AND PUBLIC HEALTH MATTER

The demography and public health of a population provide the material setting where psychiatric phenomena are found. The population's size provides estimates of how many persons are likely to show and develop psychiatric conditions, density allows estimating relative concentration, distribution tells where persons who develop psychiatric conditions are likely to be located in space, and age and sex distribution, taken with the preceding, enable estimating the likely social concentration of psychiatric conditions in segments of a particular society. With these parameters one can obtain a general picture of how visible and noticeable psychiatric conditions are likely to be and the likelihood that those closely related to victims will be affected by their behaviour. Realistic epidemiological measures along with paleo-demographical estimates provide information that allows one to visualize relatively impersonal and objective characteristics of psychiatric conditions during earlier periods of Indian history.

The science of medical epidemiology and medical ecology provides estimates of the amount and variety of all diseases in the society and their findings complement material pertaining psychiatric disorders. High prevalence of disease in a population and the morbid effects of disease are also important sources of social stress. If disease is widespread, this can undermine the vitality, social effectiveness, and the psychological wellbeing of the population at large. In contributing to physical and emotional strain and thereby demoralizing a population, high levels of general disease cause grief, anxiety, and diminished stamina and motivation. These are general factors, that, independent of specific causes (genetic vulnerability, social strain, poverty), predispose individuals to psychiatric conditions and can influence their persistence and course. Some medical diseases can directly impair brain function and psychobiological wellbeing, whereas others do so indirectly by contributing to frustration, weakness, and demoralization and by symbolizing ineffectiveness and failure. In short, the general load of disease of a population – its public health picture – should be factored into any equation designed to estimate the amount, morbidity and general significance of psychiatric condition over and above sheer level of symptoms and adverse social and cultural characteristics that impair adaptive behaviour. Again, as with demography, it would be useful to have information about public health and disease conditions during all phases of India's history and evolution. This is the domain of paleo-epidemiology, which addresses the level of disease and health of ancient populations.[191]

The careful study of demography and the public health of a society is of course a product of the modern era. Only recently have appropriate measures existed to study populations and public health. Demographers, public health physicians, and psychiatric epidemiologists have developed systematic procedures for collecting and analyzing large bodies of information about the size and structure of populations, vital statistics like fertility and mortality, and estimates of morbidity of disease as well as psychiatric conditions. Before the nineteenth century, such expertise and adequate information for study of demography and public health was simply not available. Hence, to probe these topics in an ancient society like that of India requires making informed guesses.

As to population, Renfrew and Bahn have estimated the average size of ancient large-scale, settled societies.[192] In rough terms, tribes or segmentary societies usually contained no more than a few thousand inhabitants: chiefdoms around 5,000–20,000, and states generally over

[191] Cohen and Armelagos 1984; M. N. Cohen 1989, 1998; Swedlund and Armelagos 1990.

[192] Renfrew and Bahn 1996. See also Johnson and Earle 2000.

20,000. Davis concluded that regional kingdoms and civilizations during periods of relative unification in the subcontinent of India probably contained over 500,000 inhabitants.[193] There are no helpful data for estimating fertility, mortality, and levels of public health, including morbidity, but it cannot be doubted that throughout history disease and health levels fluctuated markedly and were not dissimilar to those found in modern non-industrial societies that have been studied.

From medical anthropological studies one may presume that there were varying types of medical health care systems in ancient India. Communities had some awareness of local and even public health problems, and along with this knowledge of sickness and accepted procedures for coping with its effects. And there must have been medical practitioners of many orientations. In addition to trained Indian physicians (practising Ayurveda), one can assume lay popular healers following naturalistic herbalist traditions, conducting magico-religious rites, and practicing divination.

Some medically-oriented social scientists working in India today adopt an interactive approach to the sociology of illness and medicine.[194] They self-consciously depart from the typological tradition of Western sociology on the grounds that it exhibits an 'ideological and theoretical bias'. Emphasis is given to the effects and ways of coping with medical problems that would include psychiatric conditions. In addition, rather than stressing a dichotomy between tradition and modernity, they look for the interactions between modern and traditional approaches, between locally construed sickness conditions and biomedical disease, a perspective more appropriate to existing social and cultural characteristics of traditional Indian communities.

In attempting to visualize the demography and public health of India during earlier eras, its size and level and pattern of changed during different historical periods (evolutionary phases and transitions) it is appropriate to follow a similar interactive approach to the study of health and illness. Such an approach emphasizes that socialization and enculturation involve not only family but notably other groups as well. To interactionists, central importance is given to socialization within the system of stratification, particularly the caste and a variety of subcultures.

---

[193] Davis 1951.

[194] Gandhi 1981.

> Thus, if we view illness as a part of the interactive process of socialization and the latter as conditioned by the culture in which it takes place then it makes sense to find that the folklore of simple people in India consists of magico-religious ideas which describe diseases as caused by supernatural powers.[195]

R. S. Gandhi's assertion is relevant to public health and medical care throughout Indian history. The type of medicine an individual received varied significantly according to their position in the social hierarchy and more broadly in terms of what the population was like (density and degree of urbanization). Gandhi argues that even in ancient times medical practitioners in urban centres were beginning to apply scientific techniques that superseded magico-religious methods:

> It should be noted that the supernatural interpretation of health and disease not only relates to social hierarchy, the type of disease encountered or experienced by people and their formal education, but *the type of community*. It is well known that even in traditional India, the urban communities experienced the beginning of emancipation of medicine from magico-religious interpretation. It is in the early, pre-industrial urban communities of India that we first find the systematic philosophico-scientific explorations in Indian medicine of *Ayur Veda* ... Needless to mention that true to the diffusion of knowledge from the Great Tradition to the Little Tradition [of small communities] ... villagers of India, along with their magico-religious beliefs are quite familiar with these philosophico-scientific developments which took place in the large ancient urban centres of India.[196]

D. N. Kakar provides an additional slant on public health, general orientations to medicine, and medical practice.[197] He studied community medicine and health care practices in a development block in Ambala district of the state of Haryana. His findings support generalizations proffered by Gandhi and provide a picture of medicine in a traditional community of contemporary India that one presupposes shows traces of earlier periods of history. He conducted several studies of perceived health and use of medical services that stretched over a period of approximately ten years. The block was described as one of the backward ones of the district. Approximately one quarter of population was of scheduled castes and backward classes. The study started in 1976; its

---

[195] Gandhi 1981: 60–61.

[196] Gandhi 1981: 62–63.

[197] D. N. Kakar 1988.

population was recorded in 1979 as one million and by the end of study it had grown to 1.36 million. In Haryana village, poverty, illness and inaccessibility to routine medical care was striking. Gastrointestinal and respiratory diseases showed high prevalence and many other conditions of disease were less of concern, many not necessarily always perceived as sickness in the first place. Attribution of supernatural causes of disease was prominent in all segments of the population studied, especially among the lower social classes. Psychosocial problems were prominent, especially among the aged. However, psychiatric conditions received no special focus. Kakar and his team identified a total of 64 traditional medical practitioners who were engaged in full-time medical practice. Only nine of these practitioners were 'fully institutionally qualified', having earned a degree in ayurvedic (traditional Indian) or Unani (traditional Muslim) medicine, and ten were 'partially institutionally qualified', having earned a diploma or certificate after a short period of education. Forty-five of the sixty-four traditional medical practitioners were without any institutional training. All of the latter had worked as apprentices under registered medical practitioners for varying periods of time. The balance between traditional and non-traditional practitioners provides an index of the system of medical care in this setting.

> In addition to the 64 traditional medical practitioners, the block had as many as 600 folk practitioners, including herbalists, faith healers, spirit mediums, snake-bite curers, and bone setters.[198]

The history of medical healing in the continent, its holistic basis and religious and moral roots, and the cultural importance accorded medical practitioners are features that stand out with respect to concerns with public health and the practice of medicine.[199] In light of these considerations and the observations and findings of Gandhi and D. N. Kakar, one may suggest that since the advent of large-scale societies and after the rise to prominence of Buddhism and establishment of ancient kingdoms (Magadha, Kośala) and the Mauryan Empire, the latter half of the first millennium BCE, medical problems, including psychiatric conditions, would have been the object of competing medical traditions that included evolving practices of Ayurveda, Buddhist medicine, and local,

---

[198] D. N. Kakar 1988: 30, quote in footnote (*).

[199] Zysk, 1991, 1992, 1993. The relevance of this for the understanding of psychiatric phenomena is taken up in Chapter 7.

folk, shamanistic, and demonic or so-called magico-religious medical beliefs and practices. This was undoubtedly accentuated in later eras and especially in conjunction with the full emergence of ayurvedic and later Siddha medicine and various practices linked to Yoga after the earlier centuries of the Common Era. There has been an interaction between traditionally trained ayurvedic and Siddha practitioners and non-traditional practitioners for thousands of years. The high prevalence of poverty, disease, political exploitation, lack of knowledge about the influence general health hygiene and sanitation practices, and other social strains probably contributed to high demand for medical practitioners of all types. We may lack the data and knowledge necessary to provide a full description of the demography, public health, and morbid effects of disease in ancient Indian societies, but we can make some assumptions about the social and cultural patterns of health and medical problems in ancient times based on realistic findings in contemporary traditional societies of the subcontinent, all taken up later.

The exact mix of traditions pertaining to health and wellbeing would have depended on the size of a society and its geographic location. Disease is more prevalent and concentrated in larger societies. Where disease, pathology, and injury are more visible, there is a larger market for healers and care providers. Important in matters of medical and mental health care was the influence of large cities and sacred places associated with them (centres of pilgrimage, shrines, oracles, temples, locations of village and regional gods). These are and have been a prominent feature of India since the early medieval period, when popular Hindu sects began to flourish. Cities enclosed and/or supported nearby monasteries and temples that provided places of medical care and confinement. Cities also were likely to concentrate ayurvedic physicians and specialists in traditions of healing that had their roots in tenets of religion, morality, and spirituality. The secular medicine of India had its roots in a culture that constituted an amalgam of religion and philosophy. In villages of the hinterland and among the population at large, even in cities, there would have existed a large variety of lay and folk practitioners that addressed problems of disease, including psychiatric conditions.

NOTES ON THE HISTORICAL DEMOGRAPHY OF INDIA

Demography is a comparatively new science whose methods depend on census data that was not collected systematically until the nineteenth century. Hence, the true size of the population of India and its characteristics during earlier eras is not known. However, modern methods allow one to infer about earlier conditions. Davis indicates that:

> the first systematic attempt to ascertain the whole population of India by actually counting heads was made between 1867 and 1872.[200]

Since relevant data did not exist in earlier centuries and certainly not during antiquity, we remain in the dark about the size of earlier populations in the subcontinent, how they were structured, their size, age distribution, and relevant indices of fertility and mortality. In commenting about the modern period, Dyson states that

> it is probably fair to say that the historical demography of India is a field of academic inquiry which hardly exists.[201]

This obviously applies to antiquity with even more force.

The population of ancient India has been estimated by a number of demographers. Davis writes in *The Population of India and Pakistan*:

> In India some three to seven thousand years ago there were peoples possessing a technology sufficiently advanced to support a dense population ... Contemporary accounts of the later but still ancient historical periods ... the Brahmana literature, around 800–600 BCE, reveals that some of the villages had grown into towns and capitals with an urban mode of life ... The Buddhistic literature indicates that between the seventh and fourth centuries BCE, the economy of northern India was comparable to that of the later middle ages in Europe ... The ordinary town seemed to embrace anywhere from 30 to 1000 families, and approximately 20 cities existed in northern India alone. One tribal area, that of the Sakiyans is supposed to have contained half a million people ... So putting the evidence from archeology, literature, and history together, we reach the conclusion that before the Christian era India had a substantial population, first because of its advanced technology and second because of the fertile environment for the applica-

---

[200] Davis 1951: 4.

[201] Dyson 1989: 1.

> tion of this technology. Though great areas remained sparsely settled, some of the plains must have had a dense population.[202]

Davis surmises that by 300 BCE the population of ancient India was between 100–140 million. Many historians of ancient India concur with this estimate. The consensus seems to be that even at a remote period India was heavily populated, and observers of life in India who have left accounts in ancient literatures also describe a comparatively large and dense population.

Although these estimates refer mainly to northern India, societies in the south were almost as advanced. The population of ancient India remained at a stable level for centuries, perhaps even millennia, writes Davis:

> During the two thousand years that intervened between the ancient and modern period India's population could not have grown rapidly. It must have remained virtually stationary. The usual course was surely a gradual growth.[203]

Davis argues persuasively for a balance between fertility and mortality measures over the long haul. Undoubtedly there were periods during which population increased, but at a slow and gradual rate and only for short intervals. Periodic catastrophes such as warfare, famines, and epidemics wiped out population gains. Some historians estimate that even during the seventeenth century the population of India was still about 100 million. In the fifteenth and sixteenth centuries, Europeans were impressed with the density of population in the plains areas and in certain other regions, some considering the country overpopulated. The population of Europe, including Russia, is estimated at about 100 million in 1650. However, this covers an area larger than India. Not until after 1800 did Europe pull ahead of India in population.

Ancient India was overwhelmingly rural, with perhaps more than 85 per cent of the population living in villages and engaged in agriculture.[204] It is possible that, as in the early twentieth century, the population of ancient India was concentrated in the heavily watered river basins and coastal plains. This would mean dense population even in

---

[202] Davis 1951: 23–24.

[203] Davis 1951: 24.

[204] Basham 1954.

basically rural, agricultural communities. Even today, close to three-quarters of the inhabitants of the subcontinent live in rural, agricultural communities that are comparatively densely populated. Since very early times, then, the size and distribution of the Indian population predisposed the people to levels and types of disease that are common in non-industrial, modernizing societies today.

Although it is not possible to obtain a picture of the age composition of the population of ancient and medieval India, such knowledge would be useful because, along with fertility levels, it would allow us to infer what age groups were most affected by life-threatening diseases. It would also enable us to predict how and to what extent new disease episodes, which would have brought much strain and demoralization to families and communities, might have contributed to psychiatric conditions. In the 1940s, when data allowed more reliable analyses, the population was comparatively young, as in most non-industrial societies characterized by both high fertility and mortality. While it is problematic to equate the population of India in the mid-twentieth century with that of earlier periods, especially ancient times, comparative data nonetheless provide a rough baseline for analysis, taking into consideration the factors that would affect population size and structure at different times. The combined age pyramid for the 1940s, with the youngest group at the bottom and rising by ten-year increments, reveals a very broad base and a quickly narrowing top, is in marked contrast to the age pyramid for developed, capitalist societies, which have an almost rectangular shape.

Table 4.1.

The population distribution in India, 1940s

Persons aged	**Per cent**
10–19	20.7
20–39	32
40–59	14.9
60 and older	4.0

Such an age structure reflects the degree of dependency of various groups of the population, 'there being almost seven times as many children under 5 as adults over 65'.[205] India had less than 47 per cent of its population in the productive range of 20–60 years, compared to the US, where over 55 per cent of the population was in this range.

Dyson discusses studies of the historical demography of India that cover developments before 1872, before the census was initiated.[206] One study of rural Tamil areas during the late eighteenth and early nineteenth centuries indicated:

> There was widespread desertion of villages, abandonment and decay of both irrigation systems and cultivatable land, and general stagnation in the agricultural sector. This rural disintegration was probably most intense in the 1780s and 1790s, and it is these decades especially that may have witnessed real population decline in Tamil rural areas ... [and] negative effects persisted into the early decades of the nineteenth century; ... the undoubted faster Tamil population growth which seems to have set in from around 1830 has to be seen in the context of demographic stagnation, even decline, over the preceding 60 or 70 years.[207]

Another study addresses developments in the Doab region of North India during the nineteenth century. Here also there is evidence of depopulation in the late eighteenth century, whereas during the first half of the nineteenth century there was significant population and economic growth. This was different from the later nineteenth century, when population growth and agricultural income declined.

Dyson generalizes about the demography and general public health of India during the modern era:

> The period preceding the establishment of British rule – approximately 1760 to 1820 – was characterized by a very low, possibly negative, rate of population growth. It is certainly well established that when the British completed their hegemony of the country up to the Sutlej in 1818 they found a country in ruins, with widespread social breakdown, the results of lengthy wars.[208]

---

[205] Davis 1951: 86.
[206] Dyson 1989.
[207] Dyson 1989: 2.
[208] Dyson 1989: 8.

Dyson outlines four major phases of population change during the modern era that serve as reference points for the developments brought by Westernization. (1) From around 1760 to 1820, population remained static, and even possibly declined, because of economic disruptions and social breakdowns. (2) From 1830 to 1891, population may have grown to some extent, given a decline in mortality rates, less warfare, and increased economic stability, perhaps even growth. (3) From 1891 to 1920 was a period of significant change; population growth slowed, with an increase in epidemics, famine, and other causes of mortality. (4) From 1921 to 1960, political independence and economic development brought population growth; lower mortality was correlated with better control of disease and famine. In short, as a result of improved sanitation, water purification, and the influence of Western biomedicine, the overall size and rate of increase of the population of India has grown. It might be tempting to see these changes as resulting from the end of colonial rule. However, as Jeffery cautions, the correlation between British rule and the level of public health of the population of India is a complex topic, subject to much controversy.[209]

HISTORICAL REPRESENTATIONS OF PUBLIC HEALTH IN INDIA

The baseline of health in the Indian the subcontinent during proto- and early prehistory can be glimpsed by considering medical epidemiological studies of contemporary hunter-gatherers.[210] The latter provide a rough exemplar of what human populations were like before the advent of agriculture and this generalization can safely, although contestably, be applied to India's earliest or original inhabitants, and also the forest, tribal peoples that lived on the periphery of villages and still reside in the more isolated, less habitable parts of the subcontinent today.

A diet of vegetal items provided around if not more than two-thirds of food intake in communities living in low latitudes. Intake of micronutrients is and in past eras probably was well above contemporary recommended dietary allowances. A lifestyle of hard work was associated with high physical fitness. The risk females' cancers (breast, ovary) associated with reproductive events and pattern and number of birthing

[209] Jeffery 1988.

[210] Eaton and Eaton 1998.

is generally lower than that of modern populations. The natural indicators of overall health are generally lower among hunter-gatherers: body composition with significant less body fat, lower blood pressure, lower average cholesterol level, and aerobic fitness construed as endurance is higher. Thus, it is not surprising that hunter-gatherers have lower rates of obesity, diabetes mellitus, hypertension, coronary heart disease and major cancer killers (colon, breast, stomach). This, one can tentatively presume, was what the population of early, pre-agricultural communities was like from a standpoint of non-infectious, systemic diseases.

As a result of their nomadic lifestyle and comparatively small size, hunter-gatherers display and most probably would have displayed higher rates of infection produced by macroparasites (parasitic helminthes and arthropods) compared to microparasites (bacteria, viruses, and protozoa).[211] When plaguing human populations, and, primates in general, the infectivity of the former agents and their pattern of reproduction (life cycle, hosts, food chains) are associated with chronic infections: illnesses that they produce involve infectivity for long periods of time and level of immunization is acquired slowly and is correlated with level of infestation (amoebic dysentery, schistosomiasis). Low density of population does not protect against mainly one-shot acute infection with microparasites, like those responsible for measles, mumps, or influenza which are diseases of civilization, to be sure, but would have had analogues stemming from reservoir of viruses and bacteria carried by animals hented. Such one-shot infections produce relatively quick immunity, when they are not lethal, and tend to die out after running through a group. Thus, they do not remain in the population and of course are not endemic. Hunter-gatherers also by definition do not display domestication of animals and hence are spared infection with agents typically found in these animals, as is the case for agricultural societies.

The epidemiology of disease and level of health changes dramatically with the advent of agriculture and a sedentary style of life.[212] When Indian societies grew in size following the advent of domestication of plant and animals (a contested date), they brought on themselves a number of new diseases that produced major changes in medical ecology that are still manifest even today. Food was more predictable and plentiful, of course, and this brought an increase in population size and

[211] Kiple 1993.

[212] Kennedy 2000; Kiple 1993.

concentration. As sedentary agriculturalists, females developed more body fat and this decreased their fertility. As population in villages increased so did their medical woes as they now could host more types of disease. Kiple presents a vivid and dismal picture of health as agriculture developed and sedentary lifestyles unfolded produced their cost.

> Villages now displayed filthy conditions ... [that] that provided havens or rats, mice, ticks, fleas, and mosquitoes, all capable of harbouring and spreading a vast variety of ailments. New pathogens entered the environment in droves. The domesticated cows, pigs, sheep, cats, dogs, and goats all contributed their collections of pathogens to a swelling pool of diseases, as did domesticated fowl ... the roundworm *Ascaris* began to evolve in humans, probably from the ascarids of pigs, and joined other older heminthic parasites, such as the whipworm, pinworm, and hookworm, with the latter flourishing in the human faeces that were disposed of casually, if at all. Typhoid and other salmonella infections, along with ameobic dysentery, sprang from fouled water supplies; non-venereal syphilis passed from the mouths of dirty youngsters to other dirty youngsters and, perhaps along with leprosy, left an increasing number of disfigured and impaired individuals. Tuberculosis, a disease of animals prior to the advent of humans, was probably acquired from cattle and would have begun its insidious invasion of the human body ... Malaria and schistosomiasis took their tolls on workers where agriculture depended on irrigation.[213]

Archeologists who have concentrated on Harappan societies during the first millennium have reported indicators suggest difference in health status between hunter-gatherers and agriculturalists supporting the presumption of a trend for populations in transition to experience a lowering of public health.[214] Lukacs documents higher levels of dental pathology in women – an indicator of disrupted childhood growth and general health stress – than in men and attributes this discrepancy to a number of social and cultural practices. In addition, hunter-gatherer communities who had contact and exchange relations with agriculturalists probably underwent important biological changes as a result. For example, they could have such as supplemented their diet with foods that caused harm to the teeth; they could have acquired certain infectious or parasitic diseases that increased mortality and morbidity; and they could have suffered from genetic interbreeding. Lukacs writes,

---

[213] Kiple 1993: 360.

[214] Lukacs 1990, 1992, 1996.

> Evidence from the human skeletal record of prehistoric India suggests that diet supplementation and gene flow between settled and mobile traders has existed for at least four millennia.[215]

In short, paleo-pathological studies support the generalizations of medical ecologists and paleo-epidemiologists about differences in health status of populations living in different types of societies along a continuum of cultural evolution. They emphasize the vulnerability and high level of medically significant stress of populations in transition, especially densely populated agricultural societies like those of India.

The picture of health got even worse with the advent of cities. Larger populations led to the development of diseases of civilization. Urbanization and growth of population density led to the incubation of diseases that were intrinsic to this mode of life and that could burst out in mode of major epidemics. This included measles, diphtheria, and influenza. Furthermore,

> South Asia ... is a good suspect for being the cradle of smallpox. On the one hand, it was the first region to develop populations large enough to host the disease, and on the other, those ancient populations were the only ones wit a substantial cattle hers. When the evidence is viewed in the light of the existence in India of very ancient temples for worship of a smallpox deity and near certainty that Smallpox was practiced there during ancient times, there is clearly justification for the suspicion ... because smallpox and measles were not well distinguished until relatively recent times and again, because of the significance of the early development of large populations, it seems a good guess that South Asia and perhaps China, witnessed the rise of measles as well. In any event smallpox and measles, together with influenza, chickenpox, whooping cough, mumps, diphtheria, and a host of other diseases, arose with growing human populations. These were the illnesses that pass quickly and directly from human host to human host a need no intermediary carrier ... and began to mount assaults on human immune systems.[216]

In later sections, how psychiatric conditions are represented in classic texts of Ayurveda, the indigenous medicine of India, will be discussed. Presently, such texts can be used to illustrate the kinds of medical, physical conditions of illness that populations in early Indian society suffered from during the early centuries of the Common Era the

[215] Lukacs 1990.

[216] Kiple 1993: 362.

time when ayurvedic texts are generally thought to have been compiled.[217] While ayurvedic writings were subject to redaction and commentary during subsequent centuries, it is doubtful that essential medical knowledge lost its relevance. Thus, such writings provide photos of the kinds of problems physicians observed and dealt with.

Of course, the texts of canonical ayurvedic physicians like Caraka and Suśruta cannot be used to infer the level of disease in the population. They merely describe appearance, manifestations, and curative procedures. Moreover, depictions of clinical manifestations represent cumulative information; in other words, texts represent the compilation of experience in seeing and treating disease over a long period of time, most likely for centuries preceding the Common Era and thereafter. Ayurveda knowledge is presumed to have originated in Buddhist and other renunciant groups who had withdrawn from towns and cities and even, and who lived in the countryside observing and treating patients empirically as compared to the magical/religious methods characteristic of Vedic medicine.

Ayurvedic texts provide detailed descriptions of skin inflammations, wounds, abscesses, superficial skin growths and protuberances most likely neoplasm, as well as swelling of lymph nodes suggesting chronic infectious diseases. Such conditions were not only described vividly but also accorded specific names indicating a categorical approach to disease based on experience. Fevers, actual skin diseases resembling leprosy, and lesions of the head, face and neck are recorded. Descriptions of heart disease are not apparent but this is hardly surprising since these probably manifested in symptoms of pain and heaviness of chest that resembled gastro intestinal disturbances and manifested little in the way of specific signs. Respiratory and abdominal and intestinal disorders occupy several chapters and here again specific names are assigned to constellation of signs and symptoms based on patient's appearance, colouration, type and location of pain, and associated physiological symptoms (exudates, diarrhoea, abdominal pain, and respiratory distress).

Islamic medical texts as well as ayurvedic ones have been analyzed as a means of inferring about disease conditions that were prevalent during the medieval and pre-modern era.[218] The Mediterranean tradition

---

[217] Chakravorty 1993.

[218] Said 1993.

of medicine, comprehensively formulated by Galen during second century CE which persisted during the middle ages in Europe and Near East, was carried by the spread of Islam to central and Southeast Asia and gained foothold in India as Unani, sometimes Islamic or Arabic medicine. Its ideas and practices competed with and in some instances meshed together with Ayurveda. Epidemics are described in classic texts of Unani or Islamic medicine. Researchers infer from such descriptions that physicians during the pre-modern era were familiar with malaria, visceral leishmaniasis, leprosy, venereal disease, breakdown of liver functions, and congestive heart failure with accumulation of body fluids, termed ascites, urinary tract infections, hemorrhoids, and possibly filariasis. Smallpox, cholera, plague, and influenza, all diseases cited by medical ecologists as typical of acute infectious disease of civilizations, are also described. Analysis and interpretation of early, classical, and medieval texts demonstrate not only fidelity and accuracy of empirical description but also furnish one for a window into the morbidity of the population.

HISTORICAL CHANGES IN PUBLIC HEALTH IN INDIA

As any developing society, during its history India underwent a change in the demographic and public health features of its population, especially during its transition to modernity. A demographic transition represents a model of the change in structure of population made evident by methods of measurement and collection of vital statistics, population size, and family structure. Thus, it is a sequence of photos the representations of which describe characteristic of societies like modern Western nations, the locale where collection of such data took roots and became common practice. It is very likely that a similar pattern of demographic change took place as communities in the Indian subcontinent shifted from a mosaic pattern involving small, nomadic hunters and rural agricultural societies, on the one hand, to urban mercantile and trade societies, some of which would have included embryonic industrial features, on the other.

During the period preceding a demographic transition (the pre-transition phase) populations showed high rates of fertility and mortality, especially infant and child mortality, which together produced moderate rates of increase in size. During the transition itself death rates begin to decrease in response to changes in living conditions and health care, certainly with the promulgation of public health and sanitation efforts of the British and possibly earlier in relation to state sponsorship of ayurvedic and then Islamic medicine. The former involved not just curative medicine but a program of holistic health, which encompassed ecology, diet, exercise, and emphasize clean living conditions. Islamic medicine did also and during Islamic rule a number of hospitals were built that included facilities for the mentally ill. During a demographic transition fertility rates initially remain high because families anticipate high mortality rates in children, which only fall later with improvements in living conditions. This lag accounts for the elevated growth rates of population that is typical for developing societies. Eventually, fertility decreases in response to falling mortality that then lowers growth rates of population, typical or modern industrialized societies.

Demographers and public health practitioners describe an epidemiological transition that takes place in association with changes in population structure. It involves a change in the pattern of diseases and health profile of a population. Pre-transition phase features high rates of infectious diseases, namely, diseases that produce diarrhoea, respiratory infections, and parasitic diseases. In association with poor nutrition, this produces higher mortality rates in younger age groups. Infectious diseases then decline and children survive into adulthood and population shows and increase in life expectancy and chronic diseases that affect the older population in particular. Both transitions, of course represent exemplars or analytic abstractions and in the event population of India can be expected to have shown and continue to show variable changes depending on geographic region, ethnic composition, level of poverty, size of society and the like.[219]

Local warfare, banditry, and invasion by foreigners have been endemic throughout Indian history. Such social disruptions undoubtedly contributed to the outbreak of disease and exacerbated catastrophic epidemics. Incursions by Islamic warriors after the twelfth century, then by European colonial powers beginning in the sixteenth century, essentially aggravated these trends, but it is not possible to be precise as to how exactly these incursions affected population size and health. Warfare and epidemics periodically devastated population and public health throughout, but this was interspersed with recuperation and slow

[219] Beaglehole and Bonita 1997; Coreil 1997.

growth. However, the population of India began to increase around 1850 as a result of complex social changes and colonial public health measures.[220] Since that time, India's demographic transition has accelerated, and today it is in the midst of an associated epidemiological transition. If one assumes like demographers do that modern changes are unique and special, one can tentatively conclude that earlier population levels fluctuated and slowly increased but conditions contributing to public health were relatively stable.

As discussed earlier, in India, family-level societies (hunter-gatherers of fewer than 100 individuals) and isolated village-level societies (with populations perhaps numbering in the hundreds) clearly predated the Harappan peoples.[221] Such groups have existed in the subcontinent in isolated regions and beyond the perimeter of agricultural communities throughout its history. While hunter-gatherers tend to enjoy better public health than settled, more complex agricultural societies, members of these two types of society are in frequent contact with each other, with distinctive health consequences of a negative type, especially for the smaller ones. Paleo-epidemiologists emphasize that during social and cultural evolution, that is, societies in transition, there is a characteristic decline in health.[222]

Societies whose size, social organization, and health characteristics resembled those of Harappans and the Aryans undoubtedly existed during later millennia and into the medieval era, following the emergence of larger-scale societies, including the great empires. These smaller societies would have existed in isolated regions, far from crowded population centres. In such societies, sickness was no doubt handled communally in conformity with indigenous cultural traditions handed down over countless generations. Most likely, approaches to sickness and healing were comparatively unaffected by the emerging naturalistic, empirical approaches associated with heterodox ascetics and Buddhist wanderers before the Common Era, and certainly untouched by the academic, scientific tradition that came into prominence during this period and that was codified in the early centuries of the Common Era. Indigenous traditions of medicine will be taken up later with special attention to aspects of psychiatric conditions.

---

220 Davis 1951.

221 Kulke and Rothermund 1986; Jha 1998; Kochhar 2000; Kennedy 2000; Thapar 2002.

222 Cohen and Armelagos 1984; M. N. Cohen 1989; Swedlund and Armelagos 1990.

PUBLIC HEALTH IN INDIA TODAY

This is an appropriate point for briefly summarizing characteristics of the public health in rural areas of contemporary India. Material discussed here complements observations and generalizations of Gandhi and Kakar discussed earlier. Approximately three-quarters of the population of contemporary India are found in rural areas.[223] As noted earlier, the death rate has largely declined since the early twentieth century, but before that time it was as high as 47 per 1000. The infant mortality rate was well above 200 per 1000 live births. The mean life expectancy before 1920 was around 20 years of age. Even today, mortality among female children (34 deaths per 1000) and among women of childbearing age is very high (418 per 100,000 live births). While famine no longer takes a heavy toll, smallpox has been all but eradicated, cholera and malaria have been curbed, and widespread immunization has protected children from dangerous childhood diseases such as whooping cough, diphtheria, tetanus, and polio, these diseases have wreaked havoc on populations of India in the past. Widespread poverty and malnutrition have been dominant contributing factors. Mehta reports:

> Diseases arising from poverty, and its accompanying conditions of malnutrition, bad sanitation, lack of safe water supply, drainage or adequate housing, and low levels of immunity are still common. These include tuberculosis, gastroenteritis, malaria, leprosy, filariasis etc. (which rarely occur in the developed societies) and measles, tetanus, whooping cough, bronchitis, pneumonia, scabies, worms, and fevers (especially among children). It appears that although the average Indian may now live longer, his morbidity is only marginally less than that of his forefathers, and he continues to be prone to the same diseases as they were.[224]

Mehta's picture directly presumes the existence of similar disease pictures in ancient societies. Comparatively poor levels of public health are factors that cause physical, social, and psychological stressors that contribute to psychiatric phenomena.

The exact picture of public health varies across the regions of India. Conditions in contemporary cities are better than in rural areas, to be sure, but this merely reflects the fact that the main effects of health edu-

---

[223] Mehta 1995.

[224] Mehta 1995: 283–284.

cation programs and campaigns of hygiene, sanitation and water purification are centred in the cities. There is widespread consensus regarding the need to develop responsive primary health centres that are rooted in community participation.[225] In earlier epochs, differences between urban and rural areas may not have been so sharp; in other words, health conditions in the cities were probably also very poor. However, it is likely that the wealthy and economically secure, which tended to reside in the cities or on private estates, had better health. Today there are still marked differences in health status between the upper and middle classes and the vast bulk of the population, and these differences are strongly correlated with caste. Among the poor, 'frequent illness and untimely death are still the lot of the average individual'.[226] No doubt the same conditions that explain this high burden of disease and poor public health, such as nutritional deficiency, inadequate personal and food hygiene, and unsanitary environmental conditions, prevailed during earlier phases of history as well.

In general, over the centuries the size and structure of India's populations have changed, along with factors that affect the outbreak of disease. Nevertheless, the deficiencies of public health in contemporary India provide one way of inferring about conditions that have probably existed (with varying levels of severity and differences regarding disease type) throughout recorded history and probably throughout prehistory as well.[227] Mehta draws attention to several 'disturbing features' about the medical and health systems that were 'inherited' from the British. The 'imported model' of health care is inappropriate to India, he contends. It is top-heavy, over-centralized, heavily curative in emphasis, too urbanized and elite-oriented, costly, and tends to create dependency. In this he agrees with Banerji who, in his masterly summary of health and family services in India, reviews efforts to rectify these problems.[228] Mehta also states:

> The progress of modern medicine has unfortunately led to a devaluation of the traditional medical systems. It has also created a widespread fascination with new and magical ways of dealing with ill health rather than instilling in people the basic value of preventing ill-

---

[225] See D. Banerji 1985.

[226] Mehta 1995: 284.

[227] McKeown 1988; McNeill 1976, 1992.

[228] D. Banerji 1985.

> ness itself. It must also be mentioned that the medical establishment (that is, practitioners, clinicians, pharmacists, and drug manufacturers), which provides medical care is a part of the elite class with vested interest in aping the West.[229]

Mehta's observation is highly significant when applied to how biomedical psychiatry is being imposed in contemporary India. This is taken up in Chapters 11 and 12.

The public health condition of India is not presented here merely to analyze contemporary questions.[230] Instead, the contemporary public health picture is used as a theoretical baseline for hypothesizing about conditions and developments during the ancient and medieval periods of Indian cultural history. It is easier to appreciate the culture of health and medicine in ancient India if one has in hand a rough picture of the current level of public health, however anachronistic it may be. Levels of disease, mortality, and morbidity provide direct clues about what people confront on a day-to-day basis. The material of Gandhi and Kakar about traditional communities provides a window into conditions in earlier centuries. Contemporary data on public health also allow one to make inferences – very indirect, to be sure – about the role of disease and associated sufferings in the society and culture at large all of which contribute to levels of mental health and illness. Thus, while only presently can the sources of infection be ascertained unambiguously and there undoubtedly were differences in types of infective agents and general levels of health in earlier centuries and prehistory, the toll of epidemics and high morbidity from endemic disease can be assumed from ancient skeletal remains as discussed in Chapter 2.

PSYCHIATRIC CONDITIONS IN THE CONTEXT OF PUBLIC HEALTH

To understand the history of psychiatric phenomena in any civilization like India one must take into consideration the background of public health and the picture of mortality and morbidity from disease. In later

---

[229] Mehta 1995: 288.

[230] Present conditions reviewed naturally correlate with Westernization and imposition of the biomedical view; and by extension, the effects of this regime of medicine on beliefs and trends pertaining to mental illness. These topics are taken up later in Chapters 11 and 12.

chapters emphasis is given to the social emplacement of actual psychiatric conditions in India – where it is likely to be found in society – as well as its manifest content in light of Indian culture, religion, social and moral philosophy, world-view, and psychology. In any society, and especially in non-industrial ones, awareness of psychiatric phenomena is greatly overshadowed by physical disease and death. This was clearly echoed by the study of Kakar and is consistent with the general thrust of Gandhi's observations. Psychoses associated with behavioural dilapidation undoubtedly caused social concern and received attention. However, even the way such conditions are perceived, interpreted, and dealt with bespeaks attitudes of tolerance, accommodation, and appropriation through forms of care that blend medicine, religion, and spirituality. Kakar's observations about the anxiety and psychosocial problems of the aged in a development block located in Ambala district of Haryana suggests that such conditions, along with the myriad of physical health problems of this segment of population, tend to be overlooked and minimized. However, very poor public health in India has naturally moderated the impact and conditioned the social meaning of psychiatric conditions. Low levels of general health contribute to demoralization that, in turn, could cause or exacerbate mental health problems. The approach followed here reflects a selective bias retrospectively imposed on past societies that did not sharply separate general health problems from what today is defined as mental illness or psychiatric disorder.

Mehta suggested that public health in India has probably always been low throughout history. Epidemics, acute and chronic communicable diseases, high infant mortality, and a low average life span have repeatedly ravaged the population of India. In the modern period, a clearer picture has emerged of India's disease problems, their causes, and their consequences. It is thus not surprising that improving general public health has been a major priority in India since before Independence and prompted the development of a realistic health policy. This has included attempts to control and eradicate major communicable diseases, to establish comprehensive health programs, to improve sanitation and the quality of the water supply, and to set up comprehensive primary health centres. Since the late 1970s there has been a shift in emphasis in health care planning toward seeking community participation that involves not only the cooperation of community leaders but also their shouldering some of the financial burden. Narayana Reddy writes:

> The process of health policy in the first 35 years of independent India (1947–82) has three important phases namely: (i) phase of vertical programmes for tuberculosis, malaria, leprosy, Smallpox etc. (1947–71), (ii) phase of integration of peripheral units from uni-purpose to multipurpose functionaries (1972–77), (iii) phase of active efforts to involve the community through community health guides and related activities (1977); ... this [is the] background [of] the National Health Policy of the Government of India formulated in 1983.[231]

India's national health policy comprises a number of broad approaches that underscore the country's phase of development. In general, a country's policy about health or any other problem area is influenced by its relative position on a realistic scale of progress. More specifically, the policy is influenced by the country's resources, manpower, level of public awareness and empowerment, scientific advancements, technical skills, existing or emerging value systems, and leaders' ability to motivate the population to support needed changes. Hence, India's national health policy provides a snapshot of where it stands in the schema of improving general public health and articulating realistic and useful health goals. Among the approaches to improving general public health include: (1) a decentralized network of comprehensive primary health care services handled by the people through the organized support of volunteers; (2) training volunteers to function as health guides; (3) encouraging individual self-reliance and effective community participation; (4) establishing a referral system of adequate expertise to back up efforts at the local level, thereby avoiding a rush to city health facilities; and (5) coordinated programs for general and mental health care, including the physical and social rehabilitation of those who are mentally retarded, deaf, dumb, blind, physically disabled, infirm, and aged.

This brief description of how India conceives of its public health problems today reveals that psychiatric conditions are comparatively underemphasized. The burdens of organic pathology, disease, and disability for large segments of the population crowd out concerns with mental health and psychiatric conditions proper. Yet although such conditions do not have the same social priority as in more developed countries, there are cogent reasons for trying to conceptualize how they manifested in Indian civilization over the centuries.

---

[231] Narayana Reddy 1992: 21.

SEARCHING FOR PSYCHIATRIC CONDITIONS IN ANCIENT AND MEDIEVAL INDIAN POPULATIONS

Prominent causes of psychiatric conditions in any society include high levels of social strain, interpersonal hardships and stress, and poor public health. Vulnerable individuals succumb to emotional disturbances, behavioural irregularities, loss of morale, and weakening of behavioural controls leading on to social divisiveness. Individuals who show manifestations of such problems, when properly examined by a clinician knowledgeable of and sensitive to the language, thought worlds and habit patterns of a people will conform to psychiatric conditions. How such conditions are perceived, understood, and dealt with will reflect local standard of normality and abnormality. Such a generalization is based on comparative studies in medical anthropology and the social history of medicine in all traditional civilizations.

Like all agrarian civilizations, India has been plagued by acute and chronic infectious diseases, problems of nutrition that create vulnerabilities for metabolic, degenerative, and general infectious diseases, as well as bodily disorders and complications stemming from digestive and skin problems. To this one can add periodic crises involving famine and epidemics that take their most devastating toll on impoverished, frequently exploited populations. All of these environmental and political challenges and sources of social instability bring not only the threat of general medical diseases but also problems of morale, social suffering, and especially emotional and behavioural disturbances or anomalies.

In addition to health problems broadly conceived (both organic pathologies and psychiatric condition) that are endemic to India, societies there have also been plagued by a broad array of, in today's terminology, non-medical threats and sources of misery: warfare, banditry, crime, poverty, dependency, political coercion and exploitation, and crises stemming from moral and religious conflicts. Viewing these problems as *non-medical,* of course, reflects a secular, rationalistic interpretation of what pertains to the health and overall wellbeing of a population. Even today, many of these so-called non-medical problems are associated with manifestations of psychiatric conditions both as causes and consequences. In contemporary societies, to address such emotional and behavioural problems as psychiatric and hence medical has led to considerable criticism.[232] There are political and historical reasons tied to Western societies that involve psychiatric conditions that help explain such criticisms. However, in adopting a general posture about general physical and mental health of a population one should not disregard historically conditioned politico-economic factors that cause and condition ailments and hardship of all types any more than one can disregard aspects of meaning and interpretation. Later chapters discuss relevant cultural and symbolic factors.

Regarding real people in real communities, maladies and misfortunes associated with human suffering make up a generic category in which disease is prominent. Other sources of stress are grief and mourning, loss of morale, economic anxiety and hardships, emotional problems caused by family conflicts, guilt and self-blame caused by real and imagined religious and moral failings, and the sheer psychological devastation stemming from political and economic oppression. These misfortunes and the despair and suffering they cause are part of a civilization's cultural psychology and its ethno-medical orientation, which are interrelated. It is not surprising that anthropologists and physicians who concentrate on Indian health and specifically psychiatric problems should emphasize the holistic, integrated character of human suffering and regard misfortunes of all types as an original, traditional unity comprising both medical and psychiatric problems.[233]

In short, even speaking of a medical system or a medical representation of human suffering in the workings of an institution, in descriptions of sacred medical texts implies that problems of sickness and healing can be isolated from the rest of human experience, that they are narrowly rooted in underlying forms of disease, injury, and pathology. In reality, sickness should refer to misfortune, suffering, and absence of wellbeing, or 'dis-ease', which all signify a generic category of human distress and social maladaptation. Absorbing or integrating the 'medical' within the more generic domain of social misfortune and suffering of all types also applies to psychiatric conditions. More particularly, it is fallacious to think of placing psychiatric phenomena within the even narrower category of medical phenomena, for as the evidence makes abundantly clear, in virtually all of the traditional, indigenous medical traditions, as well as Hindu and Indo-Islamic, psychiatric conditions are

---

232 Kittrie 1971; Conrad and Schneider 1980.

233 See De Sousa and De Sousa 1984.

recognized as a species of general disease. Moreover, as we shall see later, in the broad array of India's culturally defined welfare institutions – temples, shrines, establishments of local, folk healers and wise men – and in the community at large, psychiatric conditions are always prominent concerns. However, it is not usually, or at least necessarily, conceptualized as a distinct entity, but as integral to suffering and sickness.

When analyzing how disturbances of social and psychological behaviour have been expressed in the civilization of India, one has to remember that *psychiatric condition* is a component of a larger social category of human suffering and pain. From a secular, rationalistic, and enlightened point of view, we must not confuse the cultural ontology of misfortune and suffering in ancient India with categories pertaining to different scientific ontologies such as, for example, infection, anemia, malnutrition, psychiatric disturbance, or religious doubt and demoralization. Various social scientific challenges to modern psychiatry, advances in the neural sciences and pharmacology, and political and economic contingencies tied to professional aspirations have led to a neurobiological reductionism in psychiatry, a reductionism that divides social phenomena into discrete parts and gives them different labels that refer to allegedly different, separate types of problems that allegedly call for distinctive types of solutions.[234] Nevertheless, given the frame of reference and goal pursued here, namely, to trace the configuration and enactment of psychiatric conditions across the landscape of India's social and cultural history, one cannot assume that medical conventions followed in contemporary Western societies will conform to those of traditional India. Provided clinical and cultural/linguistic frameworks of reference are integrated, one must be prepared to find psychiatric conditions not necessarily confined to the indigenous medical institutions. While traditional ayurvedic conceptions of disease incorporate conditions in many ways analogous to contemporary psychiatric ones, many such conditions when examined in cultural context are likely to be found in institutions that have nothing to do with medicine. Cultural spokespersons and experts in matters of emotional and behavioural conventions are among the individuals to whom psychiatric conditions are referred. Spiritual and moral reaffirmation, control of deviant thoughts and emotions, problems of morale, and frank disaffection from conventional thought worlds and habit patterns expected of members of

[234] Fabrega 1997.

different sects or castes are among the kinds of social psychological problems that 'non-medical' personnel, village and caste headmen, healers of different varieties, and gurus address as a matter of course. A portion of these will involve, if properly evaluated, psychiatric conditions although in local context and indigenous terms they would be viewed as problems that transgress moral, religious, and spiritual conventions.

Clear partitioning of psychiatric phenomena, a Western conceit to be sure, along medical compared to non-medical lines is not appropriate. This is justified because a large body of information, which underscores the universality of psychiatric phenomena in all human populations.[235] The ubiquity of such phenomena compels one to search for its representation (conditions and healing practices) in all corners of the social fabric of India. Provided an informed clinician's criteria are met, one is justified in viewing phenomena addressed by local non-medical constructs and practices as constituting, along with medical compounds and practitioners' establishments, a segment of the *indigenous psychiatry* of India. This term refers to the confederation of Indian institutions that are in the business of restoring and resolving emotional problems/disturbances and behavioural disaffections. In a broader, analytically imposed frame of reference, a proportion of such problems conform to psychiatric phenomena. One isolates and objectifies psychiatric phenomena for analytic purposes and acknowledges that from an intracultural 'emic' point of view, it constitutes an integral part of human suffering and understood and handled in terms of local conventions of meaning.

In summary, one can safely assume that the subcontinent of India was a setting for small-scale, nomadic hunter-gatherers, termed here 'ancient foragers', following the Upper Palaeolithic era, long before the Neolithic period of cultural evolution. Psychiatric conditions would no doubt have been handled among ancient foragers as they were in other primitive family-level societies.[236] However, little can be traced to the very earliest period. Instead, what we know as the civilization of India is assumed to have its roots in very early agricultural communities following the arrival of the Aryans – historians have discarded the idea of an invasion – around 1500 BCE. In short, problems of experience and behaviour that one can conceptualize as psychiatric conditions and that

---

[235] Fabrega 1997, 2002a. Material for India is discussed later.

[236] See Fabrega 1997.

bear the stamp of Indian culture and civilization date from before the second millennium BCE. Even before the coming of the Aryans emotional problems and disaffections of behaviour that had social consequences and implications, phenomena that one can equate with psychiatric conditions, would have conformed to popular traditions, beliefs, rituals, and myths – patterns of culture that are still found in India and in many other Eurasian societies today.

Focusing on how psychiatric condition has been realized in Indian communities, past and present, requires plunging into and examine diverse bodies of information, each of which attempts to interpret, handle, and cope with the diverse manifestations of social and psychological behaviour problems in the subcontinent. In the following chapters, I have arbitrarily compartmentalized information bearing on human problems of all types for purely expository reasons. I have abstracted material pertinent to how psychiatric conditions may have been manifested, understood, and dealt with in India out of a larger body of material pertaining to all facets of human suffering, conceived and dealt with according to local cultural ontologies and epistemologies. Readers should not assume that what is singled out as a possible variety or representation of psychiatric phenomena invariably stood apart from aspects of human maladies and sufferings that in the society and culture would have been – and perhaps ontologically and certainly social scientifically should be – seen as stemming from religious, moral, political, economic, nutritional, or purely medical considerations. It is best to assume that all types of factors played a contributing role in the creation of human suffering.

Chapter 5

Finding Psychiatric Conditions in Contemporary India

INTRODUCTION

This chapter provides an overview of psychiatric disorders and conditions in modern societies of India. Selected studies by psychiatric epidemiologists and cultural anthropologists are reviewed and discussed. The material affords two snapshots of mental illness. First, epidemiology offers a biomedical perspective of the amount and variety of psychiatric disorders. In this instance, psychiatric conditions are formulated in terms of the strict criteria of clinical neuroscience, the spawn of biomedicine. Insofar as the epidemiologists are from India, and hence conversant with the language and cultural emphases found in the locations of study, their approach gives credibility and a measure of scientific validity about the quantity of psychiatric conditions in modern context as seen from the point of view of the psychiatry establishment. On the other hand, studies conducted by cultural anthropologists provide a complementary picture; namely, how emotional and behavioural disaffections that correspond in many ways to psychiatric conditions and disorders arise from social circumstances, are understood, configured and enacted in terms of shared constructs, perspectives and meanings. The cultural slant, then, provides a glimpse of what psychiatric conditions consist of when viewed not only through a clinical lens, but through the eyes of the people themselves and in context of local circumstances.

The respective pictures of psychiatric conditions differ greatly. The material discussed is based on a selected review of literature about contemporary populations. Taken together, an epidemiological and cultural gaze allows one to appreciate in a realistic fashion the scope of the human problems that such conditions pose.[237] When communities studied are rural and traditional, and with appropriate qualifications and reservations about the interpretation of findings, one may use the material presented as clues to what psychiatric conditions may have been like in earlier periods of Indian history when 'tradition' involved standard conventional thought worlds and habit patterns. However, this method only provides a general, panoramic view. To obtain a truly Indian picture of psychiatric phenomena requires understanding additional aspects of culture, for example, aspects of Indian psychology, religion, philosophy, and medical history, all of which via beliefs, attitudes, values, moral precepts, spiritual orientation, and idioms of emotional expression provided the material in terms of which behaviour (psychiatric condition) was woven. Chapters 6 and 9 take up this part of the story.

WHY CULTURE MATTERS IN UNDERSTANDING PSYCHIATRIC CONDITIONS

In the field of cultural psychiatry and in medical anthropology more generally, a recurring theme has been emphasized on the way in which problems of health, including psychiatric conditions, are understood and dealt with across the spectrum of human societies. As discussed earlier, biomedical psychiatry is a product of Western high, scientific culture. It relies on alleged universal indicators of phenomena termed *psychiatric disorders* that are assumed to involve inherent features of such disorders and in an important way are construed as universals, being language and culture free. A disorder represents an abstract category based on such criteria as symptoms and signs – usually of physical behaviours pruned of their social meanings and interpretation – physiological changes in body function, mode of onset and duration of signs and symptoms, and the effects of all of the preceding on social functioning. A clinician confirms the presence of a disorder (uncovers it in the patient) by means of his or her examination and analysis of pertinent history. During the last ten or so years, the results of non-invasive examination of brain function have been developed that shed light on the brain anatomy and physiology corresponding to or underlying psychiat-

[237] A. K. Agarwal 1998; S. P. Agarwal 2004.

ric disorders, and it is reasonable to anticipate that when the potential of newer methodologies are perfected they will prove helpful and change diagnostic practices since a clearer understanding or clinical neuroscience is likely to require a re-formulation of the basic ontology of psychiatric disorders.

To a typical psychiatric clinician the way in which indicators of psychiatric diagnosis are expressed, communicated, and interpreted in local contexts of the individual is of little interest except insofar as it proves a hindrance to diagnosis and measurement. It may be assumed that the general demeanour, experience, and/or behaviour of an individual who 'shows' or has a psychiatric disorder (meets the required abstract criteria) will indicate this in real life in some way. In other words, the disorder may cause or be associated with a blip on the emotional and behavioural radar screen of the individual. Some aspect of the individual's life is modified in some way by the disorder. However, what this blip means to the typical clinician in the local contexts of social life of the individual (whether it is noticed, given significance, seen as negative or positive) is largely irrelevant, except insofar as overall disorder undermines or interferes with behavioural functions of the individual, in which case it can be part of the diagnosis.

To a cultural psychiatrist things are very different in two ways. Aspects of experience, emotion, behaviour, and bodily functions that figure as the *criteria of disorder in contemporary diagnostic manuals* are just as important as they are to the typical clinical psychiatrist. In fact, they are more so, because such criteria of diagnosis can illustrate in a compelling way the interplay of biology and culture; stated differently, it illustrates the pervasive influence and importance of a social science perspective in psychiatry and medicine. The cultural psychiatrist maintains that language and culture of the individual who is examined is crucially important in reaching a diagnosis. Psychiatric disorders, including their signs and symptoms, are not language- or culture-free phenomena that simply exist much like a tree or a rock formation does. Rather, they are permeated with meanings, conventions, and understandings that stem from the individual's social group, religion, social class, ethnic background, and the like. All of the preceding one may conceptualize as learned phenomena that are transmitted and expressed in linguistic terms and through meaningful behaviour. This constitutes enculturation, which is materialized in neural networks – cultural as involving brain-behaviour structures. Symbolic phenomena making up culture are the life-blood of the social sciences. It is only by carrying out observations and inquiries of an individual's mental and physiological well-being (or psychiatric status) with an understanding of their language and culture in this general sense is it meaningful to evaluate criteria of psychiatric diagnosis in the first place.

To a cultural psychiatrist, the crucial importance of language and culture in clinical evaluation constitutes but one set of considerations. Equally important is consideration of whether a psychiatric disorder has an impact on the individual's life and, if it does, what this impact consists of and how it is explained. In other words, to a cultural psychiatrist a disorder is neither a brain object, nor an entity found in nature, successfully dissected or uncovered in a patient by a clinician (reflecting a carving of 'nature at its joints'). A psychiatric disorder is a category in the language and culture of clinical neuroscience. To a cultural psychiatrist the relevant construct is psychiatric condition which involves a change in the pattern of experience, emotion, behaviour, and overall bodily functioning of an individual. It is shaped by the latter's cultural psychology which he or she has incorporated and carries along with himself or herself.[238] In local context, a clinical neuroscientist's psychiatric disorder or a cultural psychiatrist's psychiatric condition may or may not be noticed, expressed, labelled, or dealt with in any determinate way. On the other hand, if either a disorder or condition is associated with a discernible change in the individual's life that *is identified and taken into account in local context* (*intraculturally*), this can have positive or negative implications for the individual and co-members.

The important consideration for a cultural psychiatrist is not just that a psychiatric disorder involves signs and symptoms as the typical psychiatric clinician sees them. Rather, it is precisely how the individual and his or her significant others experience and see the disorder in their own (language, cultural, social) space that is just as important. Only in the light of an appreciation of what *behaviour means*, for example, ways in which sense of self, emotional experience, cognitive interpretations, and behavioural motivations are formulated and carried out *in association with or as a consequence of* signs and symptoms, that a cultural psychiatrist can come to fully appreciate the significance of psychiatric conditions or disorders. The latter cut a pathway in an individual's life, it brought change and makes an impact of some sort, but in the language

[238] Chapter 9 takes up the question of cultural psychology.

and culture of the individual this may be ignored or not given attention and whatever change it does introduce or is associated with is interpreted in terms of local conventions, standards, values, and overall meanings. As discussed earlier, what a typical psychiatrist construes as a psychiatric disorder the culturally-oriented social scientist sees as a *psychiatric condition*; namely, a pattern of emotion, behaviour, and bodily experience that, while associated with some change in the life arc of the person (a blip on the radar screen of behaviour), is fashioned and enacted in terms of cultural symbols and their meanings.

Comment

A cultural formulation of mental health problems emphasizes their meanings and social consequences. In effect, local idioms and ways of orienting to distress and social disorder shape the expression of a psychiatric condition so that it conforms to a species of disability and disharmony the local population is able to understand and handle using local traditions and concepts about behaviour, personality, sense of social reality, and the bases of human disarray. Put baldly, the social and cultural fabric of a society domesticates and configures its mental health and illness.

However, one can well enquire as to what the material content is that culture works with in fashioning its scenarios of mental disturbances. Demography and public health provide a general backdrop of the biological conditions where mental illnesses are located in a society considered as a corporate structure. The science of contemporary biological psychiatry provides an additional and crucial ingredient about the material bases of mental illness. Like demography and public health, psychiatric epidemiology, which is based on biological constructs and diagnostic indicators, is a comparatively new field of study when examined across the span of history of the subcontinent. Its science provides a descriptive picture of mental illness in contemporary Indian populations that, when examined closely, provides inklings and raises interesting questions about past scenarios of mental health and illness in societies of India. In contrast to the scientific measures of the epidemiologist, the cultural anthropologist provides first-hand accounts and analyses of the play of psychiatric phenomena in real life and in socially meaningful terms. Both pictures are needed in order to arrive at a comprehensive picture of such phenomena.

Studies by contemporary, Indian psychiatrists conducted by means of household surveys that take into consideration differences in language and cultural background are important because they bring to light our alleged bona fide disorders that are, by definition, in some way insinuated in the social fabric, but in a manner that begs explication. In urban settings, villages, communities, and sanctuaries as well as contemporary medical clinics, psychiatric epidemiologists uncover disturbances that people still conceptualize in traditional ways. When seen in local contexts of meanings and social circumstances that are considered traditional, conceptions, attitudes, and ways of coping related to the clinician's psychiatric disorders retain some of the social flavour, idiom and attire that stretches well into the past.[239] An Indologist and social and cultural historians who study India's ancient traditions characteristically rely on diverse bodies of information that span many disciplines (philosophy, literary, and contemporary ethnographies). In the context of our present concern, observations of cultural anthropologists provide information about the present, but with hypothetical exemplars or analogues of psychiatric conditions in past, traditional India as well, a topic taken up in later chapters.[240]

INCIDENCE AND PREVALENCE OF PSYCHIATRIC DISORDERS IN CONTEMPORARY INDIA

Introduction

Research psychiatrists and epidemiologists who are interested in measuring the number and distribution of psychiatric disorders in specific communities rely on the rationale and methods of epidemiology and scientific, biomedical psychiatry as their frame of reference. Biomedical diagnostic criteria of psychiatric disorders are articulated as queries and a standard questionnaire is used to interview and assess the mental status of subjects. Treated or untreated communities are sampled. Interview results establish whether subjects meet criteria for a case and when

---

[239] We will see in Chapter 11 and 12 that in contemporary Indian psychiatry this indigenous dimension is sometimes pushed aside.

[240] See Chapters 6, 7, 8, and 10.

they do questions of onset and duration enable the measurement of incidence (new) and prevalence (old and new) of cases of psychiatric disorders in a population over a given period.

Limitations of rationale and approach

For purposes of orientation, it is appropriate to clarify whether contemporary India differs from other societies in the amount and social distribution of psychiatric conditions, and if so how. Sharp cultural differences between societies could point to important differences in causality. Certain cultural parameters of Indian societies, compared to other societies, could diminish the number of conditions by creating protective zones or shields, providing social support for vulnerable individuals or religious practices that could alleviate and possibly control some of the strains or early symptoms that escalate into full blown conditions. Alternatively, conditions of Indian society and culture could actually predispose vulnerable people to develop signs and symptoms; for example, as a consequence of ill effects of modernization, social disorganization, widespread poverty, and disease, which also create emotional strains and social stressors. Analysis of demographic characteristics of Indian society, for example, the size of families and the composition of households, may help explain unique patterns of prevalence of behavioural disturbances.

Contemporary psychiatric epidemiological studies may be helpful in the study of historical change involving psychiatric phenomena. Such studies can provide a look at how traditional Indian communities of the past might have been burdened by psychiatric conditions. For example, isolated rural settings or tribal communities of India today are assumed to have preserved many ancestral social and religious practices, ways of thinking and coping, and approaches to understanding and caring for victims of behavioural disturbances. Indian social and psychiatric epidemiologists who speak native languages or dialects and are sensitive to the cultural beliefs and values of local communities are in a unique position. They can provide us with description of the manifestations (culturally realized), social landmarks and cultural idioms of conditions of psychiatric interest of traditional India. While illuminating contemporary circumstances and the magnitude of problems posed by mental illness, their results also provide rough estimates of mental health problems of the past.[241]

If social circumstances, lifeways, and the mental world image prevailing among the people of India today resemble those of earlier times with respect of causes and configurations of psychiatric conditions and disorders, then epidemiological studies could provide a way of sampling how similar matters might have appeared centuries and perhaps even thousands of years ago. In other words, since Indian epidemiologists of today are able to find psychiatric phenomena by 'looking under or behind' local attires and idioms of expression that exemplify cultural traditions with a long genealogy in the subcontinent, then they informing about phenomena likely to have been embedded in vulnerable, burdened individuals of earlier societies. Naturally, to what extent cultural, religious, moral, and philosophical traditions, as mediated by language and personality, have maintained a distinctive Hindu configuration from ancient times to the present is contestable and the enterprise aimed at clarifying such questions often challenged as misdirected. However, it is common practice among many contemporary scholars to formulate ancient mentalities and behaviours, seeking for analogues or alternatives of modern conceits with respect to the phenomena in question. Researchers in the social and cultural study of psychiatry in India seem to share a similar view that ancient communities displayed an indigenous formulation of phenomena of psychiatric interest; in other words, that problems of mental health were present and social and cultural institutions managed to provide care and healing to persons with symptoms and signs.[242]

Just as it is speculative to conjure up figures about the prevalence and distribution of psychiatric conditions during prehistoric and ancient times, the same can be said for developments since the advent of the British, when biomedical ideas and procedures began to invade and colonize India. Epidemiology is a relatively modern innovation within biomedicine. The biomedical and internationalist approaches to psychiatric diagnosis are equally new. Even if one could have conducted a field epidemiological study of disorders in India during earlier periods, methodological as well as conceptual problems would make it very difficult to obtain reliable and valid findings, for reasons already sug-

---

[241] A. K. Agarwal 1998.

[242] Balodhi 1986a, 1986b, 1987, 1989, 1991; Gautama 1999.

gested. The thought worlds, emotional architecture and habitual behaviours of pre-modern Indian peoples (what cultural psychology embodies) encased different realizations of the brain-behaviour alterations that constitute conditions of psychiatric interest. We can only make hypotheses about the character of such conditions in ancient India, guided by knowledge drawn from social biology and evolution and in light of what we know about the cultural and behavioural characteristics of ancient populations as reflected in modern traditional contexts.

In proposing to use contemporary psychiatric theory and methods, including epidemiological science, as a basis for hypothesizing about the historical patterns and changes in psychiatric phenomena in India, one takes an internationalist, universalist position about such phenomena. Such a position assumes that while cultural values and beliefs may becloud psychiatric disorders in a contemporary non-industrial society, diagnostic procedures enable the skilful interviewer to peel away cultural influences and the epidemiologist to establish 'caseness'. If researchers know something of the language and culture, these procedures are applicable and might yield reliable pictures of psychiatric disturbances. Ideally, when an analyst takes epidemiological facts about disorders and re-clothes them with their natural cultural and social apparel, thus documenting what and how such facts might look like, mean and how they would have play out in a contemporary or ancient community, he or she is configuring a representation of how traditional communities and institutions (their 'indigenous psychiatries') manage – and may have managed in the past – to incorporate and appropriate such conditions so as to re-claim the social lives of victims and their families. In other words, epidemiologists can point to cases using their criteria; but whether and if so how these cases manifest, are interpreted, and play out in a community reflects social, cultural and biological factors (brain-behaviour encasement) that are beyond the epidemiological grasp and that can only be furnished by informed observations and theoretical analysis of a social scientist and historian.

Estimate of mental illness in the US

For purposes of background, one can first look at contemporary studies in psychiatric epidemiology conducted in the US. Such an approach has limitations. An appropriate measurement in one society may not carry over to the other. This is a common problem in discussing results and involves an apt definition of a case, language translations of symptoms and signs, awareness of cultural masking of symptoms, and the social significance of biomedical psychiatry itself. However, the science of epidemiology has evolved procedures and methods for overcoming such difficulties so as to provide reasonable comparisons.

Community-based epidemiological studies in the US (household surveys of treated and untreated conditions) have yielded lifetime prevalence of psychiatric disorders. According to Robins and Regier, 32 per cent of the population report having had some disorder during their lives, with 20 per cent reporting an active disorder, a prior diagnosis of disorder plus an active symptom or an actual episode of the disorder during the preceding year.[243] Thus, according to these figures, approximately one in every three persons in the US had experienced a psychiatric disorder during a lifetime, whereas one in five had experienced one during the past year. Figures vary widely from one disorder to the next and vary according to social background (gender, ethnicity, social class, density of population). Overall, the lifetime prevalence figures for adults are given in Table 5.1.

These figures suggest that the US population has a comparatively high prevalence of formally defined and diagnosed psychiatric disorders. They exclude less serious conditions of psychological distress, social impairment and suffering, symptoms that failed to meet formal criteria of diagnosis, and disorders that respondents have forgotten or were too embarrassed to report.

The high prevalence of psychiatric disorders in the US can be used as a rough guideline against which to measure other societies. One must emphasize that these figures reflect how a psychiatric condition is defined in contemporary psychiatry. They measure prevalence of *psychiatric disorders* that by definition cause distress and produce social impairment and also impact on general medical facilities (anxiety, depression, somatization) although disorder do not necessarily preclude ability to work and even enjoy life to some extent. Most disorders do not have as poor a prognosis as schizophrenia. More important, American society has a comparatively long history of concern regarding mental illness. The stigma attached to it has been moderated somewhat through publicity about its 'medical' basis and better education about mental health problems. Finally, procedures and methods for measuring psychiatric

[243] Robins and Regier 1991.

Table 5.1.
Mental disorders in the US, 1991

Disorder	Per cent
Phobic disorder	14.2
Alcohol-related disorders	13.8
Somatization syndrome*	11.6
Generalized anxiety disorder	4.0–6.5
Mild cognitive impairment in those older than the age of 55	10.0
Affective disorder (depression, mania, mixed states)	c. 8
Antisocial personality disorder	4.0
Severe cognitive impairment over the age of 55	3.0
Obsessive-compulsive disorder	2.6
Panic disorder	2.0
Schizophrenia (the most important psychosis)	1.0
Somatization disorder**	0.13

* at least four symptoms in males and six in females
** at least 12 body symptoms in males, 14 in females

disorders in the US rely on concepts and linguistic formulations of criteria of disorder that draw largely on a common culture and are evolved from shared conceptions about personhood, psychological experience and social behaviour. As a result, physicians encounter fewer equivocal, difficult-to-diagnose cases, atypical manifestations that elude the epidemiological net, or concealment, opposition, and outright deception regarding possible symptoms.

The high prevalence of psychiatric disorders in the US can be used as a rough guideline against which to measure other societies. One must emphasize that these figures reflect how a psychiatric condition is defined in contemporary psychiatry. They measure prevalence of *psychiat-*

ric disorders that by definition cause distress and produce social impairment and also impact on general medical facilities (anxiety, depression, somatization) although disorder do not necessarily preclude ability to work and even enjoy life to some extent. Most disorders do not have as poor a prognosis as schizophrenia. More important, American society has a comparatively long history of concern regarding mental illness. The stigma attached to it has been moderated somewhat through publicity about its 'medical' basis and better education about mental health problems. Finally, procedures and methods for measuring psychiatric disorders in the US rely on concepts and linguistic formulations of criteria of disorder that draw largely on a common culture and are evolved from shared conceptions about personhood, psychological experience and social behaviour. As a result, physicians encounter fewer equivocal, difficult-to-diagnose cases, atypical manifestations that elude the epidemiological net, or concealment, opposition, and outright deception regarding possible symptoms.

Psychiatric disorders in Indian communities

Results discussed later reveal that when due allowances are made to differences in methodology, amount and distribution of psychiatric disorders in India roughly matches that of US. In general, epidemiological rates obtained in modern Western societies, as well as in modern India, could be interpreted either as maximal or minimal measurements of mental illness in ancient and medieval India. The position one adopts depends on whether one regards circumstances in earlier times as detrimental to mental health – because of poverty, unforgiving moralities, political and economic exploitation, religious oppression of social classes, poor public health – or as protective of mental health, given the absence of the ills of modernity, the power of prevailing cultural psychology to give sacred meaning, maintaining desireless purpose, and promoting rational, emotional, stoical acceptance of life's limitations. Factors that influence causation of mental illness are sufficiently complex, variable, and context-related such as to defy definitive resolution of contrasting positions. The purpose is not to obtain real levels of incidence or prevalence in traditional Indian communities but merely to provide a rough sketch of its level and distribution.

One of the earliest and most cited epidemiological studies of mental illness in India, reported by Dube, was conducted in Agra, a mixed rural-urban community of Uttar Pradesh in northern India.[244] It was a general-prevalence study that relied on home visits to rural and both industrial and non-industrial populations of 29,468 persons. Dube describes living conditions and attitudes in some settings:

> In villages, inhabitants lead a simple life living in mud-houses without proper drainage and sanitation and lack of good drinking water supply. Dispensaries are not readily available in all the villages and many diseases go untreated. Illnesses like trachoma, malnutrition, gastroenteritis, tuberculosis, etc., are fairly common. There is a considerable infant mortality rate. Rural inhabitants usually seek ayurvedic treatment which is cheaper and more readily available ... A great deal of misconception, superstition and ignorance exists in respect of mental disease. Much stigma is often attached. Mental illnesses are viewed as a visitation of evil spirits of goddess or a curse. This takes the form of exaggerated belief in mystic influences, excessive faith in the powers of saint, priest and medicament ... The medicaments, sorcerers, faith healers, priests, etc., are frequently engaged to cure cases of mental illness, snake bites, etc. There are a number of places of worship reputed as centres of treatment endowed with healing powers due to a deity. One such place in this region is Balajee, where a large number of persons from this region go in the hope of cure of mental illness. Many return disillusioned and come to Mental Hospital after other treatments have been tried.[245]

The team of investigators consisted of a psychologist, a social worker, a field investigator, and a statistician. It was a three-stage study: (1) reconnaissance, initial contact, home visits, and detection of possible cases; (2) interviews of suspected cases by a psychiatrist leading to identification of cases; and (3) compilation of data and analysis. Instances that pointed to possible cases were interviewed by two different psychiatrists. Dube defines a case as:

> A manifest disturbance of mental functioning specific enough in clinical character to be consistently recognizable as conforming to defined patterns which can be classified broadly into one of the standard categories of psychiatric illness.[246]

Active cases (during the 18 months preceding the interview) and inactive cases (earlier than 18 months) were ascertained and placed in one

[244] Dube 1970.

[245] Dube 1970: 329.

[246] Dube 1970: 332.

of six diagnostic categories: schizophrenia, manic-depressive psychosis, psychosis due to organic aetiology and epilepsy, mental deficiency, hysteria, and a category for other psychoneuroses and disorders.

A total of 701 active and inactive cases of psychopathology were counted. The lifetime prevalence was calculated at 23.79 per 1000. Females had a statistically higher prevalence rate ($p < 0.01$) than males (15.7 and 33.3 per 1000, respectively), and those with low education (illiterates or those with only primary education) had a higher rate (also $p < 0.01$) than those with more education. The highest prevalence rate was for hysteria (6.07 per 1000), mental deficiency (3.70), and psychoneuroses and other disorders (3.33). The rate for schizophrenia was 1.49. Only in the case of hysteria did education have an impact, with the least educated showing a higher prevalence ($p < 0.01$). In general, the results are considerably lower than those reported previously to contemporary America, which were obtained at a time when psychiatric epidemiology was far more advanced and applied in a modern country where methodological difficulties of measuring and ascertaining cases were less pronounced.

Carstairs and Kapur conducted an epidemiological study in the coastal village of Kota in the South Kanara district of Karnataka State.[247] Household surveys were conducted among members of three groups or castes: (1) Brahmins, the highest caste, mostly landowners, some engaged in trade, others in teaching; (2) Bants, traditionally soldiers, now agricultural labourers; and (3) Mogers, the fishermen caste. Researchers chose among many different ways of classifying psychiatric symptoms regarded as having clinical significance. One method was to develop 12 categories of disorders with similar symptoms. More than 10 per cent of respondents reported suffering from the symptoms from three categories. A hierarchical system of classification was developed, each person assigned to the class associated with his or her highest-ranking symptom and excluded from the other classes, although symptoms falling into these classes were noted. This roughly approximated a system of diagnostic classification.

The following figures were recorded:

[247] Carstairs and Kapur 1976.

Table 5.2.
Mental disorders in Kota in the South Kanara district, Karnataka State, India (Carstairs and Kapur 1976)

Disorder	Per cent
Psychosis	1.0
Epilepsy	1.0
Depression	3.0
Anxiety, worry, and other neurotic symptoms*	19.0
Somatic symptoms	10.0
Possession states and hysteria	3.0
No symptoms	63.0

* forgetfulness, poor concentration, muscular tension, restlessness, irritability

Hence, approximately one in three persons was judged to have a clinically significant psychiatric disorder. Results obtained in this study were based on very different criteria and methods of procedure and in a strict sense should not be compared with those discussed for the US or for Agra town. However, the similarity in the overall measures of psychiatric morbidity compared to the US is illuminating.

For understanding cultural factors in relation to psychiatric conditions, the foregoing study is very informative. It allowed Kapur to concentrate on comparing the role played by biomedical physicians with a psychiatric orientation, ayurvedic physicians, and other so-called folk or lay practitioners in handling psychiatric conditions. Kapur approached this problem by trying to understand what type of medical help, if any, patients who had demonstrated psychiatric morbidity in his survey had received. He points to the benefits of understanding fundamental questions about alternative medical practitioners. For example, their number, orientation, approach to patient, effectiveness in ameliorating symptoms, openness to collaborative work with a modern, biomedical mental health team, and how often they were consulted.

Kapur was surprised to find that non-psychiatrists were not 'closed' in their orientation – that is, were not rigidly wedded to their indigenous point of view – frequently referred patients to psychiatrists, and saw themselves as open to collaborative work with physicians. The physicians surveyed also had a positive, collaborative attitude toward alternative practitioners. The largest proportion of Kapur's patients had actually consulted biomedics first, which is surprising in view of information reported earlier by Dube. Results also indicated that 59 per cent of patients had consulted non-biomedics for relief since the onset of illness, and 24 per cent during the last month. Interestingly, Kapur found that only in the case of possession syndromes were biomedics not consulted first because victims preferred the folk practitioners. Moreover, a majority of such patients felt no need to receive treatment at all, presumably because they viewed their state in positive terms, that is, they may not have regarded condition as medical.

Putting aside cases of possession, and in general, the studies by Carstairs, Kapur, and Dube support a basic assumption of the universalist thesis, namely, that not only does one find individuals showing psychiatric conditions in traditional communities of India, but also that many see themselves as ill, in need of treatment, and seek help from medical practitioners, regardless of their cultural orientation. If this attitude could be generalized for historic India, it suggests that a significant proportion of psychiatric conditions were perceived as sickness or ailments and in need of medical treatment. In other words, the system of medicine of India appears to represent an important enclosure where one can find psychiatric conditions. A cultural historian of psychiatry would ask three related questions: how much of diagnosable psychiatric conditions *was perceived by respondents as not* having a medical basis? What interpretation was given to them? What was done about them?

The study of the prevalence of psychiatric disorders in India has a long ancestry and has continued to claim the attention of psychiatric epidemiologists who rely on such data to assess need for care among contemporary populations.[248] Only a few representative studies are discussed here. Of those selected, some followed a methodology comparable to that used by Carstairs and Kapur and none of those discussed

[248] Sethi, Gupta, and Kumar. 1967; Sethi *et al.* 1974; Verghese and Beig 1974; A. K. Agarwal 1998.

here adopted the methods used in the US.[249] Furthermore, different prevalence measures were reported. Indian studies generally rely on a point- or period-prevalence whereas the US studies computed lifetime prevalence and one-year prevalence. Padmavathi and colleagues reported on an epidemiological survey study of functional psychoses in an urban community in Madras, India.[250] In this study researchers relied on the Indian Psychiatric Survey Schedule (IPSS) as a screening instrument.[251] As a diagnostic instrument Padmavathi *et al.* relied on the Present State Examination, which developed at the Maudsley Hospital in London by Wing and colleagues.[252] A prevalence figure of functional psychoses of 5.56 cases per 1000 and of schizophrenia of 3.87 per 1000 was obtained.

Mehta and Verghese estimated the prevalence of priority psychiatric patients in a rural area of Tamil Nadu.[253] Researchers concentrated on schizophrenia, affective disorders, organic psychoses, epilepsy, and mental retardation, excluding disorders termed neurotic and due to personality as well as somatoform-like disorders, which were included by Carstairs and Kapur.[254] The Tamil Nadu interviews were conducted in 50 per cent of homes in 11 randomly selected villages from a total of 68. The Indian Psychiatric Survey Schedule was the screening instrument, followed by psychiatric interviews. A point prevalence of 1.4 per cent was obtained, roughly similar to that of other communities. About 75 per cent of patients identified had shown manifestations of illness for more than one year, and 36 per cent for more than five years.

D. N. Nandi and co-workers reported a ten-year follow-up study of an area approximately 50 kilometres from Calcutta.[255] A door-to-door enquiry, a different methodology from studies discussed earlier, using a check-list consisting of 70 symptoms. 'Probable' cases were given a complete medical and psychiatric examination, and the final diagnosis was decided after examinations by two independent psychiatrists. A full

---

[249] Carstairs and Kapur 1976.

[250] Padmavathi *et al.* 1987.

[251] Also used by Kapur, Kapur, and Carstairs 1974, and which resembled that described earlier for Carstairs and Kapur 1976.

[252] Wing, Cooper, and Sartorius 1974.

[253] Mehta and Verghese 1985.

[254] Carstairs and Kapur 1976.

[255] D. N. Nandi *et al.* 1986.

inventory of psychiatric disorders was considered in estimating cases at time of interview. The figure obtained by them for the same community in 1982 (8.5 per cent) was approximately the same as that obtained in 1972 (8.2 per cent).

Beliefs in spirits, demons, godlings, and other agents are part of the indigenous system of explanation of illness found in virtually all pre-modern, traditional societies. A common way in which spirits affect the wellbeing of vulnerable persons is by attacking and sometimes possessing victims. It is likely that such beliefs either predated the advent of Indo-Europeans on the subcontinent of India or were brought by them well before the time when Ayurveda medicine evolved and consolidated as scholarly, academic systems of medicine.[256] In a study conducted by Venkataramaiah *et al.* in remote, traditional villages 90 per cent of the population believed not only in the existence of such spirits but in spirit possession.[257] While illness and psychiatric condition are often explained in terms of spiritual attack or possession this is by no means always the case. Anthropological literature abounds with examples of how altered behaviour of individuals ascribed to possession can enhance the status of 'victims' who come to exert important influence among family and community.

Venkataramaiah and colleagues conducted an epidemiological study seeking to look at the prevalence of spirit possession in West Karnataka, a region that had recently experienced an 'epidemic' of such 'possession' syndromes. Subjects were drawn from 30 small, isolated villages in a setting where local folk practitioners, who themselves experienced spirit possession in the conduct of their work, practiced their brand of holistic medicine, which, of course, embraced much more than strictly physical disease. In the house-to-house survey, the head of household was the principal informant, who then volunteered information about spirit possession among members of the household during the preceding year. Subsection 10 of the Indian Psychiatric Survey was used as a guideline.[258] The cases that were identified were then examined, and every fifth one administered with an attitude questionnaire. A period prevalence of 3.7 per cent was recorded, a high figure compared to similar

---

[256] A certain class of psychiatric conditions in Ayurveda is in fact explained in terms of spiritual attack, discussed later in Chapters 7 and 8.

[257] Venkataramaiah *et al.* 1981.

[258] As used by Carstairs and Kapur 1976.

surveys in India.[259] Even when Venkataramaiah *et al.* removed from analysis individuals from West Karnataka who had been infected by the earlier epidemic because they biased the sample, the prevalence rate was still high. The majority of subjects, who were typically females under the age of 15, judged their syndromes to be 'troublesome'. The authors conclude:

> Female sex, young age, low education predispose an individual to get possessed in such atmosphere ... possession syndrome is a socio-culturally induced phenomenon used by some to become healers and counsellers (sic), by some to take up sick role and get help. Some fail to gain anything and suffer.[260]

Rajkumar studied schizophrenia in India, which, along with Sri Lanka, ranks high among Third World countries in rates of the disorder.[261] A study of functional psychoses conducted in Madras yielded a prevalence rate of 2.62 per 1000 (265 cases in a population of 101 229), and an age-corrected rate of 3.98 per 1000. These are higher than rates reported by other studies conducted in India. Studies reveal differences between rural and urban regions, but no consistent pattern appears. Nor are there evident differences between age groups. While studies in Western societies show that schizophrenia has an earlier age of onset in males, this is not demonstrated in India. Several studies showed a higher prevalence among higher socioeconomic classes, including Brahmins, than among the lower castes. According to Rajkumar, the incidence rates of schizophrenia in India are higher than in the West.

Nandi and colleagues conducted an epidemiological study of psychiatric morbidity among different tribes and different castes of communities of West Bengal.[262] This study allows us to examine how psychiatric conditions are placed in different social spaces of India and to conjecture about cultural influences. Two basic issues were addressed: are there different levels of psychiatric morbidity between different tribal and caste groups, and between different socioeconomic groups within tribes and castes? Nandi acknowledged that different 'values,

---

[259] Carstairs and Kapur 1976 reported that 26 females and 8 males of the village of Kota were diagnosed as showing a possession syndrome during the preceding six months, a rate of 3 per cent.

[260] Venkataramaiah *et al.* 1981: 218.

[261] Rajkumar 1995.

[262] D. N. Nandi *et al.* 1980.

beliefs, opinions and attitudes' went into the 'social yardstick' of what determines 'normal' versus 'abnormal' behaviour in the various groups, but these 'did not interfere with the process of case detection or diagnosis'.[263] No unusual, 'culture-bound' disorders were found, implying that the biomedical system of accounting appears to adequately cover the terrain of psychiatric conditions for India. From the standpoint of a social history of mental illness, the emphasis on tribes is significant:

> The tribal groups under survey may be taken as a replica of the people living close to nature far from the modern technological civilization. Their society is still simple, without any stratification and without any room for occupational specialization.[264]

All individuals who manifested clinically significant symptoms at the time of examination were counted as cases, except for 'hysterics' and 'epileptics', who were accepted as cases only if they had been symptomatic during the preceding year. Various types of psychiatric disorders were diagnosed, although the comparatively small size of the sample meant that some disorders could not be compared satisfactorily. Individual morbidity among the tribes did not differ; their overall rate was 2 per cent, with 11 per cent of families having one or more afflicted individuals. The lower castes showed no differences in level of individual morbidity. Their level was 7 per cent, with 27 per cent of families having at least one affected member. The morbidity level among Brahmins was 11 per cent and 54 per cent of families had at least one afflicted member.[265]

The two tribes and the lower castes were handled as two separate groups, since they appeared uniform within the groupings. They were then compared with the Brahmins, and this yielded a highly significant statistical difference. Depression was the most frequent diagnosis, with females showing a higher level in all groups, especially among Brahmins and the lower castes. Interestingly, anxiety states and obsessional disorders were not found among tribes. Among tribes and the lower castes, higher socioeconomic groups showed significantly higher morbidity rates, and a similar but non-significant trend was found for

---

[263] D. N. Nandi *et al*. 1980: 74.

[264] D. N. Nandi *et al*. 1980: 79.

[265] Because average size of family differed in the three groups, it is difficult to compare levels of family morbidity.

Brahmins. The 11 per cent level of prevalence for Brahmins was among the highest of those recorded.[266]

The higher rate of morbidity of females is consistent with other findings in social and cultural psychiatry and suggests that social role of women may constitute a predisposing factor. Differences between varieties of psychiatric conditions among the three groups caused the researchers to theorize that Brahmins exhibited higher rates of obsession and anxiety, especially females, whereas these problems did not appear among tribes, and lower-caste females had higher rates of hysteria.

> In a given cultural group certain forms of neurotic behaviour are accommodated while others are not; ... the task of the culture is to channel the symptoms of an endemic disease in such a way that the symptoms do not disrupt orderly community life.[267]

Mental health problems among elderly populations of India are common and are part of the millions of individuals that Agarwal was pointed to as in need for psychiatric care in contemporary India.[268] P. S. Nandi and colleagues confirm this.[269] They surveyed the level of morbidity of the elderly population in rural areas of West Bengal and found that 61 per cent of people aged 60 and above showed manifestations of mental illness. They conjecture that somewhere around 36 million persons in India fall into the over 60 category and that if their figures pertaining to morbidity are reasonably correct, a substantial proportion of the population show manifestations of mental illness. As is common in other studies conducted in traditional villages, it is very likely local perceptions of family did not include a category of mental illness or *unmāda*. While P. S. Nandi's data show high levels of psychiatric comorbidity, it is likely that in resort to care family sought help of local herbalists or ayurvedic physicians.

Dementia and Alzheimer's disease have recently been studied in Ballabgarh, in rural northern India.[270] Not surprisingly, the methodology of these studies relies exclusively on universal conceptions and criteria of diagnosis with respect to dementia, in keeping with state sponsorship

---

[266] The rates of other studies that were compared were 1.8–10.3 per cent.

[267] D. N. Nandi *et al.* 1980: 81.

[268] A. K. Agarwal 1998.

[269] P. S. Nandi *et al.* 1997.

[270] Chandra *et al.* 1998a, 1998b; Ganguli *et al.* 1995, 1996, 1999.

of international studies in biomedicine. Investigators worked hard to assure that criteria and methods of measurement of mental states, cognitive deficits, and functional impairment in India made sense there – that the questions asked and the tasks used to assess mental functioning were in keeping with cultural patterns of activity. For example, subjects were not asked to read any material themselves because of possible educational deficiencies. The population showed a low prevalence of incipient Alzheimer's disease and dementia. As expected, rates increased in relation to age but bore no relationship to literacy or gender. The unusually low rate of dementia could be explained by low overall life expectancy, short survival with disease, and other unspecified risk factors.

Although studies vary in their reports about psychiatric conditions in contemporary India, prevalence rates are typically lower than for Western nations. In the final analysis, this difference cannot be interpreted meaningfully because of differences in procedure and because the whole logic of community epidemiological study of mental illness – indeed, the logic of scientific psychiatry itself – is based on Western notions of human psychology and behaviour. How the thought worlds and habit patterns (cultural psychology) of traditional Indian peoples shape their psychiatric conditions, as per signs and symptoms, remains to be worked out. In general, Indian psychiatrists are committed biomedics and have been unwilling to entertain the possibility that psychiatric conditions may have a different architecture in India.[271] Simple distrust of and reluctance of traditional Indian people to share private information with their Western-trained and influenced brethren researchers may also limit the latter's access to what traditional Indian psychiatric conditions are like. In general, psychiatric disorders are defined on strict biomedical, clinical and epidemiological grounds. If the methods and procedures of an Indian study ape those of the West and reflect the latter's hegemonic status and need to establish a 'common language' irrespective of cultural differences, at the exclusion of content and meaning, then epidemiological profiles among Indian peoples will tend to by similar, differing only in narrow, quantitative ways. Stated differently: if no attempt is made to determine the effect of Indian thought worlds and habit patterns on how psychiatric conditions might be configured, a method of proceeding that requires an anthropological

[271] A topic taken up later in Chapters 11 and 12.

sensitivity about context, local values, experience and behaviour in India (normal and abnormal), it will be impossible to arrive at a realistic, valid profile of psychiatric condition in India.

Nevertheless, Indian social psychiatry has established overwhelming evidence that traditional folk as well as tribal and forest peoples show significant levels of psychiatric condition. Incorporation of such peoples into mainstream Indian civilization including religion has a long ancestry in the subcontinent and has continued through the medieval era until contemporary times.[272] Agarwal reports that:

> There will be approximately 2 million persons suffering from schizophrenia [alone] at any given time ... [and that] estimates [suggest] that 405,000 new cases of schizophrenia are being added every year.[273]

In commenting on common understanding of contemporary Indian people about mental illness Agarwal states:

> The general population believes that (a) mental illnesses are chronic and incurable, (b) mentally ill are impulsive and dangerous as they can produce physical harm to people around them ... (c) mental illness is caused by 'bad blood' in the family or due to 'bad deeds' in this life or past, (d) mentally ill cannot be given positions of responsibility as they are unreliable and incompetent ... If a person develops mental illness during service many organizations have a provision of terminating their service, (e) mentally ill are unfit to marry or remain married. Hiding the fact of mental illness at the time of marriage is considered enough ground to nullify marriage.[274]

Psychiatric disorders described in diagnostic systems of earlier modern and now contemporary psychiatry are found in urban and remote, village communities of India. Many studies have pointed to high prevalence. Venkataswamy Reddy and Chandrashekar reviewed and summarized a large number of epidemiological studies of mental illness in India and data such as these have served as battle cries for contemporary needs.[275] The logic in terms of which these studies are conducted, the sensitivity of Indian researchers to local linguistic and cultural idioms of expression and interpretation, and the widespread prevalence in

---

[272] R. S. Sharma 1983, 1991, 1995; Thapar 1984, 2002; Guha 1999.

[273] A. K. Agarwal 1998: 104.

[274] A. K. Agarwal 1998: 104.

[275] Venkataswamy Reddy and Chandrashekar 1998.

modernizing and traditional communities suggest psychiatric conditions have a long pedigree in the subcontinent.

Gururaj and Isaac have provided a comprehensive survey and summary of psychiatric epidemiological findings in modern India.[276] They describe a total of 23 studies. In rural settings prevalence rates in cases (not specified as to diagnosis) per 1000 population extend from 9.5 to 369. Of 17 such studies, ten have rates equal or greater than 15 per 1000. Urban rates extend from a low of 6.7 to a high of 72.7, and of six studies, four have rates that exceed 15 per 1000. Details about specific disorders are also presented and discussed. This review emphasizes the importance of documenting the high amount of mental illness in India for it underscores the vast need for public and private mental health services. It also points to limitations of data and further areas in need for clarification. In view of earlier discussion involving cultural masking of psychiatric conditions in real life circumstances, it is appropriate to quote one of conclusion:

> A widening gap between the 'researchers' definition of a case' and 'community perception of mental problems and needs of those requiring care' are some of the key issues not addressed in the Indian region. Even in Western countries, this debate is on the increase between science and reality. In India, it is quite clear that existing services do not even penetrate a small segment of the population, and this is obviously related to the availability and affordability of mental health services. Indian psychiatric epidemiology has closely followed international growth in this area. The majority of instruments and standardized procedures have not been tested for culture specificity and indigenous instruments are often overshadowed by Western technologies. If this gap has to be narrowed, local, culture-specific methodologies need augmentation. Any amount of research data will fail to make an impact, if it is not linked to community needs and perceptions.[277]

PSYCHIATRIC CONDITIONS IN AN INDIAN VILLAGE SETTING

While epidemiology provides a description of mental illness in a society, its picture and narrative is comparatively dry and lifeless. How psychiatric conditions are expressed in real persons, real social circumstances,

---

[276] Gururaj and Isaac 2004.

[277] Gururaj and Isaac 2004: 53.

and their implications simply cannot be appreciated. For the latter, one needs to consult the writings of cultural anthropologists. While they also speak of contemporary circumstances, they examine distressed persons whose voices, one may surmise, echo those that have been heard in the subcontinent from more traditional times.

Opler provides a window into the workings of community life in a rural area of northern India that illustrates strains and conflicts in the social fabric.[278] One can use his material as a basis for conjecturing about local conditions in earlier times. Opler concentrates on one idiom of distress, that of spirit possession. This is a token for a range of social, psychological, and physiological difficulties that his possessed subjects experienced, as well as those of many others in the village who did not claim to be possessed, or whose difficulties may not have crossed the threshold sufficiently to be regarded as problems. The theory of possession with respect to mental illness in India is taken up later.[279] Presently it is the descriptive feel of these syndromes in light of prevailing social circumstances that is relevant; and specially, the different picture one obtains compared to epidemiological studies of case.

Members of the community described by Opler live in a universe composed of natural and supernatural agents or beings. Thus the behavioural environment is comprised of human beings as well as a myriad of ghosts, spirits, demons, and godlings inhabiting a supernatural world that is believed to interpenetrate the natural one. To the people, events in one realm are caused by events in the other, and vice versa. Strains or aberrant behaviour in the natural world can raise the question of intervention from the preternatural world. Opler presents a large number of illustrative cases and six of these are selected for discussion.

> *Case #1*: A man had recently been beaten to death as a result of a political feud between antagonistic castes. His widow suddenly began to curse and snap at group mates, threatening to bite and eat them. Her attacks were aimed at a woman of her own caste with whom she had quarrelled and at members of the higher caste who were responsible for beating her husband. This was highly unusual behaviour, since she ordinarily showed respect and deference toward those of the higher caste. Others recognized her as 'possessed' and

[278] Opler 1958.

[279] See Chapter 7.

fled from her. When the woman attempted to run away, she was caught and a shaman was called. Opler suggests that this woman's behaviour conforms to a case of hysteria set in the context of one coping with understandable and 'overwhelming' anger toward higher caste individuals, the expression of which in the culture is heavily censured and unacceptable. However, Opler suggests, angry behaviour is forgivable if caused by a possessing agent. This hysteria, then, is hardly dry and lifeless when compared to the hysterias of epidemiologists discussed earlier. It is not difficult to surmise that a situation and resulting psychiatric condition such as this is likely to have been repeated countless time in earlier history of India for it hinges on universal happenings (social political strains) and biological propensities (capacity to enter altered states of consciousness).

Case #2: A man of Hindu background and from an untouchable caste left the village to work in the city. Although warned about the Muslim ghosts that 'infected' the path that he customarily took from his home to the mill, he ignored the warning. He developed a severe skin infection that forced him to leave his job and return to the village. There he became 'violent and abusive and was constantly in trouble'. He spoke out against high-caste landlords and told them he was himself a Muslim spirit, impervious to their actions. He came close to being seriously beaten by the indignant landlords. His kinfolk surmised that he had been 'possessed' by a ghost and called in a shaman. Opler suggests that upon his return to the village the man had been forced to return to the strict rules prevailing there, a contrast to the freedom he had enjoyed in the city, which put him under an intolerable strain. This case illustrates dilemmas and strains inherent in the social structure of village life in India. It suggests that individuals commonly experience psychological conflicts and tensions in the give and take of living under the strictures of *dharma*, the sacred law. In the present case, a 'brush with modernity' may have lessened inhibitions and/or sensitized the man to social injustices, resulting in his resort to aggression, as Opler suggests. Nevertheless, it is very likely that a case such as this echoes happenings that have occurred countless times in traditional India. One has only to peruse writings of Manu to be appraised of the repeated censures against those who strike higher caste persons: exhortations of the *dharma* framed in these terms were insistent precisely because the eventualities they proscribe were not uncommon, given the moral, psychological burdens inherent in the caste system. In the present case a psychotic episode was fashioned in terms of Hindu/Muslim antagonisms, a theme likely to have been common during and since the medieval period of India's past.

Case #3: A woman was convinced that the spirit of her husband's dead wife was the cause of her sense of persecution. Her burden and distress was significant enough for her to seek services of a shaman who diagnosed her condition and validated her plight. Shaman explained that the first wife had died upon returning to the village after having been attacked by 'ghosts' while living in Calcutta. As a result, she had herself become an angry ghost and was now tormenting the new wife. Opler points out that when women marry a widower they are expected to honour and worship the man's dead wife. He suggests that the woman may have been lax in her responsibilities, and her 'psychological uneasiness' about failing in her dharmic responsibilities was being realized in the paranoid idiom that Opler's account describes. Here again, one has access not only to the interiority of the social fabric of India but also to its burdens. The common theme, likely ubiquitous in traditional as well as modern times, is: social, moral strictures and expectations that in vulnerable individuals can prove burdensome and bring on a psychiatric condition. The latter's idiom 'communicates' how the social fabric is insinuated in the cultural psychology of individuals and can break out in terms of signs and symptoms of psychiatric conditions.[280]

These three cases indicate that belief in and possession by spirits furnishes the material in terms of which individuals express and communicate psychological distress inherent in village life. The manifestations of the distress involve disturbances of behaviour and conduct that go against social conventions and lead to consultation with folk practitioners. The social fabric creates strains and vulnerable individuals succumb to them through signs and symptoms that suggest indigenous varieties of psychiatric condition. Constructs and beliefs about interpersonal relations that prevail in the society ordinarily channel behaviour in conformance with social conventions. However, social expectations and

[280] Opler 1958: 561–562.

restrictions on behaviour can be onerous and when an individual's tolerance of distress is exceeded the result is a condition for which the society provides a safety valve. Two generalizations are possible: (1) deviant social conduct is taken as a manifestation of illness and psychiatric condition, often made sense of as spirit possession; and (2) violations of social behaviour norms are made sense of in spiritualist/religious discourses and controlled and regulated by the imposition and re-affirmation of the relevant norms and rituals conceptualized in medical terms. Thus, the cases illustrate what one could term a native, indigenous 'spiritualized' psychiatry or system of mental health practice.

> *Case #4*: As is usual during an epidemic, the house of a shaman was filled with women seeking aid from troublesome spirits who had 'caught' or 'possessed' them. The shaman's singing and beating a monotonous rhythm on his drum caused a woman seated at the back of the room to become 'possessed'. The shaman questioned the ghost to learn its identity and its reason for seizing the woman. Speaking through the afflicted woman, the ghost stated that it had 'possessed' her as she was returning from her father's household to her husband's village. When the shaman pressed with more questions, the ghost refused to answer. The shaman tried to persuade it leave the body of the woman, arguing that the 'possessed' woman was very poor and hardly a fit vehicle. Opler explains this episode in terms of the particular problems associated with the position of women in marriage.[281]

An important factor in this case is that when questioned the ghost indicated the problem for the woman originated during her journey from the parents' home to that of her husband. Village exogamy is practiced in the village and residence after marriage is patrilocal. Such marriages place on young brides a great deal of stress as she attempts to adjust to her husband's household and relatives. There exist constraints on movement and behaviour in her husband's village. Special forms of avoidance and politeness towards husband's kinsmen and fellow villagers are prescribed, all of which stand in contrast to the relaxed ambience and freedom the wife has in her own family's home. Hypergamous marriage is usual, with husband's family occupying a superior position

[281] Opler 1958: 561–562.

in the caste. Thus, upon marriage a bride enters a higher sub-caste as a junior and subordinate. If she has grievances she cannot easily communicate them to her husband since he sides with his own family in such disputes, and may insist she obey them.

This case points out that a woman's life during early years of marriage is fraught with anxieties and tensions and illustrates how these are channelled in the society. Failure to conceive or inability to produce a son during early years of marriage places a newly married woman in a vulnerable and precarious position. She and her husband's family will fear possible influence of a malignant ghost or spirit. In this setting, untoward behaviour on the part of the bride signals possession by ghosts and spirits that in turn elicit solicitous attitudes from her husband and his family. Opler indicates that in this and similar cases:

> Possession by ghosts may be punishment unconsciously meted out by a young woman to those about her for real or fancied reasons. A ghost or malignant spirit has a habit of persecuting a whole family, once it enters the circle of a home through an individual, and consequently its presence is most unwelcome to the whole group. Also its eradication or pacification is an expensive undertaking and often a lengthy one. It may cause still other marriage difficulties, because few families want to enter into marriage negotiations that will result in receiving a ghost in addition to a new member. A number of shamans have pointed out that a large percentage of their clients are young women who were 'caught' soon after joining their husband's families. A knowledge of the social and marital practices and the points of tension they involve goes far to explain the concentration of hysteria, possession, and trance states in this group.[282]

This case and Opler's generous analysis illustrates how the social fabric of Indian communities involving duty and obligation manages not only to control and shape behaviour but to oppress individuals. It produces the strains that culminate in a psychiatric condition. It also provides a set of precepts, guidelines, and practices that by spiritualizing conflicts and strains proyides a means for alleviating tensions and hurts in ways that still manage to maintain the social conditions of oppression.

Case #5: Ten days into a ceremony to the goddess of epidemic disease she 'possessed' the body of a woman of the grain-parcher caste.

---

[282] Opler 1958: 561–562.

> The woman screamed in a high-pitched voice that she was the disease goddess. The husband was displeased, and with the help of a fellow caste member offered to make prayers and sacrifices to the goddess. When a Brahmin priest was called for help, he offered still another fire sacrifice to the goddess. A group of men, who had gathered around the commotion, began asking questions of the goddess. One woman from a high caste questioned the goddess about the illness of her daughter-in-law, and at this the goddess 'possessing' the body of the low-caste woman became annoyed. The woman slapped the questioner, 'something that a woman of her caste could never do with impunity in normal circumstances. Yet in this setting the rebuff [was] taken calmly'. Another woman learned from the goddess that her son, reportedly sick in Bombay, would recover. The goddess speaking through the woman elicited reverential and respectful behaviour from those present.

In this case, one can presume an atmosphere of fear and foreboding, of danger and awe about preternatural intrusions. This climate of apprehension and caution underscores feelings of being controlled and a sense of limited, defenceless vulnerability. The case supports the existence of shared convictions that worldly happenings that are sources of worry and suffering are connected to and under the control of regulative preternatural agencies that monitor one's everyday actions. Thus, the case provides a compelling description of the cultural and social stage wherein varieties of signs and symptoms of psychological distress are played out in village communities of North India.

> *Case #6*: A woman married, and she and her husband took up residence in her parents' household, a move that ran counter to the norm in this patrilocal community. Cut off from his family, the man made no effort to regularly worship the family gods of his paternal line. This couple's fourteen-year-old son began to act 'strangely'; he disobeyed, cursed them, and began to stay away from the home for long periods of time. A diviner was hired and revealed that the boy was 'possessed' because an angry goddess of the father's line expected homage. A shaman was then called, and during his ritual the goddess spoke through the son, revealing her displeasure at being neglected. The mother indicated that there were actually three gods in the father's line and was worried that placating the present one

would antagonize the other two. The goddess, speaking through the son, said she would prevent the other two godlings from doing harm, which pleased the mother, since performing ceremonies is very expensive.

Opler indicated that the goddess was later installed in the family's pantheon of deities.

Comment

These cases from North India illustrate vividly and compellingly that villagers live in a world that stretches across the divide separating the natural and preternatural realms. They are plagued by an array of interpersonal and marital conflicts, tensions, psychologically troubling circumstances, and worrisome events that bring into play the intercession of spirits and ghosts who are regarded as parties to and causes of their problems. Active dialogue between the two worlds takes place through the bodies of vulnerable, sometimes troubled, and sometimes favoured and highly regarded individuals, who are possessed or attacked by spirits. They act as spokespersons for themselves and the group and allow those who are present to ask the spirit, goddess, or godling important questions of personal and group concern. The conflicts, tensions, worries, frustrations, longings, setbacks, and disappointments that are endemic to this village community – indeed, to most comparable communities of the subcontinent – are a reservoir of material that brings to the surface potential weaknesses and blemishes in the social fabric. Many cases of possession caused families to appeal to diviners and shamans, and these episodes were regarded in the community as analogous to sickness and psychiatric condition. Many were not viewed locally as sickness at all, but simply as incidents that revealed the victims' upsets, worries, and distressing circumstances, or the problems of others symbolized by their possession. Many of the latter cases, if carefully analyzed by an independent observer, might have been diagnosed as psychiatric condition.

Even if *psychiatric condition* is not an appropriate label to apply to some of these cases, they nonetheless graphically describe how social and psychological problems inherent in Indian communities are manifested and dealt with. The cases make apparent where and how emotional and behavioural disarrangements and incidents of social tension and personal distress are placed in this community. Opler observed that his cases did not distribute haphazardly in the community. When a healer called upon gods to enter and communicate with him, this was viewed as a felicitous event. Otherwise, spirit possession was interpreted as an unhappy intrusion into a person's body so as to cause sickness or misfortune.

Those who believe sickness and misfortune are due to evil forces from the preternatural world that can be targeted at them are prone to spirit possession. Similarly, those who are vulnerable for whatever reason, whether biological (such as an individual weakened by a parasitic infection) or social (such as a young wife in a precarious status in a family, caste, or community), tend to interpret a change in their circumstances or reverses as signs of spirit possession. Opler's interpretations are worth quoting here:

> On the individual level possession often can be traced to unresolved interpersonal conflict. Unpaid debts and ungracious acts tend to reappear after the death of one of the principals as intrusive ghosts. In this sense ghosts can be said to represent the standards and conscience of the community and, derivatively, of that of its individuals ... There is a rather prominent amount of projection and scapegoating in spirit possession. Not only is there a reflection of the animosities that the victim believes are directed toward him, but he tends to reveal his suspicions and unfavourable attitudes toward other groups and individuals: ill feeling toward minority groups and intercaste rancour are sometimes mirrored in his conception of his troubles ... Persons of high caste tend to be persecuted by large, dark low caste sprits and in speaking about scapegoating and projection, the tendency to attribute unmanageable and socially reprehensible sexual desires to the activities of the ghosts of others should not be forgotten ... Above all, a prevailing health anxiety is suggested by the data regarding ghost and spirit possession; ... the material ... strongly challenges the notion that the Indian village meets sickness and death with fatalism, resignation, and composure. There is, on the contrary, a determined effort through possession to anticipate and forestall disease, to deal with it when it is present, and to learn why it claimed its victims ... The mother is in terror of losing her child. It is often not only a life but her very status and future which are at stake. The family heads tremble lest the sons be stricken by epidemic disease and the line becomes extinct. Ghosts do not wander aimlessly through Indian village culture. They gather at points of

> stress and they attack the soft spots of the social order. To follow their movements is to learn a good deal about that social order.[283]

The point worth remembering is that ghosts and the supernatural provide a dominant idiom and metaphor by means of which situations of personal tension and distress articulate varieties of psychiatric conditions. This generalization, one may claim, applies to all varieties of mental illness. In earlier periods of Indian history, similar idioms of distress furnished the colouration in terms of which signs and symptoms of mental illness were played out. The idioms would have signalled local conflicts and tensions and the stories told would have provided local narratives of mental illness.

SPIRIT POSSESSION AND TREATMENT IN AN ISLAMIC RELIGIOUS SANCTUARY

The cases of possession described by Opler involve disturbances of behaviour that connect vividly to social circumstances. The disturbances are relatively transparent and revealing of the human dilemmas and entrapment of individuals in circumstances the shaman or exorcist is able to identify and resolve locally. However, such crises and their associated physiological symptoms can resist resolution. The signs and symptoms may persist and become continuing sources of behavioural disarrangement, distress, and dilemma. The condition of an individual then becomes not just a social crisis but also an identifiable and visible problem that will go away. In such cases, afflicted individuals may be taken to a temple, sanctuary, or holy site nearby or on pilgrimage further away where families can expect a more thorough and deeper approach to healing. Therapeutic centres like these exist in virtually all parts of India.

An example of healing or therapeutic centre, studied by Assayag, is the abode and sanctuary of an Indian Islamic saint in which one finds priests in charge of the tomb who are descendants of the local saint.[284] Individuals in distress are brought to the tomb of Baba Hazrat Rajnaiyyir Shaht in North Karnataka from far away and often stay there participat-

---

[283] Opler 1958: 565–566.

[284] Assayag 1999.

ing in rituals and therapeutic trances for an indeterminate period of time.[285]

In contrast to the clients or patients of Opler's village shaman, who are transparent in their causes and consequences, the characteristics and evoking circumstances of the psychiatric conditions brought to the sanctuary are more opaque and beclouded. There are many reasons for this.[286] One is simply that the individuals or cases brought to the centre are removed from local contexts. Exorcists or priests who do the healing do not initially know clients or patients brought to them, nor their circumstances. The sanctuary functions like a referral centre or retreat for resolution of indwelling problems that are more complex, acquired many ramifications in the family and community, and have compressed and materialized. Furthermore, patients brought to the centre participate in healing rites in the presence of others who they may or may not know, at least initially. Hence, the conditions brought to the saint's tomb or sanctuary are not fresh or acute, they have existed for some time and been subject to speculation, interpretation, and formulation by patient, family, and previous local healers. The use of several ethno-medical labels and constructs to explain and communicate about the conditions reflect prior intellectual attention to the malady, in this sense suggesting a degree of objectification or reification. The condition acquires an identity but its essential characteristics remain beclouded.

> Despite ... (a) plurality of perspectives and in the absence of a monotypic definition of nosological categories, the ethno-medical medium is expressed by grammatical constructions, an implicit cognitive model ... In Kannada (and in the Dravidian languages), the disease is considered as an active agent (subject) acting on a person (object) ... The verb *baru*, meaning 'to come' implies that the anger of an external agent, a 'spirit' perhaps, provoked it ... the verb *hiddide* ... with the connotation of being 'caught', evokes a sudden seizing by force: ... (a demon has caught him), or that he is touched by a (bad) dream 'falling' on him. The manner of grouping the illnesses which portend a severe or unexpected seizure, for example, 'madness' (*unmāda*), leprosy ... or bad planetary influences ... are opposed to a state of involuntary possession, when

---

[285] In the *dargah* or shrine of Jod Gomaz in North Karnataka, individuals who visit can stay living in premises up to 40 days (Parpola and Tenhunen 1998). See also Pfleiderer 1981, for a comparable study involving Muslims of India.

[286] Assayag 1999.

> the term *hiddide* is not normally used. In the case of lunacy, a very similar term '*agu*' meaning 'to come' is more commonly used.[287]

Assayag's formulation emphasizes abstract parameters devoid of social, personal content. Several factors work to render the condition an individual brings to the sanctuary ambiguous difficult to pin down clinically. When it is associated with divine or diabolical punishment, patients are simply evasive in talking about it. There exist constraints on how a condition is described. It cannot be reported (or 'conjugated') by the (first) person nor by family or friends when in the presence of the patient. This is because of connotations of responsibility or sin that attaches to the condition: to declare in a public setting insanity involves admission that individual or someone of its lineage has sinned or violated a sacred taboo. To refer to a malady by a named spirit is dangerous since its awesome and terrible powers may break loose and cause further harm to individual or those near him. As Assayag indicates, depending on circumstances, in the presentation and description of a condition and especially because of it psychological, social, and moral connotations, 'euphemism, metaphor, catachresis, and conjuration' all have a hand in how the condition is talked about all of these factors serve to becloud presentation of a condition. Furthermore, getting hold of the nature of a condition by focusing on or seeking access to a person's psychological experiences and/or bodily perceptions is deeply problematic. Language of description not only fuses constructs and domains ordinarily thought of as separate in biomedicine but merge in complex ways such as to incorporate person, ecology, and society. For example, physical weakness is associated with anxiety and, as Assayag correctly maintains, this superimposes or brings together ethno-physiology and ethnopsychology, and vice versa. Increasing heat in body or coming from outside serves as a way of describing problems of mood, such as anger, frustration, anxiety or sexual frenzy. Thermic fluxes, routine cycles, and bodily processes such as digestion, appetite, and menstruation all play a role in the regulation of the metabolic economy that is thought of as continuum of the spirit/body. Finally, emotions that a Westerner may construe as carried by and consequential to the individual in India are thought of in terms of social relations and situations and not as subjective feelings.

[287] Assayag 1999: 36.

In contrast to Opler's cases, the manifestations and ramifications of which are public and open to family, community and shaman, in the sacred abode of the saint a process of objectification or medicalization seems to have transpired. The condition's chronicity, its intellectual hardening or consolidation with more ominous religious and moral connotations, its transfer to a comparatively more impersonal setting, and social contingencies found there have now rendered a spirit possession far more awesome, mysterious, and shadowy. Assayag's analysis of the activities at the sanctuary illustrate the way that social circumstances, beliefs about the nature of psychiatric conditions, connotations associated with its spiritual causes, restrictions on the use of language and related sociolinguistic factors, and cultural meanings about body, self, and function conspire to make psychiatric conditions brought to a religious referral centre for healing and relief rather difficult to untangle.

> In a very general manner, the medical etiology is thus only a subgroup of a semantic existence which, by correlating physico-mental equilibrium to thermic homeostasy, and hence the pathology to its disorder, mixes up good health and sound behaviour, i.e. the duty (*dharma*) of the individual to conform to a social and cosmic (*dharma*) order or, more precisely, to respect the customary functions imposed upon the members of a particular caste.[288]

SPIRIT POSSESSION AND TREATMENT IN A HINDU RELIGIOUS SANCTUARY

Pakaslahti studied a family centred modality of mental health treatment at the Balaji Temple in Rajasthan.[289] Observations reported are similar to those of Assayag, but include findings that bear further discussion. In many respects, the cases observed by Pakaslahti also resemble many of the cases reported by Opler, although, as in the case of Assayag, the local context that produced spirit possession and its connections to contemporary strife in the family are not emphasized. Hundreds of devotees and health seekers are said to visit daily throughout the year and visit for a few hours of prayer and reverence. What sets this temple apart from other pilgrimage centres of northern India, however, is its

---

[288] Assayag 1999: 38.

[289] Pakaslahti 1998.

apparent specialization on problems of individuals suffering from emotional and behavioural afflictions.

Patients characteristically visit Temple accompanied by family members. The individual's distress is formulated and dealt with through ideas of spirit affliction that are culturally congenial to the visitors. Treatment makes recourse to trance states. The process of treatment is modelled as a legal hearing and trial of the evil spirits that have caused the patient harm. In essence, temple activities constitute a court of law (*adālat*) where the innocents (patients and their families) are administered justice. During the trial, the bad spirits (*bhūt*) harming the patients are subjected to cross-examination, accusation, and punishment (*saza*) by the good, helping spirits (*dūt*) that reside in the temple. These represent former spirits (*bhūt*s) who have been reformed.

Two types of professionals are found in the temple: resident hereditary priests and non-resident healers described as 'charismatic'. To the healers, who do not have any formal training, their work represents a religious calling. It often came about after personal crises in their own lives, which were 'healed' by divine help. A priest or healer each has their own guru, a religious master, not infrequently an older relative who also heals. All healers belong to higher, twice-born castes. Some are full-time well-known healers who travel in other parts of India although most are part-time with varied work and occupational background in local areas. The healers participate directly in temple worship through personal prayers, purification and devotion. Healing is not something done to the patients. It constitutes a communal project involving healer, patient, and family, a 'learning by doing' so to speak. The family, of course, has invariably provided the main impetus for treatment as is characteristic in most local popular, folk contexts of India and in requests for care from ayurvedic, Siddha, and, in many instances, biomedical physicians, including psychiatrists.

A commonly expressed reason for visiting the temple is that prior care with biomedically trained physicians have failed to provide relief and advice and counsel provided made little sense to families and to victims. Help seekers do not distinguish physical disease from psychiatric disorders, yet the impressive observation is that in fact most patients showed manifestations of psychiatric disorders.

> In presenting their complaints patients most often describe psychosomatically expressed symptoms, such as diffuse pains in the body,

> headaches, heaviness in limbs, weight on shoulders, chest pains, dizziness and vertigo, problems in swallowing, appetite and digestion. However, in more in-depth interviews, patients will also reveal emotionally experienced symptoms such as depression, dysphoria, anxiety, panic attacks and phobias.[290]

The indigenous psychiatric theory about problems and approach to treatment involves a 'divine panorama' of mythological stories and religious imagery that are prevalent in most of India and some are of provincial origin. The myths articulate a treatment rationale or scene peopled by allegorical personages with a divine provenance. They capture essential values and models of good conduct (*dharma*). The stories describe prototypical problem situations encountered by personages that articulate thought worlds and habit patterns that patients and families can identify and resonate with.

> Whatever takes place on the cosmological level of the myths is true of ordinary humans as well. The macrocosmic and microcosmic, the external and the internal are analogous, constructed according to the same patterns. The fight against the forces of chaos and destruction in the lives of patients and their families and the ways of solving their problems are modelled according to the structure and chronological sequences of the divine allegorical scripts.[291]

In this setting of popular devotion and faith or Bhakti, the stories recreated are transformed into powerful emotional experiences. The 'there and then' events of a narrative becomes 'here and now' realities of the patient and family.

Mechanisms of family centred therapeutic change involve trance behaviour on the part of healers and/or patients, which provides emotional catharsis and abreaction, and emotional destabilization and suggestion. Pakaslahti construed spirit affliction and therapy as a communication system that ties together patient, family, and healing personnel. The theory of affliction and healing found on display at the Balaji Temple bears a striking resemblance to many of the ideas discussed earlier regarding the theory found in the Vedas, Tantrism, Yoga, and even Siddha medicine described and analyzed by White.[292]

---

290 Pakaslahti 1998: 132.

291 Pakaslahti 1998: 138.

292 White 1996.

CULTURAL VIEWS OF PSYCHIATRIC CONDITIONS IN CONTEMPORARY CALCUTTA AND SINHALESE VILLAGES

The contemporary picture of how psychiatric conditions are spread across the landscape of India today depends on the perspective of the observer. If one assumes that problems of mental health and illness consist of distinctive manifestations involving thinking, feeling, and behaviour that conform to well-defined scientific criteria, then one can only see disorders that conform to contemporary diagnostic categories and criteria. However, a biomedical clinician-researcher who appreciates how these disorders are locally configured and appear to village residents, in other words, one who could decipher the culturally real landscape of psychiatric condition, sees a different picture.

A culturally sensitive portrait of psychiatric condition in India today would include patterns of distress, emotions that spell danger or dread, interference in thinking and in the conduct of everyday activities, failure to meet obligations, and sometimes frank behavioural breakdowns. Opler's cases exemplify this. Alternatively, a psychiatric condition might consist simply of conditions of bodily sickness, seemingly far removed from the traditional domain of 'mental' symptoms. The conditions, of course, would not appear fully announced as psychiatric, overt or visible, but clothed and somewhat obscured by more quotidian concerns, by the colours and shadows of explanations, rationalizations, emotions, intentions, and the run-of-the-mill circumstances that make up daily life as illustrated by Opler's findings. They might appear in contexts of family conflicts, adultery, sexual assault, unfulfilled obligations, disputes over land or access to water, or debts, all, of course, accentuated by inter- and intra-caste disputes and frustrations. A basic division of these local varieties of psychiatric condition is made on the basis of perceived causation and salience; more specifically, whether victims and families judge the maladies as a sickness requiring treatment or simply due to contextual factors and not as sickness. For example, Opler describes local problems of villagers as involving behaviour disruptions that are associated with alleged spirit possession for which shamans are consulted.[293] As discussed by Assayag, priests and exorcists who 'practice psychiatry' in religious healing centres are witness to the effects and hardenings of similar presentations, some involving spirit possession

[293] Opler 1958.

per se, others involving states of guilt and demoralization configured in terms of bodily manifestations and associated states of fatigue and diminished capacity or motivation for work. Chronicity, a degree of objectification, referral to the sanctuary, and social constraints operating there may becloud a condition's social psychological ramifications but it is reasonable to surmise that they lie buried in its history and in the experiential space of the victim. In a local setting as well, of course, conditions might remain concealed from public recognition, confined to the victim's home, with or without awareness of a sickness or malady of any sort. The biomedical psychiatrist approaching all this would find it necessary to dust away and tease apart such social distractions and or cultural encrustations to bring out what lies beneath the layers of contextual noise, namely, the indicators and criteria of universal entities, or psychiatric disorders, in operation.

Bhattacharyya provides a sensitive picture of how psychiatric condition arises in contemporary India.[294] On the basis of research in Calcutta, a city on India's eastern coast, she sought to explain *pāgalāmi* (mental illness, insanity, madness) and related native terms from the standpoint of the local inhabitants of the city. Her work is in the tradition of ethno-science and ethno-methodology, associated with anthropology and sociology, respectively, which approach a phenomenon like psychopathology as a social and cultural object – that is, from the standpoint of how native subjects perceive it and act upon it. For a year, Bhattacharyya studied the various institutions used by Calcuttans to treat symptoms of *pāgalāmi*. She interviewed patients, their relatives, and mental health professionals, and she administered the Star Questionnaire regarding descriptions of mental illness.

For Bhattacharyya, the 'psychiatric domain' of Calcutta encompassed allopathic (biomedical) psychiatric facilities and specialists and hospitals devoted exclusively to psychiatry. She also included general medical and psychological practitioners and visited institutions that did not specialize in psychiatry per se, but dispensed homeopathic medicine, Ayurveda, Islamic, or Unani medicine, and Indian varieties of psychoanalysis on through folk medicine administered by priests and temple clergy, astrologers, and practitioners of philosophical-religious rites involving Yoga.[295] Bhattacharyya delineates the structure of the external

[294] Bhattacharyya 1986.

[295] See also Kakar 1982.

system pertaining to *pāgalāmi* (psychiatric condition) – that is, how Calcutta's social structures and institutions are organized – and the internal structure of the cognitive domain of *pāgalāmi*, mental illness – that is, how it is labelled and what patients and practitioners associate with it. She identified three notions that prevail in the region: (1) *bhūta bhara* (ghost possession), (2) *tukataka* (black magic or sorcery), and (3) *mathara golamala* (malfunctioning of the head), which reflect the general categories of Ayurveda. Each is broken down into varieties. On the basis of her observations, Bhattacharyya delineated three principal, logically independent paradigms used by residents of Calcutta to make sense of psychiatric condition, each with its own terminology, aetiology, symptoms, modes of treatment, and prognosis. The characteristics of each kind of psychiatric condition – causal event, genotype, phenotype, social action of treatment, and outcome – form syntagmatic chains that indicate how each is played out in the minds of resident of Calcutta.

Bhattacharyya's method allowed her to construct a symbolic representation of psychiatric condition in Calcutta that describes the theories or explanatory models that subjects had in mind when they invoked these terms. The phenotypic *pāgalāmi*, Bhattacharyya maintains, includes observable symptoms and signs – in general, social and psychological behaviour manifestations – whereas the genotypic *pāgalāmi* incorporates the underlying psycho-physiological process and brings into play cultural developments. Each type of insanity outlined above involves: (1) a condition involving a chance possession brought on by being at the wrong place at the wrong time (*bhūta bhara*), (2) a maligned condition brought on by the evil spell of an angry person (*tukataka*); and (3) a shock to the system associated with excess bile (*mathara golamala*), which can have consequences that need not involve a psychiatric condition. They can produce divine inspiration, an accident, or physical illness, respectively. While these paradigms seem logically schematic, in actual cases subjects bring into play different paradigms and ways of proceeding. Native conceptions stray from the strictly medical and physiological ideas of insanity and tend to see it in magical, spiritual, religious, and moral terms.

Waxler conducted a study of attitudes toward psychiatric disorders among Sinhalese villagers of Ceylon, a society significantly influenced by Indian cultural values and patterns, especially those associated with

Buddhism.[296] Waxler first selected five cases of psychiatric disorder found in Ceylonese psychiatric wards whose diagnoses were consistent with those of Western psychiatrists. The narratives describing these cases focused narrowly on symptoms known to exist in the community and were framed in terms of everyday concerns and activities. Waxler then asked a sample of 102 Sinhalese Buddhist villagers living in up-country village areas their opinion of these cases. She read the narratives aloud, then asked her respondents to explain the deviant behaviour presented therein, and to recommend what should be done for each afflicted person. After noting initial responses, the interviewer then revealed more about the local, indigenous conceptions of each patient's problem. Most respondents – 93 per cent – saw the described behaviour as deviant, but judged the symptoms in various ways. There was much less agreement that the somewhat bizarre or inappropriate behaviour of a schizophrenic girl was deviance, and even fewer respondents regarded the suicide attempt by another patient as deviant. Two-thirds of the sample rated the deviance as caused by mental illness, some by physical illness, and a few attached no label to it. Fifteen per cent judged that while something was wrong, it was not illness. This show of tolerance, a marker of the difference in outlook between culture and biomedical psychiatry, was even extended in particular to the schizophrenic and the attempted suicide. Several tried to identify causes. Waxler writes:

> Several criteria enter into the decision to call someone 'mad'; ... norms ... that one should be quiet, calm, and controlled ... [means that] over-activity or aggressiveness are evidence of a mental illness; ... passivity or withdrawal are somewhat less likely to be called 'mad'. Three other criteria, however, modify this rule. Only the actions that are judged to be inexplicable and uncontrollable are called mental illness; deviant behaviour believed to be under the person's control is 'bad' or 'immoral', not 'sick'.[297]

The individual's role in society entered into the decision, as did gender. Women's symptoms tended to be viewed as either normal or immoral. For adolescents, symptoms also were normalized. Waxler explained these findings in terms of the factors that made status distinctions in the society important:

---

296 Waxler 1974.

297 Waxler 1974: 23.

> We could infer, then, that the distinctive labels of deviance given to men and women serve to confirm the status differences. When women with symptoms of mental illness are called 'immoral'; ... this definition is still another way of confirming their low status position; the label, too, serves as a warning to other women of the kind of behaviour that is most reprehensible. When women are called 'mad' and men are called 'physically ill' this confirms the belief that high status people are immune to supernatural attack; status may protect against the traditional causes of mental illness.[298]

Waxler's study shows how a community very much under the sway of Indian culture judges behaviour that, on the basis of criteria external to the culture, exhibits the symptoms of common psychiatric disorders. While 'madness' in Ceylon and *pāgalāmi* in Calcutta are lay categories for deviance and for psychiatric condition in particular, these terms have meaning and are applied in terms of concepts and rationales that have broad, important significance in the society. In India, everyone has a conception of madness, psychiatric condition, and/or psychiatric disorders. This is hardly surprising, given their universality and the deep medical roots of this class of illness in classical Indian medical and non-medical literature. Curiously, behaviours conforming to only some psychiatric disorders are likely to be called madness and insanity. Behaviour or symptoms in themselves are not the exclusive diagnostic criteria, because social roles and gender affect how madness is culturally configured.

CONCLUDING COMMENT

The findings of socially and culturally oriented medical and social scientists who study conditions of psychiatric interest in contemporary India highlight a dilemma one confronts when seeking to formulate psychiatric phenomena in ancient societies of the subcontinent. Clinician researchers have studied isolated and traditional communities as well as urban centres and have documented levels and distribution of such conditions that are within the range found in other contemporary Western societies. It would appear that there are few differences in the way psychiatric phenomena distribute in the Indian landscape today, com-

[298] Waxler 1974: 24.

pared to what one finds elsewhere in the modern world. Employing modern definitions, diagnostic conventions, and sensitivity to language and cultural orientations that anthropologists and Indian psychiatrists have essentially entered into the social spaces of different types of local communities, localities where beliefs and practices related to medicine and mental health practice show remnants of ancient, traditional beliefs and understandings, and managed to document clinical characteristics of psychiatric conditions that conform to contemporary definitions and practices. One is led to presume that given the psychiatrists' emphasis on the traditional orientation of the communities studied, and their sensitivity to the thought worlds and habit patterns of the people, they (the research psychiatrists) are in many ways providing a window into, or retrospective glimpse of, psychiatric phenomena during earlier periods of Indian history, viewed in terms of modern criteria, of course.

By contrast, studies by cultural anthropologists provide an inside look at how psychiatric conditions are actually understood and played out in Indian communities in contemporary times. Their observations bring to light the types of circumstances that cause and fashion conditions of psychiatric interest in the local fabric. The abstract measures and cases of epidemiologist are reconstituted as lived disturbances that pulsate with meanings and that give rise to efforts aimed at control and resolution of the problems and circumstances that can cause the individual and family much distress. Depending on local circumstances and where analysis takes place, psychiatric conditions are perceived and presented in different attire and with different degrees of clarity. Among real people and in real life circumstances, psychiatric conditions which Indian psychiatrists are able to diagnose in impersonal and objective terms are shown to have distinctive idioms of presentation replete with social and cultural significance.

Socially and culturally oriented psychiatrists of India, then, have little difficulty in peering through indigenous, traditional categories and beliefs about experience and behaviour and find in the psyches and behaviours of their respondents the material of modern descriptive psychopathology that enable them to diagnose contemporary varieties of psychiatric disorders. And conclusions based on formal clinical examination correspond roughly to observations made by social and cultural scientists who have actually participated in the social life of Indian communities. A reasonable counterfactual scenario is that were such well-trained and linguistically and culturally informed Indian clinician/epidemiologists and anthropologists to be transported back in time to early societies of the subcontinent with their respective tool kits they more than likely would have been able to record levels and types of conditions of psychiatric interest that resembled those found in isolated, traditional communities of contemporary India. Studies reviewed earlier and in later chapters attempt and succeed at bridging local, traditional compared to modern, biomedical frames of reference.[299] This tradition of research provides examples of how modern constructs about psychiatric condition, including the manner in which such conditions are conceptualized and expressed, contrast with traditional views about similar phenomena. In effect, work of epidemiologists and social scientists exemplify the clashes produced when inherited traditions are challenged by contemporary formulations.

Nevertheless, an analyst's dilemma is that any knowledge of psychiatric phenomena borne from contemporary conventions of diagnosis and practice and projected onto earlier societies of the subcontinent would inform us of very little of what psychiatric conditions were really like in traditional India. Specifically, although knowing that ancient peoples of India 'must have' and probably did show conditions of psychiatric interest that conform to our contemporary scientifically derived constructs, one would still be ill equipped to fully appreciate the indigenous play of such phenomena in local contexts of social life and in a cultural psychological matrix that did not bear the imprint of ideas tied to advancing modernity, modernism, and secularization. To obtain a realistic picture of the psychiatric conditions and of indigenous psychiatry as configured in earlier periods of Indian social history one seeks understanding of what such conditions meant and how they were dealt with in light of the thought worlds, habit patterns, and social resources that the culture provided for individuals experiencing emotional distress and behavioural disaffection. How that world-view bounded by its own *self-contained* social, cultural, spiritual, moral, and political boundaries contained and fleshed out psychiatric conditions is what one cannot really get at. Essentially, one would like to have confidence about two sorts of things. The first is awareness and confidence that phenomena of psychiatric interest were on display and that from the standpoint of contemporary understandings such phenomena showed similar con-

[299] Based on the work of Weiss *et al.* 1988, 1992, 2001; Weiss, Raguram, and Channabasavanna 1995; Raguram, Jadhav, and Weiss 1994; Raguram *et al.* 1996, 2001.

figurations to those recorded by trained psychiatrists. This body of information is provided by material reviewed in this chapter. Literature involving evolutionary psychology and psychiatry indicates psychiatric phenomena are universal and studies discussed earlier support this generalization for contemporary India.

A second package of information needed to make sense of earlier traditions regarding mental health and practices (the 'indigenous psychiatry') in India involves understanding what Indian societies and institutions provided for individuals and families that were burdened with psychiatric conditions. A psychiatric condition alters experience and behaviour and raises fundamental existential and moral dilemmas as these are and were construed in Indian societies. This raises a number of questions. How did attitudes, constructs, and beliefs about persons, social reality, spirituality, and philosophical world-view come together to shape psychiatric conditions and what was made of them in earlier periods of Indian history? What social practices and institutions did Indian society and culture draw on when coping with such conditions? How did religion and medicine figure as ideological and practical resources in handling of psychiatric conditions? Information obtained by clinicians and cultural anthropologists provide one only with clues as to where in the social and cultural fabric of traditional India one could have looked and expected to find such conditions and what their design (symbolic meaning) might have consisted of. Clues to some of the answers to these and related questions were inherent in material reviewed in this chapter. Obtaining a more comprehensive picture of what psychiatric phenomena was like, considered from the standpoint of conventions and understandings inherent in traditional Indian society and culture is a goal pursued in later chapters.

Chapter 6

Mental Illness in Ancient Indian Communities

INTRODUCTION

The foundations of Hindu world-view and the civilization it spawned consist of a large body of philosophical, psychological, religious, moral, and more popular literary texts. This material consists of revelations about the meaning, purpose, and obligations of human existence. They were passed from generation to generation in oral form and eventually compiled into texts. The texts describe and articulate basic conventions, standards, and prescriptions about the self, other, the nature of social responsibility, world, cosmos, and conduct of social life. They have shaped the way Indian people think and behave, imparting a distinctive colour and tone to Indian imagination and personal experience. Since a psychiatric condition involves disaffections of experience and behaviour, this naturally raises the question of how it is insinuated in and made manifest in the Indian thought world and habit patterns or 'psyche' which of necessity reflects fundamental moral, spiritual, and philosophical tenets.

Chapter 5 reviewed how psychiatric disorders are expressed, understood, and played out in *contemporary* India. In light of the innate basis and universal nature of such disorders, the material reviewed allows one to presume that analogues of them were represented in ancient Indian communities. The question one can ask is: given its presence as exemplified in the biological, physiological, and behavioural material of human populations, how were conditions of psychiatric interest configured and played out in pre-modern, traditional communities of India in terms that were meaningful to the people? On the one hand, one can assume that Indian constructions of personhood, social reality, and world-view served as the filters through which psychiatric conditions were refracted and the fabric in terms of which it was designed. On the other hand, one can also assume that those who developed such conditions manifested them in culturally meaningful behaviour and would have availed themselves of Indian social practices and institutions that had evolved to address alterations and disturbances of experience and behaviour, phenomena that comprise the material or 'stuff' of psychiatry. Clues of this were contained in cases drawn from contemporary studies reviewed in the previous chapter.

This chapter begins an examination of the medical and psychiatric past of India. Its focus is on how conditions of psychiatric interest, seen as disarticulations and problems of social and psychological behaviour that usually include visceral-somatic symptoms, were likely to have been expressed and interpreted from within traditional Indian society and culture, as well as its system of medicine. The chapter discusses the early evolution and characteristics of medicine in India. It then examines three fundamental ancient literary compilations for clues and hints about its construction of and possible influence on the expression of phenomena of psychiatric interest. Discussion involves how analogues of psychiatric conditions are represented in literary canons that are fundamental to Hindu experience and behaviour.

The texts discussed here do not concern medicine per se. Nonetheless, contemporary Indian scholars have viewed them as central to an appreciation of Indian imagination and world-view and by implication of significance to understanding phenomena of psychiatric interest in Vedic times and thereafter.[300] This material is discussed later. The ideas and beliefs that raise the question of psychiatric phenomena in the *Atharvaveda*, *The Laws of Manu*, and the *Bhagavadgītā* are examined from a broad intellectual and cultural standpoint. In subsequent chapters, attention will be given to the evolution of a genuinely medical perspective, namely, Ayurveda or the science of life.

EARLY EVOLUTION OF NATURALISTIC MEDICINE IN INDIA

Introduction

Prior to the supervention of the Aryans in the subcontinent of India, people there surely had a system of understandings and practices for dealing with general problems of health and disease. Like hunter-

[300] See, for example, Venkoba Rao 1966, 1975, 1978, 1984; De Sousa and De Sousa 1984; Somasundaram 1984; Balodhi and Chowdhary 1986.

gatherers and then the sedentary, agricultural and non-industrial peoples that have been studied first hand in the modern era, and which serve as exemplars of societies during early cultural evolutionary history, one can presume that similar groups in the subcontinent had evolved their own cultural conceptions of sickness and healing (their varieties of ethno-medicine). Ways of coping with sickness, originally based on personal experience and family lore, accumulated into pockets of local knowledge and then expanded in scope and complexity as the role of practitioners and experts evolved and their incumbents added their own experiences. Characteristics of shamanism as a system of medicine and its unfolding were on display in the subcontinent and it represented the indigenous, proto-history of Indian medicine.

Eventually, such peoples coalesced into societies of different size and complexity and developed their own more or less separate, specialized and conventional body of beliefs and systems of medical practice. One can presume much diffusion among centres of population. In addition to truly indigenous formulations, the system of beliefs undoubtedly may have included elements from regions outside of the subcontinent where major population centres had and/or were in the process of evolving. It is not unlikely that some Chinese, Turkic, Hittite, Iranian, Greek, Mongolian, or even Egyptian tenets made their way into the subcontinent during the millennium before the Common Era, carried by tradesmen who travelled the various roads and sea routes. Medical beliefs and practices that diffused throughout the region were incorporated into local traditions, further beclouding original, indigenous conceptions and practices that trace back millennia, deep into the protohistoric and prehistoric past of India.

After the Aryans came to predominate in western and northern parts of the subcontinent, India developed its distinctive trademark of philosophy, religion, moral exegesis, and general way of life. The intellectual tradition centred on and was designed to cope with the meanings and puzzles of the human condition. India's formulation of self, identity, salvation, rules of social and moral conduct, and the actual social structure and organization of communities, constitutes a distinctive and complex culture and civilization that addressed the problems of human existence in a comprehensive way. In a non-trivial way, one can conceptualize the tradition as having evolved to cope with human suffering and disorder, which would have included conditions of psychiatric interest as we understand them today.

Epistemological boundaries and the paradigm shift

The cultural legacy of traditional India involved conceptions and formulas and procedures for coping with human sufferings and maladies. It consisted of a doctrine of salvation through liberation and deliverance from karmic debts and it relied on ritual, meditation and devotional practices, and emphasis on a moral philosophy that stressed duty, obligation, caste purity, and village communalism. Because segments of this legacy addressed problems of sickness and disease, including psychiatric condition, one may think of it as Vedic medicine. Material from *Atharvaveda* involving conceptions and practices of healing of emotional and behavioural problems of psychiatric import will be discussed later. Presently, characteristics of this system of beliefs and practices are examined as medical phenomena per se; and in particular, with respect to their influence on the later evolution of Ayurveda. From a general anthropological standpoint, Vedic medicine has what will be termed a largely metaphysical basis. On the other hand, one finds in the scholarly, academic medicine of India, namely, Ayurveda, a more or less naturalistic approach to sickness and healing. It consists of comprehensive structures of knowledge and procedures that, besides being proactive with respect to health, focus curatively on specific types of diseases that span mental and physical suffering, and that formulate a naturalistic physiology and pathogenesis of disease including psychiatric conditions.[301]

As Vedic medicine evolved into Ayurveda, an epistemological divide is said to have been crossed, a paradigm shift in the history of medicine in the subcontinent during the closing centuries BCE. Scholars suggest that even in the very earliest non-medical philosophical and religious literatures (the matrix that embedded Vedic medicine) one finds echoes of a naturalistic and empirical approach to disease and therapeutics and moreover that Ayurveda contains echoes of Vedic medicine. Some of the shared aspects of healing sickness generally and psychiatric conditions more particularly involve content of ideas that were presented in Chapters 2 and 3. Looked at from a distance, aspects

[301] Chapter 7 addresses Ayurveda.

of suffering, presumptions of cause, modes of healing, and the ontology of health and sickness, while similar in some respects are markedly different in the two (Vedic and naturalistic/Ayurveda) paradigms.[302] Indian historians of science suggest that the real differences between Vedic and ayurvedic medicine are incommensurable: for example magical/religious animism (here termed 'metaphysics') compared to empirical observation and trial-and-error methods involving organic or physical phenomena (physiological/anatomic or somatic).

The seemingly sanguine relationship between the two paradigms that one can discern upon taking a closer look at the material is explained by some as a consequence of political and economic factors that resulted in the Brahmanic emphases being largely grafted on to the ayurvedic during phases of the compilation of Ayurveda texts.[303] On the one hand, the claim is that Brahmins wished to preserve Vedic tenets about medicine so as to continue to control, to exert power over, medical practice. On the other, ayurvedic physicians were willing to allow such a concession in return for official recognition of their work and enhancement of social status. Basically, ayurvedic physicians were willing to satisfy critics and improve their own political standing and appeal to the medical market. A historical formulation of the differences in these two approaches to sickness and healing suggest otherwise, namely, that philosophical ideas and related Vedic elements, including Buddhist ones, are epistemically more deeply insinuated in ayurvedic doctrines. Regardless of how one resolves the question of the origins of medical science and empiricism, contra magic and spirituality, when one looks at the philosophical foundations of the two medicines, one appreciates that the final consolidation of the Indian classical system of medicine resulted in morally based, religiously validated, naturalistic and empirical medicine. The two facets of the Indian legacy (metaphysical compared to empirical) are not necessarily independent nor is the meaning of medical, compared to psychiatric, suffering. They share epistemological assumptions although they conflict and have been the focus of dispute.[304] The question of differences in content of ideas and methods needs to be kept separate from the question of a shared structural meth-

---

[302] D. Chatoppadhyaya 1977.

[303] Taken up in a later section and in Chapter 7.

[304] D. Chattopadhyaya 1977; Roy 1986; P. V. Sharma 1992a; Wujastyk 1998, 2003; Zysk 1999.

odology of healing, the fourfold or quadrangular logic of both, and all systems of Indian healing discussed in the following chapter.

Indian medicine from a distance

The history of Indian medicine consists of three main phases. A Vedic phase roughly covers the period from 1200 to 800 BCE although material discussed earlier has already suggested that the ideas of basic texts did not just appear fully formed but were probably preceded by a long period of evolution and consolidation. A classical phase follows involving the earliest Sanskrit medical treatises by renowned physicians and covers the period from a few centuries before and several after the Common Era and includes medical treatises dating up to the Muslim invasions of the eleventh century. The final syncretic phase is marked by the influence of Islamic medicine and other non-classical writings extending to the present era.[305] In this presentation emphasis is given to the first two phases, although aspects of Islamic medicine are covered when appropriate and also taken up in Chapter 10. In light of material reviewed in Chapter 5, one needs to add a pro-historical, pre-Vedic phase to this schema. Because of lack of direct access to sources and because it is unclear whether the content of ideas and procedures displayed what later came to represent quintessential Indian features, this magico-religious system of medicine in the subcontinent is generally neglected. However, some of its characteristics can be presumed given the knowledge base of medical anthropology (ethno-medicine).

Some scholars point out that inside the moral, religious, and psychological traditions for coping with the problem of human suffering there are clues that foretell how the naturalistic medical tradition would evolve. Similarly, the sources of classical Ayurveda also reveal indications of an older religious, magical, and moral dimension to the ascendant naturalistic science, as well as a philosophical, theosophical, and psychological basis. It is undeniable that classical writings of physicians were influenced by and also influenced several of the philosophical traditions. Some scholars take a hard position and argue that Ayurveda delineates a naturalistic approach to disease, that the old theory about spiritual and supernatural influences is a later addition, and that its in-

---

[305] Zysk 1999.

clusion is evidence of a conflict with traditional priestly bodies, reflecting purely political considerations.[306]

P. V. Sharma, for example, emphasizes the significance of Vedic medicine in the Indian medical tradition by reviewing evidence from ayurvedic writings that draw on and elaborate on the hymns of the *Ṛgveda* and the *Atharvaveda*.[307] To him Ayurveda is intimately connected to Vedas since because of its antiquity it regarded as an *upaveda* and because of content as an *upāṅga* of *Atharvaveda*. During a time when the Vedas came under attack by priestly groups, Ayurveda was used to support it. Sharma also identifies a number of disease conditions discussed in the Vedas that figure in the main texts or *saṃhitās* that expound on ayurvedic medicine.

Medicine of the pre-Vedic period

The earliest documents that one may tentatively identify as having medical significance are those that came after the Harappan civilization and were associated with supervenience of Aryan people from Iran.[308] The oldest compilation of this Vedic tradition, the *Ṛgveda*, was like a liturgical book used by the Aryan priests who performed sacrifices to the gods. The scope, complexity and systematic incorporation of religious, moral, psychological, and philosophical ideas have already been discussed. As per its medical implications, the world-view and intellectual tradition embodied the indigenous medical practices from an era undoubtedly preceding entry into the subcontinent. It is reasonable to assume that its own antecedents originated in and combined aspects of shamanism, sorcery and herbal preparations, all cast in an evolving and systematic metaphysical framework. While the Vedas are presumed to have been put together into texts of different lineages sometime after migration into the subcontinent (approximately 1500 BCE), one has to assume that ideas, constructs, and beliefs seen as oral literature have a lineage that predates migration westward into the subcontinent for several centuries or even millennia.[309]

[306] D. Chattopadhyaya 1977; P. V. Sharma 1992a; Zysk 1992.

[307] P. V. Sharma 1992a.

[308] Zysk 1991, 1993.

[309] Feuerstein 1998.

However, the ethno-medicine of pre-Aryan people is of such antiquity that it is impossible to recover except very indirectly. All traditional, non-industrial peoples living in small-scale societies – not just those of India – who have been studied by medical anthropologists, are described as taking a metaphysical approach to medicine.[310] Such peoples are construed as exemplars of earlier communities pre-dating pastoralism, agriculture, and sedentary life. Of course, in some instances so-called 'indigenous' popular or folk medical wisdom and practice, observed and recorded for contemporary non-industrial societies, does not trace back to earlier pristine systems of knowledge, but rather to a more elaborate tradition, sometimes even a literate one, whose elements have been borrowed or diffused to the hinterland. Depending on geographic area, these might include borrowings from Egyptian, Mesopotamian, Hellenic, or Aztec medicine. Nonetheless, some elements of the medicine of early human societies, inferred on the basis of characteristics of contemporary non-industrial societies, no doubt hark back to the proto- and prehistoric past before the emergence of more complex and systematized systems. There are no reasons to doubt that formulation of classes of sickness, empirically tested curative vegetal preparations, metaphysical beliefs and practices, and shamanistic-like practitioners were characteristics of this protohistoric ethno-medicine of Indo-Aryan and pre-Indo-European peoples. One can assume that vocabularies and knowledge for dealing with disease in terms of ideas and beliefs found in non-industrial people of today are universal in human culture and most assuredly this generalization applies to the original settlers of Indus region and of the subcontinent as a whole.[311] In Chapter 10, material on the medical beliefs and practices of contemporary forest peoples of India will be discussed as possible exemplars of pre-Vedic medicine.

Early Vedic medicine

The Vedas provided a philosophy and spiritual conception of how the world and social order was created, what kept it going, what was required of Aryans in order to accomplish this, how social relations should be conducted, and the rationale that held all this together. It consists of sacred, revealed knowledge of great cultural significance to Aryan

---

[310] Fabrega 1974, 1997.

[311] Fabrega 1997; D. E. Brown 1991.

communities. Those texts that have been received function as landmark not only in matters of spirituality and social conduct but also in practical matters related to human misfortune, suffering, social conflicts, and problems caused by disease. It is thus not surprising that, like Sharma, many regard the Vedas if not as a textbook at least as providing a rationale for medicine and therapeutics.[312] The gods in the Vedic pantheon included deified natural phenomena and natural forces, including gods who were physicians. Specific diseases are identified in the texts along with methods of treatment. Besides prayers, the texts mention drugs (ingested and externally applied), mechanical interventions, surgical operations, and use of natural remedies such as the sun's rays, fire, water, and air.[313] Scholars also discern a preventive, public health approach in Vedic medicine. Sharma indicates that Vedic peoples emphasized integration of things physical, mental, and by means of hymns to the gods, sought a healthy longevity of the body, and mental, and moral faculties. Vedic texts also emphasize sanitation and cleanliness and a 'clean life', not only outwardly but also inwardly.

Vedic hymns were apparently intended for three kinds of cures: verbal, vegetal-aqueous, and surgical. Combinations of hymns may have been used in a formulaic manner:

> Operating together or in pairs (spells and herbs, spells and water, or spells and surgery), the threefold cures were employed as a single remedy, rather than individually against specific infirmities. [314]

There is some controversy as to whether the hymns addressing misfortunes were produced and used by members of a first (more aristocratic) estate or whether they originated with and were used by members of the third estate (people of the soil, farmers, workers) who may have incorporated Brahmin elements. In other words, it is possible that a separate coterie of priests was in charge of these 'medical' hymns and merely used ritual symbols to accommodate to the Brahmins.[315]

For Zysk, the *Atharvaveda* was the principal source of medicine during the early Vedic period and, as discussion in Chapter 7 will show, this was also the case for psychiatric conditions. Problems of an especially

---

[312] P. V. Sharma 1992a.

[313] P. V. Sharma 1992a.

[314] Zysk 1992: 333.

[315] Zysk 1992.

secular character were cast in metaphysical terms and 'solved' by magical incantations, since demons and sorcerers were viewed as prominent sources of disease.[316] Later, the Atharvanic tradition produced a ritual treatise, the *Kauśikasūtra,* which explains the rites during which the hymns of the *Atharvaveda* were to be recited. Despite this ritualistic, magical orientation, the medical sections of the *Atharvaveda* contain some ideas that are representative of the later medicine of the classical tradition, Ayurveda, rather than exclusively the medicine of the Vedic age.

The prevailing conception of health, disease, and its treatment found in the Vedas and especially in the *Atharvaveda* is complex. Medical incantations referred to the sacredness of certain plants and the cleansing powers of water, and when necessary they described actual physical procedures. However, the conception of health underlying and justifying these medical 'cures' reflects the ambiguous and transitional character of the *Ṛgveda* and *Atharvaveda.* Zysk emphasizes themes that Sharma does, namely, that concept of health has two dimensions: a 'general, non-descriptive expression of wholeness of body and mind' as represented by a word like *svasti,* which signifies 'wellbeing' and has links to the Avestan word *ha*rvatat,* which signifies 'completeness'.[317] Words that connote the obverse side of disease suggest a more differentiated and medically centred conception of health. Zysk cites specific examples of this: (1) *Āmīva* signifies a disease-demon that enters the domestic abode, seizing its inhabitants. Wholesome food was considered a form of prevention, for maintaining a state of *anāmīva.* (2) *Yakṣman* is a disease frequently encountered in the Vedas that Zysk glosses as consumption or tuberculosis. The negative of this term, *ayakṣman,* was linked to freedom from distress, or prosperity and happiness. (3) *Ātura* means suffering, or sickness both of mind and body, and its negative, *anātura,* implies wholeness and completeness. (4) *Agada* signifies wholesomeness of the body, and its negative, *gada,* means a toxin.

Thus, there are many kinds of healthy states in Vedic medicine rather than one overarching conception and he groups these into three types: (1) sound internal condition, (2) wholesome external state, and (3) a state of 'non-toxicity'. This, Zysk suggests, differs from the later Ayurveda in which one finds a more generic conception of healthy, wholesome bodily condition sufficient for all instances. Instead there are

---

[316] Zysk 1993.

[317] Zysk 1985: 312.

many healthy states depending on the particular malady that was removed.

> It was only in relation to a specific morbid bodily condition that a notion of health in the medical context emerged. Health in a positive [physiological, bodily] sense does not occur in early Vedic medicine. This fundamental dualism between disease and health, then, lies at the basis of Vedic medical diagnosis and, along with the three-fold division according to types, illustrates the very beginning of Indian scientific observation and thought.[318]

The idea that health rests not on general, abstract notions about the body or person but rather on the absence of specific and presumably well-known (culturally recognized) conditions of disease or physical affliction has interesting implications. It suggests a culture or information pool tied to, and its users burdened by, experiences with disease that were probably frequent in the population, like other calamities and disasters. Characteristics of this medicine involved explicitly articulated, indeed formulaic, treatments, which in turn entailed the mediation of socially appointed priests who implored the deities and natural forces to alleviate suffering. These suggest a socially hierarchical society already in possession of knowledge about the world, but perhaps as yet lacking an overarching, specialized system of knowledge of medicine. In other words, the society lacked an evolved philosophy or science of medicine considered as a separate, socially recognized domain. An important generalization for understanding the perception and understanding of psychiatric phenomena at this early phase of Indian history is that the 'system' of ancient Indian or Vedic medicine at this time was holistic. Its ideas and practices addressed all types of medical, psychological, and spiritual problems that were part of the human predicament posed by suffering and disorder. It also relied implicitly on a vocabulary of somatopsychic–psychosomatic integration. This was illustrated earlier in the discussion of how the concept of heat was used in the emotional language of the Vedas. On the other hand, concept of medical health also was differentiated, since the absence of specific ailments defined wellness.

In Vedic medicine demons and malevolent forces figured centrally as causes of disease. These attacked and entered the bodies of victims

---

[318] Zysk 1985: 318.

and caused morbid body conditions. Cure involved the removal of the offending (injurious, 'possessing') agent or demonic being by means of elaborate rituals. Disease 'beings', like curative plants, were deified and personified, giving rise to a pantheon of gods of disease. There is evidence to suggest that eating nutritious food was known to produce a wholesome, healthy body. This association is important because it is another link (like the classification of disease) with the later naturalistic approach to disease most fully realized in Ayurveda.[319] Magician-healers of the Vedic period relied on diverse methods, such as routines of dancing, recitation, chanting, and shaking. The hymns they chanted suggest that they knew how to prepare special herbs. Assaults to the body that signalled disease were believed to be caused by breaching taboos, by imprecations against the gods, or by witchcraft and sorcery.

Two varieties of disease are identified in the *Atharvaveda*: those marked by internal, invisible changes or causes, and those with external, visible symptoms, such as lesions, injuries, fractures. According to Zysk, internal diseases included (1) those with visible manifestations, such as a syndrome like consumption consisting of respiratory symptoms and fever; (2) those without visible symptoms, among which were found insanity and also ascites and urine retention; and (3) those caused by poisons operating either inside or outside the body. Zysk emphasizes that divination was not part of diagnosis, in contrast to contemporaneous Egyptian and Mesopotamian medicine. In keeping with later developments, causes were determined on the basis of salient and recurring symptoms, many of which, as indicated earlier, were thought of as the embodiments of demonic entities. Thus, there was an emphasis on observation, empiricism, and classification. Many types of maladies and cures were recorded, each associated with removal of noxious agents from the body.

In general, the medical practitioners of Vedic times were experts on the various hymns, used herbal preparations, and must have had some understanding of the body, but they apparently had a superficial understanding of anatomy.[320] Although they were not necessarily members of the priestly order or class and thus may not have been able to participate in certain sacrificial functions, they nonetheless drew on the ideas of the sacred texts and relied on orally transmitted procedures recorded in

---

[319] D. Chattopadhyaya 1977.

[320] Zysk 1986.

them. Through animal sacrifices, they accumulated some knowledge of anatomy and assigned terms to bodily parts that reflected a religious understanding of the body and were used in religious rituals associated with curing. These anatomical terms were used consistently and accurately, and a corresponding terminology appears later in ayurvedic medicine.

Therapy in Vedic medicine consisted of healing rites, mantras repeated in a distinctive language, and the use of amulets, talismans, and charms to expel demons and protect victims from further attack. Important elements of curing involved special naming, incantations, rhetorical questions, onomatopoeic sounds, identifying names, esoteric words or phrases, all of which focused the demon's attention on the healer, causing it to lose its grip and power.[321] The recapitulation of such stories in ritual settings connects Vedic medicine to essentially sacrificial and religious practices inherent in Vedic society.

> [During healing rites] divinities of the traditional Vedic pantheon are mentioned, usually as subordinates to the dominant Atharvavedic deity, often because their characteristics resemble those of the god being addressed. [322]

Healing rites involved recounting mythological events pertaining to plants and disease and the use of healing charms. Because like disease-demons, plant beings were also mythologized, reverence for plant life was an integral part of Vedic medicine and gave rise to an elaborate pharmacopoeia. Through these rites, disease-demons were transferred from the patient to enemies or to less desirable people, dispelled into the ground, or carried away by birds. Rituals and hymns were performed according to auspicious astrological conditions and at certain times of day.

In summary, in Vedic medicine, metaphysical or magico-religious utterances or mantras dominated and were used for both physical and emotional ailments and distress. These ranged all the way from swellings, tumours, wounds, sores, poisoning, and fever onto psychiatric conditions, as discussed below and in Chapter 7. Foundations of Vedic medicine relied on a belief in a multitude of benevolent and malevolent deities or spirits that populated the cosmos, and control of these entities

---

[321] Zysk 1989.

[322] Zysk 1991: 17.

constitutes the essence of Vedic medicine. Tenets of Vedic medicine may be illustrated in terms of psychiatric condition.

PSYCHIATRIC PHENOMENA IN VEDIC SOCIETY: THE *ATHARVAVEDA*

Introduction

The word *veda* means knowledge, and the knowledge par excellence of ancient India is contained in the compilations of sacred religious writings that go by that name. The Vedas are regarded as the oldest Indian literary documents. They describe the religious orientations and social practices of the Aryans, dating from at least 1000 BCE, although probably not written down until the end of the third century BCE. They are also known as the *saṃhitās*, which means compilations of hymns, prayers, magic songs, benedictions, and sacrificial formulas. I am here principally concerned with the fourth collection, the *Atharvaveda.* As indicated earlier, the four Vedas embody a rationale for and description of the way of life of ancient Indian communities. The characteristics of this general cultural orientation are assumed to have taken hold during the first millennium BCE and, what is more important, to have extended forward, along with additions, emendations, elaborations, through the classical, medieval, and modern eras up to the present.

All of the Vedas, even the oldest, the *Ṛgveda*, expound a distinctive world-view and vision of social order. They comprise descriptions of hymns and rituals and their interpretation. They cover construction and protection of dwelling abodes, funerary rites, sacrifices to enhance the cleansing and curative powers of water and fire, sacrifices to enhance the effects of *soma* libations, rituals of cremation, glorification of ancestors, general prayers for a happy family life, and glorification of the Brahmins.

The Vedas thus contain an image of what Aryans thought of themselves, their society, and the world. This image reflected a superior position of Vedic people in relation to other groups, which included 'servants' or 'slaves' (*dasyu* and *dāsa*) and 'foreigners' (*mlecchas*). The sociological implications of Vedic literature depict an 'introverted' and self-conscious community who thought of themselves as dominant and morally superior and who indeed exercised dominion over other inhabitants of the subcontinent and, in a considered way, could also ignore and look down on people beyond their territory.[323] They and their way of life was construed and manifested by their actual physical location in the subcontinent, their language which was construed as sacred, and their physical constitution or biology – all by virtue of their knowledge of revelation about the order of the cosmos and the structure of human society – social classes and stages of life – inherent in *dharma*.

Aryans held this view and, one can presume, lived their life in the awareness of having access to revealed knowledge about the cosmos and social world which they kept going through performance of ritual and upholding of their way of life, or *dharma*. The Vedas reflect a perspective of magical and mythical reciprocity in the maintenance of order, which embodies an inner, logical relationship between rituals, a social religious way of life of privileged people, and cosmic and natural phenomena of the world. Only members of the Aryan community could uphold and protect the identity and continuity of their society but also that of the regularity of the physical world and the cosmos.

An Aryan conception of a mythico-magical world-view that connected the daily life of obligation and rituals with maintenance and preservation of order in society and the cosmos provides one with a window into the significance of the various ways in which Vedic people conceptualized and experienced disorder and demoralization and of the central role of the concept of *dharma* in all of this.[324] This world-view also determined what was to be expected and could be done in the event of a sense of *adharma*, a failure to uphold one's responsibilities and obligation in the scheme of the world. One can conceptualize traditional Indian cultural psychology as centring individuals (mainly of the higher *varṇas*, one may presume) in a spiritual world that was philosophically complex. A person's sense of self and being, as exemplified in the reality of their social relations and concrete social station and circumstances, was created and maintained by impersonal, metaphysical actions which required and demanded their continued participation in the requirements of *dharma*. Disappointment, demoralization, depression, and distress in a person's circumstances would have registered and resonated psychologically as a disturbance and disequilibrium of the order inherent in relations between micro-, meso-, and macrocosm. It had local, concrete,

[323] Halbfass 1988, 1991.

[324] Halbfass 1988; Michaels 2004.

and prosaic dimensions and also moral, spiritual, philosophical, and timeless repercussions. Persons displaying a psychiatric condition would be unlikely to only feel anxious, be disappointed, show weird or crazy thoughts, or sense they were being persecuted. These and related symptoms and signs might be recorded by an outside analyst examiner but, in an experiential (cultural psychological) sense, they connoted and portended major and sometimes horrific alterations in their place in the scheme of things. A person's emotional disaffection was not just perceived as, but *consisted of*, a disturbance of the balance that tied them to society and to the world beyond. A psychiatric condition did not result from nor was it limited to immediate personal, concrete, and social circumstances but would have had connections to and involved happenings in the metaphysical realm; for example, as invasion of angry spirits or a shouldering of guilt over *adharma* and its implications about karmic debts. The appropriate ways of coping with emotional and behavioural disaffections included practical relief of symptoms, to be sure, but also relief of spiritual and moral anxiety for which re-education, re-affirmation, and re-connection via ritual acts of contrition, restitution, and reimbursement were necessary.

The *Atharvaveda*

Winternitz emphasizes differences between material in the *Ṛgveda* and the *Atharvaveda*.[325] In the former, the great gods of the heaven are for the most part depicted as kind and shining deities. They personify natural phenomena which the singer praises while he performs sacrifices. The sacrificer praises and prays to powerful but obliging partly sublime figures. In the *Atharvaveda*, by contrast,

> it is the dark demonic powers which bring upon human beings disease and misfortune, ghostly beings against which the magician hurls his wild curses or which he wants to appease and banish with flattering speeches.[326]

Physical metaphors, such as the heat of fire and the coolness of water, appear in these ancient texts as representations of emotions and their impact on behaviour, suggesting a kind of psychological system, a

---

[325] Winternitz 1981.

[326] Winternitz 1981: 117.

general psychology of emotions and behaviour realized in physical metaphors.[327] For example, heat gives meaning to negative emotions such as hatred and jealousy. A hymn and a charm describe the attempts of a woman to appease a jealous man by means of food and drink: 'Soothing the jealous man, and the symbolic removal of the fire of his jealousy'.[328] Love is an emotion that, when deficient, wasted, or depleted, can be heated into activity. Heat and anger are likewise dealt with together, with rituals involving water designed to cool and wash away its noxious effects on the body. Likewise, the heat of a guilty conscience is frequently suggested. In addition, there are many passages:

> In which an emotion of strong unhappiness is considered to be heat or flame in the body, particularly in the heart ... This unhappiness is here called 'misery', and where it resides in the heart it is about equivalent to 'heart-ache'. Misery is excessive heat of the body like jealousy and fever, to which it is closely related.[329]

This ancient mode of conceptualizing emotionally arousing and plaguing social situations connects not only with psychological experience but also with a person's body in terms of commonly identified physical, concrete ideas. Blair's analysis permits us to peer into the way that human longings, worries, agonies, and preoccupations were formulated and no doubt experienced, using physical concepts. It suggests a rough way of conceptualizing the effect of situations on personal experience, including the self, with implications for a sense of physical embodiment, later to be picked up in the scholarly medical tradition.

Blair finds in the *Ṛgveda* and the *Atharvaveda* a large vocabulary of meanings that equate negative emotions and associated social ills with heat and 'heated' bodily states.[330] This implies a psychosomatic, integrated way of thinking about and communicating personal distress and agony that in turn reflects a cultural psychological tendency toward 'embodying' emotional conditions, or somatization. The question of the antiquity of the *Ṛgveda* and the *Atharvaveda*, and particularly whether they are independent of Ayurveda, the science of life and medicine, or whether they preceded its oral development, are much debated. The

---

[327] Blair 1961.

[328] Blair 1961: 159.

[329] Blair 1961: 167.

[330] Blair 1961.

recent work of Zysk reaffirms the relationship between *Atharvaveda* and also provides documentation of the relationship between Buddhist medical theory and practice on the one hand, and Ayurveda, on the latter.[331] He offers compelling reasons for viewing Ayurveda as a later development of Indian medicine. While Ayurveda elaborates a somatic physiology and links body signs and symptoms with psychiatric conditions, in keeping with its naturalistic account of disease, it also incorporates emotional and behavioural aspects.

At any rate, it is clear that there existed a very ancient tendency to experience, report, and act upon manifestations of emotions, especially painful ones that can lead to psychopathology, in terms of bodily symptoms. The observations of scholars such as Roşu, Kakar, and Meulenbeld about the 'psychosomatic basis' of sickness and psychiatric condition as formulated in Ayurveda receive some confirmation here in India's very oldest canonical literatures.[332]

The magical spells and formulas contained in the hymns are directed at the gods and demons that control human destiny. All types of human misfortune were addressed by hymns and rituals conducted by a priest-magician, the two terms overlapping in meaning. Similarly, the content of the hymns makes it clear that 'sacred and auspicious' (*atharvan*) magical formulas, as well as 'hostile, black' (*aṅgiras*) magical formulas were used in the rites and invocations.[333]

Beyond general problems and concerns, hymns, spells, and rites were designed to convey specific requests and to alleviate particular sources of affliction and worry. For example, in addition to hopeful prayers such as entreaties for a good crop and success in love, the hymns reflected hatred, jealousy, general, unbounded anxiety about the malevolent actions of others, agony over a failed romantic relationship, invocation of punishment for an errant spouse, and pleas for relief from gambling debts, for removal of general and specific symptoms of disease (worms, ulcers, fever, coughs, pains, bleeding), for cure of debilitated conditions of disease, for restoration of marital harmony, and for resolution of family quarrels.

The view that Aryans held of themselves was discussed earlier. In formulating the relationship between the acts of individual and

---

[331] Zysk 1991, 1993.

[332] All taken up later in Chapters 7 and 8.

[333] Winternitz 1981.

the structure and workings of society and cosmos the Vedas exemplify distinctive thought worlds and habit patterns. One can conceptualize this as a Vedic cultural psychology. The hymns of the *Atharvaveda* thus provide one with an example of this style of reasoning and feeling. It also provides entry into how individuals whose emotions and behaviours were in a state of disarray and discomfiture were perceived both by themselves and fellow caste members. Distress and suffering were misfortunes understood to be the consequences of fault and sin. Expiatory formulas and spells for the relief of guilt and sin were integral to the same psychology that magically sought relief from physical disease and mental suffering. Failing to perform ceremonial, sacred practices was on a level with actual crimes committed knowingly or unknowingly. The sufferings, caused by sins of commission or omission, were not necessarily differentiated from one another nor were they separated from the infirmities, maladies, and physical sufferings caused by both bodily disease and mental anguish. The whole of human experience, encompassing one's own constitution and health, family wellbeing and stability, social conduct, and spiritual obligation, were conjoined in a moral-ethical framework whose perturbation caused disease conditions that overlapped with psychopathology. In summary, while many of the celebratory, auspicious hymns of the *Atharvaveda* focus on the wellbeing and status of the Brahmin elite, a substantial portion of the verses and hymns were directed at specific and very mundane human concerns, the worries, problems, burdens, and fears of ordinary people, that provide hints of a highly moral cultural psychology.[334]

Before examining a hymn in the *Atharvaveda* that deals explicitly with Vedic psychiatric conditions conceived as insanity or madness, it is useful to examine what the hymns reveal about general aspects of ancient Indian thought worlds and habit patterns insofar as they suggest how such conditions may have been experienced and understood. The following material offers illustrations of the kinds of psychological distress and suffering identified in the *Atharvaveda* that were made the object of incantations and ritual cures.[335]

---

[334] Whitney 1905.

[335] All are quoted from Whitney 1905, vol. 1, unless otherwise noted.

1. For release from evils, and for welfare:
From *kṣetriyá*, from perdition, from imprecation of sisters (*jāmí-*), from hatred (*drúh*) do I release thee, from Varuṇa's fetter; free from guilt (*-ā́gas*) I make thee by [my] incantation; be heaven-and-earth both propitious to thee. ... Thou hast been released from *yákṣma*,[336] from difficulty (*duritá*), from reproach (*avadyá*); from the fetter of hatred and from seizure hast thou been released.[337]

2. For concord:
Like-heartedness, like-mindedness, non-hostility do I make for you; do ye show affection (*harya*) the one toward the other, as the inviolable [cow] toward her calf when born. Be the son submissive to the father, like-minded with the mother; let the wife to the husband speak words (*vā́c*) full of honey, wealful. Let not brother hate brother, nor sister sister; becoming accordant (*samyáñc*) of like courses, speak ye words auspiciously (*bhadráyā*). That incantation in virtue of which the gods do not go apart, nor hate one another mutually, we perform in your house, concord for [your] men (*púruṣa*).[338]

3. For recovery of virility, using a plant:
Thee that the Gandharva dug for Varuṇa whose virility (*-bhráj*) was dead, thee here do we dig, a penis-erecting herb ... Up, the energies (*śuṣma*) of herbs, the essences (*sā́ra*) of bulls; the virility (*vṛ́ṣṇya*) of men (*púṃs*) do thou put in him, O Indra, self-controller ... I make thy member taut, like a bowstring on a bow; mount (*kram*) as it were a stag a doe, unrelaxingly always (?).[339]

4. Against jealousy:
The first blast of jealousy, and the one after the first, the fire, the heat of the heart -- this we extinguish for thee. As the earth [is] dead-minded, more dead-minded than a dead man, and as [is] the mind of one who has died, so of the jealous man the mind [be] dead. That fluttering mind (*manaská*) that has found place in (*śritá*) thy heart –

---

[336] An internal disease, often translated as consumption. See Zysk 1993.

[337] Whitney 1905: ii.10, 1, 6, pp. 51–52.

[338] Whitney 1905: iii.30, 1–4, p. 138.

[339] Whitney 1905: iv.4, 1–4, 7, pp. 150–151.

from it I set free thy jealousy, like the hot vapour from a bag of skin.[340]

5. [For freedom from fear: various prayers to bestow fearlessness, safety from enemies, for welfare, sustenance, and wellbeing.][341]

6. To remove wrath:
As the string from the bow, do I relax (*ava-tan*) fury from thy heart, that, becoming like-minded, we (two) may hold together (*sac*) like friends. We (two) will hold together like friends; I relax thy fury; we cast in thy fury under a stone that is heavy. I trample upon (*abhi-sthā*) thy fury, with heel and with foot, that thou mayest speak not uncontrolled, mayest come unto my intent.[342]

7. To assuage wrath:
We conduct away the offense (*śaráṇi*) of thy jaws, away that of thy mouth, that thou mayest not speak uncontrolled, mayest come unto my intent.[343]

8. Against evil dreams:
As a sixteenth, as an eighth, as a [whole] debt they bring together, so do we bring together all evil-dreaming for him who hates us.[344]

9. For some one's release from perdition (*nírṛti*):
The tie that the divine Nirṛti (perdition) bound upon thy neck [and] that was unreleasable; that do I untie for thee, in order to long life (*ā́yus*) splendor, strength; do thou quickened (*pra-sū*) eat uninjurious (?) food ... Thou wast bound here to an iron post (*drupadá*), bridled with deaths that are a thousand. Do thou, in concord with Yama with the Fathers, make this man ascend to the highest firmament.[345]

10. To Agni: against sorcerers and demons.[346]

11. For protection against demons and witchcraft.[347]

---

[340] Whitney 1905: vi.81, 1, pp. 293–294.
[341] Paraphrased from Whitney 1905: vi.40, p. 310.
[342] Whitney 1905: vi.42, 1–3, pp. 311–312.
[343] Whitney 1905: vi.43, 3, p. 312.
[344] Whitney 1905: vi.46, 3, p. 315.
[345] Whitney 1905: vi.63, 1, 3, p. 328–329.
[346] Whitney 1905: viii.3, vol. 2, pp. 481–486.

12. Appeals to many different gods for relief.[348]

13. Book 16 appears to have eluded accurate interpretation as to content.

Whitney suggests that these hymns resemble night time prayers to ensure sound sleep and the absence of troubling dreams. Hymn number 6 presents interesting themes:

> We have conquered today, we have won today; we have become guiltless. O dawn, of what evil-dreaming we have been afraid, let that fade away (*apa-vas*). Carry that away to him that hates; carry that away to him that curses.[349]

The hymns consist largely of exhortations, magical sayings, or mantras that had to be repeated according to a specific format, along with specific rites and references to the power and sanctity of agencies being invoked, or forces to be opposed and defeated. Zysk emphasizes the verbal content, illocutionary power, and deeply stirring emotional connotations of the language and symbolism of the hymns of the *Atharvaveda*. Here, emphasis is placed on the content and not the literary, poetic quality.[350]

Medicine and psychiatry in the *Atharvaveda*

In Vedic society, physical health and mental wellbeing was hardly the object of a separate system of medicine comprised of articulated knowledge structures and roles of medical practitioners. Depending on social complexity and culture, peoples of simple societies and those living as settled agriculturalists show an ethno-medicine, namely, medical beliefs and social practices for coping with disease that cannot easily be separated from other areas of social and political concern. Vedic people, then, showed an indigenous ethno-medicine that included an ethnopsychiatry. This 'system' of medicine was brought to bear on emotional and behavioural disturbances (psychiatric conditions), especially when

---

[347] Whitney 1905: viii.4–6, vol. 2, p. 486–498; x.1, 3, 6, vol. 2, pp. 562–567, 572–575, 585–589.

[348] Whitney 1905: xi.6, vol. 2, p. 798.

[349] Whitney 1905: xvi.6, vol. 2, p. 799.

[350] Zysk 1989.

these, in association with socially disruptive or divisive manifestations, visibly caused distress and suffering.

The sources of Vedic medicine derive from the principal religious literature. As described earlier, this involved the *Atharvaveda* in particular and to a lesser extent the *Ṛgveda,* the oldest of the four Vedas. In Vedic medicine not physiological functions but external beings of a demonic nature are held to cause disease by entering the body. Thapar suggests that many of the malevolent and benevolent spirits and ghosts described in the Vedas as injurious to health may have been initially formulated as embodiments of hunter-gatherers or forest peoples and clans and tribes that lived beyond the pale of organized Vedic social life.[351] Such demons were personified, deified, and mythologized leading to a pantheon of religious gods.[352] Plants and herbal remedies also had mythical origins and were deified and worshipped as gods. Special times and positions of the stars in heaven were auspicious times of healing, hinting at astrology. However,

> The ancient practice of divination by means other than astrology ... was not employed by the Vedic healers. Diagnosis and prognosis were rather undertaken by the isolation and identification of dominant and recurring symptoms, many of which were considered to be separate demonic entities ... illustrat[ing] the importance which the recording of observable facts played in Vedic medicine. Various characteristics of a patient were noticed, given names and recorded. Plants and herbs were also put under the same rigorous scrutiny.[353]

Cures involved exorcism by means of special rituals, efficacious words, actions, and devices all drawn from dominant local religion. The main figure in medical rites was the healer, termed *bhiṣaj,* who resorted to dancing and recitation of incantations and practices involving apotropaic and other sympathetic magical practices. Thus, an empirical medicine also involved observation and experience and helped in determination of cause and treatments.

Two varieties of insanity are represented in Vedic medicine.[354] These are classified with the internal diseases that are caused by demon enter-

---

[351] Thapar 2002.

[352] Terms found in Vedic social and medical lore still figure in the classical medical literature of India (i.e., Ayurveda) that is described later.

[353] Zysk 1985: 9.

[354] Zysk 1993.

ing the body. One variety, the translator indicates, suggests a psychiatric condition brought on by the patient through infringement of divine mores and taboos. This condition is termed *unmadita*. The second condition suggests to the translator an abnormal mental state caused by possession by demons. This condition is termed *unmatta*. A charm or verse directed at the cure of these conditions comes from the *Atharvaveda* and goes as follows:

> O Agni, for me, release this man who bound [and] well-restrained, utters nonsense. Hence, he shall make an offering to you when he becomes sane. / If your mind is agitated, let Agni quieten [it] down for you. [For] I, being skilled, prepare the medicine, so that you may become sane. / I, being skilled, prepare the medicine so that he, insane because of a curse of the gods and demented because of the *ráksas*-demons, may become sane. / Let the *Apsaras*es [other demons] return you; let Indra [and] Bhaga re[turn you; in fact,] let all the gods return you so that you may become sane.[355]

One may suggest that important parameters of these two Vedic psychiatric conditions involve disorganized, disruptive behaviour (the need to restrain and bind the subject), emotional excitement and loss of emotional control ('mind is agitated'), and altered state of consciousness brought on by curse of gods and/or demonic and spiritual possession. In general, Vedic medical theory as applied to psychiatric conditions was based on a large number of benevolent and malevolent deities and spirits that were held to populate the cosmos and could attack people. Control of these agencies was a cornerstone of this medical tradition.

The medicine of the Vedic people, when examined in terms of the healing traditions of the Indo-European peoples, is viewed as a product of learned men of the third order or estate.[356] This helps explain their ties to practical knowledge of local flora and use of magical rituals, amulets and incantations, aspects of healing best exemplified in the *Atharvaveda*. Vedic medicine, then, was a product of peasant communities and their popular, folk culture. On the other hand, knowledge and rituals derived from the highest order of priests, individuals who had access to greater cosmic forces and could manipulate the spirit world, provided healers of the third order with models for their practices and ritual performances. Initially, the latter enjoyed relative autonomy in the social order for the

[355] Zysk 1985: 63.

[356] Zysk 1993.

practice of medicine. Eventually, however, medical healers came to be shunned and excluded by the sacrificial priests of the first order. Growth in practical knowledge of disease and healing, and activities of medical healers relegated to the margins of society, was associated with a shift in medical thinking during Vedic times. There developed a shift in medical thinking. Medicine came to be devalued as a social activity.

Eventually, wandering medical healers joined and were amalgamated with mendicant Buddhist medical practitioners, and it is believed that from knowledge of sickness and treatment learned and accumulated in this larger group of medical/religious healers arose the classical science of medicine in India (Ayurveda). However, the later classical Indian medicine incorporated much of Vedic medicine. In fact, while Vedic medicine may have emphasized magical and religious healing, descriptions provided of medical conditions attest that observation, definition of medical problems, selected use of herbs and other medicaments, and mythical and religious classifications all suggest that rational and empirical approaches were also followed.

The ethno-medicine of Vedic peoples practiced by priests of the third estate addressed all types of medical problems, including psychiatric phenomena. However, such medical healers would have constituted but one segment of the system of mental health practices of the Vedic people, what one could term their indigenous psychiatry. By far most of the latter would be practiced by important spokespersons of Vedic culture, namely, individuals who were experts on inherited lore that kept the culture going. For the top three *varṇas*, this would have included persons steeped in Vedic knowledge of religion, philosophy, and morality for they articulated standard conventions about behaviour and were consulted and involved in the business of healing and rehabilitating persons who strayed away from conventional behaviour as stipulated by *dharma* and enjoined by religion and morality more generally. The lowest social grouping and the untouchables most likely resorted to folk, popular practitioners who were partly conversant with Vedic knowledge and practices and with beliefs and medical lore found among people indigenous in the subcontinent (forest and tribal peoples).

Getting behind and under textual material

Although formulated in highly evocative and poetically rich language, the verses refer to suffering and anxiety and call for help only in general terms. The details of these agonies and disturbances are not specified. The *Atharvaveda*, for example, does not contain anything that approaches a definition, a nomenclature, a descriptive typology, or a profile of behaviour that would undoubtedly have included psychiatric conditions. It is thus impossible to do more than glimpse the psychological experiences of those seeking sacred and magical relief. However, the spiritual and social concerns and even agonies of persons that cultural psychiatrists have shown correlate with psychiatric conditions and who when carefully interviewed may have met requirements of diagnosis is certainly represented in the hymns.

The need one might feel for information about the psychological, emotional, and cognitive correlates of human problems reflect one's Western, ethnocentric expectations. This is a consequence of the dominance of modern psychological language and idiom of distress. How such problems were actually conceptualized and experienced is all-important: some sort of cultural formulation, a local existentially compelling realization of suffering, must have served as the baseline of need for a mantra or hymn, as well as the end-point of treatment as formulated in ritual. Given what we know about ancient Indian cultural psychology, we assume that this need was constructed in a religious, spiritual, and moral idiom. An imaginary psychiatrist transported into the social space of ancient India would have been able to uncover, identify, or elicit symptoms and signs involving disturbances of cognition and emotions. Some of these symptoms would probably resemble the indicators of an internationalist psychiatry touched on earlier, and which, one may surmise, are relevant to contemporary Indians who in many ways are still influenced by ancient traditions. In addition, these symptoms would probably be accompanied by bodily disturbances and somatic pain.

This clinically relevant substratum of Vedic psychiatric conditions was undoubtedly integral to and explicitly acknowledged in the felt need for sacrifices and rituals. Alternatively, these more clinical features may have received additional treatment by indigenous folk-practitioners. Thus, one can assume that individuals seeking ritual counselling and relief from social and psychological sufferings and worries would have exhibited other misfortunes that would have included analogues of signs and symptoms of psychiatric conditions. The hymns and associated paraphernalia and procedures were essentially formulaic scripts enacted to alleviate general misery and suffering and/or to pursue and attain other desired ends.

Suffering, misery, worry, distress, disease, as well as symptoms of organic problems and disorders of the mind and thinking seem to be accurate and valid descriptions of the human concerns represented in the vivid poetry of the *Atharvaveda*. From today's perspective, one may surmise that social and psychological suffering often motivated people to appeal to the priest-magicians who uttered the mantras and performed the rites. However, while it is generally acknowledged that the *Atharvaveda* is a pivotal early document in the history of India's indigenous system of medicine and, by implication, of psychiatry, it is a mistake simply to characterize the concerns and problems represented in that work as psychiatric.[357] Many hymns do not even remotely involve phenomena that correspond to mental illness. As mentioned earlier, the details or symptoms and behavioural disturbances of afflicted individuals were never catalogued and hence cannot be determined. However, hints of the psychology of Vedic people can be accessed in this way and this provides a glimpse of how psychiatric conditions may have been understood and experienced.

In summary, two types of insanity are singled out for attention in the *Atharvaveda*. Each is treated by a specific charm and hymn. The first is termed *unmadita*, a demented state that afflicted one who infringed divine mores or taboos, that is, it was retribution for negative, improper behaviour; and *unmatta*, an abnormal mental state caused by possession by demons. Insanity was a condition not unlike death, in that the mind left the body and the patient exhibited distinct symptoms consisting of utterances that were regarded as either nonsensical of out of context. To return the mind to the body, the Vedic healer made propitiatory offerings to the gods in the case of *unmadita* (madness caused by infringing taboos). In the case of the second form of madness, or demonic 'possession', the healer also prepared medicines to calm the patient and to drive away the evil forces invading the body. The words of the hymn designed to treat this affliction suggests that restraints might have been used. The charm used is one of three containing names of mothers that were included in a rite for curing one 'possessed' by demons. In later Indian medicine, insanity or madness is termed *unmatta* or *unmāda*, and it is classified into various types on the basis of the theory of humours or

[357] Winternitz 1981.

doṣas. Most severe forms of insanity were included under the category of *bhūtonmāda* insanity, which was held to be caused by demons and which corresponded to the insanity mentioned in the special charm or hymn devoted to insanity in the *Atharvaveda*.

Clues about the early cultural psychology of Vedic people

The hymns of the *Atharvaveda* are designed to cope with the realm of ominous and dangerous forces that haunt and threaten to defeat everyday human strivings.[358] The positive hymns appealing for luck and benediction, as well as the negative spells or aggressive incantations designed to ward off attacks, are all integrated around the theme of protection from danger and misfortune, and they share an essential moral psychology. The word *aṃhas* (distress) also includes meanings of *trouble, misfortune*, on the one hand, and *fault, sin*, on the other. Expiation (*prāyaścitta*) is necessary for *sins* construed in general terms, explains Winternitz:

> For not paying debts, especially debts incurred while gambling, for the marrying of the younger brother before the elder one (which is forbidden by law) and in addition to prayers generally held for liberation from guilt and sin and their consequences, we find also expiatory-formulas and songs and spells associated with expiatory ceremonies by means of which mental and bodily infirmity, omens foreboding ill-luck ... wicked dreams, and sudden 'misfortunes' are supposed to be 'expiated', i.e., warded off or weakened in their effect. The concepts 'guilt', 'sin', 'disaster', and 'misfortune' run incessantly into one another ... Everything bad ... is supposed to be caused by ill-meaning demons, by wicked spirits. Just as the patient and the madman, so also the evil-doer and sinner are possessed by a wicked demon.[359]

In short, demonic agents were alive in the minds of Vedic people and exercised a controlling influence on their lives. They filtered individual's perceptions of social life and world-view. Such agents were inside their minds and in some respects it can be said that gods, godlings, ghosts, and malevolent beings of many sorts were active participants in everyday psychological life of Vedic people and in the way they planned, carried out, and evaluated themselves with respect to social

---

358 Anthropologists often refer to this realm as defining the behavioural environment of a culture.

359 Winternitz 1981: 127.

order and its moral determinants. Such agents were held to cause the myriad social ills that in our society correspond to psychiatric conditions, for example, distress and emotional pain associated with family quarrels, jealousy between lovers, marital conflicts, failed potency, and loss of sexual attractiveness. Possession or attack by spirits provided explanations of an individual's disturbances of thought, experience, and behaviour that contravened social conventions.

Winternitz's point of view matches that of J. P. Balodhi and J. R. Chowdhary.[360] These scholars follow a broad perspective in their general emphasis on the 'psychiatric concepts' in the *Atharvaveda*. They follow Indological accounts in attributing the largest proportion of the hymns (65 of 212 hymns, or approximately 30 per cent) to *bhaiṣajyāṇi*, that is, they are related to the cure of diseases and possession by demons.[361] For example, these include a number of hymns directed at enemies, demons, and witches, for 'discovery' of sorcerers, and to ensure protection.[362] Balodhi and Chowdhary assume that:

> In *Atharvaveda*, all forms of illness including mental are attributed to machinations of an enemy, malicious influence of spirits that inhabit the world around the patient and the spirit offended.[363]

In keeping with their broad point of view, they also ascribe psychiatric significance to hymns involving eroticism, different types of fear, love entanglements (spells to win a man's love), and curses. One must acknowledge that in the implications and playing out of these concerns of supplicants one would undoubtedly find staple themes of psychiatric practice today (sexual performance problems). These examples illustrate that psychiatric concepts cover situations and circumstances that involve psychological influence and concern, which are often associated with social and psychological distress and malfunction.

Looking beyond Vedic medicine toward Ayurveda

The *Atharvaveda* draws attention to the challenges and obstacles that undermined social order among Vedic people. It describes the way psy-

---

[360] Balodhi and Chowdhary 1986.

[361] See F. M. Smith 2006.

[362] See, for example, Book I, verses 7, 8, 28; Book IV, verse 36; Book VI, verse 32.

[363] Balodhi and Chowdhary 1986: 65.

chological experience was formulated, expressed, and made sense of. It also describes the efforts, sacred and profane, of the Brahmin establishment to restore social order, purpose, meaning, and moral stability when an individual's equilibrium was perturbed and caused distress and divisive behaviour. Supplicants sought protection from benevolent deities or dark, demonic powers that could bring human misery and suffering. These included everyday misfortunes and the alleged machinations of envious, evil persons and supernatural agencies.[364] Material in *Atharvaveda* records a deeply religious cultural psychology, a psychology that was in active communication with and at the behest of spiritual agencies that instilled meanings not only to common rituals and social practices that bolstered ordinary travails of everyday life but also to experiences that heralded and connoted insecurity, uncertainty, demoralization, and breakdown of experience and behaviour.

Ayurveda, the naturalistic and scientific approach to a positive, proactive health (practices involving preservation of health and rejuvenation) as well as cure of disease is often construed as discontinuous with the medicine of the Vedas. This illustrated in the account of ancient Indian medicine of Kutumbiah, who goes far to try and remove Ayurveda from ideas and practices of *Atharvaveda*.[365] Classical Ayurveda physicians are said to 'liberate' medicine from the 'stranglehold of animism'. This thesis is to some extent also exemplified in the writings of Chattopadhyaya, who even sees what little of something one might term 'animism' is left in extant ayurvedic writings as stemming from political motivations of Brahmins who sought to reinstate and perpetuate their position of authority.[366] However, as discussed later, spiritual, moral conceptions inherent in the Vedas and as illustrated in *Atharvaveda* hymns and mantras not expunged. They resonate in Ayurveda theory and practice, particularly in areas pertaining to emotional and behavioural disaffections that the medicine set apart as insanity and related psychiatric conditions.

---

[364] Later discussion in Chapter 7 will centre on more strictly medical implications of the hymns and how these fit into the evolution of the classic indigenous medical tradition of India.

[365] Kutumbiah 1969.

[366] D. Chattopadhyaya 1977.

The Dharmaśāstra

Earlier discussion has suggested that the word *dharma* has a complex meaning in Indian languages and in its psychology, philosophy, social theory, and religious world-view.[367] It can mean *ordinance, usage, duty, right, justice, morality, virtue, religion, good works,* or *function* and it also personifies a deity, and addresses the order in the world and what sustains it. The body of ideas and the theory of *dharma* originated with the Vedas and in canonical works of commentary and elaboration and other original writings that made up classical Hinduism such as the great Indian epics and the Puranas. Halbfass and Michaels are particularly lucid and cogent in tracing ideas about *dharma* starting with the Vedas.[368]

As discussed in Chapters 2 and 3, it was following the Vedic period when the construct and its full implications about social order and obligation across human groups became pre-eminent.[369] This meaning has passed through several transitions but generally always covered aspects of good conduct. The concept of *dharma* is alluded to in the precepts of the Vedas and was then elaborated, and is incorporated in virtually all of the important bodies of intellectual and popular literature such as legends, epics, moral commentaries, and writings that describe how one should live one's life and pursue righteousness. Among their many implications for Hindu thought and religion, the Puranas and the two Indian epics are exegeses about what *dharma* means and how it plays and should play out in human societies.[370] A suitable general definition includes the privileges, duties, and obligations of a person, one's standard of conduct as a member of the Aryan community, a member of a caste, and a person at a particular stage of life.[371] The word *śāstra* means rules or laws as embodied in specific texts or compilations. This would make Dharmaśāstras compilations of laws dealing with moral and legal tenets of Hindu culture and society, of which there are many.[372]

Dharma and the Dharmaśāstras constitute the essential underpinning of social order and guide to human action and conduct. They

---

[367] Halbfass 1988; Kane 1968–72; Michaels 2004.

[368] Halbfass 1988, 1991; Michaels 2004.

[369] Halbfass 1988, 1991; Michaels 2004.

[370] Brockington 1987, 1996; Nath 2001.

[371] Kane 1990.

[372] Lingat 1973; Lahiri 1986; Kane 1968–72; Doniger and Smith 1991; Chakravorti 1996; Rocher 2003.

stipulate social conduct among castes and across the various life stages of the favoured social classes. The hierarchy and its bases in transfers of material and in degrees of purity across the 'twice-born' are laid out in these writings as is also what a human lifespan should consist of, how individuals should behave during its phases starting with invocation of a commitment to the study of the Vedas. In addition to this highly personalized dimension (its representation in a Hindu's cultural psychology), throughout Indian history, even into the modern era, Dharmaśāstras have served as the foundation of Indian law. It is with reference to what these bodies of ancient truths formulate about behaviour and social responsibility that kings and rulers have sought guidance and justification in adjudicating conflicts of interest and meting out justice. Thapar's analysis of the edicts of Emperor Aśoka from the third century BCE provides a glimpse of how the spirit of the Dharmaśāstras was central to social policy and embodied in political documents during the Mauryan Empire.[373] The edicts emphasized social ethics and morality and explicitly invoked *dharma* and the Dharmaśāstras and the ruler's attempts to establish a standard of conduct throughout his empire. Āpastamba and other revered figures of Indian history, ancient and medieval writers who compiled and commented on ethical and legal precepts, are cited as fundamental to the administration of justice and regulation of the moral order in ancient traditional India.[374]

The Dharmaśāstra works do not embody a creed or religion in the traditional sense but refer to a general mode of life and code of conduct. The special slant of the various writings on behaviour and conduct is practical, admonitory, and controlling. Kane writes:

> Our dharmaśāstra works do not enter into any subtle or detailed examination of the principles of ethics or of the moral standard, nor are the concepts of duty, happiness or perfection subjected to any searching analysis. But this does not mean that the principles of ethics were passed over by dharmaśāstra works or were not highly thought of by them.[375]

Nevertheless, a broad spectrum of general morality and ethics is enjoined explicitly and implicitly in the Dharmaśāstra. Kane, for exam-

[373] Thapar 1997, 2002.

[374] Lahiri 1986; Chakravorti 1996.

[375] Kane 1990: 3–4.

ple, mentions the following: truthfulness and honesty, self-restraint, charity, forbearance, chastity, freedom from envy, and general purity of body, thought, and speech. Implicit in the writings is an emphasis on virtuous behaviour and the necessity to satisfy the conscience:

> All dharmaśāstra writers attached the highest importance to moral qualities and enjoined them upon all with all the emphasis they could command; but their main purpose was a practical on, viz., to guide people to right acts, rites and ceremonies that each person had to do with reference to his station in society.[376]

An important compilation of Dharmaśāstra is *The Laws of Manu*, comprised of 2685 verses on the social obligations and duties of the various castes of India and of individuals at different stages of life. The verses focus on duty, laws, rights, the sense of justice, social practices, rules and principles of social life – all are subsumed under the concept of *dharma*. *The Laws of Manu* were most likely composed at the beginning of the Common Era. However, as mentioned earlier the construct of *dharma* is found in early Vedas and certainly its development in later Vedic writings precede Manu's compilation. Much of Vedic literature can be read in light of the competition for social power and popular allegiance between the ruling, warrior, priestly, and merchant classes and Manu and other compilations uphold the traditional Bhrahmanic position on hierarchy and its bases in purity and pollution. *The Laws of Manu*, compiled some time after this period, were a key text of the dominant form of Hinduism.

According to Doniger and Smith, in the ancient writings that follow the Vedas and that bear a direct relation to Manu, one witnesses an attempt to infuse the very authoritarian, hostile, violent, and uncompromising tenets of the older Vedas with values based on a comparatively more humane, tolerant code of behaviour framed in principles of vegetarianism and non-violence.[377] These later writings were influenced by the highly philosophical, contemplative philosophies of the Upanishads, and the doctrines of liberation, renunciation, and release from the painful cycle of karma, that later became incorporated in heterodox sects of Buddhism and Jainism. The earliest Dharmaśāstras date to around the fourth century BCE and were written by Brahmin purist ritualists who,

---

[376] Kane 1990: 11.

[377] Doniger and Smith 1991.

in applying tenets of the Vedas to local situations, attempted to spread the new doctrine of non-violence and vegetarianism. Doniger and Smith write:

> Manu ... marks a critical moment in the orthodox priestly tradition. It is an attempt at reconciliation of an already ancient heritage as well as a reorientation of that heritage around new 'principles of life' (*dharmas*); ... the text is pivotal in the priestly response to the crisis of traditional Aryan culture.[378]

In several ways, the rules embodied in Manu provide clues about cultural psychology and its influence on psychiatric phenomena in ancient and traditional India. Problems associated with episodes of psychiatric condition, perhaps contributing to their production, are addressed in *The Laws of Manu* and other Dharmaśāstra works.[379] As indicated earlier, in an idiom of morality, ethics, and obligation they mark out the standards, conventions, and expectations regarding approved social behaviour for different social castes and during various stages of life. Details about proper behaviour between the sexes, marital obligations, social relations with one's elders and teachers, the typologies of misdemeanours and crimes, and how to conduct sacred rituals and sacrifices are only some of the themes that are taken up in great detail. Although some modifications of rites and practices are allowed, in general, all of the stipulations about approved social conduct are uncompromising in tone.[380] Explicit details of the furious and vehement punishments that would follow transgressions are stated in cold, direct language that is nevertheless emotionally arousing.

In outlining by means of lists and in detailing approved and desirable social conduct, the Dharmaśāstras generally and *The Laws of Manu* more specifically hint at and certainly connote and imply what much of the inner, experiential content of negative emotions such as guilt, shame, discouragement, demoralization, and a sense of defilement would have been like. They also stipulate, by implication, the morphology of social deviance – that is, the writings hint at the obverse of what is desirable and acceptable in areas of social life. In part, a psychiatric condition is realized and shaped, if not caused by, a person's awareness of deficien-

---

[378] Doniger and Smith 1991: xxxv.

[379] Lahiri 1986.

[380] Although sometimes inconsistent, as Doniger and Smith (1991) point out.

cies in meeting the conventions and standards of social and psychological conduct, as well as the suffering this entails. In other words, psychiatric condition is often formulated, experienced, and manifested in the real or imagined contravention of social norms, and in the present instance these would be norms stipulated by Dharmaśāstra compilations such as *The Laws of Manu*. The laws essentially delineate the semantic texture and flow that make up worry, guilt, self-deprecation, demoralization, the sense of social failure and personal anguish that can torment individuals when contemplating their current social standing and their past and future social conduct. Much of the cultural psychology inherent in *Atharvaveda* and, discussed earlier, in here expounded not explicitly with respect to spiritual agencies but the prosaic everyday world of behaviour and duty. A deeper philosophical religion that is based on concepts of karma, transmigration, and ways of liberation, through meditation or Bhakti devotion, is implicit in and imparts psychological power to Dharmaśāstra.

Comment

The Laws of Manu provide a glimpse of 'the calculus of introspection' and human psychology more generally that is reflexively set in motion when individuals fall prey to real or imagined social failures. It underscores feelings of shame and guilt that follow from transgressions and that if sustained in vulnerable persons would motivate moral re-education and spiritual re-affirmation, if not a breakdown of visceral somatic processes leading to conditions of sickness and/or psychiatric interest. Basically, vulnerable persons at risk or who are merely insecure or unsure of themselves for whatever reason, who become burdened by persistent negative emotions and self-evaluation, who seek release through appeals to prayer and liberation, or who are vulnerable to the cleansing and socially celebratory functions that are modelled by and made available through cultural patterns of states of possession, are likely to formulate, experience and play out their plight in the moral idiom of Dharmaśāstra. In other words, with respect to traditional Hindu as well Indian imagination (Indian Muslims, Jains, Buddhists, Christians, and Sikhs) the Dharmaśāstra dicta consist of analogues, if not frank representations, of the actual content of thoughts, feelings, worries, and themes of demoralization that one might expect to find in the mental experiences of a morally troubled patient plagued by a particular variety psychiatric condition. Examples of lay psychiatric conditions in different regions of contemporary North India that featured possession were reviewed earlier.[381] These provide general concepts about and glimpses of the surface manifestations of psychiatric conditions that involved local, proximal circumstances and events related to disasters, interpersonal and caste conflicts, and general sources of worry. Of course, these anthropologists describe little that is explicitly related to *dharma* or Dharmaśāstra injunctions – nor karma, or *mokṣa,* for that matter. Yet, even in this setting, the implicit cultural psychology in terms of which preoccupations, worries, and vulnerabilities of afflicted persons are understood and experience, whatever made them 'real' and meaningful, depended on a world-view and manner of thinking and feeling that was saturated with ideas of *dharma* and a sense of moral vulnerability stipulated by the standards set by Dharmaśāstra works such as *The Laws of Manu.*

For those burdened by onerous intra- and inter-caste requirements of conduct or suffering from a sense of having failed in their ritual obligations, and hence overcome with moral guilt and shame, *The Laws of Manu* hint at the inner punishment that would be felt and the ruminations, preoccupations, and self-doubt and loathing that could haunt them. Thus through or in terms of the cultural psychology that they influence and control, Dharmaśāstras point to the deep structures underlying and vitalizing how psychiatric conditions would have been and are represented in experience and behaviour. They determine and orchestrate the emotional and cognitive feelings inherent in such conditions since the latter are in part realized in negative emotions and states of feeling regarding one's social (essentially moral) standing and conduct. Viewed in comprehensive terms, then, psychiatric condition plays out in social and psychological behaviour dissatisfactions with the self, tied to awesome responsibilities that exceed what individuals might be able to muster or to the agonies of having actually failed or contravened expectations, conventions, expectations, and obligations inherent in dharmic stipulations. Given these generalizations, then, much of what *The Laws of Manu* outline are the likely criteria whereby individuals were judged harshly by significant others and by themselves, so by implication they also outline not only experiential content of, but also responses to, many incidents of psychiatric condition.

---

[381] Opler 1958; Waxler 1974, 1979; Bhattacharyya 1986; Assayag 1999.

An important theme in *The Laws of Manu* is the relative worth, social standing, and credibility of persons within the hierarchical Hindu social order. By the same token, peppered throughout the compilation are references to outcast groups of unwanted, rejected, sullied, polluted, discredited, and marginalized persons. Individuals exhibiting insanity are frequently included in these lists of human 'waste material', along with thieves, murderers, egregious transgressors of basic norms of human decency, and the like. Weiss examines explicit references to insanity as a social category in his review of moral and legal issues in the Dharmaśāstra.[382] He provides details of how persons classed as insane are to be regarded and dealt with in different social and legal situations. As Weiss points out:

> The general issues dealt with in these texts pertaining to insanity include: the victims of crimes, invalid gifts, the validity of a witness's testimony, feigned madness, prescribed penances associated with insanity, and injunctions against contact of a householder with the insane. With regard to civil law there is inheritance, contracts, debts, types of marriage, and divorce. With regard to criminal proceedings the implications of the insanity of the defendant are discussed.[383]

More specifically, in *The Laws of Manu* one finds that a condition of insanity is an excuse for nullifying marital obligations, undoing social contracts, and avoiding full responsibility in the case of slander and criminal offence. These references to insanity underscore the identity, visibility, and problematic legal and moral valuation assigned to varieties of psychopathology in ancient Hindu societies. Thus, in addition to mapping a hierarchical social order that was governed by sometimes uncompromising standards of morality, behaviour, and personal experience that favoured the higher social orders and morally policed and regulated the lower orders in matters of conduct, *The Laws of Manu* explicitly condemned but also protected those 'non-persons' who were socially recognized as insane.

---

[382] Weiss 1975, 1977.

[383] Weiss 1975: 50.

THE *BHAGAVADGĪTĀ*

Introduction

In the sacred writings of Hinduism the *Bhagavadgītā* occupies an extremely influential position. Its ideas have been important even before it was actually composed sometime around 200 BCE. Its influence is spread across sects and philosophical schools. The two epics and several of the Dharmaśāstras have had a comparable pan-Hindu influence but the emotional and spiritual power of the *Bhagavadgītā* has been greater. The influence and appeal of the *Bhagavadgītā* in the religious, philosophical, and emotional life of Hinduism has been explained as stemming from the fact that the date of compilation came during a time of social crisis when the Brahmanic tradition of Hinduism had ossified and lost its freshness and Buddhism and Jainism along with other heterodox traditions proved intellectually burdensome and too full of effort.[384]

The social and cultural context of life in India during the centuries preceding the Common Era was marked by extreme polytheism and the appeal of the *Bhagavadgītā* resided in its ability to present a direct way to the path of liberation through devotion to a personal god. The religious world of everyday life out of which the *Gītā* emerged was complex in the extreme. It not only set the stage for the appeal of the *Gītā*, but undoubtedly served as a backdrop for elaboration and consolidation of various sectarian groups and changes in medical orientation as per beliefs and practices that evolved into Ayurveda. One can presume a high degree of unrest and uncertainty, not only in the social, spiritual realm but in the psychology of the people, especially the lower castes. When a context is needed for a depiction of the emotional and behavioural disarticulation and disaffection of the period, perhaps more pronounced but certainly approximated during preceding and succeeding eras (as discussed earlier with respect to demography and public health), the setting of ambiguity, confusion, and competition among religious beliefs and practices, the shifting and conflict-ridden milieu inherent in polytheism, are worth keeping in mind. This is the context that made the *Gītā* resonant and appealing and promised and provided consolation. Here is how van Buitenen describes social conditions:

---

[384] Van Buitenen 1981.

> On the folk level the Vedic god Indra continued to be worshipped and prayed to for rain. There is evidence of a Sun cult. Fire worship of a kind persisted in the Vedic sacrifices. That there was flourishing Shiva cult cannot be doubted. Very little is known about Goddess religions, but they are likely to have existed in several forms. The veneration of ancestors was more a domestic than a social worship, but it added to the richness of religious forms. Cults of chthonic powers like snakes and Yaksas are evident. Also, a completely new god, Skanda-Kārttikeya, appears in the northern pantheon, and surely not without sectarian pressure. In Buddhism and Jainism homage was paid to the great teachers – homage that a Hindu would consider Bhakti. And then as now there undoubtedly existed *grāmadevatās* and *kuladevatās*, village and family deities. In this abounding polytheism a person needed Bhakti to find for himself his *iṣṭadevatā*, 'the god of his choice', to whom he could demonstrate his loyalty.[385]

How and why the *Bhagavadgītā* appealed

The *Bhagavadgītā* means 'Song of the Lord' and is part of the *Mahābhārata*, one of the most famous epic poems of India that is regarded as a classic of Indian literature. The attraction and influence of the *Bhagavadgītā* stems from the way it managed to appeal to the religious instincts and spiritual needs of people across all levels of the population, especially among those not encased within the Brahmanic establishment. It and the *Mahābhārata* constitute both a religious/spiritual and philosophical work and have enormous narrative, literary appeal as well. The *Mahābhārata* is a compilation of sagas, heroic poetry, and cycles that refer to famous kings and heroes of prehistoric times. The narrative itself, leaving aside the *Gītā*, is suffused with moral, spiritual, and philosophical ideas central to Hinduism. As discussed earlier, the earliest renditions of the creation and maintenance of the cosmos and society is found in the Vedas, later Brāhmaṇas, as well as in the Puranas (old legends, cosmogonical and cosmological stories, fables, myths). Such stories outline a world-view that shapes and regulates the life of members of the highest caste, who recited the Vedas and performed the rituals. The *Mahābhārata* also expounds Hindu ideals regarding personal experience and social conduct. It is regarded as a cornerstone of classical Indian culture and civilization. As indicated earlier, together with the *Rāmāyaṇa* and the Puranas, the *Mahābhārata* and specially the *Bhagavadgītā* expound upon and exemplify fundamental moral precepts and

[385] Van Buitenen 1981: 24.

injunctions regarding social conduct among the Aryans embodied in the Dharmaśāstras. They are given emotional significance and resonance through stories of ancient kings and princes.

Winternitz contends that the function of the *Mahābhārata* in Indian culture and civilization can be likened to a veritable:

> textbook of morals (*śāstra*), law and philosophy based on ancient tradition (*smṛti*) and hence endowed with indisputable authority; and since more than 1500 years it has served the Indians as much for entertainment as for instruction and sublime edification.[386]

It is

> a 'poem' only in a very restricted sense. Indeed, in a certain sense the *Mahābhārata* is not at all a poetic product, but rather an entire literature.[387]

When it was actually composed is unclear, but as indicated earlier estimates place it well before the beginning of the Common Era. It is traditionally ascribed to the ancient sage Vyāsa, but is generally assumed to have been the work of numerous unknown bardic poets and later revised by Brahmin priests who introduced segments pertaining to morality, philosophy, and statecraft.

What the *Bhagavadgītā* reveals and addresses

Besides embodying central tenets of Hindu philosophy and religion, the influence of the *Bhagavadgītā* in moulding self and identity of Indian people cannot be overstated. While a holy book of the Bhāgavatas, a Vaishnavite sect, it is also a book of worship and education for Indians generally, regardless of sect. The *Gītā* tells of a dialogue between Prince Arjuna and Krishna an avatar of god who is serving as Arjuna's charioteer on the eve of an epic battle. The prince, overcome with apprehension and rational dread, and filled with doubt and uncertainty about his mission in life at this crucial juncture – namely, at the prospect of the imminent slaughter of his people – shows reluctance and a desire to postpone or at least deflect the momentum of his role and lifepath. His imminent suffering as an agent of destruction and conflict, and the suf-

---

[386] Winternitz 1981: 300.

[387] Winternitz 1981: 296.

fering of the thousands of combatants and their families as a result of the forthcoming battle, regardless of its outcome, are cited as reasons for desisting from action and avoiding human suffering. In the process of consoling and advising the prince, Krishna presents poetically beautiful and compelling arguments for the correctness of the battle, in the process incorporating fundamental philosophical ideas involving duty or action or karmic pursuit, Yoga or selfless detachment, and the Yoga of devotion to a particular god.

Arjuna is told that the real spirit and essence of the self is indestructible and timeless, that only the mere physical body (one's temporary existence) can be injured in such a way as to cause pain, but only in a temporary way. To persist and be consumed by a temporary setback, even to die, is a small price to pay for the everlasting glory of honouring one's position and obligation as ordained by god. To desist is to invite moral shame and religious castigation. A way to proceed is to carry out an ethics of action, an economy of duty, that neutralizes one's real, moral investment in worldly affairs and outcomes; in other words, to engage in desireless action: 'do your thing, accept your circumstances, live with its inevitabilities, and do not allow mere suffering to dissuade you'.

Krishna points out to the prince that there are three ways in which one can, with certainty, overcome dilemmas, quandaries, moral floundering, and hardships derived from one's circumstances: the path of knowledge and inward reflection, the path of action and commitment to duty and obligation, and the path of love and devotion to god, or Bhakti. Moreover, it is explained that in the theosophical logic provided and urged upon him by Krishna, all three paths are integrated through and mediated by devotion to god. In short, the message is that a proper morality and theology extinguishes and trivializes whatever difficulties and hardships are linked to one's circumstances in favour of far richer and longer-lasting benefits.

This story illustrates some of the essential features of self and personhood exemplified in the Hindu tradition. The information communicated among the interlocutors not only offers consolation to the troubled but also encourages one to fulfil obligations and pursue actions that will counteract human misery and suffering. Human misfortune, in short, is to be expected as an inevitable part of pursuing one's duty and one's obligation to oneself, the world of others, and the sanctity of existence that is inherent in the social order. As we have seen, and as the narrative of Prince Arjuna exemplifies in an emotionally compelling idiom, a person's *dharma* and karma, as it were, must adhere to the dictates of the social situation, emboldened and comforted by yogic desireless detachment, the stoical recognition brought by responsible social action, and the consolation that comes from honouring god in even the most oppressive human predicaments. In short, it provides a formula that essentially spiritualizes, assuages, and transforms the realities of social and psychological maladies, even when associated with bodily ailments, into an idiom of religious comfort and resolution.

The *Bhagavadgītā* as a statement about and healing of human misery

The philosophy of life articulated by and urged upon Arjuna by Krishna and the implications of the moral philosophy enjoined reinforces influences discussed earlier for Dharmaśāstra. It provides a formulation of how inevitable setbacks and hardships should be perceived and worked through. Essentially, to stretch a point here, the prince's condition can be viewed as a prototypical example of demoralization, emotional distress, social retreat if not rebellion, and behavioural disarticulation in the face of setbacks, circumstances, and hardships resulting from and this sense imposed by one's social and moral (dharmic) obligations. The prince, in other words, personifies an emotional state whose contents would vary in relation to an individual's social position, but which exhibits a profound loss of morale and self-doubt. He is psychologically, socially, and morally floundering, overcome with guilt, emotional pain, lack of purpose and motivation, and desires to withdraw from his social circumstances, the battle of his life, questioning the principles and rationale of his role or position and of the personal hardships it may bring. He has arrived at a condition of personal distress that is framed in an idiom of philosophical and moral speculation and doubt. While it presents in poetic and literary mode the inner ruminations and burdens confronting an individual's onerous social situation and intended course of action, it also exemplifies what in a more weighing and punishing idiom would have comprised many psychiatric conditions.

Indian psychiatrists generally view the *Gītā* in positive terms. They regard the text not only as a powerful exposition of the Indian character but also as a source of religious and psychological healing replete with applications to universal themes, including those that arise in contemporary psychiatric practice. Venkoba Rao draws attention to the importance of the *Gītā* for understanding Indian psychology and as a source for therapy:

> At its fundamental level, *Gītā* highlights the Vedantic concepts of the Nature and Destiny of man; the real nature of man is divine, his destiny lies in not only knowing and realizing this divinity but also the identity of his self and universal self, which implies a state of *mokṣa* or liberation from the bondage from the material world. *Gītā* indicates the ways to realize this summum bonum. *Gītā* as a work on basic human dynamic psychology is par excellence and a masterpiece of psychotherapy. It is a recipe for a better and a higher life.[388]

Venkoba Rao reviews the myriad ways in which the *Gītā* has relevance for understanding the Indian mind and its functions, the context within which mental activities operate in human affairs generally, so different from a Western mind-set. He stresses the complex philosophical psychology implicit in the *Gītā* and how it provides a natural base for psychotherapy.

Balodhi and Keshavan outline the narrative scope of the *Gītā* in terms of principles of cognitive psychotherapy.[389] They discuss (1) a symbolic representation of universal human conflicts as exemplified in the predicament of the prince; (2) the role and function of Krishna as a 'cognitive therapist'; (3) the example of positive mental health illustrated in the character of *sthitaprajñā*, a model of one who is able to control emotions and draw on inner psychological fortitude; and (4) the *Gītā*'s 'therapeutic package' for dealing with anxiety and conflict, which includes making a rational appraisal of a situation (*jñāna*), the carrying through of karma, or appropriate action, and the importance of a mental attitude of Bhakti, or faith in execution of action. Like Venkoba Rao, these two psychiatrists see in the *Gītā* a document replete with psychiatric significance. It articulates a cultural psychology, it reviews and discusses some of the contents of psychopathology, it offers consolation and support to distressed persons burdened by social circumstances that can be defeating, and it provides an implicit strategy for shouldering the burdens of psychiatric conditions.

One can thus construe the *Gītā* as a manual or guide, if not textbook, for making sense of, rationalizing, and coping with the kind of social and psychological burdens in life generally and in contexts of psychi-

---

[388] Venkoba Rao 1984: 55.

[389] Balodhi and Keshavan 1986. Balodi's writings are discussed in later chapters.

atric condition specifically. While not a medical compilation like is found in Ayurveda or even a set of practices for the relief of spiritual, bodily ailments as in Yoga, the *Gītā* nonetheless seems to furnish the individual with a clinically compelling vision of Indian cultural psychology in context of strain and conflict, thereby exposing experiential concomitants of psychiatric conditions in traditional India. Besides offering a textual compilation of an ancient cultural psychology, the *Gītā* illustrates a broad assortment of cognitive and emotional symptoms, such as depression, anguish, loss of will and motivation, anxiety and dread, demoralization, paralysis or at least the restraint of human action, and despair in the face of trying social circumstances. While Arjuna's plight may represent a very special existential and moral dilemma, here raised to a level of profound mythical and religious importance, it also symbolizes all types of human challenges and conflicts, however mundane and prosaic they may appear.

If the message of the *Gītā* is projected across the expanse of cultural evolutionary time in India, it conveys a vision of hope and comfort that Indians have learned to rely on in the face of human suffering. One's circumstances may appear trivial and insignificant in the great scheme of things, yet the power and universality of the symbols that the *Gītā* draws on are meant to be paradigmatic for all people. Human pain, doubt, and misery are inevitable but must be endured and suffered through, if not surmounted, by means of a philosophy of duty, obligation, karmic motivation, and awe of the sacred. In this sense, a particular variety of psychopathology in a heroic, eminent, distinguished, and powerful person is here domesticated and universalized for the Indian people as a whole.

In short, besides merely delineating a rather natural and contingent reaction consisting of a breakdown of social and psychological behaviour, the story of the prince at this crucial juncture of his life reaffirms traditional Indian values and coping efforts by promoting adherence to duty, morality, and purpose. It endows human action and personality with a metaphysical dimension, as seen in the classical philosophical and literary tradition of India. In this way, the *Gītā* not only represents psychiatric phenomena in a non-medical idiom, but also expounds and articulates psychotherapeutic quests and tasks in a compelling cultural psychological idiom that attempts to mitigate the inevitability of human suffering.

Putting Hindu tradition in social context

Discussion thus far reflects an obvious bias, emphasizing a negative message – what the *Gītā* and related texts of traditional India tell us about the darker ramifications and overtones of Hindu psychology in the face of adversity and human predicaments linked to dharmic burdens, and thus what it reveals about psychiatric condition. Left out of this picture is the affirmative dimension of the story – its message of hope and affirmation of a will inherent in the courses of action it enjoins, namely, release through meditation and/or Bhakti devotionalism. The *Gītā* enjoins both courses of action as part of the experience of love of Krishna. These are usually the hallmarks of a highly positive, even ecstatic mental outlook. What an inevitably biased outsider imputes to this popular as well as theosophical Hindu classic should be balanced by what the *Gītā* promises and achieves viewed in context of human needs and imperatives.

In this regard, the moral philosophy and psychology provided by the *Gītā* brings to mind the Brahmin Chaubes of the city of Mathura, as described by Lynch (1990b). The Chaubes serve as pilgrimage priests in this sacred city which is permeated with the history and presence of Krishna and which is still a major pilgrimage centre. The tenets of the *Gītā* and other canonical texts of Hinduism are pre-eminent in the psychology of the way of life of the Chaubes. They have a social identity and embody a persona that represents a Hindu ideal: being *mast* and becoming a *mastram* – that is, a person who is happy, lusty, proud, carefree, and even intoxicated, enjoying life with a sense of physical and emotional wellbeing. This self-conscious attitude is:

> not merely a reputation for Chaubes to live up to; rather it is an ideal of personhood that tells them how to behave and how to feel when or if truly themselves ... Being *mast* is in the nature, soil, streets, air, atmosphere, blood, and culture ... especially of the Chaube.[390]

Four things are said to conduce to this state of being: marijuana, good food, remembering the Lord through prayer, and physical exercise. Lynch goes into detail about how the influence of such habitual patterns of action can have in the psychological economy of the Chaubes. In explaining the lifestyle of Chaubes and their attitude

[390] Lynch 1990b: 99.

toward life, Lynch also goes into their philosophy about thought and emotion, about asceticism and emotionalism. The seat of thought and feeling is said to be the *mān*, a word translated as *mind, heart, intellect, soul, disposition, purpose,* and *desire*. Lynch writes:

> From such a point of view, then, asceticism with its emphasis on thought and meditation, and emotionalism or eroticism, with its emphasis on feeling and emotion, are not logical contradictions: rather, they are logical contraries, two aspects of the same thing. The concern [is] to discard neither asceticism nor eroticism but rather to bring them into unity.[391]

Lynch emphasizes the many ways in which Indians are able to balance seemingly negative pursuits with positive ones so as to create a sense of integration and purpose in many areas of life.

The psychology of the Chaubes complements the clinical textbook dimension of the *Gītā*. The emphasis on a positive, upbeat frame of mind may be the object and outcome of a life formula through which many Indians not only cope with demoralization and depression but also integrate what to a Westerner might seem to be at least three disparate tendencies: asceticism and emotionalism, thought and feeling, and negative, dark constructions joined with joyful, optimistic ones. These are not opposed; they may correspond to one another and function as a unity. One concludes that a part of the Indian cultural psychology illustrated by the *Bhagavadgītā* and other influential Hindu classics involves an ability to turn one's perceptions around so as to achieve not only acceptance and resignation – transcending negative experience – but also more positive experiences, such as described by Lynch for the Chaubes of Mathura.

Caveat of limitation

Different conceptions of person or human being are evident in the corpus of the Vedas as well as in the *Bhagavadgītā* and related popular, literary texts. There is recognition that man or *puruṣa* represents a being that stands separate from the rest of sentient beings in virtue of its capacity to plan, reason, anticipate, uphold or go against *dharma*. Here, man is set apart from animals and is seen to exemplify a common heritage

---

[391] Lynch 1990b: 102.

among men of different persuasions. In this perspective man is seen as a distinct, concrete, creature of this world locked into a distinct family, village, caste, and the like. The identity of Arjuna and the circumstances that beset him fall into this perspective. This view of man and identity represents a *standard, worldly, explicit* Vedic or Hindu anthropology.[392]

In relation to this slant on the nature of identity, self, and man one can juxtapose a conception of identity or *puruṣa* as denoting something inherent, pre-eminent, and transcendent, the *ātman,* which is an expression or simply a part of the universal *Brahman* which is timeless. The *Gītā* points to this view in its real life narrative of suffering and demoralization and need for relief and liberation. Pursuit of a path of knowledge and/or ritual practice, depending on which writings or philosophical systems one consults, allows a freeing of the self (*ātman*) of the individual which is of overriding importance. This theoretical scheme is religious, philosophical and soteriological and alludes to a generic abstract conceptualization of self, identity, and man. It constitutes an *'otherworldly, implicit'* anthropology: it tells about how the Vedas and the Hindu intellectual tradition embodied and personified in the *Gītā* articulate the nature of the relationship between man and the cosmos or universe, all viewed in abstract, universal terms. Krishna's advice and consolation to the concrete, embodied and troubled Arjuna exemplifies this implicit anthropology.

The world-view of the *Bhagavadgītā* and the rest of the Hindu traditions as per conception of identity and selfhood is not without its contradictions. In both its explicit and implicit anthropology, the Hindu tradition holds that *not all human beings* have equal qualifications. Thus, in spite of the fact that all concrete humans share common features of thought and experience that distinguish them from animals and plants, for example, only selves or individuals that belong to the higher castes, the twice-born, have the opportunity to seek release from the ailments, distractions, deceptions, etc. (*saṃsāra*) of the real world that beset all concrete persons. Arjuna, after all, is a member of the higher *varṇas*, a distinguished family man, leader, and warrior. This scenario of tension posed by the implicit and explicit anthropology of the Hindu world-view excludes a significant proportion of the Indian peoples (lower castes, outsiders, foreigners) from an opportunity to benefit from its

---

392 Halbfass 1991.

moral, spiritual healing (in cases of psychiatric conditions, non-medical portion of indigenous psychiatry).

This resume and caveat makes apparent the difficulties one encounters when seeking to understand the setting and context of psychiatric phenomena in traditional India. A basic difficulty, discussed early on in this book, is that there is very little data about such phenomena in the texts to begin with. Another one, perhaps more basic, is that an analyst has very little data about the nature of experience and behaviour in real contexts and circumstances of life out of and in which psychiatric phenomena are constructed. Furthermore, putting aside information provided by cultural anthropologists about experiences and behaviour of real contemporary Indian people (as a guide to inference to traditional thought worlds and habit patterns and then psychiatric phenomena), an analyst only has access to the implicit anthropology and psychology of the Vedas and other ancient texts (like epics and Puranas). These sacred, philosophical, soteriological, and literary writings can be mined for clues of India's traditional people's conceptions of self, emotional ways of responding and thinking, and ways of behaving. However, in doing so one is crossing a shadowy, beclouded, and ontologically and epistemologically murky territory that stretches between a general, abstract view of person and identity (an implicit anthropology) and concrete selves and persons locked into everyday patterns of life and its dilemmas (an explicit anthropology). A third difficulty stems from the fact that even this abstract, philosophical, literary material only addresses a selected portion of the population anyway. The data does not inform about what one can only presume represented a very large segment of the population. One simply cannot surmise and much less ascertain what proportion of the population of traditional India enjoyed the privileges or advantages of opportunities for full understanding and participation in the Hindu ideology and religion and had access to the knowledge and ritual practices that promised liberation. One can presume that a significant proportion of the appeal of devotional practices of Bhakti and sectarian religion emanated from individuals and families outside the envelope of privilege provided by esoteric knowledge of writings. The picture of life of the less favoured and burdened lower orders provided by van Buitenen, discussed earlier, are very apropos in this regard.[393] Similarly, and in this terrain of real life dilemmas and conflicts the cases presented

[393] Van Buitenen 1981.

by Opler and displayed in temples and sanctuaries, all reviewed earlier, provide data of the commingling of general aspects of traditional culture and the messiness of everyday life and its vicissitudes. These cases provide guides to the pictures of distress, disaffection, and disarticulation likely to have prevailed in earlier epochs of Indian history among people that enjoyed part of the high Sanskritic culture of their society but were left out of its manifold of possibilities for relief and healing and had to resort to practitioners and institutions that could more directly dispense curative procedures.

TRADITIONAL INDIA AND MATERIALIZATION OF PSYCHIATRIC PHENOMENA

Having pointed to characteristics of phenomena of psychiatric interest among traditional Indian peoples, it is appropriate to turn to areas of potential social conflict and stress that may have played a role in its causation. For this, information provided by cultural anthropologists is of crucial importance. Their observations of behaviour in traditional communities comparatively less influenced by modernity provide a window into the past. What kinds of social situations and personal interactions in Indian societies may have contributed to the irruption of psychiatric condition? How were the characteristics of stress points in the culture represented in the way such conditions were expressed?

To ask such questions is not to denigrate the culture and way of life, but to merely indicate that in India, like in all complex civilizations, cultural traditions and established ways of social life, while enhancing of spiritual and mental health, can also produce strains and oppress. A psychiatric condition develops in persons who have certain vulnerabilities (inherited or acquired through developmental experiences) who are then subjected to strains and stresses that come up in their lives. As already suggested, beliefs, attitudes, values, and traditions constitute a foundational component of Indian cultural psychology. They impart a distinct resonance to experience and behaviour and, by implication, psychiatric conditions. However, what one may conceptualize as the sociology of Vedic life embodied prescriptions and commands about behaviour that one may safely assume were significant from a psychiatric standpoint.

Mandelbaum, whose observations were discussed in Chapters 2 and 3, provides many examples of the kinds of human conflicts that pervade Indian communities.[394] In describing how members of a family relate to one another, he alludes to obligations and expectations that are sometimes not met, bringing frustration and tension. Families seek to marry a daughter to a man of a higher caste, or a higher subgroup within a caste, but unfortunately when she moves into her husband's household she may be denigrated as an inferior, creating resentment, tension, and guilt, as mentioned earlier. The sheer complexity of rank attribution imposes an incessant desire to rise in the hierarchy and fear of losing status. Ranked sections of a caste are hereditary, section affiliation reckoned in different ways, and the sections of a *jāti* or caste can be made up of persons joined by lineage, of clans, villages, or territorial divisions. All of these factors create differences between the social standing of families and even between husband and wife. Members of different *jāti*s frequently coexist and work together in complementary ways (these are called *jajmānī* relations), as when a food-producing family works with families that supply them with goods and services. However, these barter exchanges can and frequently break down and cause tension. Because of social changes in modern India, such economic cooperation has been supplanted in many villages; more money is being used in village economies and modern transport now makes market exchanges more feasible. These developments can reduce the power of a dominant *jāti* and the coercive element in *jajmānī* relations, leading to new frictions and tensions.

There is always rivalry between caste groups, and even within subgroups, with respect to prestige and social standing, not to say economic resources. The prohibitions associated with the purdah places pressure on women. Arranged marriages and the inevitable sexual attraction between members of different castes create tension and unhappiness. Mandelbaum refers to the prominence of family coalitions and alliances within a village, which cannot always protect against conflict, divisiveness, and potential human distress, if not misery. Such coalitions frequently extend beyond the confines of the village. The endemic conflicts over land ownership, women, wealth, and social standing lead to the formation of alliances, and conflicts are arbitrated through them. Sometimes, more pronounced and general tensions evolved, termed by Siegel

[394] Mandelbaum 1970.

and Beals as 'factionalism', defined as: *'overt conflict within a group which leads to the increasing abandonment of cooperative activities'.*[395] Strains and tensions can escalate to the point of 'pervasive factionalism', a condition that not only involves much emotional distress and social divisiveness but frank disturbances of emotion and behaviour:

> The village seemed to lack any sense of direction or purpose. The old patterns of relationship between kinsmen and among *jātis* no longer seemed effective. Conflict among brother, between husband and wife, between different *jātis*, even between friends, seemed to be endemic. Almost every day there was a suicide, a wife beating, a theft, or a violent quarrel ... Necessary cooperation to maintain water course within the village, to repair village streets and approach roads, to purify drinking water wells, and carry on the social and ceremonial life of the village was not forthcoming.[396]

Cohn reviews the ways in which psychological, social, political, and economic tensions arising from disputes and conflicts of interest are dealt with in different types of villages and kinds of penalties that can ensue. The villages were classified in terms of number of castes and presence or absence of dominant caste and tradition-supported councils for adjudication of disputes. One of these is termed a Panchayat, a group or council, usually of respected elders, that mediates conflicts in a community or group. The focus and scope of a Panchayat meeting varies according to the problem for which it was convened. For example, the mere suggestion of proscribed relationships between the sexes can quickly summon up a council to prevent escalation and further strife in order to control the ritual peril posed by the delinquency of a few. Cohn suggests that:

> In most Indian villages conflict is the expression of structural principles in which there are many cleavages, based on caste, wealth, relation to super-ordinate political authority, kinship, occupation, patron-client ties, and ritual position, which at once unite and divide individuals and families. Dispute settling, norm setting, and norm enforcing are situational and every dispute or breach of norms involves a kind of social algebra on the part of the actors in the situation to see what lines of cleavage will be affected by what alliances they make.[397]

---

[395] Siegel and Beals 1960: 399, italics in original.

[396] Beals 1962: 94–95, quoted in Cohn 1965: 96.

[397] Cohn 1965: 97.

Many cases reviewed by him involve individuals whose behaviour suggests disorganization and distress and penalties mete out, such as ostracism, could be psychologically devastating.

Many, perhaps most, of the conflicts and tensions adjudicated in a council of elders or a Panchayat have nothing to do with psychiatric condition per se: they merely register the myriad problems that are endemic to social life and that threaten social order in communities with such a complex mixture of social and cultural elements. On the other hand, some conflicts may cause, entail, or correspond to psychiatric condition. In particularly pernicious instances and with respect to vulnerable individuals, factionalism can be expected to cause social and psychological distress, leading to psychopathology, as in cases resembling pervasive factionalism as described earlier. The result would be a pattern of symptoms and signs, such as guilt, anxiety, depression, intense anger and hostility, associated physiological symptoms, and disruption of social activities. A settled agricultural community that is relatively dense, impoverished, with massive public health problems, that is partitioned and stratified by differences that arouse strong emotions, and whose social life is governed by complex rituals and beliefs that involve both the natural and supernatural worlds, is presumably highly vulnerable to incidents of psychiatric condition. Such incidents will be manifested in the myriad conflicts of interest that are endemic to a community and when played out can involve the principal characteristics of social and cultural life in India.

HOW THE INDIGENOUS PSYCHIATRY OF INDIA WORKED

A central aim of this book, illustrated by material discussed in this chapter, is the search for the inner logic and substance of psychiatric phenomena in traditional India. Intellectual features of Indian culture are used as hypotheses with which to probe the material or content of psychiatric conditions and the social practices and institutions that appropriated them. An appreciation of the cultural roots, manifestations, and meanings of psychiatric phenomena provides a foundation for later examination of the psychiatric enterprise in contemporary India. A fundamental assumption is that psychiatric phenomena were inherent in populations of the subcontinent and that societies there had evolved comprehensible and effective ways of coping with it, modernity representing but one phase or version of India's indigenous psychiatry. Exactly how this psychiatry was done and why it was successful has not been given attention. As discussed in Chapter 1, there is large body of academic and popular literature that addresses mental health implications of Indian traditions.

Many Indian scholars have been drawn to implications of Indian scriptures for mental health. The work of Balodhi is exemplary in this respect.[398] Balodhi's study is apropos here. In it he examines the society and culture of ancient India from the standpoint of principles of community health.[399] This elaborates on his earlier discussion of the philosophical aspects of Ayurveda seen from the standpoint of mental health.[400] In this visionary essay, Balodhi selects from the expanse of Indian social and intellectual life central traditions and doctrines that he then analyses in light of a broad conception of community mental health. Using the Vedic texts, the Dharmaśāstras, the Ayurveda, and Yoga and other philosophical schools, Balodhi reviews key ideas and directives about ancient Hindu ways of life and what they imply about methods and strategies for human improvement and mitigation of problems. These documents propose cultural premises and values that organize, give meaning, provide guidelines, and offer rationales for a Hindu way of life. The doctrines also formulate how persons and communities can fail to meet the standards and conventions outlined – delineating, as it were, community ill-health. In the event of the latter, the documents he discusses prescribe ways of coping with the consequences of stress and how to restore social stability and order under adverse circumstances.

Regarding community health practices that he has derived from Vedic texts, Balodhi holds that:

> [The] recorded history of the human race clearly shows that even before the advent of any formal system of medicine, people had developed concepts about mental illness and their possible ways of management.[401]

---

[398] Balodhi 1986a, 1986b, 1987, 1989, 1991; Balodhi and Chowdhary 1986. Balodhi's study of the *Bhagavadgītā* (with Keshavan, 1986) has already been discussed. His work is taken up in later chapters.

[399] Balodhi 1989.

[400] Balodhi 1987.

[401] Balodhi 1989: 50.

He calculates that the *Atharvaveda* describes 20 types of mental illness, all of which are community-oriented. It also prescribes community rites that amount to forms of treatment: *upāsana,* or devotional worship; *namaskāra,* or bowing down in reverence; *vandana,* or acknowledging the greatness of god; *sevā,* or social service; and *arcana,* or offering gifts to god. Other forms of guidance are found in the Dharmaśāstras, which include aphorisms about social conduct; *smṛtis*, or books of conduct such as that of Manu; *śrauta, kalpa* [Śrautasūtras, Kalpasūtras], or books on ceremonial rules; and Gṛhyasūtras, or books on domestic rituals. The Dharmaśāstras he groups into rules of conduct, rules related to nature of sin and methods of expiation, rules related to social and community behaviour, and politics.

> I prefer to call them systems for community mental health, as the structure and functioning of Vedic community was based on them, which survived for ages together.[402]

All of the daily rites of the individual, those for the community at large, and 16 *saṃskāras*, sacraments or rites of passage pertaining to individuals before an event, such as a prenuptial rite involving would-be parents, across the life cycle and beyond, are discussed in terms of how they contribute to mental health. Balodhi views rituals surrounding death, for example, as patterns of psychological, family, and community activity to alleviate the pain of loss. He assesses the system of expiatory rites or *prāyaścitta* in this way:

> If a person does not perform his obligatory duties and/or his actions are directed by sexual urge, anger and greed, he commits sin and develops a sense of guilt that ultimately leads to mental problems. So, the removal of sin and guilt is essential for a person aspiring for positive mental health ... It is a kind of penance the sinner has to undergo for the purification of his mind and body and to re-integrate himself into the social order. Psychologically speaking, the system of *Prāyaścitta* is a form of social support as well as abreaction.[403]

In some respects, despite his focus, Balodhi is really not discussing mental illness or community health in ancient India but is interpreting the ancient culture itself. A hidden logic of explanation and interpreta-

---

[402] Balodhi 1989: 50.

[403] Balodhi 1989: 51.

tion underlies his efforts. He first discusses the values, traditions of behaviour, and cognitive premises underlying conventions about family, social, and moral behaviour as formulated in the appropriate texts. Next, he derives the social and psychological implications of the cultural themes he elucidates. The third stage of his analysis is to interpret the kinds of stresses and strains that apparently existed in ancient India, given the kinds of rites, mantras, and procedures for expiation found in the texts. The final stage of his interpretation is to draw a logical correspondence between the problems discovered in the society of ancient India and the modalities and institutions that are used for expiation, cleansing, liberation, purification, restoring morale, and affirming positive values and emotions. Balodhi, as it were, functions as an interpretive psychologist of the community and cultural life of ancient India. He thus complements and expands upon the work of Sudhir Kakar, who, as a psychoanalyst and therapist, limits his focus to intra-psychic aspects of self in contemporary Indian people and the transference aspects of healing.[404]

[404] Kakar 1981, 1982.

Chapter 7

Evolution of Medicine and Psychiatry in Traditional India

INTRODUCTION

Disease and its miseries were included in the Aryan solution to the problems and sufferings posed by the human condition. The way in which this was done represents a major accomplishment of what has been discussed as Vedic medical and mental health theories and practices. Upon this base of Aryan knowledge and praxis Hindu civilization went on to elaborate a body of theory and practice of medicine that was and continues to be distinctive, influential, and commanding. It resulted not only in ayurvedic medicine but also ayurvedic psychiatry since the diagnosis and therapeutics of varieties of conditions of psychiatric interest were explicitly labelled and discussed in the writings of recognized classical and medieval authorities as will become evident later.

There is virtual unanimity of opinion that Ayurveda, India's scholarly and academic medicine, represents a watershed between the approach to sickness of the Vedas and of indigenous pre-Vedic peoples of the continent as well, compared to the naturalistic academic approach of Hindu India. In its integration of both sets of factors, Ayurveda qualifies as a comprehensive medicine most fully exemplified in classical India of the Gupta period which is subject taken up in this chapter.[405] The former emphasis will generally be referred to as metaphysical or religious and involves, for example, causation by gods, spirits, or demons and related procedures such as incantations, hymns, amulets, and practices that are thought to influence and placate spiritual agencies. On the other hand, the naturalistic emphasis will be referred to as physiological/anatomical or organic (for body) and involves both causation and treatment, for example, physical environmental factors, influence of the bodily humours

---

[405] Kutumbiah 1969; D. Chattopadhyaya 1977; P. V. Sharma 1972.

and their flow or stasis in the channels of the body and into organs, herbal preparations, purgation, sudation, emesis and the like. There are three bodily humours which can become aggravated or faulted and are termed *pitta* (like fire), *vāta* (like wind or air), and *kapha* or *śleṣman* (like phlegm). A complex medical theory underlies the *doṣas*, which are explained in terms of their composition, properties, functions, affinities and harmfulness.[406]

INDIA'S EARLY HISTORY OF MEDICINE AND PSYCHIATRY: GENERAL CONSIDERATIONS

In an ideal sense a narrative of early Indian medicine and psychiatry would provide one with a picture of what preceded the approach of the Aryans, distinctive features and contributions of the Vedic solution that followed, how Vedic notions contributed to the structure of knowledge and practice that culminated in Ayurveda, and finally changes and emendations along with differences in emphasis of separate indigenous texts and traditions about health and disease that followed. Some facets of this narrative have been discussed in earlier chapters and are taken up in detail later. At the outset it should be appreciated that an ideal analysis of early Indian medicine and psychiatry is hampered by a paucity of descriptive accounts of concrete incidents of sickness as well as in-depth historical and comparative studies.

Part of the reason why formulating a social and cultural history of the psychiatric enterprise is difficult stems from the vagaries, ambiguities, and general messiness of how sickness and conditions of psychiatric interest, in particular, surface and impact on a people's way of life. In contrast to changes in brain chemistry and physiology that are its underlying correlates, *socially visible manifestations of psychiatric conditions* involve disaffections of emotion and behaviour and these do not cohere in nicely bounded universal biological categories that allow one to make clear distinctions among types nor to distinguish them from general medical conditions. Viewed in broad context, psychiatric conditions stem from the dialectical relations between population, social structure, and ecology, they situate in a public health context that includes a pool

[406] Kutumbiah 1969 is particularly lucid and comprehensive on this theory.

of general medical ailments, and are shaped, configured, labelled, and handled in terms of cultural understandings and predominating local circumstances, the functions or agendas and imperatives of which are broad. Ancient India does not appear to have a deep-rooted fascination with as well as aversion towards madness as was the case in Greek-influenced societies. This suggests that psychiatric conditions did not constitute important symbols of the culture nor made salient in intellectual and social contexts. Nonetheless, Vedic medicine and Ayurveda are comprehensive and conditions of psychiatric interest are represented in both systems. Given these generalizations, there are five points one can make about medicine and psychiatry in India: (1) concepts and principles of Vedic medicine are difficult to untangle from their precursors; (2) Vedic medicine grew into and, to an indeterminate extent, lies buried within developments that led to Ayurveda; (3) in real life psychiatric and general medical conditions do not come neatly and separately packaged but provide an amalgam that (3) is protean and ambiguous and which the categories of the Ayurveda sought to identify, describe, label, and parcel; (4) the appropriate classification of a given incident of sickness was probably subject to contestation among the diverse medical traditions that were brought into play in different localities of the subcontinent; and (5) it is not clear whether Indian societies seized on and made of psychiatric condition something of overriding social and cultural importance that could illuminate essential features of the human condition.

In many respects, as suggested earlier, India's philosophical psychology concentrated on normal, desirable, sought after goals that directed a way for individuals to connect their identity with verities about the nature of the universe and corresponding spiritual, religious, and psychological values. This intellectual tradition did not signal disease or pathology per se as a major focus. Deviations in experience and behaviour that the philosophical psychology addressed and sought to repair were not viewed as sickness in the conventional sense nor were they condemned or stigmatized. Inaccuracies, deficiencies, or anomalies of social conduct merely pointed to human limitations that needed to be overcome in order to clarify the right way of thinking and behaving and so as to promote and achieve personal liberation. The philosophical logic and behavioural prescriptions and practices of orthodox and heterodox traditions resembled a medical and quasi-psychiatric model, discussed earlier. However, they did not equate human frailties, weaknesses, or mistakes with disease per se.

The main focus of the chapter is on differences between how Vedic medicine compared to Ayurveda conceptualizes sickness generally and mental health problems, in particular. The background for these differences was discussed in the previous chapter and involves foundational documents of Indian culture and civilization. They provide clues as to the meanings and responses to conditions of psychiatric interest. However, this material is inchoate, opaque, and beclouded by philosophical, theological, and speculative psychological concerns. Neither specific manifestations nor types of human maladies, and much less, syndromes of disease and sickness, are singled out in the philosophical psychology of India. Yet in Ayurveda, one notes a distinct focus on these topics. Moreover, besides a general medical focus, one sees that varieties of psychiatric condition are explicitly set apart. These will be examined through the lens of important medical texts.

PHILOSOPHY, SPIRITUAL HEALING AND THE SCIENCE OF MEDICINE: COMMONALITIES AND DIFFERENCES

Before presenting material on the transition from Vedic medicine to Ayurveda it is instructive to examine in general, abstract terms ideas about the nature of being, human disorder, and wellbeing, as exemplified in Indian intellectual traditions and that bear on medicine and psychiatry. Interesting differences and commonalities are observed when this approach is taken. In his analysis of the relationship between Indian intellectual traditions and Ayurveda, Larson initially draws attention to its inclusion of ideas found in the *Atharvaveda*.[407] His main concern, however, involves demonstrating how the ontology and epistemology of Ayurveda was influenced by and in turn influenced traditional philosophical traditions of India (Sāṃkhya and Vaiśeṣika), a topic taken up later.

The first concern to be discussed here is not the structure of knowledge and the nature of being as this pertains to disease, seen in relation to other matter or substance of the world. Rather, it is the logic of the

[407] Larson 1987.

healing enterprise itself. In this context, putting aside obvious differences involving content of ideas and practices, Wezler, Demiéville and Halbfass have drawn attention to the shared structure of methods, procedures, and goals sought by Buddhism and other soteriological traditions and philosophies (Yoga) with respect to providing for spiritual health, on the one hand, and the same logic and methodology inherent in scientific and curative medicine of Ayurveda – and really of any system of medicine that is rational – on the other.[408]

Metaphors and similes used in both systems exemplify an instrumental practical approach of getting individuals to a desired location (across a river, to states of liberation, elimination of disease). A physician is likened to a boatman or steersman and vice versa. Philosophy is associated with metaphysical therapy, a physician as providing a rational, scientific health, and both as good teachers and advisors. In Vedantic writings and especially in Buddhist material, one finds a strong efficient therapy and medicine targeted at the *kleśas*, afflictions of greed, hatred, and illusory misperception inherent in blind attachments to worldly pursuits (*saṃsāra*). The four noble truths of Buddhism, existence of pain, its origin, possibility of relief, and a methodology for obtaining it, have an unmistakable therapeutic logic that parallels that of medicine. The similarity in the various approaches is conceptualized as constituting 'The Four-fold Division of Medicine and Philosophy' by Halbfass, which extends the formulation of Wezler about the correspondence of the 'Quadrangle Division' of spiritual methodology of Yoga with Buddhism.[409]

A question that has been asked is whether Buddhist philosophical psychology and soteriology, which with variations and modifications were adopted or echoed in several schools of Hindu philosophy, were borrowed from medicine or whether the reverse is the case. Did the logic pursued in the quest of spiritual health influence the logic of curative medicine?

Wezler and Halbfass review primary and secondary sources and not only conclude that soteriological traditions of spiritual healing did not borrow their approach from a pre-existent medical scheme but that in fact there is little if any evidence that a scheme like this existed prior to

[408] Wezler 1984; Demiéville 1985; Halbfass 1991.

[409] Halbfass 1991; Wezler 1984.

the time of the Buddha.[410] The question of whether Ayurveda medicine drew on and reflected the structural logic of Buddhism also must be answered. To what extent was the health and wellbeing sought by a physician analogous to the goal envisioned and enjoined by the metaphysical or soteriological physician? There are similarities and differences in the social logic of these two 'medicines' and they involve intention, methods employed, and target sought. In the case of medicine, the steps to accomplish this consist of definition of what the condition is (sickness), what is its cause (physiological imbalance of humours), and how the goal can be attained (herbal medicines, diet). In the case of metaphysical therapies (the soteriological traditions), they involve definition of the current state of spiritual and physical experience (unhappiness, suffering, disaffection), its cause (attachment and ignorance), and the procedures to be followed to cure the malady (meditation, inner purification, peeling away of delusions).

The end in view is important. For Ayurveda this involves, in addition to strict cure of disease, not only a return to an individual's prior state of health but an optimal if not ideal of health. As suggested by Halbfass, this involves primarily worldly health which, secondarily, allows the individual to better participate in its circumstances (following its *dharma* and coping with the inexorable burdens of karma). In the case of the soteriological paradigms, the health that is sought is predominantly other-worldly. It involves removing the encumbrances of attachments and blind presuppositions of *saṃsāra* so as to let loose and free the essential self or *ātman* of the person, that which makes him part of the universal *Brahman*. The various schools of Hindu formulate this in different ways, but they share the essential paradigm.[411]

As indicated earlier, the influence of Indian philosophical traditions on the epistemology of its scholarly, academic medicine is a separate but related topic from that involving the influence of the soteriological traditions, which of course are also philosophical systems, on the structural logic of healing. Larson points out that the dominant influences on Ayurveda come from Sāṃkhya and Vaiśeṣika traditions of philosophy, although many other traditions contribute ideas (Vedānta, Nyāya).[412] He suggests that as theories of knowledge, Ayurveda and classical philoso-

---

[410] Wezler 1984; Halbfass 1991.

[411] Wezler 1984; Halbfass 1991.

[412] Larson 1987.

phical traditions drew ideas from and influenced each other. In Ayurveda, basic substances that make up the world, the body, and disease, and the constructs in terms of which these can be perceived, are drawn from the ontology and epistemology of other philosophical traditions, especially Vaiśeṣika.[413]

The characteristics of life, health, sickness and the manner in which the mechanism of healing are thought to work come from traditional Indian philosophy. For example, ideas about the co-presence of consciousness and primordial materiality (*puruṣa* and *prakṛti*), the nature of the material subtle body and its components, what the gross body is composed of, and the influence of gross inorganic elements are Sāṃkhyan. Ayurvedic physicians knew and applied ideas from these and other schools of philosophy. This is inferred from meanings implicit in the terminology they employed. However, technical philosophical ideas were understood and used differently, which meant stretching them beyond strict philosophical conventions. Larson points out that a general set of fundamental postulates inherent in the intellectual tradition of South Asia (its *Urphilosophie*) probably preceded and inspired the later formulations of Vaiśeṣika and Sāṃkhya and these are represented in the basic epistemology and ontology of Ayurveda.[414] According to him, these include (1) the body's constituents; (2) the correspondence between the nature of the psychic apparatus and subtle aspects of the material body; (3) transmigration of the psychic apparatus across life spans which enlivens the physical body but is separate from it (a person is composed of a genetic and psychic inheritance); (4) the uniformity of ontology or being throughout nature, encompassing Western notions of mind–body and microcosm–macrocosm; and (5) the difference the self, identity or soul from the psychic apparatus, marking a distinction between mind, ego, intellect, or physical constitution and identity, on the one hand, and notions of self or soul, on the other. This philosophical and psychological schema, then, was inherent in Ayurveda, although not necessarily salient or always explicit. How this system of medicine evolved is taken up in the following sections.

[413] See also Larson 1993.

[414] Larson 1987, 1993.

THE TRANSITION FROM VEDIC MEDICINE TO AYURVEDA

Intellectual formulations about the cosmos and its influence on human affairs along with the problems of pain, misery, and suffering inherent in human existence originated in the culture and protohistoric medical traditions of other ancient Indo-Aryan and pre-Indo-European peoples. As an integral part of the philosophy and spirituality inherent in the Vedas generally, one can presume a consolidation of Vedic beliefs and practices in matters related to sickness, disease and emotional disaffection. This Vedic medicine predominated around 1200 BCE. As suggested earlier, two components of this early Indian ethno-medicine can be presumed. Brahmins, as part of their control of rituals of sacrifice and request, undoubtedly were also involved in what one can conceptualize as priestly Vedic medicine. A more popular, practical and less esoteric and intellectual Vedic medicine existed alongside priestly medicine. It drew on a rich folk knowledge and expertise that was associated with the lower, third social grouping that was involved in agrarian pursuits.[415] As time passed, learned men of this particular social order evolved and consolidated a more specialized and practical, empirical medicine than that found in priestly Vedic medicine. The latter was less removed from the details of recurring signs and symptoms of disease and more abstract and metaphysical, sponsored and promulgated by the first estate as part of their performance of sacrificial rites. Priests undoubtedly may have employed some more specific rites for purposes of healing. Those members of the third estate that specialized on disease were familiar with the flora of their surroundings and were able to learn about the medicinal properties of plants, foods, and herbs. Such medicines were used in conjunction with empirical approach to sickness based on observation, follow-up, and trial-and-error methods.

Thus, knowledge and wisdom pertaining to medicine during the Vedic period was associated with specific social classes, initially that of the priests whose words and actions were believed to bring them into contact with greater cosmic powers, and then those more practical-minded representatives of the agricultural estate. Zysk surmises that the latter were able to learn of and imitate the way of the priests, namely, how through sacrifice and ritual priests were able to manipulate the

[415] Zysk 1991.

gods and demonic influences that could cause disease and perform magical procedures and techniques to control spiritual influences.[416] Knowledge of the spirit world, combined with knowledge acquired from sacrificial cults, enabled the 'practical' healers of the third estate to establish themselves as priests in their own right, presumably centred on the peoples of this estate. The more medically specialized practitioners modelled themselves on the sacrificial priests of the first order and actually may have overlapped in status with them, as per classification of the *varṇas* as it is likely caste groupings had not as of yet consolidated. Whereas the first-order priests were conscious of social boundaries and feared contamination with the lower orders, especially in the context of disease, those of the third order immersed themselves in medical practice and observation, thereby risking invidious attacks from their competitors.

Zysk points out that third-order healers began to be excluded by the priests from making sacrificial offerings and practices linked to the first order. They withdrew from or were pushed out of organized society and were left to wander among the ascetics and common people as hermits, among whom they perfected their knowledge of properties of sickness and varieties of plants. They joined other renunciants and religiously heterodox practitioners who wandered the countryside in search of answers to the problems posed by organized society, human suffering and disorder, and which included problems posed by disease. Recall that this is the period of much social unrest and confusion during which popular, early sectarian groupings were evolving and programs for relief of misery competed with one another. It was a period rife with repercussions of much disease, poor public health, distressing urban conditions, and most likely high level of emotional and behavioural disaffection that included psychiatric conditions.

Eventually, medical healers and experts in knowledge about suffering and its associated causes and cures became associated with ascetic wise men and religious persons heavily under the sway of Buddhism. This corresponds to the troubles during the time of the Mauryas, as noted earlier. A rich tradition that combined knowledge of suffering, diseases and their cure, and the spiritual, moral, and ethical life, all became concentrated in these communities of wandering wise men who

---

416 Zysk 1999.

eventually settled into Buddhist monasteries. In turn, the monasteries became, among many other things, centres of medical knowledge and specialization.

Buddhist literatures about the nature of suffering, its causes, and relations between human beings and nature resemble that which is found in ayurvedic medical thought. This was discussed briefly earlier from a general standpoint; specifically, the four-fold or quadrangle correspondence between metaphysical ailments and their cure compared to concrete conditions of sickness and practical remedies. The art of physical healing became a salient part of Buddhism per se and put into practice in monasteries. The goal of both traditions, the empirical Buddhist and the emergent Ayurveda, was to maintain equilibrium within the body and between the body and one's surroundings. A distinctive Buddhist monastic medical tradition slowly evolved in ancient India during the centuries preceding the Common Era.[417] Later, during the early centuries of the Common Era, Brahmanism assimilated this storehouse of medical knowledge into its socio-religious and intellectual tradition, giving it an orthodox veneer. These conflicting approaches to disease are thoroughly analyzed by Chattopadhyaya, who emphasizes the attempts of Brahmins to inject a sacred and metaphysical resonance into ayurvedic medicine and the naturalistic approach to disease.[418] One can presume, however, that from its inception Ayurveda incorporated ideas and beliefs associated with Indian philosophical systems and soteriological formulation and to some extent its practices.

A characteristic that marks the Vedic–Ayurveda transition is the retention of non-human metaphysical causes and treatments *and not just with respect to psychiatric conditions*. In the *Atharvaveda,* as suggested earlier, a number of such agents were invoked as causes and treatment by means of magical charms and mantras was salient. Ayurveda, it will become clear later, retained such ideas and beliefs. In this sense, it is reminiscent of the Atharvanic tradition.

> It also retained the *daivavyapāśraya cikitsā,* which includes magical charms as remedies. Thus, though the ancient medicine in India transformed itself in Rational Medicine (*Yuktivyapāśraya cikitsā*), it could not get rid of primary beliefs and practices ['Atharvanic'] completely. It

[417] See also Birnbaum 1979.

[418] D. Chattopadhyaya 1977.

had to maintain balance between *Yukti* and *Daiva*, tradition and science.[419]

Summary comment

The road leading to a naturalistic Indian conception of disease and psychiatric condition can be subdivided into several phases. Viewed in broad evolutionary context, the road begins deep in the proto-history of life in the subcontinent and of peoples to the West of it. Of this phase, generalizations from biological and evolutionary anthropology as well as cultural and ecological anthropology can be used to provide a general narrative. Whether and if so this proto-ethno-medicine displayed Indian ideas per se is not known. Only material remains furnished by archeology and physical and physical anthropology are available, although when the Harappan script is deciphered more specific information may be forthcoming. Regard identifiable Vedic medicine, it covers a period from a few centuries before on through several centuries after the Common Era. It starts in: (1) a Vedic society already divided into classes or estates that commanded different resources and power. In this society made up spiritually sanctioned divisions their existed competing groupings of healers that addressed the myriad of maladies and disorder. The higher, Brahmanic sacrificial priests emphasized ritual and prayer and addressed the gods directly whereas the less powerful and prestigious but more practical-minded healers of a third estate of agriculturalists where immersed in the more material, concrete facets of disease. Then, (2) the latter group was able to integrate their practical knowledge of disease and herbal medicines with priestly knowledge of Vedic medicine by acquiring expertise in metaphysical practices. However, (3) in concentrating on concrete features of disease they were vulnerable to claims of uncleanness and ritual contamination. They were then (4) shunned and excluded by the sacrificial priests and lost prestige and clientele, and withdrew into the countryside. There, (5) they mingled with other hermits, ascetics, religious renunciants, and members of heterodox religions, primarily Buddhist. Eventually, the community of wandering wise and practical men became more integrated and consolidated their knowledge of disease forming a more naturalistic (compared to Vedic medicine) and empirical medicine, namely, something that led

[419] Lal Gaur 1992: 370.

the way into Ayurveda. However, Atharvanic beliefs and practices were never erased. Some have contended that such an emphasis is the result of the imposition of spiritual, religious, and philosophical beliefs by Brahmins, a process one could conceptualize as Brahmanization or Sanskritization, and that scholars construe as diminishing the scientific purity of the earlier more pristine Ayurveda. This is discussed later.

INFLUENCE OF MEDICINE IN THE BUDDHIST COMMUNITY AND MONASTERY ON AYURVEDA

Ancient Indian medicine had a distinctive Buddhist phase. Even during the life of the Buddha (early to mid-fifth century BCE), medicines were among the essential resources of the Buddhist monk.[420] There is disagreement regarding just how far Buddhism as a philosophical and religious tradition should be construed as embodying a medical framework. Some argue that Buddhism expands the concept of physical disease and suffering to apply to suffering of the whole human being that required a quasi-medical, spiritual remedy.[421] Moreover, the Buddha saw himself and was so regarded by his contemporaries as a physician of sorts. As discussed earlier, the 'Four Noble Truths' at the core of Buddhist doctrine incorporate what resembles a medical paradigm including, in particular, the nature of and how to alleviate the essential malady (human suffering stemming from psychological attachments). Much like Wezler and Halbfass, Zysk discounts the idea that epistemology of Buddhist healing rests on a pre-existent medical paradigm.[422] Yet, he emphasizes the importance in the Buddhist communities of medical knowledge and curing and healing practices. There is much documentation of this in early canons and this has parallels with information recorded in early classical ayurvedic medical texts (Caraka, Suśruta). Buddhist medicine (like Ayurveda) may have included the theory of humours, but this is not documented explicitly in Buddhist medical literature. However, knowledge and classification as well as prescribed uses of many medicines conform to tenets and precepts found in ayurvedic medical texts that did have a humoral basis.

[420] Birnbaum 1979; Demiéville 1985; Zysk 1991.

[421] This is not inconsistent with concepts of Vedic medicine.

[422] Wezler 1984; Halbfass 1991; Zysk 1991.

The Buddhist approach to healing relied on a moral-religious conception of disease and suffering that is consistent with characteristics of Hindu cultural psychology discussed earlier. Moreover, much of its knowledge was esoteric and had a strong metaphysical component. The origins of Buddhist medical knowledge and of Ayurveda as well may have been influenced by ideas and practices stemming from Tibet and China, but an indigenous Indo-Iranian or Dravidian base – even an independent Vedic, Aryan discovery – cannot be excluded.[423] At any rate, in the subcontinent Buddhist medical knowledge became amalgamated with ancient native traditions of the respective regions that were steeped in metaphysical tenets. There were probably mutual influences. In central Asia and Tibet, for example, Buddhist medical knowledge was assimilated nearly verbatim, whereas in China it was modified significantly by the native Taoist tradition.[424]

On the basis of his study of medical knowledge and therapy in the monastic code of the Pali Canon, Zysk shows a correspondence and overlap between information found in Buddhist monastic texts with that found in classical ayurvedic sources pertaining to 'the five basic medicines' (ghee or clarified butter, fresh butter, oil, honey, and molasses or treacle):

> The proper and allowable treatment for the disease suffered by the Buddhist monks, therefore, required the use of all five medicinal food provisions. There is a clear continuity between Buddhist monastic and early ayurvedic medicine, indicating the derivation of medical knowledge from a common source of medical lore.[425]

The monastic code refers to specific cases of illness and afflictions. Zysk analyses 18 case histories of affliction, documenting correspondences between clinical methods of Buddhist monks, most likely rooted in the heterodox traditions of mendicant ascetics described earlier, and the classical Ayurveda writings of Caraka, Suśruta, and Bheḷa.

One of the cases analyzed by Zysk is obviously relevant to psychiatric condition. This involves a monk who suffered from a non-human disease. Although his symptoms are not presented, it may have resembled the insanity or madness described in Ayurveda medicine:

---

[423] Birnbaum 1979; Zysk 1991.

[424] Strickmann, n.d.; Boltz 1985.

[425] Zysk 1991: 75–76.

> The non-human affliction of the Buddhist monk ... is probably a form of possession by demonic entities, perhaps the *Rākṣasas*.[426]

The treatment described in the Buddhist text involved consuming the raw flesh and blood of a swine. Zysk points out that this treatment parallels the treatment of similar ailments as documented in a text ascribed to Suśruta. The treatment represents an attempt to nourish or strengthen not the patient per se but rather the demonic agent that had 'possessed' him. Curing of the ailment in Suśruta involved a healing rite that incorporated metaphysical tenets found in ancient Vedic medicine. This case, then shows a continuity of medical knowledge across three Indian medical traditions. The medicine of monastic Buddhism involved a conception of psychiatric condition and healing that the later Brahmanic compilers of Ayurveda modified and adapted and that had been authorized in Vedic medicine.[427]

THE ACADEMIC, SCHOLARLY, AND SCIENTIFIC MEDICINE OF INDIA

General considerations

The remainder of this chapter consists of a synthesis of information discussed by anthropologists, physicians, and medical historians on the theory and practice of Ayurveda and its status as a system of medicine.[428] Somasundaram and colleagues and Sharma provide a concise description of the Siddha tradition of academic medicine; whereas White addresses Siddha as a broader tradition involving mental disciplines having tantric, yogic, and alchemical emphases as well as strictly medical/curative implications; Meulenbeld discusses concepts of Indian pharmacology; and Weiss the reconciliation between tenets of the theory of karma and aspects of explanation of physiology and disease.[429] Of

---

[426] Zysk 1991: 87.

[427] Zysk 1991.

[428] D. Chattopadhyaya 1977; Kutumbiah 1969; P. V. Sharma 1992b; Leslie 1976; Roşu 1981; Zimmermann 1987; Filliozat 1964; Jolly 1977; Obeyesekere 1970, 1977, 1982; Roy 1986; Wujastyk 1998, 2003; and Verma 1995.

[429] Somasundaram, Jayaramakrishnan, and Sureshkumar 1986; P. V. Sharma 1992b; White 1996; Meulenbeld 1987; Weiss 1980.

surpassing value as a base of reference and background are the three volumes entitled *A History of Indian Medical Literature* compiled by Meulenbeld.[430]

India developed remarkably early a naturalistic approach to medicine and disease that encompassed psychiatric conditions. As discussed earlier, previous conceptions and practices relating to human suffering and disease in the subcontinent were based largely on moral, religious, and metaphysical beliefs, only rarely introducing formulations about the natural world. Explanations tended not to connect with the person in a material and functional sense; little attention was given to how the body worked as a physical object. Of course, Vedic medicine, while predominantly metaphysical or magico-religious, contained some ideas and practices suggesting that problems of disease, including psychiatric condition, could also be viewed partly as natural problems for which were used natural remedies. In fact, many scholars find in the ayurvedic compilations ideas derived from the Vedas suggesting that the latter were deeply etched in and drawn from concrete, real life problems of sickness. Moreover, Ayurveda presents a formulation of health, well-being, and disease that includes both scientific and moral, spiritual aspects. The inner and outer realms of the person, the microcosm and the macrocosm, are not only related to each other but are interconnected and presuppose each other. This was suggested earlier in discussions about the soteriological aspects of Ayurveda and its conformance to traditional Indian philosophies.

More information on the comprehensiveness of Ayurveda and especially its commixture with essential features of the philosophical and particularly its representation of tenets of Indian cultural psychology will be elaborated later. The general scope of Ayurveda bears repeating at the outset of this discussion.[431] The *raison d'etre* of Ayurveda was not just curative as per disease but had proactive elements and soteriological resonance. It involved the promotion and maintenance of health considered in the broadest of terms, ideal constitutional health and flourishing of the individual in light of basic conceptions of Indian philosophy; for example, participation in and flourishing as epitomized in the four basic constructs of Hinduism, namely the burdens of karma and cycle of re-

[430] Meulenbeld 1999–2002.

[431] Obeyesekere 1970, 1977, 1982; Roşu 1981.

birth, pursuit of liberation, a life of ritual observances including *ahiṃsā* or non-violent action, and upholding of *dharma* in its everyday and metaphysical dimensions. More generally, the roots of Ayurveda reside in basic doctrines of Sāṃkhya philosophy of India and hark back to the Vedas. Moreover, a concern with health, longevity, and the relief from manifestations of disease, hallmarks of the medical in any system of knowledge including Ayurveda, entails in the latter an integration of or dialectical relationship between what in the West is regarded as the mental and the organic or physical body. In its medical rationale or theory, constituents of personhood are composites of elements that connect mental influences with influences linked to the subtle body. This translates as the much heralded, so-called psychosomatic and somatopsychic basis of medicine in the Ayurveda. The essential psychology and spirituality of this medicine, however, has to be appreciated as well since the very mind–subtle body constituents that are so basic to its medical holism also play a central role in the otherworldly and metaphysical sphere. Thus, while acknowledging, and thus anticipating Western notions about, the importance of unconscious mind in its conception of *saṃskāra* (unconscious constructions built into the mind or *manas*), Ayurveda also has a typically religious or spiritual reach that underlies the doctrines of Hinduism, Buddhism, and Jainism.

While Ayurveda is undeniably a naturalistic medicine (emphasis on organic factors), it also encompasses a concern with basic soteriological issues of salvation grounded in a philosophy about the nature of the mind, self, attachments to life, individuality, and spiritual identity that transcend individual lifetimes thus linking with karmic principles involving transmigration. The theory of embryology of Ayurveda, for example, deals with how constituents of mind and subtle/body also constitute the imprints or residues of previous experiences or lives. It is these repositories of self that are introduced into the material receptacle of the temporary body that is produced following conception. Traditional therapeutic concerns of Ayurveda blend matters of physical constitution, diet, and practical regimen of life with meditation on spiritual verities of mind that while addressing health and relief from disease in the present life can also, when pursued in a disciplined way, promote immortality and eventually relief from transmigration through the deliverance and liberation of *mokṣa*. Hence, it is not surprising that Ayurveda theory and practice incorporates elements of Yoga, Tantrism, and alchemy that are so central to Indian culture, religion, and philosophy.[432]

Ayurveda relies on a basic orienting framework about the nature of existence or being (ontology) that includes the idea that all forms of life experience pain and pleasure. This indicates that a 'knower' or Self has knowledge, in the form of sensations, about the 'known' – namely, the condition of a person within an environment that can produce pain and suffering. Moreover, people seek pleasure and avoid pain and suffering. These are regarded as universal givens. Thakar explains:

> Yearnings for permanent happiness and strivings for lasting freedom from pain or at least to avoid and alleviate the suffering are also eternal, being instinctive and inherently existent in all living beings.[433]

The academic, scholarly ethno-medicine of India comprises several divisions that address types of sickness and a philosophy of medicine and health. For example, it describes the causes, manifestations, and therapeutics of healthy as well as unhealthy states, spanning body, mind, and the senses. However, Ayurveda is not just targeted at conditions of disease or sickness, and especially not narrowly construed nosological entities, but on wellness compared to 'dis-ease' considered in the broadest terms possible. It is a repository of all knowledge of *āyus* (all states of the person). In this way,

> Ayurveda points out to the Man not only the ways and means to lead a meaningful life in this world but also for the same in the other world.[434]

In India, Ayurveda is a doctrine accepted by all branches of science, systems of philosophy, and particular schools of thought, and it is valid in discussions relevant to the specific topics that it addresses. It provides and rests on a theory of causation, a theory of creation (of both man and the universe), and concepts about all processes that affect human beings, from the eternal or cosmogonic (individual and universal *ātman*) to the most basic, including birth, death, digestion, metabolism, excretion, and of course pathology. Disease is viewed not only as entailing varying

---

[432] White 1996.

[433] Thakar 1992: 375.

[434] Thakar 1992: 376.

states of the individual per se, having both spiritual, karmic as well as concrete, physical determinants, but also as a condition affected and determined by the season, the region, and events in one's previous lives.

Its fundamental and more specific theories regarding health and disease are that of *pañcabhūta,* five basic elements that make up matter and the body, and that of *tridoṣa,* the three humours that in their waxing and waning and balance help to explain conditions of health and disease. The humours or *doṣas* are constantly present in the body from the moment of fertilization until death. In subtle form and within their physiological limits, the humours are called *dhātu* and they are responsible for specific functions and movements (respiration, circulation, thermoregulation, lustre and complexion). In pathological form the humours fall out of balance and accumulate in body tissues and disturb body functions. In gross form, the humours are called *kiṭṭa* or *mala* and they are eliminated as excretions. The theories of the elements and humours are not mutually exclusive, since humours evolve out of the elements, interpenetrate and compose each other, and all are implicated in health and disease.

A NATURALISTIC FOCUS ON SICKNESS

Chattopadhyaya emphasizes the differences between a naturalistic approach to medicine and a magico-religious one.[435] He outlines three fundamental presuppositions of a scientific approach to man and disease: (1) Man lives in a natural world that operates on natural principles, partakes of its characteristics, and is influenced by it in a physical, organic sense. (2) Explanations of the causes of disease must make meaningful connections between natural elements of the world and how the body functions as a physical, organic and mechanical system (devoid of influences ascribed to morality, religion, magic, or superstition. (3) Medical treatment is based on rational accounts of the world, using natural substances with naturally understood (not magic) properties and medico-surgical procedures that are physically designed to address, modify, neutralize or undo the changed mechanics of the body caused by disease.

---

[435] D. Chattopadhyaya 1977. See also Fabrega 1974, 1997; Kleinman 1980.

Some aspects of Ayurveda theory are problematic, such as its inconsistencies regarding pharmacology.[436] How the humours, the elements, the various channels of the body, and terms for anatomical organs all fit together in explanations of causes of disease is not always clear and consistent. These concepts are sufficiently ambiguous to provide latitude for explanations about the causes and pathological physiology that essentially are not falsifiable in the philosophical sense. Furthermore, in keeping with general remarks presented earlier, the compilations include frequent appeals to metaphysical and soteriological ideas that are difficult to reconcile with a naturalistic approach and optimism toward treatment.[437]

The classical writings of ayurvedic medicine, especially those ascribed to Caraka and Suśruta, are apparently transitional; they contain material that refers to older Vedic precepts and notions about the sanctity of the origins and sources of Ayurveda. Nevertheless, the thrust of these classical texts is to present a naturalistic account of disease and treatment. Scholars like Chattopadhyaya see references to the older theory of the Vedas or to magico-religious themes as later interpolations motivated by purely political exigencies aimed to protect the position of the Brahmins in the social hierarchy, and particularly their position within the medical establishment. Zysk echoes this view and amplifies by offering a narrative of how this took place.[438] Chattopadhyaya acknowledges the references to karmic debts as causes of disease but plays down their implications, and he indicates that Ayurveda essentially negates karmic theory by its emphasis on naturalistic therapies.[439] Weiss, by contrast, notes the attempts at reconciliation between science-rationalism and soteriology.[440] Roşu argues that philosophical premises should be seen in relation to psychological tenets and that all are integral to the theory of medical psychology and its comprehensive psychosomatic sweep.[441] Finally, Zysk provides details of the material on which Ayurveda is based and that it drew from Buddhism.[442]

---

[436] Meulenbeld 1987.

[437] Weiss 1980.

[438] Zysk 1999.

[439] D. Chattopadhyaya 1977.

[440] Weiss 1980.

[441] Roşu 1981.

[442] Zysk 1991, 1999.

THE SYSTEMATIC CHARACTER AND COMPREHENSIVENESS OF AYURVEDA

The dietary, ecological, and climatic underpinnings of what can cause disease and disruptions and imbalances that should be addressed in treatment, as well as its philosophical psychology and religion, are examples of the comprehensive scope of Ayurveda. So is its ecologically comprehensive formulation of what constitutes a condition of disease.[443] In its holistic conception of sickness and healing Ayurveda resembles other ancient traditions of medicine that were both comprehensive and systematic.

> We should at this point remember the context within which the doctor of antiquity practiced his art, in India as in Greece. Anatomy and physiology were quasi-inexistent, and the medical practitioner had no truly biological knowledge on which to base his actions. What pathology depended on, instead, was what the Hippocratics called *prognosis,* the science of the course taken by illnesses and of the signs that herald accident, crises, and solutions ... He was consequently less concerned to recognize the nature of a disease than to foresee its development, taking into consideration the most general conditions of life: climate, seasons, customs, postures. Ecology was an integral part of this practical context. His knowledge of the patient's environment, including the flora and fauna, enabled the doctor to anticipate the course of the disease and to take action on it.[444]

In both ancient traditions and in Greece as far back as the pre-Socratic period, political, moral, and legal considerations were tied to health. In this respect, medicine was 'a form of politics'. Compared to other scholars, Kutumbiah presents a more physiological, functional analysis of ancient Indian medicine that does not minimize its comprehensiveness nor its clinical emphasis.[445] Kakar, focusing on the emotionally sensitive approaches of ayurvedic practitioners, emphasizes the psychological sophistication of this tradition.[446]

Constructs or models about how the body functions are found in the classic *Saṃhitās* of Caraka and Suśruta. Some of these are encountered in

---

[443] Zimmermann 1987.

[444] Zimmermann 1987: 20, emphasis in original.

[445] Kutumbiah 1969.

[446] Kakar 1982.

non-medical Indian conceptions of the person and in their articulation of cultural psychology.[447] These include, among other things, constructs about (1) the five basic constituents of matter, such as the body and foodstuffs; (2) the three humours of the body – wind, bile, and phlegm – whose excess or deficiency and mutual relation is critical for health; (3) various regions and organs of the body that are connected by various channels and ducts through which substances flow naturally but in which they can accumulate and stagnate; and (4) how vitiated humours can be blocked and cause disease. Balodhi emphasizes the strictly mental health aspects of ayurvedic theory about the body and its functions.[448]

Ayurveda is an important cultural achievement not because of the validity of its ethno-physiology for explaining human disease – whether it is 'true', 'works', or compares favourably with modern biomedicine. It is a bona fide scholarly, academic and, in this sense, scientific medicine because of its comprehensive and analytical theoretical basis. This includes its ontological assumptions, on the one hand, and how these fit with its epistemic logic and claims, on the other. The naturalistic emphasis and tenor of Ayurveda sets it apart from the medicine that preceded it and makes it compatible with scientific objectivism, broadly construed. The body is understood in a wide context, in particular, as influenced by the physical environment and ingested substances such as liquids, certain plants, and animal products.[449] A regimen of personal hygiene and strain-reducing social practices having moral, spiritual elements complete the naturalistic approach to disease. Causes and manifestations of disease are classified in various rational ways, with specific therapeutics corresponding to them (geared to specific manifestations and causes) based on logically specified concepts of causation.

Indeed, classic Ayurveda is a detailed compendium of treatment practices that includes exercise, visceral-somatic practices (enemas, bladder cleansings, use of purgatives, fumigation) and procedures (bone alignments, surgical excisions), nutritional recommendations, and administration of specific medicines in complex combinations. Included in the therapeutic regimen are how to search for and prepare curative herbs and animal products, how these should be combined and in what amounts they are to be ingested or how they should be applied exter-

---

447 Marriott 1990.
448 Balodhi 1987.
449 Zimmermann 1987.

nally, for what specific diseases or phases of disease medicaments (in the broadest sense possible) they are to be used, and procedures designed to cleanse wounds and surgically repair damaged limbs and remove toxins and pathogens.

REPRESENTATION OF FEVERS IN THE *CARAKASAMHITĀ*

In order to provide a background for appreciating how psychiatric conditions (termed *unmāda* or insanity) are formulated in the *Carakasaṃhitā* (CS) material on 'fever' will be discussed. An approximate meaning of *nidāna* involves essential clinical characteristics of a medical condition. It includes cause, *pūrvarūpa* or premonitory symptoms (before the manifest appearance of the disease or incubation period), and typical symptoms once disease is manifest. Eight classes (termed causes) of fever are listed: seven involve each of the three basic humours that are faulted in disease (wind, bile, and phlegm) and their combination into pairs or all three together; and a third grouping termed accidental causes.[450] In general, factors (also termed causes) that lead to the eight classes of fever include such things as excessive indulgence in substances, procedures, actions (physical exercise), suppression of bodily urges (urination, defecation), medical procedures (enemas, purgatives), fasting, acts that lead to violent shocks, sexual congress, anxiety, grief, operations that lead to loss of blood, night-keeping, and 'disposing of the body in uneven attitudes'.[451] Humoral factors bring fever by faulting, unbalancing, overheating, or entangling (in bodily conduits or organs) the particular humours. Each class of fever is associated with a list of symptoms, which for conditions involving the humour and its pathophysiology refer predominantly to changes in the body and/or its functions.[452] CS emphasizes that a careful appraisal of the symptoms listed for each class of fever (how they present, their duration, their waxing and waning) provides the physician with a clue as to the offending fault or type of fever (which one or combination of humours needs to be considered in treatment).

---

[450] Discussed later in this chapter.

[451] In Lesson 1, of the chapter entitled *Nidānasthāna* of Volume II, one finds the statement 'Fever has, verily, its origin in the wrath of *Maheśvara*' (an epithet of Shiva, 'the Great Lord'), which the editor describes in a footnote as 'fanciful' and provides as background a mythological account of Shiva's anger. See *Carakasaṃhitā* 1996: Vol. II, 602.

[452] See premonitory symptoms discussed on page 601.

The *Carakasaṃhitā*, like all of the important medical compilations by renowned physicians, addresses many conditions of disease. Meulenbeld points out that the *Caraka-* and *Suśrutasaṃhitā* are specialized texts (internal medicine and surgery, respectively) and those that followed addressed all of medicine. Despite this generalization both of these texts include much besides their specialty emphasis. For purposes of comparison with psychiatric conditions (*unmāda* or insanity) the way the *Carakasaṃhitā* handles the class of fevers termed accidental is of particular interest. Its varieties can arise from wounds,[453] but of more relevance are those fevers due to 'companionship of passions and evil spirits, incantations, and curses'.[454] Those due to passions and evil spirits cause excited wind and bile and those borne of incantations and curses fault all three humours. The symptoms, 'growth' (unfolding or progression?), and treatment set this class fevers apart from the other seven classes (those whose 'primary' cause is a fault of humours). Both drugs and special procedures to propitiate the gods should be used in treatment for fevers caused by accidental factors.

Save for those due to spiritual attack, fevers consist predominantly of bodily signs and symptoms. A long list of these is given for each type of faulted humour. However, the characteristics of individuals who go on to develop fever due to accidental causes (their premonitory or incubatory manifestations, also termed symptoms) illustrate the holistic scope of CS. Many of these involve descriptions of ordinary body functions. They include tastelessness of the mouth, heaviness of the body, sense of fatigue, lack of desire for food, turbidity of eyes, and yawning. On the other hand, 'premonitory' symptoms of fever due to accidental causes also include aspects of experience and social behaviour. The following are listed: procrastination, inactivity or idleness and also slothfulness, disposition to thwart one's own projects or plans, condemning those owed respect and reverence, aversion to children, avoidance of responsibilities, and special food preferences. A clearly moral shadow is cast over this class of fevers.

Lesson 3 of Volume III addresses the treatment of fevers and here CS re-emphasizes essential characteristics and provides additional information about how this class of conditions is understood. The lesson begins with a mythological description and supplication from the gods

[453] This will not be considered further here.

[454] *Carakasaṃhitā* 1996: Vol. II, 600.

for knowledge about these conditions. CS then indicates that fevers involve faults of mind and body, 'for fever never seizes a person whose body is faultless'.[455] It then re-iterates and expands on a point adumbrated in Volume II discussed earlier: the origin or 'first manifestation' of fever is from excess wrath of a divine agent (Rudra, which stands for the dark, negative side of Shiva). Mental fever is introduced as a contrast set for bodily fevers, and the former are said to feature cheerlessness, absence of satisfaction, and grief or pain and the latter bodily symptoms that echo the offending humour (excitement of wind and bile leads to craving for things that are cooling, excitement of wind and phlegm craving for things that are hot). Typical symptoms of fevers caused by the humours and their combination are repeated. At this point in the lesson begins another discussion of accidental fever which is said to come in four varieties: that borne of bodily wounds (injuries that penetrate into the body resulting from whipping or weapons), lust and other passions as also the contact of evil spirits, incantations, and curses (of coercive Brahmins, mythical saint or seer). Symptoms of fevers due to excited or faulted humours are said to also manifest in accidental insanities, and here two varieties are mentioned, namely, those caused by incantations and curses.

> In consequence of the diversity of incantations, as also of curses (that may be denounced), the symptoms of fever born of incantations, as also of that born of curses, vary according to the kind of incantation that is applied, or the kind of curse that is denounced.[456]

To each of these fevers there corresponds a distinctive symptom.

Comment

How CS handles a set of conditions featured by a quintessentially physical presence illustrates the scope of Ayurveda. Its curative emphasis, specifically, its formulation of causes, manifestations, and treatments cuts across many domains. These include, for example, visceral physiology, anatomy, the mental or emotional, dietetics, ecology, and the metaphysical. Its comprehensive scope is also manifest in its proactive and general health promotion, including rejuvenation and virilization.

---

[455] *Carakasaṃhitā* 1996: Vol. III, 719.

[456] *Carakasaṃhitā* 1996: Vol. III, 730.

PSYCHIATRIC CONSIDERATIONS

How psychiatric conditions were formulated and handled in Hindu society as per Ayurveda and how this changed during subsequent eras represents an important characteristic of the social and cultural history of India. As discussed in subsequent chapter, classic medical texts of ancient India contribute to and integrate with its cultural psychology, enabling people to make sense of and cope with misfortune, suffering, pain, and misery that have been endemic in India throughout its history. As discussed eariier, problems rooted in infection, pathological anatomy and physiology, and general bodily injury are closely allied to psychological distress and suffering. Physical misfortunes could easily be accompanied by breakdowns of social and psychological behaviour that qualify as psychiatric condition, as well as by defeats of the moral imagination devolving from transgression of social and religious rules/defeats that when played out in the logic of the cultural psychology of India qualify as culturally specific versions of psychiatric conditions. Whereas it had once been approached only in moral-ethical and metaphysical terms, psychiatric conditions in India now became part of the naturalistic account of human suffering and disease.

When the material in the writings ascribed to Caraka, Suśruta, Vāgbhaṭa, and Bheḷa, the four compilations examined here, was initially formulated and then transcribed is uncertain and much contested.[457] Philological examination of the texts reveals different styles of writing, and suggests different dates of compilation. But since the oral tradition probably underwent numerous phases of clarification, emendation, and standardization, no less so than the written texts, it is fruitless to seek exact dates of origin. Although emphasis presently is given to psychiatric conditions one should not forget that classic medical texts of Ayurveda are the product of coping with a protean mix of medical conditions and related public health problems, and also grounded in a very comprehensive, holistic conception of the human being. Indeed, Balodhi argues that community and family health medicine and practice in India today have their roots in Ayurveda.[458] He finds this ancient tradition, in its cosmogonic, theosophical, moral, religious, and psy-

---

[457] Meulenbeld 1999–2002.

[458] Balodhi 1987, 1991.

chological reach, to be superior to the individualistic Western approach that is focused too narrowly at the micro level.

The holistic emphasis in Ayurveda is reflected in a broad definition of psychiatric condition that incorporates complex pictures of medical (non-psychiatric) disease. This opaque amalgam is further beclouded in local culture-specific constructions of malady, misfortune, suffering, and misery. Psychiatric condition in Ayurveda cannot be equated with identifiable central nervous system lesions or even purely emotional symptom complexes as a contemporary psychiatrist of today would expect and wish for. It covers a broad range of manifestations, and aspects of human psychology, however conceptualized, are as important as general bodily symptoms. There is a prominent somatic component to psychiatric condition in contemporary Indian populations, and this probably goes back deep in historical time and prehistory. For example, Blair observes how the concept of heat figures as a metaphor and overriding concept in explaining emotions and bodily correlates in the *Ṛgveda* and the *Atharvaveda*.[459] This emphasis on bodily physiology is re-iterated in the writings of contemporary scholars of Ayurveda.[460] Its holistic formulation of health and human function has particular relevance with respect to its formulation of psychiatric condition and mental health in general that involve a comprehensive, integrated package of human symptoms. All circumstances of the individual's life situation are significant. How diseases, classified as to types, were played out in real persons with real biographies provided the material on which Ayurveda grew as a medical science, but descriptive details of a condition's presentation in real life were expunged. Nevertheless, texts are encyclopaedic with respect to causes, manifestations, and treatment. And they present a philosophy and soteriology about misfortune and suffering which sickness accentuates. This comprehensiveness is a characteristic motif in the classic texts and ranks Ayurveda with all of the other great medical traditions, such as the Chinese, Egyptian, Hellenic, Aztec, Tibetan, and Islamic.[461]

---

[459] Blair 1961.

[460] Contemporary scholars of Ayurveda: Wujastyk 1998, 2003.

[461] Fabrega 1997.

Representations of psychiatric condition in the *Carakasaṃhitā*

Introduction

The compilation ascribed to the enigmatic mythical or real ancient physician named Caraka is arguably the most significant of all of the major basic texts of the ancient Indian medical tradition. It is viewed as a representative document of the creative phase of the evolution of medicine between 600 BCE and 200 CE.[462] Discussion of it here is based on a translation by Pandit Avinash Chandra Kaviratna compiled around the turn of the twentieth century and includes commentaries by various medical scholars. In any translation, of course, one cannot be sure of the precise meaning of the original key terms. A translator may resort to a contemporary term that he or she judges refers to a term in the original Sanskrit, both ideally referring to the same construct. This is exacerbated by somewhat outmoded terminology used by the translator. Given these handicaps, conditions as described in the translation should be regarded as rough analogues of those in the original text. The compilation ascribes its content as stemming from material revealed by a line of legendary, mythical beings and eventually compiled by Caraka. However, when the text was actually compiled and whom the individual termed 'Caraka' corresponds to, is given different identities and dates.[463] While the texts suggest a single author, according to Indologists this is contestable.

The volumes of the *Carakasaṃhitā* address far more than purely clinical considerations or what one could term curative medicine. Earlier chapters touched on the overarching theosophical, spiritual, and moral framework and these are implicit and sometimes explicit in Ayurveda. Terminology and constructs of Indian philosophical traditions are used to explain ontological and epistemological characteristics of medical diseases and states of the body. One also finds topics related to general physiology and health, characteristics of states and conditions of disease, pathogenesis, embryology, therapeutics, and medical practice and etiquette. Within its holistic compass may be found varieties of what we now call mental health and illness problems or psychiatric conditions. Many descriptions of seemingly physical conditions include psychological-behavioural manifestations as a matter of course, although the latter

[462] See Weiss 1975, 1977.

[463] Meulenbeld 1999–2002.

are not singled out in any special way. However, psychiatric condition is addressed as a separate category of disease and has its separate chapter in the volume of general medicine and in the volume on therapeutics. From a position of hindsight, descriptions suggest that what was called 'insanity' may in some instances have included other non-psychiatric medical conditions along with bona fide psychiatric ones. In other words, in the *Carakasaṃhitā*, the conception of the morbid effects of disease reflects a view of the patient that encompasses general medicine, health psychology, psychiatric malady, behavioural medicine, and psychosomatic–somatopsychic integration.

The mental apparatus in the Carakasaṃhitā

Caraka's text proclaims that man is constantly striving. It emphasizes the human desire for self-preservation, for wealth, and for a happy future in keeping with a naturalistic account of human nature. However, also included in different parts of the text is an acknowledgment of karmic debts that can affect health, although they are not necessarily immutable or vitiate the power of treatment in concert with the moral and intellectual faculties. When it comes to psychiatric condition, the mind and its various parts (senses, reasoning faculties) are the seat of concern. In relation to the strictly mental sphere, how the person functions and stands morally in the community are of critical importance.[464]

In Ayurveda generally and *Carakasaṃhitā* specifically, five types of human constitutions are singled out, resting on the properties, salience, and balance among the three humours (bile, wind, and phlegm), and these constitutions are sometimes viewed as personalities that protect, facilitate, and modify disease, including insanity. Personality types are also distinguished and are developed on the basis of food habits and morality. A complex typology of pure varieties of personality is set forth, with a number of subtypes. While aspects of general health are singled out, personality types are also conceptualized in relation to accidental or exogenous insanity that involve spiritual attack or possession states.[465] For psychiatric conditions ascribed to spiritual actions, Caraka attempts to link an individual's underlying personality and temperament to type of offending spirit and to behavioural manifestations.

---

[464] See also Balodhi 1987.

[465] Dube 1978; Meulenbeld 1997.

Indeed, in these conditions the personality and behaviour of the spirit is mirrored in the behaviour of the patient. However, even conditions that are explained in terms of a complex humoral physiology are said to be based on and show involve characteristics of the individual such as physical constitution, habits, and predominant bodily humour.

CLINICAL DESCRIPTION OF INSANITY AND RELATED CONDITIONS IN THE *CARAKASAṂHITĀ*

Insanity

Material described in this and the following sections on insanity is taken from the *Carakasaṃhitā* (CS) Volume II, involving clinical descriptions, and Volume III, involving treatment.

'A Disquisition on the Causes and Character of Insanity' provides a general definition of what in this book has been termed psychiatric condition and labelled in the text as *unmāda*:

> Insanity, it should be known, is the derangement of the mind, understanding, knowledge, memory, devotion, behaviour, acts, and practices.[466]

This definition, to the extent that it accurately communicates the original meaning of insanity, is remarkable for its focus on phenomena that are consistent with contemporary meaning of psychiatric condition. Its inclusion of devotion suggests that an individual's moral, spiritual state of mind is an important characteristic of this class of medical conditions. The passage suggests, and its contrast to descriptions of other general medical conditions in the text supports, that *unmāda* or insanity represents a separate, distinct category with its own causes and manifestations, and therapeutics.

There are said to be five varieties of psychiatric condition, four endogenous (humour-based) and one exogenous (or caused by outside forces), also termed accidental. The first four include wind-born, bile-born, and phlegm-born insanities and those produced by all three humours together. In a vulnerable person, one of weak mind, alteration in the balance of the humours can weaken or vitiate the heart (regarded

---

[466] *Carakasaṃhitā* 1996: Vol. II, 640.

as the seat of the mind) and overwhelm the ducts that transmit impressions from the senses to the mind. In a section entitled 'Treatment of Insanity', the external causes mentioned are eating improper and impure foods; attacks by the deities, Brahmins and elders; mental shocks caused by fear and joy; and abnormal efforts on the part of the individual.

Among the symptoms of all these forms of insanity one finds listed a confused restlessness and wandering of the mind and behaviour, suggesting anxiety and tension, difficulty in speaking and articulating precisely, and a sense of emptiness of the chest. The afflicted person is said to show a clouded awareness and understanding, little emotion, perhaps indifference, feeling neither happiness nor misery. The victim neglects responsibilities, lacks peace of mind, power of recall, and alacrity or sharpness. This description of the manifestations of psychiatric condition is somewhat stark. The description is objective, impersonal, and highly secular, rather like that in a contemporary textbook of Western psychiatry. All of the social attributes, circumstances, and behaviour of the person are expunged, such as morality and spirituality, and the focus sometimes resembles a malfunctioning machine. This is the naturalistic idiom that leads scholars to emphasize the break of the Ayurveda with earlier traditions of healing, medicine, and existential accounting found in the Vedas and in major religions such as Buddhism that dwell on spiritual and moral considerations. Yet Caraka's compilation never loses sight of the bigger picture of man in the context of karma, *dharma*, and moral-spiritual standing. Consequently, while the text's formulation suggests scientific and clinical 'objectivity' the context of medical discourse linked ayurvedic practice to fundamental moral and existential premises about the world and social reality and can be assumed to have been brought into play in the physician's approach. As in the case with fevers, such aspects are evident when causes and treatment are discussed.

Insanities born of the humours, also termed constitutional or endogenous, are described in detail. Vulnerability to these insanities depends on attributes of personality and temperament, specifically on the amount and balance of the humours, diet and physical health. Such vulnerability can be brought on by irreligious behaviour and negative emotions. The text of Caraka describes diverse manifestations; for example, sensation of emptiness in the head, turbidity of the eyes, loss of appetite, indigestion, strange perceptions ('diverse sounds in the ears'), possibly hallucinations, bizarre dreams, mental excitement, skin eruptions, facial contortions, restlessness of the eyes, and bristling of skin hairs. Many of these were included in description of fever. The holistic character of insanity (its inclusion of psychological and bodily symptoms) conforms to the description of psychiatric condition as formulated in this book. The descriptions also include physical characteristics that appear to have no connection to psychiatric condition (turbidity in the eyes, skin eruptions, indigestion, emaciated bodies) and may represent inter-current, co-morbid conditions of general disease.

Symptoms of *insanities* due to wind humour include unusual behaviour and experiences such as 'frequent utterance of irrelevant words', laughing, singing, dancing on unsuitable occasions, imitating sounds (echolalia?), intense anger, malice and jealousy toward those who are happy. Certain physical characteristics and manifestations are also singled out.

Food and digestion are implicated in insanities caused by bile. In general, heat and wrath are associated with bile and are said to eventually affect the heart. Restlessness, anger, abusiveness, running away (wildly?), and carelessness in dress (even going naked) are behavioural and emotional symptoms of bile-caused insanity. Volume II mentions irritability, boastfulness, anger, and striking people. The victim of bile, being 'heated', desires shady places, cold water, and refreshing food. The eyes are a coppery green or yellow colour.

Food and digestion are also implicated in insanity born of phlegm. Excess of food and lack of exercise causes food to spread from the stomach to the chest (sometimes the heart). This process is said to cause insanity by 'afflicting the understanding and the memory, and stupefying the mind'. As in the case of wind-born insanity, in Volume II a large proportion of symptoms involve unusual aspects of social and psychological behaviour, but they are different symptoms. Examples include 'rigid observance of taciturnity', 'taking short walks', social isolation, 'aversion of purity', 'an aspect that excites abomination'. Details of bodily appearance and experience are noted. In Volume III, there is again mention of taciturnity, as well as fondness for women and privacy, physiological disturbances such as disgust for food, excessive salivary secretions, gaining in strength after meals, and 'whiteness of nails and the rest'.

Insanity involving all three humours together understandably involves a combination of all those manifestations cited earlier and is said to be incurable. Volume III of the text ascribed to Caraka states: 'All the ordinances about treatment become hostile to one another, should never be taken up for treatment'.[467] Though this insanity is incurable, a large number of medicaments are recommended as remedies. As with all instances of disease and sickness, treatment also entails diet, use of herbs, behavioural hygiene, as well as psychological and spiritual pursuits. Special procedures and techniques singled out include 'striking, tying, confining, frightening, inspiring wonder, and causing forgetfulness'.

Accidental or exogenous insanities

Psychiatric conditions caused by the assault of external forces, also-called accidental insanities, are actually given greater attention than those caused by humour imbalances. They can be caused by acts undertaken in a previous life or faults committed in the current life that reflect immorality and poor judgment. Some examples include thoughts or actions that offend or show disregard for the deities, celestial beings, superhuman agents, ghostly and abominable creatures, important or revered persons, and the deceased.[468] Each kind of accidental insanity is associated with a particular category of spiritual being (dead ancestor, semi-divine agent), which is identifiable because the victim's attitude, demeanour, and actions during illness conform to what is known about the afflicting demon or power. Predisposing factors include wrath, a desire to injure the offending agent, cruel motives, a negative disposition, and dreams conveying admonitions and rebukes. Forms of attack by the attacking agent include manner of gaze, curses, physical assault, scent, and physically mounting the body of the victim. Each has a preferred method of attack. Manifestations of this kind of psychiatric condition are numerous and include 'superhuman strength, capacity for exertion, [and] prowess'.[469]

Vulnerable persons become objects of attack when they are in certain dangerous situations or they are guilty of committing acts that are provocative, immoral, or disrespectful of religious traditions. The assault comes 'when the fruits are about to manifest themselves of the

---

[467] *Carakasaṃhitā* 1996: Vol. III, 837.

[468] In ayurvedic texts they are sometimes termed *bhūtas*.

[469] *Carakasaṃhitā* 1996: Vol. II, 646.

[sinful] acts of former lives'.[470] Elsewhere Caraka's text claims that only actions viewed in the context of present morality or judgment are critical; when one is alone and in a deserted house, when one is in an impure state (such as a man having sex with a menstruating woman, or after a woman gives birth), at a time of planetary conjunction, during battles or environmental calamities, when deviating from ritual activities or dietary practices, when visiting certain locations at inauspicious times, and when performing certain physiological functions.

External agents cause accidental insanities for three reasons: to kill or wound the victim, to derive pleasure or amusement, and to elicit respect, notably regarding ritual obligations:

> These objects of those Insanity-causing beings may be ascertained from the particular indications of the conduct of the Insane. Amongst these ... the desire to kill or wound becomes manifest when the person who becomes insane enters a blazing fire, or drowns himself in water, or leaps down into holes and pits, or strikes himself with weapons and clubs and brick-bats and his own closed fists, or does other acts for destroying himself. Those cases of insanity in which the insane person seeks to destroy his own life should be known as incurable.[471]

In short, symptomatic acts that involve an attempt to injure and kill oneself are seen as causing the external agent's intention to harm the victim. A possession by the agent that has the effect of taking over the victim's will is implied. Insanities caused by the other two objectives – to gain pleasure and to elicit respect – are curable.

Volume III of the *Carakasaṃhitā* under consideration here is devoted primarily to treatment of accidental varieties of insanity. Mantras or sacred books and medicines are briefly mentioned as remedies but not elaborated upon. Very general procedures of a highly magico-religious nature include recommended readings, use of special stones or potent gems, performing auspicious and moral acts, offering sacrifices to the deities, taking vows, such as to avoid certain foods or to fast, performing ceremonies and rites, and journeying to sacred places. Interestingly, specific aspects of dietetics are not mentioned.

Insanities caused by exogenous agents may be interpreted in two ways. Because of their special character and mode of treatment, they

---

[470] *Carakasaṃhitā* 1996: Vol. II, 646.

[471] *Carakasaṃhitā* 1996: Vol. II, 647.

might seem added on to the naturalistic base of medical knowledge and practice of Ayurveda, for example, as exemplified in the endogenous varieties. Perhaps the emphasis given to these insanities reflects a response to political pressures by Brahmins to win support for the spiritual, moral strictures underlying Vedic wisdom.[472] On the other hand, these insanities point to broad sweep of Ayurveda, its comprehensive, synthetic reach into all spaces of popular life and belief. The material reviewed earlier on a quintessential physical disease like fever in which spiritual, metaphysical factors are represented support this latter interpretation. In general, an emphasis on spiritual attack or possession by deities and demons, and its basis in moral transgressions, reinforce the idea that in South Asia during late classical times and beyond, psychiatric conditions and much disease was interpreted by the scholarly medical community as a special and complex species of human malady. Its configuration, enactment, and mode of handling readily crossed the divide between mental and physical, spiritual and natural phenomena.

An individual's social, psychological, moral, and religious standing is basic to the onset of accidental insanities, or 'calamitous afflictions' having 'superhuman causes'. Victims are identified by changes in demeanour, activity, energy, and attitude that are themselves 'superhuman' (or beyond the ordinary) and that communicate knowledge of the 'scriptures and the arts'. Without materially affecting the body of the victim, the external agents enter into ('possess'?) the person. Symptoms of each type of insanity are described in detail.

The summary presented in Volume III reduces the five varieties of insanity to two: curable and incurable. Constitutional and accidental varieties of insanity can coexist and commingle, and curable properties devolve from those of the respective varieties, with the proviso that a curable variety becomes incurable if mixed with an incurable variety. The chapter ends with an interesting set of morally toned generalizations about exogenous or accidental insanities. These affirm that the final or definitive cause of such insanities is to be attributed to the acts of individuals, not to supernatural agents. Yet, virtually all of clinical description and interpretation of accidental insanities in Volume II and of their treatment in Volume III indicate that they are bona fide types of *unmāda* or insanity. This seeming inconsistency or vacillation between naturalism and metaphysics in the ontology and epistemology of insani-

---

[472] D. Chattopadhyaya 1977.

ty underscores the anomalous position of psychiatric condition in CS and Ayurveda.[473] Inconsistency of description also suggests differences of opinions among physicians about legitimacy, validity, and essential nature of syndromes of behaviour glossed as accidental insanities at the time when the text was compiled, among later redactors and commentators, or simply a politically motivated 'last word' to underscore the naturalistic credibility of Ayurveda. This topic is taken up later.

Epilepsy in the Carakasaṃhitā

A whole chapter or 'lesson' is devoted to *apasmāra*, translated as epilepsy. In contrast to *unmāda* it exists in only four varieties, each of the three humours and their combination together.[474] Metaphysical and psychological causes are not mentioned in the initial definition. Yet, epilepsy, it is said, 'appears quickly' in persons whose minds are afflicted by passion and darkness. The main emphasis in the chapter on the nature of epilepsy is on physical manifestations of body and behaviour (frothing of saliva, swooning, losing consciousness, convulsions). Nevertheless, that epilepsy did not exclude metaphysical or mythological origins is evident; for example, those who wrongly practice and carry out the stipulations of the mantras are vulnerable to epilepsy, but so are those who follow poor or injurious diets, are exceedingly lean, or in whom the humours accumulate and are inharmonious. Near the middle of this lesson, after listing once again the four (humoral) varieties, CS points out:

> Sometimes Epilepsy of the variety called Accidental supervenes upon these four (Constitutional) varieties ... special indications ... are ... the appearance of symptoms in addition to those which have already been stated ... [for the endogenous or constitutional] ... [treatment for Epilepsy involves standard correctives such as purgatives and emetics] ... When, however, the Accidental variety supervenes on any of the constitutional varieties, Mantras are beneficial.[475]

At this point in the lesson CS proceeds to describe a myth about the destruction of a sacrifice involving a deity which caused *gulma* (abdominal tumours) in 'embodied' beings who fled as consequence of convul-

---

473 We will see it repeated in the *Suśrutasaṃhitā*, discussed later.

474 But see disqualification taken up later in this chapter.

475 *Carakasaṃhitā* 1996: Lesson 8 of section on *Nidānasthāna*, Vol. II, 653.

sions of their body and later ingested copious amounts of sacrificial butter causing leprosy and out of the grief that stirred in such individuals arose the different varieties of insanity who contaminated noxious creatures and impure objects from which arose the different varieties of epilepsy. CS then includes a reference to material described earlier under fever:

> As regards Fever, it sprung from the head of Maheśvara. From the heat, again, of Fever, arose 'blood bile' (or haemorrhage).[476]

Lesson 10 of Volume III addresses the cures for epilepsy. This chapter is almost entirely devoted to special preparations and procedures used to treat epilepsy, which is acknowledged to represent a very difficult disease to treat if not incurable. It presents a clear formulation of the pathophysiology of the disease as exemplified in ayurvedic thought. Its clinical description of manifestations is brief but very vivid and addresses diverse phenomena:

> In consequence of the disappearance of the mind and understanding, the patient enters into darkness and his movements become horrid ... Of persons whose tranquillity has been disturbed by ... [humoral disturbance and who ingest wrong foodstuffs, etc.] epilepsy sets in, when their quality of Goodness is destroyed by Passion and Darkness, when their heart is overwhelmed by [movement of humours], and when their minds are afflicted by anxiety, lust, fear, wrath, grief, care, and the rest.[477]

Interpolated in the different types of dietary preparations and practices used in treatment of epilepsy and listed in Lesson 10 of Volume III of CS, as in Lesson 7 of the section called *Nidānasthāna* of Volume II on types of diseases discussed earlier, one finds a reference to the accidental variety of epilepsy once again.[478] It points out that when a physician judges that accidental variety is conjoined with and making more serious and intractable what appeared to constitute ordinary epilepsy stemming from faulted humours, he is to resort to treatments laid down for *accidental insanity*. Here follows what appears is an aside, an exegesis

---

[476] *Carakasaṃhitā* 1996: Vol. II, 653.

[477] *Carakasaṃhitā* 1996: Vol. III, Lesson 10, p. 848.

[478] It also had not included in the initial statement of causes found at the beginning of Lesson 10.

that involves recommendations of formulated by mythical or legendary physicians/wise men who passed on knowledge of Ayurveda to Caraka. This person indicates that given a conjunction of ominous, mainly physical causes (taking filthy food and drink, suppressing urges of nature, agitation of heart due to excited, faulted humours) there takes place a dim and stupefied consciousness that leads the person to apply his understanding incorrectly to things 'eternal and transitory' as well as beneficial and harmful. This constitutes a specific, severe disease called *atattvābhiniveśa,* a kind of feeble-mindedness or idiocy as noted in the footnote.

Comment

From a clinical, descriptive point of view, and in the absence of neurological confirmation, the epilepsies clearly overlap with psychiatric conditions that involve altered states of consciousness and functional seizures of various types and these two types of psychiatric disorders are sometimes very difficult if not impossible to tell apart in purely clinical, descriptive terms. Stated baldly, certain types of epilepsy produce signs and symptoms that in a descriptive sense resemble psychiatric conditions and vice versa. Finally, if one were to rely on contemporary formulations in neuro-psychiatry and the common observation of comorbidity between disorders of brain function and allegedly mental, functional problems, alcohol and epilepsy belong with the insanities (bona fide psychiatric conditions). In the logic of Ayurveda itself, as in modern medicine, alcohol-related problems, epilepsy, and other neurological conditions that show prominent mental signs and symptoms – in our society, conditions diagnosed as strokes, Huntington's disease, Parkinson's disease, multiple sclerosis, amnesic syndromes, post-concussion states – seem to be pooled with psychiatric conditions. However, some of these neuro-psychiatric disorders (Huntington's disease) may not have existed in ancient India.

Based on contemporary knowledge on the neurology of behaviour and of epilepsy, one can presume seizures, convulsions, and related changes in experience and behaviour represent human universals. Hence, physicians who contributed to the formulation of Ayurveda examined and treated some varieties of *apasmāra* or epilepsy, which overlapped with some varieties of accidental or exogenous *unmāda*.[479] In contemporary thought these conditions are construed as possession and states of mental dissociation, terms that indicated they are functional, psychological and hence not organic or neurologically based. This interpretation reflects older dynamic psychiatry thinking, involving unconscious or non-conscious impulses/thoughts, although contemporary under- standing of how the organ of attention is deployed makes them every bit brain-based.[480] Be that as it may, the broad expanse of what seizure (or epilepsy viewed in lay terms) signifies, the likelihood of hysterical or psychogenic seizures being seen in association with neuronally-based seizures, the mutual overlap of both in the context of brain lesions, the range of altered states of consciousness found in association with alcohol abuse, and the complexly structured syndromes of dissociation, all make it difficult to separate accidental or exogenous category from alcohol-based problems and epilepsy. Not surprisingly, researchers and scholars discern in these descriptions of insanity virtually all of the conditions recognized in contemporary classifications of psychiatric disorder.[481] Weiss makes an attempt to draw a correspondence between the *Carakasaṃhitā* and that of a classification of psychiatric disorders used in the US.[482]

Conditions featured by sexual manifestations

An additional variety of psychiatric condition encompassed within the *Carakasaṃhitā* compilation involves sexuality and reproduction. While a category of 'diseases of sexuality' is not singled out in the work, one finds among the tenets of the ethno-physiology delineated in the compilation the high importance ascribed to sexual fluids, particularly semen. Moreover, how sexual continence and activity fit in the economy of health is given implicit as well as explicit attention in many volumes, as is the significance of impotence as a health problem. This is consistent with the comprehensive, integrated, and holistic conception of health and the medical.

---

[479] As these two classes of disease were formulated in CS, and the other canonical texts, discussed later on in this chapter.

[480] Raz and Buhle 2006.

[481] Bhugra 1992; Haldipur 1984, 1985, 1989; Dube 1978; Balodhi 1987.

[482] Weiss 1977.

In this light, Money and colleagues examine the *Carakasaṃhitā* from the standpoint of erotic and reproductive functions and analyze the corresponding sexual practices described there in the light of contemporary knowledge about human sexual function.[483] While they underscore the admittedly masculine conception, and quite a narrow one at that, of sexual/erotic physiology outlined in Ayurveda, they nonetheless point to the emphasis given to sexuality: 50 different aphrodisiacs compounded of herbs and nutritional elements are discussed.

A similar emphasis on aspects of sexuality not only in Ayurveda per se but in what may be termed the broadly-based medical psychology of India is found in Bhugra and De Silva.[484] These authors point to the importance of sexuality in India, not only by discussing classic erotic manuals and traditions, but also medical, health-related aspects of love, impotence, and failure to conceive in Vedic medicine. They concentrate in detail on Ayurveda:

> Manufacture of semen is affected, not only by the individual's personality but also by his temperament and food intake, as well as by the climate and seasonal variations. Semen is said to be of eight varieties, and ten different types of herbs are prescribed to increase spermatogenesis. A further ten are recommended for purification of the semen; ... impotence is said to be due to both varieties [of disease, from internal and external causes].[485]

The authors discuss other causative factors, underscoring the emphasis on purely physical and psychological factors. They describe general social and psychological consequences of a preoccupation with sexual difficulties, essentially describing what today would probably be construed as a variety of psychiatric condition.

In summary, sexual activity is obviously an important component of health in the *Carakasaṃhitā*, yet the fundamental health and strength-maintaining functions that are ascribed to semen argue for a hygiene and dietetics that continually aims at its production and preservation. Here of course, Ayurveda simply mirrors other philosophical psychologies and approaches to soteriology that elaborate on sexuality in complex ways.[486] In this context, then, the precepts of the *Carakasaṃhitā* in

---

483 Money, Joshi, and Swayam Prakasam 1992.

484 Bhugra and De Silva 1995.

485 Bhugra and De Silva 1995: 161.

486 White 1996; Obesyesekere 1977, 1982.

relation to sexual practice must have reflected and/or contributed to worries and fears associated with wastage and loss of semen, conceiving of seminal fluids more generally as a symbol of health, vigour, longevity, and moral purity.

The importance of sexual continence, along with other themes prominent in India's cultural psychology, points to conceptions of healthy personhood in India. Moreover, tenets of this sexual emphasis remain salient in contemporary populations.[487] In this context, the semen loss anxiety based syndrome, or what has been termed the *dhat* syndrome, is relevant. It represents a well-recognized variety of psychiatric condition found in contemporary India. It is viewed as a more or less specific anxiety disorder found in South Asia, men presenting with weakness, debility, a sense of wasting away, and much worry and preoccupation over their perception and fixation on urinary fluids and nocturnal emissions.

The clinical manifestations of *dhat* syndrome, its presumed relationship to the prominent health and psychological concerns in the culture of India, and its epidemiology and demography are described in the medical, psychiatric, and anthropological literature.[488] The theory about the importance of semen in the economy of health and sexual function itself virtually assure that such an apparently anxiety syndrome was found in the male population. While this variety of psychiatric condition is not explicitly called or equated with insanity in the *Carakasaṃhitā*, it was very likely encountered in medical practice of ayurvedic physicians and lay, popular practitioners. The medical importance that the *Carakasaṃhitā* ascribes to sexual matters, especially loss of virility and impotence (which reinforces themes represented in the *Atharvaveda*), when seen in conjunction with its integrated perspective on general health, underscores the naturalistic conception of disease, including psychiatric condition, that Chattopadhyaya rightly emphasizes as a major intellectual contribution of Indian civilization.

Alcohol problems in the *Carakasaṃhitā*

In addition to the aforementioned medical conditions, CS discusses at length the disturbances caused by alcohol, giving a lucid account of its

[487] Daniel 1984.

[488] Singh 1985; Paris 1992.

appropriate uses and consequences of its abuse, including medical complications. The explanations offered for alcohol-related conditions and their therapeutics, resemble those of the (endogenous) insanities. Alcohol and sexually related conditions are considered as psychiatric today, but were discussed as separate from insanity in traditional India and later when CS was compiled.

REPRESENTATION OF DISEASE IN THE *SUŚRUTASAṂHITĀ*

General remarks

The *Suśrutasaṃhitā* constitutes an early and foundational text of Ayurveda. Along with the *Carakasaṃhitā* and Vāgbhaṭa's *Aṣṭāṅgasaṃgraha,* which is taken up later, they comprise the three major works of the classical era of Indian medicine. The *Suśrutasaṃhitā* involves a complete medical work but is generally regarded as making landmark contributions to surgery. Yet this text has a supplementary section entitled *Uttaratantra,* which includes additional diseases and in particular those that equate with psychiatric conditions as these have been conceptualized in this book. Fevers, which provide a good contrast case, are also included and are discussed later. Thus material discussed in what follows, namely, fever, 'organic' and 'metaphysical' insanities, and epilepsy, are found in Volume III, the supplementary treatise, also termed addendum by Meulenbeld.[489]

Fever

By far the longest chapter in *Uttaratantra,* number 39, concerns fevers. Its content is almost exclusively physiological/anatomical or somatic. It describes many, many types of fevers, their mechanisms as per the *doṣa*s and their aggravation, circulation and location of stasis in the channels or organs as well as numerous types of foods, herbs, and physical procedures involving treatment (fasting, purgation, special foods and herbs). It contains a few discussions of behavioural measures and of metaphysical considerations. For example, it is asserted that a patient convalescing from fever is recommended to avoid cold water, sleeping

---

[489] Meulenbeld 1997.

during the day, anger, exercise or sexual intercourse. It is recommended that should a patient be frightened by a non-venomous snake, trained elephants and bogus thieves at the time when a paroxysm of fever is expected to occur and food is to be avoided. A class of fevers is ascribed to malignant spirits and these should be dealt with by means of incantations, binding, and beating as is recommended for the *bhūtas*. Varieties of symbolic analogies between, on the one hand, features of a condition of fever and, on the other, behavioural measures are recommended in a few instances. For example, in the case of those suffering from 'cold-fever' a scenario of exposure to young, beautiful, voluptuous 'damsels' in the art or sport of love is recommended and they are to embrace the patient firmly until the patient feels his heat returning. Another patient who has a burning sensation is to be anointed with a special decoction and placed in a tub and when the burning goes away he should be raised out of the water, washed with cold water, smeared with soothing sandal pastes and then beautiful damsels are urged to hold the patient in a firm embrace and kiss him, but asked to leave as soon as patient feels exhilarated. In conjunction with behavioural measures, then, various organic therapies are recommended, such as various wholesome foods, purgatives, herbs and medicines.

Predominantly 'organic' insanity in the *Suśrutasaṃhitā*

Chapter 62 of *Uttaratantra* addresses insanity or *unmāda*. This is described as a disease of the mind. Its pathology involves a derangement of the bodily *doṣas*, which traverse the upper part of the body affecting channels and nerves producing a distraction of the mind. This chapter on the more 'organic' insanities contains material that parallels in many respects some of the material discussed earlier for the *Carakasaṃhitā* within its one category of insanity.[490] Whereas the latter includes five types in its chapter devoted to insanity, the *Suśrutasaṃhitā* includes six, adding mental affliction and poison, but excludes those brought by supernatural beings. The latter are set apart as different and given their own chapter, a convention that is also found in Vāgbhaṭa.

Organic insanities, then, come in six varieties. Three stem from each of the three 'deranged and aggravated' *doṣas*, one from their combination, one due to 'grief, etc. (real or imaginary)', and the last due to effects

[490] Compare material presented in the section on Caraka.

of poison. The latter variety seems added on since its regimen is said to depend on which of any of combination of *doṣa*s that are deranged or faulted. In its early stages, the last variety prior to aggravation of *doṣa*s is termed *mada*.

The *premonitory symptoms* involve purely bodily and physiological phenomena. They include such things as fits of unconsciousness, agitated state of the mind, ringing of the ears, emaciation of the body, excessive energy in action, aversion to food, eating filthy things in dreams, churning-like sensation in the body due to vital force (*vāyu*), dizziness as experienced when involved in a circling movement or moving wheel.[491] The latter symptom is part of the list: 'lying on moving wheel' are the symptoms in a patient that forebodes a speedy and impending attack of insanity.

The specific symptoms of each variety associated with deranged *doṣa*s are listed separately. All three varieties involve bodily symptoms; for example: (1) shaggy appearance, laboured breathing, emaciation of the body, joint pain and/or excessive coldness for the variety due to aggravated wind; (2) excessive thirst, perspiration, burning sensation, voracious eating, insomnia in the variety due to faulted fire *doṣa*; (3) vomiting, dullness of appetite, lassitude, and aversion to food for the phlegm variety. Each variety is also associated with behavioural symptoms: (1) use of harsh language, producing sound by clapping his hands or singing while dancing, and wandering about for the wind variety; (2) desire for shade, cold, wind, and walks by river banks, fits of anger, fancying fire in cold water and sight of stars in the sky in the day are the symptoms found in the variety caused by faulted fire; (3) aversion to food, fondness for sexual propulsion and loneliness, stupidity, somnolence, reservedness in speech, fondness for warm things and aggravation of the disease in the night mark disease of the phlegm type. The variety of insanity marked by derangement of all three *doṣa*s (termed *sannipātika*) is marked by all of the preceding symptoms and is regarded as incurable.

At this point the *Suśrutasaṃhitā* appears to introduce *two additional varieties* termed *śokaja* and *viṣaja*. These were not referred to earlier and are featured predominantly by behavioural symptoms. The first con-

[491] The following ambiguous phrase is added to the list of symptoms: 'are the symptoms in a patient which forebode a speedy and impending attack of insanity'. *Suśrutasaṃhitā* 1998–99, Vol. III, *Uttaratantra* 39, p. 606.

cerns a person (overly?) fearful of (feeling persecuted by?) thieves, officials, or his own enemies

> or suffering from any distracted state of the mind owing to a loss of wealth or from any grief (*śoka*) or bereavement or from any disappointed love.[492]

They would be likely to show a 'mental distraction' type of insanity. In such cases the patient would unconsciously talk incoherently about subjects uppermost in his mind or would sing in a stupid fashion or laugh or weep. These are the symptoms of *śokaja* insanity. On the other hand a patient showing redness of the eyes, a dull complexion and dullness of 'perceptive faculties', bodily weakness, 'extreme dejection', red face, and loss of consciousness shows an incurable insanity caused by poison.

The initial general treatment of insanity involves a series of herbal and physical procedures. They include, for example, herbs, emetics, purgatives, powders, and fumigation. Then, what one can term emotional counter-therapy is recommended.

> The patient should be made surprised with wonderful sights and the news of the death of any of his dear ones related to him. He should be constantly frightened with sights of fierce-looking men, well-trained elephants or non-venomous snakes. The patient should be threatened with being fastened with ropes or being flogged, or frightened with bundles of blazing hay, after being fastened, while asleep. He should also be pierced in his body with pointed instruments, avoiding, however, the vulnerable parts, or he should be made to reside constantly in a dry well with a cover over it.[493]

This is followed by a list of specific treatments for each type and consists of additional herbal, dietary, and physical (bloodletting) medicinal and procedures.

---

[492] *Suśrutasaṃhitā* 1998–99, Vol. III, *Uttaratantra* 62, p. 607.

[493] *Suśrutasaṃhitā* 1998–99, Vol. III, *Uttaratantra* 39, p. 608.

'Metaphysical' diseases (caused by possession of spirits) in the *Suśrutasaṃhitā*

General characteristics

Chapter 60 of *Suśrutasaṃhitā*'s *Uttaratantra* which is devoted to metaphysical insanities, also termed *bhūta* (and exogenous or accidental by Caraka), begins by describing the offending agents as 'superhuman', which refers to beings, agents, or factors 'other than' of human origin. This class of agents includes deities, demons, ghosts, monsters and even serpent deities. These 'tutelary' divinities or *graha*s are said to roam the world in search of offerings and victims. Out of intrinsic mischief or cruelty they are said to choose as victims individuals who are impure in body, mind, or actions. While of various shapes and appearance, the *graha*s are classified into eight types, some of which were encountered in Caraka's inventory. The following are singled out by Suśruta: *deva*s or deities and their enemies, *gandharva*s, *yakṣa*s, *pitṛ*s, *bhujaṅga*s (serpent deities) *rākṣasa*s (monsters) and *piśāca*s (filthy goblins).

Suśruta provides a description and opinion of these causes that while consistent with that of Caraka is more detailed. The information affords a broader look at the way of thinking inherent in Ayurveda and, by definition, how the academic, scholarly component of the indigenous psychiatry conceptualized its domain and how it worked as a system of practice.

> Austere penances and vows, self-control, truthfulness, charities and religious practices as well as the eight qualities are wholly or partially present in the *Graha*s according to the degree of their respective power. These spiritual bodies never come in contact with nor do they themselves strike human beings. Those who hold contrary opinions must be ignorant of the mysteries of demonology. It is the thousands and hundreds of thousands and hundreds of millions of the followers of the *Graha*s, who are fierce-looking and fond of flesh and blood, and who stir abroad in the night and possess the men on earth.[494]

The 'eight qualities' cited in this paragraph are translated as superhuman power to become as small as an atom at will, power of becoming light at will, expansiveness, irresistible will, power of increasing size at will, greatness, self-control, and suppression of passion.

---

[494] *Suśrutasaṃhitā* 1998–99: Vol. III, *Uttaratantra* 60, p. 591.

In this material and the paragraph quoted, the *Suśrutasaṃhitā* provides a window through which one can see what indigenous psychiatry was like during the time when it and other Ayurveda texts' formulation were regnant in the subcontinent.[495] It represents a cultural formulation of what the academic, scholarly medical traditions construed as a special class of psychiatric conditions. Viewed in broader context, the *Suśrutasaṃhitā* should be equated with Indian cultural formulations not only of the *bhūtas*, but of ordinary insanities as well as innumerable other conditions of disease such as fistulas, wasting diseases, respiratory or gastrointestinal problems. This point is taken up later.

Manifestations of victims that indicate attack or possession

In general, like *Carakasaṃhitā*, the manifestations of victims stricken with this variety of insanity resemble those of the culturally accepted characteristics of the possessing agent. However, while Caraka's descriptions were brief and incomplete, the *Suśrutasaṃhitā* provides rich examples of behavioural manifestations. Only a few examples are provided here. Each *graha* is said to have its special mode and time of attack. Those attacked by deities (*devas*) behave in a godly, spiritual, and commendable way as in keeping with the identity of the possessing agent. They appear clean, 'contented', and behave vigorously and have little need for sleep. The victim, denominated as a male, shows good command of Sanskrit and likes flowers and perfumes, grants favours to those around him, and is devoted to Brahmins. Besides showing markers of divine favour, a person possessed stares with a fixed gaze in his eyes (the only suggestive organic manifestation). One attacked by *asuragraha* (devil) speaks ill of the gods and preceptors and exhibits vicious propensities (he also perspires copiously). A *gandharvagraha* victim moves about happily and seeks lovely settings, flowers and sweet scents (he also shows copper-coloured eyes). A person attacked or struck by a malignant *bhujaṅga* or serpent-deity moves along the ground with his chest flat on the ground, always licking the corner of his lips with his tongue, much like a serpent and shows irritability and predilection for honey and milk. One attacked by a *rākṣasa* is fond of flesh, blood and various other foods and displays a heated emotionality ('ardent spirit') that includes extreme cruelty, courageousness, 'extraordinary' strength and stirs about in the night with

[495] And before, recall *Atharvaveda* psychiatry.

little regard for his appearance and hygiene, a 'blank shamelessness'. A victim attacked by *piśācagraha* shows haughtiness, garrulousness, fondness for stirring around in the night and roaming (he also shows emaciation, roughness of behaviour, fetid smell of the body).

Other syndromes of behaviour are provided. Some display unusual, objectionable behaviour, others more positive reverential behaviour and the playing out of ritual oblations, no doubt consistent with the identity and general appraisal of the attacking agent. It will be noted that manifestations just described centre predominantly on socially identifiable (symbolically meaningful, communicative) behavioural syndromes to the relative neglect of 'organic' manifestations, involving pathophysiology and anatomy.[496]

Distinguishing characteristics

These types of conditions, then, involve syndromes that are rich in symbolization. Their manifestations 'communicate' to the physician and its audience the social and cultural identity of the attacker and its standing in a scale of values. One can infer that the identity and general characteristics of these beings resides in descriptions found in the folk, popular, and mythological literature of India. Whoever compiled this text assumes that who the attacking agents are, what they stand for, and what they connote are part of the cultural information of readers and the general population. In description of these types of psychiatric conditions – the *Suśrutasaṃhitā* does not consider them insanity, but medical nonetheless – one does not find an emphasis on body considered a concrete physical entity. Physiology or chemistry is not addressed for one finds no reference to the humours involved, their flow through the body, or mechanism of bringing about a condition of insanity. Moreover, only in rare instances does the *Suśrutasaṃhitā* include indicators of dilapidated, disorganized, or incoherent behaviour in these syndromes. In contrast, his chapters on epilepsy and 'ordinary' insanities characteristically address matters of consciousness, mental focus, conceptual organization, and pathophysiology.

[496] Exceptions to this generalization were discussed earlier.

Setting medical boundaries on bhūtas

The divisions of the chapter on psychiatric conditions caused by spiritual attack (termed diseases) brought on through superhuman influences, which can be termed *bhūtas* so as equate them with other Ayurveda texts, reflect a descriptive organization that is consistent with the identity and *modus operandi* of the spiritual being. The formulation of these metaphysical 'diseases' differs from that of ordinary ones caused by and associated with organic or 'physical' causes. For example, one finds in addition to causes and manifestations involving symbolic behaviour, the preferred time when the agents are prone to attack, and appropriate treatments. In this way they resemble fevers, some of which are said to manifest during specific time periods. While descriptions of manifestation generally tend to leave the body and its physiology out of the picture, the section entitled 'Prognosis' is different and is worth quoting:

> If a person possessed by a *Graha* has swollen eyes, quick pace, foam at the mouth which he licks himself, drowsiness, staggering gait which sometimes compels him to fall down on the ground or if he is possessed by a *Graha* after his fall from a hill, an elephant, a tree or such other high place, or if he be old [in footnote one finds 'has continued for thirteen years'] he should be regarded as incurable.[497]

This paragraph sets boundary conditions for 'metaphysical' conditions contra ordinary 'organic' insanities and stipulates what in hindsight one is tempted to construe as neurological and neuro-psychiatric disorders because description suggests manifestations of permanent brain injury and points injuries that can cause it. *Suśrutasaṃhitā*'s formulation of *bhūta* as a disease entity involves a syndrome of behaviour that had resonant spiritual and cultural implications; however, the syndromes by and large did not include indicators of other diseases the manifestations of which might resemble a *bhūta* but had ominous implications. This section entitled 'Prognosis', then, represents a statement on differential diagnosis: what was and was not typical of these metaphysical conditions.

---

[497] *Suśrutasaṃhitā* 1998–99: Vol. III, *Uttaratantra* 60, p. 590.

Religious treatment of bhūtas

Treatments for these conditions involve general religious measures consisting of repetition of mantras sacred to any deity, offering of oblations to gods, and other religious rituals that are said to be carried out by a 'careful' physician. Practices of religious, symbolic nature are prescribed:

> Offerings of garland of red flowers, with red scents (such as red Sandal paste, *Kuṅkuma*, etc.), seeds (such as mustard, barley, etc.), honey, clarified butter and all sorts of victuals are the articles required generally for (propitiation of) all classes (of *Graha*).[498]

Aspects of dietetics here inserted in an otherwise religious program of therapy, are similar to those found in the 'ordinary insanities', those involving disturbance of humours and a pathophysiology. In addition, insanities caused by each of the attacking are to be administered specially prepared foods. For example, when special clothing is enjoined or recommendation involves wine, blood, flesh or milk these should be offered according to the respective liking of the specific *graha*s and on those days on which they attack their victims.

Non-religious treatment of bhūtas

An exception to the general recommendation of religious treatments that are tailored to the identity of the *graha* and reflect their preferred behaviour involves what the *Saṃhitā* describes as 'medical treatment'. These are recommended in the event that prescribed mantras that are recorded in works of demonology fail to improve the lot of the victim. Diverse animal products concocted into oils, fumigation with specially prepared incense sticks, various drugs prepared by soaking in animal fluids are prescribed as unguents and snuffs, and washings undertaken by 'experienced' physician. This section of the chapter is actually one of the longest. Dietary prescriptions and other medical procedures are used also but none of these general medical measures are recommended because of their effects on body functions per se. However, this can be inferred since treatments referred to are used for other ailments and are believed to work because of their influence on dynamics of body function. Here again, then, one finds a clue that *bhūta*s also have general medical implications.

---

[498] *Suśrutasaṃhitā* 1998–99: Vol. III, *Uttaratantra* 60, p. 592.

Final comment

The chapter on diseases caused by spiritual attack ends after a long review of standard procedures and ayurvedic medicinals that can be used with the following admonition and advice:

> Unholy and improper articles should not be employed in a case due to the influence of any *Deva Graha* (divine spirit). No hostile measures should be adopted in a case of possession by a *Graha* other than that due to the influence of a *Piśāca Graha* in as much as the mighty *Grahas*, if offended, might kill both the patient and the physician for the act. A physician, treating such a case with discretion according the rules laid down in the chapter known as *Hitāhita* [*Sūtrasthāna* 20] may acquire both fame and wealth.[499]

This quotation appears to reaffirm the medical validity of spirit-caused diseases. The chapter, a representation of the indigenous psychiatry of India as construed in the academic, scholarly sector of medicine, displays an attempt to assimilate or appropriate aspects of demonology and mythology with a naturalistic formulation.

EPILEPSY IN THE *SUŚRUTASAṂHITĀ*

The causes of epilepsy involve disturbances of contact with objects of the senses and their actions. These include, for example, contact with disvalued (filthy, impure) articles, improper regimen of conduct, harmful suppression of bodily urgings, sexual relations during menses, or mental overload of emotions (amorous fancies, fright, anxiety, grief, anger). Epilepsy, then, is formulated in pathophysiology/-anatomy or organic terms. Such factors aggravate bodily *doṣa*s that in turn affect/injure the *cetas* (mind). More specifically, the pathophysiology involves a derangement of the bodily *doṣa*s (humours of fire, wind, and phlegm) which 'overwhelm' the channels (*srotas*) of the body and lead to a predominance of the mental *doṣa*s (*rajas* and *tamas*) that bring forth unconsciousness and loss of memory.

> He writhes in agony and throws his hands and legs in convulsive jerk with contracted eyes ... and eyebrows. He gnashes his teeth, with

[499] *Suśrutasaṃhitā* 1998–99: Vol. III, *Uttaratantra* 60, p. 596.

> foams at the mouth etc. and falls to the ground with open eyes, the consciousness returning a short while after.[500]

The premonitory symptoms involve throbbing of heart, perspiration, fainting, attentiveness, 'stupid appearance', and sleeplessness. They also include emptiness or lightness that may refer to abnormal sensation in chest, possibly a reference to diminishing mental awareness since heart is held to be the seat of mind. There are said to be four types of epilepsy, one involving each of the (faulted, excited) humours and one involving their combination.

Suśrutasaṃhitā's formulation of *apasmāra* or epilepsy presented thus far is exclusively centred on the body, its ethno-physiology (abnormal humours) and anatomy (channels, heart). It then proceeds to describe the symptoms of epilepsy associated with the various humours. All are consistent with the organic emphasis. Delirious talk and utterance of indistinct, moaning sounds are present in all three varieties. However, the descriptions include the following statements:

> In the wind type ... patient fancies that a *dark supernatural being* is coming after him to seize his person and is frightened and faints in consequence with *shivering, grinding of teeth,* laboured breathing, and foaming of mouth ... In the fire variety one finds that fainting is excited by a terror of being *seized by a yellow and fierce-looking being* ... which is further marked by *thirst, increased heat of the body, perspiration,* fainting, mild tremor of the limbs and restlessness.[501]

The variety caused by abnormality of phlegm or *kapha* involves the patient's excitement:

> by a fancied dread as if a *supernatural being of white colour* is coming to apprehend him ... which is moreover characterized by ... such symptoms as shivering, nausea, sleepiness, falling prostrate on the ground and *vomiting of mucus.*[502]

This material exemplifies *Suśrutasaṃhitā*'s predominant bodily organic emphasis. However, it makes indirect reference to metaphysical factors as phenomena of the culture of traditional India of that era: *patients of each variety* are said to be fearful of or fancied by supernatural

---

[500] *Suśrutasaṃhitā* 1998–99: Vol. III, *Uttaratantra*, p. 598.

[501] *Suśrutasaṃhitā* 1998–99: Vol. III, *Uttaratantra* 61, p. 599.

[502] *Suśrutasaṃhitā* 1998–99: Vol. III, *Uttaratantra* 61, p. 599.

agents. Thus, while physicians who compiled this text appear to have excluded or expunged metaphysical factors out of epilepsy such factors remain influential in the minds of patients.[503] One notes also, that the colour of the feared supernatural agent appears to correspond to the colour of the humour (a haunting wind as dark, fire as yellow, and phlegm as white) and might be mirrored in some of the manifestations (italicized in the previous three quotes above), with shivering a feature of both wind and phlegm.

One can presume that in the minds of physicians who compiled the *Suśrutasaṃhitā*, it was body, biology, and physiology that mattered *contra metaphysics*. However, the latter may have crept into the domain implicitly. In addition to material just presented consider the following observation. Specific treatments of epilepsy, which are many, make reference only to 'physical' foods, compounds and herbs. On the other hand, medicinal agents helpful in the insanities are said to also be useful in epilepsy. Moreover,

> Medicinal measures and compound mentioned under the head of possession by the *Grahas* are also specially beneficial in the present disease' and furthermore 'The divine Rudra god and the host of his followers should be regularly worshipped and propitiated every day.[504]

The need to reaffirm organic/body factors as central to is exemplified in the following quote:

> The sudden appearance of the disease without any apparent cause and also its sudden and spontaneous disappearance after a short while without any apparent treatment, have induced several medical authorities to hold that *Apasmāra* [i.e., epilepsy] is not due to any (aggravation of the) *Doṣas*. Several authorities, on the contrary, have described, on the authority of other works on the subject, the gradual aggravation of the (suddenly) deranged *Doṣas* as well as the concomitant symptoms of the disease in its various phases with the spontaneous and speedy nature of its abatement (though only temporary). Hence it may be presumed that as seeds sprout in autumn only, when the rains make the ground ready to receive them, the shortness of time being counted as no factor potent enough to obstruct the process (of sprouting), so the deranged *Doṣas* of the body though gradually

[503] And perhaps in the minds of the physicians themselves who thought them important enough to include in the textbook.

[504] *Suśrutasaṃhitā* 1998–99: Vol. III, *Uttaratantra* 61, p. 601.

> aggravated bring on, as a matter of fact, an attack of *Apasmāra* with all its concomitant symptoms, only under conditions favourable to its appearance which may, however, be short and transitory in its duration. Hence this dreadful *Apasmāra* is certainly a disease of Dosic origin.[505]

In the case of epilepsy, then, as in case of 'ordinary' insanity, the *Suśrutasaṃhitā* appears to want to exclude metaphysical considerations yet is more than willing to include and bestow medical validity on the *bhūtas*.

VĀGBHAṬA'S *AṢṬĀṄGASAṂGRAHA*

General introduction

The *Aṣṭāṅgasaṃgraha* (AS) by Vāgbhaṭa is generally considered along with the compilations ascribed to Caraka and Suśruta one of the canonical works of Ayurveda.[506] Both the identity of the person who wrote AS and the dating of it are controversial, although the majority appears to agree that it postdates the Gupta period and a date of 600 CE has been proposed.[507] A brief review of the contents of AS, which clearly came after Caraka's and Suśruta's *Saṃhitās*, will serve to highlight a later perspective on Ayurveda as a general approach to Indian medicine and as a slant on psychiatric condition in particular.

Vāgbhaṭa's AS presents one with a comprehensive compendium of knowledge about disease and treatment. It contains reference to ideas and principles found in Caraka and Suśruta. For example, it is not merely a description of types of disease, approaches to diagnosis, and methods and procedures of treatment. It also includes a philosophical, broad-ranging formulation about wellness, maintenance of health, prevention, rejuvenation, and the role of cosmology, regimen of life, worldly causes, and happenings in previous lives that may contribute to disease. Its perspective is strongly naturalistic but alludes to metaphysical, spiritual, and/or 'magico-religious' views about causation and divinatory, incantatory approaches to healing. The broad scope and its inclusion of material on the makeup of the individual, nature of experi-

[505] *Suśrutasaṃhitā* 1998–99: Vol. III, *Uttaratantra* 61, p. 600.

[506] *Aṣṭāṅgasaṃgraha* 1999.

[507] Rama Rao 1992; Meulenbeld 1999–2002.

ence, transmigration, and appropriate conduct illustrates its conformity to India's cultural psychology which is taken up later.

A characteristic that is clearly manifest in AS, as in other texts reviewed, is the commingling of physiological-anatomical explanations (involving pathophysiology-pathogenesis) and related physical-organic therapeutic procedures and medicines. These include, for example, especially prepared foods and herbs, oils, massage, sudation, fumigation, purgation, enemas, and emesis. The timing (when in the day or night) and duration (how long) of these practices are specified and also on occasion modifications due to constitution of patient. Descriptions of disease and their treatment also include behavioural and psychological methods and techniques. Even in the analysis of the influence and treatment of the *doṣas*, a general account that excludes disease entities and concentrates on how these chemicophysiological pathogenic agents can be modified so as to counteract their aggravation or fault in any disease, one finds intercalation of behavioural-psychological methods.[508] These include for example, appropriate dwellings and exposure to pleasant surroundings and weather, 'sprinkling pure water all over', 'hearing of instrumental or vocal music which is liked', company of joyful and happy friends with similar interest, 'tight embrace by women who have slender, soft, sweet smelling body, who have put on pleasant dress ...' and the like. Examples of this holistic approach vary in frequency and content depending on type of disease and are included in the conditions selected here for discussion.

Conception and classification of disease

In Chapter 22 of Volume I, AS presents its general statements about disease. It states that as a consequence of information handed down by Ātreya and other great sages, it follows that diseases are the result of inheritance (problems with the male or female seed), congenital (defects or improper activities of mother), acquired through improper food, trauma or injury, seasonal, influential and providential (curse of gods, violation of tradition, seizure by goblins), 'natural causes' (hunger, thirst, old age). It adds that all diseases fall into two categories; they result from either activities of present life or those of previous life. However, AS stipulates that in the final analysis all diseases involve abnor-

---

[508] *Aṣṭāṅgasaṃgraha* 1999: Vol. I, Chapter 21.

mality of the *doṣas*. Diseases due to actions of present life are cured by the use of 'opposites' (drugs, foods or acts having qualities opposite to the disease). While opposites are tried and used in diseases to actions of past lives, these will be cured only after the effect of such actions comes to an end. On the other hand, the chapter also indicates that all unhealthy actions of body, speech, or mind constitute wilful transgressions and can result in disease. A careful examination of a patient is urged and described. It concentrates on observation or report of what represent predominantly physical factors (odour, taste, colour, shape, quality of faeces). It adds:

> Nature and opinion of dreams, the stellar constellation at the time of patient's birth and at time of onset of the disease, the things he hates, likes, his comforts and discomforts.[509]

Endnotes to this chapter indicate that sinful acts are considered relevant and ten varieties of these are listed (lying, bad thoughts, stealing).

AS goes on to discuss that there are several ways of explaining cause and classifying diseases. These include the following: inherited, congenital, acquired, traumatic, caused by seasonal/environmental factors, providential causes (curses, violations of traditions, spirit possession described as 'seizures by goblins and other evil spirits'), and based on natural conditions such as hunger, old age, and things that happen unavoidably or due to carelessness. Diseases can vary as to severity and as to season of year. As suggested earlier, another scheme is based on diseases produced by activities in the present life, either known or unknown, compared to activities of previous lives, definite or indefinite. Diseases due to malevolent actions of others are mentioned but given little importance; it is implied that following a moral life course renders the possibility of disease by such behaviour unlikely.

In general, AS presents an optimistic position on the course of disease and the practice of medicine. It emphasizes that by following a therapeutic regimen and 'healthy living' lifestyle it is possible that causes of disease incurred through actions in previous lives may be counteracted and defeated. The predominant view is that diseases result in or from abnormality of the three humours or *doṣas*. In the event, too much or too little of a particular *doṣa*, a negative change in its material-

---

[509] *Aṣṭāṅgasaṃgraha* 1999: Vol. I, Chapter 22, p. 314.

ity, or its stagnation in channels or organs can result from one of three conditions: (1) stimulation of sense organs by their objects; (2) wilful unhealthy modes of conduct; and (3) change of season and condition of the physical environment. Salient themes in AS are the role of 'normal' *doṣas* in the constitution of the body tissues in conditions of health, their role in the production of disease when 'abnormal' or vitiated, and ways in which they can be controlled and reversed.

Psychology and biology are implicated in causation and ontology. Three types of actions involving body, speech, and mind can cause disease. A naturalistic, more or less 'impersonal' and secular conception of disease is balanced by a moral, spiritual conception, as described above. Emphasis is given to unhealthy actions, including, besides those affecting the exterior of the body (scratching, an injury due to falling) and its 'internal' functions (overcontrolling one's breath, speaking during hunger or while eating), such things as negative emotions (fear, grief, greed, jealousy) and the ten sinful acts (stealing, unlawful sex, thinking about doing bad to others, doubting and disbelieving). As in CS, a clearly moral tone is found in basic conditions that cause disease.

Treatment is described as consisting of two general but related, mutually reinforcing approaches, those that promote health and vigour, namely, rejuvenation and virilization (each of which is among the largest of chapters in AS), and those that cure disease (mitigating cause and preventing recurrence). The three general types of treatment involve the wise use of drugs, controlling the mind (keeping it away from unhealthy thoughts), and invoking the grace of gods (chanting of hymns, auspicious ceremonies, wearing amulets). Three kinds of drugs (minerals, and vegetable and animal products) are described but treatments without recourse to drugs are listed in this section, and these include such things as exposure to sunlight and fasting as well as sacred spells, appeasing gods, charity, and inducing emotions that counteract noxious causes of disease (threatening, shocking, creating happiness).

Approaches to disease in children

A distinguishing feature of Vāgbhaṭa's AS is the emphasis given to metaphysical or spiritual aspects of medical conditions, on the one hand, and to specific diseases, namely the *bhūtas*, on the other.

The first six chapters of Volume III of AS address the medical conditions of children. Chapter 1 deals with general aspects of care and feeding and treatment of minor conditions of the newborn that are practical, physiological. It ends with the advice that:

> The body of the child should be protected from different types of evil spirits, by appropriate methods, just as a city is protected from enemies by brave men equipped with weapons.[510]

Chapter 2 concentrates on treatment of children and is similarly focused on general aspects of physiology, diet, and physical changes. It ends with the advice:

> Diseases in children arise even from evil spirits which remain concealed, therefore, it is necessary to adopt sacrifice and other ritual procedures in addition to medicinal therapies always.[511]

Chapter 3 heads full gear into metaphysical matters and is titled 'Knowledge of Diagnosis of Diseases Arise due to Evil Spirits'. AS begins this chapter with discussion of genesis of demons/evil spirits and a listing of premonitory symptoms of attack and general symptoms. It then systematically discusses 13 types of spirits that can seize the child. Chapter 4 discusses treatment of such seizures from a general point of view; it does not deal with spirits or demons separately. General measures that are discussed include protective bath, fumigation, special medicated ghee, tying of amulets, oblation, and fire sacrifices. Chapter 5 discusses the rituals and physiological methods that have to be followed in bathing the child in order to prepare it for treatment of seizure or capture by a spirit or demon. Chapter 6 systematically discusses preparation of and use of medicinal products along with rituals that need to be followed in the children who have been attacked or injured or seized by each of 12 demons.

With respect to general medicine, two chapters of Volume III deal with knowledge and treatment of diseases caused by evil spirits that affect adults. These diseases mainly implicate aspects of psychiatric condition, to be described presently. Finally, two chapters of Volume III address insanity and epilepsy, as described above. Thus, besides separating psychiatric and neurological conditions from other medical ones, AS weaves psychological and behavioural themes in most diseases.

---

[510] *Aṣṭāṅgasaṃgraha* 1999: Vol. III, Chapter 1, p. 18.

[511] *Aṣṭāṅgasaṃgraha* 1999: Vol. III, Chapter 2, p. 44.

The number of evil spirits that can cause disease is said to be 'endless'. They attack at midnight and have a 'terrifying' appearance. The principal reason for attack by spirits is 'violation of code of right conduct, either in the present life or the previous one'.[512] Reasons for this are said to be a victim's predilection to or being motivated by negative emotions like lust, anger, and greed. A long list is provided of the specific times when seizure by an evil spirit is likely to occur. They are said to produce 'disorders of the mind' and each spirit is associated with a manner of affecting a victim (touch, entering the body, emitting an odour). The habitual behaviour of persons, a kind of 'social personology', renders him/her vulnerable to specific evil spirits, each of which is said to attack on a specific day of the month and time of day. Fourteen different evil spirits are described and the set of manifestations of disease that each can cause is provided. Manifestations refer to aspects of appearance, dress, body function, state of cleanliness, and physical manifestations of motor behaviour, but by far the greatest proportion of symptoms and signs involve aspects of social and psychological behaviour. The chapter devoted to the treatment of disorders caused by evil spirits ranges over a large number of medicines, foods, and special decoctions that can be ingested, applied externally to the body, inserted nasally, burned and inhaled. These treatments are said to be useful for a number of general medical diseases but a repeated theme is aspects of insanity and epilepsy as well as disorders caused by spirits.

Formulation of fevers

Vāgbhaṭa handles diagnosis of disease in the section entitled *Nidānasthāna* found in Volume II. Fevers are classified in various ways: psychic, somatic; mild, severe; inside the body, externally on skin or other tissues; seasonal, natural and unseasonal, unnatural curable and incurable; associated with unripe or early stage and the ripe or late stage. However, these are general qualifications and the text does not carry these classifications in the chapter as a whole. Vāgbhaṭa's systematic classification includes eight varieties of fevers, seven from the *doṣa*s separately and in combination and one from external causes. Although not labelled as such, these seven varieties suggest that they are 'internal'. In these varieties, pathogenesis is explained in physiological and anatomical

[512] *Aṣṭāṅgasaṃgraha* 1999: Vol. III, 89.

terms (*doṣas*, channels, and organs). Prodromal symptoms list a number of physiological symptoms and general bodily dysfunctions but includes also psychological ones; for example, lack of faith in good advice, hatred towards children and sweets, desire for sour, salt and pungent tastes and like and dislike ('without any apparent reason') for noise, fire, water, cold breeze, shade and sunlight. Fever caused by *vāta* (faulted air or wind) leads to many and diverse physiological/bodily signs and symptoms and includes aspects of experience and behaviour, namely, grief (sorrow) and irrelevant talk. Those caused by *pitta* (fire humour) and *kapha* (phlegm humour) separately and combinations of any two of the three humours are described purely in physiological/bodily terms. Fever associated with combination of all three faulted humours (termed *sannipāta*) is also almost exclusively biological, but includes 'lack of interest in music, dance, and humour'. A good example of a 'physiological or bodily' explanation of fever in Vāgbhaṭa is the following description of one type of *sannipāta* (termed *jvara*):

> where *pitta* remains separately, either in the skin or the alimentary tract, produces burning sensation either at the onset or later; similarly *vāta* and *kapha* produce cold feeling (chills), both these fevers preceded by either burning sensation or by cold (chills, rigours) will make the fever difficult to cure. If the *kapha* is liquefied and made dry (devoid of unctuousness) there is cold (chills) at the commencement, after the cold subsides, sourness (belching), fainting, toxicity and thirst develops, if there is burning sensation at the commencement, stupor, expectoration, vomiting and exhaustion develop at the end.[513]

Vāgbhaṭa's classification of external causes of fever produces four types: injury/trauma, possession by evil spirits, worms and infectious agents, curse and witchcraft. While a prominent component of fevers caused by external causes involves metaphysical considerations, 'physical' and 'metaphysical' elements are frequently handled together and seem to be confounded; for example, possession by evil-spirits '(and micro-organisms)' include inhalation and smell of grass, flowers, poisons, emotions such as anger, fear, sorrow and lust. All of these causes produce physiological symptoms. Here are two examples of this mode of description:

---

[513] *Aṣṭāṅgasaṃgraha* 1999: Vol. II, 146.

> In fever due to the first three (possession by evil spirits, smell of pollen and poison), and in fevers due to the next three (fear, grief and lust), there is increase of *vāta*, in that due to anger, there is increase of *pitta*; those caused by curses and witchcraft will have increase of the three *doṣas* and [is] impossible to bear (or cure).[514]
>
> In fever due to witchcraft by the hymns being uttered, the mind becomes troubled first, next the body gets affected. Next follows the appearance of vesicles (eruptions), thirst, giddiness, burning sensation, fainting and increase of temperature day after day.[515]

Vāgbhaṭa's treatment of diseases (*Cikitsitasthāna*) is found in Volume II. The one on fevers focuses exclusively on modification of *doṣas* in relation to desired physiological effects. These may represent acute, short lasting fevers. On the other hand, while the chapter on chronic fevers (termed *jvaracikitsā*) is also predominantly 'physiological', it discusses additional methods and practices. These include such things as: pleasant music and aromas; exposure to pleasant physical surroundings and weather conditions; embrace of women who have well developed breasts and are adorned with cosmetics and full of youthful mirth (they are to be dismissed when the chills abate). Emotional counter-therapy as described in (the treatment of) disorders of the mind (insanity, epilepsy, etc.) is taken up later. In fevers caused by anger, a patient should be indulged and given things he desires that are comforting to the mind. Things pleasant to the mind 'cure all kinds of fever'. Recommendations of metaphysical factors are included and are clearly stated:

> The patients should offer worship to his mother, father, gods, physicians, brahmanas, Shiva and Vishnu, practice charity, control of sense, truthfulness, compassion and righteous conduct; always holy hymns, wear amulets, precious gems and great potent divine herbs.[516]

However, the following quote is somewhat ambiguous:

> In fever caused by evil spirits, use of amulets, incantations of hymns etc. prescribed in demonology should be done.[517]

---

[514] *Aṣṭāṅgasaṃgraha* 1999: Vol. II, 147.
[515] *Aṣṭāṅgasaṃgraha* 1999: Vol. II, 147.
[516] *Aṣṭāṅgasaṃgraha* 1999: Vol. II, 305.
[517] *Aṣṭāṅgasaṃgraha* 1999: Vol. II, 303.

In this instance, it is unclear if the physician himself should provide and perform these or whether treatment by an outside exorcist is recommended. At any rate, this quote and the preceding one, clearly indicates the presumed medical validity of metaphysical treatment in some cases.

Formulation of neuro-psychiatric condition

Section II of Volume II of AS entitled *Nidānasthānā* deals with diagnosis and descriptions of major disease types. In includes a chapter on *vātavyādhinidāna*, rendered as nervous disorders by translator. This chapter addresses general medical conditions that appear to affect the nervous system in a dramatic way (convulsions, tetanus, lock jaw) and attentions is focused entirely on their signs and symptoms and pathophysiology. No mention is made to aspects of psychological experience or to social conduct or comportment. This category of disease clearly is set apart from insanity yet some of its manifestations resemble psychiatric condition as this has been defined in this book. Section IV of this same volume is entitled *Cikitsitasthāna* and deals with therapeutics of specific types of diseases. Here again a chapter is devoted to neurological disease and a large number of purely physiologically-based remedies and methods or procedures of therapy are described. In both of these chapters, then, no mention is made of spirits, prayer, oblations, incantations or any other metaphysical phenomena. This is in contrast to fever, which includes such phenomena.

Aṣṭāṅgasaṃgraha's formulation of epilepsy

Epilepsy is defined as loss of an individual's capacity of remembering and recognizing things. Injury or destruction of mental activities by emotions such as fear grief, and worry are singled out as causes:

> *Doṣas* of both the mind and body getting aggravated just as in insanity spread to the mind [and] fill up the channels of consciousness in the person of poor mental stamina.[518]

They produce the seizures, signs and symptoms of which are described in detail. Treatment for the most part involves diet, medicines and bodily procedures but:

---

[518] *Aṣṭāṅgasaṃgraha* 1999: Vol. II, 119.

> In case of epilepsy caused due to seizure of evil spirits and symptoms of *bhūtas* are predominant than those of the *doṣas*, then religious methods to ward off evil spirits should be done.[519]

The epilepsies, then, appear as more organic but do not exclude metaphysical considerations.

The treatment of epilepsy is accorded a special chapter in Volume III of AS. Its content with respect to diagnosis, aetiology, manifestations, and treatment is predominantly physiological. For example, it explains epilepsy as stemming from abnormal condition and stasis of humours or *doṣa*s and movement by channels to the part of the body that causes epilepsy. This chapter makes only passing reference to what one may view as metaphysical considerations.

Aṣṭāṅgasaṃgraha's formulation of insanity

Chapter 9 is titled *Unmādapratiṣedha* and deals with the treatment of insanity. *Unmāda* is described as an intoxication of mind caused by the aggravated *doṣa*s of body and mind. The causes are varied, and include 'naturalistic' factors such as indulgence in harmful food and drink, indulgence in physical activities, and use of poisons. Also included are activities that disrespect the gods or elders and that bring shock to the mind or arising from emotions like love and hatred.

> By these [psychological and moral activities], the *doṣas* get aggravated in a person of poor mental strength, travel to all the parts of the mind, accumulate in the channels of the mind, and cause disorder in the capacity of thinking and produce insanity.[520]

A prominent model of insanity involves a seeming dilapidation of behaviour:

> The person roams about without any control, like a chariot devoid of charioteer ... without understanding either happiness or misery, right conduct or wrong conduct, and behaves without reason/aim, purpose.[521]

---

[519] *Aṣṭāṅgasaṃgraha* 1999: Vol. II, 127.
[520] *Aṣṭāṅgasaṃgraha* 1999: Vol. III, 109.
[521] *Aṣṭāṅgasaṃgraha* 1999: Vol. III, 109.

Abnormality of the *doṣas* is said to bring about insanity and vivid descriptions of each one of them are provided, with manifestations involving appearance, physiological functions, and disturbances of social and psychological behaviour. The description of insanity due to *vāta* concentrates on senseless, irrational behaviour, that of *pitta* on high energy dyscontrol and dyscoordination, and that of *kapha* on quietude, isolation and turning inward. However, there is considerable overlap in these clinical pictures. It cannot be said that abnormality of each of the *doṣas* is associated with clearly demarcated syndromes of behaviour. Neither is it the case that any of the three types conform closely to any of the contemporary disorders or syndromes recognized in systems of biomedical diagnosis in psychiatry yet each includes manifestations consistent with most of them. Perhaps the closest is that of *unmāda* or insanity caused by loss of wealth or a beloved, which resembles contemporary description of a depression disorder:

> The consequent unbearable grief lead to insanity, the person is found pale, timid, bemoans 'alas, it is lost, alas it is lost' etc. cries/weeps without reason, remembers and utters the qualities of the things lost; full of grief in mind he keeps awake always and does activities in the wrong way.[522]

A variety of preparations are described that are used in treatment of insanity. The composition of these is complex and most are used for conditions other than insanity. Non-medicinal approaches to treatment are described. If an episode of insanity results from excess or harmful emotion, then the physician should attempt to mitigate this by providing conditions that elicit opposed emotions. If the behaviour of the victim suggests that an evil spirit may be the cause (spirit possession), then a treatment that wards off that particular spirit should be adopted. Dietary regimen is another resort.

Comment

The content of the material in Vāgbhaṭa is similar to Caraka although its organization differs. In the general chapters on disease and in those related to insanity and epilepsy, the two compilations are similar in topics covered. If anything, Caraka devotes more attention than Vāgbhaṭa to

[522] *Aṣṭāṅgasaṃgraha* 1999: Vol. III, 111.

spiritual, exogenous factors of psychiatric conditions in the specific chapters dealing with insanity and epilepsy. However, the special singling out of disorders caused purely by evil spirits in Vāgbhaṭa is not found in Caraka. This emphasis resembles what is observed in Suśruta as described by Meulenbeld in his paper on ayurvedic psychiatry, a study dealt with in Chapter 8.[523] In general, in Caraka and Vāgbhaṭa, all general medical diseases can implicate psychological and emotional factors as causes and manifestations. Both compilations allow that disease and health are caused by supernatural factors. Morality, regimen, habit patterns, the *doṣas*, the seasons, and a comprehensive scheme about the nature of health and disease are manifest in both Caraka and Vāgbhaṭa. Both compilations also include harmful spiritual influences and forms of possession as relevant and the mechanisms by means of which spirits seize their victims are similar also. The actual theory, philosophy, and/or doctrine regarding the nature of disease including psychiatric condition are very similar. Finally, both compilations reflect a prevailing Indian cultural psychology that incorporates aspects of religion, metaphysics, and philosophical psychology the full implications of which are taken up in a later chapter. Differences between the compilations of Caraka and Vāgbhaṭa and their implications are also taken up discussed in Chapter 8.

BHEḶASAṂHITĀ

The original version of this text could have been compiled in approximately 1000 BCE, but the current version is said to be prepared sometime after the Gupta period.[524]

Bheḷa on irregular fever

The text reviews causes attributed to different physicians and includes the *doṣas* and their combination. It also includes metaphysical factors:

---

[523] Meulenbeld 1997.

[524] P. V. Sharma 1992a.

> Those who opine that diseases are due to the intervention of the gods presume this to be due to the tormentation (*pīḍā*) of the stars in which the person was born.[525]

The text acknowledges diversity of contemporary opinion on nature of fever. Then the preceptor (*ācārya*) of Bheḷa is quoted as follows:

> I am of the opinion that this is indeed ... due to a synergic action (of all the three aggravated *doṣas* of *vāta, pitta,* and *kapha*).[526]

A long description of the physiological and anatomical mechanism of quaternary fever follows and then a reference to metaphysical factors:

> This fever in the body of the organisms is Rudra, violent and born of Maheśvara ... Therefore the physician should attempt (his best) to quieten it down.[527]

An extended description of medicinal and therapeutic procedures follows that focus on physical factors. The chapter ends with the following quote:

> Sacrifices, rituals for peace, oblations, benedictory rituals, bathings and fastings – these quieten down quaternary fever. The Lord of the Bhūtas (or Shiva), the Undestructable and the creator of this disease of fever should be worshipped and this Lord with his Insignia of the Bull, should be approached in the cremation ground (where he stays). The quaternary fever should be destroyed by means of tying up the patient, or with other means and also by the methods of oblation and sacrifices – all as emanating from the Learning of Bhūtavidyās.[528]

Fever, a disease that in Ayurveda has a 'face' validity of physical condition is for the most part construed in organic terms but is not without reference to metaphysical ones.

The nature of insanity

Chapter 7 of *Bheḷasaṃhitā*'s *Nidānasthāna* deals with characteristics of insanity and is short. It discusses three types of insanity, due to aggra-

---

[525] *Bheḷasaṃhitā* 2000: 295.

[526] *Bheḷasaṃhitā* 2000: 295.

[527] *Bheḷasaṃhitā* 2000: 296.

[528] *Bheḷasaṃhitā* 2000: 301.

vation of *pitta* or fire humour, phlegm or *śleṣman* (no mention of wind), and combination of all three humours. It contains little information that is new. In this chapter the *Bheḷasaṃhitā* stresses pathophysiology as cause and changes in social behaviour as its manifestations. Insanity due to aggravation of fire humour is said to lead patient to sing constantly. An individual, whose constitution manifests pre-eminence of phlegm, habitually ingests foods that provoke this humour, and habitually sleeps during the day leads to an excess of the humour. As it ages or becomes faulted phlegm rises from the heart and blocks the channel of consciousness, understanding and comprehension, which is located above the palate. That person's behaviour goes awry: his sensibilities break down and he mimics 'whatever comes across or he fancies'. His mood and conduct becomes inappropriate and he sings and dances and is prone to laugh and cry. Alternatively, the individual will stay or sit in one place 'without any one whomsoever' or may fall asleep as though inert. He may also start frightening others. An aggravation of all three humours causes *sannipāta* and shows manifestations of all three humours (although the wind variety is not discussed).

Insanity can also result from unforeseen circumstances and this is Bheḷa's fifth type, described as insanity caused by 'unforeseen emergencies coming adventitiously'. It is presented, at least initially in its unfolding, as a purely psychological entity in this chapter. Brooding over a setback (loss of money) or death of a 'beloved' can lead to insanity: 'his sensibilities get deviated by (such a) brooding'. He becomes preoccupied by the ideas and feelings and this leads to brooding and talking about them. 'Shock therapy', discussed later, can cure such a patient. However, an ambiguous sentence follows this description:

> In this way the *doṣas* [humours] born in the body are confined in their scope to the body (alone). They torment the body alone as the fire does [the fuel] that has come to its own (fire's) shelter.[529]

This may represent a re-emphasis that predominantly faulted humour(s) is (are) at the root of these types of insanity. The following two paragraphs that end the chapter seem to confirm this: one asserts that spirits, gods, and demons are not responsible for insanity and that preventive measures consisting of emesis, purgation, and administration of

---

[529] *Bheḷasaṃhitā* 2000: 159.

decoctions and unctuous enemas means that 'none will ever attain the terrible diseases of insanity'.[530]

The treatment of insanity

Chapter 8 of Bheḷa's *Cikitsitāsthāna* handles the treatment of insanity. It begins by repeating its pathophysiological and psychological basis:

> These are all but (*api*) the (diverse) exertions and behaviours of *citta* (emotive or the 'heart' element), *buddhi* (intellectual or discriminative element) and *indriyas* (the senses or the elements of sensory perception) ...[531]

and their effect on the intellectual or discriminative element and the senses cause this disease. The importance of the mind as a location between the palate and the crown of the head is stressed: 'It is lordly' over sense organs and is responsible for all intellectual activities, yet *citta*, which is located in the heart, is cited (perhaps a reference to emotions) as 'the reason'. Thus the *Bheḷasaṃhitā* asserts that emotion, conceptualized as feeling/passion and the fire humour, is a basic cause. A good emotive empathy or disposition (*sucitta*) takes a salutary path while those with a poor one (*duścitta*) 'take to deviant courses'. A remarkable formulation follows: a clear analysis of the interaction of thought, emotion, discrimination, moral faculty, and *citta* are said to produce normal, acceptable, laudable behaviour.

> Intellect desires an understanding (*bodhana*) as it indulges in doing what is good and what is bad. What is to be understood is made known to a person (by such a procedure); hence a man is known as a Buddha (one who understands). That intellect is the Great Self (or God) and He is said to be in the body (of a person). It is this He that employs (the person) in (his several) activities, in accordance with what he had been doing (*kṛti*).[532]

There follows an extended explanation that weaves together the mental apparatus, *citta*, body channels and organs (the heart), which in a setting of a calamity that befalls the person leads to insanity.

---

[530] *Bheḷasaṃhitā* 2000: 160.

[531] *Bheḷasaṃhitā* 2000: 345.

[532] *Bheḷasaṃhitā* 2000: 347.

A new construct about psychiatric condition separate from that of insanity is introduced by the *Bheḷasaṃhitā*. It is termed *mada* and is equated with intoxication. When empathy and mind become deviant due to strong emotions (grief, anger, too much joy, or exhilaration, or loss of object, sadness/depression):

> As empathy (*citta*) and the mind (*manas*) (in a person) become deviant because of (excessive) grief, anger or similarly (*tathā*) because of (too much) joy or exhilaration, or because of the loss of a (great amount of) money, *mada* settles down (*nigacchati*) immediately. (In such a condition, the person) becomes moody and broods over-long (*pradhyāyati*), as a result the person weeps aloud with no reason (whatsoever), suddenly laughs out, becomes sleepy and drowsy, or does talk very little, is always anxious and upset; (he is) much tormented (*trasta*) in the body, has a miserable look, or is (ever) angry (and) has no shame whatsoever (*nirapatrapa*); (he) looks in front but does not see things as they really exist (*yathāvṛtta*); (he has) a harshness (in the body) and a turbidity in the hairs (on the body, *lomam*) and also in the eyes. He whose manifestations (*rūpāṇi*) are like this, that (state) is called *mada*. As *mada* thrives forth (*vivardhamanaḥ*), it settles (*nigacchati*) into *unmāda*. The manifestations (*rūpāṇi*) (of) this latter are accompanied with these of the (aggravated) *vāta* (biological air humour). Or (they) may arise due to the (aggravated) *śleṣma* [phlegm] and *pitta* [fire] (*doṣas*). (This) *unmāda* however (*tu*) is spoken of by the learned as being due to a synergic action (*sannipāta*) of all the three *doṣas* acting together.[533]

In this syndrome, one again sees Bheḷa's integration of pathophysiology/-anatomy with psychology in formulating the pathogenesis of insanity.

A list of physical measures involving medicines, sudation, fluids, oil, and foods are prescribed. All of the treatments recommended for epilepsy are said to be useful for insanity and are recommended. There follows an extended discussion of what one may describe as emotional counter-therapy.

> (Such a person) should be hit by whips, tied up (to a post) and also beaten. (He) should be tormented by means of an elephant or a horse (let loose on him as it were) or by means of a serpent. (He) should again be strewn about all around with fire and flames of the lit up hay (*tṛṇāgni*) or by scattering (all around similarly) the burning coals of *paribhadraka*; (he) should again be treated (*prayuktam*) with cold water thrown forcefully (*abhukṣṇayet*) against; (he) should be spread about in a flowing river and should be obstructed (immediately) from thus get-

---

[533] *Bheḷasaṃhitā* 2000: 348.

> ting spread or floating about; or (he should be) exhausted with hunger and thrown and throwing him in a well, persons bearing weapons should frighten him in unforeseen or unique manners. (In this way) physicians should torment him much by several kinds of tortures.[534]

The text goes to emphasize that 'such tormentations' if too severe would aggravate or distort the *citta* 'by the very fear' it creates, in which case it leads to a misfortune and is to be avoided. No better proof is needed that while the *Bheḷasaṃhitā* largely emphasizes organic factors it also is very 'psychological' just as it does not exclude metaphysical factors.

Dietary and herbal remedies and other procedures used in epilepsy are recommended once again. Yet, despite the largely pathophysiological basis of insanity, the chapter ends with an acknowledgement of the efficacy of metaphysical therapies:

> A physician of the mental diseases should perform rituals for peace as well as oblations (in fire). The sacrificial ceremonies specially meant for securing specific desires or *iṣṭis*, ritual for securing peace, oblations about the Vedas and they are all the works to be carried out and are destructive of Insanity.[535]

It is not clear whether this recommendation involves a referral to a separate physician priest, expert in demonology, or conjuration or whether it is assumed that the ayurvedic physician himself is expected to perform these measures. At any rated it appears clear that such metaphysical treatments are considered appropriate and are to be recommended.

Bheḷa on epilepsy

Chapter 8 of *Nidānasthāna* expounds on epilepsy of which four varieties are described. The three *doṣa*s and their combination make up four varieties. A pathophysiology is presented (not unlike that for insanity) and clear description of seizures follows. Poor diet is said to aggravate the *doṣa*s and the body:

---

[534] *Bheḷasaṃhitā* 2000: 349.

[535] *Bheḷasaṃhitā* 2000: 351.

> *Apasmāra* (epilepsy) is due only because of non-salutary foods ... [and faulted *doṣas*] ... It is not that he becomes struck down with (evil) spirits (and hence becomes epileptic).[536]

Chapter 9 of *Cikitsitāsthāna* addresses the treatment of epilepsy. The material covers pathophysiology and physical treatments. No mention is made of psychological causes or of metaphysical factors in treatment or cause. This conception stands in contrast to *Bheḷasaṃhitā*'s position on fevers and insanity.

COMMENT: THE VIEW OF PSYCHIATRIC PRACTICE IN THE SIDDHA SYSTEM OF MEDICINE

Heretofore, Siddha has been examined as one of the several interrelated traditions comprised of beliefs and practices of popular religion that were salient during the medieval era in particular. Along with Yoga, Tantra, Buddhism, and sectarian Hinduism, the Siddha tradition involved widely shared practical, oriented beliefs and methods to relieve emotional/behavioural discomfitures and disaffections in relation to everyday problems with the added twist of alchemy and iatrochemistry. Salvation, liberation, and perfected health of body and being were essential goals reached via minerals, herbal preparations, and diverse mental procedures of concentration, sometimes involving altered states of consciousness and sexual practices. However, Siddha also constituted a system of curative medicine pure and simple, although perhaps less well articulated and more shadowy as to its reach in contemporary populations of the subcontinent when compared to Ayurveda. During the medieval era in particular, Siddha medicine (sometimes considered as Tamil medicine) was a theory and practice prominent in South India. As a curative system, Siddha medicine had and may still have a distinct psychiatric component.

Somasundaram and colleagues have reviewed what they regard as the psychiatry of Siddha medicine.[537] They point out that the roots of this system are found in the 'supernatural powers' and 'school of great knowledge' associated with the 18 personages known as Nandivarga

---

[536] *Bheḷasaṃhitā* 2000: 163.

[537] Somasundaram, Jayaramakrishnan, and Sureshkumar 1986.

Siddhas.[538] The theory and practice of Siddha medicine is represented in the 'still standard text books' that contemporary Indian medical practitioners consult. Its physiology is humoral. Positive health results when its three humours (*vali*, *azhal*, and *iyam*) function as expected (gaseous control of movement and activity of body, control of temperature and metabolism, and control and stability of fluids, respectively) and form their proper 4:2:1 proportion in the body. Each humour when in excess causes its own constellation of signs and symptoms, both physical and mental. Moreover, physiognomy and temperament are related to humour function, with Siddha medicine exemplifying a somato- and behaviour/temperament-typing.

The psychiatry of the Siddha system of curative medicine has several sources among the Siddhars, individuals who achieve an exemplary religious character, the most important being Agasthivar, Voogi, and Theraiyar. Their descriptions are said include a 'phenomenological' dimension.

> The unifying factor in Siddha Psychiatry is the importance laid on the imbalance of the three humours, especially the predominance of Azhal humour over the other two. The Siddhars approved of the possible predisposition to mental illness due to constitutional make up, seasonal variation and other variables like dietetic habits, age, and sex of individuals. [539]

This bears a strong resemblance to ideas found in Ayurveda. According to Somansudaram and co-workers, there exist correspondences between the Siddha description of syndromes of psychiatric interest with disorders adumbrated in contemporary diagnostic categories (schizophrenia, mania, depression, catatonic excitement). Treatment involves herbal preparations and aspects of psychotherapy are mentioned as well. Somansundaram and co-workers conclude their presentation as follows:

> Siddha system of medicine which dates back to early BC is an excellent scientific work rendered in poetic form ... Somatotyping ... on the basis of proportion of humours ... and the temperament associated with each type is also minutely described ... classification of epileptic disorders and symptoms of various psychiatric illness [is found] ... The

---

[538] See also White 1996.

[539] Somasundaram, Jayaramakrishnan, and Sureshkumar 1986: 39.

> efficacy of their preparations stands the test of time as is evidenced by the use of Peranda Parpam for certain psychotic conditions even today ... The underlying philosophy ... is not only curative but also preventive.[540]

WHAT DO AYURVEDA TEXTS SUGGEST ABOUT PSYCHIATRIC PHENOMENA IN TRADITIONAL INDIA?

General considerations

The anatomy and physiology of the body and its vulnerability to disease and injury represent human universals. Differences in genetic factors, physical environmental factors, social environmental circumstances, and diet and other ecological factors will vary across populations, of course, but not the way in which they undermine health and cause organic disease. Hence, it is no surprise that Ayurveda's encyclopaedic texts record a myriad of such organic manifestations of disease; for example, skin eruptions or discolouration, crampy abdominal distress, vomiting of blood, respiratory distress, bloody sputum, pain or blood on urination, anal fistulas and haemorrhoids, painful and tender abscesses and localized swellings, fractures, convulsions, and gross enlargement of the abdomen and extremities (ascites and oedema). Moreover, it is bodily suffering and distress and a visible context of sickness and disability that adhere to such manifestations. They are visible to the naked eye the world over and manifest in tangible signs and clear-cut, readily identifiable symptoms. Hence, Ayurveda's description of such obvious manifestations of disease, or their representation in any society' ethno-medicine, is and would be transparent to any observer. However, how they are made sense of and explained and treated will understandably differ as a function on cultural medical beliefs and practices.

The brain, a hierarchically arranged organization of information handling systems controlling experience and behaviour, is also a human universal. Like any organ of the body it also can break down and produce manifestations, in this instance involving disaffections and disturbances of experience, emotion, and behaviour. These also are in some ways visible; for example, as per verbal report of feelings and emotions, display of attitudes and dispositions, content and organization of

---

[540] Somasundaram, Jayaramakrishnan, and Sureshkumar 1986: 44–45.

thought, and social conduct. However, disturbances such as these (psychiatric conditions) are not concretely and transparently linked to the body (although as discussed repeatedly in earlier chapters, they can be associated with general visceral somatic, and neuro-vegetative changes, but these do not transparently point to phenomena which was described above as organic). A people's ideas and beliefs about relatively intangible, and more opaque phenomena, namely, the nature of experience, behaviour (normal, abnormal, deviant or different), and how persons reflect or distort their probably altered sense of social reality (as per psychiatric condition), are brought into play to interpret and relate the resulting change in behaviour to ongoing circumstances (as per psychiatric condition).

Psychiatric conditions in the population of traditional India

What is codified in Ayurveda texts involves a cultural gloss or reading of the psychiatric conditions found in the population that *were conceptualized as medical*. The insanities of Ayurveda encompass a variety of psychiatric conditions, not just psychosis or madness or craziness. Diverse aspects of thought, behaviour and experience are included as well, phenomena corresponding to anxiety, depression, excitement, possession, mental confusion, eccentricity; behavioural inhibition, isolation, or breakdown; and paranoia. Most of the phenomena included in Ayurveda psychiatry viewed as behavioural phenomena represent human universals and much of it also is construed as abnormal or maladaptive, also cultural universals.

An important clue regarding psychiatric conditions in populations of traditional India involves the representation of *bhūta* in Ayurveda texts, namely, disturbances of emotional behaviour and social conduct that were construed as possession or attack of spirits. As material in the texts that were reviewed demonstrated, all four compilations make reference to these conditions although they give varying emphasis to them, some including them as bona fide entities some in certain respects deferring judgment as to their 'somatic' basis but including them nonetheless (Suśruta's and Bheḷa's *Saṃhitās*). Moreover, some included *bhūtas* in the inventory of insanities (given different causes, manifestations and treatments) whereas Suśruta placed them in a separate chapter and did not construe them as insanity. Nevertheless, whether placed in a special or common chapter for and named or not named as insanity the *bhūtas* are assigned a different, special cause. In this sense, they were *sui generis,* disturbances of thought, emotion, and social conduct in a class by themselves, so to speak.

The *bhūtas* can be assumed to have represented an important component of *bhūtavidyās* in Vedic ethno-medicine and ethno-psychiatry. Descriptions of *Atharvaveda* material that were reviewed in earlier chapters are consistent with the supposition that in the subcontinent the *bhūtas* (the constructs and the behavioural phenomena itself) preceded those of the Ayurveda. In the Ayurveda texts they are still described in religious terms and their causes still involve mythical, legendary, divine, and/or feared/demonic beings and treatments include religious procedures and practices. Studies in cultural and biological anthropology support the supposition that beliefs in and syndromes of behaviour about spirit possession are found in small and elementary societies the world over, and especially in societies thought to represent exemplars of earliest human social organization. In particular, syndromes such as these have been described in hunter-gatherers in the India of today.[541]

Ayurveda knowledge suggests that, in addition to academically trained physicians, the practice of psychiatry and medicine in traditional India was complemented by a range of practitioners whose beliefs and practices centred on purely metaphysical considerations. It is doubtful whether experts in demonology, witchcraft, or religion (those outside Ayurveda and mentioned in its texts) concentrated purely on disturbances of experience and behaviour (psychiatric conditions); however, by definition their beliefs and practices addressed unwanted phenomena (behaviour, disease, mishaps, blocked goals, marital discord). Because ayurvedic texts did include and address behavioural disturbances as medical phenomena seen (also) in religious terms and to varying extents amenable to naturalistic (as pathophysiology or organic) explanation they present a picture of the epidemiology of psychiatric conditions and facets of the indigenous psychiatry of traditional India.

In many respects formulation of causes, manifestations, and treatment for the diseases included under fever conform to the way such matters are formulated for insanities.[542] This is an interesting generalization. Although the overall tone and resonance of these two exemplars of ayurvedic diseases, and, to a large extent, epilepsy as well, is definitely

---

[541] Bird-David 1999.

[542] *Bheḷasaṃhitā*'s section on fever is presumed to be lost.

different, in a logical and analytical sense they show correspondence. There do not appear to be any clear criteria about emotional disaffection and behavioural disturbance (psychiatric conditions) that allows one to distinguish between Ayurveda insanities and Ayurveda *bhūtas other than their presumed and preferred explanatory model of causation*. There exist two possible exceptions to this generalization. They include *behavioural breakdown or dilapidation* per se and prominent *organic manifestations*, both more likely to be included as part of insanity but not the *bhūtavidyās*. This,. however, is a matter of degree. Only *Suśrutasaṃhitā*'s *bhūta*s and *Bheḷasaṃhitā*'s epilepsy do not, by and large, include the two classes of manifestations.

*Bhūta*s and the evolution of indigenous psychiatry in India

Spiritual, magical, religious or, as termed here, metaphysical psychiatric conditions provide one with a focus in terms of which change has taken place in Indian societies of the subcontinent. If observations of cultural, biological, and evolutionary anthropologists are taken into consideration, prior to the time when the Aryans supervened in the subcontinent the ethno-medicine and ethno-psychiatry of Indian communities was predominantly magico-religious and shamanistic. It could just as well be conceptualized as metaphysical since understanding of sickness and healing, while always including practical, 'organic' considerations, drew on knowledge and communications with unseen but real nonetheless 'other than natural' agencies (spirits, demons, ancestors witchcraft) in explaining and treating enigmatic, persistent conditions, and especially those manifesting in disturbances of experience, emotion, and the organization social behaviour or conduct. Possession and attack of such spirits figured importantly in this ethno-medicine and ethno-psychiatry. This involved not just explanation but also manifestations. In other words, psychiatric conditions were symbolic and communicative: syndrome of behaviour that encased them conformed to models of what the metaphysical domain was like, how it worked, and who were its agents.

Vedic medicine changed this state of affairs. Given larger communities, concentration of medical phenomena in light of settled communities, the possibility of pooling knowledge across generations, and especially emergence of a unique world-view, consisting of a system of religious, philosophical, cosmogonic, moral, and eschatological beliefs and directives, a priestly superstructure was added to the protohistoric, pre-

Vedic medicine. There probably was a phase when 'disciplines' or communities or schools of medicine competed with one another and selected special areas of praxis. It is reasonable to presume that medicine of Aryans like that of ancient Iranians showed different emphases and components, such as proposed by Meulenbeld:

> (1) treatment by means of iatrochemical compounds, (2) treatment by means of medicinal plants, (3) treatment by means of surgery, and (4) treatment by means of mantras.[543]

However, it is unlikely these formed nicely separate categories or compartments in the ethno-medicine and ethno-psychiatry of the period. Given what one can observe about the medicines of contemporary non-industrial, non-modern societies (and in the complementary-alternative sector of modern nation states), practitioners and clients were probably eclectic and pluralism was a regnant characteristic of their practice and in expectations of patients.

There followed the transition from a medicine and psychiatry based largely on metaphysics, or an expansion of those groups more centred on surgery and herbal, to one more organicist, namely, based more on pathophysiology/-anatomy. This was discussed earlier with emphasis given to Buddhist thought and medical practice in monasteries. The transition took place during a time of religious and social crisis in the subcontinent. The evolving medicine acquired a systematic character and it is hard to presume that this property of the evolving medicine – just like philosophy, religion, morality – was not influenced by writing, even though earliest unambiguous Ayurveda texts are not available until presumably in the earliest centuries of the Common Era.[544]

With the emergence of systematic, scholarly, academic, and textually based medicine there arose the need to incorporate explanations, practices, and descriptions of actual conditions of sickness that were and had been prevalent in the subcontinent for centuries if not millennia. These involved the 'metaphysical' domain, exemplified by the *bhūtas*. It is possible that purely politico-economic factors involving re-affirmation of Brahmanic power were factors that led to incorporation of 'metaphysical' medicine in an otherwise organic medicine. *Suśrutasaṃhitā*'s placement of such conditions in a special volume is consistent with this

---

[543] Meulenbeld 1997: 183.

[544] Goody 1977, 1986, 1987.

explanation,[545] but in the *Carakasaṃhitā* 'metaphysics' seems to be interwoven into the fabric of the texts of the insanities, fevers, and epilepsy, suggesting that the psychiatric conditions in the population were driving factors, and probably had been earlier.

Given the availability of more textual material, the fate of the *bhūtas* following the early classical phase of Ayurveda is somewhat easier to document as is also their influence as a marker of the subsequent history and evolution of Ayurveda psychiatry.

ON THE ACCOMPLISHMENT OF AYURVEDIC PSYCHIATRY

From the standpoint of a general, world history of psychiatry it is easy to take for granted the immense accomplishment of Ayurveda. It essentially demarcated and objectified the territory of what has been referred to here as psychiatric phenomena, namely, conditions of impaired mental health and their medical interpretation and treatment. From the holistic and global sweep of Vedic medicine in the domain of psychiatry, Ayurveda managed to articulate a distinct territory comprised of discrete and articulated sets of concepts and empirical tenets pertaining to behaviour, pathophysiology, diagnostics, and therapeutics. These were brought to bear on individuals whose inner complexity and outer interconnectedness with nature, the social fabric, the spiritual, and the cosmic and timeless, were never slighted.

A protean and inchoate material alluding to forms of behavioural and medical suffering in Vedic medicine gave way to types of admittedly loosely defined but epistemically differentiated syndromes of abnormal experience and behaviour. A network of causes that is comprehensive is brought to bear on varieties of human abnormality that are by definition, replete with complicated forms of abnormal, deviant experiences and behaviour that continue to elude classification and understanding even today in the era of international aspirations for a universal psychiatry. In other words, in this system of medicine one finds an attempt to place in one bin a myriad of disaffections of emotion, behaviour, and bodily functions that modern medicine still equates as psychiatric. Greek and Roman medicine may have provided what on first in-

---

[545] Termed an addendum by Meulenbeld 1997.

spection appear to represent more specifically identifiable 'modern' and bona fide psychiatric disorders. However, some of the relevance of this psychiatry results from continuity of descriptive language found in the Western history of psychiatry. Sanskrit vocabulary of psychiatric phenomena is not today part of international psychiatry as is Greek and Roman medical vocabulary, in many ways an accident of history, geography, and political economy. Yet, phenomena covered by both ancient systems of psychiatry overlap and equally cover the complex territory of psychiatric phenomena. With respect to how systematically a naturalistic domain of health, sickness, and medical practice is set apart, ayurvedic medicine and especially its psychiatry seems in most ways the equal of that of the traditions of the Mediterranean societies of antiquity. Furthermore, mainly in Ayurveda does one find a self-conscious compartmentalization of the psychiatric domain. In Ayurveda, causes link to manifestations and these to principles of diagnosis that themselves stipulate specific guidelines pertaining to therapeutics equal to the task of the tradition's broad and comprehensive sweep. A Greek physiology of a quasi-psychiatric condition (epilepsy or 'the sacred' disease) is also found in the Hippocratic texts.

Ayurvedic medicine and psychiatry thus constitute a milestone in the cultural understanding and control of psychiatric conditions not only in the subcontinent but also in a world history of medicine. It consolidated theories of diagnosis and healing and provided an organized framework of understanding about mental health and illness. In this sense it was an advance over what preceded it: a new phase in the cultural evolution of psychiatric phenomena not only in the subcontinent but perhaps in the world during early parts of the first millennium BCE when Ayurveda was probably consolidated. During the time of its formulation, a predominantly metaphysical conceptualization of abnormal experience and behaviour was reconstructed and reconfigured; in hindsight, we can refer to these as mental health and illness problems. Ayurvedic psychiatry comprised an epistemology and therapeutics based on Indian medicine that was rooted in careful observation, description, empiricism, and naturalistic forms of reasoning and evaluation.

In a fundamental sense, the *construction of psychiatric phenomena* changed. A vocabulary and idiom that was based on a naturalistic and systematically differentiated approach to abnormal experience and breakdowns of behaviour was added to the prevailing ones that encompassed general tenets linked purely to spirituality, religion, philosophical psychology, and folk wisdom. This of course is one facet of the general evolution of psychiatric phenomena: how syndromes, their victims, and treatments they obtain situate and move about and through the social fabric changes as modes of their interpretation change. In other words, as a consequence of the spread of ayurvedic psychiatry, a change takes place in *gaze and approach* to abnormal experience and behaviour and in the *social trajectory* of victims.

Devotional behaviour and ecstatic, mystical states of spiritual insight and longing can present dilemmas of interpretation to one who charts the path of psychiatric phenomena across any social landscape and this is no different for India. The influence of myths about 'divine' madness and actual behaviours of 'madness of saints' indicates that models of psychiatric condition play an important role in Indian religious psychology and social life.[546] Whether 'mad behaviour' constitutes a medical condition or religious inspiration represents a paradigm case of the dilemma of generalizing about psychiatric phenomena cross-culturally, a dilemma played out in the actual lives of saints (discussed in detail in Chapter 10). In India, material detailing how devotees and intelligentsia dealt with seemingly inspired but disordered members of the congregation makes it clear that a 'naturalistic, ayurvedic psychiatry' was one of the idioms that competed in contests of interpretation.[547] The material reviewed by McDaniel, of course, centred on developments during the modern era. However, there seems to be little reason to doubt that the idiom of ayurvedic naturalism was used since the beginning of the Common Era in order to make sense of persons showing extreme changes of experience and behaviour wherever they may have occurred.[548] Depending on the community's size and position in the geography of a society, the ayurvedic challenge would have probably differed in tone and emphasis. But it would have been represented nonetheless, although surely challenged later by Islamic, Western, and other doctrines of medicine. However, Ayurveda's power and salience through the centuries has been unchallenged until the modern era.

As societies and cultures evolve, so do the idioms for making sense of psychiatric conditions, as these surround crisis points and situations of a society that stress vulnerable individuals. This leads to changes in

---

[546] Kinsley 1974; McDaniel 1989.

[547] McDaniel 1989.

[548] Kinsley 1974.

the perceptions and understandings of victims as well as audience. In a fundamental sense, the latter are challenged to respond to the actions of victims showing a syndrome of fractious, divisive, or distraught behaviour. In effect, a contest between competing systems of meanings takes place. If a naturalistic viewpoint gains ascendancy, then, in a basic sense, one can claim a change in the social and cultural constitution of the syndrome. Experience and behaviour do not take place in a social vacuum. Rather, they are interactive and iterative as a result of attributions by symbol wielding members of a significant group who by definition are linked to each other in complex ways. Social and psychological behaviour, then, springs from and resonates in a culturally shared context of symbols and their meanings about the nature of social 'reality' including normality and abnormality. The general point is that (1) symbols and idioms about psychiatric condition are subject to historical change; (2) in relation to this, the perceptions, interpretations, and alternative responses of group mates also change, and along with this the victim's own conceptions and behaviour; (3) Ayurveda imposed a partly empirical and naturalistic epistemology of medicine; and as a result (4) *essential descriptive aspects as well as interpretations of psychiatric condition* in the subcontinent were modified. Still, one may surmise that the distinctive cultural psychology of the Indian people continued to be influential in interpretations of psychiatric condition.

FINAL COMMENT

Exactly where and when in the subcontinent Ayurveda took hold as an alternative approach to sickness and psychiatric condition is impossible to ascertain. To take hold does not mean to negate or nullify alternative interpretations. Ayurveda broadened and deepened the manifold of interpretation of psychiatric conditions. It did not displace but complemented pre-existing frameworks of meaning. Material reviewed earlier suggests that an important setting was in cities and among the prosperous elite. However, in villages and rural hamlets, and perhaps even in tribal areas, people may have had access to ayurvedic physicians and especially to their ideas and methods of treatment. This is the case because one cultural domain to which it spread was places of formal religious worship such as temples, monasteries, shrines, centres of pilgrimage and other localities that housed gods and saints. In these localities one would have found diviners and priests along with practitioners of humour-based folk medicine. Some physicians trained in Ayurveda were located in these centres, others were given land grants in their proximity and still others would have simply been attracted to them. Persons afflicted by intractable, debilitating, and religiously ominous medical problems would have been taken to these sacred places. Results of empirical studies reviewed earlier that are based on populations attending or housed in religious establishments suggest that in earlier centuries one would have found there persons showing delusions, hallucinations, recurring episodes of altered states of consciousness, irrational anger, depression, anxiety, and other kinds of psychological suffering. Whatever the immediate cause, these aberrations would have been explained in the new naturalistic medical idiom. However, as material discussed earlier indicates, even physicians practicing early Ayurveda tenets would have had recourse as well to a religious and philosophical psychology idiom – for example, sickness and psychiatric condition as stemming from transgressions against sacred, moral traditions and rules of conduct. Even if not seen as retribution by spiritual agents, the conditions would be thought to require a spiritual understanding and form of healing.

In time, the new naturalistic approach to sickness and psychiatric condition probably grew in influence in the first centuries CE. It complemented but did not necessarily invalidate the pre-existing, parallel one that was permeated with magic, religion, and spirituality.

With the advent of Ayurveda, the cultural evolution of psychiatric phenomena in the civilization of southern Asia entered a new developmental phase. A medical naturalism became important in diagnosis and treatment. It spread to the family, caste, village, and hinterland. The tradition evolved as compilers of medical wisdom, theoreticians, and renowned physicians commented on and reinterpreted key tenets of ayurvedic theory. In other words, as explanations and interpretations of sickness and psychiatric condition changed and elaborated, so also did the conditions themselves: for physician observations, queries and treatment emphases were communicated to patients and family who learned new ways of making sense and experiencing their maladies. In time, and in South India, the academic, scientific indigenous tradition of Siddha medicine became an important component of Indian medicine. It drew from Dravidian culture and Tamil literature, but had obvious connections with the ayurvedic main stalk.[549] Siddha medicine, and the traditions of the perfected religious adepts termed Siddhars, embodied complex features of Tantra, Yoga, and alchemy.[550] Later, during the middle ages, to this amalgam was added Islamic or Unani medicine (largely Galenic), and eventually Western biomedicine. The cultural infrastructure of psychiatric phenomena by and large retained its religious/spiritual and moral/ethical character but a superstructure of professional and secular interpretations acquired significance in some social spaces.

---

549 Somasundaram, Jayaramakrishnan, and Sureshkumar 1986; P. V. Sharma 1992b.

550 White 1996.

Appendix

Characteristics of Psychiatric Condition in the *Carakasaṃhitā*

DEFINITION OF INSANITY OR *UNMĀDA*

Insanity, it should be known, is the derangement of the mind, understanding, knowledge, memory, devotion, behaviour, acts, and practices.

Vulnerability factors

Viewed as 'psychological' by contemporary conventions

- Timidity or vulnerability to fear;
- Abnormal invocation of tantric ordinances;
- Other abnormalities of religious practices (reciting śāstric texts in a crematorium, remaining with head downwards for several hours;
- Harbouring feelings of lust, wrath, cupidity, joy, fear, grief, worries, anxieties.

Viewed as 'somatic' by contemporary conventions

- Abnormal levels of the humours. Ingestion of food mixed with impurities that has spoiled (vitiated), poorly digestible, prepared without regard to harmony of combination and without attending to traditional considerations of *prakṛti*, karma, *saṃyoga*.
- Those whose bodies show emaciation.

Viewed as 'psychosomatic' by contemporary conventions

With affliction of wind and the understanding being disturbed, the humours get aggravated and provoked; they settle in the heart causing obstruction in the channels through which the mind operates, they beget insanity.

Incubatory symptoms of the disease

Viewed as 'psychological' by contemporary conventions

- Thoughtfulness with regard to matters that do not deserve to be thought of;
- Toiling for objects that no way deserve toil;
- Wondering at things that should not excite wonder;
- Anxiety about objects that are of no interest;
- Constant excitement of the mind;
- Restlessness of the eyes so that the gaze is now directed towards one object and now towards another;
- Diverse sounds in the ears [possible auditory hallucinations];
- Diverse and unusual dream imagery [beholding objects that are whirling around or disgusting, mounting on oil machines that are circling around, feeling that one is sinking in strong eddies of dirty water];
- Frequent horripilation [bristling of hair, flesh, or body as in gooseflesh or terror].

Viewed as 'somatic' by contemporary conventions

- A sensation of the head being empty;
- Turbidness of the eyes;
- Discharge of watery secretions from the mouth;
- Loss of appetite, and disgust for food;
- Indigestion;
- Facial contortions;
- Pressure on the chest (as if some heavy object is placed on it);
- Appearance of eruptions on the body like *urticaria evanida*.

The distinctive symptoms of each of the humoral insanities contain a mixture of elements

Wind insanities:

- Stretching of the lips, the shoulders, the cheeks, the arms, and the legs, without any cause;
- Frequent utterance of irrelevant words;
- The emission of froth from the mouth;

- Indulgence in smile, laughter, dancing, singing, and playing on instruments, on unsuitable occasions;
- Imitating the sounds of *vīṇā*, flutes, conch-shells, and *saṃya*, and striking of palms against each other unmelodiously;
- Bedecking the person with such things as are never used for ornamentation by others;
- Fierceness or fury of disposition;
- Malice or incapacity to bear the sight of other people's happiness;
- Emaciation of the body;
- Roughness of the body;
- Redness of the eyes, which seem, again, to come out.

Insanity born of the bile:
- Incapacity to bear the least annoyance;
- Exhibition of wrath;
- Indulgence in boastfulness;
- Rushing at relatives or strangers, with weapons, brick-bats, whips, clubs, or closed fists, or striking them therewith;
- Excessive heat of the body (accompanied by burning sensation);
- A coppery, or green, or yellow colour of the eyes, which besides become steadfast.

Insanity born of the phlegm:
- Sitting in one place (for long hours and from day-to-day);
- Rigid observance of taciturnity;
- Discharge of salivary and phlegmonous secretions from the mouth and the nose;
- Desire for solitude and privacy;
- Excess of sleep;
- Dropsical swellings on the face;
- Paleness and fixedness of the eyes, which, besides, become covered with filthy secretions.

Insanity should be known as born of all the three faults when the symptoms presented are those, in a combined states, of each of the faults (as enumerated above). Such insanity is regarded incurable by those who are well-versed in the science of medicine.

Accidental types of insanity

Description

That variety of insanity is called accidental, which is characterized by causes, incubatory indications, and pronounced symptoms, differing from those of the fault-born [humoral] varieties.

General characteristics

- Some say that the evil acts of previous lives are the cause of this variety of insanity (that which is called accidental).
- The truth is, this one (the person afflicted by accidental insanity) does evil by disregarding the deities, the *ṛṣi*s, the *pitṛ*s, the *gandharvas*, this *yakṣa*s, the *rākṣasa*s, the *piśāca*s, seniors, men of advanced years, the *siddha*s, preceptors, and others deserving of worship; or commits some other sinful acts of this kind.
- The afflicting deities and others make such a person, already afflicted himself, insane.

Incubatory symptoms

Of one who is about to be afflicted with accidental insanity having for its cause the wrath of deities and others, the incubatory symptoms are these:

- A disposition to injure the deities, kine, Brahmins, and ascetics;
- A wrathful temperament;
- Cherishing cruel purposes and intentions;
- Absence of contentment;
- Morbidness of *ojas*, complexion, lustre, strength, and flesh;
- Admonitions and rebukes administered, in dreams, by the deities and others;
- Instigations, by those beings, to particular acts (in dreams).

Agents causing accidental insanities

- It should be stated here that the following are the several acts, with regard to persons who are about to be afflicted with insanity, of the several orders of superhuman beings who bring about insanity.
- The deities generate insanity by directing their gaze (to the persons with whom they are offended).
- Seniors, and persons of advanced age, and *siddhas*, and *ṛṣis* cause it by enouncing curses.
- The *pitṛs* bring it about by forcible assaults.
- The *gandharvas* do it by touch.
- The *yakṣas* do it by entering into the bodies of the persons.
- The *rākṣasas* bring about insanity by causing the persons to inhale their scent.
- The *piśācas*, again, bring about this disease by riding on the necks or heads of the persons and using them as convenient beasts.

Manifestations

The following are the symptoms of insanity that is accidental (caused by the influence of deities and others:

- Superhuman strength, energy, capacity for exertion, prowess, apprehension, conservation, reproduction, speech, knowledge, and science.

The time, again, is not fixed for the exhibition of the fits of insanity.

Verily, of deities and *ṛṣis* ... and those who bring about insanity, the following are the occasions when persons become objects of assault.

- At the commencement of sinful acts;
- At the time when the fruits are about to manifest themselves of the (sinful) acts of former lives;
- At the time when one remains alone in a deserted house;
- At those places where four roads meet, during the morning and the evening twilight;
- At those times when one remains in an unguarded (unclean or impure) state;
- At times of sexual congress if such act is indulged on the joining hours of *parvan* days;

- At the time when one has sexual contact with a woman in her menses;
- On occasions when improprieties creep into the performance of such acts as the study (or recitation) of the Vedas, the dedication of offerings to the deities, rites of propitiation, and the pouring of libations on the sacrificial fire;
- At those times when one swerves from religious observances and vows and *brahmacarya*;
- At such times when the great planets course from one sign to another;
- As regards women, when they are about to bring forth children;
- At such times when one touches different kinds of inauspicious creatures (as dogs, jackals, vultures, etc.) and impure things (as hair, ashes, bones, etc.);
- At such times when one vomits or purges or has discharges of blood from one's body;
- At such times when one goes in a state of impurity or condition of negligence in respect of dress, speech, etc., to the vicinage of a sacred tree or the temple of a deity;
- At such times when one remains impure after having eaten flesh, honey, sesame, treacle, and wine;
- At such times when one remains in a state of nudity;
- When one goes, during the hours of night, to such spots in towns and cities where four roads meet;
- When one goes, during such hours, to gardens and pleasure-groves and cremation grounds;
- At such times when one insults and humiliates Brahmins and seniors and deities, and *yatis* and others that are deserving of reverence;
- At such times when defects occur in the recitation of religious treatises;
- At the commencement of unrighteous acts.

There are three objects for the attainment of which the superhuman beings spoken of cause insanity.

- These are (1) the desire to kill or wound; (2) the desire for pleasure; and (3) the desire for obtaining respectful worship.
- These objects of those insanity-causing beings may be ascertained from the particular indications of the conduct of the insane.

- Amongst these three objects, the desire to kill or wound becomes manifest when the person who becomes insane enters a blazing fire, or drowns himself in water, or leaps down into holes and pits, or strikes himself with weapons and clubs and brick-bats and his own closed fists, or does other acts for destroying himself.
- Those cases of insanity in which the insane person seeks to destroy his own life should be known as incurable.

On the morality of accidental insanities: Neither the deities, nor gandharvas, nor piśācas, nor rākṣasas nor others afflict a man. The truth is that, man afflicts himself.

- This affliction is not on account of those deities and others who pursue the man, for the latter (in reality) is afflicted by his own acts.
- Indeed, in the matter of this affliction, the deities and others have no direct agency.
- When the disease is generated by error of judgment, an intelligent person should regard it as born of the diseased man's own acts. He should never name the deities, or the *pitṛs*, or the *rākṣasas* as the cause.
- One should regard one's own self as the agent of one's own pleasure and pain. Hence, one should betake oneself to the path which leads to what is good, and never swerve from it.
- Contributing to the gratification of the deities and others, practice of all that is good, and avoidance of everything that leads to a disagreement with them – all these are within one's own competence.

Chapter 8

The Scope of Mental Health Practices in Traditional India

INTRODUCTION

In a general, analytical sense mental wellness or health designates an unspecified, open human universal. The construct refers not just to the absence of emotional pain or social distress, but something positive in a personal and behavioural sense. However, how mental health is defined, experienced, expressed, and sought out depends on systems of meaning or culture. In relation to India, and as construed in this book, mental health involves a person's sense of overall wellbeing conditioned on satisfaction with social station and moral standing viewed in relation to local situations and circumstances (family, caste) and spiritual, other-worldly concerns. It encompasses optimism, confidence and hope as well as a positive morale fundamental to effective coping and comfort with an individual's place in the scheme of things as he or she sees them. An important indicator of how well a society or civilization succeeds as a human enterprise depends on the extent to which it promotes mental health or welfare in a population. To do this it enables its members to successfully (positively) overcome (existential, social) factors or impediments that undermine optimism, hope, and coping abilities and this includes, but is not limited to, manifestations of conditions of psychiatric interest.

The emergence and achievement of Ayurveda contributed to mental and physical health positively through its provision of a body of theory and practice that improved wellbeing in a general sense. It also marks a positive change in understanding and handling of conditions of psychiatric interest in the subcontinent as well as a major landmark in the history and theory of medicine that includes psychiatry. The cultural and political significance and intellectual power of Ayurveda as a naturalistic medicine slowly modified but never effaced old, purely Vedic ways of thinking with respect to disease generally and conditions of psychiatric interest more specifically. Because Ayurveda constitutes a blend of Vedic 'metaphysics' and traditional, pre-modern science it has earned its high place among the learned and intellectually unique accomplishments of Indian civilization. The challenge and promise that Ayurveda introduced in the social life of India around the beginning of the Common Era came to be appreciated more fully with the passage of time and was then assimilated. Efforts of modern scholars and theorists to critically examine and understand the theory, claims, and scope of Ayurveda insights as per psychiatric condition are discussed in this chapter.

The range of human problems addressed by Ayurveda directs one to examine how it set about to ameliorate them and why it was or was not successful as a body of theory and practice. One can think of such an assessment as examining the medical validity of Ayurveda or any discipline that functions to relieve suffering, pain, misery, and social disorder. Such an examination and analysis leads one to clarify what is unique about Ayurveda and raise the question of other bodies of theory and praxis that influence mental health. This question is relevant because Ayurveda is not the only learned Indian institution that has had a major impact on the mental health of pre-modern Indian societies. This chapter also discusses factors that need to be considered in an assessment of how and why Ayurveda worked in pre-modern India and ways in which it differed from but also resembled other institutions that dealt with problems of mental health and conditions of psychiatric interest.

To accomplish this successfully it would be desirable to understand the medical theories and practices of accomplished adepts referred to as *siddhas*. The study of Siddha medicine brings to mind an emphasis on physiology, much like Ayurveda, but with a predominant emphasis on iatrochemistry or alchemy.[551] It has its own psychiatric dimensions that will be taken up later.[552] A concerted and sustained anthropological inquiry involving Siddha medicine in modern India was not entirely satisfactory and fruitful, for reasons about which its own expositor remains unclear.[553] While Siddha as medicine is construed as a parallel or spin-off from Ayurveda having a strong alchemical emphasis, its iden-

[551] P. V. Sharma 1992b.

[552] Somasundaram, Jayaramakrishnan, and Sureshkumar 1986.

[553] Hausman 1996.

tity as a purely curative discipline now and perhaps in pre-modern India is less well defined than Ayurveda.

However, viewed in broad context, Siddha covers far more that curative medicine. It should be lumped with the more influential and long lasting Tantra and Yoga as disciplines and institutions constituted of knowledge and practice that achieved high profile in medieval India, the mental health implications of which are enormous. These movements emerged in more visible form around 600 CE, but drew on and elaborated earlier thought and praxis of the Vedas, 'popular' Hinduism, Buddhism, and the various philosophical schools.[554] Siddha, Yoga, and Tantra involved practices of concentration and meditation aimed at focusing the mind and leading to release of the self from attachments and the cycle of rebirth. These movements or traditions involved far more than just curative medicine and their mental health implications also strayed well beyond the realm of conditions of psychiatric interest. Furthermore, while converts, devotees and adepts may have represented a selected, arguably more urban, group committed to exploring purely intellectual as well as soteriological pursuits, many of their clients or followers were concerned with village-centred dilemmas of everyday life of the common folk. This is especially the case because communication of ideas and practices of *siddhas*, yogins, tantrics, gurus, and practitioners of related movements and traditions, in association with ideas richly exemplified in epics and especially the *Bhagavadgītā*, had a massive influence on sectarian religion.[555] The latter is not limited to purely spiritual or eschatological and soteriological considerations but also encompasses everyday, concrete concerns as well, what Mandelbaum describes as transcendental and pragmatic aspects of religion, respectively.[556] In this context the more religious, spiritual, Bhakti-oriented traditions, along with Ayurveda, contributed in a major way to mental health and healing of conditions of psychiatric interest.[557]

A study of the scope and influence of Ayurveda in pre-modern India necessarily leads in two directions. The first is to probe its constructs and theory and examine its validity as a medical and mental health discipline. The second is to map its contours in the social fabric

---

[554] Dasgupta 1922; White 1996; Feuerstein 1998; Whicher 1998.

[555] Mlecko 1982.

[556] Mandelbaum 1966.

[557] Fields 2001.

and examine how it differs from, yet also resembles, other traditions and movements comprised of theory and practice that, while not strictly involved in the business of curative medicine, nevertheless had profound influence on mental health and practice. These matters are also discussed in subsequent sections of the chapter.

Commonalities and differences between Ayurveda and Tantra, Yoga, and Siddha tell one part of the history of mental illness in the subcontinent. Besides its tie to strictly non-medical disciplines, how Ayurveda differed from Islamic tradition of medicine and the mutual influences each had on the other represents an additional chapter of this story of how indigenous psychiatry and the psychiatric enterprise worked in traditional India. Ideally, one hopes to clarify the extent to which the configuration and enactment of psychiatric phenomena changed in the subcontinent following the wake of Islamic influence. This would lay the groundwork for developments that come to pass with the advent of modernity and the spread of biomedical psychiatry. But these topics are taken up in subsequent chapters.

THEORY AND CLASSIFICATION OF MENTAL DISORDERS IN AYURVEDA

Standard compilations of Ayurveda provide a reasonably clear and consistent picture of how conditions of psychiatric interest were defined and conceptualized in this tradition. This provides a baseline for critical analysis. Ramu and co-workers discuss why Ayurveda should properly be understood as a scholarly, academic, and scientific theoretical system of medicine.[558] They rely on root linguistic terms, derived from classical sources, which they have translated. This means that when rendered in another language, these terms have been visualized through an indeterminate degree of editing and transformation involving judgments not only between linguistic systems but also between two semantic domains or conceptual frameworks, the ancient Indian one and the contemporary psychiatric-psychological one. According to these scholars, the appropriate way in which to appreciate the depth and focus of ayurvedic psychiatric condition is not only or simply as *unmāda*, madness, but rather

[558] Ramu, Venkataram, and Janakiramaiah 1988.

as *manovikāra* or *mānasavikāra*, mental disorder. Such terms, like that employed here, namely, 'psychiatric condition', better comprehend the power of the ayurvedic vision of the psychiatric domain. According to them, when one unpacks the ayurvedic psychiatric territory six varieties of mental disorder come into view: (1) impairment of general mental functions (*mānasa* karmas, such as disordered perception and motor control in the absence of organic problems), inability to make decisions, loss of memory, responsiveness, and desire, aberrant conduct, temperament, and psychomotor activity; (2) weak psyche (*alpasattva*) in the genesis of the illness; (3) disorders of the humours, which are responsible for physical, physiological, and psychological functions and behaviour patterns; this includes disorders of the two psychological aspects of the mind governing activity (characterized by excessive talking), egoism, anger, arrogance, and jealousy); and inertia (characterized by fear, ignorance, excessive sleep, lethargy, and tastelessness); (4) involvement of both body and mind, or mind alone; (5) either classic mental disorders or mind–body disorders; (6) vitiated 'pores' or 'conveyers' of material aspects of mind, which operate throughout the body.[559]

Ramu *et al.* agree that psychosis (*unmāda*) as defined in the *Carakasaṃhitā* is an appropriate covering prototype of mental disorders, since one or more of the basic aspects of mental function and behaviour are affected by it. These consist of aspects of mind, decision, memory, desire, habits and temperament, psychomotor activity, conduct, and orientation and responsiveness. In their analysis of the epistemology of Ayurveda, a weak psyche and vitiated anatomical organs and channels explain a disorder's manifestations, course, progress, natural history, severity, and prognosis.

This, in essence, is the basic conceptual structure of disease as well as psychiatric condition in ayurvedic medicine. Diseases are classified in various ways, according to aetiology, zone of resort, organ of genesis, prognosis, severity, the humours involved, and the bodily channels and anatomical sites where the humours collect. Classification can be based on the degree of involvement of any of these factors. While from our contemporary logic some diseases, including psychiatric condition, can appear primarily mental, rather than bodily, and some as mind–body, body–mind unities, such a classification is not feasible in Ayurveda:

---

[559] Often this refers to the head, brain, and heart, which are most closely related to mental functions.

> Since all diseases affect the living body, which is a combination of *sharīra* [body], *indriya* [senses], *sattva* [psyche], and *ātmā* [self] wherein, even if one of them is disturbed, the remaining three are also affected.[560]

Although the classic sources hint at intricate ways of classifying diseases, Ayurveda physicians do not actually provide a classification of them or of mental disorders. For example, in addition to concentrating and sharpening causation, as in the case of endogenous (humoral physiology) compared to exogenous varieties of insanity (spirit attack), Caraka essentially presents an encyclopaedic account of clinically relevant facts for generic categories of disease. Having studied the classic sources, Ramu *et al.* propose a way of equating ayurvedic psychiatric condition with modern concerns: (1) abnormal emotions, such as passion, anger, infatuation, envy, pride, arrogance, grief, anxiety, worry, fear, exhilaration, anguish, jealousy, and meanness; (2) abnormalities caused by an imbalance of one of the three humours, such as auditory hallucinations, withdrawal, confusion, sadness, anguish, excessive loquacity, insomnia, fickleness, hypersomnia; (3) mental disorders with body-to-mind involvement, such as psychosis, epilepsy, obsession, hysteria, intoxication, alcoholism, fainting, coma, toxic psychosis, and hydrophobia; and (4) mental disorders with mind-to-body involvement. Ramu *et al.* describe two complex syndromes in depth: *udvega* and *viṣāda*, roughly comparable to anxiety and depression.

The *Carakasaṃhitā* can seem overwhelming in its detail, variety, and redundancy of material. When its many categories and concepts are teased apart and distinguished, it appears to provide a system of constructs and theoretical principles in terms of which virtually any known syndrome could be diagnosed and categorized. One who studies ayurvedic psychiatry seems to be transferred back over the millennia, to enter the mind of a competent, but hypothetical, to be sure, diagnostician and practitioner. The journey provides one with a tutorial and its slant on how what the modern student now defines as psychiatric condition was conceptualized at that time. The scheme of Ramu *et al.* may in fact reflect the collective mind of a fully knowledgeable, hypothetical ancient ayurvedic diagnostician-practitioner, as embodied in the complete system of diagnosis and theory of mental illness obtained from classical texts. On the other hand, their scheme may merely reflect the

---

[560] Ramu, Venkataram, and Janakiramaiah 1988: 42.

knowledge of these contemporary reviewers who are steeped in the modern science of psychopathology and clinical psychiatry. The modern formulation of Ramu *et al.* is their own model of Ayurveda, and arguably it is unlikely to have been explicit in the mind of practitioners but certainly implicit.

Ramu *et al.* provide an interesting account of ayurvedic psychiatry. However, can the schema be productively used or applied today as a system of diagnosis and classification? Here there are problems. Some concepts are ambiguous and imprecise, even redundant. Other concepts may be impossible to measure, since they are abstract and metaphysical. Nevertheless, some key concepts might be reliably measured and then subjected to further testing to enable diagnosis and classification in the ayurvedic way. This might be the next step in resurrecting ayurvedic psychiatry and testing its power to classify and heal modern varieties of conditions of psychiatric interest.

Not surprisingly, and in keeping with the modernity influence that Ramu and co-workers reflects, their description and classification of psychiatric condition is abstract, generic, and impersonal. It contains little of the posited cultural psychology of India, the contents of which have been alluded to earlier and are taken up in detail in the following chapter. These academics focus pretty much on clinical aspects of conditions of psychiatric interest as are conceptualized in today's Western culture dominated epistemology of the reigning secular psychiatry. The cultural tenets that colour and give nuance to experience, thought and behaviour are left out of their clinical calculus. This, to be fair, is what even the canonical texts of Caraka, Suśruta, Bheḷa, and Vāgbhaṭa tend to do and Ramu and co-workers have followed suit. Except for the exogenous varieties and the demon/spirit-caused conditions (*bhūta*),[561] hints and clues in the classics about how actual clinicians may have formulated social, interpersonal, and experiential factors in their patients are left out of focus. Their approach to healing-on-the-ground disturbances of experience and behaviour that tapped into humanistic, social, and moral concerns are simply ignored or played down in the classics. In this respect, these scholars resemble Chattopadhyaya, who emphasizes purely general, naturalistic aspects of ayurvedic medicine, extolling its scientific breakthrough and minimizing remnants of ancient traditions, this time of purely magico-religious and metaphysical

[561] See discussion in the following section.

ideas.[562] With respect to the alleged secularism of Ayurveda, one has to keep in mind that patients of ancient ayurvedic practitioners would have been enmeshed in any number of social relationships, burdened by distress and emotions linked to their obligations in the world. They suffered from true psychiatric disorders, as defined in biomedicine today, or from general stress-related effects tied to structural factors of the society, neither of which the religious wing of the indigenous psychiatry could appropriate and assimilate. Vulnerable individuals who suffered from allegedly 'secularized' and antiseptic conditions of psychiatric interest only made sense in light of their cultural psychology, world-view and ongoing concerns. In other words, echoes of what their symptoms meant and implied in the moral drama of their lives – present, past, and future – would have unquestionably formed part of the clinical picture. However, the classification system given us here contains no categories that could take into account such broader and indeed vital existential concerns.

In the schema of mental disorders proposed by Ramu *et al.*, cultural values and social concerns sometimes appear, but in a muted way. For example, emotional disorders make reference to passion, anger, infatuation, envy, and pride – social emotions that if properly examined would entail aspects of cultural psychology played out in consequential Indian social realities. However, in the schema proposed, they appear merely as 'signs', largely devoid of existential import. Mental disorders caused by exclusive involvement of one of the three biological principles (*vāta, pitta,* and *kapha*) make reference to 'sadness-anguish' and 'fickleness'. These, again, carry faint echoes of persons caught in human existential dramas, but they connect to clinical concerns of ayurvedic psychiatry in a most tangential and sanitized way. The other two main classes of mental disorders contain even less reference to culturally significant themes.

In noting this style of diagnosis, one may ask whether ayurvedic psychiatry is as reductionistic as the biomedical psychiatry of today. In a society and culture as deeply spiritual, moral, introspective, and concerned with metaphysical and soteriological questions as that of ancient India, was there really in existence an objective, impersonal system of psychiatry, as modern biomedical psychiatry tries to be? Were humane aspects of psychiatric care and practice in ancient India characteristically

[562] D. Chattopadhyaya 1977.

a part of practitioner–client, physician–patient relationships? Did the ayurvedic system of abstract, impersonal diagnosis and classification of disease mean equally objective and impersonal rules of practice? Did ayurvedic physicians view the maladies of their patients shorn of their connections to the social, ethical, and spiritual circumstances and everyday concerns? Earlier discussions have emphasized the integrated character of Ayurveda, the tendency to encompass the whole of the patient's life. Hence the seeming objectivity and reductionism of the classification and epistemology proposed by Ramu *et al.* is puzzling. Kakar provides examples of contemporary clinical encounters that strongly challenge culturally sterile ayurvedic psychiatry.[563]

A CRITICAL LOOK AT AYURVEDIC PSYCHIATRIC CONSTRUCTS AND PRINCIPLES

Introduction

The writings of Indian medical authorities record not only how practitioners and theorists formulated medical topics but also how consumers of this medical tradition – patients, family members, the literate community, and folk or popular practitioners influenced by scholarly ideas – probably interpreted, handled, and, in a way, construed psychiatric condition. All of a practitioner's patients would have presented a complex assortment of symptoms and signs, feelings, worries, and sufferings rooted in specific social circumstances and expressed in an idiom shaped by and expressive of the ethno- or cultural psychology of India. The content and implications of this psychology are discussed in the following chapter. However, at least from the way in which renowned physicians seem to boil down sickness and the psychiatric in their compilations, there is a suggestion of objectification of the medical encounter. This mode of representation may be a consequence of sheer demands for spread of textualized knowledge and emphasis on theory, rather than of how knowledge was actually applied and processed in interactions with real patients.

Early in the social history of India conditions of psychiatric interest had a predominantly 'magico-religious' (termed metaphysical) meaning

563 Kakar 1982.

involving an individual's social condition and possibility of possession and spirits. However, following Vedic medicine, it is probably the case that in seeking treatment and as a result of interactions with physicians, a proportion of patients and their families may have come to view at least some of their maladies (their social and psychological distress) in ways that resembled the professional, naturalistic language of the new medicine. In other words, dry and impersonal ayurvedic theory and needs for direct and efficient practical considerations of curative medicine probably operated as factors that influenced the naturalistic language which physicians used and consumers learned. However, as discussed earlier, a purely naturalistic or organic approach does not appear to describe the way conditions of psychiatric interest were understood and handled.

Rather than addressing ayurvedic psychiatry in a general way as many researchers have done, others opt for specificity and detailed analysis.[564] Meulenbeld has examined the whole tradition of Indian medicine in historical context, that is, from the point of view of early classics and later additions and emendations by acclaimed physicians.[565] He also has brought the broad sweep of Ayurveda to bear on psychiatric phenomena per se.[566]

Psychiatry as an ayurvedic medical discipline

Psychiatry represented a principal division of ayurvedic medicine. The creation of a special category on insanity and of other conditions of psychiatric interest involving spirit attack attests to this. *Bhūtavidyā* as listed in the *Chāndogya-Upanishad* is one of the disciplines of knowledge and involves spiritual, demonic elements.[567] Meulenbeld indicates that of the eight branches of Indian medicine, one involved treatment of insanity and epilepsy, which he glosses as *bhūtavidyā*. Other branches included internal medicine, paediatrics, surgery, toxicology.[568] Retention of the term *bhūtavidyā* suggests that this branch of medicine was once con-

[564] Dube 1978; Haldipur 1984, 1985, 1989; Bhugra 1996, 2001.

[565] Meulenbeld 1999–2002.

[566] Meulenbeld 1997.

[567] Lal Gaur 1992.

[568] Meulenbeld 1997. Meulenbeld opines that in ancient times each branch of medicine had its own specialists.

cerned with disorders attributed to spirit possession. Meulenbeld assumes that it was a carryover from a religious tradition of medicine, as described in the *Atharvaveda,* because the term *bhūtacikitsaka* means an exorcist or religious healer. For Meulenbeld, the meaning of *bhūtavidyā* came to influence and may in fact have changed to include all types of insanities or conditions of psychiatric interest. In association with this process, the metaphysical, possession *bhūta*s were reinterpreted as having if not actual natural causes certainly natural correlates in the system of physiology that involved somatic processes, humours, and their circulation and contamination or congestion in bodily organs.

In some compilations of medicine, this possible root base of the mental disorders is retained as *bhūtonmāda,* which, along with *unmāda* (insanity) and *apasmāra* (epilepsy), make up conditions of psychiatric interest. Earlier, attention was given to the differences in the way four ayurvedic texts handled fever, insanity, epilepsy, and related conditions of psychiatric interest and diseases caused by evil spirits. While differences in emphasis were found between these types, the logic or analytical focus for these conditions was similar. This brings up the question of possible change in emphasis and tone between Ayurveda texts that were compiled during different periods, starting roughly 200 to 600 CE. Discussion in the previous chapter suggested that when examined in their entirety, writings on essential characteristics of psychiatric condition in India point to changes in terminology and meaning, namely, to different styles as well as different representation of psychiatric, and of course, general medical, phenomena. To the extent that medical compilations stand for ideas and practices implemented by physicians in real life but in different historical and cultural circumstances, changing representations of knowledge indicate cultural change and evolution in the theory, practice, and institution of medicine including psychiatry.

As suggested earlier, it is reasonable to assume that change in emphasis and in writings of acclaimed physicians corresponded not only to change in scientific and clinical understanding but to changes in the popular view of psychiatric condition. This probably worked in two ways. Physicians taught and spread new academic knowledge insofar as they were agents of an important cultural institution holding considerable social power. Thus, they influenced ideas and beliefs of people across all levels of society and regions of the subcontinent. On the other hand, ayurvedic physicians were also educated, clever, and insightful learners of popular or folk medical traditions and were in the position of learning its tenets. It is reasonable to assume that insights gleamed from popular medicine made their way into the formal texts. Indeed, as material discussed earlier indicates, Ayurveda itself owes its existence to insights and observations of renunciants and scholar monks who during the centuries preceding the Common Era were deeply insinuated into the workings of popular medicine and religion of their times.

Commonalities and complexities in psychiatric knowledge

Meulenbeld's analysis, when placed in an evolutionary context, suggests similarities and differences in the way psychiatric condition was conceptualized in ayurvedic compilations across centuries and even millennia.[569] One complex issue, already discussed, is the tension between 'metaphysical' and 'organic' or 'somatic' factors. This centres on the influences of evil spirits, the supernatural in general, and actions carried over from previous lives compared to aspects of natural body functions (like digestion especially) and the role of the humours or *doṣas* as affected by happenings in the individual's current life. Another one is the influence of such things as regimen of diet and physical characteristics and activities as compared to aspects of social and psychological behaviour including emotions, the morality of behaviour, the motives and impulses that describe a person's general orientation. Unfortunately, Meulenbeld does not examine in any detail the question of whether there is a clear and systematic progression in tone and emphasis in the way conditions of psychiatric interest were conceptualized across the span of medical compilations. His massive compilation of Indian medicine contains the relevant information but combing it so as to measure changes in details or is prohibitively cumbersome and probably impossible given the intellectual variation and messiness of texts and emendations. Meulenbeld's general point seems to be that Indian medical literature grappled with a series of topics of relevance to psychiatry. A unitary and somewhat static general tradition of great variety and complexity is suggested – echoes of what Ramu *et al.* emphasize, as discussed earlier – that is, a waxing and waning in the importance attributed to factors and concepts originally described in the classics of Caraka, Suśruta, Bheḷa, Vāgbhaṭa and many other renowned compila-

[569] Meulenbeld 1997.

tions. Themes and variations rather than a clear movement toward a consolidation are what Meulenbeld's analysis suggests.

Explanations of how a psychiatric condition arises (its pathogenesis) in Ayurveda are also complex and inconsistent. Generally, the various substances and processes that explain psychiatric condition in naturalistic terms are said to operate not in the brain per se, but in the heart:

> In Indian thought in general, mental processes are usually not regarded as connected with the brain, but, instead, with the heart (*hṛdaya*).[570]

But the Suśruta compilation mentions the mind (*manas*), and not the heart, as the locus of pathology.[571] As already indicated, Bheḷa holds that psychiatric condition is the result of corrupted humours reaching the *manas*, which he places between the cranium and the palate (at the base of the brain?), where the corrupted *manas* cause disorders of two psychic organs, the *citta* and the *buddhi*. Most generally, however,

> insanity develops, according to the generally accepted classical theory, when corrupted humours reach the heart and obstruct the channel transporting the *manas*.[572]

The following concepts are important causes of psychiatric condition in the Ayurveda tradition. The three bodily humours or *doṣas* (wind, bile, and phlegm) have already been discussed. There are two similar substances, also termed *doṣas* or *mānasadoṣas*, which affect the mind and are termed *rajas* and *tamas*. Ideas about the three constituents (*guṇas*) of the universe are also part of the Ayurveda conceptual apparatus. As suggested in earlier discussions of Sāṃkhya philosophy, all of these terms and constructs and many more can be construed as the ideological component of the cultural or ethno-psychology of psychiatric condition.[573] However, as noted, the various medical compilations are confused and inconsistent regarding the functions of the humours and the relations among the various other substances and world elements. A tradition of such antiquity, with an initial basis in verbal communication, is inevitably subject to this kind of confusion and incoherence.

---

[570] Meulenbeld 1997: 189.

[571] This refers to a psychic organ that actually is located in the heart.

[572] Meulenbeld 1997: 190.

[573] Dasgupta 1922; Obeyesekere 1977, 1982.

A principle of psychosomatic–somatopsychic integration clearly operates in the way conditions of psychiatric interest are formulated in Ayurveda. Bodily-based diseases cause mental symptoms, and mental symptoms lead to or cause bodily disorders. There is even a correspondence between the symptoms caused by the bodily *doṣa*s (humours) and the *mānasadoṣa*s (mind-affecting substances similar to the humours). Both sets of pathogenic agents bring about insanities or *bhūta*s with diverse manifestations that do not easily conform to contemporary models of psychiatric disorders. The *Carakasaṃhitā* lists selected manifestations found in *unmāda* and some of its varieties.[574] Manifestations are segregated into the more mental compared to bodily categories. Taken together, the information as well as the manifestation labelled 'psychosomatic' in the Appendix of Chapter 7 attests to the holistic, integrated character inherent in the way *Carakasaṃhitā* construes conditions of psychiatric interest. This way of construing conditions of psychiatric interest applies to conditions brought on by metaphysical agents and it characterizes all of the text discussed in the previous chapter. This pattern clearly sets Ayurveda psychiatry apart from our, contemporary preoccupation with the 'psyche' of psychiatric disorders.

The pathophysiology of Ayurveda conditions of psychiatric interest (*unmāda* and/or *bhūta*s) is no less complex. However, there are commonalities. Earlier review of material indicated that there are first of all the types caused by the three humours individually and by all three humours together. According to Meulenbeld, surveying the whole expanse of Indian medical literature, food intake and digestion serves an important theoretical and temporal fulcrum linking psychiatric condition caused by the humours and their clinical manifestations. A clue about a condition is often the colour of the skin. While no larger theory links skin colour to psychiatric condition, this bodily marker is important in Indian medical writings. It was mentioned in the descriptions of conditions discussed in the last chapter. Meulenbeld points this out to emphasize the uniqueness and complexity of the epistemology of Ayurveda regarding the role of humours in conditions of psychiatric interest and partly to counter the generalizations of Weiss, who posits a correspondence between humoral types of insanity and disorders in the Western classification system of psychiatry.[575]

[574] See Chapter 7, Appendix.

[575] Weiss 1977, 1980.

Meulenbeld concurs that conditions of psychiatric interest brought on by possession and strong emotions do not reach the magnitude of psychosis. As discussed in the previous chapter, manifestations of the *bhūtas* have a different emphasis (more socially communicative, symbolic) and also appear to represent more serious conditions than the 'pure' humoral types. This is actually very difficult to validate, given the variety of symptoms listed. However, in general manifestations suggesting behavioural breakdown (psychosis) seem to be more in evidence in the humoral types, and especially when aggravation, or faulting of more than one humour is involved. Seven emotions are important: anxiety, grief, and frustrated love predominate, but anger, greed, envy, and excitement are sometimes added. As suggested earlier, the *Bheḷasaṃhitā* is exceptional in the way in which it handles emotions in relation to conditions of psychiatric interest. To begin with, it locates the mind anatomically and describes its characteristics and/or mode of operation (e.g., perception, thought, emotion). The *Bheḷasaṃhitā* goes on to emphasize how a concatenation of intellectual and emotional setbacks can cause of rising of bodily (i.e., physiological) disturbances upwards such as to overwhelm the person's adaptive abilities in which case the syndrome of *mada* gives way to *unmāda*. Commentators differ regarding psychiatric condition caused by intense emotions as opposed to the humours, some emphasizing the distinction, and others attempting to combine them (excited emotions lead to an excitement of the humours).

The *bhūtas* are discussed in different, and inconsistent, ways in the compilations. Some authorities hold that spirit possession actually takes place; others that the basis of the possession lies in the similarity between the pathological manifestations and the characteristic behaviour of the offending spirit, with afflicted persons adopting these patterns voluntarily; and still others that possession psychopathologies are caused by the spirits' glancing at or cursing the patient. Caraka, Suśruta, and Vāgbhaṭa relate the onset or recrudescence of symptoms to a particular day in the lunar cycle, and this 'pathognomonic sign', according to Meulenbeld, clearly separates these conditions from the humoral ones, whose symptoms relate to eating and digesting food.

The *raison d'etre* or pathogenesis of the *bhūtonmādas* is also disputed with respect to the actions precipitating an attack of spirits, which in turn causes the malady and eventually the faulted, aggravated humours. Here, the ambiguity involves whether spirits punish for bad action in past lives, which would imply that treatment would be ineffective, at the behest of past actions of others – and sometimes both views are found in the same collection – compared to moral transgressions stemming from inter-current defective insight and behaviour in the present life. Finally, there is inconsistency in that both the *bhūtonmāda*s and the humoral conditions are sometimes treated differently. For example, in the *Carakasaṃhitā* there is no distinction between mild drugs and religious measures, and it does not specify special treatments for the various *bhūtonmāda*s, whereas the *Suśrutasaṃhitā* does.

Ontology of personality and its pathologies

Psychiatric conditions per se, as discussed earlier, represent a significant focus of ayurvedic curative medicine. A characterology or theory of personality types is also found in some treatises, but its medical implications and relationship to conditions of psychiatric interest in particular are not entirely clear. There are many inconsistencies in the way the texts handle personality or character types.[576] In the medical texts of Caraka, Suśruta, Bheḷa, and Kāśyapa, the link between character types (termed *sattva* or *kāya*) and the various *bhūta*s is very prominent and the latter manifest and are explained as exaggerations of the 'normal' character types.[577] However, many character types are described in the medical treatises and they are 'actually innumerable' given combinations and gradations. They are not all represented in different varieties of possession. The term *sattva* carries the same meaning as *manas* (mind), a psychic organ. Yet the character types refer not only to psychological mental dispositions or behaviour manifestations but also have a physical basis.

Character types are classified according to the three Sāṃkhya constituents (*guṇas*). These include *sattva, rajas,* and *tamas* and yield three classes of character types, *sāttvika, rājasa,* and *tāmasa,* which are further subdivided into many types that are named in terms of gods and living beings. Interestingly, *sattva* types apply not only to humans but also to animals, especially horses and elephants, and thus are integral to Indian veterinary medicine. Meulenbeld discounts the importance of character types in medicine.

---

[576] Meulenbeld 1997.

[577] Meulenbeld 1997.

> That the elaborate typology of human beings does not belong to the central parts of Ayurveda is attested by the fact that human character types are of no importance to the practice of medicine.[578]

Yet, while exaggeration of the features of the various characters including that of *sattva* is equated with vulnerability to possession and can mark its manifestations or characteristics, the treatises also assert that *sattva* (as compared to the two other *guṇas*) does not lead to organic disease. While it is not a '*mānasadoṣa,* only *rajas* and *tamas* are', the treatises are unclear about this since the *guṇas* contain mixtures of each other. Meulenbeld opines that the various *sattva* types are like the *bhūtas*: they exemplify phenomena that are ambiguous and that Ayurveda as a system of naturalistic medicine equivocated on.

The Sāṃkhyan basic constituents of the universe (the three *guṇas*) form but one of the many typologies of individual differences that is important in Ayurveda. Many others are found and have distinctive properties. For example, some are based on the three humours, which give rise to seven types of combinations into constitutions and which are featured by mental and bodily or 'physical' characteristics. Second, types are based on *ẹlements* of the body (*dhātu*). The constitutions are called *sāra* of which there are eight, although differently represented in the treatises. These constitutions also have mental and bodily characteristics and persons can be endowed with more than one variety. Various features of an individual's resistance to disease and overall health are ascribed to mixtures and types of *sāras*. Third, the *Suśrutasaṃhitā* points out that a typology of character types based on preponderance of one of the five *mahābhūtas* as elements of *prakṛtis* is found among medical authorities. These *prakṛtis* consist of mixtures of mental and bodily characteristics. The elements of wind, fire, and water are regarded as identical to windy, bilious, and phlegmatic constitution and thus are not used, only ether or space and earth. However, according to Meulenbeld, a commentator in Suśruta indicates that some physicians identify as many as 31 constitutions based on mixtures of two, three, four, and all five *mahābhūtas*. Fourth, types are based on the three *guṇas* and called *sattva.*

[578] Meulenbeld 1997: 198.

A neuropsychiatric focus in Ayurveda

Contemporary psychiatry is currently under the sway of a neurobiological reductionism. The push is toward the neural sciences rather than the psychological and social sciences, a situation not unlike the nineteenth-century tension between the psychosomatic and the organic emphases in Europe.[579] Today there is even a sub-discipline of neuropsychiatry that handles the behavioural difficulties related to neurological diseases and disorders caused by brain injury. Thus, it is refreshing to note that Ayurveda reflects a similar explicit overlap with respect to characteristics of epilepsy – a neurological disease to us today – and conditions of psychiatric interest involving disorders of consciousness that may not necessarily be based on cerebral organic pathology but certainly can resemble and overlap with them in actual cases.

As mentioned earlier, the possession syndromes of Ayurveda are examples of conditions that conflate neurological and psychological factors. In some instances Ayurveda links disorders glossed as epilepsy and those due to metaphysical factors and 'possession'. This was manifest in the texts of Caraka, Suśruta and Vāgbhaṭa. However, it will be recalled that this was not the case in the *Bheḷasaṃhitā* and that Vāgbhaṭa's *Aṣṭāṅgasaṃgraha* has a category that includes neurological conditions and no reference was made in that section to aspects of metaphysics or psychological factors. To Bheḷa and Vāgbhaṭa, then, epilepsy and neurological disorders are clearly conceptualized differently from Caraka and the *Suśrutasaṃhitā*. Perhaps the root of this ambiguity or inconsistency is that convulsions or seizures and motor behaviour abnormalities can have either organic or psychological causes, sometimes both. Even today, in many cases, only an electroencephalographic reading during an actual convulsion or altered mental or behavioural state can establish that the episode has a neurological basis. The later ayurvedic literature introduces other classes of disorders that in complex ways involve the emotions, body symptoms, unusual posturing, involuntary movements, hysteria-like manifestations, mental instability, and trembling, resulting from head injuries and accumulation of fluid in the head. Although these are not well described, they illustrate the broad sweep of Ayurveda and its tendency to distinguish among disorders

---

[579] Fabrega 1992a, 1992b.

that in a complex way involve body and mental-behavioural problems.[580]

Three other conditions of psychiatric interest reveal the ambiguity and inconsistency in descriptions of pathogenesis. The first is a class of grave disorders called *mahāgada* or *atattvābhiniveśa*, the two names reflecting the ambiguity of its definition and analysis in the various compilations. In some instances it is not included at all. The *Carakasaṃhitā*, for example, mentions it only under the treatment but not the aetiology of epilepsy and it appears to be interpolated by certain followers of Caraka. Its description conveys the flavour of how conditions of psychiatric interest were handled by Ayurveda:

> When, made corrupted by various corrupting factors, the humours reach the heart, corrupt the vessels transporting *manas* and *buddhi*, and stay there in someone whose mind is covered by *rajas* and *moha* [*tamas*], this person, whose *buddhi* and *manas* are covered by the increased *rajas* and *tamas* and whose heart is bewildered by the humours, becomes confused and his *cetanā* (consciousness) diminishes; his judgment is impaired with regard to things eternal and transient, wholesome and unwholesome; the authorities call this major illness *atattvābhiniveśa*.[581]

This disorder is treated by drugs and by the psychological support of steadfast and wise friends.

The humour-based disorder termed *mada* provides another example of the complexities and inconsistencies in Ayurveda psychiatry. Caraka presents this as one of three severe illnesses, *mada*, *mūrchā*, and *saṃnyāsa*, caused by the humours in those whose minds are affected by *rajas* (excitement) and *tamas* (darkness). All three entail mental confusion (*moha*) caused by damage to the channels transporting consciousness (*samjñā*). Vāgbhaṭa links these disorders to alcohol abuse. Meulenbeld points out that some authorities simply fail to give it a distinct identity. Caraka distinguishes four types based on the humours but indicates that they can also come about as a result of blood, alcohol, and poisons. According to Caraka and Vāgbhaṭa, signs of *mada* include bodily and mental changes due to the humours, although the *Carakasaṃhitā* also includes disorders arising from *mānasadoṣas* (substances related to the *doṣas* that affect the mind). Caraka also uses *mada* to refer to arrogance associated

[580] Meulenbeld 1997.

[581] Meulenbeld 1997: 202.

with alcohol intoxication and indicates that intoxication with other substances can have the same result. He regards it not only as a disease, but as a symptom of other diseases, including psychiatric condition. Bheḷa uses *mada* to mean conditions of psychiatric interest caused by intense emotions.

A similar enigmatic construct with neuropsychiatric resonance is *mūrchā*, described as loss of consciousness preceded by visual disturbances. According to Caraka and Vāgbhaṭa, four varieties caused by the humours are described, one resembling epilepsy. Meulenbeld interprets it, termed *saṃnyāsa*, as fainting spells or temporal lobe epilepsy, recovery from which requires formal treatment. However, the link to general medicine and sickness is evident once again since the term is also used to designate fevers stemming from disturbances from all three humours. In *saṃnyāsa* the individual loses consciousness suddenly and remains in an apparent comatose state for a long period of time. It is likely that this condition referred to cerebral hemorrhage or ruptured brain aneurysm, but in some instances it may have pointed to altered states of consciousness having a psychological basis. Meulenbeld singles out several other disorders that have a predominantly neurological character, perhaps in some instances with neuropsychiatric overtones, namely, *apatantraka, apatānaka, ākṣepaka, daṇḍapatānaka,* and *pratānaka.*

Dreams provide another theoretical focus for connections between brain and mind. One supposes that Ayurveda's emphasis on connection between psychology, sickness, and psychiatric condition would have included attention to dreams. However, it appears that few medical authorities regarded dreams as useful to physicians. However, a relation between emotions, poisons, and disease was recognized, as mentioned earlier. Suśruta included both, but, according to Meulenbeld, Caraka, did not mention poisons and handled strong emotions ambiguously. In Bheḷa's compilation, strong emotions are responsible for an altogether different variety of psychiatric condition; they are termed *mada,* and not *unmāda.* In general, explicit relationships were drawn between emotions and humours, on the one hand, and somatic disorders, on the other. Sleep disorders and sexual disorders were also understood to have a possible relationship to psychiatric condition. Disorders associated with alcohol consumption were also related to the humours in complex ways. And finally, epilepsy was seen to entail the humours, the vessels around the heart, and movement toward the brain. In some instances, a variety of epilepsy is linked to possession, but this is disputed or not mentioned in other compilations.

VISUALIZING EVOLUTION OF AYURVEDIC PSYCHIATRY

From the standpoint of the evolution of the medical segment of premodern India's indigenous psychiatry several trends can be inferred from a careful analysis of Ayurveda generally and aspects of Indian psychiatry, more specifically. A starting point is that there existed a popular, folk medicine in the subcontinent, partially represented in the Vedas, especially the *Atharvaveda*. This facet of psychiatric phenomena was covered in earlier chapters. Many scholars have indicated that the emergence of Ayurveda constituted a major transformation in the approach to disease and its mode of handling in the subcontinent. In referring to the way conditions of psychiatric interest were conceptualized, Meulenbeld uses the idea of 'demystification' of magical, religious Vedic material and, like Chattopadhyaya, he seems to view the evolution of a naturalistic approach to medicine, compared to a 'supernatural' or 'metaphysical' approach, as a momentous development in the world history of medicine.[582] The work of Zysk, discussed earlier, certainly presupposes the achievement of Ayurveda but provides a fine-grained narrative of how and why it evolved as a system of medicine.

Meulenbeld stresses that the very earliest compilations of Ayurveda knowledge consisted of specialized works in any one of the major divisions of medicine. The established tradition included nine divisions: internal medicine, surgery, diseases of the head (ears, eyes, nose, mouth), diseases and problems of females (obstetrics, gynaecology, paediatrics), of children, the treatment of mental disorders (termed *bhūtavidyā*), toxicology, the science of longevity, and the science of aphrodisiacs. The *bhūtavidyā*s are important, as the term indicates that originally these disorders were treated chiefly by *daivavyapāśraya* measures (derived from religion). This is certainly consistent with what Zysk indicated and some of his case examples of Buddhist formulation illustrate this. Very little remains in the way of documentation of this very early phase of emphasis on specialization and Zysk's analysis is the most up to date.

---

[582] D. Chattopadhyaya 1977.

Vedic, Buddhist, and related magico-religious medical tenets were interwoven, and, in some instances, replaced by the compilation of general medical textbooks that, while perhaps starting as specialized treatises, expanded to cover the whole of medicine.

The compilations of Caraka (initial emphasis on internal medicine) and Suśruta (initial emphasis on surgery) are the earliest general Ayurveda works and constitute the classics to which later physicians and scholars returned to, emended, redacted, and commented upon. Two of these were discussed in the previous chapter. Later works on Ayurveda depart from these classics. In them there is no trace of an initial specialized emphasis and in effect they cover the whole of medicine and function as veritable general textbooks. Tensions and inconsistencies in the classics tend to be smoothed over and harmonized in the later textbooks. Since this evolutionary trend affects Ayurveda as a whole it obviously involves also the traditional Indian medical approach to psychiatric phenomena since it was included as a major component of disease.

A second major area of cultural change of psychiatric phenomena involves the way the specific types or varieties of the *bhūta*s were conceptualized. Here, a central point of change involves disorders attributed to non-human, spiritual attack or seizure, what came to be termed the *bhūtonmāda*s, viewed in comparison to the other relatively unproblematic varieties of *bhūta*s, namely, epilepsy (*apasmāra*) and insanity (*unmāda*). The classic texts differ in their approaches: while they both handle epilepsy and insanity as separate entities – they are placed in different chapters or divisions – Caraka deals with spirit-related disorders within the chapter on (and as a variety of) insanity, whereas Suśruta deals with these disorders as though they were different altogether (*bhūtonmāda*s and insanity and epilepsy are placed in separate chapters). This is the way the spirit possession disorders are conceptualized and classified in Vāgbhaṭa's *Aṣṭāṅgasaṃgraha*. On the other hand, the general compilation of Bheḷa, a work more or less contemporary with Vāgbhaṭa, reflects an unusual, conservative, conceptualization. As discussed in earlier chapters, it gives the *bhūtonmāda*s minor attention and acknowledges that exorcists and religious means are the appropriate way of dealing with these disorders.

In general, however, later texts of Ayurveda continue to include the *bhūtonmāda*s as integral to naturalistic medicine. Spirit possession disorders are included and handled as real medical entities. Moreover, while later texts accept spiritual factors in aetiology and allow for magical ritualistic modes of therapy, they also incorporate a humoral approach to spirit possession. Implied is the idea that in the final analysis these disorders, like epilepsy and insanity, come to involve the humours or *doṣas*. This is mentioned explicitly or implied, since associated with their treatment are preparations and medical procedures that are used not only with epilepsy and insanity but also a whole range of other medical, seemingly organic conditions. However, Meulenbeld points out that later textbooks shift between containing and restricting *bhūtonmāda*s within the more generally established category of insanity or handling them more liberally as a separate variety, as does Suśruta and also Vāgbhaṭa. A growing number of types of possession appear in the later compilations and Meulenbeld holds that these were probably borrowed from popular beliefs and also influenced by Tantrism.

Meulenbeld lists the number of supernatural agents that are associated with causes of conditions of psychiatric interest and the types of *bhūtonmāda* represented in selected ayurvedic and medical texts. One can use this information in attempt to clarify possible change in relation to time. Table 8.1 lists relevant information taken from Meulenbeld's study. In the left hand column of the table, selected Ayurveda texts are listed in chronological order. Accurate information on dating is difficult to obtain. Dates are for received texts, not date of when a compilation may have first been compiled. Meulenbeld's best judgment of date is used as a basis of chronology listed in table. I have placed the *Bheḷasaṃhitā* after the *Kāśyapasaṃhitā*, because dates given for it extend for centuries beyond the latter's seventh century. The middle column records number of *unmāda*s or insanity listed in the texts for which information is available. The third column lists the number of non-human agents or *bhūtonmāda*s that are held to cause conditions of psychiatric interest.

Inspection of this table shows that the number of insanities remains roughly the same across the historical period listed, between five and eight types. This suggests that the Ayurveda classification of types of conditions of psychiatric interest glossed as insanity remained relatively stable. It may well be the case that other facets of Ayurveda knowledge about the insanities changed and became more systematic and extensive (and, in this, may have evolved); for example, descriptive specificity of types, explanatory formulation or pathophysiology, treatment regimen, or prognosis – all categories employed in the *saṃhitā* described in the last chapter. However, information such as this, even for the four *saṃhitā*s discussed in the previous chapter, is very difficult to obtain. Inspection of the table shows that the number of non-human, 'metaphysical' agents is variable. It ranges from eight to 27. This variation suggests that as far as Ayurveda psychiatry was concerned, the influence of metaphysics never lost its level of salience. Moreover, since the number of agents appears to increase as one moves down the entries of column three, it might have been the case that beyond the classical era (*Carakasaṃhitā* and *Suśrutasaṃhitā*) such agents increased in salience. Indeed, when one moves into the later medieval era, there is a progressive increase. Vāgbhaṭa's 18 agents, while qualifying as an outlier, can also be taken as marking the beginning of the medieval era. Interestingly, high representation of non-natural causes in medical texts, starting with those of Vāgbhaṭa's dates, coincide with the period of Indian history when classical Yoga, its spin-offs and associated disciplines (Tantra, alchemy), and sectarianism and Bhakti devotionalism became a predominant feature of social, cultural life.

Analyses by scholars such as Meulenbeld, Chattopadhyaya, and Zysk and also Weiss provide one with a window that affords visualization of the cultural change of psychiatric phenomena in India.[583] While Ayurveda is an important Indian tradition, these and other scholars (Dube, Haldipur, Kutumbiah) make it clear that it does not present one totally coherent picture of psychiatric phenomena. Laying aside the matter of possible evolution, the material suggests that there are many representations of psychiatric phenomena as scholars of Indian ayurvedic medicine and psychiatry have pointed out. There is much overlap and a core of shared knowledge among exponents of the tradition, although their commentators and interpolators have introduced important differences. They recorded their observations at different times, although exact dates for the orally transmitted collections, their transcriptions, and works by various commentators and interpolators are difficult to determine.

Many competing schools of medicine existed during traditional, classical, and later medieval eras, as the collections were copied, interpreted in the light of new clinical experience and knowledge, and modified. The ayurvedic tradition was an evolving tradition of medicine reflecting how literate, scholarly, academic physicians thought about psychiatric condition over a long expanse of time This cultural interpretation of psychiatric condition was undoubtedly taught to patients and

[583] See Weiss 1977, 1980.

Table 8.1.
Ayurveda texts by approximate date in the Common Era

Name of Ayurveda document	Approximate date centuries CE	Types of *unmāda* no.	Types of *bhūtonmāda* no.
Carakasaṃhitā	1–3	5	8
Suśrutasaṃhitā	1–3	6	9
Vāgbhaṭa, *Aṣṭāṅgahṛdayasaṃhitā*	6	6	18
Vāgbhaṭa, *Aṣṭāṅgasaṃgraha*	6	6	18
Bheḷasaṃhitā	7	5	?
Mādhavanidāna	8	6	8
Kāśyapasaṃhitā	7	5	?
Kalyāṇakāraka	9	5	8
Hārītasaṃhitā	10 (800–1200)	8	21
Tantrasārasaṃgraha	12	?	27 (18 *mahāgrahas*, 9 *grahas*)
Gadharasaṃhitā	14	6	20
Amṛtasāgara	18	16	

their families, who must have disseminated its tenets. To this diffusion of naturalistic knowledge into the popular social spheres was added the interpretation of local (non-ayurvedic) practitioners like priests, diviners, tantric and yogic specialists, and herbalists, who themselves appropriated wisdom of authorities and classical writings.[584] All this under-

[584] Discussed in later sections of this chapter.

scores the fact that psychiatric condition as a cultural objects formulated by Ayurveda evolved over centuries, even millennia, and interacted with other traditions of medicine - folk, popular, and religious – which in complex ways complemented the scholarly and scientific one.

Similarities and differences between exogenous and endogenous conditions of psychiatric interest no doubt posed an enigma and conundrum to practitioners of Ayurveda and folk traditions of medicine. It is not merely incidental that Ayurveda should reflect a struggle regarding the ontology and epistemology of the *bhūtonmāda*s compared to the endogenous, humoral classes of conditions of psychiatric interest. The struggle has a social aspect: the views of the elitist, scientific, scholarly community of ayurvedic physicians would seem to be opposed to the popular, religious and non-scientific ideas about insanity – that is, between explanations based on allegedly scientific, objective, impersonal concepts involving natural phenomena, as against superstitious, magical ones involving idiosyncratic, supernatural phenomena. But, as we have seen, Ayurveda does not fully exclude the latter; in fact, to many treatises metaphysical conditions of psychiatric interest are clearly relevant, although there are inconsistencies regarding the causes of conditions of psychiatric interest in general.

In many ways, the inconsistency and competition as to hegemonic authority within ayurvedic medicine and in relation to practical, popular or folk medicine is not unlike a major dilemma in contemporary psychiatry. This has two related formulations: (1) are psychiatric disorders 'real' diseases or merely illness syndromes? And (2) are the disorders best conceptualized as organically rooted disturbances or merely psychological, functional changes? These two interrelated positions are often associated with types of psychiatrists, between whom invidious comparisons are made. The philosophy of science applied to psychiatry would see the competing views about the character of psychopathology as based on a fruitless dualism about the nature of reality, including human behaviour, associated with Cartesian philosophy. Indian intellectual theory is said to be monistic and unencumbered by dualism, yet the ambiguity and inconsistency between the humour-based conditions of psychiatric interest and those caused by possession (*bhūtonmāda*s), between the functions of the bodily and mental humours as causes of psychopathology, between the functions ascribed to physical organs and vessels as against a mental organ (*manas*) in bringing about psychiatric condition, and between the allegedly mental and sensory entities that are carried, blocked, or released in the physical body and that account for the manifestations of psychiatric condition, quickly convince one that Ayurveda also struggled with psychiatric phenomena in ways not unlike Western medicine and psychiatry. Neither of these two clearly formulated academic systems of medicine which seek to explain conditions of psychiatric interest can easily avoid the dilemma of having to explain how disturbances of phenomena as 'physical', as the body and brain, can result in disturbances with such patently mental, cognitive, and behavioural manifestations. They bridge our domains of mind and body descriptively and logically (and unproblematically) and are not burdened by having to account for complexities of crossing what have and continue to constitute major Western frontiers or spaces of brain/body and mind/behaviour.

PSYCHIATRIC PRACTICE AS AN OUTGROWTH OF PHILOSOPHY

There is a tendency to view Ayurveda as the only learned, scholarly variety of Indian medicine that was relevant to conditions of psychiatric interest. These also were general medicines applied to both bodily and mental problems that would have been relevant to treating conditions of psychiatric interest. Siddha medicine as a curative practice of medicine has been discussed in general terms, but has not been fully articulated as theory and praxis.[585] It achieved prominence during the medieval period especially in South India. Islamic or Unani medicine, brought to India by Turkish, Arab, and Mughal overlords during the later medieval and early modern period, has also not been systematically described. Consequently, there is not much information about their way of handling conditions of psychiatric interest in India. The Buddhist tradition, discussed earlier, provided a bridge between Vedic medicine and Ayurveda, and was also applied to conditions of psychiatric interest. Among other religious and philosophical systems, Yoga has proven particularly fruitful.

Yoga, an integral part of Siddha medicine, was and continues to be important in the diagnosis and treatment of psychiatric condition. Balodhi, who studied the relevance of Yoga for psychiatry and mental health, regards the system of *rājayoga,* articulated by Patañjali (*c.* 200

[585] P. V. Sharma 1992b; Hausman 1996.

BCE), as a picture of Hindu clinical psychology as it stood 2000 years ago.[586] Although classed as a system of philosophy, it was also a practical discipline for self-growth and transcendence. Yoga involves certain body manoeuvres – breathing techniques, symbolic gestures and postures, blocking organ passages by muscle contractions, cleansing techniques – and experiential techniques such as 'restructuring' the cognitive and analytic apparatus of the psyche for personality expansion and growth. The former is associated with *haṭhayoga* and is associated with Hindu Tantra writings. These techniques have been applied to a number of general medical conditions such as hypertension, anxiety states, and stress. Balodhi sees the 'experiential' component of Yoga as fostering cognitive growth and transcendence of the self. The physical techniques of *rājayoga* have influenced many systems of Indian philosophical psychology. They are generally not just applied alone for the purpose of controlling physiological processes, but used in association with different theories that pertain to a particular school of philosophy. Patañjali's well-known classic, The *Yogasūtra*, unified a number of traditions. Its representation of Yoga philosophy understands the psyche (*citta*) as comprised of mind (*manas*), considered as 'a supersensory system for semantic and symbolic interpretation of features of the world', ego (*ahaṃkāra*), and intellect (*buddhi*).[587] These three aspects of experience are integrated in *citta*, 'habitually fickle and unsteady', and they interact in a complex way that is 'uncontrolled' and seemingly without a directed destination. Balodhi explains that there are five ways in which the *citta* operates: in states of tension and restlessness (*kṣipta*), in 'stupefied/infatuated states' of intense emotions such as sexual excitement and anger (*mūḍha*), in a 'fickle and partly calm manner' (*vikṣipta*), in states of focus and 'one-pointedness' (*ekāgra*), and as orderly, tranquil, and stable (*niruddha*): or highly ordered, stable, and tranquil.[588] The first three states wherein *citta* functions are implicated as causes of psychiatric condition in the Yoga system, whereas the fourth and fifth states are used in the pursuit of higher and altered states of consciousness and functioning.

Nine varieties of conditions of psychiatric interest of psychological afflictions are described by Patañjali: somatic disturbances, gloominess, doubt, procrastination, sloth, craving for sensual pleasure, hallucination,

---

[586] Balodhi 1986b. See also Hartranft 2003.

[587] Balodhi 1986b: 134.

[588] Balodhi 1986b.

failure to concentrate, and instability. Eight steps must be followed and practiced in order to be free of these afflictions, a method of therapy that is a total and radical change from any Western style of life, takes years to master, and (Balodhi assumes) the longer and deeper the training the better it works for serious mental health problems. Balodhi emphasizes that Patañjali's conception of mind and its afflictions and the practices he perfected involve a co-operative interaction between mind and body. The therapy it promotes involves a comprehensive change of the individual, involving transformation 'of socio-ethical, physiological and psychological outlook'.[589]

General mental health implications of Yoga as a theosophical tradition are discussed later.

SOTERIOLOGICAL AND CULTURAL PSYCHOLOGY OF HEALTH AND SICKNESS

Gupta's *Psycho-pathology in Indian Medicine: With Special Reference to Its Philosophical Basis* stresses the theoretically integrative character of Ayurveda.[590] Like other observers, he also focuses on metaphysical as well as clinical, empirical questions.[591] Ayurveda, Gupta emphasizes, is a synthesis of the Sāṃkhya, Vaiśeṣika, Nyāya, and Vedānta systems. It incorporates virtually all of the major schools of philosophy of India. However, like Balodhi, he gives special attention to the system of Yoga, in which one finds aspects of mind, experience, being, and organic constitution brought into play in relation to questions of spirituality.[592] Not surprisingly, Gupta finds the roots of many of these representative ideas in the *Atharvaveda* and in *Kauśikasūtra,* which he views as the 'divine lineage of Ayurveda'. He emphasizes that Yoga and the quest for liberation are complementary in the pursuit of health:

> In Ayurveda, therefore, the life surpasses the limits of the complexity of cells and tissues, but also covers the transcendental plane of life, an

[589] Balodhi 1986b: 137.

[590] Gupta 1976.

[591] See Roşu 1981; Ramu, Venkataram, and Janakiramaiah 1988; Balodhi 1986b, 1987; Kakar 1982.

[592] Balodhi 1986b.

> essential component for the fuller development of human potentialities, and for achieving the highest order of harmony in life. Besides the concept of life, Ayurveda as well admits the happiness of senses, mind, and soul to be the essential condition for an ideal health. The humoral and systemic equilibrium are not only sufficient for health, but these should be consistent with the perfect wellbeing of a man in the complete sense of psychological and spiritual aspects of life, and only then a person may be called as healthy ... So the foundation of *darśanas* and Ayurveda are laid on the common ground. If dyspepsia and insanity are the physical and mental disorders, the cycle of birth and death is certainly a spiritual disorder, and Ayurveda is fully conscious of this spiritual disorder, and it directs every man to overcome this cycle of birth and death by attaining liberation (*mokṣa*).[593]

In discussing spiritual and mental remnants of karma and their relationship to the development of the foetus, Gupta holds that Ayurveda incorporates an evolutionary conception of the individual. Evolution here is meant to refer to how persons are believed to have originated in the remote past and how their essence continues across lifetimes.[594] Karmic influences as composites of experience and primordial matter are transferred to individuals following conception and, in conjunction with maternal and paternal influences, which Gupta equates with genetic influences, contribute to human development. He shows how conceptions of mind in Ayurveda correspond to ideas found in various philosophical schools about things mental as opposed to physical, many of which were discussed earlier; for example *dravya*, Caraka's substratum of action and qualities and a co-existent cause of things, including mind (*manas*), one of the nine forms of this substratum, *prakṛti* or matter, *puruṣa* or spirit, which is but a counterpart of matter. In Ayurveda, the three constituents or *guṇas* (*triguṇa*) are related to the Sāṃkhya notion, which is used to designate the three principles of material being, namely, *sattva* (light), *rajas* (excitement), and *tamas* (darkness), and that these are integral to the constitution of mind. The metaphysical identity of the *triguṇas* rests in writings of the Sāṃkhya-Yoga school. Primordial matter (*prakṛti*) is part of the way the triad of *guṇas* interact with one another. The quiescent of *prakṛti* is broken by the impact of *puruṣa*. This disturbs the prior equilibrium. Gupta surmises that, in spite of its metaphysical roots, the concept of *guṇas* refers to psychological constitution.

---

593 Gupta 1976: 25.

594 See also Weiss *et al.* 1986.

The importance of these concepts to Gupta is that they underscore how metaphysical, ontological, and indeed spiritual phenomena are interrelated in the inheritance of individuals and in their physical constitution. Hence, they are integral to states of health and sickness. In other words, the universal constituents (*guṇas*) are implicated in the production of mental symptoms of disease. Recall that to Kakar the *guṇas* are essential elements of the unconscious and of *citta* (one of the psychic organs), which play important roles in his psychoanalytic interpretation of the Hindu world-view. Gupta agrees with the purely mentalistic, psychoanalytic views of Indian cultural psychology and Ayurveda.

A concept found in Ayurveda to which Gupta gives considerable attention is that of personality which was discussed earlier in relation to the work of Meulenbeld.[595] Gupta shows that what this concept refers to encompasses far more than mental and psychological phenomena. As already discussed, in ayurvedic medicine the person has a spiritual, metaphysical dimension, given its roots in karmic influences, as well as a physical dimension. Gupta' discussion of this is more comprehensive than that of other scholars reviewed earlier. Basing his formulation on the compilations of Caraka he points out that karmas can be divided into two portions, one of these refers to actions undertaken in previous lives, while the other to actions undertaken in the present life. When these are in a condition of *sama,* or wholesomeness, this lightens a disease but when in a condition of unwholesomeness they lead to the emergence of disease. Thus, Gupta sees Ayurveda as joining metaphysical ideas about the nature of being, as given in Yoga, with notions of human embryology and anatomy that lead to the human physical constitution and states of health or sickness. Gupta provides an explanation of where mental aspects of personality are located in the body. As part of the conception of personality, Ayurveda considers the individual's location, life habits, station in life, and morality. All of these factors affect types of personalities, which in turn play a role in the kinds of diseases individuals are prone to develop. Personality, then, embraces physical aspects of the self, partly inherited from previous lives, partly formed by social circumstances including moral behaviour, and partly reflected in how the body is organically constituted. This imparts a distinctive tone and quality to disease, which physicians corroborate by means of various investigations.

---

[595] Meulenbeld 1997.

Gupta provides information on the many factors that can cause disease, such as diet, habits, seasons of the year, geography, and aspects of mind and personality brought forward from previous lives. He provides an account of symptoms and signs and general methods of treatment. A theme that surfaces repeatedly is one we have already encountered: the presence of bodily symptoms in so-called mental diseases and so-called mental symptoms in bodily diseases. By underscoring the metaphysical and spiritual components of mind and personality that affect the physical constitution of the foetus, Ayurveda provides a much expanded integrative (psychosomatic and somatopsychic) approach to health and sickness.

In summary, Gupta underscores the quintessentially philosophical and religious ayurvedic construction of health and disease. He places conditions of psychiatric interest firmly within its holistic and integrated perspective on human adaptation. This perspective exemplifies the religious, philosophical cultural psychology of India. Its view of the mind and personality, embodied in the transmigration of karmic influences that make up the embryology and anatomy of the foetus, is complemented by, an almost unitary conception of body, mind, and personality in the context of health and disease.

The Hindu conception of life and personhood, a conception in which yogic notions of *mokṣa* and *citta* play central roles, reveals that for the people of India a 'romantic', 'ironic', and 'childlike' yearning for integration of the self with the 'other' brings a longing and quest for things spiritual and moral.[596] This yearning characterizes the thought of elite intellectuals no less than the devotional lives and private beliefs of the common folk. Shweder and co-workers point out that such themes are inherent in the cultural psychology of India.[597] They are consistent with the presuppositions about the inner rationales of devotional practices as well as the longings and experiences of devotees described by McDaniel, that have played such an influential role in the relationship between madness and religiosity in India.[598] All these scholars remind us that Ayurveda, while perhaps path-breaking in its emphasis on the natural-

[596] Kakar 1981.

[597] Shweder 1991, 1993; Shweder *et al.* 1997. See also Menon and Shweder 1994, 1998; Miller 1997, discussed in the following chapter.

[598] McDaniel 1989.

istic basis of disease, is nevertheless rooted deeply in the cultural psychology, philosophy, and religion of India.

INFLUENCE OF THEOSOPHICAL TRADITIONS IN INDIA'S INDIGENOUS PSYCHIATRY

Ayurveda presents a clearly manifest source of information for one seeking to understand what scholars describe as India's academic or scholarly system of mental health practices. There are many reasons for this. It is by definition health promoting, curative; it categorizes its medical targets, draws together manifestations that appear to match contemporary conditions of psychiatric interest, resides in a distinct and finite number of texts one can consult, and its information as per manifestations of disease and modes of practice allows one to infer how specially trained physicians thought about their domain and how its clients did also. Moreover, Ayurveda's spiritual, philosophical, and moral roots allow one to appreciate its texture in the cultural fabric of traditional India. It is true that only in hindsight and at the cost of committing sins stipulated by strict cultural relativism and historical anachronism (Whiggish history) can one conceptualize Ayurveda as indigenous psychiatry or speak of Ayurveda psychiatry. The warrant for this has been discussed in earlier chapters and would include Ayurveda's own medical focus and function.

However, Ayurveda is not the only account of academic, scholarly thought and practice in pre-modern India that addressed problems of mental health and conditions of psychiatric interest as these are construed in this book. There are many others that did and still do the same. They do not present to one as self-contained systems of medicine or appropriate exemplars of indigenous psychiatry as does Ayurveda. As suggested earlier, their link to actual presentations of disease and conditions of psychiatric interest is more opaque and equivocal. For examples of scholarly, academic but non-medical traditions involved in mental health one can consider once again Yoga, Tantra, and Siddha and add Buddhism and Jainism. Siddha has its strictly medical 'hard core' and its yogic, philosophic, religious 'soft core'.[599] The other four – and Siddha,

[599] Siddha, a daughter of Ayurveda: see P. V. Sharma 1992b; Hausman 1996; White 1996.

viewed purely as a discipline with iatrochemical designs on the mind and body – are not primarily or essentially curative (or medical) disciplines at all. When used for such purposes, they do not focus on specific types of disorders or disease. In other words, the traditions while having a textual basis are far from simple medical compendia per se. However, all five disciplines and practices would undoubtedly have been sought or used curatively for real conditions of disease, on behalf of practitioner himself or a client/devotee. When masquerading as medical systems their focus appears more to be, and would have been, general conditions of 'physical' or 'mental' ailments and maladies; conditions one can gloss as 'dis-ease'.

The *raison d'etre* of Yoga, Tantra, and Siddha and also Buddhism and Jainism is primarily proactive, the latter two not emphasized in what follows. They seek not only to enhance health and wellbeing and promote longevity and sexual vigour in this life. They are also transformative disciplines and practices, promoting wellbeing for eternity. They aim to enable individuals to more directly connect with their essential self so as to free 'it' and themselves from the suffering and ailments of participating in the recurrent cycle of worry, disappointment, and unfulfilled expectation all of which devolve from the illusion or deceptions inherent in the world of everyday concerns. In this sense, they represent systems of mental health practice in broad, humanistic and spiritual sense. They accomplish this by purifying the body and mind and allowing the self or *ātman* to achieve union with the Universal Being or *Brahman*. Stated baldly, the three disciplines as they were construed and constructed socially as praxes in *traditional* or pre-modern India were primarily soteriological.[600] Nonetheless, viewed from the perspective followed in this book, in their original context – hypothetically, analytically construed, to be sure – the three disciplines were medically and psychiatrically relevant. They represented components of traditional India's indigenous psychiatry that straddled the continuum between medicine and non-medicine, the latter prominently involving religion in the philosophical psychology as well as sectarian sense.

The disciplines and practices, then, are medical/psychiatric in two senses. They exemplify the 'quadrangle' organization of soteriological

---

[600] The word 'traditional' is italicized because in modern society, including and especially the West, these disciplines, along with Ayurveda itself, have come to represent seductive panaceas of practice for modernist emotional and bodily aches and woes. See Langford 2002; De Michelis 2004; Alter 2004. For contrast, see Fields 2001.

theory and practice shared with medicine, which was described earlier. And, given their intrinsic focus and the high prevalence of real suffering in traditional India including that associated with conditions of psychiatric interest, the traditions would have been directed at real problems of mental health as conceptualized in this book. However, Tantra, Yoga, and Siddha, and also Buddhism and Jainism, are in some ways similar to and yet in other ways very different from Ayurveda. In two ways each of the three hardly constituted a simple unity, as Ayurveda, one presumes, did.[601] Each is constituted of many schools or traditions of knowledge and systems of practice; and they do not represent separate social, cultural, or institutional entities. Each also articulates and seeks to promote a way of fulfilling and completing one's life: its essential communication and benefits are meant to be life-long. Yoga and Tantra, and probably also the Alchemical Siddha, are incorporative: they indoctrinate and appropriate individual, prosaic 'psyches' and selves, form communities, organizations, and movements and seek pursuits that add up to lessening the ailments of its devotees.[602] In this incorporative sense, they appear to have differed sharply from Ayurveda, although ideas and practices of the latter undoubtedly were appropriated by yogins, gurus, and practitioners of the higher traditions.[603]

Tantra, Yoga, and Siddha share many other characteristics. These include, for example, foundational ideological verities of Indian and eventually Hindu civilization (Vedas, Upanishads, Buddhism) and extra-Indian sources and outflows (indigenous cultures of the subcontinent, China, Tibet). Their period of ascendance and social evolutionary history are similar: they gained prominence starting around the sixth–seventh century CE and became increasingly more visible and influential in succeeding centuries.[604] Each tradition is hardly unitary. They all are constituted by many movements, groupings, and sub-disciplines. Here they also appear to differ from Ayurveda since the latter's practitioners were identified as trained, educated elites in the practice of medicine who of course were subject to legal regulation.[605] Moreover, Tantra, Yoga, and

---

[601] For a modern critique of this position, see Langford 2002, and, for comparison, Fields 2001.

[602] It is unclear to what extent these three traditions and Jainism met needs of females and the lower orders of society, whereas it appears that Buddhism did.

[603] Discussed later on pages 377–378.

[604] Buddhism and Jainism got started much earlier, of course.

[605] Discussed in Chapter 10.

Siddha are hardly separate from each other. They share ideas, beliefs, and practices. It would be very difficult to tease apart the original roots, sources, mutual influences, and different ideas and items of belief that separated Yoga, Tantra, and Siddha from each other, and for that matter, Buddhism and Jainism. The constructs, methods and techniques of the three exemplify complex philosophies of being and soteriology that address the body, the mind, the self, and spirituality. Tantra, Yoga, and Alchemical Siddha have a strong pedagogical emphasis: they rely on yogins, wise Siddha experts, and/or gurus in the promotion of their way of life.[606] As indicated earlier, as social institutions and exemplars of indigenous psychiatry, the three do not stand apart from one another. They overlap producing hybrids, which encompass differing tenets and practice regimens and emphasize different parameters. The metamorphosis that Yoga and Tantra, and also, for that matter Ayurveda, have undergone during the modern era is similar. Today, the three traditions' comprehensive, totalistic program of life, the emphasis on all aspects of self and salvation via release from earthly, suffering existence, has broken apart and fragmented into more or less formulaic procedures designed to cope with stress and improve wellbeing as practical exigencies that reflect a flare of the exotic and 'other'.

All of these traditions become identified and influential during the early centuries of the Common Era.[607] All five involve philosophical psychologies many of the ideas about which scholars have been able to trace back to those found in revealed orthodox, classical, Vedic Brahmanism.[608] They also make up, feed into, and influence sectarian, devotional religious movements that gather momentum during centuries starting around 700 CE. In other words, the evolutionary history of Tantra, Yoga, Siddha and sectarian religions in India are roughly similar.[609] They not only share a common historical pathway, but constitute an ideational amalgam. It would seem extremely difficult, if not impossible, to describe Hinduism as a composite of innumerable sects without having to draw on ideas exemplified in these five traditions and it

---

[606] Mlecko 1982.

[607] As indicated earlier, Buddhism and Jainism many centuries before.

[608] Feuerstein 1998; White 1996, 2000; Whicher 1998; Fields 2001; Flood 1996; Michaels 2004.

[609] And here again they are distinct from Ayurveda, which was influential starting even before the Common Era, although contemporary medical texts are not available to document this.

would also be difficult to trace each one's ideas in distinct and separate historical pathway.

In their religious ramifications the three traditions accomplish and go well beyond their personalized and strictly soteriological journeys. In other words, they modify and deliver more than pure release from the cycle of suffering and karma via practices and procedures designed to purify and free the body and mind (their transcendental function). In addition to, and sometimes as a substitute for, such ideas and practices the traditions introduce and give emphasis to devotion, love, and union with god and promise salvation in this world. All of these traditions, except Buddhism, become prominent in the religious, philosophic, and cultural psychological thought worlds and habit patterns of life in the subcontinent during the medieval period. And all sectarian groups, communities, and traditions, one can argue, become profoundly influential as systems of mental health practice in their own right, distinct from but in many instances undoubtedly supplementary to and synergistic with Ayurveda.

As scholars have pointed out, each of the traditions, including the major sectarian religions, have their orthodox, Brahmanic representations as per householders; their renunciant splinter groups; and draw from and merge into popular, folk, shamanic, and religious ideas and practices which involve meditation, trance, divination, dissociated mental states, and spirit possession. It was at the village level when this social structure first emerged in a particular region of the subcontinent during prehistory and then spread widely. At the village level one can also best visualize the social and cultural influence and power that sectarian religion has exercised on the population of the subcontinent at the grass roots or mundane level of everyday problems. At this popular and populist level the protean amalgam of yogic, tantric, and Siddha ideas, rituals of health and devotional faith and love of gods, goddesses, saints, and demons merge in what earlier was described as the 'popular sector of medicine', namely, the body of knowledge, practices, and influences on mental health of non-ayurvedic medical and non-medical practitioners, although the latter sector would have contained ayurvedic ideas and practices. Mandelbaum discusses transcendental and pragmatic aspects of religion and this exemplifies the two prongs of these traditions: soteriology and salvation compared to practical health/malaise/ disorders.[610]

The point to emphasize is that Yoga, Tantra, and Siddha represent important non-medical scholarly, academic traditions of knowledge and practice that when played out in different regions and status levels of the population influenced and appropriated the thought worlds, emotional imagination, and habit of peoples of the subcontinent. Like Ayurveda, their roots go back to Vedic times. However, they only become distinctive traditions of thought and practice well into the Common Era whereas Ayurveda did well before this. While both medical and non-medical traditions aimed at different targets and end points, only Tantra, Yoga, and Siddha concerned themselves primarily and constitutively with questions of being and spirituality. They also functioned as movements that incorporated *devotees* into a program of life, very different from Ayurveda which relied on *clients and patients* who stood on different platforms of the social hierarchy. Ayurveda rested on premises and were facilitative and promotional of traditional religious, philosophical, and moral pursuits and values. It shared these with Tantra, Siddha and Yoga, although these and to varying degrees were more heterodox and inclusive than orthodox and exclusive. On the other hand, in spite of its other-worldly, metaphysical vision and goals, practitioners of the three traditions borrowed worldly medicinal and dietary precepts and practices from Ayurveda. It was perhaps as the three traditions provided direction, momentum and energy to sectarian religious movements after around 700 CE that they achieved their most powerful effects on mental health. At this village level and among diverse peoples and castes, one would have found that Yoga, Tantra, and Siddha to different degrees, depending on family, village, region, constituted a popular, populistic body of beliefs and practices conducive to and restorative of mental health in which Ayurveda practices were also operative. It is not unreasonable to conceptualize many individuals vulnerable to or manifesting frank conditions of psychiatric interest appropriated and enrolled in careers and programs of life articulated by this amalgam of traditions that gave direction, meaning, and alleviated signs and symptoms.

---

[610] Mandelbaum 1966.

MEDICAL VALIDITY IN ANCIENT INDIA

Introduction

It is hardly surprising that questions of medical efficacy and validity constitute a fundamental and compelling concern of all medical traditions. Besides causing pain and suffering, sickness implies danger and potential loss of life. It leads to a sense of disconnection with abrogation of ties to social, interpersonal, and material objects that underlie and maintain social order. Consequently, sickness elicits dependence, gives rise to need and hope and leads to placing trust and confidence in healers. The sense of vulnerability and fear engendered by sickness is what underpins and gives urgency to questions of authenticity and potential exploitation by healers. Counteracting doubt and instilling trust is a basic desideration of any system of medicine that seeks to establish itself as official or acceptable. This is why in scholarly treatises one finds, besides presentation of details of theory and treatment, emphasis on personal morality of physician and formulation of standards of care and medical ethics. Such statements imply that the care offered by physicians of the tradition is good, honourable, and correct.

The importance of health and the uncertainty and danger posed by sickness also helps explain the fact that in non-modern, traditional societies like India a system of medicine is based on ideas and beliefs central to religion, spirituality, and morality. If not specifically constituted as an enterprise that involves metaphysical and possibly sanctified transactions, a system of medicine certainly draws its inspiration and power from widely shared world-views and traditions that exemplify such overarching concerns. A recognized healer who expounds the regnant system of ideas and beliefs about sickness can be viewed as a clerical, ministerial and certainly humanitarian figure. The trade-off between modern medicine and one found in pre-modern societies involves an exchange between trust in a system based purely on secular concerns generated by the scientific method and one based on the power of philosophical, spiritual and moral traditions that happen to inform a system of practical knowledge about sickness and healing and that are exemplified in the persona of a practitioner. A theory that references impersonal mechanisms situated in and affecting the physical body replaces a doctrine in which ultimate and sacred values are conceptualized as integral to healing. In modern medicine explanations about the governance of cosmology and the physical world (macrocosm) are based on a science that is not only consistent but also equivalent to the way persons and bodies, and health and sickness, are explained (microcosm). This holds equally so for Ayurveda and the strictly non-curative medicines, which have psychiatric import, the difference being that ultimate transcendental questions about the world rest on theosophical beliefs.

What constitutes an effective treatment for an ailment is a central concern of members of any society. Medical healing is the province of practitioners who, depending on the type of society, practice their art and science under varying degrees of regulation. In contemporary Western societies formal and official guidelines based on the scientific method determine medical validity. Not surprisingly, given the economic and political stakes of medical validity, it is a topic associated with considerable tension and conflict.

Biomedicine has evolved a unitary, conceptualization of medical validity based on strict procedures most fully realized in results of the randomized placebo-controlled clinical trial (RCT).[611] Besides constituting an evolved method or protocol, RCT is also a culture pattern having a distinct history in Western societies. An analysis of medicine as practiced in ancient India provides an alternative perspective on the question of medical validity.

The elite scholarly sector as a locale of valid medical practice

In ancient societies like India there existed what one can term a more or less official, elite, politically influential and dominant medicine. This sector consisted of educated, experienced, and influential physicians steeped in the philosophical and spiritual canons as well as in the medical classics of Ayurveda. As discussed earlier, the practice of medicine and the indigenous psychiatry of India had fuzzy boundaries. Viewed in broad context, the reigning approach to sickness and healing was in some establishments more 'organic' and in others more 'metaphysical' but in all of them it had spiritual, religious, and moral resonance. The practitioners who drew on the amalgam of beliefs and practices that made up India's indigenous psychiatry exemplified a form of benevolence. The scholarly medicine was based, on the one hand, on natural philosophy; for example, the *doṣas*, dietetics, practices of meditation, and

---

611 Lilienfeld 1982.

alchemy as per the Ayurveda and Siddha traditions of India; on the other hand, scholarly traditions also incorporated fundamental philosophical, spiritual, and occult (magical, ritualistic) tenets of the culture. And the other non-medical, but also medical, component of the system of mental health practices featured similar pursuits although with contrastive emphases.

Considering Ayurveda alone and in its own terms, an approved and institutionally well-established course of education and socialization mediated and validated a student's entry into a quasi-religious and quasi-scientific body of physicians who claimed expertise in the prevailing system of medical knowledge. The physician apprentice came under the tutelage of an established, publicly validated ayurvedic expert – a recognized and successful expert. In many instances and during different historical eras the elite practitioners functioned under the patronage of kingly, private, bureaucratic, or city personnel under some form of political backing and control.[612] The three traditions discussed earlier produced adepts and specialists whose training was in spiritual and self-purification training programs that progressively advanced their knowledge and expertise as per clarity of insight about the large metaphysical questions involving human flourishing and wellbeing. Their institutional backing rested also on private benefactors and here also experience and expertise counted. However, probably to a much greater extent than with a would-be physician enrolled in a program of medical apprenticeship, what counted was an ability to achieve and charismatically communicate valid insights, and not knowledge in the traditional sense, acquired in the ascent towards bodily, spiritual purification and release (the devotee's personal, religious transformation).

In broad context and with respect to both systems of practice, an appropriate amalgam of textually recorded or orally transmitted ideas and practices as well as a form of politico-economic approval could be said to have sanctioned and validated the society's system or method of scholarly, academic medicine and its psychiatry. Physicians and gurus formed schools or lineages that were based, either on their slant on medical canons and scriptures or, alternatively, on their command of knowledge and especially practice in the realm of metaphysics, soteriology, meditation, and self-purification. In both settings, to varying extents and during different stages of learning and ascent towards validity

[612] The role of physicians-as-spies will be covered later in Chapter 10.

as practitioner or guru, success in communication of expertise in areas of theory and practice, honed in the light of challenge and disputation, played important roles.

A sacred, holy trust and conviction that healing constituted a form of goodness that brought spiritual as well as social rewards nourished teacher–student, master–disciple relations in ayurvedic medicine and no less can be said of success in the more religious, spiritual traditions when these are examined in the secular light of psychology and sociology.[613]

In late classical and medieval India, the followers of the two early classic physicians, Caraka and Suśruta and later Vāgbhaṭa, established a tradition that has persisted through millennia in a comparatively integrated way.[614] During the medieval era, Siddha's iatrochemical medicine grew as a branch of Ayurveda, mainly centred in South India and involving a greater emphasis of alchemical methods.[615] Differences in details of medical knowledge and continued commentaries and reinterpretations of basic items of theory and practice, such as, for example, the relative importance of surgery, characteristics of regimen and decoctions, causes and mechanisms of pathophysiology, and approaches to spirit-caused disease, bear testimony to the vitality and ferment of the tradition. Ayurvedic medicine drew on scriptural authority and perfected a holistic system of healing that was based on a blend of natural philosophy, trial-and-error learning, and religion. In the case of Tantra, Yoga, and Siddha it is possible to also trace their unfolding but mainly as religious, metaphysical, and philosophical traditions and intellectual institutions.[616] It is more difficult to connect them with distinctive ensembles of aches and pains, namely, 'real, hurting people who are on the ground', as it is for Ayurveda, given its anchoring in the face validating details of symptoms and signs. As discussed in previous chapters, it is in the writings of cultural anthropologists of contemporary India that one can appreciate details of what hurts and what needs fixing, not only in the body, but also in mind.[617]

---

[613] Kutumbiah 1969; White 1996; Fields 2001; Alter 2004.

[614] D. Chattopadhyaya 1977; P. V. Sharma 1992b; Meulenbeld 1999–2002.

[615] P. V. Sharma 1992b; Hymavathi 1993; White 1996.

[616] Feuerstein 1998; Michaels 2004; Flood 1996; White 1996; Whicher 1998; Fields 2001.

[617] See also papers in White 2000.

In general, physicians who expounded and enlarged upon the scholarly tradition formed a select group in society. Yet, no less can be said of wise practitioners, moral and textual experts, gurus, and yogins. Among the latter, success and validation was obviously more local, sacral, based not on knowledge and success in healing distinct constellations of signs and symptoms but in moving distressed and suffering individuals of the community, sect, or movement closer to release and cleansing of existential woes. In a secular, sociological sense, all practitioners acquired expertise and renown by treating distressed, troubled individuals. Physicians may have written treatises, commented on inherited written texts (the received tradition), attracted disciples, and formulated the boundaries of acceptable, orthodox and valid medicine in an open most likely urban setting. On the other hand, the practitioners of the more religious approaches to and guardians and promoters of ways of achieving mental health based their status on more intangible facets of experience and wellbeing, and certainly no less important, as these impacted on more closed communities.

The relevance of Tantra, Yoga, and Siddha as distinct philosophical systems of self-improvement and healing and especially their influence on the practices of sectarian and popular religion are more encompassing, powerful, and energizing in areas of mental health and human flourishing although perhaps more opaque and ambiguous when viewed through the prism of medical validity as this has been generally construed. Nonetheless, they should not be allowed to distract from the accomplishment of Ayurveda as a system of medicine. It is rightly regarded as constituting one of the oldest naturalistic traditions of medicine. As described earlier, it slowly and haltingly attempted to acquire independence from the priestly, more magical, and politicized medicine of the Brahmins that was based on the religious Vedas and also from Buddhist tenets.[618] In late classical India, there is a suggestion that associations or schools of physicians followed traditions of one of the classicists; earlier, prior to the era when general comprehensive approaches to medicine gained ascendancy, physicians probably grouped together around one of the specialist branches of Ayurveda.[619] Historians of Ayurveda emphasize the importance of argument, disputation, and

---

[618] D. Chattopadhyaya 1977; Zysk 1991, 1993.

[619] Meulenbeld 1997, 1999–2002.

the intellectual arts in the forging of medical knowledge.[620] The tradition of medical scholarship integrated naturalistic knowledge about body functions and pathological processes with ancient tenets pertaining to morality, spirituality, and philosophy. In antiquity, Ayurveda and its physicians constituted strong support for the system of moral conduct and operated as a pillar of duty and obligation that the state not only endorsed and promoted but also actively used as agents of colonization and governance.[621]

In summary, in traditional India participation in scholarly medicine meant involvement in and promotion of valid, effective, and trustworthy medicine. This is the setting where old knowledge was examined, challenged, and refined. Medical training involved a period of apprenticeship and the sources indicate the existence of institutions analogous to actual medical schools. In these particular settings, the master–disciple relationships were of overwhelming importance. Social historians of medicine emphasize that apprenticeship was featured not only by the transmission and learning of knowledge but also by the inculcation of basic philosophical, moral, and spiritual values of the civilization. Furthermore, behaviour that contravened sacred traditions and moral precepts was held to cause disease. In short, the education of physicians, their functions as social agents, and the theory of disease they relied on all worked together to promote behaviour enjoined by philosophical and religious traditions. This general tone influenced happenings in the popular sector.

The popular medical sector

The knowledge of elite and influential practitioners of Ayurveda about causation, diagnosis, and treatment percolated downwards in the society. It reached and affected activities of folk, popular, and religious practitioners. There, items of information from establishment medicine mixed and competed with those of extant traditions of local, folk medicine, some of it of probable pre-Vedic origin. In any one setting or therapeutic context it would have been difficult if not impossible to untangle the practice of popular medicine from that of popular religion and popular counselling. They all might involve recourse to advice, spirit

---

[620] Kutumbiah 1969.

[621] Sternbach 1965.

possession, negotiation with feared spirits, and/or divination pertaining to a range of problems. For example: solution of problems involving general health, sickness, family worries, suspicion of bewitchment or other forms of malevolence, spiritual reprisals, guilt involving rituals of ancestors, marital conflicts, infertility, missing or stolen property, disturbing dreams, social exclusion, wayward young adults, fearful forebodings, karmic worries, failures in local business or schooling ventures, unemployment, debt – and many more of the sundry intellectual dilemmas and emotions constituting demoralization and disillusionment stemming from poverty, marginalization, and politico-economic exploitation. This constellation of more secular, practical, everyday problems should be seen as analytically different from but in a concrete, practical, and experiential sense as embedded in the strictly more spiritual, religious concerns integral to the numerous sects that in different regions and time periods appropriated ideas and practices of Yoga, Tantra, and Siddha.

In an official and communitarian but no less individualized sense, sectarian religions provided comfort through practices involving adoration, love, and devotion to local or regional gods (*bhakti*). On the other hand, popular medicine and counselling relied on techniques and practices that strayed into magic, divination, witchcraft, and shamanism but while personalized and idiosyncratic also were also exercised in a public group setting where anonymity and privacy were traded for the promise of relief.[622] At village level and in marginal sectors of towns and cities among the very poor, unemployed migrants, the handling of these and related problems exemplified popular religion, ritual, and magical beliefs and practices, the 'little', less Sanskritic or more popular, folk traditions of society.[623] In urban centres, and village communities, this medicine was usually associated with the less affluent members of the population, individuals who were politically, economically less influential and sometimes marginalized if not exploited.

The practice of medicine and handling of conditions of psychiatric interest in small towns and villages was unregulated. A large and complex group of diviners, would be yogins, tantrics, and Siddha experts, herbalists, practitioners of black magic, sorcerers, shamans, and itinerant peddlers of medical lore competed in the folk, popular medical sector

---

622 For contemporary examples, see Kakar 1982, Pakaslahti 1998, and Erndl 2000.

623 Redfield 1955, 1956; Singer 1972.

with no supervision or overarching system of formal evaluation and regulation. As mentioned earlier, this popular medicine should be construed as different from activities followed in the sectarian religions. In populous villages each caste or sub-caste probably had individuals with experience in healing who were consulted and it is likely that in many instances medical practice involved crossing caste boundaries such as to preserve purity and avoid pollution. Besides caste affiliation, a default requirement in many cases, practitioners earned their reputation based on psychological and charismatic influences, relief of symptoms and signs, and the perceived morality of the practitioner. These and related factors served as criteria in terms of which practitioners plied their trade and held on to practice their trade. Similar loose, ambiguous criteria of validity and efficacy obviously operated in the elite sector as well, although in the latter formal medical education, official patronage, professional standing, subsidy or employment by the state, and participation in political, religious rituals were also taken into consideration. In a broad sense, many if not most criteria brought to bear on the official, recognized, public standing of a practitioner's competence and validity are shared across human societies.

Association with and very often membership of folk religious sects and temples were factors that contributed to choice of practitioner and influenced level of prestige and validity. Even professional and academic physicians had associations with strictly religious institutions like temples and monasteries. In India, for example, many physicians were provided with land grants and assigned to and practiced in cities near centres of pilgrimage related religious establishments.[624] There also existed wise men and specialist diviners, often associated with religious devotional cults as well as exorcists, who, while not physicians in the scholarly, elite, and establishment sense, were nevertheless knowledgeable of Ayurveda and commanded respect and admiration, if not awe and fear.

What constituted an effective and/or valid medical treatment at the popular, folk level was ultimately moot, decided on trial and error, and trust. Culturally, it depended in part on the sanctions afforded by popular religion and scriptural authority and partly on the cleverness and acumen of practitioners as reflected not only in how they used medical knowledge, but also in whom they selected to treat. Even in

---

[624] Hymavathi 1993.

elite, scholarly medicine, it should be emphasized, there existed guidelines for the avoidance of patients deemed to be terminally ill. From a scientific standpoint, psychological influences in healing obviously played an important role and this was the case also among the influential establishment physicians of the scholarly tradition. The unregulated conditions of medical practice existing in villages, sections of large towns and small cities situated far away, in a social sense, from where elite, scholarly physicians practiced were replicated in rural communities of the hinterland. It should be emphasized that medical happenings and practices taking place in agricultural settings and among village and small town dwellers are not described in received texts and were probably little known and less evaluated by courts of kings and princes who exercised jurisdiction. Historical sources are generally silent about everyday life and coping at the popular, religious level. Only for contemporary times and by cultural anthropologists have on-the-ground folk, popular medicine practices been studied in traditional, village settings. Ayurveda and Yoga have been the objects of study in context of modern developments in India and its relationship to the West.[625]

As suggested earlier, the assessment of validity of a tradition of medicine is hampered by natural diffusion of ideas pertinent to theory and practice. There is the matter of selective, mutual borrowings and testing of ideas between and across 'great' traditions, most notably between Ayurveda and Islamic or Unani medicine during the medieval era. Keeping aside diffusion across such traditions, the focus presently is diffusion between elite and popular sectors of any one society that, in some instances, amounted to an interpenetration of ideas. In general, complex societies under the influence of ancient traditions showed a pluralistic system of medicine. Clients of literate, scholarly physicians of India also sought the services of popular, religious practitioners who were found in villages, larger towns and cities. These physicians were aware of procedures and treatments (rituals and herbal preparations) found in the popular, religious sector and were not averse to using them, factoring effects of their use and general knowledge of the treatment into the equation of what worked with their own patients. In time, this popular knowledge of treatment efficacy came to be incorporated in the canons of materia medica. Hence, what passed as the official body of established, valid, efficacious treatment contained elements originally

[625] Langford 2002; De Michelis 2004; Alter 2004.

evolved empirically and frequently validated partly on ritual, magical grounds in the popular sector. And, to complete the circle, many procedures and agents that prevailed in the latter came originally from the scholarly classical and elite sector; that is, from the body of naturalistic medicine generated by academic physicians who inherited old knowledge, tested it, and elaborated upon it on the basis of their observation of clinical work and discussion with colleagues and disciples.

What does medical validity mean anyway?

From a comparative standpoint, all systems or traditions of medicine fulfil various functions in society in a way that a modern scientist would construe as valid, and not all of which are strictly curing sickness. Traditions differ in how well they perform in the light of the various functions of medical traditions that include much more than just success in treating disease.[626] However, the present focus is on the question of medical effectiveness or validity viewed in broad context. This would have to include a consideration of the advantages compared to disadvantages of any system or tradition of medicine, viewed in comprehensive terms (i.e., as phenomena *sui generis*). One can anticipate that a synthesis and analysis of information drawn from the study of comparative medicine or ethno-medicine, for example, medical anthropology, social history of medicine, and sociology and epidemiology of biomedicine, would lead to a formulation of what the overarching goals and functions of any medical system or tradition should be (e.g., that of traditional India, China, biomedicine). How well any one system or tradition fares or performs in such a schema of accounting would necessarily involve calibration along the lines of optimality theory (i.e., trade-offs between benefits and costs).

Several points, with their qualifications, can be mentioned. One is that an approach to medical diagnosis and an agent or procedure of treatment that persists in and validated by an ancient, non-Western scholarly tradition of medicine like Ayurveda should be granted a provisional measure of clinical validity. The mix of diseases is influenced by size, density, and demography (birth rate, mortality, age structure) of the population, the diet and hygienic practices, sanitation and public facilities, the level and distribution of wealth, and the politico-economic

[626] Fabrega 1974, 1975, 1976a, 1976b, 1997.

organization of the society. The prevalence of acute infectious and chronic diseases can be expected to have been quite high for reasons already discussed. However, the prevalence of chronic disease like diabetes, cancer, and cardio- and cerebral blood-vessel disease is not at all clear. The protocols of medical practice in the respective societies evolved under prevailing conditions of social and medical ecology, a mix of cultural ambience, physical environment, diet, pattern of social life, and genetic structuring of the population that created distinct patterns of immunity and pictures of bodily health to which practitioners oriented and against which they evaluated efficacy. Obviously, hindsight informs of the powerlessness of many ancient medical traditions in the fight against infectious diseases and especially epidemics. It is against the backdrop of very high mortality and relative ineffectiveness with these diseases and an appreciation of mixed conditions of sickness moderated by social ecology that the more or less effective and valid elements of healing and specific treatments of a non-Western tradition of medicine should be gauged.[627]

That validity goes with longevity of a system of treatment would certainly apply in a negative way. Thus, knowledge that a treatment was patently harmful would spread rapidly in a society by the process of cultural selection and the result would be its rejection by medical consumers, an important and very often final audience of judges and arbiters of the validity of medical treatments. Knowledge in comparative medicine points out that rarely if ever over the long haul have medical practitioners acquired such social power that they could literally enforce or coerce patients to follow medical regimen that was culturally established in the respective community and perceived as health endangering or productive of increased mortality and morbidity. In hindsight, even treatments endorsed by establishment Western-based physicians of the modern era have proven ineffective, some harmful, of course; but the question at issue is the cultural persistence of treatments known to be ineffective and especially harmful.

Generalizations about positive medical treatments are more difficult to arrive at but some can also be proffered. As indicated earlier, distinguished physician scholars in India functioned not only as clinical standard bearers of excellence, but also as prominent and influential educa-

---

[627] Fabrega 1997.

tors of orthodox practitioners of the society. In traditional times, practitioners developed knowledge of sickness based on clinical observations across time in their dealings with patients. On this basis they refined methods of treatment, learned about the effects of material from animal and plants, prepared herbal remedies and drugs, and refined techniques of surgery.[628] Ayurvedic physicians were not only spiritually high-minded and of impeccable morality but were, in addition, acute observers of the medical beliefs and practices of their time. This would have included knowledge of the more purely symbolic and frankly magical practices found in the popular sector. The physicians incorporated such ideas and treatments into the official canons of the scholarly tradition when evidence of healing efficacy asserted itself. In this context, one should recall that untangling empirical and even scientific tenets of medicine from magical, ritualistic, or psychological influences presents many theoretical problems when evaluating theories and practices of pre-modern non-Western and Western traditions of medicine.[629] It is simplistic and also erroneous to assume that only European physicians of the nineteenth century, who had access to the bodies of their dead patients, were concerned about, evolved and practiced what on general grounds one can term a clinical science.[630]

How a 'great' tradition of medicine like Ayurveda arrived at a corpus of established and more or less valid pool of medical information is not fully known and may never be satisfactorily explained. The very earliest observations and practices that on hindsight can be loosely conceptualized as analogous to informal clinical trials and experiments of medical healing that led to acceptable and probably valid treatments in India have not been systematically recorded, much less codified. Most of the inventory of a literate tradition's treatments, for example, those pertaining to pharmacological preparations, diet and health habits, and surgical procedures, are simply recorded in medical texts after they have been developed, used, and deemed efficacious. Following this, they are further analyzed, refined on the basis of clinical use and experience, and contribute to the generation of newer and presumably better theories of sickness and healing.

---

[628] The narrative provided by Zysk (1991) involving evolution of Ayurveda exemplifies this process of learning and establishing medical validity.

[629] Lloyd 1979; Lindberg 1992.

[630] Kutumbiah 1969; D. Chattopadhyaya 1977; Meulenbeld 1999–2002.

Records of physician's case histories that cover a course of treatment provide a window into clinical reasoning and afford a way of studying the question of medical efficacy and validity.[631] For India, although actual case histories of ancient ayurvedic physicians have not to my knowledge been studied and may simply not be available, the attention paid to refinement of concepts and elements of treatment by compilers, redactors, apprentices strongly suggests a no less rigorous quest for medical knowledge of efficacy and thus for a 'clinical science of medicine' in India.[632] It was here, after all, that arguably the earliest naturalistic medicine evolved.[633]

From a contemporary scientific standpoint, establishing medical validity of ancient treatments is a major problem because in cases of sickness usually a large number of treatments were used conjointly. Three major textbooks of Ayurveda, as an example, *Carakasaṃhitā*, *Suśrutasaṃhitā*, and Vāgbhaṭa's *Aṣṭāṅgasaṃgraha*, all list a large number of items of dietetics, regimen, and decoctions derived from animal and plant material that serve as the basis for treatment.[634] In addition to natural end points of sickness or remissions and the influence of purely psychological factors, any benefits that accrued to a clinical regimen of therapy could have resulted from any one of the several or many treatments that were used conjointly. While this pattern of general diversity and opacity regarding the effects of clinical care may be a concomitant of unregulated medicine generally, it constitutes a special problem in the evaluation of the efficacy and validity of the theory and practice of medicine in a 'great' tradition such as Ayurveda.

Several factors, then, contributed to the forging of medical validity in ancient civilizations like India. Among these one can include the following: participation in historically evolved, accepted and prestigious scholarly, academic traditions of medicine; an ideological ambience governed by humanistic and humane values that conformed to traditional spiritual, religious tenets of the society; the operation of formal and informal but rigorous educational institutions that authorized expertise through examinations of clinical proficiency in the context of trial-and-error methods of practice; clinically-based, and slowly evolved treat-

---

[631] For Greek medicine, see Grmek 1989.

[632] Meulenbeld 1999–2002; Kutumbiah 1969.

[633] D. Chattopadhyaya 1977.

[634] *Carakasaṃhitā* 1996; *Aṣṭāṅgasaṃgraha* 1999.

ments that were subjected to careful observation, study, disputation and challenge among physicians carefully selected for their intelligence and ethics who were not only jealous to uphold their social status but desirous also of achieving moral, spiritual approbation as well as socioeconomic success. There did not exist an official state agency or body that could be said to have tightly regulated and controlled the practice of medicine and much less an established, formal protocol or set of guidelines that was used to validate medical treatments. Nevertheless, several factors suggest that the practice of ayurvedic medicine was not unregulated. Virtually all treatises of medicine describe and emphasize signs of untreatable disease counselled non-involvement with such patients. The presumption seems reasonable that physicians were advised to avoid dealing with terminal conditions because this would bring them to the attention of authorities. Physicians were employed and supported by state and private organizations and in some instances employed for programs of free care for the needy. The way in which private or public physicians where selected, favoured, recompensed in monies and food, spared politically onerous responsibilities and the like – their standing as social agents of health control – reflected a system of regulation and control. In addition, hearsay, the informal communication about medical expertise, the market place itself, overall clinical success formally or informally evaluated, and the prevailing canons about acceptable medical knowledge and practice as expounded by educated, renowned members of an ennobled, sacred profession in their conjunction created a culture of expertise and a system of knowledge about medical validity. The writings and activities of scholarly physicians, their strictures and condemnations about heterodox and disreputable practitioners, served to delineate the boundaries of acceptable and orthodox medical treatment.[635] In this sense, public and especially moral opinion as applied in the respective communities that made up societies influenced by ayurvedic medicine played an important role in validating treatment. Furthermore, aspects of validity of medicine do not just reside in actions of physicians. It is reflected in support of programs to distribute medicines, and provide places of confinement and hospitals for those suffering from acute diseases and chronic diseases all of which described major population centres of traditional India.

---

[635] Fabrega 1997.

Conceptualizing the medical validity of Ayurveda

In a scientific context, the question of medical validity of Ayurveda with respect to general diseases is little different from that pertaining to validity in the treatment of conditions of psychiatric interest. Regardless of how the basic sciences of medicine conceptualize and explain the mechanisms underlying conditions of mal-adaptation including general disease or psychiatric condition, from the standpoint of medical validity, it is how well Ayurveda reverses, cures, and/or rehabilitates and restores the victim that counts. Thus, virtually all of the generalizations about validity that were reviewed earlier apply to incidents of psychiatric condition.

Psychiatric conditions by definition incorporate the spheres of social and psychological behaviour in a special and significant way and its manifestation usually compromise and can undermine an individual's stability in the order of its life. One can thus assume that a system of medicine and healing that depends heavily on cultural meanings that key into an individual's understanding of the world and seeks to harmonize its place with traditional values will prove especially relevant and in many instances efficacious. The manifestations of psychiatric condition, it has been repeatedly emphasized, are configured and enacted in a manner or idiom that reflects the cultural psychology of India.[636] This same cultural psychology is integral to premises in Ayurveda, first and foremost, about persons, of course; but in relation to them, to the character of sickness generally. However, in the case of general diseases prominent somatic signs and physical symptoms (swellings, bleeding, fever, marked debility) predominate. On the other hand, with respect to conditions of psychiatric interest, bodily phenomena take a back seat. However, they are not absent. Nonetheless, as emphasized earlier, aspects of emotional experience and social behaviour predominate and they roughly involve precisely those areas heavily affected by ideas and traditions that make up the cultural psychology of India. The persistent and gnawing presence of the *bhūtavidyās*, as markers of suffering that embrace personal identity connected to social and spiritual relations, support these generalizations.

Further examples can be provided. Earlier in this chapter, the formulations of Meulenbeld, Gupta, and Balodhi all attest to the integral tie

---

[636] Taken up in detail in the following chapter.

between ayurvedic views of psychiatric condition and underlying traditional philosophical and religious values of the culture of India. These reviewed the way conditions of psychiatric interest are conceptualized in the compilations of Caraka and Vāgbhaṭa. The vulnerability (moral standing, karmic debts), manifestations (characteristics of social behaviour), and the causes (karmic debts, environmental contingencies, and numerous types of spirits whose attack relate to a person's characteristic previous behaviours), all richly tap into the ideas, values, world-views, and philosophical-moral traditions that constitute the cultural psychology. Material taken up in the following chapter will elaborate on the importance of social meanings, religion, moral conduct, spirituality, and general intellectual and cultural traditions in shaping the manifestations (symbolic content as well as signs and symptoms) of psychiatric condition. Because Ayurveda constitutes a tradition of healing emanating from and richly elaborative of the cultural psychology of India it can be expected to have a powerful bearing on how conditions of psychiatric interest are influenced via its program of healing since such conditions are socially constructed in terms of symbols and meaning integral to that psychology.

It is precisely aspects of experience and behaviour that can be expected to permeate an incident of psychiatric condition. And, to complete the logical web, it is precisely towards this amalgam of experience and behaviour that the comprehensive body of theory and praxis of Ayurveda is directed, among others, of course, like human physiology. It is also the case that the psychological influences of any system of medicine, including in particular its psychotherapeutic features as formulated in modern psychiatry, are especially realized in the practice of Ayurveda.[637]

In summary, even the RCT that is entrusted with scientifically certifying medical validity in contemporary biomedicine acknowledges the power of psychological influences as per the placebo response. While in biomedicine, the latter functions pretty much as a mere hurdle that a treatment needs to surmount in order to qualify as valid, that it depends on brain-behaviour mechanisms created by expectancy, sets under the regulation of systems of healing that evoke powerful psycho-physiological responses is generally assumed to be axiomatic. At the very least, then, these powerful, seemingly innate mechanisms of brain-behaviour

[637] Kakar 1982; Balodhi 1987, 1989, 1991.

mediation can be expected to have operated in contexts of ayurvedic healing, especially those directed to conditions of psychiatric interest. One need only simply to add that psycho-physiologically mediated brain-behaviour mechanisms are activated by a meaningful, symbolically rich ensemble of beliefs and rituals that determine the expectations, hope, and anticipations that bring about relief and improvement. The sense of vindication, justification, moral rehabilitation, and social integration that victims experience as a function of ayurvedic healing adds another layer to the validity of Indian medicine in the context of psychiatric condition. These generalizations apply with equal, if not greater, relevance to the traditions discussed earlier that while not construed as medical or curative per se, nonetheless came into play in pre-modern India as components of its indigenous psychiatry. Additional material bearing on the validity of Ayurveda will be discussed later. Studies by contemporary Indian psychiatrists will be reviewed that provides empirical support in favour of traditional herbal, medicinal products associated with Ayurveda that have been used in the treatment of psychiatric disorders.

INDIA'S INDIGENOUS PSYCHIATRY COVERS MORE THAN AYURVEDA

A comprehensive understanding of psychiatric phenomena cannot be had by limiting one's study to contemporary societies, regardless of how advanced and probing are one's theory and methods. Because psychiatry constitutes first and foremost a cultural institution of modern society it is only its domain there that is available for examination. Moreover, even within this very limited slice of human social and cultural history we are profoundly ignorant of basic information about how psychiatry functions as an institution of society.

This generalization may appear highly controversial. For example there is a large body of information in the sciences and disciplines contained within psychiatry the precise focus of which involves the description and analysis of the way psychiatric disorders are distributed and handled not only by the clinical arms of psychiatry but by diverse systems and institutions of mental health practice. When one grafts this body of knowledge with that involving the neurobiology, psychopharmacology, and results of comparative efficacy of treatment modalities it can properly be said that how 'psychiatry as a social institution is functioning' is not only relatively well understood but also that its accomplishments are substantial.

Yet all knowledge that psychiatry and allied sciences have accumulated applies to modern ecologies, social circumstances, and politico-economic conditions. Anyone seeking to understand the wide range of human problems involving emotional and behavioural disaffection – that one can gloss as conditions of psychiatric interest – in a comprehensive way has to take into account how such problems were configured, understood, and handled in other eras by means of institutions governed by differing regimes of knowledge and practice. India is a test case for such an analysis. How well its institutions were able to quell the pangs of emotional suffering and help stabilize associated interpersonal strife involves crucial information about Indian culture and for understanding the interplay of psychiatric phenomena and society.

One seeking to formulate and understand what psychiatric phenomena were like in earlier societies of the subcontinent has available several bodies of information on which to draw. One involves compendia of Ayurveda by the great physicians of India (Caraka, Suśruta, Bheḷa). Psychiatric conditions, as discussed earlier, form one category of disease that is discernible in these compendia and the way in which its varieties were conceptualized leaves little doubt that such conditions were known to physicians and displayed characteristics (signs, symptoms, and behavioural manifestations) that parallel those found today. However, the compendia are comparable to textbooks pure and simple, and no case illustrations are to be found in them. They record how physicians viewed and thought about the signs and symptoms of conditions of psychiatric interest and disorder, but tell virtually nothing about how abstract clinical material figured in the lives of victims and their families. One remains comparatively uninformed about real narratives of human suffering, about how psychiatric phenomena played out in the daily life of individuals and families, and the way physicians negotiated the translation of the formal 'theory of physic and practice' into the language of suffering, distress, and tensions of social life from and in which psychiatric phenomena originated.[638] Nevertheless, one conclusion that

[638] The findings of contemporary medically-oriented cultural anthropologists, taken up later, are windows into related phenomena in pre-modern societies of the subcontinent.

can be drawn from scholarly compendia of Ayurveda is that psychiatric suffering, construed in terms of experience, emotion and behaviour, resembled what psychiatrists of today still have to appreciate, understand, and handle. In other words, viewed through the prism of bread and butter descriptions of medical classification and diagnosis, one sees in ayurvedic texts signs and symptoms of conditions of psychiatric interest that still ring true today and may, in fact, constitute universals of any system or tradition that encompasses and appropriates such conditions (i.e., ethno-psychiatric enterprise considered in *sui generis* terms). We have seen that the influence and longevity of this system of medicine, not only its science, but resonance with the core philosophical psychology and spiritual values of Hindu culture, provides a measure of its validity.

The handling of conditions of psychiatric interest viewed as clinically relevant distress and feelings of social and moral disarticulation is exemplified in the writings of contemporary anthropologists and cultural psychiatrists whose interests take them to traditional settings and people of India as well as other places where one finds indigenous systems of medicine and psychiatry (i.e., ethno-medicine and ethnopsychiatry). Some of this material was reviewed earlier. It describes and analyzes what actual syndromes of behaviour of psychiatric relevance are like, visualized in terms of the real, context-specific concerns of individuals coping with vicissitudes in their lives. One sees in such writings conflicts between generations and marital partners, frustrations of relationships of love, pangs of shame and guilt associated with forbidden sexual desires and ritual failures, animosities borne of invidious jealousies or contaminations with social relations involving caste identity, feared malevolence and sorcery, emotional distress stemming from inability to conform to strictures of morality and obligation as dictated by *dharma* and caste, burdens caused by still unpaid karmic debts, and much more besides. Syndromes of emotional and behavioural disaffection that play out in such social dramas will persuade anyone that reads about them that the stuff of conditions of psychiatric interest, the social, existentially relevant material that plague individuals in distress, resemble what one can witness in any psychiatric clinic or mental health treatment setting of today. Dilemmas and disappointment such as these represent in part human universals, although certainly are not necessarily construed as abnormal or as sickness worthy of medical attention or consultation with a diviner. It is usually when such syndromes of affliction produce unwanted or untoward changes in consciousness (mental dissociation or confusion, unexplained possession), behavioural adjustment (social paralysis, eccentricity or ineptitude of conduct), and/ or bodily symptoms of stress reactions (visceral somatic and neuro-vegetative signs involving digestion, sleep, sexuality, weakness and debility), that they elicit special attention from appropriate practitioners depending on local context.

Material highlighted by cultural anthropologists and Indian social psychiatrists comes from observation and study of communities where one finds traditional beliefs and values, communities saturated with ways of life that are presumed to resemble those of centuries past. Consequently, one may take some comfort in assuming that the material provides a window on psychiatric phenomena as it burdened, compromised, and played out in syndromes of personal affliction that have a long history in the subcontinent. Information of this type, projected on to the past with due allowance of biases of observation and context stemming from modern thought worlds, provides one with a complement to the information provided by ayurvedic texts. The former describes lived realities of personal pain and misfortune and the latter shows how it was represented as medical academic material pertinent to practicing physicians.

However, when syndromes of affliction and fully articulated conditions of psychiatric interest emerge today they are obviously dressed in attires the content of which differs. Anthropologists have described this very well and so have non-Indian as well as cultural and Indian psychiatrists.[639] However, not everything one finds in contemporary clinical descriptions of psychiatric phenomena among traditional peoples can be assumed to represent uncovered pre-modern exemplifications of such phenomena. After all, mental health problems and conditions of psychiatric interest that anthropologists and Indian social psychiatrists study today should be viewed at least in part as behavioural ailments and swellings not only shaped with respect to content, but to an indeterminate extent as behavioural phenomena produced, broken apart, and extruded by the profound clash in values and world-views wrought by modernism and modernity including conceptions of personal identity and social and spiritual reality. In other words, modernity as culture, even though it does not eradicate pre-modern world-view or concep-

---

[639] Fabrega 1997. See also discussion in Chapters 5 and 11.

tions of personhood, does furnish a vocabulary in terms of which individuals learn – from the communication media, more educated and secular family members and acquaintances – how to label and talk but perhaps not fully understanding about their sense of distress and disarticulation. Thus depending on when or where contemporary data about native behavioural syndromes of psychiatric import are collected, and although they might retain seemingly traditional or pre-modern 'fossils' of ideas and beliefs (cultural meanings) about why and how a psychiatric condition hurts or disturbs personal stability, they nonetheless will reflect modern conceptions of what such conditions mean in modern vocabularies. To an indeterminate extent, then, modern culture and history considered as thought worlds and habit patterns nuance, hide, distort, contextualize, and/or add material to the ensemble of behavioural phenomena that one observes in the clinic, village setting, or urban environment of today. One does not obtain pristine, pre-modern material but its deformation. It is self-evident that cultural and historical material, when played out in social scenarios, will appropriate syndromes of affliction and frank conditions of psychiatric interest into any number of institutions or settings, be they an ayurvedic establishment or shrine or temple where religious practitioners of different persuasion (tantrics, yogins, *siddhas*, gurus, local saints, deified avatars) play out their role.

An important source of information that complements Ayurveda in the indigenous psychiatry of India, and which makes assessment of its validity difficult if one adheres to traditional medical criteria of efficacy, involves the ethos permeating thought worlds and habit patterns of Indian peoples. It includes, more specifically, material on India's philosophical psychology and spiritual tradition. Along with the body of work on moral obligation on which it was rationalized and practiced, this idealist and religious philosophy was inherent in the basic logic (presuppositions) of Ayurveda and in the non-medical quasi and bona fide religions discussed earlier. A *raison d'etre* of disease derived from Vedic lore and its various schools of philosophy and spin-offs was to explain human hardship. Why there was disease? What important proximal factors brought it to the surface, and which factors explain it and could be harnessed to treat it were not only consistent with but ultimately rationalized tenets that had their origins in spiritual, moral, and religious psychology. The distress of a psychiatric condition, which featured conflicts devolving from relations of everyday life, and manifested as psychological and bodily dysfunctions, in one way or another, bore the imprint of transgressions surrounding norms, values, obligations, and spiritual pursuits inherent in everyday life.

Spiritual and moral concerns are germane to the indigenous psychiatry of India not only in a negative or even passive way; that is to say, just as a benchmark of expectations regarding conventional behaviour, deviations from which could cause, shape, and fuel signs and symptoms of conditions of psychiatric interest. In a more positive and direct way, Indian moral, philosophical and spiritual striving among the learned and wise as among the lay, village-level folk addressed ways of improving and alleviating the mental lives of a person. Discussion earlier, as well as the writings of Balodhi, reviewed, exemplifies this proposition. To repeat the point: in a general sense thinking, believing, and doing religion in religious settings of India, as perhaps in all religions, involved not only connecting with and entering into the mental lives of a person. It also involved manipulating and normalizing its manifold discords. Prayer, meditation and other spiritual/philosophical undertakings associated with religious ritual and practice (Bhakti devotionalism as practiced by common folk through the many sects of Hinduism), on the one hand, and the more formal and structured exercises designed to purify the mind, control bodily processes, and so realize detachment, if not release, from everyday miseries, on the other, involved induction and manipulation of altered levels of consciousness. Thus, the material that registered the psychological burdens of conditions of psychiatric interest was essentially the same as that targeted by traditional, folk, orthodox and heterodox, and the more learned, elite forms of meditation and prayer. One thing that Hinduism delivered, in short, was melioration of the suffering and personal misery of conflicts and crises of social life. Relief of this same set of experiences was the aim of ayurvedic physicians.

Constructs, beliefs and values embodied in the religions and medicine of India permeate its culture as a whole.[640] One is hard pressed to draw a boundary between what is of otherworldly, religious import compared to what is purely secular, worldly. This is richly exemplified in India's literary traditions as recorded not only in religious documents per se but in the great epics and Puranas, which abound with myths, legends, and moral teachings that are integral to Hinduism generally

---

[640] W. N. Brown 1966; Singer 1972; Hoch 1993; O'Flaherty 1984; Kakar 1982.

and construction and pursuit of right conduct more specifically. An important theme of this literature, one of particular relevance to relief of conditions of psychiatric interest, involves its handling of and play with one's sense of reality, that is, what an individual can bank on as certain. This literature displays a preoccupation with dreams, illusions, delusions, and other imaginary happenings.[641] The nature of what is real is frequently shown not to be real at all. What appears certain and accessible to the interpretation of one's condition and apparent prospects in social life changes is impermanent and problematic, subject always to possible modification and nullification as when reformulated as seemingly real happenings in a dream or illusory transformation or awakening as promoted by gods, godlings, or demons. Moreover, the drama of one's circumstances may constitute but a staging ground of what one carried forward from previous lives, or will take one, may carry into future ones. One implication that a person may derive from a thought world that shapes and contours a shadowy and inconstant world of experience, of what reality is and portends, then, is to soften and devitalize the pains and misery that appear so commanding and compelling about one's social circumstances. Obviously, what religion brings directly as per relief of human suffering through active contemplation and identification with the divine is complex. Devotion, prayer, and meditation centred on the numinous and divinity itself take place in association with a transformation of experience and behaviour of suffering. This is a consequence of believing, expecting, and experiencing that which ails and pains the individual in context of medical suffering or sickness. The source of such experiences, whether real, imaginary or illusory is a moot point. They all involve forms of malady that are targeted by agents which are thought to personify divinity and demonic agency. An effect of spiritual, religious action is a modulation, acceptance, or re-interpretation of experience. In either way, this means that commitment to and participation in the Hindu way of life has the effect of promoting relief from the miseries associated with social life.

Consistent with such influences one has to consider the influence of altered states of consciousness as exemplified in religious practices. Stated baldly, Indian spirituality, mysticism, and devotional and meditation practices promise and deliver direct relief and deliverance from worldly secular ailments and the world-view it promotes and reinforces

---

[641] Hoch 1993; O'Flaherty 1984.

has as a principal dictum that life and its effects are less than real and maybe illusory after all, or at least likely to change, with the result of attenuation and depletion of the effects of those ailments.

VISUALIZING CULTURAL CHANGE OF PSYCHIATRIC PHENOMENA

Different types of societies have existed in the subcontinent extending from hunter-gatherers or family-level societies of prehistory through settled agricultural societies, tribes, kingdoms, states, and eventually empires and whole civilizations. This represents a full evolutionary continuum.[642] With respect to changes in its configuration and meaning, one seeks to understand how conditions of psychiatric interest have been configured and enacted in these different types of societies and how all of this changed in relation to society, culture and ecology. To a contemporary psychiatrist attuned to its neurobiological formulations and internationalist scope, psychiatric disturbances are unchanging, because signs and symptoms are overt and compelling, discoverable through careful examination, and hence not beclouded by local meanings and values. It has been argued here that from a cultural standpoint, conditions of psychiatric interest in India have taken shape in light of its distinctive cultural psychology, reflecting a particular world-view, religious and philosophical psychology, and conception of life plans and goals.

One may depict changes in psychiatric condition across types of society in a purely analytic way. A family-level society, for example, manifests a fairly distinctive set of culture patterns, subsistence practices, and social relations in a blend of relatively undifferentiated political and economic arrangements. As social entities, conditions of psychiatric interest would be interpreted and handled in a relatively homogeneous and culturally distinctive way. An approach involving their change in meaning and enactment presupposes that, as biomedical phenomena, conditions of psychiatric interest, even among very elementary societies, are inevitable and recurring. Their universality as disturbances of information handling systems of the brain is a primitive given in any theory of culture, society, and mental illness. Based on this formulation,

[642] See Johnson and Earle 2000; Fried 1967; Sahlins 1972; Service 1975; Kennedy 2000; Kochhar 2000.

one assumes that in different types of societies along the evolutionary continuum, there are different ways of socially and culturally interpreting and handling the epidemiologist's various formulations of psychiatric disorders which, of course, are unlikely to correspond to Indian constructions as condition. Beginning with the Vedic age, a new and recognizably Hindu phase of evolutionary continuum is set in motion. The culture of this era, represented in ancient philosophical, religious, moral, and literary texts, allows one to extrapolate how different types of culture patterns may have been incorporated in conditions of psychiatric interest, as has been discussed earlier.

A culture and civilization has many types of knowledge structures and, within each there are many canonical texts or documents. Each text covers a long period during which ideas change and evolve. Moreover, texts often contain commentaries that record ongoing changes in the way problems were addressed and understood. Canonical texts dating from later periods renew the cycle of representation, modification, and evolution of ideas. When this body of information is examined, the resulting picture records a phase of social and cultural change. Since conditions of psychiatric interest are shaped by cultural influences that address social and ecological stressors and conflicts in personal relationships, their formulation also helps one to visualize their change and evolution.

Following the Vedic period of Indian history there was substantial social change culminating in the rise of kingdoms, states, and empires (the Maurya and Gupta and others). Each was associated with (1) systems of social hierarchy and cultural orientation that differed as to ethnicity and language; (2) different levels of social and politico-economic complexity and social organization (size and density of urban centres and villages; and (3) groups of literate Brahmin scholars and individuals who functioned as caste leaders, each of whom contributed to knowledge production and cultural change in matters relevant to human experience and behaviour and its problems and deviations (psychiatric condition), and how to deal with them. At each point along this evolutionary continuum there would be a different way of understanding and coping with conditions of psychiatric interest prevalent in the society generally, and in particular subgroups, and in different regions. Vedic influence would have remained salient. Following this era, as discussed earlier, growth and expansion of religious sects took place, along with changes in attitudes and values expounded in the Puranas and epics, and institutionalization and change in Ayurveda.

Differences noted in Ayurveda texts and about problems of mental health and illness paint another picture of cultural change of psychiatric phenomena. Compared to earlier models, the advent of Ayurveda consolidated, standardized and narrowly circumscribed earlier viewpoints dominated by traditional and popular religion. Emphasis has already been given to the way later compilers of Ayurveda amended, broadened, and sharpened the canons. However, the introduction of change in the ayurvedic pool of information as a result of scholarly interpretation is difficult to measure. The classical focus remained influential, undergoing relatively little change even when confronted with Siddha, Unani, and early Western medicine. Ayurveda ideas and theories spread across the social fabric and no doubt influenced local folk and popular religious approaches. And, here again, it provided a narrow and more conservative cast to approaches and practices of popular and sectarian religions and of non-medical theosophical traditions and movements exemplified by Tantra, Yoga, and Siddha.

The concept of cultural change and evolution covers a vast expanse of time. Even over one generation, more or less subtle changes in emphasis and meaning may be found in relation to culture patterns affecting perception and expression of conditions of psychiatric interest. If one extends the amount of time covered from one generation to, say, five generations, there would be far more noticeable changes in the configuration and enactment of such conditions, including their insinuation into the social fabric of society and contributing to a culture pattern. Different labels for aberrant behaviour is likely to emerge, or at least different interpretations of distress, suffering, the makeup of maladies of spirit and body, and their putative causes. There would take place changing social values or levels of stigma or acceptability assigned to discredited feelings and impulses (or symptoms), different appreciation of bodily symptoms or how to resolve conflicts raised by an individual showing a psychiatric condition, and different levels of salience among competing systems of medicine – folk, popular, demonological, astrological, religious, and scholarly.

No society, except possibly the most elementary, understands conditions of psychiatric interest in only one way.[643] Syndromes are too

[643] Fabrega 1997.

malleable, complex and problematic for this to be the case, especially in societies as fractured by differences in religion, language, ethnicity, caste, and regional culture as those of India. Even the centuries predating the Common Era, and carried forward through the medieval era (even, one might add, up to the present), one would find pre-Vedic, magico-religious beliefs and associated religious and/or demonic practices in remote villages, late Vedic concepts of karmic debt, moral and spiritual failure, and religious mystical reaffirmation in other areas, towns, and cities. Formulations of distress based on ayurvedic conceptions of the body's disorders involving the humours and body elements would obviously also be found, not only among the more affluent and sophisticated elite, but among folk whom they influenced.

In cities located along trade routes or at ports that specialized in trade and commerce, there would have been greater variety in the configuration and enactment of conditions of psychiatric interest owing to the impact of foreign cultures. For example, the Arabs brought with them an entirely different tradition regarding caste, religion, social behaviour, morality, duty and obligation, aspects of cultural psychology, and, of course, different systems of medicine. The Portuguese and eventually the British introduced different traditions and culture patterns derived from their own history and their own varieties of psychiatric condition that came with them. However, beneath or alongside the more recently imposed Islamic and early European influences, anciently rooted Hindu culture and social practices continued to evolve along with indigenous varieties of psychopathology.

In summary, the social and cultural change of psychiatric phenomena in India was spread across a broad terrain covering a vast expanse of time. This terrain can be visualized in two ways. One is provided by biological psychiatry, which enjoins similar if not identical behavioural signs and symptoms based on the idiom of scientific, internationalist medicine. It would be claimed that a hypothetical contemporary biomedical psychiatrist who understood the local cultures and languages and who entered the evolutionary terrain would have had relatively little difficulty in spotting various psychiatric syndromes that continue to exist today. This view of the terrain assumes a universality of material phenomena, given the universal sameness of the neurobiological determinants of psychiatric condition. Actual cases might appear fanciful and exotic, given the variety of meanings and interpretations that were assigned to disordered cerebral processes and mechanisms. However, while the cultural and religious phenomena would differ, the phenomena looked at through the gaze of modern psychiatry would not. This picture celebrates the power of modern biological psychiatry and endorses its increasing influence in communities throughout India.

The second picture also underscores the commonalities in psychiatric phenomena over the centuries, but realized from the vantage point of cultural psychology, which includes ayurvedic medicine. Cultural models of experience and behaviour, along with their meanings and connotations, would have been configured in the language of philosophical psychology and religious world imagery that have long comprised the cultural psychology of the region. Because this language entails basic concepts about obligation and morality, it is invoked when the standards that they authorize are thwarted by manifestations of conditions of psychiatric interest. A closer look at the cultural picture, however, would reveal differences. This applies to ayurvedic interpretations and to the way revealed knowledge and tenets of popular religion have been enacted, as in the traditions of Bhakti devotion and religious mysticism.

Each epoch inherits a common cultural psychology, subjects it to reinterpretation and elaboration, and manages to achieve integration and balance. In the modern and especially the contemporary eras, the picture and fate of conditions of psychiatric interest in India seem far less optimistic. It is not clear what the end point of the evolutionary, cultural trajectory of India's psychiatric enterprise (or ethno-psychiatry) will involve. How well India manages to integrate its ancient wisdom about conditions of psychiatric interest with its borrowing of modern clinical neuroscience psychiatry is not entirely clear and remains to be seen. The modern narrative involves an invasion and contamination of the indigenous world-view by the magical bullets of modern medicine and psychiatry. These promise radical cures but do not necessarily provide existential resonance, and much less for spiritual solace and even less for liberation. It is modern psychiatry's invasion, imposition and colonialization of traditional constructions of psychiatric condition that comprise the most recent phase of its cultural evolution in India and in the world at large.

Chapter 9

Influence of Cultural Psychology on Psychiatric Conditions

WHAT IS CULTURAL PSYCHOLOGY AND WHY IS IT IMPORTANT?

Background

There are two general ways in which psychology in relation to culture have been studied and they are usually referred to as culture and personality and cross-cultural psychology. Anthropologists, psychologists, and psychoanalysts are involved in these studies seeking to understand and compare thinking, feeling, and acting among peoples from different cultures. Anthropologists predominate in the field of culture and personality. Although not centred on the study of personality itself, any sensitive cultural ethnography of a people provides information for one to appreciate how individuals see their world, their sense of social reality and their perception and understanding of themselves and others. A cultural anthropologist's participant observation of the life of a people and inferences and testing of how they think, feel and behave in social situations provides them and those of us who study their ethnographies with a window through which to infer the people's basic view of their world and their sense of self. As anthropologists, culture and personality theorists build on these basics and proceed to more directly examine psychological phenomena usually by means of interviews, surveys and testing procedures. A particular interest has been the typical personality, often referred to as 'modal personality', of a society or culture.

Cross-cultural psychology includes both anthropologists and psychologists and studies diverse aspects of experiences and behaviour in different cultures via analysis on controlled observation and testing of groups, but this time to compare psychological phenomena in at least two cultures. Descriptive characteristics of the way personality traits manifest and are played out in social settings are frequent topics of interest: for example, the influence of value orientations, drives for achievement, or preferred modes of social relationships. Such characteristics are compared between cultures. Psychoanalysts are clinicians first and foremost and work with patients or clients undergoing intensive psychotherapy, who are interested both in modes of experience and behaviour approached from the standpoint of the organization of the personality viewed as a structural arrangement of parts that can come into play in different situations and in different ways because of systems and organization of cultural meanings. Instead of empirical, controlled studies of groups, the usual approach to data of culture and personality and cultural psychologists, psychoanalysts study single cases and report on individual characteristics derived from intensive anamnesis and the method of free association. The organization and mode of operation of intra-psychic structures constitute the frame of reference of psychoanalysts. Interests and theories of researchers in these three fields obviously overlap, their shared presumption that all psychological traits, and personality as an organization of them are, in an analytic sense, human universals but significantly affected by culture in ways that create observed differences between members of different societies with respect to experience and behaviour.

Cultural psychology

A different but certainly not unrelated slant on the relationship between culture, experience, and behaviour is found in the field that goes under the term 'cultural psychology'. It involves anthropologists and psychologists. By and large they do not rely on the methods and oftentimes the assumptions of culture-and-personality theorists, cross-cultural psychologists, and psychoanalysts. They dispute the idea of a sharp dichotomy between human psychology and personality, on the one hand, compared to culture and society, on the other. They may grudgingly agree that psychological traits are universals, but at a level so abstract as to make claims about behaviour vapid and empty. Universals are not meaningful things that are simply shaped or moulded differently by different cultures and societies. Instead, to cultural psychologists, the human mind and human culture mutually incorporate each other. The way of life of a well-defined, self-contained group – a community, tribe, or society – is associated with its own, distinctive psychology.[644] To a cultural psychologist the psyche and the system of meanings (culture) of a people are fused into an amalgam that must be examined as a totality in its own right. There is a different cultural psychology for the people of India, for example, as compared to the people of China or North America. They do not just simply perceive and/or respond to phenomena of the world or formulate it in their imagination differently.[645] For different peoples the phenomena are constituted differently.

Cultural psychology places strong emphasis on cultural content as meaningful behaviour and guides the self in action. Thought worlds and habit patterns are formed in terms of culture and shared among those who are members of a cultural community. From the perspective of this book, a people's cultural psychology (the cultural psychology of pre-modern Indian peoples) resides in arrangements of information handling systems of the brain: enculturation (learning, internalizing culture) is assumed to be represented in culturally distinctive networks that traverse between cortical (pre-frontal, cingulate, and temporal lobes) and sub-cortical centres of brain.[646] This is a way of emphasizing that *symbols and their meanings* associated with a group and shared by its members *are encoded in the brain* where they influence, on the one hand, basic cognitive operations, such as attention, perception, and reasoning, that are central to experience and behaviour and, on the other, associated appetitive, conative responses (activities of the neuro-vegetative, visceral somatic brain) that involve emotion, motivation, and sense of embodiment. Stated baldly, a people's cultural psychology is rooted in organic templates, because the learning of culture or the process of enculturation involves the shaping and wiring of plastic brain networks during development.

Cultural content involves mundane concerns (such as food preferences, personal hygiene) to the sacred and esoteric (such as metaphysical assumptions about the self). How a people ask and answer basic existential questions, the symbolic meaning or content given to fundamental aspects of social and psychological life, are of paramount importance to cultural psychology. This includes, for example, the kinds of questions and answers a people have evolved about law, morality, duty, obliga-

---

[644] Shweder, Mahapatra, and Miller 1990; Shweder, 1991, 1993.

[645] Nisbett *et al.* 2001.

[646] LeVine 1990.

tion, responsibility to others, emotions, the nature of the self, the ends and purposes of life, and the sacred or divine. Staple themes of cultural psychology are symbolic behaviour, social practices and behaviours seen in relation to cultural meanings, including ways of feeling, thinking, perceiving, categorizing, and communicating. All of the preceding are reflected in and played out in innumerable prosaic ways of everyday behaviour.

Cultural psychology also emphasizes the meanings implicit in behavioural practices that are institutionalized, some as rituals and artistic performance. Institutions and rituals are significant primarily in terms of the cultural values and meanings they exemplify and have projected onto them. More private patterns of behaviour, such as rules governing sexual relations, courting, preparing and eating food, sleeping arrangements, care of the body, and relations with parents, are also important. Indeed, the core of a people's cultural psychology, its meaning and content, is revealed precisely in response to questions about the reasons for and intentions behind institutionalized forms of behaviour such as these.

An important aspect of cultural psychology is how persons are construed. There is a substantial literature on this topic.[647] A basic assumption is that a person's sense of self and his or her standing in the social reality of a particular society is pervasively influenced by culture (shaped, fashioned, constructed). This can involve person as an object in the ideology or system of beliefs of the group. It also includes cognitive styles and modes of reasoning in real world situations.[648] A more appropriate formulation for our purposes is that persons and selves, viewed as feeling, thinking, moral, and embodied beings (selves in action not just self as part of an ideology) are constituted differently as a function of enculturation.[649]

---

[647] Shweder and LeVine 1984; Marsella, DeVos, and Hsu 1985; Berry *et al.* 1992; Moore and Mathews 2001.

[648] Nisbett *et al.* 2001; Nisbett 2003.

[649] Lutz 1988; Shweder, Mahapatra, and Miller 1990; LeVine 1990; Csordas 1994.

Why cultural psychology is relevant to the study of psychiatric phenomena

Unfortunately, literature in cultural psychology contains relatively little work on the influence of cultural ideas and beliefs pertaining to persons, on the one hand, and the actual manifestations of conditions of psychiatric interest, on the other. One would presume that in societies that stress the individual over the group (*individual selves*), interpretation and actual manifestations of psychiatric condition are more likely to draw on explanations involving will and human agency, personal dispositions, sense of separateness, and individual responsibility. On the other hand, in societies where *sociocentric selves* predominate (stress on group over individual), like those of the Indian subcontinent, the presumption would be that conditions of psychiatric interest would reflect beliefs and attitudes framed in social terms, for example, involving family and kinship relationships and moral obligations to them. In other words, self as connected to others and self as a separate being would be exemplified in how conditions of psychiatric interest are constructed in these two types of society. In India, for example, one might expect the victim to seek help from others, remain integrated in the group, and try and resolve difficulties in local contexts with ideas of *dharma* and karma predominant whereas in Western societies signs and symptoms would be configured and played such as to reflect an individual's sense of ownership of its difficulties and lead them to seek help alone. These are not unreasonable assumptions. However, putting aside observations of psychoanalysts, usually although not always confined to literate urban Indians, very little research has examined the relationship between cultural notions of persons and descriptive features of psychiatric condition.[650]

If information linking self and characteristics of psychiatric condition were available for many different societies, one would have information with which to build a broad picture about how psychiatric phenomena might or might not differ as a function culture. And if one were to compare peoples of societies featured by different social and politicoeconomic organizations, for example, exemplars or types of society placed on an evolutionary continuum, then one might be able to draw generalizations about how sociological and ecological factors and his-

[650] Kakar 1968, 1981; Hoch 1993; Roland 1988. The work of psychoanalysts is discussed later.

tory change the configuration of conditions of psychiatric interest. With respect to the Indian subcontinent relevant questions one would want answers for include: In what ways did modes of apprehending and relating to the world and to one's co-members change as hunter-gatherers or 'forest peoples' were incorporated into Aryan society? Did the systems of meanings pure and simple (pre-Vedic compared to Vedic) make a difference or was the social organization (size, mode of subsistence, organization into tribes) a significant factor and if so how? In what if any ways did thinking and feelings (cultural psychology) change as Brahmanic societies evolved into Hindu societies? Was the cultural psychology of an Indian learned savant different from that of the average person in a village? Yoga meditation or Bhakti devotion certainly involves different sets of beliefs and disciplines about ways of existential release and salvation, but do they exemplify different constellations of cognitions and feelings about the self in action (do they alter Hindu cultural psychology)? What impact did Muslim ideas about the nature of being, and later still, British ideas, change cultural psychologies in the subcontinent?

Such questions are formulated in this book in terms of cultural psychology. Indian cultural psychology constitutes a system of networks insinuated into the architecture of the brain. It constitutes a neuropsychological representation as well as a filter or screen through which signs and symptoms of conditions of psychiatric interest are experienced, formulated, shaped and expressed as sheer behaviour (thinking, feeling, social conduct, perceived bodily changes and their meanings). Consequently, the questions raised earlier are equally relevant to conditions of psychiatric interest. These are questions for which solid answers are not really possible but they serve to give a feel for the slant given to relevant phenomena.

In summary, cultural psychology provides a fruitful perspective from which to examine how mental health problems are configured and expressed in a civilization. It serves not only as the idiom of expression of conditions of psychiatric interest, but as an *organ of experience* and constitutes some of their essential properties. The content and meaning of a people's mental health problems or conditions of psychiatric interest should be examined in relation to how experience and behaviour are shaped, experienced, and enacted taking into account their traditions, values, myths, and religions. What a clinician might regard as the real signs and symptoms of a people's conditions of psychiatric interest, disturbances of experience, thought, behaviour, and bodily function, do not just burst forth as self-evident natural or organic phenomena that are discrete and scripted in the universal idiom of biomedical, clinical neuroscience psychiatry. Instead, they are incorporated in and played out in terms of the tenets of their psychology and sense of embodiment, all considered as cultural programmes and structures encoded in the brain.

Cultural psychology will serve as the framework for understanding the behaviour of the people of India. Discussion will focus on some of the basic characteristics of Indian culture and civilization as they are expressed in people's perceptions, attitudes, orientations, assumptions, and ways of feeling and behaving. Elements of this psychology have a very long history in the subcontinent. Perhaps some of these go back even before the advent of the Aryans and were later incorporated in or appropriated into Hindu civilization. Regardless of origins, once this cultural psychology emerged and took shape, and here the influence of the Vedas and especially the Upanishads played a fundamental role, it has endured with amazing predominance to this day. Ways of perceiving and thinking have naturally been modified by developments during the classical and medieval periods going on to include cognitive categories associated with Westernization and secularization. This is hardly surprising: belief in ancient traditions about obligation, morality and philosophy can dramatically coexist with modern scientific conceptions about politics and health.[651]

PROLEGOMENON: IS A RELATIONAL EPISTEMOLOGY INDIA'S ORIGINAL CULTURAL PSYCHOLOGY?

Among many evolutionary and biological anthropologists, isolated small nomadic societies that hunt and gather for a living exemplify the mode of life of the very earliest societies after the emergence of anatomically modern humans. There are, of course, many factors tied to the political economy of modern, capitalist nations that impact on such peoples and the condition of some of their characteristics, challenging the rather simplistic idea that they are pristine examples of early anatomi-

[651] L. Cohen 1992; Prakash 1999.

cally modern humans but these are not relevant for present purposes. Putting such matters aside, one can regard anthropological descriptions of contemporary hunter-gatherers as useful exemplars of the earliest inhabitants of the subcontinent, pre-Aryan, indigenous peoples like the ones that later coalesced into the very earliest agricultural, animal husbandry settlements.

In this light, contemporary studies of hunter-gatherers are of particular interest for one intending to clarify the indigenous, pre-Vedic exemplars of psychology and indigenous psychiatry. If the studies involve peoples *of the subcontinent,* so much the better. One can imagine them and their way of life, (aside from their relationship to nearby agricultural people who show Hindu culture) as echoing similar phenommena of being and behaviour that existed in the subcontinent in times past. The studies provide a window into the cultural psychology of unacculturated peoples of India, not fully assimilated and influenced by popular Hindu culture as exemplified by the Puranas and epics.[652] In speaking about the Nayakas of South India, Bird-David (who incidentally has also used her observations to make evolutionary interpretations) remarks:

> These 'hunter' gatherers of South India, and their forefathers before them, going back hundreds if not thousands of years, have been living within a Hindu environment ... to some extent their practices coevolved with those of the Hindu people and [one can] anticipate resemblances.[653]

The bulk of the material discussed in this section involves the Nayaka people by Bird-David.[654] Much of this analysis is pursued using the work of Gardner and Morris on other forest peoples from South India as background and support.[655] Their work is also cited where appropriate. The Nayakas live in the lower northwestern slopes of the Nilgiri Hills in the jungle areas of South India, in the border areas of Tamil Nadu, Kerala, and Karnataka. The total number of the Nayakas is around 1000 distributed in small groups which have little if any contact with each other. They conform to descriptions of very elementary social

---

[652] Nath 2001.

[653] Bird-David 1996: 270.

[654] Bird-David 1990, 1992a, 1992b, 1994, 1996, 1999.

[655] Gardner 1982, 1991a, 1991b; Morris 1981.

groups classified as 'immediate return'-type of hunter-gatherers. They forage and hunt for immediate purposes and do not store foodstuffs. They follow a life of hunting and foraging but from time to time have relationships with nearby agricultural peoples who are Hindu.

The culture of these South Indian foragers is described as elementary and uncomplicated. They have few myths and their religion is based predominantly on natural objects of the environment, such as hills, rock outcroppings or trees that are considered the abode of spirits and in fact as supernatural entities in their own right. Spiritual beings also include the ghosts of dead ancestors and these also figure in their rituals. The gods of nearby Hindu agricultural peoples are also represented in their religion but tend to play a minor role. Bird-David finds many commonalities between thought worlds, habit patterns, and rituals of spirit possession among the Nayakas and other forest people of India reported by Gardner and Morris.[656] They all involve relating to spirits as real, immediate beings, making offerings to them, sharing food, and a day-long event framed in context of everyday activities.

Bird-David has formulated the theory or cognitive model of the Nayaka world-view. How they construe themselves, persons of the group, spiritual beings, and physical objects of the habitat involves a shared relatedness and sense of immediacy. They participate with, in and through communication and relationships with animate, inanimate spiritualized beings and spirits of dead ancestors. What essentially involves the ethno- or cultural psychology of the Nayaka people has been termed by Bird-David a *relational epistemology*. It describes a self in nature and the spiritual world which involves reverence, awe, respect, appreciation, shared participatory relatedness, and sense of immanence about the world. In a general sense, the religion, world-view, and psychology of the Nayakas could be described as animism. However, to use such a label is not only pejorative ('primitive' stage of religion), but misses the general point about the sense of self, social reality, and spiritual dimension of mind set of these forest peoples.

They have the same relationship with themselves as they have with spiritual beings of the habitat. A sense of shared, immediate participation is displayed in rituals of spirit-possession. Thus, Nayakas do not think of themselves as persons or beings that are ontologically separate from one another. Instead they view themselves as connected to each

---

[656] Gardner 1982, 1991a, 1991b; Morris 1981.

other, group members and the group, and the spiritual beings that include ancestor and personified objects of environment. In fact, this 'relational epistemology' is exemplified in matters of sickness and death. For example, the class of serious, problematic disease, termed *batha*, is *construed together with misfortune, which encompasses the group*. The bodily identity of these ailments actually involves an *intercorporeality*, which involves not only the person who is sick, but the bodies of group members and spirits.

> *Batha* highlights the 'inseparable many', predicated as it is on a sense of 'us' and 'we' (more than 'self/selves', whether as a single agent or a series thereof). Although Nayaka can, clearly, observe the suffering of the individual body, the concept of *batha* ... directs attention to joined humans and non-humans, who together are constructed as 'our relatives'.[657]

In context of visitation of spirits that involve the group deities come to possess and speak through a member in trance and answer questions from interlocutors about ongoing concerns. A matter-of-fact, personalized yet group-shared give-and-take relationship is observed between interlocutor and spirit speaking through the person possessed. During rituals spirits become family members or kin and they are immediately present and available to the Nayakas, regardless of whether they are ancestral or spirits of the objects of the physical environment: 'Nayaka shared with ancestral spirits *because* they were kin, and with other spirits to make them kin'.[658]

During spirit possession rituals objects that belonged to kin (knives, bracelets, cups) often functioned much like icons for the Nayakas. After the death of a relative such objects were important. They stood for their owners and during the first year ensured the presence of the deceased relatives. Thereafter, the spirits could approach and communicate through possession and so could also spirits that personified physical objects of the environment. This contributed to the highly informal and personal characteristic of Nayaka rituals of spirit possession. For them, relations with spirits as per ritual of possession are

> in some ways an extension of this world of kinship and domestic sharing. It draws the spirits into this world by occasioning domestic

[657] Bird-David 1999: 327.

[658] Bird-David 1999: 271.

> sharing with them ... verbal exchange with the spirits – rather than consultation in higher powers – often took the form of chatty, leisurely talk ... making offerings was framed as sharing ... Nayaka and the spirits nagged each other and demanded things, stressing their needs and the moral duty of kin to care for each other.[659]

As indicated earlier, during Nayaka spirit-possession rituals objects with special meanings were used and they functioned like icons. This raises the question of how the Nayakas construed Hindu icons, which often were also used in their rituals, compared to their own icons of physical objects of relative or environment. Bird-David points out that there are in fact several similarities between Nayaka rituals of possession and the spiritual offerings or *pūjā* of popular Hinduism. For example, in popular Hindu worship icons are dealt with as real, divinized beings; they are undressed, bathed, decorated. They are often entertained by music and dances and offered special foods, water, and lighted incense sticks. Even spirit possession can be an accompaniment of Hindu devotional practices. The question then arises as to whether Nayakas read their own meanings into the rituals they share with Hindus or retain and bring to bear their own ethos as forest people. The Hindu icons used in Nayaka spirit possession rituals were conceptualized both as Hindu deities and as objects that a relative had purchased. While for a Hindu a religious icon is regarded as divine, this is not the case for the Nayakas. In devotion a Hindu devotee seeks to come close to the divine, thereby for a short period of time becoming divinized. 'By contrast, Nayakas in their ritual sought to bring spirits into their kinship realm and, so, 'socialize' them'.[660]

Many queries and answers between entranced performers, spirits, and observers involved a sickness that may have resulted from some fault on the part of the sick person or relative. The Nayakas asked for information so as to make amends. Verbal exchanges during ritual point to the shared, immediacy ethos and reflected an emphasis on social harmony.

> The 'faults' ... varied, ranging from interpersonal offences to transgression of tradition ... the 'guilty' person (or the performer on his behalf) only had to promise making offerings to the spirits in the next coming celebration; this, instead of attending to the fault ... the important thing

[659] Bird-David 1999: 271.

[660] Bird-David 1999: 273.

> was to mend relationships thereafter, not things that had been done in the past.[661]

When faults are identified, then, Nayakas promise to make offerings rather than undo the 'fault', because from their standpoint this reaffirms kinship bonds and such bonds are what bring and maintain the good will of spirits/kin.

The Nayakas view and feel themselves as intimately connected, showing what is described as 'we-relationships' and a sharing perspective.[662] Their model or construal of each other involves kinship. They share and participate together in social activities as they do with the gods and this is particularly evident during religious ceremonies where spirit possession among members – those able to achieve mental dissociation as trance – is on display. Exchanges with the possessing spirit reflect the same sense of immediacy and exchange.

The mode of life of hunter-gatherers of the subcontinent does not appear to involve representations of persons as separate, responsible, and autonomous beings. Not the self or *ātman*, not the impersonal, supreme Other, and not release and salvation through an identification of the two in pursuit of soteriological aims shape the psychology of the Nayakas. This ideological self does not appear to command their concern and religious, moral life as it would for a Hindu. The self in action is what counts, but this 'self' is relational and interconnected with diverse beings, animate, inanimate, live, and dead. Data about the Nayakas and other South Indian forest peoples, together with ethnographies of contemporary hunter-gatherers from different regions of the world (arguably the best models for early human social behaviour), would lead one to presume that during the millennia before the Common Era groups were small, nomadic, stable, and members highly interdependent. Sharing and a group-centred psychology together with egalitarianism constituted distinguishing social characteristics. In some reports, the self-sufficiency and self-reliance of individuals is also emphasized along with the shared participation emphasized by Bird-David. Mechanisms were at work in the culture to level individual differences and promote integration of social relationships, in cooperative problem solving efforts. Anthropologists have argued that dynamics of sociality

---

[661] Bird-David 1996: 266.

[662] Bird-David 1994.

in small groups create distinctive constructions of self in relation to other beings. On the one hand, an 'egalitarian syndrome' describes group efforts among small groups to actively equalize status and thwart attempts of an individual to promote itself or gain power and, on the other, a 'relational epistemology' underscores the behaviour of sharing, relatedness, and connectedness between individual not only with group mates but with physical, and spiritual beings of the environment.[663]

Unfortunately, studies of hunter-gatherers do not include much information about their ethno-medicine and much less about their indigenous psychiatry.[664] With respect to South Indian forest peoples, findings of Morris, Gardner, and Bird-David point to similarities in religious beliefs and practices, the way spirits and gods are consulted and used, the actual manner in which they make their presence felt (by possession of some group members who serve as conduits for special advice), the sense of relief and satisfaction that possessing beings bring to members of the group (besides answering questions and giving advice), as a form of catharsis. South Indian forest peoples exemplify easy access to gods and other spiritual beings and the latter show a readiness to communicate about the sources of illness, disorder, and human suffering. These characteristics represent pillars of their system of mental health practices.

> There is ... a complex interplay, articulated through these spirit possession séances, between Hill deities, misfortune and transgression of certain norms ... Their help is sought in times of distress and they are looked to for protection – as having essentially a concern for the welfare and wellbeing of the Hill Pandaram ... the neglects of certain norms is linked ... [to] misfortune ... deities are believed to be angered by such neglect or by the transgression of such customs.[665]
>
> Nayaka turned to the spirits when they did not recognize and illness and its causes.[666]

Not all individuals of these Indian forest peoples are able to trance and serve as mediators between worldly and otherworldly affairs – 1 in 8 adults among the Hill Pandarams; 28 per cent of adults among the Paliyans. Moreover, it does not appear as though these forest peoples

[663] Boehm 1999; Bird-David 1999; Ingold 1987, 1993, 1995, 1999, 2000.

[664] Fabrega 1997.

[665] Morris 1981: 207.

[666] Bird-David 1996: 265.

have identified special persons of their group as more gifted and insightful about dilemmas of health ('physical or mental') although only some serve as conduits of the gods, which the group and not only they invoke. While anthropologists employ the construct of shamanism, they do not imply by it a well-defined individual known and distinguished by group members as an actual expert in communication with gods, merely individuals of the group who can become possessed.[667] The role of shaman per se does not seem to have emerged in this rather elementary ethno-medicine. Morris, Gardner and Bird-David all provide rich descriptions of possession behaviour and healing among the Hill Pandarams, Paliyans and Nayakas, respectively.[668] They underscore the central importance of states of mental dissociation in healing, but the common theme is their sociality and the informal interpersonal climate of these certainly not purely medical, psychiatric 'treatment' sessions. Incidents of possession are often requested by group members, not necessarily the person who becomes possessed. With exceptions in the cases described by Gardner, specific syndromes of behaviour displayed one possessed by and serving as conduit for a spirit or god do not seem stylized; they do not conform to stereotypes, well established cultural categories, nor are they named.[669] In this sense, indigenous psychiatry is loosely represented in the social life of South Indian forest peoples. It is unclear to what extent the peoples turn to practitioners of the nearby agricultural peoples for help in cases of sickness or psychiatric condition.

GENEALOGY AND THE SCOPE OF INDIAN CULTURAL PSYCHOLOGY

Foundational texts of India's culture and civilization were described in Chapter 2. They range over political ideas and institutions, legal and moral tenets about duty and social obligation as exemplified in the Dharmaśāstras, cosmological, soteriological and eschatological notions about the sacred and divine and the nature of being, forms of religious worship, rationales and practices about how to achieve psychological and spiritual liberation, tenets about the immediate and long-term con-

[667] Gardner 1991a, 1991b.

[668] Morris 1981; Gardner 1991a, 1991b; Bird-David 1999.

[669] Gardner 1991a, 1991b.

sequences of one's actions (the theory of karma), and also more secular texts explaining how the body functions and how to maintain physical wellbeing.[670] Taken together, this material articulates a sense of self and social reality and ultimate purposes of life in a distinct cosmological world. Theosophical ideas that give meaning to life and provide a sense of what it is individuals can do to realize their spiritual and moral standing in this and future lives constitute what one may conceptualize as an *Indian cultural psychology*. A cultural psychology implies that an individual sees the self and world in a culturally distinctive way; that ideas, beliefs, and values that are regnant in the society are entrained or enculturated in the individual during development and reinforced throughout life. Indian thought worlds and habit patterns are also influenced by folk beliefs and practices, particularly as they pertain to the many popular sects that make up Hinduism. Both cultural anthropologists and clinical psychologists have explored this topic.[671] It is difficult not to take into consideration this ideological self which is based on Vedic ideas and influences (especially later developments in Upanishads) when attempting to make sense of psychiatric phenomena during the first millennium BCE, a topic covered earlier.

A problem that hinders one's understanding of Indian cultural psychology is that native subjects handle as similar notions that in Western psychology are handled separately (body–mind, self–family).[672] On the other hand, their systems for classifying sociological and psychological concepts are extremely elaborate. Marriott early on provided an alternative formulation to Dumont's very influential idea about Hindu cultural psychology.[673] He has gone on to emphasize the complexity of Indian conception of personhood and behaviour. Indian conceptions of experience and behaviour are so numerous, complex in meaning, and overlapping in content that they defy easy integration.

> There are widely known classical lists of three 'strands' (*guṇas*), three 'humours' (*doṣas*), three + one 'human aims' (*puruṣārthas*), four 'classes' (*varṇas*), four 'stages' (*āśramas*), five 'elements' (*bhūtas*), five 'senses'

---

[670] Winternitz 1967; R. S. Sharma 1991; Zimmermann 1987; Keyes and Daniel 1983; O'Flaherty 1980; White 1996; Chakravorti 1996; Doniger and Smith 1991; Dumont 1970.

[671] See Wadley 1975; Daniel 1984; Mandelbaum 1988; Justice 1997; Kakar 1981, 1982; Bharati 1985; McDaniel 1989.

[672] Daniel 1984.

[673] See also Marriott and Inden 1977.

> (*indriyas*), five 'sheaths' (*kośas*), six 'savours' (*rasas*), eight + one 'sentiments' (*rasas*), eight + one 'feelings' (*bhāvas*), and so on. Lists bearing such titles respectively suggest specialised metaphysical, biological, moral, economic, developmental, physical, psychological, and aesthetic subject matters ... these lists describe what are felt to be concentric domains: they are understood as differently labelled, but approximately congruent overlays on a common underlying set of processes whose complexity is less than its many surface appearances would suggest.[674]

The 'philosophical' resonance of the cultural psychology implied by Marriott covers a complex body of knowledge described earlier and elaborated later.[675] The point needing emphasis here is the essential link between matters pertaining to religion, spirituality, philosophy, and aspects of human psychology. The perceptions of the world, the orientations to community life, ideas about social conduct as based on morality, and major milestones in an individual's life are all imbued with a sense of spirituality and obligation. The roots of this connection are found in the Vedas, as well as in the later body of traditional knowledge that continued to articulate a moral, spiritual approach to life, the overcoming of inherited burdens, ritual disciplines and practices to liberate the self, and more specific ways of obtaining salvation through love and devotion to god.

THE CULTURAL PSYCHOLOGY OF MORAL BEHAVIOUR IN INDIA

A sense of what is right and wrong, obligation, and duty are central foundations of social order and a pre-eminent source of values in all non-modern societies. This is especially the case for India. Constructs that in India provide meaning and coherence to self, experience, and behaviour and in doing so articulate its cultural psychology have a moral basis. These include, for example, *dharma*, karma, caste, *āśrama*, and Bhakti. Morality and ethics are of predominant importance in shaping thought worlds, habit patterns, and emotional opinions and reactions in peoples of the subcontinent. This has been repeatedly

---

[674] Dumont 1970: 16.

[675] See also Marriott 1976.

emphasized in previous chapters. How such directives are construed and valued and what implications adherence or transgressions have with respect to conditions of psychiatric interest (culturally constructed phenomena) cannot be overstated. Strictures about behaviour are what give direction and valence to actions conducted in culturally meaningful spaces. However, intentions and actions all too often miss or simply disregard moral targets which in turn bring anguish and related painful emotions and social isolation or condemnation. The melioration of feelings of moral deficiency and fault constitutes fundamental rationales of India's indigenous psychiatry. That is why moral behaviour is of such central importance to the social sciences and psychiatry.

The characteristics of what is considered moral and right behaviour in India compared to the US and how such views are acquired by children was the subject of a comprehensive study by Shweder and coworkers.[676] They administered a lengthy and detailed interview to children ages five to 13 years of age, and both male and female adults from Brahmin and untouchable families in the orthodox Hindu temple town of Orissa, India, and from Judeo-Christian families in a secular university neighbourhood of Chicago, Illinois. Questions covered diverse areas of behaviour where culture can be expected to be influential. Responses to a total of 39 questions about a range of family and social practices were collected and analyzed. Questions were selected to sample a set of existential issues that in the researchers' opinion have to handled and dealt with by any society: personal boundaries, sexual identity, maturity, autonomy, ethnicity, hierarchy, and how the burdens and benefits of social life should be distributed. Questions included the following: kinship avoidance, forms of address between superiors and inferiors, sleeping arrangements, manifestations of incest avoidance, appropriateness of diet in different circumstances, forms of dress, marriage and remarriage, personal possessions and private property, begging, nepotism, monogamy, wife beating, physical punishment for children, division of activities within the family, inheritance of property, protection of people from harm – psychological as well as physical – funeral rights, and practices surrounding birth of a child. A language of right and wrong framed each question, such as, for example, 'Is it wrong for ...', 'How serious is ...', 'Is it a sin to ...', 'Would it be best if ...', 'What if no one knew that such and such was done ...', 'Would it be right for a people to

[676] Shweder, Mahapatra, and Miller 1990.

change a rule about ...', and 'Do you think it is wrong if such and such does so and so?' Answers about the morality (the rightness or wrongness) of each of the 39 practices were followed up with the following standard questions: how serious was the violation, whether it was sinful, whether secrecy of violation mattered, whether it should be upheld by all people, and whether people should be stopped from violating a practice and be punished. Basically, answers to such questions point out why seemingly innocent questions (cooking while menstruating) elicit such strong emotional responses; why 'innocent' questions mean so much to Indians that are not apparent to an observer, on what lines of reasoning are moral situations evaluated.

Results showed that in each group, Americans and Indians, there was marked consensus in responses to the 39 practices and there were no important sex differences. There were cases on which Indians and Americans agreed and on which they disagreed.

> Of the 39 practices or cases, Brahman and American adults display similar judgments of right versus wrong concerning ten practices and opposed judgments concerning 16 practices. For 11 other practices there is disagreement about what's right or wrong within one community or the other, although never in both.[677]

One basic orientation of the study was to determine whether rights and wrongs were perceived as being based on social conventions or on a natural, moral order. The researchers were not able to distinguish substantive views on social practices along this dichotomy. The idea of a conventional obligation played some part in the thinking of older American children and especially adults but it is almost non-existent way of thinking among Orissa subjects. A *moral* and *not conventional* point of view or emphasis in India

> is on the natural duty to respect the truths of *dharma,* which concern the justice of received differences and inequalities, the moral implications of asymmetrical interdependencies in nature (for example, parent–child), and the vulnerabilities and differential rationality of social actors.[678]

[677] Shweder, Mahapatra, and Miller 1990: 173.

[678] Shweder, Mahapatra, and Miller 1990: 160.

With respect to the matter of enculturation, namely when and how elements of a cultural psychology get implanted in brain, it is highly significant that young children by age five are expressing culturally distinctive opinions about what is wrong and right: 'Oriya children sound very Oriya, and the American children sound very American'.[679] However, this is not to say that the *capacity* to feel 'disgust', 'stained', 'pure', 'elevated', or 'sinful' is culturally acquired but rather that what it is that children feel 'about X', 'because of Y', 'towards Z', or 'at' any other moral situation reflects a judgment that is in place at an early age, even if not consciously articulated or verbally accessible. Conversely, one must look for developments taking place during the first four years of life if one hopes to find a universal moral code that is

> spontaneously generated independently of participation in social practices. By age five, children around the word do not typically agree with each other about what is morally right or wrong.[680]

In a general sense the results of the study by Shweder and co-workers support and broaden the generalizations of Bharati and Roland, discussed later, about features of the Indian self and the importance of metaphysical tenets. In some respects, however, the results cut against these results most basically in suggesting that the idea of different selves can only be taken into consideration in a largely analytical sense. In a fundamental way and with respect to discretely articulated social situations, what is right or wrong spiritually, in the best interests of the individual, and in conformance to values and expectations exemplified in the family social morality and obligations sit in one pocket of Indian cultural psychology. What is spiritually right, what should be done and what one feels about a social situation, and how one reasons logically about such phenomena have spiritual and familial dimensions. The questions posed required subjects to bring into play social and individual considerations and in this sense, but to a lesser extent, it brought into play their individual and not just their social selves.

The results of the study support a cardinal assumption about conditions of psychiatric interest exemplified in this book. That is, that emotional disaffections, habit patterns, social and anti-social behaviour, sense of embodiment and visceral somatic dysregulation, and what a

---

[679] Shweder, Mahapatra, and Miller 1990: 183.

[680] Shweder, Mahapatra, and Miller 1990: 183.

psychiatric condition entails at a general level of abstraction, are human universals. All peoples display conditions of psychiatric interest just like they display patterns of disgust, approval, condemnation, and valuation of intimate behaviour including sexuality. However, how such phenomena are constituted can differ markedly across cultures. Moreover, because social, emotional strictures feel so right or wrong and are in place so early and so pervasively one has to anticipate that behavioural phenomena that exemplify the consequences of transgressing moral strictures, the diverse patterns stipulated by *dharma*, will show common patterns in Indian communities not only in moral contexts but with respect to conditions of psychiatric interest. The study shows commonalities in moral behaviour but does not comment on why and how infractions can be transgressed and what the consequences are given extenuating circumstances. In other words, the result present a general map but far from a concrete picture of how and why transgressions might carry greater or lesser significance given differences in social, economic, familial, and village level structures of caste.

MORE ON COGNITIVE ASPECTS OF INDIAN CULTURAL PSYCHOLOGY

Some psychologists who have worked in India focus on ways of thinking, feeling and behaving in local contexts of meaning. Their emphasis is not on theoretical constructs and beliefs as represented in scriptural sources.[681] As noted earlier, they are experimental psychologists. Building on a study of Lawrence Park, one of Shweder's collaborators, their body of work draws attention to three ways in which people across the globe explain misfortune and suffering – a category that prominently includes medical problems and, thus, psychiatric condition.[682] Such 'cultural ontologies of suffering' include interpersonal relations (envy, ill will toward others), moral concerns (personal transgressions, immoral behaviour), and scientific-biomedical considerations (impersonal, 'objective' factors, beyond responsibility and agency). Different peoples draw on these ontologies to differing degrees. Although Shweder and

---

[681] Shweder 1991; Shweder, Mahapatra, and Miller 1990; Shweder *et al.* 1997; Menon and Shweder 1994, 1998; see also Miller 1997.

[682] Shweder *et al.* 1997.

co-workers focus on everyday happenings in terms of lay, folk knowledge and beliefs, they emphasize that there is apparently a universal tendency to fall back on moral and interpersonal ontologies when explaining human catastrophes and disasters.

The Shweder group examined how Indians explain misfortune and particularly health problems by studying the cultural psychology of moral attribution in the city of Bhubaneswar, Orissa, discussed earlier. On the basis of analysis of extended explanations of why and how the 39 cases represented moral transgression, Shweder and co-workers identified 16 general moral themes. By means of statistical analysis they were able

> to distinguish three clusters of conceptually linked themes and to identify the degree of saturation of each incident by ideas from each cluster.[683]

Results pointed to an *ethics of autonomy* that draws on concepts involving rights, harms, and justice to emphasize the discretion that individuals can exercise in pursuing their personal preferences. Here, then, something resembling Western individualism is a variable, but seen in a highly moral, duty-bound, and even sacred context that ascribes to each individual's soul a special essence. The *ethics of community* emphasized duty, interdependence, and social hierarchy and stressed the moral integrity of the categories of social roles that make up the community. Morality and duty were thus centred in respect for community values and responsibilities. Finally, an *ethics of divinity*, which drew on concepts about sacred traditions, the character of the divine, sin, and pollution, seemed geared to protecting spiritual aspects of the human agent from degradation. Clearly, these three ethics bear a close resemblance to constructs of self as described by Roland.[684]

These three clusters of ethical imperatives are mutually reinforcing discourses about morality; alternatively, they are symbol systems used to describe any aspect of human experience, such as psychological phenomena and health. The three discourses are integrated and produce three different types of 'goods', which as we have seen, are held to coexist in the Hindu imagination and approach to behaviour. An ethical world-view inherent in the cultural psychology requires all three direc-

---

683 Shweder *et al.* 1997: 138.

684 Roland 1988, 1994.

tives or ontologies. In contrast to Western societies (especially for the US), notions of autonomy and individualism are in the background in India while notions of community and divinity are in the forefront, more salient, and institutionalized.

The various ways of conceptualizing social responsibility in Orissa

> represent an expanded repertoire of discourse for construing the grounds of obligation, the nature of particular obligations, and the consequences of failure in matters of obligation ... an expanded discourse for considering the social, psychological, and behavioural context of health maintenance.[685]

With some imagination and intellectual tolerance for anachronistic excesses, one might suggest that Shweder and co-workers, in conformance with the observations of Bharati and Roland and of Kakar, are pointing to aspects of consciousness, experience, and behaviour that were manifested and perhaps crystallized in the minds of Indians long ago and reinforced vigorously as far back as the reign of the emperor Aśoka when his service and welfare administrators sought to not only reinforce but impose dicta stipulated in *dharma* for the pecple as discussed by Thapar.[686]

In another study, Menon and Shweder document the understandings and meanings of an important and ancient cultural myth of India concerning relations between the sexes and symbolized in the activities of the gods.[687] The myth and uses made of it are grounded in Indian cultural psychology and involve social norms about emotional regulation and the morality of shame and emotional control. By measuring the degree to which subjects internalize the significance of the myth, the researchers could measure their degree of cultural competence and social praxis in an area of everyday relationships. By examining earlier writings on the myth, researchers attempted to ascertain its canonical interpretation. The Menon–Shweder study supports with empirical data an important facet of Indian cultural psychology discussed earlier, namely, how contemporary subjects understand a historically ancient and culturally important tale about the gods and their behaviour, and its

---

[685] Shweder *et al.* 1997: 150.

[686] Thapar 1984, 1997, 2002.

[687] Menon and Shweder 1994.

relationship on how they themselves should behave in circumstances in which expressions of emotion have moral implications.

In India the theory of karma plays a fundamental role in underwriting the essentially moral basis for conceptualizing misfortunes, especially medical problems. The idea that individuals and those close to them are affected by the moral impact of feelings, thoughts, and actions is deeply embedded in the Indian cultural psyche. Moral transgressions can have immediate as well as long-term consequences – that is, both during one's mortal life and in another life after the transmigration of the soul and rebirth in other forms.[688] There is an obvious connection between ideas about moral values (exemplified in *dharma*, or obligation, law, duty) and the theory of personal responsibility for one's actions (*karma*). To these researchers belief in karma seemed to create a feeling of conviction and inevitability a person's actions have a measured and proportionate consequence for an individual.

> It lends a motivational force to the felt obligatoriness of the many demanding practices in Indian domestic, social, and ritual life.[689]

When seen in relation to the three discourses about morality and responsibility discussed earlier, the bank account of merits and demerits that one accumulates as stipulated by the theory of karma creates an inexorable burden that gives meaning to every facet of one's life. Bad conduct and neglect of stipulations inherent in *dharma* that are covered by any of the three moral codes described (autonomy, community, divinity) bodes harm, predicting suffering that includes 'physical illness or pain, psychological suffering, and social disharmony'.[690]

Comment on the moral fabric of Indian conditions of psychiatric interest

One can use the framework of cultural psychology of India and its realization in the morality of behaviour as a way of providing one with an exemplar of conditions of psychiatric interest in the subcontinent. To begin with, how a psychiatric condition originates, its fundamental

[688] As already discussed with respect to the theory of Ayurveda and Yoga.

[689] Shweder *et al.* 1997: 150.

[690] Shweder *et al.* 1997: 154.

causes and materiality, is a moot point. Also, perhaps it is not really possible to answer ultimate questions such as these. The root causes can involve genetic vulnerabilities involving the disorganization and function of information handling systems of the brain (networks) or disturbances or discomfitures arising in the social environment and experienced existentially. These two factors involve the strands or filaments of a psychiatric condition and they cannot but come together. One might think that neuroscience promises a road to brain and genetic determinism as a way of understanding psychiatric disorders, but it does not. Brain disturbances seen in such disorders don't exist as ready-made markers of impersonal, objective, or easily measured phenomena but in *individuals selected beforehand because their ways of thinking, feeling and behaving conform to cultural models of abnormal behaviour*. Furthermore, they can only be made sense of if they can be related to the social, cultural behaviour and circumstance of the person whose brain is being examined.

In India, one can pre-suppose that environmental determinants and the coming together of brain and behaviour vulnerabilities of brain function in relation to psychiatric condition involve something having to do with *dharma*, debts or carry-overs linked to past karmic actions, one's relative position in the programme of liberation or salvation and the like. In other words, the sorts of things Roland and Kakar identified in their work with Indian patients and Shweder and co-workers with their subjects. What, why, and how a condition surfaces in a vulnerable individual can involve dilemmas of a purely worldly nature, for example, resulting from eating a particular food at the wrong time, displaying too much familiarity with a younger sister-in-law, failure to properly honour one's ancestors in performance of a ritual. All of these resonate with moral implications.

Cultural learning during childhood and throughout life involves sensing, perceiving, and handling meaning filled information which is then processed in hierarchically interconnected levels of the nervous system. In other words, the system of social symbols and their meanings (i.e., culture) gets encoded and carried in the brain. Enculturation results in establishment of networks that span and link prefrontal and temporal neocortex and subcortical structures which regulate perception, conception, and emotional/motivational processes. Rules, injunctions, and values encoded in brain when psychologically represented and experienced are what account for or determine the moral fabric or texture of a psychiatric condition. In India this arrangement or design will involve impulses, actions, emotional responses, disappointments, social withdrawal, or the pursuit of new directions or emphases in one's course of life so as to atone, set things right, or deepen commitment to mental disciplines and devotional exercises. Here again, questions of right and wrong, of how to handle and resolve moral dilemmas loom all important. Perhaps it will involve renewed dedication to ritual, more intense efforts at meditation so as purify mind and body, a more intense loving and devotion to a god or a goddess, or a greater motivation to work with one's guru or advisor. Prayer to one's ancestor might work or resort to divination or demonology (depending on matters of felt anger versus victimization). If the unfolding psychiatric condition continues to plague the individual and there does not appear that resolution is possible given its situation, then the amalgam of thought, feeling, and need/requirement for cognitive, emotional, and physical cleansing can trigger a change in level of consciousness, a mental dissociation that can be expressed via experience of possession or bewitchment. The fabric of India's culture articulates many patterns or avenues for communication via a syndrome of *bhūta*s or *unmāda*.[691] Even if one were to conceptualize a psychiatric condition as basically involving the turning on or off of energy, drive or instinct, level of intensity or activity, or emotionality, culture and morality come into play since these forms of expression are necessarily configured in an idiom and vocabulary, which reflects and communicates in a field where morality and questions of right and wrong operate.

The final design, scenario, plot or portrayal of a psychiatric condition in India, then, will have a moral resonance or dimension. Its parts and colours may involve coming on too strong or not strong enough to a widowed aunt that is not strictly following the right tone in her clothing, touching a person from a lower caste, not paying the proper respect to one higher in the hierarchy of caste village, or family, wearing the wrong type of clothes at a local shrine, eating with a husband's older brother, falling in love with a person of the wrong caste, visiting a temple at the wrong time, not disciplining and, if necessary, beating a disobedient wife or child, or cooking when one is not supposed to. The concrete, overt scene of worldly disarrangement exemplified in a psychiatric condition will reflect questions of morality linked to family and

[691] Described earlier in Chapter 8.

social environment whereas its deeper, more private, and pervasive disaffection and discomfort will involve how the concrete, surface phenomena play out in the spiritual, metaphysical design to which the individual feel compelled and obligated to conform.

IDEOLOGICAL SELF AND SELF IN ACTION: ASPECTS OF INDIAN CULTURAL PSYCHOLOGY

In Bharati's opinion Hindu India has concerned itself primarily with 'self' as a thing in itself that exists through time and gets perfected in spiritual terms.[692] Such an ideological view of self, grounded in metaphysics and philosophy and in virtually all systems of Indian thought, constitutes for Bharati 'the' central theme of Hindu culture and civilization. He emphasizes that this is only part of the story of what from my standpoint is a crucial feature of Indian cultural psychology, a feature that he somewhat reprovingly describes as engagement in 'retrospective Indology'. He attempts to differentiate between this abstract 'cognitive' self from the conative sphere of striving, acting, and motivated action of 'flesh and blood' Indians in real life circumstances.

To an informed Hindu scholar, a pandit, the self is exemplified and worked out conceptually in Advaita Vedānta, the monistic doctrine alluded to earlier which was first exhibited in canonical Upanishads of the eighth century BCE. Bharati contends that this doctrine and world-view was best articulated by Shankara in eighth century CE, who founded the Daśanāmi Order of the sannyasis, generally regarded as the most esteemed religious order in Hindu India. Advaita literature is monistic, concerned to enable the adept to connect with his inner *ātman*, which is part of the universal *Brahman*, by breaking through the delusion of multiplicity and plurality. This is accomplished not by bookish reading, discourse, and/or contemplation, but in a mediated way as per disciplined instruction with a guru. The self an adept seeks is abstract; for example, it is said that one cannot describe it or be object of experience; it consists of virtually all phenomena and is the controller of all. Bharati juxtaposes this cognitive, ontological self to the empirical self; in other words, the 'self in action' in everyday worldly affairs given different

---

[692] Bharati 1985.

settings and circumstances. The empirical self was not of interest to scholars of the Hindu tradition as it has been and still is to anthropologists, psychologists, sociologists, and psychoanalysts. Scholars reject, assimilate, or denigrate the ontological status of the empirical self. For them a metaphysical construct is what it is important, Self with a capital 'S'. The closest thing to an empirical self is denoted *jīva*, which not only consists of undesirable traits (lust, anger, egotism) but it is constituted by them (it 'is' such negative strivings).

Bharati points out that a natural expectation is that the highly intellectualized, cognitive self is found only among the religious and intellectual elite. One would think that a non-scholarly Hindu had a down-to-earth idea about self in action, the domain of Bharati's empirical self.

> Such an intuition, however, would be wrong. Hindu thoughts and perceptions, Hindu values – all Hindu values – have been thoroughly informed by these seemingly recondite concepts ... Hindu notions of the self were generated and are being perpetuated from that metaphysical-speculative base just like Western notions of self were generated and perpetuated by empirical epistemologies ... [of Greece and Christianity].[693]

To the ordinary Hindu, just like for the pandit intellectual, everyday decisions and actions are prompted by ideas tied to karma, which are linked to the metaphysical self.

Work with patients in India has persuaded Roland to include in his formulation of self and behaviour categories that encompass and are not inconsistent with those of Bharati.[694] He sees Indian cultural psychology as embodying three selves: the spiritual, familial, and individual. The latter involves ideals of autonomy, agency, and personal striving and their associated conceptions about persons and social relationships that are freely entered into and largely contractual, a perspective typically associated with Western culture and that Roland has also observed in his psychoanalytic work with Indian patients – mainly urban, educated. This will not be discussed further here.

For Roland, a *spiritual self* involves the sense of spiritual reality that is 'inside' a person and comes to the fore as a lived experience in different circumstances. Very much like Bharati, Roland contends that in

---

693 Bharati 1985: 190.

694 Roland 1988.

India the spiritual self is expressed 'through a complex structure' of gods, goddesses, rituals, and practices, and disciplines of meditation. It corresponds to the self that Bharati formulates as the cognitive, ontological, and metaphysical self. Roland emphasizes that 'the' ultimate goal of life of a Hindu is pursuit of subjective, pure consciousness via different disciplines and gurus, pandits who can guide the devotee. This involves a progressive and gradual dismantling of ordinary mental constructions such as attitudes, values, and ambitions borne in the everyday reality of individuals but of lesser salience in their psychic lives.

Nevertheless, Roland gives more attention than Bharati does to the empirical, interactive self and regards it as extremely important for understanding Indian cultural psychology and conditions of psychiatric interest. He emphasizes the emotional and social enmeshment of an individual in one's family, kinship network, and secondarily in caste. He finds that in Indian culture a person's sense of self and social identity is profoundly influenced by the family. Nevertheless, cross-cutting this important vector Roland notes that persons and selves are construed in highly particularistic terms, embodying differing natures from others because of their inherent qualities (*guṇa*), powers (*śakti*), and dispositions devolving from actions in previous lives (*karma*) and associated attachments (*saṃskāra*). Because of these inner natures and because of structural arrangements within family, village, and caste, persons are not viewed as equal to each other. There is a built-in tension then between status and identity based on the hierarchy of sheer structure and power and one of inner qualities. The differences reflect a theory of Indian cultural psychology. Roughly, it involves differences between cultural conventions of behaviour stipulated on the basis of 'who is boss in the family' compared to 'who is really a good person', an echo from the duality of metaphysical worth compared to worldly value/accomplishment, discussed in detail in earlier chapters. This theory creates alternative and complex ways in the way in which the empirical self relates and the conflicts, dilemmas, and emotional hardships it causes as per relations based on hierarchies of structure compared to quality.

Besides a spiritual self, then, Roland draws attention to what he terms the *familial self* as an important component of how persons are shaped in Indian culture and how they behave in social situations (Indian cultural psychology). He sees it as constituted of several psychosocial dimensions; structural hierarchy, hierarchy by quality, and qualitative of hierarchical relationships. Basically, with respect to the third dimension, Roland appears to suggest, but is not entirely clear, that family relationships in form of hierarchy are associated with a mode of thinking, feeling, and engaging in social relationships.

One psychosocial dimension of the familial self involves more or less formalized stipulations based on structural hierarchy. It devolves simply from the hierarchical way in which structures of power and relationships of the family are supposed to work out in practice. There exist different social, psychological, and behavioural spaces that family members occupy that are based on age, gender, and marital relationships. Such traditional values of the culture are learned from older women of the family.[695] They call for ideals of solidarity and cooperation, understanding, and emotional expression, in line with traditional customs and norms of the family and in the way conflicts are supposed to be resolved. Women are often entrusted with socialization of such modalities and values of social relations.

> These older women recite the vitally important mythology from the two major epics ... [popular literature] ... and proverbs and folktales appropriate for a great variety of relationships and situations, thus giving meaning to the myriad hierarchical relationships through clear images of good and bad. Timeless models become crucial for living in traditionally defined, multiple hierarchical relationships in the extended family and other groups.[696]

Roland emphasizes the numerous conflicts, tensions, and signs and symptoms that can result from the demands inherent in the structural hierarchy of the extended family and the carryover of such expectations into the workplace or other relations among persons outside the family, where family models of reciprocal give and take do not work and cause much consternation.

Besides family relationships based on a psychosocial dimension of structure and power (structural hierarchy), Roland draws attention to a hierarchy based on quality. The qualitative dimension of the familial self is governed by the qualities judged to inhere in different individuals. Relations based on hierarchy of quality are highly personalized and emotional and communications in them take place largely non-verbally. The psychosocial dimension based on structural hierarchy involves def-

---

[695] See also discussion of work by Kakar, taken up later.

[696] Roland 1988: 216.

erence, subordination, and loyalty towards the superior. In the dimension based on hierarchy on quality the inner quality of superior persons earn them respect, veneration, and idealization. These styles of relating and feeling are termed by Roland as 'modes of interaction'. The quality meriting veneration might reflect standing in the structural hierarchy but it might not. It can accrue to a younger member and even to a non-family acquaintance such as a maid, including untouchables. Superior quality here is based on the qualities, powers, and inherited karmas of an individual mentioned earlier.

The third psychosocial dimension of hierarchical relationships found in Indian culture involves what Roland terms 'the qualitative' mode and by this he means the subjective side or emotional feel of relationships. His label for this dimension introduces some ambiguity since one of the hierarchical relationships is based on 'quality'.[697] With respect to emotional repercussions and possible behavioural phenomena of psychiatric import this psychosocial dimension of family relationships and of those found outside the family for that matter, since relationships in the latter are often modelled on the former, is particularly relevant. Its description illuminates and makes explicit much of the work of cultural anthropologists discussed in earlier chapters.

> The qualitative mode of these highly personalized extended family hierarchical relationships can be characterized by an intense emotional connectedness and interdependence with a constant flow of affect and responsiveness between persons; by a strong mutual caring and dependence with an intensely heightened asking and giving in an emotional atmosphere usually of affection and warmth, with expectations of reciprocity; and by highly empathic sensitivity of to one another's feelings and needs without expression of them ... qualitative mode primarily takes place on a non-verbal level and has to be felt empathically to be understood. When intense expectations are not fulfilled, considerable hurt and anger are experienced ... feelings disruptive to the hierarchical relationship, especially ambivalent ones that may be experienced by the subordinate, are most often contained, inhibited, or defended against through a variety of unconscious defence mechanisms in order not to disturb the relationship.[698]

---

[697] It is unclear if Roland makes a distinction between the qualitative mode of relations based on structural compared to quality hierarchy.

[698] Roland 1988: 220–221.

Relationships based purely on structural hierarchy relating to questions of authority and power can give rise to inconsistent and plaguing emotions, felt and privately held, contra overt communications in public setting. However, in relations of hierarchy based on quality there is generally consistency between what interactants feel, say, and seek to implement. In family settings discontinuities between demands, expectations, feelings, and actions undertaken in these two hierarchies (structure and quality) can give rise to emotional conflicts and tensions as Roland documents from analysis of sessions in psychotherapy. In keeping with his psychoanalytic orientation Roland posits several intra-psychic landmarks of the familial self that enable an individual to function effectively in the various psychosocial dimensions of hierarchical family relationships. These will not be discussed.

Roland, then, offers one a lucid and systematic way of visualizing Indian cultural psychology as exemplified in his three selves, namely, the spiritual, the familial and the individual. One can view the spiritual self as providing a basic anchor for an individual's experiences and behaviour, his or her sense of self and his or her position in the scheme of religion, morality, and cosmological placement. The ideas, beliefs, world-views, and philosophical psychology of the spiritual self contextualizes and articulates the ultimate meanings inherent in being and the ways of fulfilling dharmic expectations in accordance with metaphysical verities and considerations devolving from theory of karma. As Bharati contends, and as the work of anthropologists support, even today a Hindu's sense of self and wellbeing as to status and social conduct somehow resonate with such metaphysical beliefs. Roland tends to see these as important but less central aspects of Indian intra-psychic structure and function. On the other hand, the self considered in terms of roles, obligations, especially everyday family social relations, mundane preoccupations and personal concerns and strivings are predominant aspects of Indian cultural psychology. It is the aspect of the Indian self that brings it happiness, satisfaction, and misery and suffering.

Roland's patients were burdened by conflicts emanating from the way stipulations dictated by the familial self were thwarted. Hardships and setbacks experienced by the familial self predominated in their conflicts and signs and symptoms. For example:

> Sons, with normal expectations of the Indian familial self, identified with their fathers' values and tried to gain their fathers' respect and re-

> flect well on their fathers. This frequently resulted in their depreciating Indian culture and, therefore, their more core self, which was closely associated with indigenous culture through the earlier maternal relationships.[699]

However, even among such largely urban, educated persons whose individual selves were better defined and functional, relevant feelings and concerns devolving from their spiritual 'self' resonated and could cause suffering and misery. To account for the importance of the spiritual self in contextualizing and sometimes dominating signs and symptoms of otherwise normal, functional, and socially competent patients, Roland was forced to make adjustments in his conception of how intrapsychic structures and self-object relations were structured and functioned in Indian cultural psychology.

> Related to hierarchical relationships are ... facets of the familial self ... termed [by Roland] 'symbiosis-reciprocity', in contrast to the Western stress on separation-individuation. The experiential sense of self ... is much more of a we-self than the individualistic I-self of Westerners, a we-self that varies more with relationships.[700]

DEVELOPMENTAL AND INTRAPSYCHIC ASPECTS OF INDIAN CULTURAL PSYCHOLOGY

Introduction

Earlier the work of Bharati was discussed and Roland in particular examined the Indian self, considered in social psychological context as well as in terms of ideology and spirituality. Although Roland is a practicing psychoanalyst, his formulation was derived from work with patients, and thus framed in the theory of personality of psychoanalysis, it was mainly his interpretation of the give and take of Indian selves in social, interpersonal and especially familial context that was the focus. In this section use of traditional ideas of psychoanalytic theory as per Indian personality are taken up in more detail.

A psychoanalyst is interested in understanding the way in which a people's personality, behaviour, and social functioning acquires its char-

---

[699] Roland 1994: 363.

[700] Roland 1994: 373.

acteristics. He or she seeks to understand how early relations with parents, especially with the mother, shape an infant's evolving sense of self. This involves an analysis of how individuals managed developmental milestones, deal with environmental contingencies, mother–infant interactions, and the goals and challenges associated with early life and adolescence. The constructs on which psychoanalytic theory is based are derived from conventions about the behaviour of individuals in Western, scientific culture and this gives rise to the two issues touched on previously. First and most obvious, the rationale and theory of psychoanalysis is based on Western conventions, not only about knowledge and reality but, more specifically, about the object of study: Western notions about mind, experience, behaviour, and personality or selfhood. Because the analyst usually shares the world-view and conceptual nexus out of which his or her theory or epistemology evolved, it is very difficult, if not impossible, either to question these conventions or to go outside them to examine the workings of a psychology based on different conventions and assumptions about self and behaviour that can prevail in another culture.[701] Ideally, an analyst should have a good understanding of another's culture that renders its mental (cultural psychological) representations real and compelling, shaping how an individual responds, feels, interprets, behaves, and copes with one's surroundings. Furthermore, analyst should seek to understand the individual's mental structures and how they work in light of the individual's culture, independent of what the theory presupposes. This is a complex task that has occupied culture-and-personality theorists for well over 50 years. Secondly, having identified characteristics of an individual's cultural psychology, for example, preferred defence mechanisms, ego ideals, construct of person, and when and how to express emotion, the analyst must seek to understand how all of these and related characteristics were learned and internalized in mental structures during the course of development, a process that has been termed *enculturation.*[702]

The task is easier if the analyst shares the cultural beliefs and practices of the patient. This is specially the case if the analyst happens to construe psychoanalytic theory as applying to peoples of all cultures (as universal) and interprets his or her data with little regard for cultural differences involving personality structure. If this is not the case, then

---

[701] Roland alluded to this difficulty and was able to modify important assumptions.

[702] LeVine 1973, 1990; Shweder and LeVine 1984; LeVine and Norman 2001.

analyst should indicate modifications of psychoanalytic theory based on cultural psychological particulars, as suggested earlier with respect to the work of Roland.[703] In either case, a culturally sensitive psychoanalytic interpretation of human psychology requires a delineation of the salient characteristics of a culture as these are reflected in the inner life of individuals.

With respect to the aims pursued in this book, a caveat is in order. To formulate human psychology psychoanalysts draw on the verbal associations and observations of real, contemporary people. The cases from Roland and Kakar were largely urban, educated persons. Obviously, aspects of modernity colour what subjects talk about and cope with mentally, and on what psychoanalysts based their formulations. However, the task proposed here is to use such insights, as much as this is possible, in order to understand the cultural psychology of traditional, pre- or non-modern Indian populations. An assumption one relies on is that it is reasonable to draw on culturally specific psychoanalytic generalizations – exemplars of Indian psychology today – and apply them across the expanse of Indian history if such generalizations are formulated on the basis of generic and fundamental parameters that affect how the Indian mind is constructed and works, including, for example, behaviour traditions, conceptions of persons, developmental experiences, myths, folklore, legends and tales, proverbs, and characteristic role models of figures drawn from ancient, canonical literatures. To the extent that psychoanalysts' generalizations about cultural psychology are based on generic and archetypal patterns of experience and behaviour found in Indian society, one is allowed to draw on them to make sense of Indian experience and behaviour across larger expanses of time. This includes psychiatric phenomena: specific concerns, preoccupations, circumstances, events, and situations played out on the stage of Indian history that configure and enact emotional and behavioural discomfitures and disaffections of psychiatric interest. Obviously such phenomena differ vastly when seen across historical epochs. However, the paradigms, stereotypes, basic themes, rationales, and generic abstract representations of the 'plays' of conditions of psychiatric interest reflect changing, but more or less stable, characteristics of personality, conduct, and human relationships. Consequently, paradigms and stereotypes that can be formulated on this stage are grist for the mill for examining the

[703] Roland 1988, 1994.

cultural history of psychiatric phenomena in traditional, pre-modern India.

Psychoanalytic configuration of Indian personality

Sudhir Kakar, a Western-trained Indian, is a practicing psychoanalyst interested in culture and behaviour and well positioned to cope with problems of intercultural analysis of experience and behaviour.[704] In his formulation of Indian cultural psychology he not only draws on work with patients but also upon knowledge of traditions, world-views, and concepts of experience and behaviour inherent in ancient literatures. His goal is to formulate how the average Hindu constructs a sense of reality, orients to social circumstances, pursues a life course, meets challenges and obligations, seeks worldly goals, and strives after fundamental Hindu ideals about the meaning and purpose of life.

Kakar's analysis involves the interrelations among three fundamental characteristics of the Hindu world image: (1) the theme of fusion as exemplified in the concept of *mokṣa*; (2) the theme of an appropriate life task and life cycle as exemplified in the concept of *dharma* and its analogues (*svadharma* or life task, *āśramadharma* or human life cycle); and (3) ideas of time and destiny as featured in the unconscious and as moderated by the concept of karma.

All of these religious and philosophical concepts have been mentioned earlier. Kakar formulates in intra-psychic, psychological terms. To begin with *mokṣa,* the ultimate aim of existence in Hindu culture, refers to *self-realization through transcendence.* Salvation comes through a release from worldly involvement and *direct experience* of the fundamental unity between an individual and the infinite, including the 'other' and the holy (*samādhi,* or attainment of oneness). The ideal of *mokṣa* gives the average Hindu the possibility of a *mystical experience in life* and to Kakar it becomes a reality when the experience of 'I', *pure consciousness* or the centre of awareness that pervades all experience, becomes manifest in the selves of others as empathy and complete identification. He explains that until a Hindu's composite self or sense of 'I' and generalized 'other' is established and maintained he or she lives in *avidyā,* namely, ignorance or false consciousness. Only one who is liberated from karmic debts *knows* true reality. Until then perception and sense of self remains

[704] Kakar 1968, 1981, 1982.

an illusion or deception (*māyā*). A sense of reality is achieved when processes of sensing and feeling are in touch, as it were, with fundamental rhythms and harmonies of the universe as conceptualized in the Hindu world image. To Kakar, the conception of an 'ego-oriented' *māyā* helps explain the average Hindu's interest and respect for the occult. Astrologers, soothsayers, *sādhus*, fakirs, and shamans in general are individuals who seek to transcend the limitations of *māyā*.

Kakar naturally construes Hindu cultural psychology in psychoanalytic terms. He opines that to the Hindu, a basic sense of reality does not inhere in structures that make up the ego (pre-conscious perceptions, unconscious defences, rational principles) but in the 'id', an organism's instinctual drives, the deeper and phylogenetic much older structure of personality. Reality can be appreciated largely in terms of such archaic, unconscious, pre-verbal processes of sensing and feeling. Based on psychoanalytic theories, contrasts between Hindu and Western cultural psychology are emphasized:

> The distinctions between reality and *māyā*, between *vidyā* and *avidyā* – true and false consciousness – illustrate a fundamental difference between Hindu and Western world images, as well as a discrepancy in the modes of thought and apperception, which even the best-intentioned movements of cultural ecumenism cannot hope to bridge satisfactorily. The maintenance of ego boundaries – between 'inside' and 'outside', and between 'I' and 'others' – and the sensory experiences and social relations based on these separations, is the stuff of reality in Western thought and yet *māyā* to the Hindus. The optimal discrimination of this reality of separateness, expressed in terms of heightened ego functions such as reality sense, reality testing and adaptation to reality, is the stated goal of most Western psychotherapies, but of paltry importance in the ways of liberation.[705]

To the elect and disciplined, the task of liberation is reached through the practices of Yoga and Kakar sees provocative parallels between Hindu and psychoanalytic conception of mental life as exemplified in such practices. An object of Yoga is connecting with an individual's *citta*. According to Kakar, this denotes the fundamental concept in the Hindu model of the psyche and is closely related to the notion of the id in psychoanalysis. However, the *citta* actually contrasts sharply with the id of psychoanalysis, which is seen as involving instincts that are undirected

[705] Kakar 1981: 20.

and maladaptive, always seeking indiscriminate discharge. The psychoanalytic view posits opposition between the ego and the id, with the former always on guard and geared to the latter's control. In Hindu cultural psychology, a permanent opposition between the two psychic systems is not in evidence. While recognizing that the *citta* has a restless and driven character, their psychology attributes to it a purpose inherent in human life and not at odds with it. In contrast to id, rather than exclusively denoting the dark, ominous, and unruly, however, *citta* is a potential reservoir of positive human striving that an individual seeks to transform toward a final 'one-pointed' form involving an altruistic union of the 'I' with the 'not-I'. Kakar indicates, in orthodox psychoanalytic fashion, that this interpretation of the unconscious and what Yoga practitioners pursue is actually consistent with some of Freud's writings. Sexuality is an important reservoir of *citta* energy that, according to Hindu religious teachers, must be gathered, concentrated, and transformed:

> *citta* is attached to the organs of the body and exists restlessly in scattered and darkening forms ... Only in radical acknowledgement of *citta*, by diving deep through its calm waters, can man realize *mokṣa* and thus comprehend true 'reality'.[706]

Thus, the Hindu vision of reality as exemplified in the practice of Yoga offers what Kakar calls a romantic quest to achieve something like a mystical union with the absolute. While the esoteric practices of *rāja-yoga* are used by a small religious elite and disciplined few, there are myriad sanctioned ways for the majority of Hindus to achieve this ideal state. Kakar includes intense devotional activity (the way of Bhakti), the way of *karmayoga* or selfless work, and the cultivation of the capacity to distinguish between the real and apparent or *jñāna*. However, all Hindus realize that reaching the ideal of liberation is improbable in any one lifetime. For Kakar the details and possibilities of the fusion experience are less important than the *mokṣa* as an ideal, a basic and specific form of Hindu religiosity and cultural psychology. It provides motivation and purpose to a Hindu that, while actively striven for, *mokṣa* should be patiently awaited through life cycles, if necessary. Here is his psychoanalytic formulation:

---

[706] Kakar 1981: 25.

> *mokṣa* – and by implication, the possible transformation of *citta* – is a cherished fact; ... [it] persists as the main element in the 'ideology of the superego', providing an unconscious ethical direction to the course of life ... [an] altruistic longing ... the universal beacon of 'higher feeling' in the lives of most Hindus, cutting across class distinctions and caste boundaries.[707]

Kakar holds that *mokṣa* as a goal of life was exquisitely conscious and freely articulated in ancient India, and he implies that it continues to be an important feature of the Hindu inner world image. He examines artistic Indian traditions and finds there the characteristic longing and fusion with aspects of the unconscious and *citta*:

> Man, not as a discrete presence but absorbed in his surroundings; ego, not in opposition to the id but merged with it; individual, not separate but existing in all his myriad connections: these versions of human experience provided the main thematic content of Indian art.[708]

Interestingly, and in keeping with a theme discussed earlier and that we will encounter later, Kakar relates this trait of Hindu cultural psychology to a unitary vision of body and psyche, phenomena ordinarily separated in Western intellectual life and psychological experience. He draws on the experiences of therapists and theorists who have studied psychosomatic aspects of medical problems in Indian patients, the latter holding views about self and experience by means of their body organs. The theme of psychosomatic integration is indeed foundational in Hindu psychology and medicine and has already been mentioned earlier in discussion of writings on Ayurveda by Roşu. In Kakar's estimation, the following passage from the writings of Swami Sivananda echoes themes that resonate with the 'classical Hindu view' about mind–body relationships in the context of disease:[709]

> The body with its organs is no other than the mind. The physical body is the outward manifestation of the mind ... Whatever you hold in your mind will be produced in the physical body. An ill-feeling or bitterness towards another person will at once affect the body and produce some kind of disease in the body. Intense passion, hatred, longstanding bitter jealousy corroding anxiety, fits of hot temper, actually destroy cells

---

[707] Kakar 1981: 30.

[708] Kakar 1981: 32.

[709] Sivananda 1974.

> of the body and induce diseases of heart, liver, kidneys, spleen and stomach. When the mind is agitated, then this body also is agitated. When both the body and mind are agitated, the Prana flows in a wrong direction. Instead of pervading the whole body steadily and equally, it will vibrate at an unequal rate (unrhythmically). The food is not digested properly. Diseases originate. If the primary cause is removed, then all diseases will disappear.[710]

Kakar holds that the essential psychological feature of Hindu culture is the polarity and conflict posed by fusion, which entails a loss of identity and autonomy, and separation or autonomy, which raises the fears of aloneness and isolation. He views these psychoanalytical verities as intimately related to the human fear of death and he maintains that Hindu cultural psychology attempts to confront and resolve the fear of death in its elaboration of the theme of *mokṣa* as a fundamental goal of human life. Hindus, in Kakar's estimation, deal with the fears of death as realized in conflicts about fusion and separation by attempting to move toward the goal of *mokṣa* slowly and deliberately through a full life lived in *dharma*, the second important concept in the Hindu cultural psychology and world image. An individual's *dharma*, or right action, is embodied in a life task (*svadharma*) that stretches over the human life cycle (*āśramadharma*). Four coordinates of action realize the content of one's *dharma*, and these are given by the culture (*deśa*, lit. 'locale'), by the historical period (*kāla*), by the efforts required during different stages of one's life (*āśrama*), and by the innate psychobiological traits (*guṇa*s) that are the heritage of one's previous lives.

Kakar conceptualizes *dharma* as a Hindu moderator or version of the superego, the mental agency responsible for maintaining standards learned from the culture. In other cultures, the pressure of the superego gives rise to a need to alleviate the pain caused by transgressing rigid 'thou-shalt' and 'thou-shalt-not' axioms, whereas for Hindus this is accomplished by *dharma*. Throughout one's life, more permissively and gently than the superego, although ambiguously, *dharma* prescribes 'thou-canst-but-try' precepts. This creates a kind of ethical uncertainty and indeterminacy that Kakar terms an ethical relativism. A result is that from early childhood a Hindu acquires a sense of doubt and uncertainty as to the wisdom or efficacy of individual initiative.

---

[710] Quoted in Kakar 1981: 215.

> To size up a situation for oneself and proceed to act upon one's momentary judgement is to take an enormous cultural as well as a personal risk. For most Hindus such independent voluntary action is unthinkable.[711]

Hindus increase their sense of psychological security by acting in conformity with how their ancestors acted in the past and as one's social group does at present. Right action, then, translates as traditional action in conformity with dictates of one's *dharma* as formulated by family, kin, and caste. Kakar sees Hindus as basically suspicious of innovation and thus conservative. Effort and achievement in the world outside is important, but also so is effort and achievement towards the realization of one's *svadharma,* namely, preparation 'inside' that brings the individual closer to an inner calm and wisdom that are the prerequisite for *mokṣa.*

Psychoanalytic formulations of Indian life course

The image of the life cycle in India is given by *āśramadharma.* To explicate this concept, Kakar draws on ideas of an ego-psychology version of psychoanalytic theory, most completely realized in the work of Erik Erikson.[712] Kakar equates the Hindu life cycle plan, which he describes fully, with the epigenetic principle applied to human development in relation to society.[713] The Hindu world image, which stipulates a directed course toward the ideal of liberation, is provided by the individual's *āśramadharma,* a social plan that gently yet progressively moves the individual forward to a state of connectedness and fusion with the godhead.

The third fundamental theme of Hindu psychology is derived from the implications of the concept of karma. Kakar sees the path to *mokṣa,* one's life goal, which underwrites the individual's formulation of his *dharma,* right action, to be impeded by one's inheritance from past actions. Here Kakar draws on the Hindu principle that the newborn infant is not a blank slate but rather a bundle of inherited characteristics that are a unique mixture of three fundamental qualities, or *guṇa*s. These qualities, Kakar theorizes, are the individual's unconscious; indeed, insofar as they are exquisitely fashioned from Hindu images of the world

[711] Kakar 1981: 37.

[712] Erikson 1950.

[713] Kakar 1968.

and experience, they should be regarded as something like a cultural or ethnic unconscious.[714] The three qualities of the *guṇa*s that make up this cultural unconscious are *sattva* (clarity and light), *rajas* (passion and desire), and *tamas* (dullness and darkness):

> In the Hindu idea of destiny the unconscious has an innate tendency to strive towards clarity and light, just as *citta*'s aim is to mature from its scattered and darkening forms. Yet the other two qualities of the unconscious, passion and darkness, are concurrent and omnipresent, their relative strength differing from one infant to another; ... an individual may, by reason of his innate *guṇa* constellation, need to expend much more conscious and unremitting effort to live in *dharma* than another whose unconscious is characterized by a more 'propitious' mix. In any case, a constant intimacy with the unconscious together with a recognition and control of impulses and fantasies ... are essential aspects of living in *dharma*.[715]

A Hindu, then, begins life with a mixture of positive and negative aspects of mind and being, the components of the unconscious. The mixture of *guṇa*s bestowed at birth charts the beginning of a journey toward *mokṣa* by means of a relativistic *dharma* that one has arrived at in conformity with social circumstances. Given these limitations, and prodded by a gentle albeit ambiguous dharmic plan, the individual is given several lifetimes in which to finish the journey. The character of the individual's unconscious as realized in the mixture of *sattva, tama*s, and *rajas* plays a determining role in this journey. Kakar explains:

> The *karma* theory, as it unfolds, assures the individual that none of his efforts has been wasted, for he will start the next life with the balance of *guṇas* attained at the close of his previous existence. The unconscious, then, occupies a central place in the Hindu world image and theory of the meaning of human life; the origin and constitution of the unconscious are not biological but *metaphysical*, its nature depending upon the 'actions' (in the widest sense of the word) of a previous life.[716]

Through the idea of karma, Kakar weaves together the main threads that make up the Hindu image of the world and the purpose that guides individuals through the life plan. A unique conception of time and destiny, one that stretches across the individual human lifetime, and a

---

[714] Devereux 1956.

[715] Kakar 1981: 47–48.

[716] Kakar 1981: 48, emphasis added.

unique conception of an altruistic goal of liberation and fusion with the godhead or the 'other' give meaning and purpose to the Hindu's everyday pursuits. In Kakar's formulation, then, karma is not merely transmigration or fatalism but promises hope. A Hindu's innate and unconscious movement towards light (*sattva*), in combination with personal striving through their vision of *dharma*), means that karma need not hinder attainment of *mokṣa*, although setbacks and hurdles may be interposed along the way, requiring more than one lifetime.

> For the average Hindu ... such ideas are not based on a logic of extension or linear reasoning, but are absorbed as a kind of dream-like intuitive inner orientation early in life.[717]

Kakar's clinical experiences convinced him that such ideas have considerable influence in the everyday lives of Hindus. Individuals are prone to oversee themselves, ever conscious of their *saṃskāras*, their more or less innate constitutional dispositions. In fact, so ingrained is this propensity that it operates as a culturally specific form of resistance in psychotherapy.

Psychoanalytic interpretations of gender differences

Kakar discusses mother–infant relations and construction of gender in particular, a topic covered earlier. He acknowledges that women in India generally show a relatively low social position. Despite the inequities suffered by females and the dominance of males in Indian society, Kakar points out that one does not find heightened female hostility and envy toward males, or a pronounced antagonism between the sexes. He acknowledges that one possible consequence of the unequal position and treatment of women could be that in a patriarchal society like India girls and adult women are likely to direct aggression towards themselves, in the process turning cultural devaluation of women into feelings of inferiority and even worthlessness.

> There is scattered evidence that ... hostility towards men and potential aggression against males in fact are often turned inward, subsumed in a diffuse hostility against oneself, in a conversion of outrage into self-deprecation.[718]

---

[717] Kakar 1981: 48.

[718] Kakar 1981: 59.

Kakar argues that the strong devaluation of girls and women imposes a psychological burden and perhaps creates a greater vulnerability to mental health problems among females in India. He offers some support for this possibility by referring to his clinical work with upper middle-class female patients. However, he is reluctant to offer this as a generalization covering all of Indian society. To argue that women show a 'widespread depressive pattern', one would have to prove that two conditions exist. First, that behaviour and attitudes toward infant girls by parents and other adults is fully consistent with female self-devaluation. Second, that women have no opportunity or sphere of influence (living space) in which to express and realize their abilities apart from those attached to males (develop feminine identity through intimacy and collaboration with other women). However, these conditions do not exist, mitigating the effects of the discrimination and inequities toward women caused by patriarchal institutions in India.

The sources of Indian behaviour lead Kakar to analyze the relation between basic tenets of the culture, as reflected in ancient lore and tradition, and aspects of contemporary cultural psychology and personality. As a psychoanalyst he is able to demonstrate how themes, concepts, standards, and the behaviour of key figures in the great epics are used as a basis for the construction of the inner self. In intimate, everyday mother–child relations, in family exhortations regarding moral conduct, in the performance of daily rituals, and in setting guidelines for proper behaviour in relation to the various stations of life, fragments of wisdom from scriptural tales are fed to individuals, and in this way they enter into the psychological constitution of what it is to be a good daughter or wife, or a brave and honourable man.

This point is illustrated by the legend of Sita and Rama in the *Rāmāyaṇa* epic, one of the important Indian epics. Kakar pays great attention to the ego ideal of femininity that is embodied in the character and behaviour of Sita, the epitome of self-sacrifice, abiding devotion, and repeated commitment to her lover despite innumerable challenges and tribulations. Kakar relates Sita's personality and behaviour to the Indian ideal of the perfect wife. He uses themes of the Sita legend to construct a psychosocial and psychoanalytic formulation of the influences that crystallize a Hindu woman's identity and character. He also considers how the legend helps women to assuage feelings of guilt and anxiety. Kakar sees women, especially mothers, as pivotal in maintaining communal and family solidarity, and he attempts to show how the Sita legend helps women adjust to the social realities of their culture. He stresses that he is pin-pointing essential and generally accepted features of female gender identity in India that

> in spite of many changes in individual circumstances in the course of modernization, urbanization and education, still governs the inner imagery of individual men and women as well as the social relations between them in both the traditional and modern sectors of the Indian community.[719]

Kakar draws on many characters and their situations and behaviour as depicted in other legends and epic tales to show how they influence not only conceptions of femininity and masculinity, but also notions of duty, obligation, morality, and even religious devotion which have already been discussed. Such tales serve as role models for Indian children and adolescents. Functioning as ego ideals or as negative 'identity fragments', they are drawn from legendary sources that themselves are framed in ideas about social and moral order that hark back to scriptural canons. Kakar formulates his conclusions very widely so that his generalizations about the behaviour of boys, girls, and adults of different stations of life in contemporary India could, with a little imagination, be applied to earlier epochs.

Many examples are provided of behaviour within Indian families that indulges infant sensuality and sexuality and the problems this indulgence brings later in childhood, adolescence, and especially adulthood when the individual must learn to be aloof and distant and must shut off close, potentially physically intimate relations with members of the extended household. Psychoanalytic observations and inferences about infancy that contribute to a pleasurable sensuality are shown to relate to unconscious fantasies and fears, affecting both males and females, which are based on interpretations of scriptural lore. All of this is found in everyday social relations associated with emotional conflicts between men and women. Mandelbaum's work, reviewed earlier, is also rich in illustrations of how social patterns reflecting gender role differences contribute to emotional conflicts within families, communities, and especially the caste system.[720]

---

[719] Kakar 1981: 68.

[720] Mandelbaum 1970, 1988.

Much attention is placed on the negative psychological influence of the mother in Indian culture. Kakar attributes what he sees as characteristic Indian passivity and dependence in part to the universal wish to avoid isolation and in part to the influence of the extended household – specifically, the need to share responsibility for one's life with others. This is less an 'oral fixation' than cultural acceptance and encouragement of these needs. Obviously, this behaviour sharply divides India's ideal models of human relationships from those of the West. Kakar also indicates that separation anxiety is more pronounced and common in India than in Western cultures. This is not attributed to the mother 'spoiling' her children, however:

> In India the anxiety that may fester around the theme of separation stems at least partly from that moment in later infancy when the mother may suddenly withdraw her attention and her presence from her child. And indeed, retrospective accounts of adults as well as anthropological observations of child-rearing practices suggest that this is a widely used method of disciplining young children in India.[721]

It is common to discipline children by frightening them with stories of punishment by ghosts and goblins and by locking them in a dark room – threats of abandonment and isolation. Yet it is not the means of reprimand and punishment or the intense connection between mother and infant that Kakar singles out in the image of what has been termed by others the 'bad mother'. To him, rather, the important factor is the danger of inversion of emotional roles, a situation involving loving maternal behaviour that affects males in particular. Mothers usually perceive a son as a godsend and indulge him with love, appreciation and 'even reverence'. They unconsciously expect and demand that sons behave as objects of their own 'unfulfilled desires and wishes' and they in turn feel compelled to behave as their mother's 'saviour'. As a consequence of repeated unconscious demands and expectations sons can develop a sense of inadequacy, anxiety, and conflict over their mother's 'overwhelming nearness' and their own ambivalence (inability or unwillingness) to resist and 'get away'.[722]

For a variety of reasons stemming from characteristics of female psychosexual development in India, a woman's sexual longings are dis-

[721] Kakar 1981: 88.

[722] Kakar 1981: 89.

placed from her husband to her son. This poses 'one of the most difficult problems for a boy to handle'.[723] Kakar sees the effects of this displacement not only in actual verbal associations of Indian patients whom he and his colleagues have treated, but also in countless proverbs, myths, and taboos drawn from legends of the canonical literatures. He explains many aspects of traditional Indian culture on the basis of interpretations from psychoanalytical theory – for example, a 'mildly phobic' male attitude toward women who are sexually mature, the unusual disparity in age between the sexes at the time of marriage, and a heightened fear and actual higher incidence of impotence. In his customary fashion, Kakar supports all of this by an extensive review and analysis of traditional cultural themes found in myths, legends, situations, and exemplary and negative behaviour models of characters in the great Indian epics.

Female identity: complementary observations

Ashis Nandy also uses psychoanalytic formulations of Indian culture in his critiques of the political psychology of India and of the roles played by its leading reformers.[724] While primarily interested in recent political figures and events, Nandy provides interesting commentaries on general aspects of Indian cultural psychology, particularly as it has been affected by the colonial experience. His orientation follows the approach to the interplay between society and personality established by Erikson and carried forth by Kakar.[725] In analyzing the life of Rammohun Roy, the early nineteenth-century reformer who is credited with bringing to an end the practice of *satī*, the suicide of widows, Nandy draws attention to the importance of family relations in shaping the adult personality and to the potential negative influence of mothers on the psychology and behaviour of their sons. He comments on the 'egalitarian' influences of a typical joint household in India. On finds in such families a tendency for the growing child to be exposed more than one adult authority and discouragement from or at least ambiguity about distinguishing between 'near' and 'distant' relations amongst those authorities. An 'emotionally exclusive' loyalty to the individual's own nuclear family is discouraged. In a large, joint family authority is diffused and responsi-

---

723 Kakar 1981: 91.

724 Nandy 1980, 1983, 1995.

725 Erikson 1950; Kakar 1981.

bility spread across more than one adult member. The actual father of the child is distant and plays a non-committal role in family relations and decisions. His influence as a direct and intimate authority towards his children is blunted. The result is that boundaries within nuclear units are fuzzy.

Nandy indicates that because Roy's childhood was 'distorted by the process of nuclearization', it influenced his conception of the problems of society. His ambivalent relationship with his mother was centrally important in his commitment to social change affecting women, particularly criminalizing the traditional support for and practice of *satī*. The basis and rationale for this social institution is ascribed to features of Indian cultural psychology. Among other sources for the negative influence of mothers, Nandy draws on the work of Kakar on the themes of aggression as found in Indian folktales. He also stresses that any father–son distance or emotional restriction do not apply to child–mother relationships. The culture ensures that the 'primordial intimacy' of the child with the mother leads to her constituting the principal if not 'only' effective person and role within the family. In relationships with family members the son's sexuality and age are what delineate their social identity, but it is the mother who provides a feeling of individuality. This intimacy is strengthened since woman as mother is idolized, but woman as wife actually devalued. As the main source of power during early childhood mothers come to symbolically personify ultimate authority but this comes to target them for feelings of anger and defiance. Nandy indicates that a result of this is to produce ambivalence towards mother since the idea of maternal authority is linked to that of one who is unreliable and likely to betray and aggress. Nandy sees this psychodynamic script played out in legends and myths as well as personal fantasies and it helps explain the aggression and devaluing of women that the institution of *satī* symbolizes.

Cognition and Indian cultural psychology

For Kakar, a highly significant feature of Indian ego development as embodied in maternal behaviour is that it deprives Indian children of the many gradual frustrations and disappointments that would come naturally as a result of imposition of controls and that would lead them to recognize a mother's limitations harmlessly over time. According to Kakar, this pattern of child rearing and mother–infant relations could have far-reaching implications in the way cognition is structured in Indian cultural psychology. He believes ego–id and child–mother differentiation is structurally weaker and comes rather late in development compared to the West. As a result, the symbiotic relationship between mother and child has a larger influence on structures of Indian cultural psychology.

The result, for Kakar, is the accentuation and persistence of so-called primary process thinking by which analysts mean thinking in terms of feelings, impressions, representations, and visual and sensual images, as opposed to secondary thinking which is characteristically seen in language and which involves causality, rationality, abstraction, and logical mental operations. Kakar claims that compared to their counterparts in the West, Indian children are encouraged to continue to live in a mythical, fantasized world for a comparatively long time, in a world where objects, events, and other persons are seen not as objects with an existence of their own but as phenomena related to the self and its mysterious moods.

> Animistic and magical thinking persists, somewhat diluted, among many Indians well into adulthood. The projection of one's own emotions onto others, the tendency to see natural and human 'objects' predominantly as extensions of oneself, the belief in spirits animating the world outside and the shuttling back and forth between secondary and primary process modes are common features of daily intercourse.[726]

This is equated with psychopathology since it perpetuates into adulthood a persistent form of infantile behaviour. It is reflected, Kakar claims, in the tendency to minimize order, categorization, and logicality in favour of direct, 'primary process' thinking and perception as seen in the yogin's meditation, the artist's intuition, and the general belief that to reach one's goals one must enlarge the inner world and not act on the outer one. It is reflected also in the injunction of the karma doctrine to accept and use outer reality for inner development and the tendency of Indians to admire gurus and shamanistic preceptors rather than eminent scientists and professionals. Kakar traces these aspects of cognition and general social demeanour and orientation to styles of upbringing, and he sees them reflected in the social fabric. Persons, and especially mothers, function as the important agents of socialization and they embody and

[726] Kakar 1981: 105.

communicate to the child prevailing cultural ideas and practices as well as meanings of social institutions and organizations all of which result in the (brain-based) enculturation of a sense of responsibility. The child, as it were, is said to function as a passive receptacle and the mother and her cultural resources as the vehicle. In traditional India early on the mother functions as the child's ego ideal or model, 'mediating his most elementary experiences' and this goes on until the age of four or so. Then, controls and directives that function to monitor and integrate reality for the child are taken over by to the other family members and social institutions. The result is that the family at large and not the child itself are involved in reasoning and making decisions about everyday concerns.

From features of mother–infant relationships that hark back to ancient, traditional aspects of Indian belief, religion, morality, folklore, and ideal models of behaviour, Kakar, and, to some degree, Nandy, explains many characteristics of the Indian mode of thinking, behaving, and psychopathology broadly conceived. However, while Kakar's claim that parental forms of rearing can influence patterns of thought is interesting it is also controversial. It does not explain, for example, the accomplishments of Indian scientists and mathematicians or the clear logical reasoning in complex waters of thought of intellectuals like himself and Nandy. How well individuals reason in 'secondary' areas requiring logic, rationality, and science is likely to be a function of a number of cultural, psychological, socioeconomic, educational, as well as purely intellectual factors, and it would be surprising if mother–infant indulgence per se has such a determining influence. It is true, nonetheless, that both Kakar and Nandy are able to derive and in this way explain a number of aspects of Indian experience and behaviour from a predilection for 'primary process' experience. While Kakar does not state this explicitly, it would seem to follow that a predilection toward primary process thinking, if it exists, might predispose an individual to enter states of dissociation such as trance and possession, as mentioned earlier, that are important means by which psychopathology is expressed in Indian villages.

More on the cultural psychology of Ayurveda

Ayurveda presupposes and grows out of philosophical and religious texts that are landmarks and foundations of Indian culture and civilization. These provided Ayurveda with cultural, psychological resonance and the framework in terms of which it achieved influence and authority in Hindu societies. For these and related reasons, Ayurveda has often been construed not only as practical curative medicine or a general science of life. It has also been viewed as a body of knowledge that was handed down from gods to legendary physicians and then to man and which told what sentient beings were supposed to do in order to maintain wellbeing, thereby enabling it to meet moral obligations and reach soteriological goals (stipulations of the Dharmaśāstras, neutralization of karmic debts).

One view is that of Thakar, who points out that the Ayurveda is mentioned as a lesser or complementary subsection of the *Atharvaveda* and should be regarded as a fifth Veda.[727] She maintains that hymns or *mantras* of the Vedas were integral to the evolution of a naturalistic conception of medicine and are well represented in ayurvedic texts of the classical era as discussed earlier. Thakar holds that the compilations of Ayurveda 'fall somewhere in between' the Brāhmaṇas and the later great epic poems and Puranas. The point here is that the main medical texts of India, those that refer explicitly to culture-specific, medical varieties of conditions of psychiatric interest (and disease in general), that outline the philosophy of health and disease and formulate the 'what, how, and why' of the medical component of indigenous psychiatry in India, are consistent and in fact reinforce intellectual foundations of Indian culture. In short, Ayurveda theory about person and wellbeing exemplify themes central to Hindu morality, philosophy, and religion, and by extension, the ideological component of its cultural psychology.

Ayurveda also displays a distinctive theory of the human body as well as mind. It encompasses a number of concepts and schemas that are integral to India's cultural psychology considered in material, medical-biological terms.[728] The approach is rooted in a broad, integrated conception of body and spirit that derives from the doctrines of Sāṃkhya, one of the principal orthodox systems of Indian philosophy.

The philosophical doctrine of *saṃskāra* includes not only a theory about psychological, spiritual, and material aspects of human beings, but also aspects of disease and how the manifestations and causes of

[727] Thakar 1992.

[728] Roşu 1981; Obeyesekere 1977, 1982.

disease are related to one's life experiences, broadly conceived.[729] Technically, *saṃskāra* refers to unconscious residues that are built up in the mind (*manas*) and consists of ideas, perceptions, including past impressions, and active imprints of past actions associated with world experiences that one has accumulated. *Saṃskāra* is a repository of ideas, memories, and character traits, an amalgam of past psychic residues and actions. It can be conceptualized as mental phenomena that describe the individual, as well as the burden that individuals carry with them through their lives and even into future lives. These psychic embodiments of individuality are active in the mind, which also embody *sūkṣmaśarīra* or aspects of the 'subtle' immaterial body. Together, the residues of mind and the immaterial body participate in transmigration to future lives and bodies. Roşu suggests that vital manifestations of the immaterial body (termed *liṅga*) might reflect dynamic imprints of the unconscious mind (termed *vāsanā*).

> Whether or not this is true, the Sanskrit medical texts use the word *liṅga* for the signs as manifestations of vegetative and psychic life.[730]

Bodily and psychological elements of disease, then, are here equated in some way with the components and residua of the subtle body and the repository of psychic impressions and memories that individuals have acquired and which can contribute not only to personal identity but also disease.

The amalgam of immaterial bodily and psychical essences is what carries the residual impressions of past karmic debts. Through transmigration, this material passes into a new body, which it infuses with its past, acquired individuality, despite the new body's own physical and genetic identity and constitution. As discussed earlier, Hindu tradition adds to this formulation an ontological substratum in the psyche, giving mind an additional spiritual principle or 'soul' (*ātman, puruṣa*). One would presume that such an elaborate sense of self and mind was integral to beliefs and attitudes of adepts and serious, learned clients and members of higher castes. Among them, the material, tangible component of self supports the more ideological, philosophical psychology and theosophy. This cultural psychology describes the classical Hindu ideo-

---

[729] Roşu 1981.

[730] Roşu 1981: 207.

logical self and at the same represents a potential medical burden or load to the new body. In this way, the transmigrant material operates as an essential problem for Yoga that is a psychological technique or set of techniques designed to rid the individual of this karmic inheritance. Practices of Yoga are designed to control mind and body towards the aim of a person's salvation and quest of the Absolute.

> At the physiological level one can control the life function of breathing (*prāṇāyāma*) and at the psychological level, the mental states. Both have their basic explanation in ayurvedic doctrines.[731]

A key attribute of this highly theoretical cultural psychology, here merely highlighted, is its connection to mental and bodily phenomena. One sees again the connection that Ayurveda, a science of health and medicine, has with fundamental aspects of India's philosophical, cultural psychology. The theory gives importance to residues of contemporary experiences and past actions, it stipulates that the body's functions are influenced by current as well as past actions, and indicates that spiritual matters bear integrally not only on morality and behaviour but on bodily health and mental existence. Ayurveda's psychosomatic doctrine is very comprehensive. It stipulates a sense of Hindu embodiment. It integrates the body with the mind, to be sure, but the cultural psychology of India here fuses the preceding not only across present, past, and future time but also across the divide between what the West calls science and religion, or the natural and supernatural realms. The doctrine that rationalizes the makeup of *saṃsāra*, a complex mixture of conscious and unconscious material of the mind, which along with the character of the subtle, immaterial body reflect all previous experiences and actions, provide a context and interpretation for manifestations of bodily malfunctions, which reflect not only immediate physiological changes but also the effects of prior karmic action carried into the present that weaken the body's constitution. Stated succinctly, the philosophical substratum of India's cultural psychology encompasses morally evaluated human action, karmic debts, representations of mind and of the immaterial, subtle body, transmigration, vulnerability to disease, manifestations of disease, and a health psychology and medicine focused on herbal pharmaceutics and meditation.

---

[731] Roşu 1981: 209.

Neki formulates a different, more practical way of delineating the philosophical aspects of India's cultural psychology, one that gives emphasis to the concept of mental health.[732] He relies on the concept *sahaja* that subsumes the *triguṇa* theory of personality of Sāṃkhya. According to his formulation, there are three qualities or modes of living, three *guṇas*, which consists of (1) *sattva*, consciousness and striving for insight and harmony; (2) *rajas*, passion, which connotes activity and excites desire; and (3) *tamas*, darkness and gloom, which contributes to apathy, inertia, and resistance. These qualities are found in all individuals, and the personality of any one being is a composite of the three *guṇas*, one of which can sometimes dominate the others. Neki describes an elaborate typology of Indian personality based on the composites of the *guṇas*. By transcending the three-mode states that govern the ordinary experience and behaviour of those dictated by their respective personalities (transcending the *triguṇa prakṛti*), a person enters a transcendent state, *sahaja*, that involves 'an unruffled state beyond mundane pleasures and pains ... Life is spontaneously good and creative and, thereby, purposeful'.[733]

Yoga theory describes three levels of consciousness. These are awakeness, dreaming, and deep sleep. The highest yogic state of consciousness is termed *samādhi*, a consciousness beyond ordinary levels in which consciousness can function without perturbation. Yogic procedures and methods are designed to enable the individual to reach *samādhi*. Assumptions about causality are what govern the appearance of reality. Behind the multiplicity of the perceived world lies a cosmic reality (*Brahman*), and beyond the so-called empirical self lies the real self (*ātman*). The deceptions and ambiguities created by adhering to mundane assumptions, illusions, and views dictated by ordinary states of thinking and feeling are broken by achieving liberation or *mokṣa*, which resembles the state of *sahaja*. Neki elaborates on the Sikh concept of *sahaja* that in effect transcends the states defined by Sāṃkhyan, Yogic, and Vedantic concepts of self-transcendence. He indicates that the state or condition of *sahaja* contains 'elements of illumination, equipoise, spontaneity, freedom, and harmony [that] spell a state of positive and robust mental health'.[734] Neki's study nicely contrasts the Western notion of mental health and the psychiatric – with its emphasis on worldly,

---

[732] Neki 1975.

[733] Neki 1975: 3.

[734] Neki 1975: 5.

practical, individualistic, and biographical considerations yet strangely minimizing, if not disregarding, things laden with material bearing on morality and commentative of the self – with that of India, which implicates transcendence, metaphysics, spirituality, and salvation, and a notion of the sacred – one in which techniques of concentration and body control, that is, features germane to medicine, as above – though yogic methods are relevant.

A cultural psychology that exemplifies and unites aspects of body and mind in a formulation of experience, behaviour, and mental and physical health is obviously germane to formulation of psychiatric condition. As repeatedly emphasized, the latter involves disturbances of social and psychological behaviour that are associated with bodily symptoms. One of the important generalizations of modern clinical psychiatry is that a large class of disturbances – for example, anxiety, depression, and the many somatoform disorders – as well as traditional categories, such as neurosis and psychosis, include prominent signs and symptoms affecting the body. Identifying these disorders, and distinguishing between them, especially in non-Western people, is notoriously difficult largely because of the presence of bodily signs and symptoms that do not fit the dualistic epistemology about the person in which Western psychiatric practice of diagnosis is anchored. This was illustrated in our description and analysis of Caraka's inventory of symptoms and signs of conditions of psychiatric interest. In biomedical theory, manifestations of disorders can include reports of pain, fatigue, lack of motivation, decreased ability to experience pleasure, impaired physiological functions, and changes in sleep patterns, diet, and sexuality, all of which are classic 'bodily' phenomena. We see in Ayurveda a theoretical framework that asserts the unity of mind and body in conditions of disease and that echo fundamental philosophical and religious conceptions but that appear to shape phenomena (symptoms and signs) differently from that of the West. Emphasis on significance of the body in conceptions of mental health ironically underscores validity of criticism about the myth of mental illness, since the term *mental illness* is usually taken to apply only to psychological, emotional phenomena, ignoring the unity between body and mind.

The medical organically-based system of ayurvedic physiology and therapeutics embraces mental and emotional factors and general conditions of 'dis-ease' framed in system of meanings that shape experience, behaviour, and personhood. It constitutes Ayurveda's contribution to

Indian cultural psychology. This helps to explain the broad scope, appeal, and power of Indian traditional medicine. It is an academic, scholarly, and in this sense scientific tradition that conceptualizes and handles disease including psychiatric condition as a component of a general, holistic medicine. A generalization in modern psychiatry that has emerged largely as a result of weathering the digressive excesses of a reductionist neuropathology and psychoanalysis through the chaotic and shaky (though pivotal) formulations of a psychosomatic medicine is confirmed by a tradition of medicine that emerged around 2000 years ago.

INDIAN CULTURAL PSYCHOLOGY AS A REFRACTIVE MEDIUM FOR PSYCHIATRIC PHENOMENA

There is a long tradition in psychiatry that involves the study of the effects of culture and society on psychiatric disorder. An important question is whether disorders are the same the world over. The controversy involves whether official criteria of diagnosis represent essential and universal as compared to purely Western tenets of human psychology and behaviour. Universalists explain cultural variation in terms of concept of plasticity, the flexibility and indeterminacy of wiring or patterning of neuron connections and 'neural nets' that under-gird information handling pathways found in higher levels of the nervous system function. A culture-free language is said to enable an experienced examiner who understands the influence of culture to diagnose psychiatric disorers anywhere. Official diagnostic indicators, in other words, 'carve nature at the joints' or disclose the weak points where and how all human beings regardless of culture break down as a consequence of inherited vulnerabilities and local stressors and circumstances. The work of Indian psychiatric epidemiologists reviewed earlier reflects an internationalist viewpoint and illustrates its relevance and applicability for India.[735]

The emphasis of cultural relativists, on the other hand, is different. To them, consistent with ideas about a cultural psychology, each well-defined and self-contained group of people probably manifests its own

[735] The implications of this for a 'full' account of psychiatry in India is taken up in Chapters 11 and 12.

'indigenous' conditions of psychiatric interest. The claim can involve that even the neurobiological correlates of disorders when examined carefully are likely to show features that correspond to mental, cognitive representations inherent in brain networks that during enculturation go to make up a cultural psychology of a people.[736] Putting aside aspects of brain function, cultural relativist would argue for an Indian system of disorders, taxonomy, and corresponding diagnostic system, just as they would for a Chinese versions of the same, each based on indigenous cultural psychologies and, the argument goes, appropriately indigenous modes of treatment. The relativists' claim is that conditions of psychiatric interest (as realized and perceived in natural communities), disorders (as professionally, scientifically formulated), and psychiatric phenomena that would include indigenous forms of therapy all should reflect the verities of thought worlds and habit patterns of a people.

For purposes of understanding the history of psychiatric phenomena in a civilization with a rich cultural and scientific tradition like India, it seems inappropriate to be limited to the universalist and internationalist perspective. A psychiatric condition involves a general category encompassing all forms of social and psychological behaviour problems and breakdowns that include body-related symptoms and signs. Left unspecified as to cultural features, such conditions are found wherever human populations coalesce, across historical and geographic boundaries. The Western scientific classification system represents one possible and highly influential slant on conditions of psychiatric interest. Material reviewed in this and earlier chapters suggests that in India the expression, perception, and understanding of psychiatric phenomena was based on a distinctive cultural psychology, the roots of which can be traced far back into the history of the subcontinent.

There is controversy regarding when one may assert that Indian cultural psychology took shape. Foundational Indian literary classics, including Ayurveda texts, were first articulated and then transcribed. The *Ṛgveda* came first, of course, but this concentrates largely on religious beliefs and ritual practices and reveals comparatively little about the inner thought world of Vedic people. The later Vedas (like *Atharvaveda*) and the accompanying manuals and texts (Brāhmaṇas, Upanishads) came next, followed by the two epics, voluminous popular com-

[736] LeVine 1990; Mezzich *et al.* 1996.

pilations of Puranas, the moral texts and code books (*The Laws of Manu*), and still later the rich religious literatures and lyric poetry of sectarian groups. The time of and preceding transcription of Hindu revealed truths about the world is contested.

The meaning of key constructs of the philosophical religious writings about the nature of soul and self clearly had explicit psychological implications. Similarly, while the inner thought world of an individual per se was not an explicit focus of later religious and popular literatures, it is clear that their portrayal of life had a psychological dimension.[737] A basic point is that Indian conceptions and psychological structures involving the nature of personhood, health, wellbeing, and the conduct of life extend far back into early medieval era and well beyond that event perhaps into prehistory. This Indian cultural psychology describes essential characteristics of Hindu experience and behaviour. Concepts and beliefs were modified in relation to historical circumstances – for example, the emergence of Bhakti devotionalism in the medieval era, the growth of regionalism, Islamic influences, and Westernization. However, the essential core of Hindu conceptions about self, including concepts of the body and sense of embodiment, world-view, and a general orientation about the conduct of life, have remained relatively securely anchored deep in the Indian psyche. Since cultural psychology is the screen or space wherein essential characteristics of disturbances of experience and behaviour are registered (conditions of psychiatric interest), this means that it can be used as a window through which one might glimpse how varieties of conditions of psychiatric interest were likely to have been configured and played out in real communities from ancient times up to the present.

The psychoanalytic vision of Indian cultural psychology, formulated by Kakar and Roland as well as Hoch and Nandy, complements and deepens observations reviewed earlier by cultural anthropologists, psychologists, and medical theorists such as Shweder and Roşu. Together, these ideas provide a picture of how Hindus construct and structure social life and experience its inner meanings. They indicate that aspects of morality, feeling, distress, and mental representation of the social world as well as conceptions and representations of the body–mind ensemble exemplify Indian conceptions that connect with cultural and literary essence of Indian civilization. In essence, because they give content

[737] See the earlier discussion by Kakar and Nandy.

to experience they also provide a window into how strains and frustrations are likely to be perceived, formulated, and expressed.

A psychiatric condition can be examined from any number of standpoints. As reviewed earlier, the characteristics of the problems for which priests were consulted in ancient India, as described in the *Atharvaveda*, constitute one vision of psychiatric condition. Similarly, the exhortations found in the *Bhagavadgītā* about the meaning and purpose of life suggests how conflicts encountered in meeting social obligations were likely to be coped with. Ayurveda provides still another vision of psychiatric condition. It brings to bear a more secular and naturalistic interpretation for an essentially medical disease model on experience, behaviour, and human health problems. In all of these refractions, it is Indian categories about the self, body, morality, world, and cosmology that are centrally represented.

For the most part, a medical, secular, or naturalistic vision is found in the Hindu world image described by Kakar. However, this does not apply to his observations on psychosomatic medicine among Indian patients where one finds how Indian bodies are represented and experienced. The studies of cultural anthropologists reviewed earlier provide a largely psychological vision. What all of these researchers describe is a vivid picture of a religious, spiritual, moral inner dimension of human striving and longing and suggest how emotional distress, behavioural disaffections, and bodily disturbances were likely to be experienced, conceptualized, and enacted. Implicit in the writings of Kakar, Shweder and Nandy, as well as Roşu, is the idea that while life plans do have a social and cultural rationale in India, ordinary life is arduous and trying for most people. Paths to goals are blocked by frustrations, limitations, deprivations, and insecurities that make it hard to pursue right action and reach the mystical and religious end points identified by the culture. They eventuate in disturbances of experience and behaviour, including bodily experience viewed through the prism of the regnant cultural psychology.

Virtually all who address Indian cultural psychology (Thapar, R.S. Sharma, Kakar) underscore the rigors of *dharma* and the social order it expounds and sanctions. They emphasize that a basically 'religious' and 'moral' way of life was inherent in the social fabric, even regulated, controlled, and enforced by the state. Given the facts of caste, poverty, and politico-economic exigencies, dharmic and associated caste requirements could pose strain and conflict and exact a high psychological price. This suffering component of social life must be viewed as the consequence of having encountered so many disheartening impediments to fulfilling one's life goals and the karmic burdens from previous lifetimes. Regardless of what label a Hindu peasant or housewife may give to misfortune and suffering, whether a medical one or one invoking spiritual punishment, they experience personal distress and demoralization in their attempts to meet everyday obligations. A Hindu religious, moral image of the world, then, is the basic material of psychiatric condition.

Emptiness and anxiety, caused by recognizing one's deficiencies in the scheme dictated by *dharma,* karmic debts, and the pursuit of liberation, obviously do not equal psychiatric condition. On the other hand, regardless of how one conceptualizes the latter – as personality conflicts, personal distress, impaired fitness, signs and symptoms, behavioural inefficiency or impairment, neurotransmitter imbalances – one surmises that in traditional India its formulation and realization as a syndrome of emotional and behavioural disaffection (experienced and expressed in idiom of cultural psychology) is rationalized in a religious idiom. In many respects, the basic language that captures the essence of psychiatric condition in India is provided by conceptions of how life is construed and constructed morally from within and reinforced in the social order.

This inside, psychological space is where one can look in order to find essential symbolic characteristics of Indian conditions of psychiatric interest. The insights of Kakar, Bharati, Roland, Shweder and co-workers, Hoch, Nandy, and Roşu help to articulate what such conditions mean and how they are felt and expressed, psychologically, in bodily terms, and behaviourally.[738] At the same time, one must consider the influence of spirits, godlings, demons that, as Opler and Freed and Freed, as well as Kakar, show, stand ready to invade, attack, and possess individuals, with adverse health consequences.[739] Moreover, as Kakar suggests, they may be characteristics of the Indian personality and ways of thinking and responding to the world derived from maternal and family influences during childhood that have resonance in the literary classics and thus go far back in history.[740] The comment by Shweder *et al.*

[738] Kakar 1981; Bharati 1985; Roland 1988, 1994.

[739] Opler 1958; Freed and Freed 1964; Kakar 1982.

[740] Kakar 1981.

about contemporary times could be applied to circumstances prevailing centuries and even millennia ago:

> In Orissa, persons who are suffering from an illness or misfortune may consult sacred specialists, holy persons, or oracles to ascertain the karmic cause of their suffering; ... [these] may not only diagnose karmic problems but also prescribe remedial actions. This is especially true for illnesses or misfortunes that are not amenable to 'immediate' or proximal remedial interventions (medicine, magic, or astrology).[741]

The latter caveat underscores that 'proximal' considerations are not necessarily primary; rather, ultimate, long-term implications of illness and misfortune are important. Similarly, they emphasize that indigenous diagnoses of moral maladies and prescriptions of therapy entail measures related to charity, support of religious institutions, worship, sacrifice, personal austerity, discussing the scriptures, personal hygiene, and ways of maintaining personal sanctity:

> The fundamental presupposition is that traditional codes of ethics are part of the *divine and natural order of the universe* and are established for the purpose of enhancing the wellbeing of persons in their *worldly existence as well as the afterlife*. In this view, morality and obedience to the obligation and limits of ... ethical discourses directly affect physical and mental health.[742]

J. P. Balodhi, a professor of Sanskrit literature at the National Institute of Mental Health in Bangalore, examines ancient Hindu culture from the perspective of contemporary psychiatry.[743] He makes a succinct and yet comprehensive formulation of the cultural approach toward health problems that is manifested in the culture of ancient India as reflected in scriptural texts and traditions. Having reviewed the various folk, lay, and more scholarly approaches to medicine, including forms of treatment from using medicinal herbs to psychological procedures, he concludes that the social perspective manifest in Hindu culture is one of sharing among individuals in ever more inclusive, incorporative groups. For example, the individual is related to family, then with extended family, the village, the caste, the community at large, and eventually the

---

[741] Shweder *et al.* 1997: 154–155.

[742] Shweder *et al.* 1997: 156–157, emphasis added.

[743] Balodhi 1991.

gods. Psychiatric illness, according to Balodhi, in a sense belongs to the community

> is considered as the fault of the whole community and if one individual is subject to it this time, some other will be a victim another time.[744]

Thus Balodhi conceives of Hindu communities as embodying cultural values and social practices that reflect a communitarian orientation that is consistent with the principles of contemporary community psychology and psychiatry.

---

[744] Balodhi 1991: 103.

Chapter 10

An Odyssey through Indian Systems of Psychiatry

PROLEGOMENON: MENTAL HEALTH PRACTICES OF INDIA'S FOREST PEOPLES

A historical tour over the territory of psychiatric phenomena in the subcontinent naturally conjures up characteristics involving how conditions of psychiatric interest were understood, enacted, and dealt with there. This ranges over communities in the process of coming under the influence of and later consolidating a Hindu identity and thereafter. Some of the landmarks of this territory have been discussed and additional ones taken up later. Medieval developments involving indigenous medicine and psychiatry and later influences stemming from Islamic and Western influence would complete the tour.

However, it is important to include in this odyssey phenomena of psychiatric interest as displayed and enacted among contemporary simple, egalitarian hunter-gatherers, in India referred to as 'forest peoples'. In some respects, such peoples could represent remnants of non-Vedic indigenous ways of life in the subcontinent. They exemplify approaches to sickness and behaviour and possible echoes of interactions Hindu communities have had with non-Hindu peoples since the former supervened in the subcontinent. One cannot doubt that the population of premodern and modern India included and still includes not just peoples of predominant Aryan descent (whatever that might mean) but innumerable descendants of forest and indigenous peoples of diverse ethnicity. Over millennia such peoples have assimilated and acculturated to Hindu culture and been incorporated usually as lower castes sometimes appropriated as fully organized, segmentary tribes and sometimes accorded high status.[745] Ethnic and genetic mixing are prominent features that obviously have marked the unfolding of Hindu populations, culture, and society.

It would be impossible for one to tease apart and determine what proportion of ideas inherent in the vast puranic and other popular literatures of Hindu India originated in Vedic, Brahmin ideas as compared to more indigenous sources, namely, ultimately stemming from the thought worlds and habit patterns of what today are termed forest peoples. Popular, folk religion and culture in India, especially in the south, cannot but reflect these indigenous influences. Morris, who worked with forest peoples of the subcontinent, echoes this point by indicating first that indigenous hill deities have been 'synchronized or identified with' metaphysical beliefs drawn from Hindu ideology.[746]

> Many hill deities ... [combine] the personification of a specific natural phenomenon with a religious conception, which has wide cultural significance. There is indeed a graduation in the degree to which the hill deities are, as it were, incorporated into wider Hinduism.[747]

Given this interplay and exchange between village Hindu society and neighbouring hunter-gatherers, where the latter acquire but a surface layer of terms and constructs, it behoves one to examine how phenomena of possible psychiatric interest, namely, the original or 'real' indigenous psychiatry of the subcontinent – the earliest realization of the psychiatric enterprise there – were understood and enacted. Arguably, the forest people provide the best slant on such matters.[748]

The work of Gardner, Morris, and Bird-David provides information that one can use to at least set the contours of indigenous psychiatry of forest peoples.[749] Attention was already given to the sense of immediacy, shared participation, and pervasive, almost spiritual relatedness of these

---

[745] Nath 2001; Thapar 2002.

[746] Morris 1981.

[747] Morris 1981: 213; Gardner 1991a, 1991b.

[748] The word 'real' is placed in quotation because indigenous psychiatry has generally been used as a cover term for all systems of mental health practice in the continent, medical and non-medical, ayurvedic and non-ayurvedic, scholarly and popular, 'great' tradition and 'little' Tradition, and such religious and philosophical, largely non-medical movements as Yoga, Tantra, and the tradition of the accomplished yogins termed Siddha.

[749] Gardner 1982, 1991a, 1991b; Morris 1981; Bird-David 1990, 1992a, 1992b, 1994, 1996, 1999, 2004.

people with objects of the physical habitat, protective spirits that personified them, ancestors, and indeed with each other. While such a cultural psychology was most evident for the Nayakas, Bird-David found support for a similar relational epistemology among the Paliyans and Hill Pandarams, and other hunter-gatherers not of the subcontinent studied by biological anthropologists. In broad context, one can view relationships involving spirit possession and the functions, advantages, and benefits spirits and gods furnished these forest people with a means of easing emotional tensions and promoting wellbeing (mental health). In times of need, puzzlement, worry, anxiety and demoralization, not just in relation to conditions of physical disease or need for advice on mundane yet significant matters, but on far more gnawing concerns, spirits were called upon. Members congregated and formed groups, followed by dancing and music, and an invocation of spirits on the part of those present resulted in the trance behaviour of a few selected members of group.

The gods and spirits made themselves known in the behaviour of the possessed and available for consultation and/or healing. They were then interrogated by members in attendance about problems and worries and the gods responded in language and behaviour – via possessing and acting through selected or appointed members – in accordance with whatever requests and needs were communicated to them. These group encounters varied as to tone and resonance. In all of the three groups, the relationship between gods and group members could be informal, engaging, sometimes humorous, and fully egalitarian. The exchange was described by Morris as a 'benign cosmology' and he viewed the Hill Pandarams as a 'secular people' in view of the absence of ceremonial, iconic forms, and ritual.[750] The 'relational epistemology' described by Bird-David included relations with spirits via possession and it too had its informal, entertainment dimension besides representing a setting for healing.[751] In other instances, and especially among the Paliyans, exchanges with the gods could be more intense, emotional, and permeated with awe and reverence, surrender, and even apprehension.[752] In all groups the encounters often took place at night, were private as per selected group members as participants, and lasted several hours. Simi-

[750] Morris 1981.

[751] Bird-David 1999.

[752] Gardner 1991a, 1991b.

lar cathartic, stimulating, tension releasing 'dances' or 'group therapy sessions' have been described for other hunter-gatherers, not just for those of the subcontinent.[753]

Nothing of what has been described thus far for these forest peoples reflects psychopathology, sickness, or indigenous psychiatry per se. With few exceptions, ethnographers make no mention of phenomena of psychiatric interest. The material reviewed simply involves culture at work, people behaving in terms of cultural beliefs and practices that address general human concerns and in which altered states of consciousness and mental dissociation as per spirit possession figure in a central way. Only in a very general sense could the bulk of these dialogues with spirits be construed as indigenous psychiatry (focus on conditions of psychiatric interest, relationships involving therapy for group or individuals).

> A sort of dialogue goes on day and night between these 'visitors' [spirits] and the celebrants in the course of which the former are made to promise to look after the health of the latter, and the later promise to look after the needs of the former and follow the forefathers' ways.[754]

Morris emphasizes that any connection between hill deities and moral injunction among Hill Pandarams, as typically observed among agricultural communities, is 'extremely tenuous'. Moral transgressions countering supernatural sanctions among agricultural people are not seen by the Hill Pandarams as related to personal or group misfortune. Indeed, Morris suggests that morality is itself a tenuous construct among these people. During spirit possession encounters with hill deities moral infringements are not a topic of discussion. When Morris questioned Hill Pandaram people they did not appear to reflect

> any clear moral concepts associated with theft, murder, adultery or incest. They certainly resent theft [a rare phenomenon given their meagre resources of value] and adultery but this is primarily because they are felt to be infringements of an individual's rights rather than because they are infringements of any ethical or religious principle. Incest with close kin (for example, a man co-habiting with his daughter or sister) – as permanent liaisons and not merely as involving casual

[753] Fabrega 1997.

[754] Bird-David 2004: 330.

> sexual encounters – seem to be freely tolerated, while murder seems to be unknown in the society.[755]

His descriptions suggest that the Pandarams simply show seemingly institutional behaviour in and around spirits and little of indigenous psychiatry per se, save perhaps for the comfort derived from being healed by them for concerns he unfortunately does not elaborate on.

The best example of cultural behaviour that enters the 'genuine' domain of indigenous psychiatry for these forest peoples is provided by Gardner for the Paliyans.[756] He describes three syndromes of behaviour involving spirit possession but only two are taken up here. The first involved several individuals becoming possessed and presentation of personal needs of nine persons, which were dealt with by the possessing spirit. Most of these were described as serious although a few were frivolous. The behaviour of the possessed person toward the supplicant in need of comfort and understanding communicated a direct healing function. One case involved removing 'all the ailments' from the body of a person who eight to nine days previously, while bathing at a cistern had heard the screeching of a white lizard who had frightened the woman and made her feel feverish. Here, one may surmise, emotional and behavioural disturbances, as well as bodily ailments that persisted and occasioned much grief, shaped around the significance of the lizard and its behaviour, constituted the psychiatric condition. No further details of healing, divination, or outcome were discussed with respect to this case.

Gardner then went about collecting information on cases involving spirit possession of Paliyans settled in agricultural labour outside the margin of the forest. These subjects retained native ways, but one could argue that they were more acculturated to Tamil and Hindu popular ideas, beliefs, and influence than those discussed earlier. Gardner observed several cases of spirit possession. They followed an incident involving an attempt on the part of the son of an official to modernize the 'political structure' of the Paliyans by conducting an election. In retrospect, this was interpreted by Gardner as a significantly upsetting incident that disturbed the emotional and social equilibrium of these peoples. During early hours of the morning following this incident Gardner was awakened by music and sounds from flutes and drums

---

[755] Morris 1981: 209.

[756] Gardner 1991a, 1991b.

and incoherent outbursts of a person who was possessed by a spirit, the first of seven who experience possession. Five possessions took place simultaneously, three of the persons becoming violent, needing restraint or calming, but only two of the seven became 'mouthpieces' for the spirit. One could argue that these cases represent examples of stress-related acute emotional disaffections or anxiety framed in Paliyan cultural patterns of behaviour. The two main performances had many similarities, an initial 10–20 minutes of sobbing, onlookers loosening the hair of possessed person, intense and dramatic movements of torso and arms, dancing. Characteristics observed in these cases included the tying of a sash about the waist of the possessed person, vigorous self-administered whipping of lower legs, 'singing in well metered, often rhyming couplets', shrill noises by one person, use of regular dance steps, simultaneity, and extensive mechanical divining by the spirits. The demeanour, verbalizations, and action of those possessed suggested conventional rules and some patterning of behaviour.

> In addition to being performed with distinctive pitch, held breath, and run-on phrases, invocational prayers are replete with uniquely Paliyan figurative words, expressions, and phrases ... meanings of the latter are quite unknown to those [with] competence in the forest dialect ... they represent private and somewhat cryptic Paliyan knowledge ... it is manifestly clear that we are confronted by a highly distinctive area of cultural performance in both content and form.[757]

I would suggest that in these cases one sees culture at work in shaping, constructing, rationalizing, and appropriating material of stress and anxiety into a form that appears to border on institutionalization, both the syndrome, the resort to healing, and the exchanges that constituted healing.

The principal focus of Gardner's study is to provide a formulation of the 'pragmatic meanings' inherent in events involving possession by spirits that are of high cultural importance to the Paliyans. He identifies five meanings and implications that were exemplified in the behaviour and communication of these spirits via spirit possession of selected persons. Gardner describes the latter as 'mouthpieces' and terms them shamans but it is clear that this refers mainly of their ability to trance and serve as conduit for the gods.

---

[757] Morris 1976, 1981: 380.

> Given the importance of shamanism in the culture, it is a testimony to the adequacy of the general safeguards against prestige acquisition that shamans in a Paliyan community do not stand off from others. Even on an informal level, no prerogatives are accorded to Paliyan shamans, they have no de facto badges of office, and they are not socially distinct (indeed, their characteristic personal behaviour runs the full range, as does that of non-shamans.[758]

In this report Gardner suggests that these shamans, while themselves responding to stress, via syndromes of possession that had violent overtones, are also engaged in the business of healing the emotional discomfitures or anxiety of group mates who are burdened by their own separate problems. One can presume that in the context described, and while healing others, the shamans are themselves being healed by giving meaningful order, purpose, and release to their (and the group's) pent up feelings that are burdensome; for example, a sense of outrage and anxiety of being forced to participate in a politically intrusive exchange with an administrator's son. All of this smacks of indigenous psychiatry being played out via the fabric of Paliyan culture.

From the standpoint of indigenous psychiatry, in addition to the mental healing, just described, it is the importance of the *samis* (i.e. gods), and not just the shamans, that is significant. The *samis* were conceptualized by Gardner as having five major influences in Paliyan culture: they are indulgent, demanding, selective and authoritative, belonging to a formal realm, and wise. He discusses all of these but only one is dealt with here. Of considerable psychiatric relevance is the indulgence of the *sami*. Gardner emphasizes that 'too an unusual' extent, Paliyans feel they each should manage their own affairs. An affront or injury from a group member should be followed by self-control and voluntary retreat.

> In sum, a person is expected to be autonomous as an individual and to avoid disrespect toward anyone else. The code applies to all adults and it applies so strictly that people avoid recourse to, or even recognition of, human experts and authorities, and they make no claims of expertise themselves.[759]

It should be noted that the proposition just quoted is in conflict with that of Bird-David and indeed that of many other biological anthropolo-

[758] Gardner 1991a: 381–382.

[759] Gardner 1991a: 377.

gists who stress the importance of shared participation among group members and group connectedness of the self in communities of hunter-gatherers such as the Paliyans. They stress that the environment (worldly and other-worldly) is an integral part of the thought world and habit patterns of the people (their cultural psychology). I suspect that what Gardner is stressing (autonomy) is merely egalitarian behaviour and requirements of self-reliance and independence, commonly said of hunter-gatherers, and not a description of cultural psychology per se, not a sense of self or conception of the person as a separate, autonomous being.

Be that as it may, the psychiatric significance of Gardner's proposition is that with their *sami*s Paliyans behave in a manner that is the obverse of their self-reliance and self-sufficiency. For example, they bow and supplicate, make much of their personal deficiencies or difficulties, or prostrate themselves at the feet of the possessing *sami* whence they ask for help and protection.

> With visiting *samis* cast thus, in an indulgent guardian or parental role, the Paliyans can escape momentarily, if they wish, the burden of behaving responsibly as adults ... Paliyans find the availability of the *samis'* knowledge and judgement especially helpful, for theirs is a society lacking purely human super-ordinate controls and justice.[760]

It is Gardner's opinion that a factor inherent in the behaviour of *sami*s is a conscious or non-consciously perceived laxity of behaviour on the part of some Paliyans. They seem to 'need' the *samis*' visits for, as some informants indicated, Paliyans show increased interaction with outsiders and the attendant adoption of alien or improper practices. This breakdown of acceptable behaviour of a Paliyan is something that displeases the *sami*s. *Sami*s are said by Gardner to 'prescribe' moral behaviour, monitor compliance, and punish acts, which are socially, morally offensive; for example, having sexual relations prior to making offerings or praying to the *sami*s. Sessions with the *sami*s reveal their concern about specific, recent family quarrels and they are said to chastise and punish disrespect and violence.

> One young man's disabling boils on his leg were interpreted to be punishment for disruptions, which followed from his making his

---

[760] Gardner 1991a: 377.

> mother pregnant. While the baby born of this union was welcomed, the act of incest offended the mother's current husband and it eventuated in a temporary ... marital separation. The young man, believed to have been the one to initiate the incest, was also said later to have been punished for 'ruining the earth'.[761]

Here again, one sees social phenomena that enters the domain of indigenous psychiatry: a syndrome of behaviour (inappropriate incest) that violated prescriptions of 'appropriate' (consensual) incest, was followed by condemnation and social breakdown or disorder in the group, probably causing the individual who instigated the incest some emotional discomfiture, and that in turn might have aggravated his condition of disease.

In summary, forest peoples of contemporary India exemplify a culture and way of life that stands in contrast to that of agricultural Hindu communities that live nearby and with whom they interact, sometimes participating in waged labour. They show awareness of nearby popular religion but beliefs, ideas, and actual spiritual beings of Hindu communities are not deeply represented in everyday life and they play a minor, surface role in religious practices including those relevant to mental health.[762] What is described here as the indigenous psychiatry of forest peoples is part of their ethno-medicine: problems of health, sickness are intermixed with gnawing emotional and behavioural concerns that cause a 'disturbance' in the social fabric rationalizing a medico-religious healing. No names attach to the ailments that the gods can heal and global medical problems are their focus. The psychiatry is also exemplified in the way gods are used generically: they provide advice, support, healing, and help regulate behaviour. No specific agent or role is identified that functions as a central figure. In this sense, the indigenous psychiatry is little differentiated from the society and culture at large. This exemplar of sickness-emotional behaviour, disturbance-healing provides one with a window into an early phase of the evolution of psychiatric phenomena in the subcontinent.

---

[761] Gardner 1991a: 378.

[762] Discussed in Chapters 7 and 8.

EARLY EXPRESSION OF INDIAN CIVILIZATION

Introduction

The virtual absence of information about characteristics of social life and culture of peoples of the so-called Indus civilization, which after its apparent heyday (approximately 2500 BCE) experienced a decline of some sort the cause of which is unclear, means that one is left with many questions and no answers about the early cultural evolution of psychiatric phenomena in the subcontinent. One has no access to the peoples' beliefs, values, religious orientation, mythology, or philosophical worldviews and no less about their ways of coping with social crises, disorder, and misfortune and disaffections of experience and behaviour. One must reserve judgment about the influence of Indus civilization on the thought worlds and habit patterns of the people and the societies that followed.

However, one cannot ignore the assortment of ideas, beliefs, worldviews, and practices that are relevant to *behavioural syndromes of psychiatric interest* that were indigenous in the subcontinent. It prevailed among all varieties of social groupings, whether hunter-gatherers, pastoralists, and part- or full-time agriculturalists. This material involved what has been termed in this book ethno-medicine and ethno- or indigenous psychiatry. Earlier, cultural ethnographies of contemporary forest peoples provided a possible window into the lifeways of indigenous approaches in matters one can gloss and popular or practical religion, medicine, and mental health and healing. These beliefs and practices were life-sustaining and organizing, inseparable from culture considered as a system of symbols and their meanings. An important function of this array of ideas and practices addressed human disorder, sickness and 'dis-ease', suffering, misery, demoralization, and the like – material that either embeds a psychiatric condition or helps bring it into being. Such phenomena predated the Aryans and were played out in folk or popular medicine, shamanism, witchcraft, sorcery, everyday religion, and forms of adjudication of social conflicts. All of these practices and institution served as localities where psychiatric phenomena were on display.

The basic point needing emphasis presently is that indigenous cultures found in the subcontinent prior to the Aryans had rich resources for coping with phenomena of psychiatric interest. In the history of

India right up to modern times, this assortment of beliefs and practices *never went away*. Literate documents that exemplify the Vedic and Hindu traditions and that were composed during the centuries preceding the Common Era document ideas, thought worlds, and habit patterns of interest to psychiatry that had long existed in the subcontinent and probably in Iran. Such material becomes more visible in documents during the medieval era, but it did not just surface or originate out of nothing at that point in written history. It has a long prehistory and was in the subcontinent long before the Aryans came into prominence.

Moreover, one can safely presume that some of beliefs and practices the Aryans brought into the subcontinent *already included* what has been termed indigenous material of psychiatric interest, only in this instance it was of Iranian sources. Such material can be construed as exemplifying part of the culture not only of South and Eastern Asia but of Western Asia as well, including Asia Minor and the Near East. The texts that were later evolved and that exemplify Vedic and Hindu culture represent a world-view and literate culture of enormous intellectual scope and beauty that is the equal of any that was evolved elsewhere in the ancient civilizations. However, in an ultimate sense, it drew from, incorporated, reworked, and rationalized ideas of indigenous peoples of Iran and the subcontinent.

Life in the subcontinent and the advent of the Aryans

The period during which the Aryans supervened in the populations of the subcontinent marked a major transformation in the way of life of people there. To be sure, what life was like during Vedic times (roughly post-1500 BCE) is hardly transparent. As suggested earlier, one must read in between the lines of sacred texts and popular compendia, all of which *began to be written* centuries later and even then after a period of oral transmission, standardization, and redaction and emendation. These are by and large compilations about cosmology, spirituality, philosophy, religious ritual, and valued and acceptable ways of being and behaviour, on the one hand, and folklore, legendary tales, conventional stories, and expositions of social, moral, and popular values, on the other. They are ideological and ideal formulations about experience, behaviour, and social life and popular and entertaining narratives about how the good and bad, the real and fanciful, the acceptable and unacceptable, were construed and played out (material that is of 'psychiatric interest').

In the best of scenarios, data found in later literatures depicts the desirable and the conventional high ground. What everyday life was 'really' like among Vedic peoples is not known and, more importantly for our purposes here, one is also in the dark about what life was like for the multitude of other peoples of the subcontinent all of whom were historically mute and also not spoken for and possibly not really understood by the wise and the adept who compiled their narratives about the standards for desirable and commendable behaviour.[763] Yet it is precisely this undoubtedly much larger proportion of the population of the subcontinent, starting with the Aryan, Vedic era and continuing through the rise and consolidation of Hinduism in the classical and medieval period and into the present, that should be taken into consideration if one intends to obtain a coherent and comprehensive understanding of psychiatric phenomena in India.

One presumes, then, that following or coterminous with the decline of the Indus Valley civilization, the Vedic peoples established a very different social order and way of life. Archeologists and historians suggest as much.[764] One must also presume that the culture of the Aryans, exemplified in the Vedas, Brāhmaṇas, and the Āraṇyakas and their popular spin-offs of practical knowledge, represented a major shift in the way problems of health, misfortune, and human suffering were construed and handled.

During the early Vedic period (1500–800 BCE) societies of the subcontinent were comparatively larger and composed of socially differentiated groupings in ranked schemas of prestige and social power. Priests of major rituals that sanctified the society and brought it into harmony with the universe together with other priests involved in mediating relations between gods and human concerns in more private ways represented two categories of experts that could be recruited in matters of sickness and emotional, behavioural disaffections. There existed local, popular groupings of people of lower station whose needs in area of mental health and for treatment of conditions of psychiatric interest were met by religious cum medical, cum psychiatric practitioners.

---

[763] Although this is doubtful, given the indigenous roots of Aryan knowledge discussed earlier in Chapters 2, 3 and 8.

[764] Kennedy 2000; R. S. Sharma 1995, 1996; Stein 1998; Thapar 2002.

Knowledge filtered from the Vedas, drawn from indigenous oral traditions, and from the expertise of shamans whose position in communities was well defined, complemented the more established 'great' traditions' approach to sickness and healing found in the *Atharvaveda*.[765] No strong separation of classes of ailments or specialist healers was found and all types were consulted for all types of ailments.

In effect, the advent of Brahmanism and later of classical Hinduism marked a major turning point in the history and evolution of indigenous psychiatry and in the way conditions of psychiatric interest were construed and handled in the subcontinent.[766] Indigenous peoples have a long history in the subcontinent. They lived in comparatively socially undifferentiated small groups (hunter-gatherers, pastoralists, horticulturalists, or small-scale agriculturalists). Egalitarian, informal and sometimes inegalitarian and more differentiated practices of ethno-medicine and shamanistic mental health among such peoples represent a possible exemplar of baseline of health/medical beliefs and practices that predated the Aryan entry into the subcontinent. On this ethno-medical and ethno-psychiatric template were imposed Aryan and later Hindu ways, although such indigenous beliefs and practices (to an indeterminate extent) were probably slowly appropriated and contributed to the evolution of the structure of the early Vedic way of life that has been described earlier. As already indicated, this is a comparatively beclouded period from the standpoint of documentation of behavioural phenomena, settlement of disputes, adjudication of social political conflicts and the healing disturbances of physical and mental health except in the most general terms, teased out from later documents particularly the major epics, Puranas, as well as the Vedas.

Towards classical Hinduism

Michaels refers to the period stretching from 500 to 200 BCE as the era of ascetic reformism, which was followed by classical Hinduism that extends through the first millennium CE.[767] The first great and influential empire in India arose during the fourth century BCE, a period during which heterodox religions (Buddhism, Jainism) took hold. Through

[765] See Chapter 3 and especially Chapter 6.

[766] Michaels 2004.

[767] Michaels 2004.

military force, the early Maurya rulers achieved political supremacy over a large part of the subcontinent, all but the extreme south. In addition to the growth of cities and administrative centres, Maurya control evidently extended to remote parts of the country. The history of the Mauryas is recorded in a compilation of social, political, and economic practices, the *Arthaśāstra*, written by Kauṭilya, an influential minister of the court; in the *Indika*, written by the Greek ambassador Megasthenes; and in inscriptions of edicts issued by Aśoka, the great Maurya ruler who presided during the mid-third century BC. Buddhist influence during the Mauryan period was very strong, and dispatches from Buddhist clerics to neighbouring regions and satellite territories are influential landmarks in the religious history of India and Southeast Asia more generally.

Proclamations by the emperor Aśoka appear to have been aimed at regulating not only political and economic life, but also social, moral, legal, and religious behaviour, and by extension, virtually all types of interpersonal relations.[768] The freedom to pursue a life of ascetic religious contemplation and duty, for example, was apparently regulated so as to screen out all who were not yet beyond childbearing or still had obligations to their families. All of this suggests that at the time there existed a strong push towards 'dropping out'. This involved a strong current of impulses for and attractions towards unconventional, antinomian, and subaltern ways of life that were deemed disorderly, disreputable, and dangerous. To control and regulate these segments of the population, the arms of administration and state representatives intervened in ways that undoubtedly involved a measure of coercion. Besides ostracism, seclusion in religious hermitages, banishment or incarceration, measures included taxation, forced labour, and forced migration and settlement of new territories for agricultural exploitation. The state maintained a monopoly over mining and metallurgy. In areas of settled agriculture, there was intense regulation of the four main castes, with the lower castes particularly marginalized and excluded.

Sharma and Thapar have provided interpretations of life and society during this period of time during which Hindu polities were centralized and took on the fundamental shape and characteristics of civilization in the subcontinent.[769] Sharma specifically describes the harsh character of

[768] R. S. Sharma 1995; Chakravorti 1996; Thapar 2002.

[769] R. S. Sharma 1995, 1996; Thapar 1997, 2002.

social life, providing something of a theory about social organization and control of the political and economic order during Aśoka's time and later. He indicates that 'primitive' ideas and practices from Vedic times were borrowed, refined and elaborated to serve the cause of Brahmanism. All classes, Sharma surmises, subscribed to 'these superstitions' that functioned like an ideological cement that contained class conflicts and social tensions, leaving people with few causes 'for grumbling'. This ideology was later emphasized in the epics, Puranas, law books, and other influential traditional literatures and effectively 'driven home to the Hindus through oral and written 'propaganda'.[770] Sharma's classical India is an oppressed society, with higher orders intent on maintaining their hold and power in the polities. The common, folk peoples were manipulated and coerced by a relentless administration under the priestly activities of the most prestigious Brahmanic caste that functioned at the behest of its close allies, the political ruling class and their supporters among the military.

Mental health during the period of ascetic reform

Thapar supports Sharma's generalizations, extending the picture to cover how the Mauryan society might have contributed directly and indirectly to social strain and conflict and, by implication, to the cause of social stress and emotional disaffection.[771] Aśoka's reign was characterized by centralized power, with a king who was the supreme arbiter of society, state bureaucracies for controlling society, and even a system of spies spread throughout the communities. The Brahmins gained in social, religious, and moral authority and power, and the caste system of society was crystallized. Thapar draws heavily on Kauṭilya's *Arthaśāstra*, whose validity as a historical account of the Mauryas is controversial, so the following generalizations are contestable.[772] Thapar presupposes that the policy of *dharma*, related to Dharmaśāstras and Dharmasūtras, was largely a creation of Aśoka. It was in its application in Mauryan India that one finds 'the true achievement' of Aśoka. To him, *dharma* was a secular teaching that emphasized respecting religious authorities and

---

[770] R. S. Sharma 1995.

[771] Thapar 2002.

[772] Thapar 1997.

family elders. It advocated liberality and charity toward others, warned against killing animals, and promoted a sense of social ethics.[773]

Another civic improvement, or coercive measure depending on one's point of view, was the creation of a new service system staffed by a group of functionaries, termed *dharmamahāmātras*, who were empowered to spread the *dharma* and explain its relevance and state policy implications. Thapar indicates that such officers and the services they provided were new to Indian administration.[774] While originally their functions were predominantly related to human welfare in general, gradually the power of such officers increased until they influenced the workings of various sectarian and secular institutions.[775] In many ways, state systems of social, political, and economic control were instituted that applied throughout the empire, with highly efficient administrative machinery, and which 'extended to the very details of daily life'.[776] Thapar suggests that government officials and welfare officers probably introduced 'too much' regulation and control in social life and 'must on occasion' have oppressed and restricted life of the average citizen.

The high degree of social stratification and coercive control during this period, and the obvious social disorder and misery that prevailed and that set it in motion, suggests that in the population many people would have experienced disabling health conditions of all types.[777] For political and social reasons, attempts were made to standardize thought worlds and impose more structured habit patterns and social relations by means of an imposed moral ethos. This included a formal system for adjudicating conflicts and strong disapproval of straying from an approved code of conduct. Such a potentially oppressive, punitive order would have likely caused conflicts in social relationships and moral strains regarding acceptable conduct, perhaps even encouraging the role of sickness and emotional disaffection if not causing conditions of psychiatric interest.

Aśoka's more than three-decade-long reign during the Mauryan Empire represents the first well documented period of Indian history.

---

[773] Thapar 1997: 163.

[774] Thapar 1997.

[775] Thapar 1997: 118.

[776] Thapar 1997, 2002.

[777] The interplay of public health, epidemiological hardships, and social stress in matters pertaining to mental health and psychiatric conditions was emphasized in Chapters 4, 5 and 8.

His conversion to Buddhism, his promotion of Buddhist ideas, practices, and establishments, the overall missionary activity during his reign, and his general humanitarian disposition is legendary. Did these personality traits or his temperament transfer in some way to actions that in a *concrete sense* led to the promotion of health? Aśoka's concern for the welfare of his subjects led him to import medicinal plants and, where needed for both men and animals, to dig wells and establish rest-houses at regular intervals along roads in various regions of the empire. Aśoka's commitment to Buddhism and the latter's logical ties to healing of all types of ills and ailments would be consistent with a notion that he may in some tangible way have moved in the direction of state support of medical health (and religious, of course) healing. Be that as it may, one of the benefits found in Mauryan India is said to be the active promotion of health through provision of resources and habits of behaviour that probably improved the health of populations. If this is true it can be construed as a sanguine development, although perhaps a response to 'unsanguine' conditions of life to which the state itself had contributed. To obtain a more complete picture of health in relation to social conditions and problems, one is again forced to read between the lines of the official reading of documents produced by the religious, political, and economically influential upper orders. One might ask where one would have found those showing constellations of signs and symptoms of genuine conditions of psychiatric interest and others located in the penumbra of mental health ailments and sufferings that consisted of equally painful and demoralizing emotional, behavioural disaffections. Answer: certainly, places of incarceration, asylum in religious establishments, intentional entry or indoctrination into antinomian religious movements, pure retreat and social withdrawal within family enclaves or sojourn in the countryside as itinerant beggars, taken together represent locations in the social fabric where conditions of psychiatric interest would have been emplaced.

To one interested in the cultural history of psychiatric phenomena in India, these generalizations provide clues about the character of social life as it bears on causes and prevalence of emotional distress and behavioural strain in local communities. It raises two ways of thinking about where the 'indigenous psychiatry' of early pre-classical Hinduism times was situated and how it worked. Strain and stress pushed vulnerable individuals over thresholds of adaptive behaviour that, given mind–body integration, was manifested in bodily and emotional signs and symptoms that conformed to Buddhist and early ayurvedic exemplars of conditions of psychiatric interest. These required services that could have been provided by several types of more medically-oriented practitioners: monks, travelling mendicants and renunciants with expertise in medicine, and physicians conversant with knowledge and expertise later to emerge as Ayurveda. Persons with special knowledge about plants, herbs, and ways of handling bodily and behavioural syndromes (psycho-physiologically based disturbances) were part of this medical segment of indigenous psychiatry. Some shamans should be included as well, especially those who were more expert in sickness and healing, and whose secular knowledge complemented expertise in mediation with spirits. These settings and transactions within them realized the more medical component of indigenous psychiatry.

On the other hand, one has practitioners involved in the non-medical, religious-healing approach to psychiatric phenomena. These would have included higher caste ritual experts versed in the Vedas; agents of the state or spies promoting *dharma;* accomplished gurus associated with emerging more popular soteriological movements and emergent sects; those adept in psycho-energetic pursuits who served as tutors for initiates, *sādhus* or religious mendicants; tricksters who traded on the sometimes perplexing and disorganized nature and understanding of 'social reality'; traditional shamans primarily involved in spiritual journeying and possible forms of divination; custodians of religious temples and shrines and other persons versed in the art of witchcraft and demonic disciplines. Many individuals in this complex mixture of talent, religious insight, expertise in meditation, charisma and communicative skills, moral conviction and persuasiveness, and motivation to enthral and manipulate, were participants and instrumental actors that in subsequent centuries would be labelled as yogins, tantrics, and spiritually adept *siddhas*. All of the preceding involves beliefs and practices of psychiatric interest, material rooted in and evolving from Vedas and indigenous substratum of practical knowledge. In addition, villages or clusters of them undoubtedly had access to indigenous material per se, namely, popular medical and purely religious practitioners as well as local or lineage elders versed in the art of settlement arbitration and adjudication of social conflict. The latter also represent localities or settings to which persons with conditions of psychiatric interest would have been taken by family.

Many individuals in need of indigenous psychiatric care would find temporary domicile in temples, hermitages, and monasteries. Upholders of morality and behavioural standards along with medical and religious practitioners all participated in social spaces to which persons with emotional, behavioural, and bodily symptoms were taken by family for diagnosis and healing. Besides the use of curative procedures, experts of different persuasion functioned also to reinforce traditional values, and to reform and rehabilitate individuals unable to cope with social demands. In effect, all of these personnel made up the non-medical component of the indigenous psychiatry.

This division, of course, is purely analytic. As emphasized in earlier chapters, in traditional India, and indeed through the medieval period and prior to the emergence of the pre-modern era, persons sought the services of and were attended by a holistic system of mental health practice. It is probably not the case that there was a sharp differentiation made between what our conception of sickness construes as a 'physical, somatic symptom picture' compared to what I have singled out in this book as a 'condition of psychiatric interest', which our conceit is to view as a mental or emotional entity. Not the body/mind, the medical/religious or natural/supernatural dualism was part of the understanding of impaired sense of wellbeing in traditional India. A hallmark of this medicine was that it was holistic: it construed sickness as a biopsychosocial amalgam that exemplified spiritual and moral considerations as well. Rather, a medical–non-medical–religious *amalgam* of beliefs and practices constituted a society's indigenous psychiatry. Even during the period when Ayurveda was well established and its eight branches were differentiated conditions of psychiatric interest and their treatment had secular, moral, and religious dimensions. This integrative composition and formulation of disturbances of health and wellbeing is a reflection of the fact that two dualisms so important in contemporary Western societies simply had no important presence: mind–body dualism and a secular, natural contra spiritual, moral emphasis in matters of sickness.

Historians like R. S. Sharma and Thapar point to the rise of several religious sects starting around the Mauryan period and especially during the centuries that followed into the Common Era. Eliade and White, whose focus is on developments in philosophical psychology and soteriology that gained visibility and momentum during the medieval era, emphasize a long period 'since time immemorial' during which popular, sectarian, unorthodox, exotic movements and practices were striking in laying the groundwork for the evolution of Yoga, Tantra, and the Siddha traditions.[778] This substratum of religious pluralism reflected the search for meaning, emotional release, and a need for a positive re-affirmation, in relation to problems of morale and sense of oppression stemming from poverty, kingly exploitation, the social imposition of *dharma* and the regulations carried out by agents of the state who sprouted after breakup of the Mauryan era. At the same time, the rise of new sects very likely contributed to social tensions and conflicts, as well as psychological predicaments.

Sharma emphasizes the important appeal of the main philosophies and religions of liberation, Buddhism and Jainism. These grew in influence during the centuries before the Common Era. Buddhism in particular, with its emphasis on social equality, had a special appeal to the lower social orders. A fabric of ideas carried the population forward and provided intellectual meaning to the populations. It included Vedic doctrines about being, existence, salvation and revelation (*Ṛgveda, Atharvaveda,* Brāhmaṇas, Upanishads), traditions, guidelines, examples of moral behaviour, emerging rules propounded in, or later incorporated in, early Dharmaśāstras and imposed politically by the kings and emperors, and wisdom literature and regulations propounded in folklore, myths, legendary accounts, hagiographical stories about deified saints and the like that provided the background for later popular writings (the great epics, the Puranas). Religio-moral hegemony of the Brahmin caste along with members of the political elite presided over and imposed interpretation and validation through ritual of what moral behaviour was expected to involve and lower orders had their antinomian, subaltern, seditious, popular, sectarian modes of obtaining liberation and salvation. A complex, diversified ensemble of ideas and practices describes thought worlds and habits of persons during the period that predated the classical era.[779]

This is a picture of complex and potentially divisive religious pluralism with roots in the past and stemming from a diversity of languages and ethnicities, not to say social castes and classes. These sources of discord appear to have come into sharper focus during and especially following the Mauryan period. For example, there were several deities and religious ideas that differed from those found in the Vedas. Promi-

[778] Eliade 1964, 1969; White 1996, 2000.

[779] Jha 1998.

nent sacred personages, originally of non-Aryan origin, appear to have been incorporated into the Brahmanic canon. Ways of paying homage to these varied deities

> anticipated the theistic sects which later became popular in the various parts of the country. Evidence of the popular belief in malevolent spirits, magical practices, and superstitions of all kinds also find mention in the *Arthaśāstra* and perhaps formed part of the popular culture.[780]

THE TRANSITION INTO THE CLASSICAL ERA

The high degree of social turmoil described by Jha, Thapar, and Stein and suggested by Eliade and White has implications for phenomena of psychiatric interest.[781] A period of turmoil offers competing and perhaps inconsistent answers to vital questions about the meaning of existence and social life in general. The competition stemming from religious differences also involved ethnic and economic differences all of which one can presume translated at the level of individuals and families as mental confusion, emotional unrest and tension, shifts in allegiances productive of hopeful optimistic moods alternating with demoralizing, pessimistic ones. This can contribute significantly to strains in the population. In vulnerable individuals, this would have contributed to the production and higher incidence of various psychopathologies.

The centuries preceding, during, and following the Mauryan period social tensions such as these waxed and waned in communities that came increasingly under the influence of centralized systems of politico-economic, ideological, and cultural control. While originating in metropolitan areas and directly enforced there, such instruments of social, moral, and political control were exported to the hinterland where regional administrative units brought the oppressive system to bear on the social life of rural communities, with consequent strains. Many tribal peoples were persuaded if not coerced to incorporate in the official Hindu way of life. They formed or were forced to live as new castes, all of which contributed to social and ethnic pluralism. The push towards acculturation, assimilation, and meaningful social participation directed to such groupings, no doubt increased economic and political competi-

---

[780] Jha 1998: 104.

[781] Stein 1998; Eliade 1964, 1969; White 1996, 2000.

tion, invidious comparisons and ambitions as per caste status, and contributed to social tensions all of which were registered in psychiatric casualties.

Aśoka has been singled out in the earlier account because his reign exhibits features of the social fabric of early societies under the influence of the formative phase of Indian civilization. This period is also well covered by social historians, whose work has been discussed. The social characteristics of Aśoka's reign can be emblematic of many contemporary and later kingdoms that may not have been as large and politically powerful, but were similar in form and function. Characteristics and the regional spread of these kingdoms are well documented in the work of Thapar and the historical accounts of Kulke and Rothermund, and Stein.[782] Many of the social, political, and religio-moral traditions of the Mauryan synthesis endured into later societies and were most likely featured in the golden period of the Guptas and beyond. Generalizations about social life of this period, along with inferences about emotional distress and behavioural disaffection based on writings about Aśoka and the Mauryan Empire, are thus applicable to societies and empires that followed.

Comment

This discussion suggests that Aśoka expounded upon and emphasized the tradition of the *dharma* in the context of a society seriously divided by caste, religion, ethnicity, and economic standing. It is true that Aśoka is held to have promoted his policies by means of edicts emphasizing toleration, non-violence, respect, and a heightened sense of the dignity of the individual. They emphasized virtuous behaviour, ethical and social responsibility, toleration toward all beings, and interdependence among members of all social groups and classes. These edicts can be viewed as a tribute to the intentions, emphases, and accomplishments of a great king who promoted morality, social organization, and stability.[783]

Thus, because Aśoka converted to Buddhism and helped promote that religion in India, his reign might be thought to have promoted a 'softer' social policy with a less punitive policy toward wrongdoing, but this is only a conjecture. However, the emphasis on regulating behav-

[782] Thapar 2002; Kulke and Rothermund 1986; Stein 1998.

[783] Thapar 1997.

iour and coercive implementation could reflect political oppression, signalling great social disorganization, instability, and misery that needed not only formal attention but also political control.[784] The traditions present during the time of Aśoka, which he built on, consolidated and then stipulated as policy, had roots deep in orthodox tradition, being integral to the Vedas and related scriptures and texts. These are traditions that competed with Buddhism and that Aśoka and his advisors probably wanted de-emphasized or set aside. Moreover, one can assume prevalence of other religious, soteriological traditions that sharply conflicted with Buddhism. Aśoka's motives may have been politically inspired, to diminish conflict and unrest among his subjects. However, they were also controlling, uncompromising, and in some respects obviously coercive. While the heavy emphasis given to social-political and especially ethical-moral principles, as stipulated in the Arthaśāstra and Dharmaśāstra codes, and the tenacity with which they were enforced as quasi-political legal dicta, can be viewed as contributing a homogenizing, hardening influence on Hindu culture, their pernicious consequences for mental health cannot be overlooked. Implications of all of this for understanding conditions of psychiatric interest during the classical period are taken up in what follows.

JURIDICAL AND LEGAL CONSTRAINTS ON AYURVEDIC PSYCHIATRIC CARE IN ANCIENT AND CLASSICAL INDIA

Introduction

As cultural universals, conditions of psychiatric interest were certainly a feature of all human communities of the subcontinent of India during the ancient and classical period. It was emplaced in many social spaces, undoubtedly more prominent among impoverished, marginalized social and occupational groups who would have been significantly more strained from a medical, physical, and political standpoint. Since such conditions constitute human problem replete with special social and existential implications, they made connections with many different types of social institutions, medical, moral, religious, and legal. However, concentrating purely on the spectrum of medical avenues of care,

[784] R. S. Sharma 1995.

ayurvedic practice must be regarded as an exception of how conditions of psychiatric interest were dealt with in traditional India. As discussed earlier, a not inconsiderate number of conditions would have connected with medical and spiritual stations operated by moral educative, religious, ritual, and generally recognized wise persons found in the three higher *varṇas* for sure and more than likely in groups across the hierarchical landscape including tribals and the socially excluded. Such types of practitioners and healers and many others (shamans, witchcraft specialists) made up the non-medical component of the indigenous psychiatry of Hindu cities, towns and villages. These were not individuals trained in the evolving corpus of information carried forth by leading physicians who espoused, or whose writings were later incorporated in the major medical canons of Bheḷa, Caraka and Suśruta. However, they may well have been familiar with ayurvedic ideas, principles, and philosophy. The interpretation of psychiatric condition and healing, observed in any station or setting of this loosely organized indigenous assemblage of religious/spiritual healing beliefs and practices, varied. It was, naturally, influenced by local factors such as caste membership and religious/spiritual affiliation of popular practitioners, related personnel, and clients. Nevertheless, it can safely be assumed that regardless of predominant focus, a variable mix of religion, spirituality, and rational/secular/materia medica approaches would have prevailed. However, it is exclusively ayurvedic medical care for psychopathology that is given attention in what follows.

If by psychiatric care one means the self-conscious resort to and administration of healing, counselling, and procedures of medicine for a separable class of disorders accorded special identity, then psychiatric care generally, and ayurvedic psychiatric care more specifically, did not exist in the subcontinent prior to the modern era. But within the compass of traditional medical practice, ayurvedic care of Indian varieties of psychiatric condition certainly did delineate an indigenous system of mental health practice. A review of ancient classical writings discloses this. For purposes of exposition, one is allowed to describe these diagnostic and healing dialogues as constituting ayurvedic psychiatry. One can venture to hypothesize that virtually all forms, but obviously not all instances, of psychiatric condition at some point in their evolution and history would come under the influence of and sometimes connected with ayurvedic establishments.

In what follows, attention is given not to chronic, dilapidated conditions of behavioural breakdown (psychoses, dementia, insanity, madness) but instead to relatively fresh, acute cases of sickness that fulfilled criteria of psychiatric condition. What needs emphasis presently are the kinds of social constraints that affected the ayurvedic care of new and/or acute, cases of psychiatric condition (anxiety, depression, disorientations due to stress, episodes of dissociation and possession) *as a consequence of the legal, juridical status surrounding the practice of ayurvedic physicians.*

The sociology and legality of ayurvedic practice

To better understand aspects of ayurvedic psychiatric practice in traditional India, it is useful to consider first some of the characteristics and constraints surrounding the practice of medicine as represented in ancient Indian law.[785] To begin with, physicians in Ayurveda were viewed as members of a sacred lineage of highly respected, noble, venerable, sagacious, almost god-like personages. They were defined as individuals whose primary means of subsistence was diagnosis and the practice of promoting a long life that included the giving of remedies and prescriptions. The writings of the great physicians as well as the various moral/ethical/religious *śāstra*s described the characteristics and qualifications that a student of medicine should possess and these included such things as cleanliness, modesty, intelligence, intellectual probity, and exemplary behaviour. Around the age of 16, students meeting these moral and intellectual traits could apprentice with a physician guru, provided he was of the higher castes; persons of the lowest order or *śūdra*s caste and of mixed caste were apparently excluded.

A set of qualifications involving knowledge of the medical and other scriptural texts as well as high moral, ethical standards was expected of physicians who functioned as teachers. Once accepted by a physician-teacher, an initiation marked the beginning of studies as a consequence of which students were expected to renounce negative attitudes and dispositions (anger, lust, avarice, folly, vanity, deception) and follow the regulations stipulated by the teacher in a number of areas befitting a physician that involved appearance, demeanour, conduct and habits. Learning the texts, acquiring practical skills of therapy that embraced surgery, and living a life free of sin constituted requirements of the edu-

---

[785] Sternbach 1965: Chapter VIII.

cational enterprise. A period of intense theoretical learning and practical experience in caring for patients and performing medical procedures, as well as meeting exacting social, moral, and psychological standards of behaviour qualified a student as passing his educational hurdle.

Medical writings but not the various Dharmaśāstras indicate that one who passed the rigors of education and training had to obtain permission from the king or ruler in order to practice medicine. This, in some respects, was the equivalent of a medical license at least, apparently, as authorized or recommended by the orthodox medical community. These same medical writings drew a strong distinction between such morally, intellectually qualified and licensed physicians and those who failed to meet these qualifications, and instead of functioning as 'saviours of life', simply chased after diseases, destroyed life, and were self-promoters and seekers of pure monetary success.

A complex assortment of laudable, morally valued behaviours and habits served as guidelines to clinical practice; this body of medical ethics spanned aspects of sheer diagnosis and treatment decisions as well as conduct with patients, their families. With few qualifications, the role of the physician was a positive one and occupants were esteemed and expected to obtain remuneration for their work. It was also explained in medical texts that many classes of patients should be treated free of charge. These texts also stipulated the avoidance of patients of ill repute and of low, polluting occupations and households and enjoined the treatment of patients who in the estimation of physicians were curable. Because of the potentially polluting nature of the practice of medicine, in some instances this appears to have diminished the role of the physician and lowered his social esteem among members of higher castes.

Legal, medical, and juridical texts suggest that in some respects physicians and ayurvedic medicine functioned as agents of the state and as arms of the polity, respectively. This complements material discussed earlier about social, political characteristics of the tenor of societies during the Mauryan period and those influenced by its mode of governance. In the first place, physicians were often induced to migrate to regions where they were rewarded with special land grants and expected to serve people in need. In some respects, they here functioned as state agents promoting colonization and helping to create conditions that attracted peasants or at least made their forced migration more tolerable in the state's efforts to drain and secure reclamation of land for agricultural use. These gifts of land to the physician could not be sold or mortgaged, but could provide income and migrant physicians received the usual wages in addition to their land.

More suggestive of state control and regulation was the fact that all physicians had a duty to inform administrative authorities with respect to aspects of their practice. In the event of patients dying, physicians who had undertaken such perilous medical enterprises without properly informing authorities were subject to fine. Indeed, whom someone chose to treat and the medical condition treated came under a form of state regulation. According to Kauṭilya's *Arthaśāstra*,

> in order to safeguard himself from a possible penalty, the physician had to inform the corresponding office ... of treating a grievous case which might cause death. If he did not ... and death occurred, he was liable to [a fine]. The physician had also to inform the [administrator] immediately in case when he was called to a patient suspected of concealing his whereabouts. If the physician gave medical treatment to any such patient, whether for a wound or an excess of unwholesome food, he was liable to the same penalty as the patient. Anyone sheltering such a patient was also liable to the penalty.[786]

As indicated earlier, the medical and scriptural texts certainly depict the role of the physician as highly esteemed. To administer treatment with the welfare of one's patient at heart was said to lead to virtue, wealth, fame, and heaven; and physicians should be worshipped as gods were worshipped and respected like kings. However,

> Kauṭilya [putative author of *Arthaśāstra*] turned the high esteem and honour attributed to physicians to his own advantage and to the better use of his Machiavellian purposes ... we find very often mention of physicians used as spies ... in order to ascertain the nature of the intrigue prevalent among parties favourably disposed to his master, as well as the conspiracy among hostile factions, and in order to determine whether people were loyal or disloyal to the enemy ... Spies disguised as physicians, could in addition, be ordered to make a 'seditious' minister, or another person 'of seditious character' believe to be sick, and cold contrive to poison him while prescribing medicines and diet.[787]

---

[786] Sternbach 1965: 291.

[787] Sternbach 1965: 298–299.

Considerable attention was devoted in legal and juridical texts to the responsibility of physicians for the conduct and outcome of medical care. In instances when the outcome of care could be equated with malpractice, it was neither the patient nor his or her relatives who were the object of primary concern or protection. Heirs of the patient, for example, were not indemnified in the event of death. The focus of litigation was the physician: as a general rule all physicians who acted improperly were subject to punishment. They were liable to penalties for their careless medical treatment and the fines collected by the king or state. In assessing blame and culpability and hence in levying fines, a number of subtle distinctions were made between selfish and dishonest actions, careless actions, actions devolving from lack of standard medical knowledge, negligent actions motivated out of greed, and 'honest' errors of judgments or decisions resulting from confusing disease pictures whose symptoms overlapped and could not be known for sure.

> The question arose as to whether a physician ... acted either improperly i.e. dishonestly or erroneously that was falsely. In any case he was responsible for every dishonest or improper act, including carelessness ... If, however, his actions being the sequel to misapprehension, appeared to be false or wrong i.e. when the physician imputed 'that' to what was 'not that', and gave a wrong diagnosis and treated his patients according to it, in such a case there did not arise any [fault] ... consequently, it would seem that, in case of such a misapprehension the physician could not be held responsible even if his medical treatment proved to be without success ... [In cases] due to false recognition of certain symptoms common to two or more different diseases and at the same time this false recognition was not caused by ignorance but was due exclusively to an error (misapprehension) the physician was free from responsibility for his medical treatment.[788]

Implications involving traditional practice of ayurvedic psychiatry

Psychiatric conditions by definition involve personal distress manifested by disturbances of emotion, thinking, attitude, and behaviour along with associated bodily symptoms. An individual's suffering and disability would have manifested in outward fractious, socially divisive behaviour (jealousies, anger, sense of victimization or persecution, avoidance and rejection of family or community residents) that contra-

[788] Sternbach 1965: 312–313.

vened social conventions and caste regulations, as these are enshrined and stipulated in the various moral and legal codes. Another venue of expression of psychiatric condition involved experiences of anguish, inward fears and morbid preoccupations (anxieties, obsessions, depressive feelings, altered states of consciousness, delusions and hallucinations). Alternatively, features of both of these scenarios could have been found together. Given the stress level placed on integrative structures of physiological and psychological function inherent in a psychiatric condition one can anticipate that 'clinical pictures' included signs and symptoms involving body. While an ayurvedic slant on such manifestations would have emphasized unbalanced humours, blockages and stasis, and circulatory disturbances in context of conditions of ecology and life habits, the philosophy or general perspective of the physician would nonetheless have, at least implicitly, reinforced traditional ideas and values about morality and social obligation (see below).

However, material discussed in the previous chapter suggests that, putting aside concrete bodily disturbances, an individual's condition was exemplified in the distinctive Hindu cultural psychology. In other words, a purely clinical and more or less objective or secular representation of psychiatric condition constitutes an abstraction. It favours the idea that Ayurveda represented a major scientific breakthrough in the history of human culture and society. This conception is certainly not wrong, although it is incomplete. In Hindu civilization and society, how clinical parameters of psychiatric condition were interpreted, expressed, and dealt with bore the imprint of the prevailing philosophy, morality, religious, and ideational presuppositions in terms of which individuals were enculturated.[789] The meaning and interpretation accorded conditions of psychiatric interest was framed in a distinctive idiom of constructs and beliefs about spirituality, morality, obligation, personal psychology, and metaphysics, all of which are hallmarks of Hindu civilization and culture.

Furthermore, Ayurveda was a science of health and disease, including psychiatric condition, which was rooted in scriptural authority. A naturalistic formulation of sickness, empirically-based procedures of diagnosis, and a broad array of carefully rationalized therapeutic practices rendered Indian medicine a showcase of its science. However, a unique slant of Ayurveda was that it not only supported but promoted

[789] Freed and Freed 1964; see LeVine 1990, for general exposition.

general social, cultural, and religious viewpoints about the nature of personal experience and moral/religious conduct. To make contact with an ayurvedic physician, one may assume, was to seek and obtain reinforcement of traditional values and directives about the conduct of life in a context of suffering, uncertainty, and vulnerability associated with sickness and brought about by different types of stress. In some respects, to promote health and undo disease by recourse to ayurvedic medicine was to re-establish and strengthen if not seek actual re-instatement in the acceptable mould and pattern of approved behaviour and conduct.

AYURVEDA AS A SYSTEM OF SOCIAL REGULATION

In light of what conditions of psychiatric interest involve, material presented above about the administrative or 'statist' character of Ayurveda raises interesting questions about the social functions of this and other systems of academic medicine of ancient societies and civilizations. In contrast to general states of sickness in which bodily ailments predominate, psychiatric conditions not only highlight but also uniquely constitute signs and symptoms involving the experiential and social behavioural world. Such conditions often result from and/or lead individuals to a questioning and undermining of their commitment to the social order. This encompasses adherence to the values placed on interpretation of pro-social, moral, religious behaviour. Thus, turning to an ayurvedic physician cannot be viewed simply as reaching for, nor the anticipation of receiving ministrations from, an impartial, neutral, unconditionally supportive and accepting ally.

Ayurvedic physicians were indoctrinated in the unique and highly moralized cultural psychology of traditional India and, it would appear, its political psychology and ideology. They were promoters and exponents of its values in all areas of life, including the potentially socially divisive and psychologically alienating experiences that victims of psychiatric conditions could and must have experienced. The sponsorship and outright appropriation of the role of the physician by the state in the service of maintaining social order and control, especially given the lack of a purely secular, rationalistic, objective ethos which might possibly not have punished (and perhaps tolerated) alternative forms of (possibly even deviant) behaviour, undoubtedly reinforced in the society at large a view of the physician as an upholder of the status quo.

In light with this line of thought one is prompted to ask the impertinent question of whether in some respects Ayurveda constituted a social medicine and its agents perceived in part as 'medical policemen'. This supposition, of course, runs counter to contemporary descriptions by anthropologists of the humanism and sensitivity of ayurvedic practitioners; however, it must be acknowledged that the latter describe medical happenings in a very different world than that of ancient India, a world influenced by enlightenment ideals and in which modern ideas about medicine are pre-eminent.[790]

How might the ayurvedic physician's social control functions have played out in medical dialogues of traditional India? Provided a warrant for this was part of the medical culture (not a trivial consideration as discussed later), one consequence would be fear of telling the doctor one's 'real' or 'private' story about their condition and associated local circumstances and reactions to it. For example, the (natural?) tendency of psychosis to undermine, challenge, and interdict socially acceptable standards of behaviour, indeed, the tendency for behaviour to dilapidate and stray beyond the bonds of acceptability, would have been met with potential disapproval and stricture, couched perhaps in a paternalistic, supportive, but no less socially controlling if not coercive, tone. Desirable social behaviour would have been enjoined by what in effect also represented moral arbiters and supporters of the values of the family/state/community (the socially appointed physician).

Indeed, one is motivated to raise more fundamental questions about characteristics of the cultural presuppositions that contextualized medical care in ancient India. Ayurveda, like other traditional Indian systems pertaining to physical and emotional disaffection, was (and still is) proactive: it was not just curative but sought future wellbeing of the person as emphasized in earlier chapters. In India this had and still has broad implications leading one to ask a number of questions: Was Ayurveda a truly secular, rational, or naturalistic medicine, a medicine that favoured the individual and promoted his or her personal strivings if not individuality as per health? Were private ideas and beliefs about self and body likely to be shared with a healer? Was this personal domain constitutive of what an individual was expected if not enjoined to bring to

[790] Kakar 1982.

and talk about in the 'doctor–patient' relationship? Could a culture of medicine that favoured dispassionate and objective review of highly private doubts and personal woes in relation to sickness really have existed in the world of traditional India? Could guardians, if not enforcers and preservers of the sanctity of the societies' cultural psychology and morality, individuals who in practice seem to have been regulated and in some respects controlled if not coerced by the state, have functioned as impartial allies and supporters of persons who were plagued with divisive thoughts, feelings, impulses (along with their somatic correlates)? Was an individual's and a physician's formulation and treatment of a condition of psychiatric interest framed in terms of concern for sheer relief of signs and symptoms or was it conditioned and channelled if not manipulated towards the maintenance of social values and principles about moral, political order contingent on endorsement of cosmological, soteriological, and eschatological commandments?

The answers to these questions are not available to us. But it is not unreasonable to suggest tentatively that answers would be 'not completely' or 'probably not' or 'both' directives featured physician patient dialogues. (One should keep in mind that the structure of the therapeutic moment in traditional India did not ordinarily comprise just physician and patient, but the latter's family and sometimes other patients waiting to see physician.) But to deny ayurvedic psychiatrists a possible role as (anachronistic modern) healers and psychotherapists is hardly to disqualify their humanity or minimize the support and caring that they offered their clientele. In the ethos of the time, ayurvedic psychiatrists, perhaps like agents or practitioners of several other social institutions of ancient India that handled conditions of psychiatric interest, undoubtedly offered and provided relief and understanding to victims. To what extent there really existed a warrant for truly emancipated thought, for dispassionate review of private conflicts and impulses, the toleration of attitudes and sentiments that contravened foundational assumptions and traditions of the culture, and the like, is an open question.

Indeed, such an ideal (and ethnocentric) formulation of a psychiatric enterprise, redolent with the scent of modernity as it is, might fail to be realized in any indigenous psychiatry, even in those of contemporary nation states. Such questions get at the heart of what a system of medicine evolves to do, who its patrons and clients are, the concerns it addresses, and how these are culturally formulated. It is providing answers to such questions that make it very difficult to obtain an 'impartial' evaluation of efficacy or validity of a system of healing, for it has many functions beyond pure cure, functions that encompass metaphysical considerations as well as sociological ones.

Another slant may be taken with respect to the interplay between Ayurveda tenets, cultural expectations, and maintenance of social order. It could be the case, for example, that the moral, spiritual, and religious character of the cultural psychology of India may have minimized or even blocked the emergence of socially, politically contrary thoughts and dysphoric emotions about the social and spiritual order itself. More specifically, among vulnerable individuals experiencing stress, some of which displayed psychiatric condition, there may have existed cultural prescriptions that militated against the generation, experience, and communication (certainly to ayurvedic physicians) of signs and symptoms embodying consciously formulated spiritual doubt, lack of confidence about prevailing ideology, deviant, antisocial, immoral feelings and impulses, and the expression of associated actions which one can assume were at least implicit in the context of somatic symptoms (as per psychiatric condition).

As material reviewed in Chapter 5 disclosed, it is to be expected that an informed analyst would have 'diagnosed' some clinical manifestations of conditions of psychiatric interest in traditional India. In fact, such conditions are assumed here to constitute human, cultural universals. However, there may have existed cultural psychological factors that militated against the framing of emotional, spiritual, morale-related, and behavioural disaffections in the language of complaint and social divisiveness (psychological distress framed in cognitively oppositional if not perverse ideas, and impulses and behaviours signalling social deviance).

Taken at face value, as an overarching characteristic of Indian culture and ayurvedic medical practice this possibility can be rejected outright. The feelings and actions condemned in the *Atharvaveda*, the consistently uncompromising injunctions found in the various Dharmaśāstras, and emphases recorded in ancient legal documents together underscore the reality and compelling nature of such 'negatively framed' emotional and behavioural problems and suggest the gnawing prevalence of antisocial, divisive, and socially undesirable tendencies and behaviours. (Of course, not all individuals showing such a syndrome of behaviour would have necessarily met criteria for diagnosis of a psychiatric condition.) Furthermore, the bulk of literature in cultural psychiatry and medical anthropology argues for the universality of socially, morally deviant, devious, and discreditable feelings and impulses in the context of sickness and/or psychiatric condition.

One could maintain that in no ancient non-modern society and civilization would one have found a secular purely naturalistic, non-spiritual medical tradition. Cultures and societies of antiquity did not articulate nor promote ideas and values authorizing 'objective inquiries' about health in an ethos that involved individuality, autonomy, and self-centred personal striving. They were not modern! Conditions of sickness, physicians and medical compounds and even religious sanctuaries and temples where the healing of medical ailments took place were simply not sites for 'open' politically-oriented dialogues. The ethos of professional and folk healing did accept, approve, and much less promote open expression of doubts that challenged definitions about the character of virtue, conduct, and the fairness of the social, political order. Such modes of inquiry and dialogue may have possibly been nascent among philosophers of Greece and the Hellenistic Mediterranean. But even among them as well as physicians, the framework that supported this medicine (as the one of traditional China and India) exemplified the view that health, wellbeing, and sickness were matters involving the harmony or balance prevailing in the divine order of the cosmos.

In general, systems of medicine in ancient societies and civilizations upheld moral traditions, social values and ideas about social order. Their theories underscored the negative effects of contravention of social conventions contra legitimization of them as merely 'potentially harmful'. Models and narratives about sickness that punctuated medical dialogues did not as a matter of principle welcome, and may have actually worked against the generation and expression of ideas, impulses, and feelings that went against normative moral psychology and behaviour and which could wreak havoc with somatic wellbeing.

Returning again to India the evidence from scripture and texts that condemned antisocial, individualistic forms of conduct and experience hint at ways of thinking and feeling that contravened norms and traditions. However, a significant question is at what level of incidence and prevalence was this socially contrary material found and was it an acceptable and accepted part of medical dialogues?

It can be assumed that in traditional India (and in other ancient societies and indeed in any society) persons displaying conditions of psychiatric interest were not just experiencing signs and symptoms purely as burdensome psycho-physiological 'facts' nor were their conditions unrelated to antinomian sentiments and perception and reaction to politically harmful circumstances. Sickness generally and conditions of psychiatric interest in particular can be presumed to embody socially, politically contrary emotions, beliefs, and impulses as well as frank anti-social, immoral behaviours. Indeed, one can plausibly maintain that such a social, cultural, political, and moral and in the conceit of biomedicine 'non-medical' amalgam of ailments is in fact one of the universal features of conditions of psychiatric interest even though not necessarily formulated intraculturally in this way (it is implicit and covert).

In this context, one may be allowed to take the position that perhaps it was a unique character (genius?) of traditional Hindu culture to strongly shape and configure psychiatric conditions, or at least rein them in, along traditional, acceptable channels of social and moral discourse. This would imply that ayurvedic psychiatry functioned as an important pillar of influence, at least among the elite, gentry, and economically better-off layers of society that more than likely constituted its principal consumers. However, juridical and administrative functions of Ayurveda reviewed earlier raise the question of a possible source of politically motivated social stigma of conditions of psychiatric interest and need of gatekeepers (including ayurvedic physicians) to dampen or push aside if not discredit their manifestations as per moral, political implications.

PSYCHIATRIC STIGMA IN ANCIENT STATE SOCIETIES OF INDIA

There is much material that indicates conditions of psychiatric interest are highly stigmatizing in contemporary India.[791] However, while concern over disclosure and shame regarding mental illness has been studied empirically, and its many ramifications discussed, the origin of these rather strong and pervasive feelings is unclear.

Spiritual and demonic residues

Ayurveda is based predominantly on naturalism and reflects a very organic view of *unmāda* and *apasmāra*, insanity and epilepsy respectively.

[791] Chowdhury *et al.* 2000; Raguram *et al.* 2001; Weiss *et al.* 2001.

To the extent that this avenue of thought and healing prevailed in the society at large one would surmise that such conditions were not stigmatizing. However, an important category of insanity or madness in virtually all of the authoritative medical compendia (Caraka, Suśruta, Bheḷa, Vāgbhaṭa), termed *bhūtavidyā,* involves spirit attack, possession, or agents that had a malevolent intent and effect on the person. As discussed earlier, these conditions originally constituted a separate branch of Ayurveda, but in later compilations this was less emphasized, perhaps as a political concession to or desire to placate Brahmins.[792] Nonetheless, such causes still represent a major division of conditions of psychiatric interest classified as *unmāda.* They have different characteristics and some consist of behaviour involving possession, the occult and malign influences that by definition would have had negative implications in traditional times. However, it is not possible to tell whether other than strictly natural remedies were resorted to in treatment, although different compilations make reference to ritual prayer and religious observances. Spirit-related varieties were certainly also construed to have an organic basis. Yet, the presence within ayurvedic psychiatry of a division into a class of insanities that carried negative connotations, unquestionably an inheritance from much earlier thought and practice but still prevalent in settings where Ayurveda was practiced during traditional times, suggests the possibly of a society wide stigma with respect to some classes of conditions of psychiatric interest.

The moral burden of conditions of psychiatric interest

The Dharmaśāstras, ancient moral, ethical, and religious wisdom about social life, stipulate and provide guidelines regarding all facets of comportment. Their emphasis is on duties and obligations in social relations and in conduct of rituals in activities and rounds of daily life within household, in community settings, and with respect to some devotional practices. An important theme in these laws is the relative worth, social standing, and credibility of persons. They map a hierarchical social order that was governed by sometimes uncompromising standards of morality and behaviour. The laws favoured the higher social orders and morally policed and regulated the lower orders in matters of conduct.

---

[792] D. Chattopadhyaya 1977.

Peppered throughout the various compilations are references to outcast groups of unwanted, rejected, sullied, polluted, discredited, and marginalized persons, castes, and occupations. Individuals exhibiting insanity are frequently included in these lists of human waste material, along with thieves, murderers, egregious transgressors of basic norms of human decency, and the like. Weiss examines explicit references to insanity as a social category in his review of moral and legal issues in the Dharmaśāstras.[793] He provides details of how persons classed as insane are to be regarded and dealt with in different social and legal situations. As Weiss points out:

> The general issues dealt with in these texts pertaining to insanity include: the victims of crimes, invalid gifts, the validity of a witness's testimony, feigned madness, prescribed penances associated with insanity, and injunctions against contact of a householder with the insane. With regard to civil law there is inheritance, contracts, debts, types of marriage, and divorce. With regard to criminal proceedings the implications of the insanity of the defendant are discussed.[794]

More specifically, in *The Laws of Manu* one finds that a condition of insanity is an excuse for nullifying marital obligations, undoing social contracts, and avoiding full responsibility in the case of slander and criminal offence.[795] These references to insanity underscore the identity, visibility, and problematic legal and moral valuation assigned to varieties of psychopathology in ancient Hindu societies. The *Laws* explicitly condemned but also protected those non-persons who were socially recognized as insane.

Earlier, the high regard of ayurvedic physicians in Indian society was emphasized. Their doctrine had roots in the Vedas and, while addressing naturalistic concerns over health it also had a religious resonance. Furthermore, in affirming morally acceptable behaviour, physicians functioned to uphold and promote social order. Thus it is interesting that legal, medical, and juridical texts suggest that in some respects physicians and ayurvedic medicine were used politically. The legal and outright control functions of ayurvedic physicians suggest they may also have worked to accentuate stigma of conditions of psychiatric interest.

---

[793] Weiss 1975, 1977.

[794] Weiss 1975: 50.

[795] Doniger and Smith 1991.

A more fundamental set of questions can be raised. It involves the possible influence that Hindu cultural psychology had on the moral tone of conditions of psychiatric interest. It could be claimed, for example, that the moral, spiritual, and religious character of the cultural psychology of India may have, in the first place, minimized the generation of deviant, antisocial, immoral feelings and impulses and the expression of associated actions among victims of conditions of psychiatric interest. In other words, while signs and symptoms singled out by an outsider clinician-observer would have been found, one might suppose there existed cultural psychological constraints against their expression as psychological perversity and social deviance. Taken at face value, this possibility can be rejected outright. It contradicts essential characteristics of human nature and the disorganizing effects that psychiatric condition have on experience and behaviour. In addition, the bulk of literature in cultural psychiatry and medical anthropology argues for the universality of socially deviant, devious, and disreputable feelings and impulses and not necessarily in the context of sickness and/or psychiatric condition.

Furthermore, the received sources contradict the suggestion that social norms and cultural values of Indian society prevented expression of divisive manifestations of conditions of psychiatric interest. The feelings and actions condemned in the *Atharvaveda*, the consistently uncompromising injunctions found in the various Dharmaśāstras, and emphases recorded in ancient legal documents all together underscore the reality and suggest the relatively high prevalence of antisocial, divisive, and socially undesirable tendencies and behaviours.

It is true that Indian philosophy and culture did not support and indulge truly secular dialogues that questioned the character of virtue, conduct, personal experience, and individuality. Support of selfish, economistic interests and values was not emphasized. The apparent lack of a mainly secular conception regarding experience, behaviour and individuality, like in Greece and Rome, may have been a(n indirect, unconscious?) factor that potentially constrained expression of unruly and insubordinate manifestations of conditions of psychiatric interest in ancient India. A highly moralized, religiously slanted cultural psychology could have worked to retard or at least tone down ideas, impulses, and feelings that contravened normative psychology and behaviour. Again, however, the evidence from scripture and texts that (implicitly and explicitly) condemned selfish behaviours that contravened traditional forms of conduct and experience indicate that divisive behaviours were hardly unheard of, for one finds there ways of thinking and feeling that contravened norms and traditions and that needed to be pacified and overcome.

One can assume, then, that victims of conditions of psychiatric interest in ancient India were not devoid of socially perverse experiences and impulses and acted in transgressive ways. Given the moral tone and religious resonance of the culture, misbehaviours inherent in some conditions of psychiatric interest would have brought condemnation and been associated with psychiatric stigma. Indeed, one can plausibly maintain that a social, cultural, and non-clinical feature of many conditions of psychiatric interest is that they elicit censure and discredit individuals. In this context, one may be allowed to take the position that perhaps one of the unique elements (the genius?) of traditional Hindu culture was at least to attempt to shape and configure conditions of psychiatric interest, or at least rein in their manifestations, along traditional, normative and acceptable channels.

An element of modernity emphasized earlier (individualism, autonomy) was attenuation of traditional values and institutions (religion, spirituality, morality). These influences, which in any society provide external controls on experience and behaviour, need to be buttressed by internal (cultural-psychological) controls. Many of the contravening features of 'problem populations' of nineteenth-century Europe, which included conditions of psychiatric interest, undoubtedly devolved from purely politico-economic changes but some of them must be construed as resulting from the loss of external controls and the opening up and requirement for inner controls that a modern view of the world entailed. Traditional values and institutions of traditional societies of India, then, help constrain, control, and direct manifestations of conditions of psychiatric interest along channels that are acceptable, compatible, and supportive of social order. Herein lays an advantage discussed earlier.

This line of argument implies that ayurvedic psychiatry functioned as an important pillar of influence, at least among the economically better-off layers of society that more than likely constituted its principal consumers. However, its basic tenets, norms and traditions embodied social values and moral controls inherent in the culture at large. In this account of the matter, Ayurveda, the scholarly medicine of traditional India was in the business of not only healing conditions of psychiatric interest but also restraining and upbraiding unruly manifestations. This does not mean that manifestations of conditions of psychiatric interest were not reproved. But it provides an explanation of why traditional Indian societies were not confronted with the dilemmas of social order posed by problem populations and conditions of psychiatric interest compared to Western ones.

A SNAPSHOT OF MEDIEVAL INDIGENOUS PSYCHIATRY THROUGH AN AYURVEDA LENS

Tibetan ayurvedic medicine

The content of the approach taken by Ayurveda with respect to conditions of psychiatric interest has been discussed in previous chapters. It will be recalled that both somatic and metaphysical factors were represented. A general comparison was made of the way knowledge of *unmāda* and *bhūtavidyā* was represented in ayurvedic texts based on information provided by Meulenbeld.[796] It showed a relatively similar distribution of types of *unmāda* across classical and medieval eras but a trend towards an increase in types of *bhūtas*, namely, conditions of psychiatric interest in which spirit attack or possession was salient. A foundational text of medicine and especially indigenous psychiatry was taken to Tibet from India and translated there in seventh century CE. This text, *The Four Tantras* by Candranandana, is said to be based on Ayurveda.[797] Inspection of this text affords one an opportunity to get a glimpse of how conditions of psychiatric interest were formulated in the milieu of this era.

Clifford discusses the characteristics of Tibetan Buddhist medicine and psychiatry using this seventh century as a base.[798] However, her review reinforces the organic and metaphysical components of medical epistemology that were discussed here in earlier chapters about Ayurveda. She also has extrapolated material from a section of Buddhist scriptures termed Abhidharma. These two foundations, Clifford suggests, constitute the backbone of Tibetan thought about phenomena of psychiatric interest. An elaborate theory of sickness and psychiatry is

---

796 Meulenbeld 1997.

797 Chandra 1984; Clifford 1984.

798 Clifford 1984.

found in Tibetan medicine not all of which will be discussed here because this ethno-medicine and ethno-psychiatry falls outside the scope of this book.

It is the material drawn from the founding ayurvedic text that is of primary concern since it gives a portrait of psychiatric phenomena in the subcontinent during the medieval era (seventh century CE). In a very general way Tibetan medicine and the ayurvedic text indicate that there are five causes of conditions of psychiatric interest: karma, grief-worry, humoral imbalance, poison, and evil spirits. These are all causes we have encountered previously.

Of particular interest presently is Clifford's translation of three chapters from *The Four Tantras* by Candranandana, which address what one can safely presume involve *unmāda* or insanity and the *bhūta*s, although she does not employ this nomenclature.[799] Another Tantra discusses causes of epilepsy but is not translated. Chapter 17 enumerates the ways to cure evil spirits, which cause disease fall into five groups and that Clifford equates with types of diseases as understood in the contemporary medicine of that era.[800] These include: elemental spirits, madness-causing demons, amnesia-causing demons, planetary spirits that cause epilepsy and serpent spirits that cause leprosy. Right away, then, one notes that conditions of psychiatric interest are glossed with medical diseases that are behaviourally disruptive and socially divisive or alarming, suggesting how such conditions may have been valorous in social context.

The conditions that bring or motivate elemental spirits to attack involve negative actions by the victim, poisons, and/or presence of strong negative, painful emotions. Characteristics of these conditions involve the spirit's residence in the victim's body and mind and the spirits' control of the individual's behaviour. Eighteen classes of elemental spirits are identified and are said to bring an abrupt change in a person's behaviour. On the basis of her own knowledge of Tibetan, ayurvedic, and Buddhist medicine, Clifford provides a brief description of all of these spirits. I have summarized these using language of Clifford: god-demons, jealous or anti-god demons, scent-eater demons, serpent-spirit demons, harm-giver demons, pervasive-spirit demons, cannibal demons, flesh-eater demons, hungry-ghost demons, vampire-ghoul de-

[799] Clifford 1984, referring to Candranandana, Chapters 77–79.

[800] And in Tibet presently, for that matter.

mons, evil-curse spirit demons, mental-agitator demons, zombie demons, ancestor-spirit demons, guru demons, sage demons, respected-elder demons, and accomplishment-emanation demons. The manifestations of conditions of psychiatric interest caused by the elemental spirits bring on a discernible and 'abrupt' change in behaviour reminiscent of descriptions of spirit-possession described earlier. The manifestations of spirit attack reflect the character of attacking or invading spirit. Those possessed by the demonic effects of the guru, the sage, the respected elder, and the accomplished emanation are all consistent in their paths of action and diet. They befriend all children, go naked, and cannot stay in one place. They have wild hair, unhappy minds, and feel long abandoned.[801]

Clifford elaborates that in the case of guru spirit possession, demon and presumably victim behaves like a spiritual teacher and likes to perform acts of devotion whereas magical-emanation spirit demon is brought on by a *siddha* who has tantric powers and leads the victim to imagine or behave accordingly and, finally, respected-elder attack leads the victim to assume posture of old men and prefer quiet places. The cure of these conditions is largely metaphysical (burning incense, reciting Tantras, reading scriptures, meditation). In additions dietary factors are used.

Chapter 78 and 79 will not be discussed in detail here. They are similar to material discussed about humoral causes of *unmāda,* their manifestations, and treatment. Causes stem from poor diet, a feeble mind (the heart which houses cognition and feelings), and inadequate diet. They arise from excesses or faults of each humour, their combination, mental distress, poison, or demonic influence. Each humour causes its own constellation of bodily and behavioural signs and symptoms, necessitates is own type of cure. The latter are predominantly medicinal and dietary. In cases of depressed spirits cure involves the wealth of the *dharma* and sweet conversation so as to elevate and re-invigorate moral commitment and psychological morale. Very little material is available for Chapter 79 addresses primarily problems of consciousness and memory associated with what appear to be neurological conditions.[802] Causes, manifestations, and cures are similar to conditions found in Chapter 78.

---

[801] Quoted in Clifford 1984: 189.

[802] Although this category is separate from that of epilepsy, which is described later, but is not translated by Clifford.

Comment

The Three Tantras by Candranandana (and probably a fourth on epilepsy) provide one with a slant on psychiatric phenomena in India that one can draw on to complement discussion so far. It is true it addresses ayurvedic medicine during the seventh century CE, well after the period of ascetic reformism and into the period of classical Hinduism. However, it parallels ayurvedic texts discussed in earlier chapters about the prevalence of metaphysical perspective on conditions of psychiatric interest during earlier centuries CE. Its relevance at this point is that it underscores, reinforces, and seems to elaborate on the influence of spirits. Specific details of what these spirits bring about, namely, behavioural manifestations, are more sharply etched. The extent to which metaphysical aspects of indigenous psychiatry are represented in the academic sector of medicine is clear. One can surmise that Candranandana is recording and reporting on the intrusion of phenomena of psychiatric interest described earlier as originating and most fully (perhaps) exemplified in indigenous peoples and peoples of the lower orders. This fundament of beliefs and practices about metaphysical dimension of India's indigenous psychiatry can be explained in two ways: it represents but a documentation (or acknowledgement) of the importance of metaphysical factors in understanding phenomena of psychiatric interest 'from time immemorial' as academics have contended; or, it records and documents recent changes in the evolution of psychiatric phenomena in India; in other words, the spread, expansion or greater visibility of religious ideas and their fashioning of conditions of psychiatric interest. It should be noted that most of the spirits mentioned in these Tantras involve cultural categories germane to aspects of religion, popular thought, and popular medicine and also represented in classical Hinduism. In this sense one can say that indigenous ideas and beliefs about psychiatric phenomena of India's 'little' tradition has been 'Sanskritized' and entered the 'great' tradition.

CULTURAL DIVERSITY AND MEDICAL PRACTICE IN THE MEDIEVAL ERA

Introduction

Ritual and secular popular medicine, oftentimes glossed as folk or 'magical', soothsaying and divination, sorcery and the black arts, and practices one can gloss under the overused and fuzzily delimited category of shamanism in its many varieties are all prevalent in regions of contemporary India. As emphasized earlier, such practices have a long ancestry in the subcontinent. They were integral components of Vedic medicine as exemplified most clearly in *Atharvaveda*. Sharma reports that this component of religion and medicine as realized in social practice and culture became a prominent landmark of early medieval India.[803] Eliade, White, and Feuerstein support this although they often describe such beliefs and practices under the rubric of 'popular religion' a term that is also overused and the meanings of which vary and overlap.[804]

As discussed by Bell, 'popular religion' is sometimes (1) used as 'little' or folk to contrast with the 'great' or elite tradition; (2) stands for textually represented and ritually enacted (Sanskritic) compared to everyday (popular) social experience and practice in local, usually village levels; (3) has been used to designate a shared and common body of beliefs and practices of *both elite and common villager*; and (4) can signify a part of the structure and culture of a society (religion as a fully embedded system of meaning or culture).[805] There is contestation indeed about what popular religion 'is'. No one meaning covers the way in which the term has been used earlier and will be used later in this chapter. The context should make clear which meaning or meanings are appropriate. Emphasis is placed on social phenomena and cultural meanings of religious, spiritual nature and indigenous psychiatric import that are *widespread in society*, covering peoples practicing Brahmanic rituals in towns and cities (and villages as well), sometimes more cultic sectarian Hinduism as classically seen in village settings, and sometimes heterodox traditions including Buddhist, tantric and yogic ideas and methods of meditation and devotion. Many scholars have thought of popular,

---

803 R. S. Sharma 1995.

804 Eliade 1964, 1969; White 1996, 2000; Feuerstein 1998, 2006.

805 Bell 1989.

local, everyday religion as constituting beliefs and practices that funnelled into Yoga, Tantra, and movements led by accomplished adepts termed *siddhas*. These three traditions and a range of religious sects all are said to have gained momentum during centuries surrounding the turn in to the Common Era but reached visibility as per textual documentation during the medieval era. Histories of Hinduism all suggest as much.[806]

Sharma points out that today illiterate priests of the lower castes provide devotees of various mother goddesses in the countryside with answers to troubling questions and help to resolve problems that include physical illness, 'possession' by spirits or demons, and conditions of psychiatric interest. The cases of Opler,[807] results of epidemiological studies that document traditional ways of understanding psychiatric phenomena, and the broad survey of Fuller involving popular and practical religious approaches to everyday problems posed by misfortune among contemporary Indians attest to the survivals of ideas and practices that originated and functioned in centuries well before the Common Era and became incorporated in heterodox and sectarian popular, widely shared religions during the early medieval eras (roughly, the early centuries CE).[808] Belief in demonic influences, spirit possession, and spell casting, discussed in earlier chapters, examples of lifeways found among city and village dwellers alike throughout all of Indian history. Each village, moreover, has its literate Brahmin priest who often functions as an astrologer; he prepares horoscopes and is consulted about the most auspicious times for any number of social events. Soothsayers, diviners, and priests involved in astrology can be found even in large cities. Sharma contends that these practices are carryovers from the medieval period. He contends that a preoccupation with fate, omens, portents, and divination were not prominently represented in Vedic texts yet one cannot doubt that such beliefs and practices, perhaps not astrology per se, were prevalent then and in preceding eras among peoples indigenous to the subcontinent. Moreover, various heretical sects are believed to have traded in such ideas, promoting the belief that human fate is determined and beyond the influence of free will or human agency, although the future can be foretold. Whereas

---

[806] Zaehner 1962; Flood 1996, 2003; Michaels 2004.

[807] See Chapter 5.

[808] Fuller 1992.

astrology as known in the West may have originated in central Asia and Greece, the first important Indian work on astrology was written in the sixth century CE:

> From Gupta times onward astrology emerged as an important factor in the mental make-up of the common people.[809]

The ancestry of the Puranas and the epics is contested but material in them extends backwards well below when they were finally codified. This literature played an important role in popularizing ideas of magic, religious healing and astrology,

> which were meant for the instruction of women and the lower orders, in other words, for the illiterate masses which formed the overwhelming majority of the population.[810]

Consistent with conventions adopted earlier, and for purposes of concision, this large assortment of beliefs and practices will be construed as involved in the business of 'metaphysical mental health therapy' or 'metaphysical healing' and it contrasts with 'organic or somatic healing' it being understood that these constitute analytic categories and that 'on the ground' they overlapped considerably. Metaphysical healing includes popular religion, fertility cults centred on local gods and goddesses, movements devoted to the adoration of and salvation through the love towards god (*bhakti*), movements and disciplines led by adepts or gurus and their disciples and devotees that involved philosophical psychology and theosophy (psycho-energetics of mental concentration and meditation).

Many of these metaphysical traditions involved beliefs and practices that during the early centuries of the Common Era exemplified a blend of Buddhism and Hinduism and later came to be incorporated in Yoga, Tantra, and Siddha, taken up later. They are construed as movements and traditions that came to the fore and are identifiable in texts (popular, philosophical, sectarian) written starting around 600–700 CE. The general point is that while metaphysical healing is a social, cultural and historical phenomenon largely construed as emerging and consolidating during the early medieval era, its roots can be presumed to have started well before the Common Era, as discussed in previous chapters.

---

[809] R. S. Sharma 1995: 134.

[810] R. S. Sharma 1995: 135.

Societies and populations

Societies of the medieval era varied in size and complexity, from villages and hamlets largely devoted to agriculture, but with representative members of any number of occupational groups, to towns and cities that grew up around political, commercial, and religious centres and that featured a large variety of craft and artisan specialists as well as merchants and shopkeepers. Kingdoms and principalities and states and even empires served as politico-economic centres of influence and domination.[811] In the hinterland and regions far from settled villages forest or tribal peoples, and hunter-gatherers were found. A diversity of social organization and institutions of different scope and size, societies exemplifying 'great' and 'little' traditions were to be found. The social practices and institutions for handling human problems of sickness and conditions of psychiatric interest were no less varied. One seeks answers about questions involving what sort of mental health problems were found, how they were configured and construed, and where they were located in the social fabric.

One venue involves the sheer problems of interpersonal behaviour. Places where habitual criminals, antisocial characters, and malicious persons were confined or ostracized to would have represented one locale for varieties of conditions of psychiatric interest. Another locality would involve settings where human conflicts and tensions disrupted social order of a degree and type that gave rise to the need for arbitration. In small, rural communities, local village headmen and caste representatives handled disputes and conflicts of interest in a local and focused manner, with disputants and victims making personal appearance along with their agents and patrons. Village councils called together for arbitration of competing claims and adjudication would have dealt with conflicts centred within and across families, within and between competing castes, and among hamlets of a village. In cases of inter-village conflicts, regional councils were convened. The kinds of problems taken there would have involved theft, destruction of property, disrespect and physical acting out, and property disputes. Putting aside egregious disturbance of social conduct likely to result in incarceration, physical punishment or banishment, village level conflicts, like those reviewed, are the bread and butter concomitants of village life

[811] Stein 1998.

which are 'to be expected' in the course of events.[812] Nonetheless, such conflicts and strains can so disorient, incense, demoralize, arouse impulses, and yield to dyscontrol of passions that on occasion may come to reflect or at least push vulnerable persons into conditions of psychological misery that include some manifestations an external observer would qualify as a psychiatric condition. Besides ordinary run-of-the-mill misunderstandings and conflicts, cases reaching the jurisdiction of councils for arbitration and settlement would have also included problems of temperament, character, and personality, and related dispositions closer to the traffic of emotionally saturated interpersonal relationships, all of which today we are more conditioned to regard as a potential locus of phenomena of psychiatric interest. Cases of this type include inter-caste rivalries and infractions regarding normative, expected behaviour, marital conflicts, runaway wives, cases involving ruthless and merciless treatment of newly married women by mothers-in-law or husbands, and frank brutalization of the weak and powerless by those of the higher orders. Cohn provides a very useful picture of the conduct of law and of conflict resolution in village communities of the modern era and suggests that these legal arrangements and practices, while obviously not commanded by 'up top' colonial administration of Mughals and British, have a long ancestry in the subcontinent.[813]

An obvious category of phenomena of psychiatric interest was fashioned, not in legal attires, but in medical and religious terms. These have been discussed already in considerable detail. One can merely suggest that the few local practitioners found in nearby, local village were versed in several techniques and methods of healing, stretching from mundane, secular practical ones (herbs, dietary) on through involvement with preternatural agencies, as exemplified in activities of local priests, sectarian cult managers, shamans and including individuals skilled in the black arts. Misfortune, disorder, and social and psychological crises were addressed via a blend of secular and popular religious tenets. The respective practitioners aimed at cure or relief of concrete signs and symptoms (demonic possession, chronic depressions or acute anxieties). However, as repeatedly emphasized, the manner in which practitioners of popular, folk religion and medicine conceptualized and dealt with problems which were brought to them involved

---

[812] Parpola and Tenhunen 1998.

[813] Cohn 1987.

negotiation, manipulation, and persuasion in realms of social and psychological behaviour.

In regional centres and larger communities, one would have found a much more varied grouping of metaphysical healing, including priests, diviners, spiritualists, herbalists, and, later, astrologists, as indicated by Sharma previously. Similarly, an emphasis on medical diagnostics and therapeutics that grew out of the community of mendicant, itinerant herbalists and healers described by Zysk, would have ushered in by the early medieval era what in many respects one can realistically and fairly describe as a form of naturalistic, scientific, and academic medicine.[814] Classical texts of Ayurveda, the native tradition of medicine of India, date from early in the first centuries CE, but are generally assumed to have existed even in textual form during earlier periods.

What is important to emphasize, then, is that during the early medieval period one would have seen in place of the brand and flavour of organic, secular medical and related metaphysical healing that are distinctive of the civilization of India. The various texts and characteristics of the way they formulated conditions of psychiatric interest were reviewed earlier. Pushing away from their purely somatic attire or emphasis, and to round out the picture of psychiatric phenomena, one can make explicit problems involving loss of hope, demoralization, disaffection, moral disarticulation, and downright emotional suffering in relation to social, politico-economic conditions generally and the more specific problems involving interpersonal conflicts and tensions. All of the previously mentioned facilities, personnel, and rationales are relevant here as well. They handled existential problems that might punctuates psychiatric condition or simply prove debilitating.

Most or virtually all problems and conditions were contained within and dealt with in the family. Other settings that would have attracted and emplaced psychiatric condition included the establishments and compounds of healers and practitioners as well as those of priests and diviners associated with temples and centres of religious worship.

Models and knowledge of patterns of behaviour of the type that configured conditions of psychiatric interest and related syndromes of behaviour were inherent in the culture and not just in ayurvedic compendia as per *unmāda* and the *bhūta*s. As indicated earlier, such texts merely codified what was widespread in the population. Moreover,

[814] Zysk 1991.

what physicians saw and treated represented but the 'tip of the iceberg' of mental health problems. Knowledge of *unmāda* and *bhūtavidyā*, of behavioural irregularities, of the emotional consequences of moral-ethical breeches of conduct, and of forms of dissociation and spirit possession would have been commonplace among the population generally and in the minds of health practitioners. This included the mainly medical, naturalistically-oriented physicians and the mainly religious, spiritual, metaphysically-oriented personnel. In other words, general knowledge of behavioural breakdowns or disturbances an analyst would equate as psychiatric phenomena would have been widely dispersed in the population at large and not just known to ayurvedic physicians. However, specialist knowledge about these matters would have been concentrated among persons of influence to whom victims of mental health problems were taken.

A direct, strictly curative approach to the treatment of concrete signs and symptoms of the bodily, physiological components of psychiatric and stress conditions, along with more disabling behavioural, emotional disturbances, would have taken place in the establishments of local and regional herbalists, diviners, experts in witchcraft, folk medical practitioners and physicians with some exposure to ayurvedic knowledge, as well as those who had successfully completed their apprenticeship. However, when such approaches failed, more extended forms of treatment were sought. Renowned practitioners of cults, and priests, scribes, or attendants at monasteries, temples and shrines were the persons and locations to which families would have turned. There, social, religious, and moral therapies that were emotionally and spiritually charged were available for families *as well as* the identified 'patient'. Such individual, family, and group psychotherapies could restore equilibrium and balance in the lives of afflicted persons. The therapies brought a sense of rearrangement, re-affirmation, restoration of moral connectedness, and emotional and spiritual support.

A distinctive hierarchy of resort described the sequence of efforts families undertook in attempting to cope with emotional and behavioural problems that were not amenable to easy solutions. They would have included conditions of disease and psychiatric condition associated with prominent displays of suffering and extensive ramifications in the affairs of families and villages. Attempts at coping started with family and local hamlet residents and moved from there to more experienced and better recognized healers and spiritual advisors found in nearby villages or centres of religious worship, culminating in the towns, cities, and regional centres of commerce, temples, and monasteries where the full display of medical and mental health disciplines would have been found. In a general sense, all centres and all healers would have manifested a blend or eclectic mix of spiritualist-religious (or magico-religious) healing rationales and practices, on the one hand, with a growing naturalistic base of knowledge pertaining to bodily physiology and function, on the other. Ayurvedic physicians, or at least ayurvedic principles of diagnostics and pharmaceutics, would more than likely have played a major role in this system of medical and psychological/spiritual healing.

UNTANGLING THE ROOTS OF PSYCHIATRIC PHENOMENA DURING THE MEDIEVAL PERIOD

Introduction

Previous discussions have underscored the point that how conditions of psychiatric interest have been construed and dealt with in the subcontinent has a long and complex genealogy. The evolutionary trajectory of psychiatric phenomena in India has involved three overlapping narratives. The first is that of the intellectualist tradition beginning with the religious Vedas and continuing onto refinements of philosophical psychology and soteriology. This tradition, rooted in an oral and later a textual tradition that extends to around the second millennia BCE, addressed basic existential questions involving the nature of being that comprehended cosmology, but had application to personal disorder and suffering as per mental health concerns. It was applied to a variety of experiential, emotional, and bodily ailments that locate inside and around the borders of what has been termed a psychiatric condition; and, the tradition evolved a way of comprehending and healing it in its own terms, as a spiritual and material phenomenon. Vedic psychiatry as Brahmanic practice had its corresponding analogue in popular settings where it influenced and was influenced by the other traditions enveloping what one can term practical or popular religion, discussed below as the third component of India's medieval system for coping with mental health problems or indigenous psychiatry.

The second narrative is the far more practical, empirical but still theoretical account provided by Ayurveda, which, of course, cannot be completely separated from Vedic and traditional philosophical schools. In general, Ayurveda formalized psychiatric phenomena as a natural, medical object with its own ontology in anatomy, chemistry, physiology, and psychology and it did not exclude but actually admitted in and gave a distinctive form to the spiritualist and philosophical emphases in mental health practice.

The third narrative is more heterogeneous and diffuse. It draws on beliefs and practices indigenous to the cultures of the subcontinent, popular and later sectarian Hinduism, and early medieval Buddhist influences.[815] It includes in particular what Strickmann in his monograph on Chinese magical medicine describes as tantric Buddhism.[816] In India, this third stream had tributaries from Brahmanic and popular Hinduism and in turn contributed to secular medical practice.

Viewed in sheer intellectualist terms, this leads one to the illusion that the three wings of medical mental health related beliefs and practices can be easily distinguished. This is hardly the case even in a purely analytical, philosophical sense, as already suggested. Furthermore, textual studies that trace the spread of ideas and practices and the relationship between religious and secular views on sickness and healing including conditions of psychiatric interest, as disorganized behaviour, demonic possession, depict a picture that a purist analyst would conclude was very messy and inchoate. Ideas involving spirit possession, a common gloss for ailments of all types including madness, are clearly depicted in early Buddhist writings. These show borrowings of and connections to categories and ideas and practices described in *Atharvaveda* and later thought of as popular Hinduism and became incorporated with material of Tibetan and tantric origin only to reappear in later texts of Yoga.

Practical and popular religion and medicine

When compared to Brahmanic and ayurvedic academic medical traditions, it is hard not to conclude that at a practical popular level religious ideas and practices were emotionally resonant: they were seminal,

---

[815] Fuller 1992.

[816] Strickmann 2002.

dynamic, potent, and far-reaching with respect to social impact and influence on behaviour. In fact, viewed in historical and evolutionary context, popular or practical religion and medicine constitute a complex amalgam that can safely be construed as the most enveloping, invasive, and comprehensive although perhaps less coherent system of mental health care. The medical, religious, or magical narrative described earlier tells the inchoate and largely unknown story about the implications of popular religion, sectarian religion, folk psychology, folk philosophy, ethno-medicine and the more immediate longing/aspiration towards health as a physical, ethical, and spiritual phenomenon.

Further emphasis is needed presently on the influence that metaphysical ideas and practices of healing had during the medieval period and how they fused and interconnected at local levels and contexts. This involves discussing disciplines and practices of Buddhism, Yoga, Tantra, and Siddha. With respect to Buddhism, Strickmann finds it difficult to untangle from the amalgam of ideas about mental illness and health practices of medieval India and China, and also Japan and Tibet, what corresponds to Indian Tantrism as compared to Indian Buddhism and, of course, Chinese Taoism.[817] He discusses the influence of Buddhist ideas during early centuries of CE and perhaps earlier as well in setting the foundations of textual ideas that became influential centuries later during the medieval era proper in texts and compendia aimed at healing sickness, bewitchment, spirit possession, demonic attacks and the like, which included madness. Because of the uncertainty about origins and fluidity of ideas, he desists from setting clear boundaries within India and, of course, China, his principal focus, between things tantric, Taoist, and Buddhist and opts for the term tantric Buddhism when referring to magical medicine and healing.

Fuller's monograph summarizes cultural anthropological work in contemporary India that addresses how Hindu and Buddhist ideas come into play in religious contexts in local settings throughout India.[818] This monograph addresses many facets of popular Hinduism as it comes into play in local contexts; for example, types of gods and goddesses, sacrifices, rituals of kingship and villages, and devotion. It also addresses problems of relevance to current concerns: pertaining to disorder and misfortune including sickness and spirit possession in particular. Many,

---

817 Strickmann 2002.

818 Fuller 1992.

if not most, beliefs and practices that Fuller discusses echo material that Strickmann presents in his review of the medieval era, attesting to their durability. Both of these compendia describe the rich interplay of ideas that have origins in Hinduism and Buddhism with respect to questions of 'socio-cosmic' disorder, personal suffering, and conditions of spirit possession, the inventory of manifestations of which suggest conditions of psychiatric interest. Fuller makes abundantly clear the diverse assortment of beliefs found in different parts of India with respect to causes of ailments and approaches to healing that one can presume represent modern embodiments of religious, magical medicine and healing that go back millennia. He stresses the fluid relationship that is found in local settings between the prosaic, divine, and mundane worlds, all of which are peopled by malevolent ghosts, godlings, spirits, and demons. Sorcerers, local priests, guardians of tutelary village gods, and other types of religious practitioners of diverse conceptual and spiritual orientation address problems involving demonic possession that bring diverse signs and symptoms.

> Malevolent ghostly spirits almost always harm people by possessing them. They enter their victims to take control of their bodies and minds so that they fall ill, go mad, become unable to bear children, or find themselves thwarted at every turn.[819]

Yoga, Tantra, and Siddha

Viewed in social context, ideas and practices discussed by Strickmann and Fuller that carry a heavy load of practical Hinduism and Buddhism are difficult to define and demarcate, for their ideas and practices flourished during the medieval period overlap with one another. Moreover, during this same period and at local levels and contexts, the Buddhist-Hindu amalgam appears to have melded with Yoga, Tantra, and Siddha. These latter three can qualify as traditions, movements, philosophies, and forms of spiritual quest and bodily purification. Psychological, spiritual, and health-related behaviour may appear to represent the principal targets of all of these confederations of ideas and practices. However, it needs to be kept in mind that although in some ways addressing phenomena analogous to our 'psyche' in the indigenous cultural psychology the phenomena in question were (and in many

[819] Fuller 1992: 231.

ways still are) construed in material and bodily terms. It should be emphasized that the association of bodily signs and symptoms with emotional and behavioural phenomena classically thought of as psychiatric is not just a conceptual or cultural gloss that India places on problems of health. In strict clinical neuroscience terms information handling systems responsible for psychic or higher cortical functions are hierarchically interconnected with systems that regulate motivation, emotion, and visceral somatic functions found in sub-cortical centres of the brain. Prior to the advent of modern psychiatry conceits of theory and practice, of course, it would have been difficult to untangle psychic from somatic signs and symptoms as earlier analysis of Ayurveda texts has indicated.

In the most general terms, Yoga refers to ascetic disciplines and practices involving mental concentration and meditation. In this attire, Yoga is inherent in the thought worlds and habit patterns of Indian culture and civilization, ideas and disciplines that had their origins in the Vedas and that some see as, arguably, predating them, as indigenous or pre-Aryan. At the other pole of abstraction and specificity, classical Yoga refers to one of the six major philosophies of India that first took definitive shape in the *Yogasūtra* of Patañjali, which is thought to have been compiled sometime during the first or second century CE[820] classical Yoga holds to the view that the world is real but the product of the illusion or enslavement of the individual, who is unable to apprehend the true nature of mind and spirit inherent in the cosmos. Its practices are designed to bring about a full understanding of this illusion though meditation and bodily perfections aimed at perfecting its spiritual material. However,

> side by side with this classic Yoga, there are countless forms of popular, non-systematic Yoga; there are also non-Brahmanic Yogas, (Buddhist, Jainist); above all, there are Yogas whose structures are magical, mystical, and so on.[821]

Tantra personifies another style of spirituality in India that took shape and became influential during the early centuries of CE. Its masters contributed to the compilation of the Tantras, works comparable in importance to the sacred writings of sects involving the worship of

---

[820] Whicher 1998.

[821] Eliade 1969: 4.

Shiva and Vishnu. Tantrism is distinguished by its emphasis on the feminine psycho-cosmic principle (*śakti*). It also construes experience as a reflection of the divine, timeless energy that maintains the cosmos. However, its practices and rituals seek to 'appropriate and channel that energy, within the human microcosm, in creative and emancipatory ways'.[822] Tantrism also has deep roots in Indian culture. Goddess worship is central to many tantric schools but can be traced to Vedic times. The scope of the Tantras is enormous. They cover cosmogony, activities and functions of many male and female deities, and ritual practices involving their worship. They also involve magic, sorcery, and divination and techniques for purifying mind and body and expositions about the enlightenment, which includes consideration of sexuality.[823] Tantrism originated in areas of India little influenced by Hinduism, where indigenous peoples represented the counterculture or antinomian presence. It also involved exotic, foreign ideas and myths. Its greatest influence is arguably Tibet where Buddhist Tantrism along with Ayurveda represents the background of Tibetan medicine and psychiatry.[824]

One of the Indian foundations of Tantrism involves Hindu sectarian groups that came to be called the Siddhas. Although appropriating beliefs and practices that predated Tantrism, this spiritual tradition did not achieve prominence until the twelfth and thirteen centuries. The Siddhas formed a loosely structured religious community in medieval India whose influence has exceeded and outlasted the tantrics.[825] A *siddha* refers to an individual, an accomplished, perfected adept or practitioner, who is regarded as having realized superhuman powers and bodily immortality. However, as a sectarian movement, Siddha encompasses many groups including early Buddhist tantrics, devotees of Shiva, alchemists from Tamil Nadu and medieval India – the Rasa Siddhas – and a North Indian group known as Nath Siddhas.[826] Siddha incorporated tantric, yogic, alchemical and other elements into its practices. It evolved to a cult of demigods that mediated between human aspirations and supernatural, divine beings. The cults displayed a 'popular' soteriology which differed from and in many ways countered the 'author-

[822] White 2000: 9.
[823] Feuerstein 1998.
[824] Clifford 1984; Epstein and Rapgay 1989.
[825] White 1996.
[826] White 1996.

ized' soteriologies inherent in the Vedas and classical Hinduism. With the Siddhas one is

> dealing with a movement of considerable importance ... highly popular after the twelfth century ... the point of convergence for a large number of religious, magical, and alchemical traditions and practices, most of them Śivaistic, but some Buddhist.[827]

Comment

The indigenous psychiatry of medieval India embodied all of these disciplines, traditions, and practices. Only Ayurveda qualifies as a medically authenticated Indian psychiatry in virtue of its emphasis on specified syndromes, modes of diagnosis, formulation of causes, ethnophysiology and ethno-anatomy, and description of manifestations. The others, as emphasized earlier and in Chapters 6 and 7, are medical only in a very general sense. They are based on a soteriological model of medicine whose ailment or malady involves the suffering or dis-ease of demoralization, anomie, and impaired wellbeing, the signs and symptoms of which varied. Yet, all these traditions have three things in common: they draw on and have relevance to the 'psychopathologies of everyday life' as well as bona fide conditions of psychiatric interest, their reach into, engagement with, and effects on mental health of populations of India are prodigious; and they achieved prominence during the medieval period when it seems, as inferred by received texts, that metaphysical ideas involving health prominently displayed syndromes marked by spiritual (spiritual possession, *bhūta*s of Ayurveda) and somatic components both of which were represented in the methods and practices of the traditions.

RELIGIOUS BEHAVIOUR AND THE FABRIC OF PSYCHIATRIC CONDITIONS IN INDIA

Introduction

This section discusses the relevance of religious systems of meaning for understanding the character of psychiatric phenomena in the subconti-

[827] Eliade 1969: 302.

nent of India. Cultural psychology, as discussed earlier, represents an internal, posited structure of ideas, beliefs, and emotional dispositions and attitudes 'carried in the head', a structure, which shapes experience and behaviour. In traditional India this psychology involves constructs and beliefs the content of which span philosophy, morality, religion, and medicine. It is responsible for the meaning inherent in the thought worlds and habit patterns of traditional Indian peoples. One can add here that Indian cultural psychology shapes what have been referred to as conditions of psychiatric interest which amount to disturbances of level of consciousness (e.g., as per dissociation), emotion, behaviour, and *embodiment*, which refers to feelings linked to and explained by prevailing ethno-physiological ideas, beliefs, and nuances of perception tied to the body.

Experience, emotion, sense of self and social understanding, and the programs of behaviour, which all of the preceding constitute, represent biologically conditioned cultural phenomena. The Hindu thought world and cultural outlook imparts a distinctive symbolic and affective resonance to disturbances of behaviour and sense of bodily wellbeing. The whole is embodied in neural networks and brain information handling systems which are responsible for shaping and producing 'normal' Indian behaviour (depending, of course, on such factors as linguistic preference, region, caste, and religion). This same cultural psychology is responsible for moulding and shaping syndromes of altered behaviour and of sickness viewed as a biopsychosocial amalgam, all of which equate with conditions of psychiatric interest which are forged in a Hindu cultural psychological mould.

Possession states in India

Spirit possession has figured in earlier accounts about cultural meanings, in other words, as part of everyday 'normal behaviour', and as conditions of psychiatric interest per se. Its high prevalence in contemporary India and its long history in the subcontinent have been emphasized. In concentrating here on the importance of such conditions and how they have been configured and played out in different historical contexts it will prove useful to discuss their ontology and epistemology.

To enter a state of possession is to experience a species of mental dissociation. This refers to a psychological mechanism or process that produces a discernible alteration in a person's thoughts, feelings, or actions so that for a time the victim cannot associate or integrate certain pieces of information with other information in a normal or logical manner.[828] Put another way, dissociation is a special, 'altered' form of consciousness in which events that are ordinarily connected are divided. Thus it is usually viewed as a disturbance or alteration in the normally integrative functions of identity, memory, or consciousness. The capacity for dissociation is most likely a human biological universal.

The ability to enter states of trance and possession – that is, to experience dissociation – are also cultural universals. Thus the biological capacity for dissociation is related to a cultural category or trait that assigns specific meanings to such altered states of consciousness, usually states equivalent to trance and possession, thereby situating the behaviour in question in a context that makes sense in the culture. Alternatively, we can say that culture embraces patterns of meaning and rationales that allow dissociation to be played out in distinctive ways. It provides a script for behaviour for dissociations. Trance and spirit possession are integral aspects of divination and healing by shamans that have nothing to do with conditions of psychiatric interest per se. The altered state of consciousness is believed to provide access to the supernatural realm where the origins of human maladies are found and where effective healing interventions must take place. The diviner, shaman, or spiritist essentially undergoes a controlled dissociation in the service of his or her curative functions. Possession involves the takeover of a person by a spirit or godling. It entails a culturally specific theory about the cause, contents, and significance of altered states of consciousness.

Possession states were features of ordinary social life as well as of healing rituals and ceremonies in classical, medieval, and early modern Western societies. They are still found in some societies and are relatively prominent in India today and undoubtedly were also in earlier millennia as discussed earlier. Victims or postulants, whatever the case may be, characteristically undergo altered states of consciousness (dissociation) during which a spirit is said to enter the body and to use it for purposes of revelation, communication, or harm. Very often, the state of possession or trance allows the expression of otherwise socially, morally, and politically suppressed thoughts and sentiments, as illustrated in cases cited by Opler.[829] 'Possession' states should not be viewed as neces-

[828] Hilgard 1986.

[829] Opler 1958.

sarily pathological in either an intracultural sense (that is, from an emic standpoint, from the point of view of cultural standards and labels) or a clinical, biomedical sense (that is, from an etic standpoint, from the point of view of Western, medical conventions).

Behaving as though one is possessed can be a culturally appropriate way of resolving strains in the social system. It certainly constitutes a cultural category, almost a social role, which individuals can draw on or use to resolve social conflicts. Possession states and syndromes are also a cultural institution for coping with stress. The various descriptions of the *bhūta*s point to and codify standardized varieties of spiritual attack which one can presume stemmed from an individual. Some occurrences of possession are viewed as disturbances, if not illnesses, and receive medical attention. The various descriptions of the *bhūtas* discussed earlier point to and codify standardized varieties of spiritual attack. Multiple personality disorder (MPD) is a Western variety of psychiatric condition in which dissociation serves as a cultural psychological template for creating alternative selves, or other 'personalities'. In Western societies, in which the self is held to be a separate, autonomous, wilful, independent, individual phenomenon, a victim of this kind of dissociation, when expressed in this pathological form, can seem to embody a number of different, highly individualized personalities that wilfully take over and 'run' the person. The victim of MPD, no longer a unique, singular identity, gains new identities. On the other hand, in non-Western, pre-industrial societies not dominated by an individualistic ethos, which are more group-oriented, the capacity for dissociation, if it becomes pathological, leads to conditions that demonstrate that supernatural spirits have 'invaded' from without and thus have 'taken over'. One does not gain in psychological richness and complexity by acquiring alternative selves, rather one is temporarily displaced by spirits; when they depart, they leave the individual intact, albeit very often cured of an 'ailment' whose symptoms had consisted of the indwelling presence of or communication from the spirit. Persons who repeatedly experience possession by a spirit can acquire considerable social prestige and political, cultural power as spokespersons for deities.

In summary, disorders such as MPD and 'possession' are produced by (1) a biological capacity for dissociation of consciousness; (2) an alteration, exaggeration, magnification, or pathological expression of this capacity; and (3) a culturally inherited code pertaining to selves, persons, beings in the world (the kinds of beings that are held to be real, authentic) whereby a victim of stress plays out the pressures and anxieties that brought about the dissociation episode in the first place. Thus, psychological stressors that are due to inconsistencies and strains in one's personal situation can lead to disorders of personality and identity.

Trance, 'possession' states, and disorders expressed as dissociation prove that people learn to behave in ways that are deemed possible and acceptable by their culture. The culture, as it were, provides models for dissociation; the culture stipulates the kinds of identities that one can take on. In a disenchanted, secular, rationalistic, and individualistic culture such as that of postmodern West, dissociation means the acquisition of 'alternative' selves, whereas more spiritualized, transcendental, and socially centred cultures like those found of India, in contemporary times and throughout the civilization's history, assume the existence of supernatural entities. Alternative personalities and supernatural spirits come to 'dwell in' the individual in ways that conform to cultural regulations and norms. 'Possessing' spirits and alternative personalities are perceived by their audience to be what they are because of the symbolic codes of the culture. Societies thus provide different cultural scripts through which the individual can resolve crises affecting the self.

In the official psychiatric diagnostic system, so-called dissociative disorders include episodes in which individuals are said to lose their identity and become possessed, to be ruled by an alternative self, or they simply enter states of altered consciousness during which they can appear normal but later have no memory of the experience. Actual possession syndromes (as by a spirit) are relatively uncommon in Anglo-American and other Western societies yet are relatively common in India and neighbouring countries such as Bangladesh, Nepal, Pakistan, and Sri Lanka. These syndromes, as elaborated below, very often affect female adolescents and involve the temporary takeover of the self by spirits, usually at a time of crisis. In their incarnate form, the spirits often make demands and express feelings to which family members acquiesce. On the other hand, MPD is relatively common in the US, yet very rare in India and other countries of the region.

Adityanjee and colleagues report three cases of MPD in India that had accumulated over a three-year period.[830] All three cases involved adolescents, two of whom were females. Each case presented only one

---

[830] Adityanjee, Raju, and Khandelwal 1989.

alternate self, and in each case the transitions between personalities occurred suddenly after waking in the morning. Psychosocial stresses involving sexuality were prominent in all three cases. The authors elaborate that in Indian culture, dependence and interdependence are crucial in identity formation – rather than dependence *versus* independence, as in Anglo-American and European culture. In many respects, these Indian cases of MPD are somewhat atypical and rather conventionalized. This is not surprising, insofar as the culture's code regarding autonomy, voluntarism, and separation hardly could be said to foster an awareness of or to provide a strong possibility for full individuation, as is expected in Western-influenced societies. By contrast, the Indian culture posits the existence of numerous spirits that can provide vehicles for the expression of wishes and actions, and these seem to play important roles in resolving psychological, interpersonal and intrafamilial stress in cases of spirit possession.

RELIGION, MADNESS, AND SPIRIT POSSESSION AS HISTORICAL TEMPLATES FOR PSYCHIATRIC CONDITION

Introduction

Madness is a construct that is often loosely applied to some Hindu gods. Their spiritual and moral resonance seems to stem from the power of their personalities and the awesome actions they can display. They are sometimes portrayed as wild, chaotic, frenzied, uncontrolled, and unpredictable. Their behaviour can violate social conventions; mythological descriptions of Shiva, for example, present him as unkempt, untamed, and living on the moral boundaries of society.

> He is frequently said to mock 'establishment' values and institutions ... He wanders the cosmos naked, minimally dressed, or attired in wild-animal skins; he haunts cremation grounds, covers his body with ashes, and is frequently said to be accompanied by an entourage of ghouls.[831]

Kinsley quotes that he can sing, dance and laugh in ecstasy, leaps, gapes, and weep, speaks like a madman or a drunkard. These and many

[831] Kinsley 1974: 274.

other aspects of behaviour of Shiva and other gods are portrayed in hymns and popular literature. Together these descriptions exemplify that a theme of divine madness is prominently insinuated into the culture and social fabric of India. Indeed, one can view this general pattern as involving a celebration of madness in Indian society in context of religion. The gods, then, provide culturally valorized models of madness, for they break out of ordinary constraints of normality, do not consistently act in conformance to acceptable conventions, and appear as insane or intoxicated.[832]

Holy madness

While Kinsley's formulation is based on textual analyses, McDaniel has studied the topic through observation and interviews of religious devotees as well as analyses of accounts of historical personages.[833] She offers further evidence for the central role played by madness in religion and spirituality. We can turn this proposition upside down: what role does religion play in shaping and interpreting potential varieties of psychiatric condition? McDaniel describes culturally expected and accepted behaviours of individuals that are interpreted as madness, from the author's standpoint and from the standpoint of community members. Like Kinsley, McDaniel uses the term *madness* in an ordinary sense, referring to behaviours that are disordered, disturbed, distressing, and disorganized. In a general sense, the term could be glossed as *craziness*. What is more important, McDaniel's *madness* is also used to qualify and give meaning to behaviours that are otherwise viewed as religious, spiritual, and devotional. Ecstasy, ritual meditation, religious longing, and altered states of consciousness (states of dissociation) figure importantly in the syndromes of religious and 'mad' behaviour that she studies. While it is mainly centred on religious traditions, on persons regarded as holy, and on followers or devotees she encountered in a number of sects of South India and particularly Bengal, McDaniel makes it clear that the roots of the phenomenon she studied are to be found in ancient India and that related beliefs, practices, and institutions exist throughout India. To her, *madness* sometimes covers disturbances of behaviour that suggest states of dissociation. She points out, however,

---

[832] Kinsley 1974.

[833] McDaniel 1989.

that in India the behaviour is interpreted in various ways – most saliently, in either a medical or socio-cultural frame of reference, but religious implications are her primary focus. Personal conflicts of individuals that might have a predominantly civil, secular, or nonreligious basis and which may not only affect manifestations but causation of disordered behaviour are slighted in favour of explicitly religious interpretations and meanings.

Psychiatric condition as conceptualized in previous chapters clearly embraces McDaniel's *madness.* They encompass concepts covering feelings, beliefs, and actions as well as frank disturbances of behaviour of a variegated character that can and have had diverse cultural interpretations. McDaniel reinforces a theme implicit and explicit throughout earlier material – the religious, spiritual, philosophical, moralistic, and supernatural dimensions of psychological being, experience, and behaviour in India. This amalgam of Hindu culture is rooted in material found in authoritative texts. When internalized in structures of meaning that shape cultural psychology, one can assume that it has and continues to shape expression and certainly interpretation of psychiatric condition in traditional contexts. One cannot learn about Vedic medicine in context of psychiatric condition without concluding that from early prehistoric times, problems of social and psychological behaviour have been cloaked in religious and spiritual attire.

Kinsley and McDaniel argue that psychiatric condition and religious ideology of India are closely interwoven. Devotional and ritual practices associated with meditation, spiritual longing, seeking personal salvation through integration with deities, and practices aimed at liberation from oppressive worldly circumstances and liabilities are pervasive; cultural universal, in other words. India has many devotional communities and sects that, while they conflict in some details of belief and practice, share many basic assumptions about characteristics of the divine, the personality of deities, elements of religious knowledge, and practices of devotion and spiritual quest. The roots of this Bhakti devotionalism were discussed earlier.

The concept of religious or divine madness (*divyonmāda*) includes manifestations that on general grounds and in the local culture are considered attributes of psychiatric condition or ordinary, secular madness. Examples include auditory and visual hallucinations, acts of seemingly hostile, violent, self-destructive, and otherwise inappropriate behaviour (laughing, singing, dancing, trembling), bodily distortions and contortions, speaking nonsense, and other uncontrollable motor behaviours. The lives of revered saints as described by their biographers and the experiences and activities of devotees as well as contemporary holy persons, many of whom McDaniel interviewed, clearly raise the question of pathology. Ecstatic longing for and participation with sacred personages is shown to be central to devotional practice, and all such practices involve manifestations of what an outsider would call madness. Even the so-called secular, naturalistic, and academic medicine in India, we have seen, has a spiritual basis. Indeed for McDaniel the medical tradition called Ayurveda, or the knowledge of long living, merely re-labels and medicalizes an old religious tradition. It uses a new idiom, new descriptive conventions, and makes healing recommendations that encompass diet and a secular pharmacopeia, but is founded on ancient devotional and religious practices.

The close relationship between religious culture and psychiatric condition is exhibited in McDaniel's discussion of the lives of saints and holy persons in India. It echoes the models of madness adduced by Kinsley and discussed earlier. Virtually all saints have led unusual and socially isolated lives and claim to have experienced visions and visitations from deities. Even as children and adolescents they were considered mad, and their parents sought help from exorcists and treatment by ayurvedic physicians. Besides hallucinations, eccentric behaviour, and strange seizure like thrashings, at various times they engaged in unproductive behaviour toward peers and family members. Many collected strange objects, preferred the company of animals and shared their meals with them. They visited cremation grounds to commune with deities, dressed in ragged, dirty clothes, sometimes ate dirt, and smeared themselves with dirt and even faeces. Many experienced frank social and psychological breakdowns, entering a deteriorated condition not unlike that of psychotic persons diagnosed with schizophrenia. Some holy persons were never able to behave normally, and their actions raised the question of feigned religiosity. Experts and respected authorities were sometimes convened to validate the authenticity of their claims to religious inspiration, to distinguish their behaviour from ordinary madness or deception. Nevertheless, despite a social career made up of grossly unusual, bizarre, if not pathological behaviour, viewed on strict clinical grounds, most of these holy persons and saints were consistently and repeatedly declared to be genuinely inspired by spiritual forces and their actions were given a religious interpretation.

A secular Western-oriented observer may conceptualize a psychiatric condition abstractly as a 'disturbance' or abnormality of behaviour. However, it would appear that in India it has for a long time constituted a disputed territory of social and cultural life. In the modern period, religion and 'science' variously conceived (ayurvedic medicine, exorcism, astrology) all claim to interpret the territory labelled *madness*. This reflects a deep-rooted and ancient approach to experience that combines the natural and the supernatural realms of existence. What it suggests is that during very early prehistory, notions indigenous to India and perhaps similar to those found in Indo-European-based societies of the West, provided an initial idiom for making sense of psychiatric condition, including explanations of disordered individual behaviour and social life more generally.

Given the original cultural material or social fabric from which psychiatric condition was modelled and interpreted in ancient India, the territory of pathology was clearly difficult to identify, let alone demarcate and analyze as a separate category of behaviour. At a later time, aspects of specialized, possibly Aryan concepts of cosmology, religion, and spirituality came to be applied to this contested territory of social life. Whatever corpus of social symbols and meaning existed to define the realms of medicine, morality, religion, and the law, a prominent sector was used to make sense of disturbances of behaviour one may label psychiatric condition. Authority over the realm of mental pathology would have been drawn from revealed Vedic knowledge, moral traditions that stipulated appropriate behaviour for members of the various social classes and orders, astrology, and assorted animistic and magico-religious beliefs and practices. Soon thereafter, in the centuries just preceding the Common Era, a more naturalistic approach to sickness and wellbeing – ayurvedic medicine – was also applied to uncover the mysterious meaning of anomalous and disturbed experience and behaviour.

Holy madness is more than just a rich illustration of how conditions of psychiatric interest are fashioned and understood in Indian society. It also represents an important cultural category that became prominent during the medieval period. The idea of holy madness does not just have implications for one's understanding of psychiatric phenomena 'on the ground' but also as religious, artistic, literary, and general intellectual symbol and tradition. Feuerstein has discussed the influence of an idea or symbol like 'crazy wisdom' or 'crazy adepts' in all major religions.[834] In India it has served as a mode of acquainting and implanting an authentic religious vision via radical and 'irreligious' confrontation so as to shock devotees into appreciation of the bizarre, unreal, counter-intuitive and enigmatic visions that stand behind or on top of conventional religious and moral precepts.

Holy fools in some ways fulfil a role in Indian society. Their real or legendary prototypes reject customary behaviour and criticize and ridicule the views of the orthodox religious establishment. They dress in bizarre ways or go about naked. They are subversive and antinomian but in India they have not only been tolerated, but sometimes deified. The cases described by McDaniel are good examples of the genre although only a few achieve sanctification.

> When we look at the ... [crazy adepts or holy mad] ... past and present, we see phenomenal feats of renunciation. We also see behaviour patterns that border on the psychotic, at least in terms of Western psychology. Some [of them] sometimes puzzle over their own experience, wondering whether it was not in least in part 'sick' ... they certainly cannot help behaving the way they do ... They have entered a new frame of reference, in which transcendence of the conventional reality looms uppermost. They experience reality differently.[835]

Holy madness as a social category filled with religious and literary implications runs deep in the history of the subcontinent. The behaviour of crazy fools revolves around the *avadhūta*, a designation that came into vogue during the Common Era in association with the rise of Tantra as exemplified in some of the traditions subsumed under Buddhism, Hinduism, and other sects. Such individuals, real or imaginary, serve as focal points for cults and sects. They are objects of adoration that personify wisdom and enrichment for they can reduce or negate the mundane and burdensome worries and pain. In making light and folly of ordinary conventions, they lift up spirits and this is one basis of their power as a component of indigenous psychiatry. In medieval Tibet tantric *siddha*s were institutionalized and proved a target of much literature and art.[836]

The cultural pattern or template of Indian crazy adepts, then, illustrates once again how deeply the design of indigenous psychiatry fabric

[834] Feuerstein 1998.

[835] Feuerstein 2006: 49.

[836] Linrothe 2006.

weaves together popular religion and psychiatric condition. It is not just the case that individuals whose manifestations in behaviour conform to the exemplars are understood and handled in largely religious, spiritual terms. Rather, it is that their behaviour or role is institutionalized in areas of religion, art, literature, and mental health healing.

COMMENT ON RELIGION AND PSYCHIATRIC CONDITION

A discussion of the cultural history of psychiatry in India covers a great sweep of time from prehistory to the present era. Emphasis has been given to the importance of sacred ancient canonical works and to the tradition of Bhakti in governing Indian concepts of behaviour and well-being. Ideas about health are inextricably linked to spiritual ideas, and this blend of religion and concepts of psychiatric condition as madness can be projected backward in time several millennia. Consequently, attempts to understand the meaning of psychiatric history in India requires one to slice through cultural and religious history.

How successful the naturalistic approach to medicine termed Ayurveda was in claiming jurisdictional authority over the territory of psychiatric condition is an open question. The seemingly formal tie between Ayurveda and the canonical scriptures suggests a continuing religious and moral influence. The soil from which the science of health and disease sprouted incorporated quasi-scientific concepts and assumptions, as well as a spiritualized, religious, magical, enchanted world-view. Some see this scientific medicine as totally victorious over competing interpretations, whereas there is evidence to suggest that even during its classical phase, Ayurveda was less successful in appropriating the territory from its rivals and had to make concessions to prevailing religious, magical and folk traditions.[837]

The exogenous or accidental insanities of Caraka consisted essentially of spirit-caused varieties. After this early phase, and throughout later periods, the ayurvedic tradition of medicine continued to be highly influential in efforts to cope with psychiatric condition and its consequences. However, especially in village and tribal communities, and undoubtedly in urban centres as well, the territory of surrounding

[837] D. Chattopadhyaya 1977.

mental illness remained highly contested. As discussed earlier, by the time of Vāgbhaṭa and Candranandana, whose compilations were influential during the early medieval period, spiritual influence and possession syndromes had become important features of ayurvedic psychiatric knowledge and practice. This might represent an accommodation to the prominent religious, spiritual influences affecting contemporary interpretations of sickness generally and particularly psychiatric condition. In other words, the soil out of which grew native varieties of the adjustment and health problems that on hindsight one labels as psychiatric, was permeated by notions regarding spirits, ghosts, conflicts in religious tenets, and the interconnection between worldly and otherworldly agents and happenings. One cannot but assume that actual manifestations of conditions of psychiatric interest were expressed in conformance to representations of learned cultural models. Later, tenets from the Islamic tradition were added to the competing interpretations of psychiatric condition and eventually, in the modern era, biomedical psychiatry entered the fray.

MEDIEVAL INDIAN MEDICINE AND THE ISLAMIC INFLUENCE

Introduction

The expansion of Muslim rule in India brought with it an influx of Muslim scholars and merchants from intellectual centres in Baghdad and Egypt. This had an important influence in literature, the arts, and architecture, as well as in religion and law. It also had implications for medicine, public health and, to some extent, for how conditions of psychiatric interest may have been handled. The Islamic system of medicine, termed Unani, became important especially in the courts and cities that housed centres of administration. The writings of Galen and the Mediterranean tradition of medicine linked to the Greek and classical world of Europe constituted the backbone of Islamic medicine.[838] This tradition complemented and in some ways challenged native Indian medical traditions such as Ayurveda and Siddha.

---

[838] L. I. Conrad 1993; Dols 1984, 1985, 1992; Ullmann 1978.

General background

Throughout pre- and recorded history, one would have found in the Indian subcontinent a mixture of medical problems. While infectious and general degenerative diseases of all types, including disorders linked to gestation and parturition as well as 'paediatric' problems may have constituted the primary base of medicine, varieties of psychopathology would have been included. Material reviewed earlier indicates that in contemporary surveys of medical problems handled by lay, popular, 'traditional' practitioners – those not learned or professionally trained – one usually finds representation of so-called neurotic and psychosomatic problems as well as frank psychiatric disorders.[839] There are no good reasons for doubting that such a state of affairs would have also prevailed in India following the Vedic period and would have continued into the ancient, classical era and beyond.

What one today may term ayurvedic physicians, during earlier times would probably have been conceptualized as learned, wise men with special expertise in the promotion of health and diagnosis and treatment of disease. Ayurvedic physicians practiced predominantly among the well-off and especially among the elite, either at the courts of the rulers and kings, in urban mercantile centres, or near and around religious shrines. However, physicians would have also been found in villages since they were often the recipients or 'donees' of land and sets of villages, the revenues from which were used to support the running of temples, monasteries, religious educational institutions, and the medical clinics and hospitals that provided care to the populace including all groupings and castes.

Ayurvedic physicians, scholarly, and to some extent 'professional', were attached to these religious establishments. In the medieval period one would have also found more religiously-oriented priests and diviners who were linked to the various sects that became prominent during this era and who were well-versed in secular as well as religious, spiritual medicine. In general, persons burdened by chronic general medical sicknesses related to infection, malnutrition, degenerative conditions, old age, bowel problems and respiratory ailments would have predominated in medical clinics and religious establishments and temples. How-

[839] Shukla and Mishra 1991.

ever, a not inconsiderable proportion of persons would have manifested conditions of psychiatric interest.

Alchemy and the Siddha tradition

The genesis of Ayurveda, the dominant native tradition of medicine of India, is found in the medical ideas and practices of pre-Vedic and Vedic times. A system of knowledge that contributed to the fuller realization of Ayurveda was that of alchemy generally described as *rasāyaṇa* and *rasacikitsā*. This system played an important role in the Siddha tradition, one of the four lines of development of professional Indian medicine described in previous chapters. Siddha medicine is prevalent in Tamil Nadu, is of Dravidian origin, and its literature is in the Tamil language. Like Ayurveda, it also traces its roots to mythological and religious events and situations.

Siddha medicine is generally viewed as branching out of Ayurveda and while comparatively of small influence in contemporary India played an important role in the medical context of the medieval period.[840] White discusses in great detail the rich lore and connection to alchemy and yogic practices of the Siddha tradition during the medieval period.[841] The ideas associated with this tradition are worth examining in some detail.

The word *siddha* refers to an individual who has received an 'extraordinary merit of power'. It entails disciplining the mind through meditation and disciplining the body through the ingestion of metals. Several of the influential practitioners and theoreticians of Siddha medicine visited China and Tibet, where they presumably learned special techniques in association with tantric cults. Sharma writes:

> These cults aimed at perfection of man not only on spiritual level but also on the physical level. To achieve the former, yogic practices were formulated and for the latter mercurial formulations were evolved which formed the nucleus of *Rasaśāstra*. Some of them were also engaged in transmutation of base metals, which is alchemy proper.[842]

---

[840] See Hausman 1996.

[841] White 1996.

[842] P. V. Sharma 1992b: 447–448.

Many of the concepts of Siddha medicine parallel those of Ayurveda. The humours, the elements, the correspondence between macro and micro worlds, and pharmaceutical preparations used in treatment are conceptualized in similar ways, although given different emphasis in Siddha. Its distinguishing properties, most of which devolve from tantric sources, are the use of metals and minerals in treatment, particularly mercury; special pharmaceutical preparations; examining the pulse in diagnosis; and a highly developed technique of examining urine. In mental diseases, a preparation made of human skulls and the skulls of dogs, termed *pārada bhasma,* was used.[843] White reviews the medieval Siddha traditions of Hindu alchemy and *haṭhayoga,* two important fields of Indian tantric mysticism.[844] He traces developments in the phenomenology of mystical experience as well as the promotion of health by alchemical means. While the practice of medicine per se is not a focus of White's study it is of great relevance to understanding Siddha medicine. It underscores the special influence of meditation, alchemy, psychophysiological practices, and sexual concepts and practices on pursuits of longevity, spirituality, and health status. It would be highly unlikely if specialists in Siddha devotional practices did not treat persons who were ill, including those with conditions of psychiatric interest.

Indian officials have recently tried to bring the Siddha tradition to life in contemporary India as an alternative to Western medicine. Formally trained Siddha practitioners of general medicine, including specialists in paediatrics and orthopaedics (fracture specialists), were interviewed by Hausman, who sought to uncover the distinctive characteristics and hidden lore of the tradition.[845] He noted the comprehensiveness and uniqueness of the Siddha tradition, how the accumulated wisdom of ancestors is preserved by families and confirmed by empirical practice, especially the use of special pharmaceutical preparations. However, the dedicated and enthusiastic practitioners of Siddha today mainly practice general medicine, and Siddha appears to constitute but a branch of Ayurveda in South India.

Rasacikitsā and Siddha medicine along with alchemy, then, continue the tantric tradition of Indian medicine.[846] While the origins of alchemy

[843] P. V. Sharma 1992b.

[844] White 1996.

[845] Hausman 1996.

[846] White 1996; P. V. Sharma 1992b; Ramachandra Rao 1985.

in India hark back to China during the centuries before the Christian era, some of its preoccupations (prolongation of life, transmutation of base into noble metals) were represented in the Vedas. However, alchemy never produced a true system in India until three or four centuries after the beginning of the Christian era.

> In support of the superiority of this system [alchemy], it is claimed that while other systems of philosophy describe the state of emancipation (*mukti*) as possible only after death of the physical body, the alchemic system advocates the obtainment of this highest state even while the physical body is functioning.[847]

Ramachandra Rao also describes interesting relationships between mercury and sulphur in Indian alchemy, the preparation of phallic icons (*rasaliṅga*), and in the practices of *karmayoga* and medical healing more generally.[848]

Polavarapu Hymavathy has written a history of Ayurveda in South India during the late medieval period (fourteenth to seventeenth century CE).[849] Many of the individuals cited as exemplary physicians followed principles of Ayurveda, as well as Siddha. The high esteem with which physicians were regarded during this period in Andhradesa is a repeated theme in Hymavathy's monograph. Most physicians were from the higher castes, *brāhmaṇas*, *kṣatriyas*, or *vaiśyas*, but some were said also to belong to the fourth caste. Physicians learned from their families and/or underwent periods of apprenticeship. Great care went into the choosing a proper guru or preceptor as well as student. Exemplary personal characteristics were a requirement.

> But it was always regarded compulsory to gain scholarship at least in Sanskrit and Telugu languages and the knowledge of *Dharmaśāstras* [code of moral behaviour] to become a doctor.[850]

Medicine in general was an esteemed branch of scriptural knowledge as princes, the sons of ministers, and generals also underwent periods of training although they did not undergo the actual practice of medicine, although generals stood to gain from this knowledge in help-

---

[847] Ramachandra Rao 1985: 11.

[848] See also P. V. Sharma 1992b; White 1996.

[849] Hymavathy 1993.

[850] Hymavathy 1993: 149.

ing military physicians to better care for their troops during war. Physicians were also appointed as high officials of the state.

Many categories of physicians were recognized in Andhradesa during the late medieval period. They included physicians steeped in Ayurveda and Siddha, those employed by royal houses and the military, those associated with the various sects, 'a good Shaivite physician serving the people', those situated in temples and monasteries where they ran clinics and hospitals, country and common physicians of different orientation, and learned laymen. A category of physicians that may have been special to the region is mentioned. It is termed *parahita*. These are individuals or possibly families and hereditary physicians who pursue the medical profession in large part so as to promote the welfare of living beings. Hymavathy recounts a tale about an individual linked to this tradition, who was said to have treated a live snake on whose jaws was jammed a small animal. *Parahitas* are equated also with individuals who do not accept payment for the treatment of bites by snakes and scorpions.

> We should not overlook a fact that not all physicians were called as *parahitas*. The term ... seems to be an honorific title given to certain individual physicians who were scholars in all aspects of medicine and who dedicated their lives for the public service without expecting any monetary benefit from the people.[851]

An incipient specialization among the class of physicians is alluded to. Individuals with special expertise in general medicine, surgery, and ophthalmology are mentioned. All Indian physicians, as already suggested, espoused a holistic orientation that included a consideration of bodily and emotional and psychological factors. A form of hypnosis was said to constitute a technique that was frequently used to treat disease. Moreover, conditions of psychiatric interest were included in the corpus of medical diseases treated by ayurvedic physicians. Hymavathy mentions that physicians had grown sophisticated in reading the condition and course of illness from paying close attention to the moods, expressions, postures, and demeanours of the actual messengers from families and patients who were the ones seeking advice and consultation from the physician.[852] Writings are cited that describe a possible specialty of

---

[851] Hymavathy 1993: 88.

[852] Hymavathy 1993.

medicine or 'cadre of physicians' who may have concentrated on certain varieties of psychiatric condition. These physicians dealt with medical problems attributed to spirits and possession. They were described in one text cited by Hymavathy as apparently distinctive, in terms of their apparel, paraphernalia, and countenance:

> The *Bhūta* had the Vibhutil marks on the forehead and in between the two eyebrows he put on a big saffron mark; he wore amulets to both the arms; a serpent-cane and a box with shelves to [sic] small compartments in one hand; he was very fearful to look at. It is further indicated ... that the *Bhūtas* followed strict rules and regulations in their profession. The people believed that the *Bhūtas* were endowed with great powers to drive away the demons and evil spirits and to cure the mental diseases.[853]

These physicians were said to treat not only run-of-the-mill persons showing manifestations of conditions of psychiatric interest but also 'the soldiers who lost the mental balance in the battlefield'.

The Islamic influence in medicine

During the medieval period, to the already pluralistic system of medicine of India was added the medicine of the Near East including Turkey. Unani medicine, a synthesis of Greek and Arabic medical theories and practices, had an important presence in the subcontinent of India during the medieval period. Its peak influence was during the Islamic conquest of northern India and establishment of the Sultanate of Delhi and later during the period of the rise and fall of the Mughal Empire, roughly between the eleventh through the eighteenth centuries.[854] Unani physicians practiced an academic, scholarly and textually based tradition of medicine that was brought to the subcontinent from centres in central Asia, especially Iran. Unani medicine would naturally have been represented primarily in settings where Muslim political, intellectual, and trade influences were prominent. More than likely, these are the same as or similar to the settings where Ayurveda had been and undoubtedly continued to be prominent.

Many historians have studied the development of medicine in India during the medieval period, with an emphasis on Islamic influ-

[853] Hymavathy 1993: 168.
[854] Bagchi 1997.

ences.[855] Scholars have reviewed the general medical documents that were translated during the reigns of various Muslim rulers, the construction of general hospitals in large cities, the close cooperation between native ayurvedic and Unani physicians, whose traditions were said to be complementary and mutually enriching, despite the differences in epistemology between the Ayurveda, Siddha, and Unani medical traditions. These writers also describe support for the various medical traditions by the rulers, the relation between traditional medicine and private clinics, and how physicians were trained – which by and large involved family influences and periods of preceptorship in hospitals.

For the most part, most scholars have not dealt systematically with changes introduced into Islamic medicine as a result of its contact with Ayurveda. Kutumbiah discusses developments in medical theory in medieval India, but he concentrates exclusively on Ayurveda.[856] Conrad covers the history and aspects of theory and practice in Islamic medicine but does not touch on developments in India.[857] Needless to say, none of these authors deals with the problem of conditions of psychiatric interest in India viewed from within the system of Islamic medicine. For this, one has to consult Dols who concentrates on developments predominantly within Islamic societies.[858]

When Arabic, Persian, and Islamic influences in medicine were preeminent in the continent, Ayurveda and Unani physicians functioned as a principal means of medicine for the political elite, the rich merchants, and the economically well-off of the subcontinent. However, both Ayurveda and Unani ideas and practices would have diffused vertically and horizontally across social spaces, away from the cities and clinics visited by the elite and wealthy to reach poorer and illiterate segments. Two factors would have accounted for this. First, academic physicians who were favoured and recognized by the powerful were accorded prestige and likely to be endowed with positions of administration over hospitals and clinics located in important cities where the powerful resided. Stipends were often provided to them to support their services in administering to the medical needs of the poor of the city. They also

[855] See Bala 1982; Siddiqi 1981; Israili 1980; Jaggi 1977.

[856] Kutumbiah 1969.

[857] L. I. Conrad 1993.

[858] Dols 1992.

enjoyed lucrative private medical practices. Some physicians were granted portions of land and control over villages with the proviso that they were to operate medical establishments where the poor could visit.

The second complementary factor accounting for the spread of academic, scholarly medical theories of Ayurveda and Unani was more nearly purely an ideational and ideological one. Those in the employ of and actually servicing the rich and powerful would have learned about the scholarly, elite traditions of medicine directly and used the ideas. The availability of texts, usually produced by academic scholarly physicians themselves, would have provided a repository of ideas about disease that the less educated and even semiliterate could learn about directly or through intermediaries. Some of the principles of medical diagnosis and therapeutics most fully realized in the academic, scholarly traditions would have spread and diffused and been mined by segments of the pluralistic medical community who practiced a more local, folk and popular medicine. In short, one can assume that some of the ideas of Ayurveda and Unani medicine, for example, that involving not only diagnosis but especially materia medica, would have been assimilated by practitioners who lacked the training and prestige of the elite physicians.

Unani medicine

This tradition was an amalgam of Hippocratic, Galenic influences and those stemming from Arabia and Persia. Bagchi points out that even in traditional Arabic centres Ayurveda had an influence and contributed to the flowering of Unani medicine.[859] Ali Ibn Rabban at-Tabari, for example, was an Arab physician of the ninth century who is regarded as an important figure who promoted the incorporation of ayurvedic ideas into Unani medicine. He and others were influential in establishing connections between the two traditions.

> Many Vaids [Indian ayurvedic physicians] were invited to Baghdad in the early Abbasid period and several ayurvedic works were translated into Arabic by order of the Caliph, and students and practitioners of Unani medicine were acquainted with them.[860]

---

[859] Bagchi 1997.

[860] Bagchi 1997: 56.

Many of the famous physicians who practiced the Unani scholarly tradition in India had received their training and experience in the main educational institutions of Baghdad.[861] They were brought to or called by the courts of the various Muslim rulers of India. During the Mughal Dynasty in particular (1526–1748) Unani physicians played important role in the medical affairs of the courts and in social, community medical activities. Their personalities and accomplishments as practitioners and scholars are amply recorded in historical accounts of the era. Most Muslim rulers and even some wealthy merchants built hospitals in many urban centres of the subcontinent during the medieval period. Unani physicians usually ran these hospitals and it is highly likely that ayurvedic physicians practiced in them as well.

Bagchi emphasizes that in India Islamic influence played an important role in the development of Unani medicine.[862] Lucknow, Delhi, Hyderabad, Jaipur, and Lahore are renowned centres where Unani influence flourished. In them were established many distinguished families of Unani physicians of India. Their founders had come from Shiraz and Gilan in Iran and had emigrated to India during the medieval period. Some of the male descendants of these physicians were not only famous and respected practitioners but were also influential in translating and publishing Unani medical texts in India. While primarily identified with Graeco-Arabic medical traditions, scholarly medicine of the era as promoted by influential Unani physicians included material from Ayurveda. Thus, while it is probably the case that at least in Muslim political and intellectual circles ayurvedic medicine was somewhat overshadowed by Unani medicine, it would appear that Islamic physicians were heavily committed to scholarly and academic traditions of medical learning and made a point of including ayurvedic principles.[863]

---

[861] L. I. Conrad 1993, 1995.

[862] Bagchi 1997.

[863] The status of Unani medicine in the complicated terrain of competing medical systems in India during the early part of the twentieth century is discussed by Liebeskind (2002).

INTERACTION AND COMPETITION AMONG SCHOLARLY TRADITIONS

It is difficult to get a first-hand picture of how the pluralistic system of medicine of India functioned in real communities. Most of the historical information that is available has an academic, intellectual focus that is purely descriptive. It is also heavily flattering to physicians around whom discussions centre. Besides describing happenings in an abstract, laudatory tone, it also provides details of the perceptions and points of view of mainly the intellectual and political elite. One has to rely on information provided by modern cultural anthropologists on medical practice in colonial and non-industrial societies in order to derive hypotheses about competitions between literate, academic traditions, on the one hand, compared to non-literate, folk, popular and shamanistic traditions, on the other.

Earlier chapters discussed relevant material pertaining to this facet of competition and interaction among approaches to diagnosis and treatment. While these studies obviously focus on the interplay between Western biomedicine and traditional indigenous approaches, with a little imagination generalizations observed can be projected backwards onto earlier historical periods. In previous eras, it would have been Ayurveda, Siddha, and Unani medicine as compared to biomedicine that was hegemonic in a political and intellectual or 'scientific' sense whereas a blend of ideas and practices associated with herbal, spiritual, divinatory, astrological, shamanistic, and sometimes outright demonic influences would have constituted the 'alternative', 'complementary', or 'non-orthodox' approach. In general, the sources are silent about the ebb and flow of medical care and practice as it pertains to indigenous, non-academic traditions. This is true not only for general medical problems and diseases but of conditions of psychiatric interest in particular.

The scholars who write about Unani and ayurvedic medicine in the medieval period and the sources that they describe tend to emphasize the more sanguine aspects of medical interaction between the two traditions.[864] The mutual respect that physicians had towards their respective colleagues tends to be emphasized along with attempts to integrate aspects of diagnosis and treatment whenever possible. The physicians are described as tolerant, interested in advancing medical knowledge,

---

[864] Bagchi 1997; Bala 1982, 1984a, 1984b, 1991; Siddiqi 1981.

and willing to cross boundaries so as to learn from the rival tradition. Nothing resembling mutual distrust, criticism, or antagonism is even suggested. Yet, Bagchi and historians like Mujeeb point out that persecution of Hindus was not uncommon during various phases of Muslim hegemony in India and that this included the burning of sacred books that must have included at time writings on medicine.[865] Similarly, to the extent that physicians practiced in a limited market, one can anticipate that economic competition must have marred the otherwise friendly and mutually respectful relations between practitioners of the two traditions of scholarly medicine.

A window into the way the system of medicine functioned in relation to the educated and economically well-off social classes of India is provided by writings of foreign visitors and tourists to different parts of India including in particular Goa.[866] The Portuguese began to exert influence in the Mughal court sometime after Jahangir's accession to the throne. However, even before that many European travellers passing through Goa are reported to have commented favourably about the 'medical performances' of ayurvedic physicians and about the prestige that they had acquired in the community.

Jan Huygen van Linschoten lived in Goa from 1583 to 1588. He is quoted as saying

> that *vaidyas* [name applied to ayurvedic physicians] were held in esteem and were honoured by the people ... [they] did not only cure their own people, but the Portuguese also. The viceroy, the Archbishop and all the monks and friars put great trust in the vaidyas than the early European physicians.[867]

Bagchi quotes the observations about the practice of medicine in India made by Francois Bernier, a French tourist who toured various localities and also visited Goa in 1560.[868] Details of ayurvedic medical regimen and differences compared to how similar medical problems were dealt with in Europe are described. Bernier describes the practice of 'Gentiles of Hindustan' (presumably, ayurvedic physicians) to rely on

---

[865] Bagchi 1997; Mujeeb 1967.

[866] Bagchi 1997.

[867] Quoted in Bagchi 1997: 109–110.

[868] Bagchi 1997.

abstinence and 'no great nourishment' for conditions of brain fever and resort to occasional bloodletting.

> I shall only remark that they are successful in Hindustan and that the Mogol and Mahometan physicians who follow the rules of Avicenna and Averroes (Unani physicians) adopt them no less than do those of the Gentiles, especially in regard to abstinence from meat broth. The Mogols ... are rather more given to the practice of bleeding than the Gentiles, for where the apprehend the inflammation just mentioned, they generally bleed once or twice, not in the triflig [sic] manner of the modern practitioners of Goa and Paris but copiously like the ancients, taking 18 or 20 ounces of blood, sometimes even to fainting; thus frequently subduing the disease at the commencement according to the advice of Galen and as I have witnessed in several cases.[869]

The Frenchman Charles Dellon reported on the practice of medicine in Daman and Goa in the 1670s. He remarked on the lack of an anatomical focus and the extensive reliance if not dependence of ayurvedic physicians on 'recipes' from their ancestors. Dellon describes them as being 'very timorous', tending to let a patient die rather than running the risk of using a remedy which might not be sufficiently approved by experience or of doubtful value even though they judge the 'distemper to be mortal or incurable' without the medication. Yet he acknowledges that ayurvedic physicians 'by their long experience' are more successful than 'the most learned foreign physicians' who are in some instances forced to follow in 'their footsteps' in order to succeed in the climate of the region. The following quote provides an interesting view of the dynamics of the contemporary medical practice of the time in India compared with Europe:

> Letting blood is much used ... without the least reluctancy [sic] to be observed in patients who never grumble here at what their physicians do but are exactly observant of their orders much beyond what is practiced in most part of Europe, where the patients, their friends and the nurses proposed their own remedies before the physician's prescriptions.[870]

John Fryer, an English physician of the East India Company, was stationed in India during the seventeenth century and also visited Goa

[869] Quoted in Bagchi 1997: 110–111.

[870] Quoted in Bagchi 1997: 112.

in 1675. As is not untypical, he painted a negative picture of the native Indian traditions of medicine compared with the European. His comments, however, widen the scope of medical practice during the medieval period.

> Physick here is now, as in former days, open to all pretenders, here being no bars of authority or formal graduation, examination or proof of their proficiency but everyone ventures and everyone prescribes on former experience descending in their families, not considering either alterations of tempers or seasons but succeeded well to one they apply to all.[871]

MEDIEVAL MEDICINE AND PSYCHIATRIC CONDITIONS

The preceding discussion presents a general picture of how medicine was practiced in medieval India primarily as viewed from the standpoint of Western visitors. Direct observations and comments reviewed above applied principally to the educated, intellectual community and concerned the practices of physicians of the two scholarly traditions. A comparatively secular, rational medicine is described. Unfortunately, the sources generally do not deal with the handling of general medical cases and certainly less so with cases of mental illness or conditions of psychiatric interest.

Since Unani medicine was based on the writings of Greek and Hellenistic physicians, especially Galen, it was rational, academic, scholarly, and comprehensive. Various types of conditions of psychiatric interest were recognized in Galenic medicine; for example, hypochondria, melancholia, hysteria, and mania. An important feature of both Galenic and Islamic medicine, which was most likely also true of Unani medicine, was that conditions of psychiatric interest were handled in naturalistic terms. The relatively 'objective', impersonal, and rational gaze of Ayurveda, with reservations noted, had certain parallels with the somewhat similar non-religious, secular gaze of the Islamic and, presumably, the Unani traditions. At the same time, the medicine of medieval Islam was also strongly influenced by Prophetic Medicine, which consisted of folk traditions native to Arabia and elaborated upon in the writings of the

[871] Quoted in Bagchi 1997: 114.

Prophet and his followers. To what extent this medicine operated in the subcontinent is not known.

In the main, however, Unani medicine continued the rationalistic approach to disease, including psychiatric condition, found in Greek medicine.[872] To provide an example, Ivanow describes a 'witch case' that occurred in a fourteenth-century Muslim community in India.[873] A victim developed an enigmatic,

> serious indisposition of illness ... so that his appetite entirely departed from him and he for several days neither ate any food nor drank water.[874]

Ivanow describes the community's beliefs about dreams, sorcerers, bewitchment, and rites performed at gravesites to counteract the effects of a certain suspected witch. Before these procedures were carried out, local physicians were called – presumably Unani practitioners. After examining the victim's pulse and urine, they found no abnormalities and 'retired helpless'.

It can safely be assumed that varieties of psychiatric condition of an acute nature that occurred among the clientele of Unani physicians would have been diagnosed and dealt with pretty much like the run-of-the-mill 'organic' type of sicknesses typically described in Ayurveda. In other words, both of the literate, scholarly traditions espoused a highly medical, naturalistic approach to psychiatric condition that stressed its physical or organic character. In addition, this perspective would have also been applied to varieties of psychiatric condition associated with states of possession and dissociation, incidents that today tend to be conceptualized more in functional, psychological terms rather than as 'organic'. To what extent Unani medical theory accommodated to spiritual and folk-based notions about possession like Ayurveda did is not clear but one may assume an eclectic base of knowledge. Dols makes clear that Islamic physicians wrestled with religious, magical interpretations of sickness in general and mental illness in particular.[875]

Cases of chronic and more disabling varieties of psychiatric condition would have been hospitalized. The historical sources are clear in

---

[872] See Dols 1992.

[873] Ivanow 1923.

[874] Ivanow 1923: 47.

[875] Dols 1984, 1985, 1992.

their emphasis on the importance of hospitals in medieval India. While these institutions undoubtedly were used to address acute and chronic disabling medical and surgical conditions requiring intensive care and support, they would also have been used to treat and perhaps also to temporarily house cases manifesting behavioural breakdowns and dilapidation caused by organic neuro-psychiatric disorders that involved brain lesions, dementia, degenerative neurological disorders, as well as the functional conditions of psychiatric interest (individuals showing depressions, paranoid states, schizophrenia, panic disorders).

Most of the hospitals found in the various urban centres and sponsored by the rulers provided care and facilities to the poor as well as the economically better-off. Bagchi discusses the relevance of Islamic approaches to general medicine, the use of hospitals, and to the management of conditions of psychiatric interest for the reign of Firoz Shah Tughlaq (1351–1388).[876] His comments are useful for they emphasize common approaches to social and public health present in other reigns although the matter of the handling of mental illness is not mentioned.

> Under his orders, a medical compendium ... was compiled ... [He] established a hospital in Delhi for the relief of the sickness among natives and strangers. Able physicians were appointed to run the hospital and provision was made for the supply of medicines, food and drink form the state exchequer. He also endowed some fertile land to provide them with their running expenses ... He had ordered that everyone suffering from insanity should be arrested, incarcerated and kept in the hospital and treated with medicines prescribed by himself, which were useful. He also ordered that all the mental cases had to be provided with special diet as recommended by the Sultan himself. It appears that the Sultan had established many mobile dispensaries and city hospitals, and appointed competent physicians to each of them.[877]

This picture is consistent with material discussed earlier. In particular, the humanitarian effort to provide care for the medically indigent, although here tempered by incarceration and arrest, the heavily organic-medical approach to conditions of psychiatric interest, and the generally paternalistic and controlling posture adopted towards the sick by the rulers and their physician agents and clients.

---

[876] Bagchi 1997.

[877] Bagchi 1997: 74.

Dols concentrates on fundamental aspects of Islamic culture that made conditions of psychiatric interest significant from a medical, intellectual, literary, and religious standpoint.[878] However, it is difficult to apply his generalizations specifically to Indian communities. Some of the culture patterns, beliefs, and modes of social interaction Dols describes may have been present in Indian communities. However, he makes virtually no direct reference to the interplay, much less conflict, between Islamic patterns of culture and Hindu ones. One must assume that victims of psychiatric condition were confined and cared for in the numerous hospitals built under Islamic influence in India, but whether they handled native Indian subjects or converts to Islam, as compared to members of the entourage of the rulers, cannot be determined. In general, given the predominantly secular, rationalistic, and humour-based, Galenic approach of Islamic medicine to sickness generally, as well as to conditions of psychiatric interest, one can conclude that physicians under the sway of this tradition who had migrated to India adopted and applied it to all of their patients. Since they not only practiced medicine among the ruling class but also had private clinics in the community that were open to the public – sometimes sponsored by royal patronage – one can assume that Unani medicine contributed a secularizing influence on the approach to behavioural breakdowns and emotional disorders.

Social and cultural historians report that during the medieval period there were native medical establishments for the sick and that some housed mentally ill patients.[879] Unfortunately, little is known about these establishments, which functioned like our hospitals or hospices for the care and treatment of the insane. India also has an ancient legal tradition that exercised virtually all of the secular functions of modern jurisprudence – as well, of course, as enforcing moral and religious norms of behaviour that is quintessentially Hindu. Moreover, since the earliest times, deviants and those who threatened social order were confined and incarcerated. Given the difficulty of separating manifestations of conditions of psychiatric interest from criminal, and civil behaviour problems, many victims of psychiatric condition must also have been legally restrained with other deviants.

---

[878] Dols 1984, 1985, 1992.

[879] Somasundaram 1984.

All complex societies have to provide for the chronically sick, the destitute, and the mentally ill. In earlier centuries, the resources and influence of the extended family, the social cement provided by *dharma*, and the solace of religious traditions were called upon to help victims of chronic, deteriorating forms of psychiatric condition. Indian societies must have had institutions to protect and control those who were unable to care for themselves, socially marginalized, or a danger to others because of debilitating and chronic mental illness. If they were not confined in 'mental' hospitals, medical, religious, and civil establishments would have served as places of confinement in Indian societies for troubled, even violent victims of psychopathology whom family members could not care for.

Punishments administered by judges and rulers could be harsh indeed in ancient India. While chronic, socially well-established varieties of 'insanity' clearly could be cited as mitigating factors in assigning blame and responsibility in contractual and criminal law, as reflected in the Dharmaśāstras, for example, those suffering from many lesser varieties of psychiatric condition – or behavioural breakdowns and dilapidations – would have been banished, beaten, branded, trampled by elephants, their heads shaved, their property confiscated, and tortured in prison-like establishments.[880] However, given the moral and religious basis of India's cultural psychology and the ethos supporting social order in India, frankly antisocial and criminal behaviour stemming from psychiatric condition may not all have been punished by the state-operated welfare and criminal justice systems, as in other ancient civilizations. Many victims would have been dealt with locally, in keeping with the community-centred ethos of traditional India. Suspicion and fear of centralized authority would have led to finding local solutions, even local punishment, for problems caused by local behavioural disturbances.[881]

Most varieties of psychiatric condition, especially those falling short of behavioural dilapidation, would have remained connected to everyday concerns and activities but would have involved a transgression of local norms of behaviour. The extended family would have played a major role in containing and modifying behavioural disturbances that contravened traditions and standards, just as the family had primary

---

[880] Sen-Gupta 1953; Lahiri 1986; Chakravorti 1996; Lingat 1973.

[881] Moore 1985.

responsibility for caring for dysfunctional members. Local problems of conduct and behaviour would have been arbitrated, sorted out, and resolved in community assemblies or Panchayats. Local healers, sometimes from within the caste, would have been consulted by caste elders for advice or divination. Victims of conditions of psychiatric interest would also have been referred to village councils that adjudicated conflicts of interest between members of different castes.[882] Royal police and courts having both religious and criminal jurisdiction would have been official backup forces empowered to regulate behaviour.

[882] See Moore 1985.

Chapter 11

Modern Psychiatry in India

INTRODUCTION

In earlier chapters the problems of mental health have been examined from within the confines of traditional Indian ideas, beliefs, and practices. While the material analyzed has been Indian, the analytical framework has involved general anthropology, from the standpoint of which modern and Western ideas about conditions of psychiatric interest have been examined retrospectively in an Indian context. Analysis has involved looking backwards into Indian history and culture and seeking to describe the Indian attire and meanings of what have been termed here 'conditions of psychiatric interest'. The lens of Western ideas about psychiatric disorders and treatments was used to point to those sickness pictures, emotional behaviour disturbances, and/or spiritual moral crises of adjustment which in diverse social spaces of early Indian society and culture were dealt with through various forms of healing. It should b. kept in mind that such 'conditions' when exhibited in cultural terms, regardless of setting (e.g., medical, religious, moral educative), can *only in a restricted sense* be equated with psychiatric disorders as formulated in Western medical nosologies and nomenclatures. A signal characteristic of 'conditions of psychiatric interest' is that, depending on setting or locality where they were found, they may or may not have been construed as pathological or abnormal and most assuredly did not carry the heavy moral baggage associated with 'mental illness' in modern societies. Of course, ayurvedic formulations of *unmāda, apasmāra,* and/or *bhūtavidyā,* which in a descriptive sense (and by convention adopted here) represent conditions of psychiatric interest, do happen to be considered pathological in the local culture since they are described in medical texts that contain many other impairments of wellbeing and sickness. Setting aside Ayurveda, information about Indian world-views, religion, philosophical psychology, and related human welfare ideas and practices were used to infer how mental illness and mental health practices were formulated and handled.

In this and the final chapter, the story of mental illness in India has a different focus although the same analytical framework is followed. Examination of the contemporary Indian scene allows one to see psychiatric phenomena directly. This is the case because during the modern era and especially since Independence in 1947, modern ideas and practices about conditions of psychiatric interest have spread and taken root in India. Moreover, the central government and medical profession have taken a beneficent, ameliorative and directive posture towards problems posed by such conditions. Historical material provides documentation of this diffusion of Western scientific and political ideas. One can see Western medical psychiatric ideas and beliefs being assimilated by administrators and professional experts and applied to behavioural phenomena now seen by Indians themselves in this new idiom of clinical neuroscience psychiatry. Thus, the focus here shifts away from the question what psychiatry might have been like in a traditional India. The new focus is how modern India has assimilated modern psychiatry and what course did its ideas and practices take there and what effects were produced.

Discussion of *modern psychiatry in India* also allows one to examine how the traditional conceptions and institutions involving problems of mental health have fared under this new hegemonic 'regime' of psychiatric knowledge and practice. More specifically, yoking a comparative anthropological and historical perspective with modern psychiatry allows the clarification what influence, if any, traditional Indian understandings and modes of handling emotional and behavioural problems have had in the clinical neuroscience program of psychiatry that is commonplace in Western nations and regnant in India today.

MILESTONES AND LANDMARKS OF MODERN PSYCHIATRY'S SPREAD INTO INDIA: A BRIEF EXCURSUS

Introduction

The influence that Western medicine had in the imperial project of the British in India has been the topic of numerous studies.[883] Health problems of personnel of the British East India Company and of civil servants and military stationed in India later were a major concern. Effective management of colonial administration policies required control of infectious diseases and improvement of public health. Epidemics of smallpox, cholera and plague along with high levels of diarrhoeal diseases, tuberculosis and malaria posed major obstacles that had to be and were overcome. Maintaining the health of British residents was of overriding importance. A major result of this effort was the rise to influence of tropical medicine as a distinct discipline. Western medicine did not merely diffuse into India where it found a willing and passive client. The spread was interactional and dialectical: India presented political and medical obstacles with which the British had to contend.[884] Moreover, in many respects, knowledge of disease, medical care practices, and epidemiology that exemplify biomedicine evolved in response to challenges posed by the physical and biotic environment of India.

The care of British subjects who were mentally ill was of secondary importance to the colonialist goal of maintaining optimal levels of health among its personnel. This is hardly surprising for a number of reasons. In the colonialist context, incidence and prevalence of mental illness and psychiatric disability was not taken into consideration, in part because the science of psychiatry during the eighteenth century and even later lacked a framework that allowed the conception of mental illness other than as dilapidated behaviour (insanity). More to the point, mental illness, even broadly conceived, posed levels of morbidity and disorder that were overshadowed by public, physical health especially infectious disease.[885] However, when one looks at this general problem of possible

---

[883] Jeffery 1988; Arnold 1993.

[884] Arnold 1993.

[885] Awareness and sensitivity about the wide prevalence and significant burdens imposed by mental illness is a phenomenon of the latter third of the twentieth century; it reflects modern sensibilities about human coping and forms of suffering and, furthermore, had to wait for developments in the sciences of diagnosis, statistical survey analysis, and psychiatric epidemiology.

neglect of 'mental illness' and insensitivity to human sensibilities of Indians in the colonialist context, the morbidity, mortality, and overall burden that general medical diseases imposed on a people were far greater than those devolving from conditions of psychiatric interest.

Finally, it should be remembered that modern psychiatry is largely a development of the twentieth century and that early during the preceding century especially *social and political and not medical problems* posed by the mentally ill were a major concern in Western Europe. Of course, conditions involving behaviour that one can retrospectively formulate as psychiatric were identified and occasioned much intellectual, philosophic discussion in societies of the Mediterranean basin during the classical era of European history. Phenomena of psychiatric interest as recorded in drama and philosophy were construed in a broad scientific and intellectual context that also involved medicine as forms of disease. During the so-called Dark Ages and on through the pre-modern era of European history, medicine and philosophy, including particularly religion, psychiatric phenomena had a tangible presence in intellectual and social life that never lost its connection to medicine. However, the important point is that not until the nineteenth century unfolded in Europe did psychiatric conditions acquire a naturalistic identity, as phenomena in themselves. State- and later university-sponsored efforts were made to understand and cope with such conditions as distinct medical problems but not until well into the twentieth century can one see in these efforts something resembling psychiatric understanding in the modern sense. Parenthetically, in analogy to the cultural evolution of Western psychiatry as rooted in its own intellectual and historical circumstances, one may be allowed to anticipate that modernization of Indian psychiatry will reflect a unique blend of its own Indian indigenous traditions of mental health as well as Western ideas.

One may well ask what this brief digression into European history of psychiatry has to do with our concern here, namely, the spread of modern psychiatry into the Indian subcontinent. The answer is that while the care of the seriously mentally ill – cases of behavioural breakdown and dilapidation construed as insanity, including possible hospitals and asylums – had a presence in India well before the entry of the British, it appears to have been irregular, unsystematic, purely custodial, and geographically variable in the subcontinent. It was not until the British entered the scene that modern psychiatry showed a presence in India and this took place in association with developments that were unfolding in Europe *at roughly the same time* and that involved increasing awareness and concern about the plight of the mentally ill *in European nations*. Psychiatry was simply not sharply configured on the radar screen of human problems during the time the British East India company was hegemonic; and, even when the Raj assumed ascendancy in mid-nineteenth century, Western psychiatry was mainly concerned with establishing and maintaining humane asylum conditions and care, the science and historiography of modern psychiatric conceptions of psychopathology beginning to unfold during late nineteenth century achieving focus and cogency during the early twentieth century.

Colonialist psychiatry rode into India on the coat-tails, or simply the tail, of colonialist medicine. In contrast to the latter, control and treatment of psychiatric conditions does not appear to have played a significant role in the imperialist agenda compared to general diseases. To repeat, it was not until the late nineteenth and early twentieth century that one can discern modern psychiatry taking roots in India. However, it should be understood that what in earlier chapters has been formulated as indigenous psychiatry of India continued to flourish and one can hardly expect otherwise: a system of traditional mental health practices is deeply woven into the fabric of Indian society and culture. Nevertheless, as earlier discussions have suggested, during the modern era much of this indigenous psychiatry (popular religion, Brahmanic Hinduism, 'modern' Yoga, Ayurveda) has been influenced by circumstances created by challenges posed by colonialism to which the Indian intellectuals have responded.

Pre-Independence Indian psychiatry

The mental hospitals of India today stemmed from British conception although there are reports of earlier indigenous places of confinement.[886] Pre-Independence psychiatry involved the establishment of modern 'lunatic asylums' in India starting during late eighteenth century and continuing into the mid-nineteenth century. These were set up in centres of British rule and for the care of British subjects. The British Lunacy Act of 1858 laid down guidelines for new construction of asylums and set procedures for admitting mental patients. These were modified for India including elaborate instructions for admitting individuals who were

[886] S. P. Agarwal *et al.* 2004; Rama Rao 1975; Somasundaram 1984.

mentally ill and had pending criminal charges. In general, asylums and places of confinement were set up, less for care of those who were mentally ill and much more to protect the public. After the commencement of British governmental control of India, more hospitals were constructed but these followed the same admission requirements and policing functions. The idea of housing British subjects with native Indian patients was an important concern of British administration.[887] Twentieth-century developments prior to Independence involved transfer of control of Indian asylums from centres of prison administration to health services administration and later the passage of the Indian Lunacy Act of 1912, which followed growing concern about the health conditions of those hospitalized in asylums.[888]

S. D. Sharma identifies the period just preceding Independence (1920–47) as involving a movement away from places of confinement, marked in shift in terminology from asylum to hospital.[889] This period saw growing appreciation of need for occupational therapy and other rehabilitative services, recognition of the relevance of psychologists and other social scientists for treatment, first efforts to educate psychiatrists and psychiatric nurses, and beginning efforts to establish links with families of patients through family units in hospitals. All of these emphases mirror what was happening in contemporary Western psychiatry. Specialists in mental illness became full-time officers in some hospitals.[890] The first conference of proto-psychiatrists (termed alienists at the time) in India was held in January 1939.[891]

Early post-Independence psychiatry in India

Developments in modern psychiatry of India are a direct outcome of the humanitarian, intellectual, scientific, political, and professional motivations of many physicians and psychiatrists. These efforts grow out of, contribute to, and are intellectually a part of the efforts of numerous politicians and renowned figures, which had aimed to establish a self-standing, self-sufficient, and self-respecting modern Indian polity. Much

---

[887] McDowell 1897.

[888] Somansudaram 1987.

[889] S. D. Sharma 2004.

[890] Shaw 1932.

[891] Bhugra 2001.

like political figures whose focus was to work towards independence through assimilation of Western political ideas, the psychiatric intelligentsia's focus and motivation was to bring modern psychiatry to India. In both contexts, a perhaps idealistic position to take is that such Western cultural ideas and beliefs would be culturally refracted so as to represent indigenous political, spiritual, and medical wisdom. This topic is well beyond the perimeter of this monograph. However, the turn to modern psychiatry should be seen not merely as a consequence of efforts of this intelligentsia, but also in context of a changing ecology of disease and human health problems broadly conceived.

Contemporary India still faces many health problems tied to traditional life in village and city and disadvantages stemming from its traditional approach to public health and sanitary practices. To these vulnerabilities one has to add the load and burden stemming from the effects of major politico-economic changes in the structure of society associated with migration, urbanization, industrialization, capitalism, and secular democracy. All of these changes have supervened in a fashion that challenges traditional habit patterns, family structures, occupational opportunities, values, mental thought worlds, moral imperatives, and the general resonance of interpersonal relationships. Modernization through colonialism involved an added major transformation in way of life, morale, and emotional health resulting from social, moral, and general psychological indignities. One can argue that the most pernicious effects of this political regime on the cultural psychology of Indians were early on predominantly focused on urban and educated Indians. It is on this segment of the population that British colonialist policy was directly imposed involving new political imperatives and requirements for education for effective participation in bureaucracies as well as for social and intellectual accommodation.

Since Independence, the scope of social change has increased and slowly come to affect other segments of the population. It has attracted and/or pushed peasant from village to city for want of resources, facilities, and opportunities with consequent negative health implications. However, other developments involving sanitation of public facilities, public health programs, and control of infectious disease have changed the ecological picture of demography and health conditions of Indian populations. Changes in mortality, fertility, and population size, termed the 'demographic transition', and changes in the profile of disease from acute and chronic infections to more systemic, chronic disease (heart disease, cancer), a shift that is referred to as the 'epidemiological transition', has led to a relaxation of the vice that squeezes high levels of medical morbidity and mortality. This has meant that since Independence India's major public health problems became less intractable and better controlled. In relation to this changing ecology of disease, psychiatrists slowly acquired a window of medical opportunity, and the luxury, to press the need for a modern and effective understanding and treatment of problems of mental health and illness.

Modern ideas about diagnosis of mental illness and approaches to inpatient and outpatient mental health care, and later the explosion of drug therapy, came to India not long after they supervened in the West. Indeed, the growth of modern psychiatry in Western nations began during the 1950s and especially 1960s, the same period during which modern psychiatry took hold in India. There are big differences in the way this development played out in India compared to the West, however. Changes leading to modern biological medicine and psychiatry in the West had especial historical momentum, because it was there that modern medicine evolved. In Western societies, world-views and systems of practice were grounded in and involved a progressive departure from and eventual disconnection from popular, lay, traditional approaches to sickness and mental illness.[892] In India, the attack and marginalization of indigenous psychiatry by the British was concentrated on Ayurveda. The advent and heyday of Indian colonialist biological medicine in this century was associated with a direct denigration and systematic marginalization of ayurvedic physicians, a development well documented by American cultural anthropologists and sociologists.[893] In general, save for the animus directed at Ayurveda, the other facets of indigenous psychiatry discussed in earlier chapters do not appear to have been targets of denigration neither by the British or large segments of India's intelligentsia, including its medical elite.[894]

An emphasis on research in clinical psychiatry and its basic science and efforts to document need for in- and outpatient mental health services was part of the shift in medicine that resulted from relative success

[892] However, it is clear that the modern version of traditional 'popular' medicine as alternative and complementary medicine thrives as an industry in Western nations.

[893] Leslie 1974, 1976; Leslie and Young 1992; Nunley 1992; Hausman 1996; Langford 2002; Arnold 1993.

[894] How assiduously, persistently, and effectively modern Indian psychiatry utilizes its indigenous psychiatric resources is taken up later.

in efforts to prevent, control spread of, and treatment of communicable diseases. Following Independence, many mental institutions have been built, and facilities and resources of individual institutions allocated for development of services. The quality of service in custodial institutions was up-graded in quality. In some institutions, as suggested earlier, family members of patients were involved in comprehensive services and participated in therapy, hospitalization care, and preparation for discharge. An important development involved general hospital psychiatry. A few beds were set aside in hospital wards for acutely ill psychiatric patients and outpatient units or divisions of psychiatry were developed. While the first unit was first set up in 1933, the 1960s witnessed a sharp increase in their number. During the 20 years following Independence, approximately 90 units were developed.[895] Innovative services in non-custodial settings were set up in a few psychiatric hospitals and in some instances involved using indigenous mental health practices, such as Yoga, and drawing on traditional mental health healing relationships, termed *guru–celā*.[896]

Planning for education and manpower development began soon after Independence. The Indian Psychiatric Society (IPS) was set up in 1949 and in the same year the *Indian Journal of Neurology and Psychiatry* was inaugurated. At the eleventh meeting of IPS, it was renamed *Indian Journal of Psychiatry*. The All India Institute of Mental Health was set up in 1954 in Bangalore and later termed the National Institute of Mental Health and Neurosciences (NIMHANS) and became the main centre for education of psychiatrists, clinical psychologists, and psychiatric nurses. Instruction of psychiatrists and clinical psychologists began in 1955.

Indian research involving mental illness has gone through several phases. Initially, research was predominantly conceptual and psychoanalytical aimed at elucidating and improving individual psychological functioning. There was little emphasis on the phenomenology of illness or on epidemiology. This changed during the period from 1960 to 1972:

> Research publications became broader in their orientation and moved from individual psychopathology to the interface between the individual and society and group·behaviour. The cross-fertilization of ideas between sociology, psychology and psychiatry was very benefi-

---

[895] Sarada Menon 2004.

[896] Neki 1973, 1975.

cial from a public health perspective, thus sowing the seeds for community-oriented research and program planning.[897]

Major psychiatric epidemiological studies involving Indian populations were launched during the 1970s. Some of these results were discussed in Chapter 4 for the purpose of providing background about mental illness in traditional populations of the subcontinent. Indian psychiatric epidemiology has matured in tandem with the psychiatric epidemiology of Western academies. The following statement echoes this generalization:

> India has not lagged behind the growth of psychiatric epidemiology. The period between 1950 and 2000 has seen tremendous growth of this discipline across India with studies getting more and more refined and advancing clearly.[898]

The new sensibility – modern clinical neuroscience – about psychiatric conditions places the level of serious mental illness at 1 per cent of the population and approximately at 5–10 per cent of moderately serious psychiatric disorders needing psychiatric care. One the other hand, it appears to be the case that in contemporary India less than 10 per cent of those in urgent need of psychiatric care are receiving it given the level of existing services, and the burden of unmet mental health care is worse in rural India compared to cities. Furthermore,

> A simple extension of the present system of care will not be able to ensure adequate services to the vast majority of the Indian population in the near foreseeable future.[899]

One is compelled to ask how much of this burden of psychiatric disorder reflects verities likely to have existed in previous eras of Indian history; how much is due to conditions imposed by residua of colonialism and persistent ramifications wrought by modernization; and how much merely reflects different, postmodernist conceptions and values about what is problematic in the human condition. Rhetorical questions such as these bring into focus a persistent dilemma emphasized in earlier chapters: what conceptual issues are necessarily raised when one

---

[897] Sarada Menon 2004: 34.

[898] Gururaj and Isaac 2004: 40.

[899] Murthy 2004: 76.

seeks to understand psychiatric phenomena in a cross-cultural, cross-historical, and indeed inter-species and human evolutionary frame of reference.[900]

It is not appropriate or necessary to further summarize continued milestones and landmarks of the evolution of modern clinical neuroscience psychiatry in India since Independence. A 'taking stock' of where psychiatry is, should be, and can expect to be in the near future in areas of professional and lay education, comprehensive clinical care services, and research has been done in an admirable way in the recently published *Mental Health: An Indian perspective, 1946–2003*, edited by S. P. Agarwal and others.[901] This has been accomplished at a level of acumen, cogency, probity and comprehensiveness that is not likely to be exceeded by any other nation. However, the details of where India is in its mission to improve mental health of its population, and its success in these efforts, are not a concern of this monograph. The focus here is in tracing the history of psychiatric phenomena in the subcontinent considered in social, political, religious, philosophical, and general cultural terms. To accomplish this satisfactorily, to the extent possible in one monograph by one individual, necessitates examining the entry and spread of modern psychiatry in India as simply the latest chapter in a long story whose roots go back to its rich intellectual tradition.

PUTTING INDIA ON THE ROAD TO THE MODERNIZATION OF PSYCHIATRY

Under British colonial rule, dating from the eighteenth century, India experienced a major transformation in social philosophy and values, political economy, social governance, and political and social psychology. These developments, as discussed earlier, were naturally associated with profound changes involving secularization, Westernization, and, in some instances, a heightening of Indian nationalism including Sanskritization in Indian communities.[902] British medicine's interaction with ayurvedic and Unani (Islamic) medicine in India is but a chapter of the long story that involved a pattern of mutual influence that had

---

[900] Fabrega 1997, 2002a.

[901] S. P. Agarwal *et al.* 2004.

[902] D. E. Smith 1963; Srinivas 1966; Nandy 1980, 1983.

existed between indigenous physicians and European practitioners of medicine starting in the sixteenth century.[903] In contrast to the apparent cordial and mutually beneficial enrichment of the respective medical traditions, this chapter tells a less than sanguine tale and does not have a happy ending for Ayurveda.

A first impediment to the evolution of an effective program of modern psychiatry in India was the generally low level of public health in the nation. Ideally, in order to estimate the extent of a society's mental health and illness problems, it is desirable to be able to exclude general medical conditions because these can cause, mimic, or becloud diagnosis of psychiatric conditions. A high prevalence of medical conditions, along with social factors that compromise general health, can hinder clarification of levels of psychiatric morbidity. In India, as in many non-industrial, traditional societies, it has been difficult to demarcate a separate sector pertaining to mental health and illness problems. Jeffery provides a historical account of India's massive public health problems and discusses issues relating to development of an effective and responsive native health policy.[904] The quest to meet effective public health program requirements and associated social and mental health measures is ongoing in India as the nation seeks to modernize its medical system by inculcating a secular, scientific philosophy about medicine that can effectively compete with the sacred, value-laden one inherited from the traditional past.[905]

Ideally, an imperial, colonialist enterprise seeking to promote social welfare and health in its client or partner strives to encourage acceptance and growth of the best of the patron's science and medicine that respects, complements, and expands on native traditions.[906] Given the characteristics of India's ethno-medicine and indigenous psychiatry, an important step in the movement to achieve improvement in mental health as clinical neuroscience psychiatry construes this target was to work with Indian perspectives and sensibilities. However, this effort was marred by the competition between biomedicine, a social system under state sponsorship, and the prevailing cultural approach to health. Exponents of indigenous Ayurveda and Siddha traditions of medicine

[903] Patterson 1987.

[904] Jeffery 1988.

[905] S. P. Agarwal 2004.

[906] Basalla 1967.

sought recognition, empowerment, and official representation in state-sponsored medical affairs. However, after 1835, Western medicine was construed as the hallmark of a superior civilization and its implementation as a moral obligation to limit if not thwart the ignorance and barbarism of India's indigenous medicine:[907]

> By the 1850s and 1860s attitudes (towards ayurvedic medicine), never universally enthusiastic ... hardened. As Western medicine grew in confidence and political authority, as it freed itself from the humoral pathology which had earlier kept it in touch with the principles of ayurvedic and Yunani medicine, and as it began to take upon itself responsibility for Indian and European health and thus to see indigenous medicine more clearly as its rival, it also exhibited a growing tendency to dismiss indigenous medicine and its practitioners, almost without qualification.[908]

Scientific medicine won this political skirmish with Ayurveda by political mandate since it was sponsored by the state. It did so well before psychiatry had achieved definition as an enterprise with well-defined scientific and social goals. Left unchecked, British colonialist policy would have paved the way towards dominance of clinical neuroscience psychiatry. An irony here is that after Independence, it has been Indian (and not British) psychiatrists, with state backing, who have achieved hegemonic control for this quintessential brand of psychiatry. On the other hand, a vibrant indigenous medicine and psychiatry integrates general medical and mental health related problems and conceptualizes them in traditional and holistic terms. As suggested earlier, ayurvedic physicians were and still are deeply involved with psychiatry, managing syndromes of emotional and behavioural disaffection that in the society at large are conceptualized in general health and/or spiritual-moral terms.[909] Resort to popular and indigenous physicians can hinder the evolution of a truly separate conception and mode of handling of psychiatric problems. Thus in many respects, physicians and psychiatrists seeking to promote their vision of what is best are sometimes forced to downplay, if not marginalize, competing medical and psychiatric traditions regardless of how sacredly and vitally they (religious, *dharma*-rooted) may answer to the call of ancient pleadings. Many have

---

[907] Arnold 1993: 57.

[908] Arnold 1993: 52.

[909] Fields 2001; Langford 2002.

described this clash between allopathic-cosmopolitan and indigenous medical traditions in India, the principal attention being given to Ayurveda.[910] As Hausman notes, it is difficult to find the roots of the Siddha tradition of medicine and healing in contemporary India, because of competition from other indigenous traditions, notably Ayurveda, as well as modern biomedicine.

The battle to establish a clearly delineated psychiatric domain is ongoing.[911] There is continuing tension and competition over the legitimate basis for the care of victims of psychiatric conditions among representatives of the various scholarly traditions of indigenous psychiatry. As argued in earlier chapters, in addition to ayurvedic physicians, indigenous psychiatry embraces efforts of gurus, wise men, religious figures, local folk practitioners, priests in charge of temples, and modern exponents of Yoga, Tantra, and respected Siddha figures.[912] All of the preceding is challenged by practitioners of the black arts (magicians, witchcraft experts, and sorcerers) and, to some extent, all compete with clinical neuroscience psychiatrists for the market for mental health services in today's India.

When the basic goals of public health, especially control of infectious diseases, are satisfactorily met in a developing society, then general medical causes of disease, debility, and demoralization are brought under some control. The result is that many important causes of psychiatric conditions are controlled. An improvement in general public health due to elimination of medical diseases can lead to the general spread of modern specialties of medicine, including psychiatry. This opens up opportunities that enable psychiatrists to more effectively and economically apply their expertise and bring it to a position of dominance. At this point, public health conditions begin to approximate those in other modern societies in which psychiatry evolved its special expertise.

SCIENCE AS A CULTURAL FORCE IN MODERNIZATION

The period of major colonial British influence in India occurred following the emergence and consolidation of the modern concept of disease

---

910 See Leslie 1976; Leslie and Young 1992; Jeffery 1988; Hausman 1996.

911 Bhattacharyya 1986.

912 Besides Fields 2001; Langford 2002; Barth 1990, see also Kakar 1982.

and the growth of biomedical theory and practice. It was also a period during which there evolved a general awareness in Europe about the plight of the mentally ill.[913] In general, British administrators in India played a major role in improving public health and establishing baselines of statistical knowledge for estimating it. However, they took a dim view of indigenous traditions of medicine. They were less sceptical of Unani medicine. Its Galenic roots could be related to early modern antecedents of biomedicine. While they attempted to infuse native traditions with tenets of the evolving modern approach to disease, they did not contribute to their independent growth. Jaggi, Jeffery, and Bala discuss the modern history of medicine in India, with an emphasis on reactions and interactions between Western and native traditions.[914] Hausman, who chronicles an attempt to understand the native Siddha tradition of medicine in India, is particularly informative about British scepticism and condemnation toward native medical traditions.[915] He discusses major proposals and efforts of the British to reform local medical colleges by appointing Western-trained physicians who could be relied on to make changes in curricula. All of these developments are also dealt with in Arnold's discussion of colonial medicine in India.[916] He sees the latter picture as a chapter, albeit very special because of circumstances involving medical ecology and colonialist imperatives, in the modern state's control over the body via diffused disciplines of power.

A dominant motif of the transformation of society during the modern period involved the entry and spread of science in Indian communities. Prakash provides a spirited and critical analysis of these social, cultural, and political developments involving the initial staging and then actual internalization and enactment of science in India.[917] The groundwork for this eventual transformation in matters related to physical and mental health can be traced to developments starting in the late eighteenth century. However, this really took root in earnest during the first half of the nineteenth century. It was during the second half of the nineteenth century that the emergence and functioning of science as a form of cultural authority in most colonial parts of India became evi-

---

[913] Fabrega 1997.

[914] Jaggi 1977; Jeffery 1988; Bala 1991.

[915] Hausman 1996.

[916] Arnold 1993.

[917] Prakash 1999.

dent. Educated elite, mostly of Brahmin background, played a very influential role initially. An enthusiasm for science as a form of social reform and re-vitalization was eventually manifested in major urban metropolitan centres, in particular. Genuine intellectual curiosity was part of this revolution, to be sure, but so was a spirit of reform of society and religion through an inculcation of natural laws over native superstitions.

The city of Calcutta occupied the initial strategic centre of this movement involving the general distribution of the discourse of science. It played a major role as an instrument of social and cultural renewal manifested in an enthusiasm for science as a language of reform. Many reform organizations were established and:

> The[ir] objectives ... varied – the diffusion of new forms of knowledge, religious and social reform, female education, the promotion of vernacular literature, the improvement of agriculture ... all of them [the organizations] were formed by and functioned with a sense of the rediscovery of reason. As science was part of this rediscovery, the popularization of its authority emerged as one of the key aims of such organizations.[918]

The exercise of the authority of science in the discourse of the native elite was first manifest in Bengal, but after the mid-nineteenth century was also observable in other provinces, especially in North India. By the late nineteenth century the 'pervasive deployment of science's persuasive power' in North India was evident in the cultural milieu that developed around Hindi language and literature and a Hindu revivalism, more generally. Much thought and effort went into the making of Hindi a language for the production of scientific knowledge.

An intellectual attraction for science has culminated in a passion and a more general, associated social and cultural intoxication that has influenced attitudes and approaches to native medical traditions. It was and is manifest in the way Western-trained Indian physicians and then psychiatrists took to conceptualizing aspects of sickness and psychiatric condition. As described earlier, an Indian medicine and psychiatry was manifest in the subcontinent stretching back to the classical and medieval period. A balanced integration or an amalgam of spirituality, religion, and naturalism, came into conflict with the increasingly totalistic

---

[918] Prakash 1999: 54.

and reductionist medicine and psychiatry of the modern, contemporary period. A key question in a study of the social and cultural history of psychiatric phenomena in India is the way that native, indigenous modes of thinking about and dealing with psychiatric conditions were affected by this invasion of foreign and modern thought, and, given its industrial capitalist momentum, highly seductive brand of medical psychology. While the Indian traditions were holistic, personalized, and concerned with all facets of human biological, psychological and spiritual experience and function, biomedicine and its child, neurobiological psychiatry, was reductionist, impersonal, and secular. A prominent clash of medical traditions can be surmised.

COLONIAL MEDICINE AS A MODERNIZING FORCE – WHERE WAS COLONIAL PSYCHIATRY?

There were many non-medical sciences that benefited from the colonization of India, for example, botany, geology, chemistry, and linguistics. However, medicine by far played a more important role. Indeed one can say that but for imperial medicine it is doubtful that the British could have exercised the degree of politico-economic control and moral hegemony that they achieved. Western medicine was a state medicine. The administrative and bureaucratic apparatus that sustained colonial rule was kept functional partly because of the work of Western medical practitioners who took care of British personnel and military troops all of whom experienced many infectious diseases and general health hazards. Colonial medicine also contributed to the health of the Indian population, not so much from a curative standpoint, but through imposition of sanitary and public health measures that blunted the onset and limited the spread of infectious diseases.[919]

One can propose that just as Western medicine colonized Indian ethno-medicine, so did Western psychiatry colonize India's indigenous psychiatry. However, this was not a nineteenth- and early twentieth-century phenomenon. It took place after Independence, but has gained momentum during the last decades and is now in full force. Moreover, there are many other factors that distinguish the colonial medical thrust

---

[919] Arnold 1993.

and the entry and spread of psychiatry. Western medicine as a body of ideas, curative and preventative practices, and as an institution with social power, was aided by colonization. Knowledge of disease increased. Factors that contributed to epidemics, the ways in which infectious diseases spread, their effects of metabolism and physiology, along with their natural course and prognosis were made clearer by observation and slow, controlled application of knowledge about biomedicine in India. The medicine that the British could bring to bear during the late eighteenth and early nineteenth centuries was radically different from that of 1900 and this difference, while dependent on scientific knowledge gained in the European and Anglo-American world, was partly earned by the ordeals of coping with cholera, plague, malaria, tuberculosis, leprosy, small pox, diarrhoeal diseases of children, and health problems of females of childbearing age. The British were able to define and begin to effectively control these medical problems as a consequence of having to cope with them first hand. Vague Western ideas about the influence of climate on physiological constitution and vulnerability towards disease were sharpened during the nineteenth century colonial regime. The basic sciences of medicine gained momentum including in particular microscopy and microbiology at the end of the nineteenth century.[920]

An advantage that colonial medicine had was that it could largely ignore social and cultural characteristics of Indian populations and limit attention to demographic factors and matters of disease and public health. Of course, initially, the British medical presence was enclavist. It catered to enclaves of state administrators and military troops, all of whom were quarantined and needed but brief excursions into the social and cultural spaces where the population lived. This changed as the nineteenth century wore on, as colonial administrators were forced into a more dialectical, interactional relationship with Indian populations, as management and control of epidemics became a prominent concern. However, this effort did not require understanding and appreciation of the influence of cultural ideas and beliefs on sickness and healing. Moreover, Western medicine is reductionist. Except for impersonal, objective or mechanical behaviours that involve possibility of transmission of disease, exposure to vectors, or access to water supplies, colonial, state medicine needed to know little about the content and meaning of

[920] Arnold 1993.

the Indian psyche, culture and behaviour. They could afford to show, and did so, repugnance and disdain towards it.

An early exception to neglect, avoidance, and ridicule of native ways was colonialist interest in Ayurveda and its practitioners.[921] As indicated earlier, this attention, however, seems to have been entirely practical and exploitative and hardly one of coming to understand and appreciate meanings, thought worlds or thought patterns about sickness, health, or medical care considered as cultural phenomena. Ayurvedic texts were translated and efforts made to learn about diseases of Indians and indigenous ways of controlling them, namely Ayurveda materia medica. This proved less than rewarding. Western physicians and public health officers then resorted to using ayurvedic practitioners as informants about health conditions and treatments, but this effort was not productive. While attitudes towards and interest in Indian ayurvedic and Unani medicine and their respective practitioners were generally positive during the early decades of the nineteenth century, by the 1850s and 1860s the tide had changed. In the interim, colonial authorities had put in place a Western medical school in 1835 with education to be conducted exclusively in English.

> Western medicine after 1835 was taken as the hallmark of a higher civilization, as sign of the moral purpose and legitimacy of colonial rule in India, just as indigenous medical ideas and practices could be casually equated with ignorance and barbarism.[922]

Psychiatry was spared the ordeal of having to cope with health problems that hindered the hegemonic mission of its patron as well as the benefits that accrued to general medical and public health practitioners who helped it. For one thing, at the end of the eighteenth and beginning of the nineteenth century psychiatry was hardly defined as a discipline over which it had expertise and could control clinically. A science of diagnosis and treatment of mental illness was nowhere to be found. Psychiatrists per se did not exist, only general physicians who took care of the very psychotic and demented that families, community welfare resources, and jails and workhouses could not handle. The abysmal state of knowledge and understanding about mental illness and its treatment was made apparent as inquiries, commissions, and reform

[921] Arnold 1993; Langford 2002; Ernst 2002.

[922] Arnold 1993: 57.

movements in Western nations inquired about the living conditions of the mad and insane. Psychiatry's social role during the nineteenth century was largely custodial, split between places of public confinement for the behaviourally dilapidated victims who were poor and socially marginal, and a private trade in lunacy for the better-off who could afford supervision in comfortable homes or establishments. It was only well into the nineteenth century that something resembling a language of psychopathology and description of separate psychiatric conditions took shape. There did not exist a conception of community mental health nor an appreciation of the influence of social, cultural factors in the causation and unfolding of psychiatric conditions. A comprehensive vision of psychiatric conditions as embodying diverse social and cultural as well as medical and neuroscience factors was a development of the second half of the twentieth century.

Thus as colonial medicine and its patron thrust its imperial tentacles into India and achieved control, power, and prestige there, psychiatry was nowhere to be found. Physicians as custodians of the mad in India, British subjects or Indian personnel, were the only ones that represented a semblance of psychiatry and they were of course not influential in the growth of knowledge for a clinical science and discipline of practice that did not yet exist. Psychiatry in colonial India was not in a position to appreciate and benefit from learning about social, cultural influences that impacted on psychiatric conditions nor about Ayurveda psychiatry and the non-medical segments of the indigenous psychiatry of India discussed here. It is true that late in the nineteenth century some academic, university-affiliated German psychiatrists began to show interest in psychoses in non-Western nations. However, a social and cultural psychiatry, the perspective exemplified in this book, only began to take place in America during the 1960s.

Moreover, as a Western-oriented Indian psychiatry took shape, it had to address mental health problems that unlike infectious diseases, overt signs of internal physiological disturbances, or visible lesions, for example, did not form easy targets to magical bullet treatments that were the hallmark of Western medicine. The tangible, empirically self-evident conditions addressed by general medicine, surgery, and public health were far different in appearance and expression compared to the more protean and less well defined conditions targeted by psychiatric treatments. Such organic and visible manifestations of disease processes provided clearer criteria for efficacy. Thus general medicine was seen as more effective and may have enjoyed greater legitimacy than psychiatry the domain of which more readily (perhaps) crossed over into emotional, moral, spiritual concerns. What Western-trained psychiatrists saw in their clinics and hospitals were not pre-digested presentations of sickness as per biomedicine but disturbances of thought, experience, behaviour, and bodily ailments that the people had understood in terms of the ideas, beliefs, and practices that have been termed here as 'indigenous psychiatry'. The ideas of mental health and illness that one found in the populace, then, especially among the poor and in villages, were completely discrepant and largely unacculturated to Western conventions. As biomedicine matured in India and success in prevention and treatment of disease achieved public recognition, mentally ill persons were taken to establishments of Indian psychiatrists with the families' expectations that magical bullets would be dispensed, as they had with infectious diseases. Of course, really effective pharmacological agents for the treatment of psychiatric disorders were really not available *in the West* until after the 1970s. This line of thought implies that biomedical psychiatry's colonization of India proceeded in a path whose terrain was marked by very different landmarks from that of general medicine.

MODERN PSYCHIATRY IN INDIAN SOCIETY

Introduction

From an anthropological and sociological point of view, modern psychiatry is a cultural institution that evolved in Western societies in relation to a large class of emotional and behavioural disaffections and breakdowns that had come to pose major social and politico-economic problems in Western societies during the late eighteenth and especially the nineteenth century.[923] Integral to this evolution was the development of a scientific rationale and associated methods, procedures, and medicines in terms of which such problems were construed and dealt with. The enterprise of Western psychiatry grew out of efforts to make sense of psychiatric conditions in context of changing ideas and conditions in the demography, social organization, institutional fabric, and political economy of industrial capitalism.

---

[923] Fabrega 1989c; Scull 1989, 1993.

The impetus and ambition of world capitalism pushed Western nations beyond their geographic boundaries and pressed them into an imperialist and colonialist enterprise. Imperialist expansion got underway well before effective knowledge of disease prevention and control and associated public health measures had evolved. However, as the modern sciences of medicine acquired expertise, their practical value as instruments for the control of dangerous health territories became obvious. It fed into, sharpened, and made more effective the thrust of imperialist expansion during the nineteenth century and thereafter.

Modern medicine evolved in concert with maturation of imperialism. As this happened, medical ideas and practices came to affect the thought worlds and habit patterns of indigenous populations wherever colonialism took roots. Western ideas came to affect an important area of social life of client populations, namely, their own medical ideas and practices. However, psychiatry played a relatively small, albeit overtly repressive, role in the colonialist regimes of the nineteenth century. The maturation of modern psychiatry is a phenomenon of the twentieth century. Its diffusion outside the perimeter of Europe took place well beyond the initial period of colonialist exploitation and domination.

As the British efforts evolved and were pushed into involving nation-building in India it prompted critical examination of Indian science and medicine as potential resources for more effective regulation and control of populations in selected parts of the subcontinent.[924] Like the effects wrought by the sciences of public health and general medicine during the nineteenth century, the spread of psychiatry during the twentieth century brought about a collision with alternative, indigenous traditions and practices.

Barriers to a regime of colonialist medicine and psychiatry

Introducing modern, secular biomedicine into a traditional culture is an enterprise strewn with many complexities and having wide-ranging ramifications. Ideally, a goal might be to rely on and enlarge upon the reservoir of folk and popular knowledge and social practices of medicine, and to integrate them, as much as is reasonable, with modern conceptions and practices so as to constitute the resulting package of medicine in an idiom that is understandable intellectually, and emotionally

[924] Arnold 1993; Inden 2000; Prakash 1999.

resonant to a people undergoing modernization. However, in practice, the colonial enterprise is sometimes forced to peel away and set aside what the modern science of medicine all too often regards as old-fashioned, fanciful, superstitious beliefs and practices. Indigenous ways are said to becloud and interfere with the goal of improving health as an instrument of political and economic control. In a clinical context, traditional ideas about health and human fate may clutter clinical presentations of disease as sickness, more specifically, what patients report and think about their sickness; and they can interfere with adoption of modern practices and programs of health promotion.

Most branches of modern medicine have been successful in bringing about a changed world-view about disease, which they formulate in impersonal terms. In the science of biomedicine, disease stands outside the moral perimeter of the self. Furthermore, many diseases can be cured or prevented cleanly and effectively. The body and its physical attributes constitute the focus of the biomedical idiom. Its idiom addresses the body in mechanical and impersonal terms. The body can be examined and probed by means of technical devices that, in theory, leave the person as cultural being (beliefs, values, personal concerns) out of the picture of sickness.

Psychiatry has travelled the same evolutionary path as other medical disciplines and one might anticipate its targets (psychiatric disorders or diseases) have evolved the same sort of concrete material ontology. Indeed, if the disorders falling within the purview of psychiatry can also be reduced to physical, mechanical structures and substances and if its subject matter is equally secular and authorizes the same exclusion of self, local culture, religion, and spirituality, then the spread of psychiatry into India is simply an addendum to the spread of biomedicine worldwide. However, this cannot happen for a number of reasons.

First of all, even in Western societies psychiatric conditions are special entities replete with moral implications about the self.[925] They never represented impersonal, objective things and never will either. Even if psychiatric disorder as per clinical neuroscience could be reduced to disturbances of networks that handle information processing in the brain as its ontology, a vaulted neuroscience cannot avoid having to immerse itself in the messiness of social conduct. Brains may be mapped objectively and non-invasively but they belong to individuals who are

---

925 Fabrega 2006a.

selected because of their psychiatric condition and all of its diverse cultural ramifications. Moreover, and especially relevant to our focus here, ideas of clinical neuroscience cannot be expected to simply float into Indian culture and take root there, like ideas pertaining to communicable disease. As discussed earlier, psychiatric conditions and indigenous mental health practices, when brought into play as per a given individual have a unique, special tie with foundational ideas about being, experience, social reality, and cosmology. This makes the attempt to impose a new, reductionist clinical neuroscience psychiatry in India particularly disruptive.

The space into which psychiatry intrudes in a non-Western country is similar to that generally encountered by all of Western medicine. However, because of the highly visible, morbid effects of general medical problems and because of the availability of procedures and medications that operate like magic bullets or surgical excisions because of their precision, speed and effectiveness, objections to the colonial imposition of general medicine and programs of public health are more readily rationalized. On the other hand, given that psychiatric conditions in India are rooted in a complex cultural psychology and its manifestations bring into play widely influential religious, moral, and philosophical beliefs and practices, the magical bullets of modern psychiatry are aimed, not only at inexact targets, but also potentially can cause collateral disruptions in ways of thinking, feeling, and behaving that are psychologically, socially, morally, and theosophically compelling to personal wellbeing.

Psychiatric conditions involve complex phenomena deeply embedded in a society's social structures, institutions, and cultural territories. Their signs and symptoms are often mysterious and frightening and their explanations resonate with ideas about morality, the meaning of existence, and sense of historical and cosmological placement. By definition psychiatric conditions involve emotional distress as well as functional impairment in the performance of an individual's basic roles and responsibilities. Although those who promote the idea of an international system of psychiatric diagnosis argue that from a strict clinical point of view criteria for disorders are reducible to a finite set of pancultural, universal signs and symptoms, from a social and cultural standpoint they are far less objective or impersonal and much less easily set apart from ongoing concerns.

Aberrant behaviour, emotional suffering, disturbed thinking and feeling, and related bodily maladies make up incidents of psychiatric conditions. Their manifestations are configured and played out through social routines that reflect or can lead to alienation and anomie, often in violation of norms pertaining to acceptable behaviour that are authorized in terms of cultural patterns and values. Although exhibited in individual behaviour, these manifestations are handled through social practices and institutions involving the family and the community. While conditions can divide and disrupt the fabric of family ties and mutual obligations among those linked by blood and marriage, such conditions are also a community phenomenon.[926] When they cannot be handled by the family, they impact on other institutions and structures of the society the function of which is to alleviate suffering, arbitrate conflicts, control behaviour that contravenes acceptable norms, and generally repair breaches in the social fabric caused by such conditions.

Impact of modern psychiatry in India

The dissemination of the ideas of modern clinical neuroscience marks the final phase of the social and cultural history of mental illness in India. This encroachment, which began in the late eighteenth and early nineteenth centuries under British colonial rule, has been described as the imposition of a Western system of social control.

Ernst argues that the establishment of institutions for handling problems of mental illness in India was part of the enforced consolidation of British rule in selected territories of the subcontinent.[927] This included the creation of courts of law and the establishment of police forces and jails that could guarantee imperial control over public life. Public hospitals, termed police or pauper hospitals, were erected, along with workhouses, dispensaries, and licensed brothels. The salient instrument of psychiatry at the time was the asylum, largely used for warehousing and thereby containing those guilty of behavioural disturbances that threatened social order. Ernst writes:

> It was within this context, that it was decreed by the Court of Directors of the East India Company in 1802 that lunatic asylums for the recep-

---

[926] Opler 1958; Freed and Freed 1964; Bhattacharyya 1986; Waxler 1974, 1979.

[927] Ernst 1987, 1988.

> tion of both criminal and freely wandering insane Indians ought to be established in Bengal. The measure had been necessitated by the authorities' concern with public peace and order, which had frequently been disturbed by mischievous Indian lunatics committing violent actions. As the Courts of Circuit in Madras and Bombay expressed a similar worry about stone throwing and otherwise dangerous lunatics, in those Presidencies too the erection of lunatic asylums for Indians was sanctioned.[928]

By 1820 a number of native lunatic asylums for Indian patients had been established. Similar institutions were set up for the European insane. Conditions in these asylums led to inquiries about their operation and regulation.

While major milestones and landmarks that punctuate the evolution of official psychiatry in India are known, actual details about how ideas and practices of modern psychiatry sought entry into the cultural and social fabric of Indian society are lacking. Information about its competition with indigenous or native rationales and practices remains to be adequately documented, just as in the case of how Ayurveda and Islamic medicine, and psychiatry, interacted at grass root levels of social practices of healing during earlier centuries. This contrasts sharply with the wealth of research in the social history of psychiatry in European societies.[929]

European history provides ample evidence of the complexities attending the identification and growing understanding of the problems posed by mental illness. This involved, among many considerations, the play of professional interests and ambitions and the clash of traditional views of madness and insanity with humanitarian impulses that urged a reform of social institutions devoted to caring for the mentally ill.[930] In Western societies, there has been a slow but steady rise of psychiatric knowledge to a position of high visibility, if not dominance, over social welfare policies designed to help victims of psychiatric conditions.

The enormous size and scope of problems of psychiatric disorders has come to light only in relatively recent times and as a consequence of the maturation of the field of psychiatric epidemiology. Prior to this time, developments in the theory and practice of psychiatry as a medical

---

928 Ernst 1987: 170.

929 Dörner 1981; Castel 1988; Foucault 1965; Porter 1987; Scull 1984, 1989, 1993.

930 Fabrega 1997, 2000.

discipline in European countries, including England, involved a slow but steady progress in the definition of psychiatric disorders and their separation from general medicine and neurology in particular.[931] In the population at large, the steady rise of psychiatry to a position of medical influence was partly based on increasing awareness in the population of the kinds of widespread emotional and behaviour problems that were ascribed to maladies and disturbances of the mind and to socially marginal populations.[932] The details of this process have been discussed previously and need not be gone into further detail here.[933]

The important point is that in the history and evolution of mental illness in pre-modern India one cannot identify a fully secular, scientific movement toward understanding psychiatric conditions, as was the case in the West. This is a factor that explains why Western ideas have been hindered by the valuation and intellectual resonance, and hence, impenetrability, of indigenous cultural psychology and social traditions about mental health and illness discussed earlier. Here, one must include not just Indian medicine per se but also a number diverse philosophical, spiritual, theosophical, and moral traditions and practices. Not only do these traditions conceptualize and handle mental health problems differently, but also they can impede efforts to change and modernize deeply entrenched notions about being, metaphysics, and cosmology that constitute what mental health means in India.

Colonial initiative built into the enterprise of colonialist medicine has given higher priority to other social problems, in particular, the threat of infectious disease, infant mortality, and the generally low state of public health, poverty, and low take-up of education. Coping with these problems effectively consumed efforts of administrators and resources at their disposal not only to manage a hegemonic colonialist regime, but also to promote the growth of scientific understanding of disease, especially in tropical India. As a consequence, notwithstanding differing time horizons and time lags, from its inception the early spread of modern mental health principles and scientific psychiatry has been impeded by a lack of understanding of mental illness and by a dearth of economic and technological resources. An associated problem has been lack of appreciation of modern conception of mental illness and the

[931] Berrios and Porter 1995.

[932] Porter 1987.

[933] Fabrega 1992a, 1992b, 1997, 2000.

small number of committed advocates of improved mental health practices compared to European societies.[934]

A central problem during the period when biomedicine became incorporated into Indian society and supervened as an instrument of state policy involved what was to be done about the indigenous ayurvedic, Siddha and Unani systems of medicine. This involves a tale that can only be mentioned briefly in route to a description of the main focus here, namely, the fate of modern psychiatry in India. As suggested earlier, spread of colonialist medicine involves a complex story of deemphasis and disregard, if not denigration, of the cultural and social, as well as medical importance that indigenous traditions of medicine have always had and continue to have in Indian civilization. Each one of the three traditions and especially Ayurveda had evolved a well-established position about disease including mental illness as secular and natural phenomena. Indians historians of science and medicine extol this scientific vision in contrast to ideas of folk, popular practitioners who are viewed as exponents of what are euphemistically termed magico-religious.[935] In reality, as earlier chapters have made clear, Ayurveda and, indeed, all pre-modern scholarly systems of medicine, are consistent with and owe their cultural validity precisely to fundamental social, moral, religious, and soteriological ideas about nature of existence.

Non-literate, non-academic, folk and popular traditions of holistic healing were part of the social fabric and texture of the cultural psychology, philosophy, and religions of India that nurtured its indigenous psychiatry. To qualify them simply and dismissively as magico-religious or as involving forms of faith-healing is to reflect not only a modern, Western ethno-centrism but to completely miss the power, meaning, and vitality of indigenous medical and psychiatric traditions. They represent impediments to the spread and imposition of modern psychiatry, not only in India proper, but across the spectrum of non-industrial, modernizing societies.

The ideal of a culturally sensitive psychiatry is to blend the best that modern scientific knowledge has to offer about psychiatric disorders. This requires an appreciation of how individuals and families are affected by and cope with psychiatric conditions in light of their own cultural psychology and world-view. And, to complete the line of thought,

---

[934] B. Banerjii 1981, 1985; Arnold 1988; Mehta 1995.

[935] D. Chattopadhyaya 1977.

efforts to medically and psychiatrically modernize India involve appreciation of its population beyond the educated and urban sector to resort to indigenous ayurvedic physicians as well as local, popular magico-religious practitioners.

The slow movement of modern Western ideas and practices about mental illness into the India of the late nineteenth and early twentieth century is but a faint echo of related developments in Britain and Europe. In the West, owing to special cultural and historical antecedents, developments in treating behavioural and emotional problems were given a cultural rationale and hence a social license of authenticity, as well as a relatively open field of operation. Basic assumptions, categories, and practices that enabled modern psychiatry to achieve social influence in Europe and Britain grew out of distinctive social, cultural, politico-economic, and historical conditions that rationalized how mental illness and its control were to be constructed. In India, comparable developments had to contend first with the obstacle posed by basic problems of disease and public health and second with the challenge posed by a complex web of very different traditions and values surround psychiatric phenomena.

In the West, liberal, modern, secular ideas about the nature of experience, behaviour, and social, politico-economic order developed in concert with the social philosophy of biomedicine and the nature of psychiatric phenomena. Development of secularization, loss of religious meaning and values, disenchantment of social reality, and massive dislocation, under the impetus of industrial capitalism, of structures that maintained psychological stability and social order are examples of phenomena that problematized psychiatric conditions and made them objects of public concern in the West during the nineteenth century. In actuality, pre-modern notions about the nature and being of personal and social identity began to change during the eighteenth century. Such notions slowly yielded to liberal modernist ideas during the nineteenth century. However, in India a comparable transformation of pre-modern thought worlds and habit patterns did not evolve at a measured pace of social validity and influence as it did in Europe. Moreover, one can argue that while liberal, rational ideas of the Enlightenment did not spread across the whole of India as it did in the territories of modern Western nations, their effects on the transformation of Indian lifeways has wrought more disruption precisely because of their abrupt imposition and deep roots and wide expanse of traditional ideas embedded in cultural psychology and social institutional life.

Obstacles encountered

Following the Mughal Empire and up to the modern era emotional and behavioural breakdowns were handled by cultural traditions and practices, medical as well as non-medical, which were more or less in balance. Ayurveda involved the academic and scholarly medical component of the indigenous psychiatry. Popular medicine complemented it. In addition there existed a range of non-medical personnel who could provide aid and comfort to those burdened with emotional distress and behavioural disaffection. Signs and symptoms of psychiatric condition were amenable to non-medical means of healing. Afflicted persons and their families had access to village elders, regional court administrators, experts in the theory of *dharma*, temple priests, leaders of devotional sects, and local persons in charge of sanctuaries. At the pinnacle of the indigenous psychiatry, the loose confederation of mental health institutions stood scholarly physician-practitioners of Ayurveda, Siddha, and Unani medicine.

Undoubtedly, non-medical personnel were limited in their knowledge of the many ramifications of psychiatric conditions. The problems of children and juveniles, who did not conform to acceptable standards of behaviour or who posed problems to families and communities, may not have been amenable to traditional forms of religious influence and social persuasion. Recalcitrant cases may have been met with harshness. Those who transgressed community boundaries of social control or committed antisocial criminal acts were handled through the justice system, with little attention given to possible mitigating factors. And finally, the unfair and harsh treatment of women in a misogynistic society and the oppression of disfavoured castes did not easily get defined as systems of oppression that caused enormous stress and psychological trauma. Thus, there existed harsh social practices in the society at large as well as deficiencies, even outright abuse, of many individuals and groups, not only those vulnerable to psychiatric conditions.

However, negative characteristics of the society have to be viewed in context of the strengths and mental health promoting features of Hindu traditions. The diverse set of beliefs that enabled individuals to make sense of the human situation and promoted hope through philosophical understanding, meditation, devotion, and philosophical release also provided diverse practices and personnel who could instruct, guide, and restore. Hinduism, of which Ayurveda is an integral part, encompasses diverse tenets and practices that are conducive to the promotion of emotional and physical wellbeing and restoration of health and morale when adverse conditions threaten to push vulnerable individuals over the threshold of toleration.[936] Furthermore, not only was the indigenous psychiatry of the subcontinent, not inadequate or wanting, but that which was to follow was not all beneficial or sanguine in its implications. The limitations, biases, insularity, and partiality of modern secular beliefs and practices inherent in modern psychiatry and mental health need to be appreciated. In many respects, they fit poorly and inappropriately in relation to Hindu traditions. One must also take into account the potential damage that biomedical psychiatric colonization can bring through its often insensitive and pernicious disregard for time-honoured and tested traditions of mental health. Western-trained social planners are intent on bringing the best of modern psychiatry to the subcontinent, but their goals can sometimes obscure the way it can undermine morale and hope.

Politicians, social reformers, policy makers, and influential physicians and psychiatrists of India have sought to create an awareness of the problems of mental health so as to develop an effective policy since before Independence in 1947. The Health Survey and Development Committee, known as the Bhore Committee, surveyed mental hospitals in India in the 1940s. Besides calling for improvements in the nation's 17 mental hospitals, the Committee's report of 1946 also recommended placing a system of mental health under a director-general of health services and demanded more trained personnel. At Independence, India is said to have had fewer than a dozen mental health professionals and only 10,000 psychiatric beds.[937] The Bhore Committee's recommendations led to the establishment of the All India Institute of Mental Health in Bangalore in 1954. Since then, special committees have emphasized the need for more mental health services, hospitals, training facilities, and research pertaining to all kinds of behavioural disorders, including social psychiatry. A draft of the Mental Health Act was prepared by the

---

[936] Wujastyk 2003.

[937] Murthy 1998.

Indian Psychiatric Society in 1949, and, because of political delays, the bill was not passed until May 1987.[938]

Developing an effective mental health policy and a responsive system of health care has been difficult. Narayana Reddy, who examines the road to an effective mental health program in India, emphasizes that mental health services have long been neglected in the country.[939] Although the ancient system of ayurvedic medicine gave mental health equal importance with bodily health, more modern credos about disease and mental illness have failed to do so. Moreover, those whose interest lay in rapidly modernizing an inherently tension-ridden society have pushed to segregate mentally ill persons in institutions for maintaining public order. In short, while the growth in understanding and treating physical health problems has been relatively fast and impressive, mental health services in India have lagged far behind, because of the antiquated misconceptions of politicians and administrators who assume that mental illness is uncommon, treatment is ineffective, rehabilitation is impossible, and segregation and confinement necessary.

Currently there are calls for change in attitudes toward mental health in contemporary India. Murthy notes the effects of stress, the close interplay of mind and body in all forms of disease, the pernicious effects of psychological trauma, recognition of suicide as a mental health problem, the mental health needs of women and children, the importance of child development, and the adverse social and psychological consequences of rapid social change.[940] Shah addresses the current and future status of forensic psychiatry in India. Traditional systems for coping with mental health, he notes, covered all aspects of social conduct, from religious devotion, which was often inseparable from obedience to norms of proper behaviour, to duty, morality, and obligations to family and neighbours.[941] Traditional institutions also included the criminal justice system, which was characterized by uncompromising strictness that ignored mitigating factors pertaining to psychopathology.[942] Recall that the Dharmaśāstras regarded madness and insanity as nullifying a contract. These codes did not take the afflicted

[938] Narayana Reddy 1992.

[939] Narayana Reddy 1992. See also Murthy 2004.

[940] Murthy 1998.

[941] Shah 1999.

[942] Chakravorti 1996.

person's plight into account, or recommend care, compassion, and understanding.

Shah calls for moral, legal, and clinical awareness of the plight of the mentally ill in India. Using European history for comparison – for example, legislation covering the insane, recognition of the special needs of the criminally insane, and the campaign to reform asylums, Shah takes stock of where India stands and where it needs to go, as a democratic nation, in legal and clinical areas, in teaching and training, and in research. He calls for mental health legislation, especially measures recognizing the crucial role of treatment for the mentally ill, judicial safeguards for patients' rights, such as the disposition of the property of allegedly mentally ill persons. Measures are needed to protect children and juveniles from unwarranted cruelty and restraint. He covers the insanity defence in criminal trials, substance abuse, and suicide, emphasizing the viewpoint and standards of modern psychiatry.

INDIAN PSYCHIATRIC CONDITIONS THROUGH THE PRISM OF MODERN PSYCHIATRY

Restraint and caution should be shown when analyzing differences in community prevalence of psychiatric condition in India compared to Western nations. There are obvious limitations in the findings because of analytical problems as well as differences in procedure. The cultural psychology of India plays a distinctive role in how psychiatric conditions are understood and expressed in socially meaningful behaviours. It is difficult to accept all of the assumptions underlying the universal, pan-cultural point of view regarding psychiatric diagnosis: first, that psychiatric disturbances are reducible to the same forms, once distracting cultural trappings are removed; and, second, that language and culture play a comparatively unimportant role in shaping manifestations of psychiatric conditions and that problems can be overcome by merely translating concepts and terms that capture the Western-based criteria of diagnosis.

There are two important questions about the character and emplacement of psychiatric conditions in India that need to be considered. On the one hand, general medical health problems are strongly associated with symptoms and signs of psychiatric condition; furthermore, many victims of such conditions do not seek the help of psychiatrists and instead go to medical outpatient clinics as well as to religious establishments. Both of these realities echo the emphasis in Vedic and ayurvedic medicine on the mind–body and natural–metaphysical integration of human suffering. Physical signs and symptoms are commonly associated with social, psychological symptoms in clinical syndromes of psychiatric condition; moreover, people's perceptions, beliefs, and general interpretation of their maladies are typically seen in spiritual, moral, and religious terms.[943] The four Vedas (especially the *Atharvaveda*) and the Ayurveda are early statements of these ideas, and they continue to shape the cultural psychology of India.[944]

Weiss and colleagues document the overlap in bodily and 'purely' psychological symptoms among contemporary samples of patients suffering from medical and psychiatric disorders.[945] Indeed, bodily manifestations of many psychiatric conditions (a finding ordinarily construed as somatization) are common and compelling among the mass of people in India, like many other indigenous and ethnic groups around the world. This finding supports the idea that there is a negative bias in the internationalist psychiatric diagnostic systems in favour of emotional and other mental characteristics and against bodily problems per se. This has been called the psychologization of psychiatric condition, devolving from how mental illness was dealt with in European societies, ultimately based on mind versus body thinking.[946] In modern psychiatry somatization is frequently viewed as a contamination of physical symptoms in what should be a psychological-emotional domain. That bodily signs and symptoms are prominent components of human suffering in India comes as no surprise. An integrated, psychosomatic and somatopsychic language for describing distress and suffering existed as far back as the *Ṛgveda* and the *Atharvaveda*.[947]

Sen studied the prevalence of psychiatric disturbances in three primary health care clinics in Calcutta.[948] The Clinical Interview Schedule (CIS) was used to determine psychopathology. This is a standardized

---

[943] Opler 1958.

[944] See Kakar 1981.

[945] Weiss *et al.* 1986, 1988, 1992.

[946] See Kirmayer 1984; Kleinman and Good 1985; Kleinman 1988.

[947] Blair 1961; Roşu 1981.

[948] Sen 1987.

semi-structured inventory that was used in Brazil. With a 95 per cent confidence interval, the figures estimated total morbidity for psychiatric condition to be 41.5–59 per cent. In other words, virtually half of persons being seen in the primary health care showed a diagnosable psychiatric condition. Interestingly, only 1 of 101 patients identified had received prior psychiatric treatment, whereas all had sought care from traditional mental and physical health practitioners.

Of 500 adult patients, not acutely ill, chosen randomly from a general medical outpatient, non-psychiatric department in Bombay, 57 per cent received scores on the General Health Questionnaire (GHQ) that indicated psychiatric morbidity.[949] From this number, 50 randomly selected patients were given a direct psychiatric evaluation, and of these 50 per cent were found to be suffering from a mental illness. Finally, Prakash and Murthy demonstrated a high prevalence of psychiatric caseness, particularly depression among menopausal women from an outpatient gynaecology clinic, women who presumably also showed bodily symptoms.[950] These studies show that many general medical outpatients, ostensibly seeking care for a self-defined physical problem, often manifest a clinically significant psychiatric condition.

Finally, there is the question of psychiatric condition, including somatization in non-medical populations that one can presume to be at risk for social and psychological problems. Sharma and colleagues studied individuals who had been legally confined for begging in a beggars' colony of Bangalore.[951] They reported a period prevalence of 13.1 per cent for serious neuropsychiatric morbidity, some replete with somatic symptoms, including functional psychoses, epilepsy, organic psychoses, mental retardation, and schizophrenia. Moreover, even more common conditions, which were associated with bodily symptoms, such as neurosis and somatoform-like disorders, were not even searched for.

Satija and colleagues randomly selected 20 subjects from five rest houses who were in attendance at the famous temple of Rajasthan, in Mehandipur Balaji.[952] Those in the sample were young, educated, and comparatively well-off. Direct clinical interviews found that the vast majority (92 per cent) suffered from psychiatric ailments as against

[949] Bagadia *et al.* 1986.
[950] Prakesh and Murthy 1981.
[951] P. S. V. N. Sharma, Muralidhar, and Gopinath 1985.
[952] Satija *et al.* 1981.

purely physical problems (8 per cent). Of the former group, most suffered from neurotic (48 per cent) and psychotic (28 per cent) disorders.[953] Entering a state of trance was assumed to be requisite for obtaining benefit, but only about half of the subjects were able to enter such states. Results indicated that approximately one-quarter, mainly the psychoneurotics, showed different degrees of recovery following trance experiences. This led authors to conclude that in cases of spiritual treatment of psychiatric condition, a fair proportion of subjects are able to find relief. More generally, these results suggest that many of individuals and families, perhaps of a more traditional orientation, who seek spiritual help for fulfilment and who undertake a period of rest and residence at religious temples may exhibit high levels of psychiatric morbidity, all of which can be expected to include somatic symptoms and be thought of by the afflicted individuals as simply medical or physical. These findings support generalizations discussed earlier: a medical idiom consistent with tenets of Ayurveda and Siddha provide the model or exemplar of sicknesses that include psychiatric condition.

The overlap of bodily and mental symptoms and signs in psychiatric syndromes is only one element in how Indian culture and society shapes manifestations of psychiatric condition. Equally important is the question not of whether but of how manifestations of psychiatric disorders that are the staples of international diagnostic systems (depression, mania, and anxiety) are shaped and moulded by Indian cultural psychology. The potential influence of culture on psychiatric condition in India is revealed in how moods and emotions are experienced, described, expressed, and interpreted. Psychological phenomena are not static entities, but complex responses to social circumstances and biological perturbations that are perceived in culturally patterned ways and played out in cultural scenarios of meaning. They are psychological events that tell complex cultural narratives with subtle subjective nuances. The metaphors and other conceptual models used by a people to make sense of social reality and its effects on experience and behaviour vary significantly across cultures and languages. This takes place despite the obvious anchoring effects of body structure and spatial orientation that function as universal grids on which thought and experience are configured and accounts for the differences in how emotions

---

[953] Satija *et al.* 1981: 250.

are registered and experienced, including emotional disturbances.[954] How this applies to psychiatric condition in India has not been tackled in any systematic way.

One might expect the Hindu world image and Indian cultural psychology to have an influence on behavioural breakdowns and psychiatric disturbances dominated by thought and emotion. Any category of the internationalist diagnostic system could be used to test the universalist hypothesis prevalent in psychiatric practice today. Kulhara and co-workers provide numerous examples of the testing of cardinal feature of schizophrenia in Indian populations. Kulhara's work in the field of Indian and world psychiatry is exemplary from a clinical, epidemiological, and research standpoint, but what bears consideration here is what he leaves out of his gaze.[955] He argues that schizophrenia is not affected by the characteristics of specific cultures, and is sceptical about comparative studies.[956] He points out that extensive research involving the phenomenological features of schizophrenia – templates of experience and thought which come from Germany and later England – that has been conducted in developed as well as developing countries is not comparable to that of the West and hence suspect because it has not been based on structured or standardized methods of interviewing.[957] In other words, Kulhara assumes that schizophrenia has a standard definition and essence. He shows the Western view of what schizophrenia is and his goal is to study its transcultural aspects as described by traditional European sources: first-rank symptoms, delusions, and hallucinations. In his survey of diagnostic criteria and classifications of schizophrenia, Kulhara never touches on the possible influence of the cultural psychology of India on expression of signs and symptoms. Basically, he reviews how Western-defined parameters of schizophrenia in Western populations fit in with, or might differ from, those of Indian populations from a quantitative standpoint.

---

[954] Lakoff 1987; M. Johnson 1987; see also Lutz 1988; Kleinman and Good 1985.

[955] Kulhara 1994; Raj, Kulhara, and Avasthi 1991.

[956] Kulhara 1994.

[957] Kulhara 1994.

TRADITIONAL PSYCHIATRIC CONDITIONS IN MODERN ATTIRES

Introduction

Earlier chapters discussed the influence of cultural psychology of India on the construction of psychiatric conditions. To appreciate this one would like to be able to summon real-life psychiatric conditions as these were expressed in traditional times. In contrast to descriptions of presumably real case studies as these are preserved in Chinese traditional medicine these are not available for India. For the most part one has medical encyclopaedias and texts such as those described earlier. However, material gathered by cultural anthropologists on contemporary populations sheds light on traditional concepts and beliefs about self and experience and these are relevant to psychiatric conditions. Material obtained from studies by psychiatrists is usually biased by their emphasis on contemporary definitions of clinical phenomena and by overall changes in world-view of the people that stem from the political economy and psychology of modernity. However, many studies make a point of concentrating on respondents or patients that show traditional life styles. The accessible material provides snapshots of preserved constructs and beliefs that reflect, however imperfectly, what things may have been like in earlier eras.

Spirit possession through a clinical lens

In Chapter 4 attention was drawn to the high prevalence of beliefs in spirits and spirit possession in contemporary India.[958] It is very likely such syndromes and related psychiatric conditions have a long pedigree in the subcontinent. Opler's cases discussed earlier illustrated social contexts and cultural enmeshment of spirit possession. Echoing the importance of this phenomenon is the study by Varma and co-workers, who draw attention to the high prevalence throughout India of what they also term 'possession syndrome'.[959] They made observations during an epidemic of measles or chickenpox that caused a 'religious frenzy' and aroused 'mass hysteria' in the village setting in the vicinity of

---

[958] Venkataramaiah *et al.* 1981.

[959] Venkataramaiah *et al.* 1981.

Ranchi Mansik Arogyashala. The clinical manifestations of the viral infection is generally not viewed as an illness in the villages but is thought to result from a visit by a goddess.[960] A possession by the goddess or one of her seven sisters is thought to bring on the eruption. Strict rituals of quarantine, physical care, prayer, and feeding were carried out in the family following an outbreak.

The high number of cases of acute infection set in motion an 'epidemic' of spirit possession syndromes. These began when a girl of 11 felt a peculiar sensation entering her body and her right upper extremity grew heavy. She entered a trance and showed possession by spirit through dramatic changes in the tone and content of her speech, apparent altered state of consciousness, and body contortions and seeming convulsions. This incident of possession spread to other females and a boy aged eight.

The run of cases prompted Varma and co-workers to describe characteristics of possession syndrome as these manifest in local settings. During the possession the victim is thought special, shows behaviours that contravene social conventions, and is treated with deference and caution.

> People pay respect and prostrate before her. Her predictions are believed and her forebodings are awaited with a good deal of anxiety and apprehension. She speaks as if she were the god or goddess herself. In this state of her mind, she has no respect for her elders and treats them like her children. The episode lasts for a few hours ... Many of these ... do not come to us for treatment as they are not considered mentally ill by our people but occasionally, however, the excitement does not come down within a few days or ... becomes so unmanageable ... that they are brought to the hospital for treatment.[961]

Varma and co-workers proceeded to review cases brought to hospital over a 12-year period. Of over 42,000 admissions, 400 suffered from possession syndrome. It was possible to assign a diagnosis of psychiatric disorder to the patients. The demographic features, social and religious background, and clinical characteristics of the patients were discussed and analyzed. It is evident from this study that relatively few cases of possession are seen in this modern, biomedical centre; however, the possession cases that are seen also exhibit a bona fide psychiatric disor-

[960] Varma, Srivastava, and Sahay 1970: 59.

[961] Varma, Srivastava, and Sahay 1970: 62–63.

der. The researchers did not make clear that the possession behaviour itself was conceptualized locally as illness, but resort to biomedical care suggests this. It is very likely that many more 'possession syndromes' are found in the hinterland served by the medical centre but just not taken there.

Teja and co-workers studied in depth the clinical characteristics of 15 possession states brought to the attention of psychiatry department of the All India Institute of Medical Sciences in New Delhi.[962] This study included circumstances of admission and manifestations and provided insight about social context and cultural fashioning. The first case, for example, involved an unmarried Hindu girl of 18 who was brought to the emergency service in an excited state. Her 'present illness' included periods of unconsciousness with violent bodily movements, episodes of barking like a dog, talking as though possessed by a brother of hers who had died before she was born, and neglect of personal care. The patient had been taken earlier to a faith healer and ayurvedic practitioner. Other cases are described in terms of age, sex, and social background. Characteristics of these cases that illustrate the influence of social and cultural factors on the development and expression of psychiatric conditions are the following: past histories of social strain and conflicts with relatives and/or spouses, the 'naturalness' of beliefs in spirit and demonic possession, precipitating stressors in the life circumstances of the victim and family, symptoms and signs of diagnosable psychiatric disorders present in association with possession episodes, interweaving and accommodation of possession behaviour in the dynamics of family and community life, past histories of possession behaviour and of psychiatric conditions not accompanied by possession, and prior treatment by a variety of local, popular practitioners who appeared to function as the initial resort to care outside family.

Along with a range of other signs and symptoms, possession appears to constitute a common means for the expression of psychiatric conditions in India. While possession need not connote illness in a society and culture nor exemplify a psychiatric condition in the first place, the cases discussed by these research psychiatrists provide compelling evidence that such syndromes can and do register effects, correlate with, or actualize manifestations of psychiatric conditions, however these might be construed. Taken together, the prevalence of constructs and

[962] Teja, Khanna, and Subrahmanyam 1970.

beliefs in something like a 'possession syndrome', a culture pattern, the interpersonal tensions and conflicts, inevitable and recurrent in any social system, from and in which a syndrome arises and is enmeshed, and the interweaving of its dynamics and effects in the system of meaning suggest a long ancestry in populations of the Indian subcontinent and in nearby societies of Southeast Asia.

Obeyesekere, for example, has offered an in depth account of the idiom of demonic possession in a female living in a village in the Western Province of Ceylon who was possessed by *mala yaka,* an inferior spirit of a dead ancestor and who was brought to treatment to Buddhist monks.[963] Obeyesekere makes it abundantly clear that the culturally complex character of the way mental illness is understood and played out in this Buddhist society, pointing out in particular how social constraints and pressures impacted on the victim and how manifestations reflected her plight and appeared to cope with her predicaments.

All of this material involves contemporary varieties and enactments of psychiatric conditions. However, their setting, form and meaning leads one to infer that they demonstrate historically rooted and hence traditional ways in which social tensions, hardships, and oppressive dilemmas have been coped with in the subcontinent for generations. Altered states of consciousness, in this case involving possession, are and have been one idiom for the expression of psychiatric conditions in traditional India.

That states of mental dissociation are important in the way psychiatric conditions are fashioned in India is illustrated also by the study of Alexander and Das.[964] This study illustrates also the protean character of mental dissociation in India. The researchers draw attention to the inadequacy of the contemporary system of psychiatric diagnosis in international psychiatry as a means of properly classifying syndromes of dissociation. They studied 36 inpatient cases admitted over a two-year stretch with a diagnosis of dissociative, conversion disorder to one psychiatric unit of the Kasturba Medical College in Manipal. Not surprisingly, in keeping with the holistic expression of psychiatric conditions and the 'naturalness' of a somatic idiom, most of the patients were initially seen in the outpatient departments of neurology, cardiology, and general medicine and not brought to psychiatry. Alexander and Das

---

[963] Obeyesekere 1970.

[964] Alexander and Das 1997.

draw attention to a special form of psychiatric condition in India that they termed brief dissociative stupor.[965] Eighteen of the 36 patients were assigned this diagnosis. It consists of recurrent, short episodes (less than one hour) of profound interference in motor functions and responsiveness not associated with speech or spontaneous and purposeful movements, which are virtually absent.[966] The syndromes were usually followed by amnesia. Interestingly, in the sample of cases they studied none showed trance and possession disorder. Approximately one-fifth of the 36 patients showed dissociative convulsions.

How mental dissociation manifests, how it is handled, what family members believe is the appropriate course of action, the influence of education and social background on such views, and where they are referred to and why are factors that are undoubtedly changing in relation to the impact of modern society and culture. However, that psychiatric conditions bearing the imprint of mental dissociation have a long lineage in Indian communities is difficult to refute. In general, spirit possession and dissociative states often exemplify psychiatric conditions as contemporary psychiatrists define them as well as a traditional idiom of *unmāda* that goes back to ayurvedic times and undoubtedly into the Vedic era. One feature of a vibrant cultural psychiatry seeks to interpose contemporary constructs of psychiatric conditions with traditional ones.

A cultural phenomenology of psychiatric conditions?

In the way a psychiatric condition is understood and expressed in symbolic behaviour, one obtains a window into its cultural meanings and social implications. In any contemporary setting the resulting picture of behaviour will naturally reflect the impact of modernity, and in a nation like India whose traditional past still lives in thought worlds and habit patterns, modernity brings clashes in thought patterns and lifeways. 'Modernity' here involves, for example, politico-economic upheavals, high levels of urbanization, poverty, challenges to traditional meanings, values, and coping resources, and the cultural significance and social implications now associated with psychiatric conditions. Viewed in abstract terms, some of these factors are trans-historical: likely to have been present in earlier historical epochs. All peoples, and especially

[965] Alexander and Das 1997.

[966] No convulsive-like phenomena in this type of dissociation.

those of the Indian subcontinent, have been subject to repeated stressors and clashes of traditions, religious emphases, and ethnic differences. At least in part, colonialism and modernity is the last of a long list of social upheavals, albeit unique, momentous and with enormous implications. Nevertheless, viewing circumstances from afar, by examining the psychosocial characteristics and dynamics of contemporary cases of psychiatric conditions one may be able to extrapolate and hypothecate about related characteristics during traditional eras.

The Explanatory Model Interview Schedule (EMIC) consists of a protocol of questions that enable a clinician or researcher to tease out the inner meaning of a sickness condition. It was devised and refined by Byron Good, Arthur Kleinman, and other anthropologists and cultural psychiatrists of Harvard University.[967] The material this interview format seeks to recover exemplifies the quest of cultural psychiatry at its best and contrasts sharply with the usual way in which modern psychiatrists, including Indian psychiatrists, handle clinical phenomena. It has been applied to the study of clinical depression in India.[968] The interview schedule allows clarification of clinical profile, patterns of distress, perceived causes, and conventional help-seeking behaviours.

A common finding and assertion of researchers who study depression is that language of body – weakness, lassitude, pain, gastro intestinal malfunction – is an important idiom in terms of which psychiatric conditions like depression are conceptualized and expressed. Researchers were able to verify that in Indian cases of depression somatic complaints are frequently 'up-front' in the way patients present to a caretaker. However, by following up with questions that sought to elaborate on personal meanings they found that language of feelings and emotions was relevant and seemingly no less important in the cultural and psychosocial equation of psychiatric conditions.[969]

Here are three examples of the phenomenology and behaviour of psychiatric disorder of depression elicited by these researchers. It is not unlikely that in a traditional context and past era some of the phenomenological components of depression discussed below would have been embodied in a psychiatric condition, analogous, perhaps, to a depres-

---

[967] Weiss *et al.* 1992.

[968] Raguram *et al.* 1996, 2001.

[969] At least as the researchers, all clinically minded contemporary psychiatrists, viewed the matter.

sion disorder of today. However, since descriptions of symptoms are formulated in light of modern assumptions of self and experience, they may not necessarily have been 'up-front'.

> Whenever I sleep with my husband I get headaches like this. If I object to having sexual relations with him, he gets angry with me. The days he sleeps away from me, I am happy. But I cannot do that. This is my problem ... I have done some Karma to suffer like this. God has given me food, shelter and money. But he has not given me health. It must be written on my forehead. It is my fate to suffer like this. If this continues, I may even die.
>
> We have financial problems because we are not getting rains properly. Our crops are suffering because of this. The land has become dry. If we grow well we can earn. My mind (*manas*) always worries about how to manage the household if we don't get the rain. Before five years I did not have any problems at all. The rains were plenty and we were happier also.[970]
>
> *Nara* [the perceived cause of the patient's 'nerve illness', termed *nar kayile*] starts from the head and travels all over the body. This *nara* and the blood vessels are different. My depression [an unlikely gloss, condition, sickness, or *nar kayile* the likely label here] may be due to *nara* coming to a knot in the head. [At this point the patient demonstrated the process with her fingers.] See, the *nara* gets twisted like this in the head. My sadness may be due to this *nara* problem. Something must have gone wrong with the *nara* in my head. That is why I am having this problem.[971]

The way in which these psychiatric conditions are formulated and framed undoubtedly reflects the imprint of modern constructs and culture. In the quotes above, attention is drawn to how contemporary formulations of depression may reflect modern ideas (the mind as a separate repository). One may add that the tone of objectification and unvarnished presentation of intimate personal details might be the result of acquired modern ideas about sickness, social relations, the assumed 'natural domain' of psychiatric disorders, and female empowerment. Nonetheless, it is difficult to negate the view that the phenomenology and behaviour of these conditions were likely occurrences in traditional contexts and eras. The three cases, in other words, provide glimpses of

---

[970] In this case, 'difficulty in meeting our needs' may have been preferred idiom rather than idea of money or financial; 'I feel so distressed and worried about our situation', may have been preferred idiom, rather than idea of mind as a separate space.

[971] The three examples are quoted from Raguram *et al.* 2001: 40–41.

how psychiatric conditions were likely to have been emplaced in the categories of thought, emotion, calculus of social relations, and strains of everyday life.

An interesting idea that these researchers posed, studied, and obtained supportive evidence, for in a separate study was that a preferred somatic language for depression was the result of social stigma associated with mental illness in India. In general, psychiatric stigma has a long history in India.[972] In his dissertation on *unmāda*, for example, Weiss indicated that from ancient times marriages could be annulled should one of the participants develop this condition or, more to the point, was suspected to have harboured it prior to the marriage. To this day, researchers have shown that psychiatric stigma is manifest in primary care workers and caretakers who look after patients with chronic psychiatric illness.[973] It continues to represent an important topic in applied social and cultural psychiatry.[974] Further aspects of psychiatric stigma in contemporary India are taken up later. However, it should be pointed out that the genealogy of psychiatric stigma in traditional India as per victims of psychiatric conditions, the roots and sources for this, and its influence in contemporary societies over and beyond those who care for psychiatric patients needs full explication.[975]

Returning now to the idiom of somatization as studied by Raguram and co-workers, they demonstrated that cases of depression in which emotional, psychological signs and symptoms were more predominant compared to somatic ones were associated with a higher score on a stigma scale. The researchers found a positive association between the prominence of what they regard as essential symptoms of depression (emotional distress of various types) and scores on a stigma; whereas a negative association obtained between stigma and prominence of somatic symptoms. They conclude that in their conceptualization of a typical depression, 'symptom expression is governed by the perceived stigma attached to psychological problems'.[976]

These researchers imply, then, that depressions that 'hurt in the mind' are associated with more sense of social shame or stigma, whereas

---

[972] Raguram *et al.* 1996.

[973] Chowdhury *et al.* 2000.

[974] Weiss and Ramakrishna 2006.

[975] For the scope of the problem in one region, see the study by Raguram *et al.* 2004.

[976] Raguram *et al.* 1996: 1047.

those that are contained within and mainly 'hurt in the body' are less likely to bring, or be associated with, stigma. Somatization in depression, they suggest, shields against stigma and may represent a (voluntary?) defence against the stigma that comes with revelation of emotional symptoms. This conclusion may be valid, but the researches failed to control for severity of the depression as a whole (compared to prominence of specific types of signs and symptoms). In other words, it may be the case that in more severe depressions emotional framing of illness is more prominent and simply elaborates or 'spills over' into and may even entail stigma as a social psychological component of the condition.

Raguram and co-workers are compelling in their analysis of what psychiatric stigma is like in India in the contemporary period. For example, they point out:

> The social meaning of somatic symptoms is less distressing because they closely approximate experiences that everyone has from time to time. Depressive symptoms [those which they regard as central to the modern disorder], on the other hand, are considered to be private and even dangerous. They are experienced as socially disadvantageous; they might interfere with marriage, diminish social status, and compromise the self-esteem required to perform effectively in society.[977]

This cannot be questioned and their data support this.

However, for purposes of understanding psychiatric conditions in a broadly comparative and evolutionary frame of reference, several questions are relevant: did something like our contemporary psychiatric disorders involving depression present in the traditional eras as psychiatric conditions predominated by somatic symptoms? Were the psychological manifestations regarded today as 'essential' of depression disorder (felt, expressed, and communicated sadness, fear, anxiety, worry) components of psychiatric conditions analogous to them in traditional settings of the past? Could it have been the case that emotional components of psychiatric conditions were predominantly somatic in presentation and that social stigma of the emotional was an important cause for this? Could it not be the case that depression as diagnosed today merely reflects conventions about self, mind, and body and that in a trans-historical, evolutionary sense 'depression', or however else one might want to label this chunk of the psychiatric phenomena carried by

---

[977] Raguram *et al.* 1996: 1048.

traditional Indian populations, is best seen as complex psycho-biological ensemble of manifestations.

The topic of somatization bears an obvious relationship to the Hindu conception of self as discussed by Kakar. He describes a unitary vision of body and psyche and contrasts it with the belief of dualism as found in Western societies.[978] He draws on the experiences of therapists and theorists who have studied psychosomatic aspects of medical problems in Indian patients. The latter, it is claimed, think about themselves and their experiences by means of their body organs. The theme of psychosomatic integration is indeed foundational in Hindu psychology and medicine and has already been mentioned. In Kakar's estimation, the following passage from the writings of Swami Sivananda represents the 'classical Hindu view' about mind–body relationships in the context of disease:

> The body with its organs is no other than the mind. The physical body is the outward manifestation of the mind ... Whatever you hold in your mind will be produced in the physical body. An ill-feeling or bitterness towards another person will at once affect the body and produce some kind of disease in the body. Intense passion, hatred, longstanding bitter jealousy corroding anxiety, fits of hot temper, actually destroy cells of the body and induce diseases of heart, liver, kidneys, spleen and stomach. When the mind is agitated, then this body also is agitated. When both the body and mind are agitated, the Prana flows in a wrong direction. Instead of pervading the whole body steadily and equally, it will vibrate at an unequal rate (unrhythmically). The food is not digested properly. Diseases originate. If the primary cause is removed, then all diseases will disappear.[979]

In summary, markers of psychosis, madness, insanity, and or behavioural dilapidations certainly posed a heavy social and psychological burden on those who suffered from them and their families in traditional India.[980] However, it is unclear whether such conditions predominantly shifted onto or away from a language of emotional distress and ills, and whether they were stigmatizing in that era. It is possible to argue that in light of the important influence ascribed to spirit possession, personality, and emotional manifestations in ayurvedic medicine, it

---

[978] Kakar 1981.

[979] Quoted in Kakar 1981: 215.

[980] And probably in all societies, for that matter, see Fabrega 1993.

is unlikely that such manifestations of a psychiatric condition were condemnatory, although it is certainly the case that such conditions were explained in somatic terms and deeply marked by somatic signs and symptoms. What this line of argument suggests is that psychiatric conditions, including depression disorder, are best conceptualized as psychobiological wholes, not just of the 'psyche', with disturbances found across systems of the individual, and that whether they were stigmatizing in earlier eras remains an important research question.

Opportunities for clarifying a theory of psychiatric condition

The study of Ayurveda leads one to the conclusion that the language of sickness distress incorporates dysfunctions of psyche and body, forming a natural amalgam. Medical facts formulated as somatization signal a dilemma of modern medicine and psychiatry.[981] This has been created by the meanings, pre-suppositions and models that Western theory of disease and medical practice has evolved. What 'somatization' stands for results from the fact that individuals when they seek relief for a 'sickness problem' often, or usually, depending on culture and society, enter a modern system of biomedical practice where ambitious and knowledgeable researchers of medicine are found, or they are contacted by epidemiologists conducting field studies in their homes. As a result the categories of information gathering and systematization of Western-trained clinician/researchers get applied to raw 'sickness problems'. The constructs and inquiries based on them proceed to delineate, shape and label sickness phenomena, providing a cultural (biomedical) slant on it. Exactly which station of the biomedical care establishment is contacted by the individual patient is critically important in establishing the future ontology, being or type of its condition. The basic point is that except for individual and, perhaps, significant group members, a sickness problem construed as a raw experience of a person has little or no name, ontology, identity in the biomedicine system prior to its entry there; and even thereafter, it will continue to have at least dual meanings, that of physicians/psychiatrists and that of patient, who has to cope with the perspectives offered by the physician.

It needs to be appreciated that a characteristic of stress-related maladaptive behaviour, especially when protracted, involves the production

[981] Fabrega 1989a, 1989b, 1989c.

of visceral somatic dysfunctions. Constructs inherent in the growth of modern biomedicine, a phenomenon which represents a cultural, historical development that among many things involves constructions about the body and about the self and its sense of embodiment, have stipulated different 'realities' to experiences, feelings, sensations, perceptions, and/or communications about the body. References to the body are said to represent 'real' or organic manifestations of disease pathology whereas other references are ascribed to psychological or mental disturbances that are described as also somatic in nature. In other words, somatization as a manifestation of psychiatric condition reflects imposition of a biomedical, historical and cultural bias: some bodily symptoms are real, whereas some are not; or alternatively, some are really in the body whereas others are not, but in the mind. Furthermore, one should keep in mind that the evolution of modern medicine and psychiatry has involved a selective, culturally biased rule or stipulation that removes some of the parts of a clinical picture of sickness – real somatic signs and symptoms – and assigned them to other medical diseases. For the most part, modern psychiatrists diagnose and treat a selected, medically screened population of sickness problems, not a natural population of psychiatric patients. Thus, when other medical, organic diseases have been ruled out from their population of patients, psychiatrists cope with biomedically enigmatic bodily symptoms and signs by construing them as somatization. A medical selection of this type would obviously not have been possible in ancient, traditional settings of India where ayurvedic physicians practiced, although cultural slants of different types would have been found.

It follows from this line of thinking that the data collected by Weiss, Raguram and co-workers based on ethno-scientific methods of elicitation in anthropology (emic) make this generalization about the cultural moulding of sickness phenomena abundantly clear. However, their analyses and conclusions at times fail to control for the bias of their medical training, a system of categories about the biomedical nature of disease. Indian medical and psychiatric problems, like those studied in traditional settings of India and reported by Indian psychiatrists, provide opportunities to clarify essential attributes of sickness and psychiatric condition. This is so because such problems and conditions are configured as different cultural ontologies and phenomenologies. When patients of ancient India saw ayurvedic physicians they would have highlighted their problems in terms of a blend of what they perceived and felt as per their native, traditional categories of meaning, on the one hand, and one the basis of their conception of what was appropriate for the examiner to know (what the latter expected or wanted to hear), on the other. Contemporary Indian psychiatrists, then, can be urged to listen to their traditional patients so as to better articulate characteristics of Indian sickness behaviour.

The influence of indigenous formulations of self and body

Several of the cases reviewed earlier illustrate how Indian conceptions of sickness (as involving knots, karma, *nara*) influence the interpretation and expression of the signs and symptoms of psychiatric condition. Basically, the latter consist of perturbations of experience, bodily function, and behaviour. Cultural formulations of self and body provide the material that configures them. This cultural embedding is illustrated by the importance given the way concepts of bodily fluids or substances are formulated in Indian philosophy generally and in the medical theories of Ayurveda more specifically. Vital ingredients of body are termed *dhātu* and each of seven of these is a refinement of the previous one. Zimmermann points out that chyle is concentrated into blood, which is then concentrated into flesh, then into fat, bone, marrow, and eventually into semen.[982] The word *dhātu* appears to be favoured for semen, the most perfect and powerful bodily substance. This is the case for both men and women, although the nature, amount, viscosity and the like of semen in the sexes differ. Many beliefs, rituals, and meditation practices linked to religion and philosophy are based on the need to preserve vital essence and guard against its dissipation. These range over diet, environmental factors, patterns of exercise, nocturnal emissions, turbid urine, masturbation, and the amount of sexual activity.

Thus, it is hardly a surprise that actual or perceived loss of semen is regarded as a potential health hazard, a source of worry and frank anxiety, and is regarded as causing an illness that can have grave consequences. The theory dealing with semen loss is found in the earliest ayurvedic texts. A psychiatric condition found in India today, termed the *dhat* syndrome, features anxiety, depression, and preoccupation with bodily functions and habits in relation to semen loss.[983] The following

---

[982] Zimmermann 1987.

[983] For its antecedents, see Raguram, Jadhav, and Weiss 1994.

signs and symptoms are observed: sense of weakness, fatigue, palpitations, insomnia, headaches, anxiety and depression, and loss of appetite. Patients are said to feel that they have aged prematurely and worry about the condition of their hair and skin.[984] What holds together this cluster of emotional and bodily distress is the fear, and sometimes delusional conviction that their semen is being depleted.

The so-called *dhat* syndrome, then, is an example of a psychiatric condition rooted in ancient cultural beliefs central to Hindu culture and ayurvedic theory of health and disease. Its core meanings are woven into Indian culture and psychology and are often accompanied by other psychiatric conditions.[985] Since this syndrome has been described in many ancient medical literatures of the world it is very likely not only to have been seen by practitioners of traditional India but by practitioners of other societies. Bottero, for example finds descriptions of similar preoccupations and syndromes for China and the Mediterranean basin.[986] In China it is termed *shen-k'uei*.[987] The syndrome illustrates how universal psychiatric phenomena – genetic or developmental vulnerability, anxiety and depression associated with social environmental stressors, ethnic formulations of body function – come together and in context of specific constructs and beliefs shape distinctive varieties of psychiatric conditions. Raguram and colleagues have reviewed the genealogy of beliefs about *dhat* syndrome in India but also discuss its prevalence in non-Asian populations and suggested that in America this condition shared behavioural and symptomatic features with neurasthenia.[988] They provide a broad, interdisciplinary, holistic framework for understanding syndromes that may reflect cultural varieties of a universal diathesis and vulnerability. Sumathipala and colleagues provide an excellent review of psychiatric conditions similar to *dhat* but framed in world context also.[989] They centre their discussion around the construct of culture-bound syndromes, namely, psychiatric conditions that allegedly are observed in relation to culture-specific beliefs about illness. They challenge

---

[984] Bhatia and Malik 1991; Singh 1985; Bottero 1991; Edwards 1983; Raguram, Jadhav, and Weiss 1994.

[985] Joshi and Money 1995; Raguram, Jadhav, and Weiss 1994; Mumford 1996.

[986] Bottero 1991.

[987] Wen and Wang 1981.

[988] Raguram, Jadhav, and Weiss 1994.

[989] Sumathipala, Siribaddana, and Bhugra 2004.

the isolationist account of such syndromes using *dhat* as an illustration of a psychiatric condition, where the content transcends national boundaries and is target of differing interpretations based on local conventions of meaning. Despite its cosmopolitan pedigree, something resembling *dhat* most likely has had a long presence in the subcontinent of India.[990]

Not just psychiatric conditions, but means of treating them are found reflected in the indigenous system of mental health practices of India. Emphasis has been given already to religious practices and ayurvedic textual representations or 'medicines' and systems of meditation. Three additional examples can be provided. Vahia and co-workers culled and streamlined essential elements of ancient medical and philosophical literatures an applied them with beneficial results to a sample of Indian psychiatric patients in a hospital in Kaiwalyadhama, a centre in Lonavla, near Bombay.[991] The study by R. V. Reddy and colleagues conducted among a semi-nomadic ethnic group found in Cuddapah district of Andhra Pradesh provides additional material.[992] They identified 14 plant species available in the locality used for the 'folklore' treatment of epilepsy, hysteria, fits of madness, and insanity. Here in this aboriginal group, in other words, such conditions are not only set apart and classified, but they have served as objects of speculation, study, and empirical treatment. Finally, Kulaichev and Ramendic studied the psychological and electroencephalographic correlates of meditation with the ancient tantric ritual drawing termed *Śrīyantra* that was used in ancient India.[993] This physical drawing and the practice of meditation associated with it was used by religious devotees for purposes of obtaining mental clarity, emotional stability and harmony, and a clearing of emotional distractions and worries linked to everyday life in religious communities. Most likely, monks and other practitioners prescribed the same practice for individuals experiencing religious, medical, or emotional distress found in association with psychiatric conditions. The elements of *Śrīyantra*, the researchers concluded, seemed precisely adjusted to mechanisms underlying perception, neural activation, induction of special psycho-physiological states, and heightening

[990] As discussed in Chapter 4.

[991] Vahia, Vinekar, and Doongaji 1966; Vahia 1969.

[992] Reddy, Lakshmi, and Venkata Raju 2000.

[993] Kulaichev and Ramendic 1989.

right cerebral hemisphere synchrony. It is reasonable to surmise that ritual practices such as these have a long pedigree in India.

Comment

All of the material reviewed in this section gives access to psychiatric phenomena of peoples of the subcontinent of India during traditional times. When one peels away incrustations wrought by modernity in all of its manifestations, one finds preserved in contemporary beliefs about sickness, traditions of philosophy and medicine, and methodologies of healing the impact of psychiatric conditions in traditional India. The social, psychological, and symbolic resonance of manifestations of such conditions can be appreciated. The way in which they were understood, formulated, and handled are archeologically recorded in the material reviewed and all point to the challenge such conditions posed to traditional society and the intellectual, scientific, and broadly humanistic framework of healing and social and cultural appropriation.

One should recall that persons of social and spiritual authority in ancient Indian communities influenced how psychiatric conditions were understood and dealt with and were thus highly influential in what happened to a victim. In Vedic times, Brahmin priests functioned as moral arbiters, ritual specialists, and healers and would have been consulted for their advice. Many of the hymns of the *Atharvaveda* suggest how such consultations were conducted. Anthropologists and psychologists provide illustrations of how healers in India today deal with patients exhibiting emotional and social behaviour problems and they provide windows of past efforts to heal psychiatric conditions. Kakar and Obeyesekere discuss the kinds of psychological insights offered by healers in India and other South Asian countries to whom victims of psychiatric conditions are taken.[994] No doubt such healers are representative of the types of healers that have existed in the region since medieval times and possibly even since classical times. In establishing that an afflicted person's psychological and behavioural difficulties are caused by bewitchment, sorcery, spiritual attack, or merely the jealousy and envy of group mates, healers can validate and thereby shape how a psychiatric condition is understood by others. Finally, as discussed earlier in relation to religious madness, devotional communities and the leaders

---

[994] Kakar 1982; Obeyesekere 1977, 1982.

and respected elders associated with them played an extraordinarily important role in how others relate to those showing manifestations of psychiatric conditions. Religious careers sanctioning ecstatic experiences, prophetic visions, meditation, and other ritual and devotional practices can be fashioned for persons who, on secular grounds, might otherwise be viewed as ill.

In these and other ways, then, those who debate the meaning and significance of a psychiatric condition must have exercised a strong influence on its configuration and enactment. At various times in different social and economic spheres, local, popular healers, priests, village elders, and leaders of a devotional community or sect have all influenced the course of an individual's psychiatric condition, having participated in the debate over the meaning of disturbed behaviour. In appropriating its significance they have domesticated such conditions and thus determined the fate of victims.

CAN AN AUTHENTIC INDIAN CONSTRUCTION OF PSYCHIATRIC CONDITION EMERGE?

The march of biomedicine across the cultural landscape, with mainstream psychiatry tied to its coat-tails, is the final chapter in the story of the evolution of sickness and healing.[995] It is indisputable that factors other than purely scientific validity and therapeutic power over the control of psychiatric condition per se explain the spread, invasion, and seeming victory of biomedical psychiatry over its traditional rivals in the battle over interpretation and treatment of psychological maladies and suffering. Powerful political and economic factors tied to world capitalism, profit-driven directives of pharmaceutical organizations, the personal drive of state officials for power and influence over local affairs, and the professional aspirations of emancipated, Western-acculturated psychiatrists all play a role in the spread of biomedical psychiatry. This is not to denigrate the intrinsic value of its scientific theories and demonstrated effectiveness of clinical procedures and medicines in alleviating much suffering. But a careful analysis of international psychiatry's spread should take into consideration several factors.

---

[995] Fabrega 1997.

As a civilization, India possesses its own authentic, unique version of medical psychiatry and a related confederation of social, religious, moral, and welfare-related institutions capable of withstanding the blandishments of Western biomedical psychiatry. The indigenous tradition is intellectually rich, diverse, spiritually sensitive, holistic, and grounded in an ancient cultural psychology. Biomedical psychiatry, objective, impersonal, rationalistic, scientific, and steeped in an individualistic view of man and society, is a product of another culture.

Each culture has its own versions of emotional and behavioural disaffections. What gets institutionalized as a system of mental health practices to cope with them includes many types of social institutions, not just medical (popular, academic). How a society exemplifies the psychiatric enterprise (its indigenous psychiatry), namely the nature and confederation of institutions, involves the promotion and maintenance of mental health, reflects salient properties of its history and culture. National versions of even the official medical component of an indigenous psychiatry can endorse the tenets of a pernicious political order, as illustrated in Soviet society, which created special varieties of schizophrenia that included indicators of oppositional, 'uncivic behaviour'. However, in a civilization where spirituality, religious devotion, and the concept of social obligation or duty are an integral part of the way being and personal experience are constituted, and where democratic institutions and values have taken root in spite of class distinctions, a humane, effective, and culturally authentic psychiatry is a real possibility.

Western biomedical psychiatry per se, or the seductive power of its ethos and political economy, exercises a strong influence in contemporary clinical studies of psychiatric condition in India. Derasari and Shah, for example, compared clinical pictures of depression in India and the US.[996] The authors coded a large set of symptoms for subjects in the two nations, mainly related to body complaints. Given that diagnostic criteria rely significantly on actual symptoms of emotional experience, the clinical method of diagnosis assures a fair comparability of symptom pictures between the two societies. Indian psychiatrists, with exceptions noted above, do not ordinarily handle patients showing depression in a way that facilitates the delineation of culturally specific manifestations in mood and affect. Thus, if these particular researchers had used indigenous criteria of experience and behaviour as a way delineating an

[996] Derasari and Shah 1988.

Indian exemplar of depression and compared it to depression among US patients, they might have explored another dimension of cultural differences. Instead, they relied on a preconceived, essentially closed, biomedical and Western model of the disorder.

Furthermore, because a non-traditional formulation of experience and behaviour was employed, respondents may have not volunteered essential elements of their suffering. Nevertheless, the study reveals interesting differences in the proportion of symptoms in the two samples. When patients were asked to volunteer up to five complaints, a request designed to elicit indigenously formulated descriptions of experience and culturally authentic symptom pictures, Indians mentioned five symptoms of a somatic nature, whereas US patients cited only one. Furthermore, on an inventory of 50 somatic symptoms, on 35 of these Indian patients reported higher levels, and on thirty of these the difference was statistically significant, at least to less than the .05 level. On four of the 15 symptoms in which US subjects showed a higher level, the difference was statistically significant.

There were no compelling differences when psychological symptoms were compared between the two groups, although personal experiences of depressed patients were expressed differently. Core symptoms of depression were similarly distributed in the two samples, which is hardly surprising, given common diagnostic criteria. However, in discussing the differences, the researchers draw largely on information from previous medical studies but include passing references to the cultural psychology of India. This study, then, illustrates the seductive power of biomedical psychiatry, in that its logic of diagnosis was imported wholesale without any attempt to elicit and induce a truly authentic yet comparable clinical entity for purposes of comparison. Yet it is tantalizing, in that it suggests how depression might be configured differently in India.

A similar lack of interest in delineating authentically Indian representations of psychiatric conditions is found in Kulhara and Prasad Rao.[997] They studied obsessive-compulsive neurosis in northwest India. US psychiatric diagnosticians working with US populations evolved the diagnostic criteria although ultimately the criteria stemmed from

---

[997] Kulhara and Prasad Rao 1985.

German psychiatry.[998] Thus, it is interesting that an almost exclusive Western theoretical psychology was used to make sense of the phenomenology of this disorder among Indian subjects. No attempt was made to probe into the content of obsessions and compulsions, let alone the personal distress and social behaviour of these burdened patients, to uncover something authentically Indian. Left out of focus, then, were ideas about the possible fit, lack of fit, even conflict, between sociocultural defences and psychological defences and the consequences for the character of obsessive-compulsive phenomenology of this psychiatric condition in India.

Finally, there is the topic of manifestations of schizophrenia, mentioned earlier in a general way. Several studies have analyzed important phenomenological attributes of schizophrenia, namely, delusions and hallucinations.[999] Kala and Kala studied the phenomenology of psychotic jealousy, a clinical feature prominently associated with schizophrenia.[1000] Again, these authors all use a standard logic and methodology but did not probe aspects of experience and behaviour that might reveal clues to an Indian analogue of schizophrenia. Kulhara and colleagues and Arora and colleagues all essentially follow the same format: an excellent rationale and methodology of biomedical psychiatry that is almost completely lacking in interest in the possible cultural aspects of psychiatric phenomenology in India.[1001] The same can be said for Susser and colleagues on the symptomatology of transient psychosis.[1002]

Gopinath and Chaturvedi concentrated on carefully diagnosed schizophrenic patients and inquired as to the kinds of symptoms that family members found distressing and difficult to cope with.[1003] The researchers grouped manifestations of schizophrenia into several clusters in terms of meaningful content. For both diagnosis and symptom content, they relied on standard measures derived from the international community and made no attempt to derive categories from the standpoint of an Indian understanding of psychiatric condition, behaviour, or

---

[998] Seven structural varieties of obsessions, six involving the content of obsessions, and two structural varieties of compulsions.

[999] See Kulhara *et al.* 1986a, 1986b; Ramanathan 1982.

[1000] Kala and Kala 1981.

[1001] Kulhara *et al.* 1986a, 1986b, 1989; Arora, Avasthi, and Kulhara 1997.

[1002] Susser *et al.* 1995.

[1003] Gopinath and Chaturvedi 1992.

cultural psychology. The biomedical template was thus the grid through which they peered into how schizophrenia is or should be shaped and formulated in India. The commonest behavioural disturbances were signalled by an inability or refusal to work (64 per cent), not doing household tasks (56 per cent), poor personal hygiene (53 per cent), and a general behavioural slowing (53 per cent). Individuals that were not aggressive or psychotic but were sluggish and failed to care for themselves proved especially burdensome to family members. The authors occasionally commented on the differences between Indian perceptions and those of the West. They invoked cultural factors in one instance – a belief that supernatural factors might have caused the disturbances reduced the family's concern about aggressive and psychotic symptoms – and socioeconomic ones in another, because of widespread poverty in India, dependent relatives found it particularly distressing when victims avoided work.

An important theoretical issue in the study of schizophrenia involves the factors associated with or that might exacerbate symptoms and cause patients to return to the hospital. How relatives talk and relate to a patient whose disorder is in remission has received attention in the West, since the character of 'expressed emotion' in these exchanges has sometimes been shown to exacerbate the illness. Researchers have noted relatives' critical comments, hostility, excessive involvement, as well as displays of warmth and positive remarks to evaluate the possible impact of such remarks on patients' symptoms. This theoretical approach to studying the dynamics of schizophrenia *in situ*, that is, in actual interactions between patients and family members wherein fundamental elements of cultural psychology are visible, cuts to the core of the controversy between schizophrenia as a universal phenomenon or a culturally relative one. A theory developed in Britain specifies that a natural disorder like schizophrenia is exacerbated by Y types of family interactions that are reducible to sets of utterances measured by Z types of variables. A 'universal' science of psychiatry would assume that certain types of interactions and utterances between Indian patients and their relatives should produce the same results as in British samples, if measured appropriately.

Wig and colleagues, for example, studied the effects of expressed emotions by relatives of Indian schizophrenics, comparing results from Chandigarh, India, with those of Aarhus, Denmark, against the general background of British and US studies.[1004] A number of interesting differences were observed. Indian researchers attempted to standardize ratings in India and found it difficult not to 'drift away' from conventions established in England. Some measures could be 'satisfactorily transferred' from English to Hindi, such as critical comments. Remarks expressing hostility proved difficult, but researchers judged that these assessments were 'also likely to be transferable across the linguistic frontiers without significant distortion'[1005]. Reliability and transferability of the measures of relatives' over-involvement were 'less satisfactory', those of warmth 'clouded', and those of positive remarks 'peculiar'.

Despite these obvious difficulties, the researchers nevertheless compared Indian samples with patients from Britain and Denmark using standard instruments. They focused on relatives who had spent large amounts of time with patients, since their remarks were assumed to carry the 'negative weight' of expressed emotions. Interesting differences were obtained, too numerous to discuss here. Most of these differences were quantitative, reflecting different levels of a particular measure. However, measures of warmth were positively correlated with criticism in Indian families, whereas in Danish and most British families these factors were negatively correlated. This combination of emotions was judged troublesome not only because it was viewed as anomalous, but also because it was problematic in light of the theory about schizophrenia and its course.

In general, in the studies reviewed, the researchers explained in great detail the methodological difficulties of cross-cultural measures of psychiatric conditions, as well as the results of comparison between samples. In all instances, these explanations were intended to preserve the validity of the experimental rationale, the method of procedure, and the overall theory about schizophrenia and its course. That a particular type of emotion may not only be expressed differently from one culture to another, but actually have an entirely different meaning to those expressing them and to patients, was not taken into serious consideration. In other words, the experimenters do not consider the possibility that the cultural psychologies of India, Britain, and Denmark might differ substantially – which in turn might explain differences in what constitutes schizophrenia in those countries and its course generally – to say

---

[1004] Wig *et al.* 1987a, 1987b; see also Leff *et al.* 1987.

[1005] Wig *et al.* 1987a: 158.

nothing of what family communications consist of in an 'expressed' emotional sense. One should appreciate the subtleties and context-based differences involving emotional expression and how they may support, encourage, displease, discourage, or undermine patients diagnosed with schizophrenia.[1006]

Similarly, a rather quantitative and universalistic calculus – one might say bureaucratic and rationalistic – seemed to govern how relatives were identified and the evaluation of their role in the course of illness. Recall that relatives were chosen for assessment by the amount of time they spent with the patient. The definition and overall meaning of the roles of relative or patient could have been more fully developed, and the respective roles might have been subordinated to the overall meaning of the person who was the patient or relative. Similarly, the authors could have recognized that intra-family dynamics might differ between the two cultures, that one might be more family-centred and the other more person-centred, all of which affects how family members interrelate under the pressure of psychopathology. Similarly, using the amount of time spent with a patient as a critical measure of who qualifies as a significant relative reflects the ethnocentric notion that 'time matters and is of the essence', a quantitative view of family relations typical of industrial capitalist, Western societies. In other words, the quality of relations or communications, seen in the light of cultural values, and traditions can be equally important, if not more important, than time spent with a patient, but this again was not considered. Culturally sensitive parameters of family relations and of expressed emotion might reveal differences in what really matters to persons afflicted with schizophrenia.

The cross-cultural study of schizophrenia reveals interesting differences in the course of the illness and prognosis that have been staple themes in cultural psychiatry.[1007] On the other hand, because of its pancultural distribution and consistent prevalence across societies, along with its neurobiological features, schizophrenia has become a classic exemplar for those who seek to formulate phenomena of psychiatric interest in evolutionary terms.[1008] Unfortunately, Indian psychiatrists adopt a narrow and exclusive international perspective on the diagnosis

[1006] See also Shweder 1991; Lynch 1990a, 1990b; Lamb 1993.

[1007] Waxler 1979; Kleinman 1988; Verghese *et al.* 1989; Thara *et al.* 1994.

[1008] Fabrega 2002a.

of schizophrenia, although biomedically defensible, and even when given the opportunity to explore its potentially unique manifestations of cultural psychology, they fail to take full advantage of it. The special burden of stigma that this disorder places on females and which is felt by primary caretakers who look after them has been emphasized. A culturally sensitive definition of schizophrenia should ideally incorporate indigenous, traditionally shaped and construed signs and symptoms, even if they don't match official criteria. This would provide for a therapy to take place in a more culturally meaningful and satisfying way.[1009]

CLASH OF TRADITIONS: PSYCHIATRIC TREATMENT IN UTTAR PRADESH

Following its penetration into Indian society and civilization, and with its consolidation into the Indian system of medicine, modern psychiatry acquired a huge territory covering disorders that took different guises and shapes. As a social movement, psychiatry had to compete with cultural institutions and practices under the governance of various experts who had social credibility as upholders of traditional ideas and values relevant to mental health care in India. The insinuation of psychiatric concepts and methods into the indigenous system of psychiatry gave rise to sharp conflict of world-views.

Nunley concentrates on the rationales, procedures, and clinical practices of psychiatrists in inpatient wards and outpatient clinics of the leading university hospital of Uttar Pradesh.[1010] His study records the accomplishments of a quintessential, bona fide sponsor of modern scientific psychiatry in India, as well as describing some of the difficulties and conflicts encountered as a result of a clash of traditions. Over a period of 18 months in 1989–90, Nunley studied the social practice of modern psychiatry on a daily basis, observing interactions between psychiatrists and patients. He interviewed selected staff and faculty psychiatrists of the hospital, including residents in training. Some practitioners saw private patients in community settings, and interviews with them furnished information about the private practice of modern psy-

---

[1009] Thara and Srinivasan 2000; Thara *et al.* 1994; Thara, Kamath, and Kumar 2003.

[1010] Nunley 1992.

chiatry. Nunley also conducted a mail survey of the 1130 members of the Indian Psychiatric Association, comprised of psychiatrists who had finished their residency training, and received 318 replies, a response rate of approximately 30 per cent. Questions addressed respondents' views of psychiatry, their practice, and the position of psychiatry relative to other aspects of scientific medicine.

Nunley found that a strong sense of 'scientism' characterized the orientation of psychiatrists to their work. Conceptions of psychiatric condition and its care were integrally allied to views of the march of science in general, particularly biomedicine. Psychiatrists seemed to approach their work, deal with patients, and actually communicate their ideology and rationale about psychiatric conditions and its treatment with moral zeal. He suggests that this type of educational, almost missionary stance may have been a reaction to the negative view of psychiatry held by both the medical and the lay populations, where there was a prominent social stigma associated with psychiatry and its practitioners.

Nunley concludes that while there are exceptions, in general 'top' medical candidates in India usually do not choose psychiatry. Moreover, psychiatry seems to be devalued as a medical specialty by other physicians. The strong stigma attached to 'mental illness' in India seemed to 'infect' those who treated these conditions, for Indian psychiatrists often mentioned the condemnation surrounding the practice of psychiatry and psychiatrists. While these attitudes about treating 'crazy' patients are part of the profession in all modern societies, it is much stronger in India. He indicates that a stigma against psychiatry as found in Western societies is more pronounced in India, perhaps because identification with one's occupation is much stronger. As exemplified in the caste system, there is the belief that an individual absorbs qualities simply by contact with other persons and objects. This view is almost literal among the less educated but also present in a more subtle way among the educated and elite who ostensibly reject it.[1011] A factor contributing to stigma is that in India the boundaries of the self are thought to be permeable, 'open' to outside influences; aspects of other persons and indeed objects and agents of the behavioural environment (including psychiatrists) are

[1011] Nunley 1992.

thought to be able to 'move in and out' of the self and 'pollute' it, even to become incorporated in a person's constitution.[1012]

Nunley provides a graphic and illuminating picture of the clash between several traditions and practices involving medicine in India, particularly problems surrounding mental illness. For example, he notes psychiatrists' perceptions of other Western-trained physicians and how they viewed psychiatry and mental illness. The statements of psychiatrists about the activities of 'faith healers' (an unfortunate term, see below) provide a glimpse of psychiatric practice in the community where, although practitioners generally follow a humane approach to mental health care (providing support and advice, having discussions with family members, using humoral medicines), they also routinely perform some brutal, destructive procedures based in demonology and witchcraft.

Information about tenets and traditions of medical practice of indigenous practitioners, mainly ayurvedic, gave Nunley a profile of another system of medicine, suggesting how psychiatry was practiced in contemporary eastern Uttar Pradesh. The practice of academic, scientific medicine in India by biomedics and physicians of indigenous medical traditions serves as a comparison for how modern psychiatry was practiced. Nunley emphasizes the diversity of medical traditions in India that seem to play a role in the treatment of psychopathology, drawing attention not only to the biomedical tradition (which he terms the *allopathic* tradition) but also to homeopathy, biochemical medicine, astrology, and Yoga. In short, many practitioners who may not specialize in treating mental illness routinely see such patients in their practice. Nunley also emphasizes that this feature of psychiatric care sets India apart from Europe and the US.[1013]

However, Nunley calls 'faith healers' the principal 'competitors' of psychiatrists. This is an unfortunate term that covers the heterogeneous collection of practitioners who are not physicians but who follow local traditions of healing based on spiritual, religious, and humoral ideas and practices. Indeed, he describes faith healers as the first to be consulted not only for common, 'soft' varieties of psychiatric condition (depressions, anxiety, obsessive disorders, general run-of-the-mill neuroses, and psychosomatic ailments), but also for 'hard' varieties: The

[1012] Lamb 1993; Marriott 1976, 1990; Daniel 1984.

[1013] Nunley 1992.

'faith healers' were usually first in the line of resort of families whose normal life was undermined by signs and symptoms of a psychotic member. On the whole, Nunley found that psychiatrists were not hostile to 'faith-based' practitioners. The latter often referred patients that the psychiatrists encountered in their practice. While psychiatrists gave them mixed reviews, some psychiatrists frequently saw themselves as working in concert with local faith healers. However, while the more traditional, indigenous popular approach to psychiatric condition exemplified by faith healers shares certain characteristics with those of modern psychiatry, they also differ in important ways. This allowed Nunley to better explain some of the obstacles and difficulties attending the consolidation of modern psychiatry in contemporary India.

Nunley reports that during the period in which he made his observations of psychiatric practice in eastern Uttar Pradesh clinicians seemed to follow an 'epidemic' view of mental illness. By this he means that psychiatrists usually responded to his questions:

> in terms of the numbers of persons who are afflicted, treated, or recovered from mental disorders, as opposed to answering my questions with stories about particular cases.[1014]

An epidemic view also characterizes how psychiatric conditions are enacted and dealt with in this region. Such conditions are prevalent and psychiatrists are required to see an extremely large volume of patients on a daily basis. A first-come-first-served standard was followed in the clinic, meaning that practitioners of institutional psychiatry in outpatient settings sometimes saw more than thirty patients in one to two hours, thus spending no more than five minutes with each one. In inpatient settings, a family member is hospitalized along with the patient and helps with care and feeding, a practice necessitated by limited resources and the paucity of mental health personnel. Patients who are virtually incapacitated by (usually psychotic) symptoms are hospitalized, but the pressure of families and the need for patients to resume employment or return to household responsibilities usually means a relatively short hospitalization and a quick return home.[1015]

[1014] Nunley 1992: 320.

[1015] The equivalent of US state hospitals that provide backup residential, custodial care, but Nunley does not describe them.

Not surprisingly, drugs and shock therapy were the principal modes of treatment. Psychiatrists were personally supportive while taking histories, advising, and administering treatment. However, time constraints severely limited the possibility of even a supportive kind of psychotherapy. Problems caused by family dynamics, interpersonal conflicts, and/or clashes between traditional and modern ways of thinking and solving problems could not be effectively dealt with in an outpatient clinic because of sheer lack of time. Therapeutic transactions amounted to documents that record diagnosis and prescriptions for psychoactive agents. These documents authorized pharmaceutical agents as possible magic bullets, seemed to be stamps of approval and certification of modern psychiatry's newly acquired power. Medical documents validated its identity, meaning, scientific wisdom, and therapeutic power.

However, psychoactive drugs are readily available in India and do not require a prescription by a psychiatrist. Other biomedical and indigenous professional physicians may recommend them, and they are easily purchased in pharmacies. There is said to be a large underground market for these agents. The 'epidemic' conception of psychiatric condition and the pressure to 'do something tangible' that characterized psychiatric practice in this region of India thus extended beyond the work of psychiatrists. Drugs were an integral component of treatment not only among psychiatrists, but also among a large penumbra of practitioners and institutions, which applied them in an effort to control the high prevalence of social and psychological behaviour problems in modern India. The credo of modern psychiatry that relies on a medley of psychoactive agents is now seen as a panacea for the evils that modern culture has brought about in effacing older traditions of meaning and value.

An epidemic approach to psychiatric condition is also manifested in how diagnoses were discussed and drugs prescribed by psychiatrists. A 'shotgun' approach seemed to prevail. Psychiatrists were forced to 'cover' their activities by formulating alternative diagnoses and prescribed many clinically standard types of psychoactive agents not only to counteract side effects but also to allay complex sickness pictures that, from a strict diagnostic standpoint, were often ambiguous and could not be fully worked out, given time limits. Psychiatrists responded to the puzzles posed by patients' histories almost in a formulaic, textbook manner. Limited time and resources, and no doubt vast differences in education, seemed to rule out the psychiatrist's considering the personal, idiosyncratic subtleties that underlay patients' symptoms and problems instead of standard, textbook scripts for diagnosis and treatment. In other words, it is as if the repository of ancient traditions about the 'stuff' of psychiatric condition, how it was exemplified and interpreted in light of India's cultural psychology, the character of suffering, and existential implications, were simply cast aside and totally neglected. Perhaps it is the case that these psychiatrists really know that traditional methods have proven of no use and this authorizes their urgency to help patients who seek their services.

It would appear that a mix of culturally relevant factors are simply taken for granted in the quest for a 'quick fix' that promises to relieve miseries that now have acquired a new and illusory identity simply because they can be named with a new sacred vocabulary. Nunley comments:

> To act like a doctor in India is to take an epidemic view, deal rapidly with a huge patient load, quickly make provisional disease diagnoses, and prescribe drugs. To handle problems that are brought to them in any other way would make psychiatrists less like other doctors and more like gurus, spiritual counsellors, or faith healers, which are not what psychiatrists in India want to be.[1016]

Nunley opines that a traditional humoral approach to medical problems in India, a heritage not only of indigenous academic traditions but also of many types of folk practice, seemed to explain why psychopathology was viewed as a physical disorder for which equally physical modes of treatment were required. According to psychiatrists, patients espoused a somatic philosophy as a result of their medical experiences generally, although this perspective was probably how modern biomedical psychiatry and its disorders were being portrayed in the media and by psychiatrists. An epidemic conception of psychiatric condition in the minds of Indian psychiatrists thus seemed to correspond to the 'commodification' of medicine and medical practice in the minds of patients and their families. Nunley draws on the ideas of cultural anthropologists about general medical orientations in India.

An epidemic view of psychiatric condition and of its treatment also characterizes how victims of mental illness are identified, distributed in the community, and taken to clinics, and what happens when they meet

[1016] Nunley 1992: 434.

a psychiatrist. In general, as mentioned earlier, cases brought to the clinic have already been seen by an assortment of popular medical and religious healers, for example, priests, diviners, shamans, and local wise men as well as physicians of different persuasions. Acute problems seem to predominate, although in many instances these are associated with chronic conditions and pernicious family and social influences that psychiatrists feel powerless to contend with.

Physicians studied by Nunley usually prescribed a short-term supply of medications. This strategy was designed to save money, to be sure, but also 'puts out the fires' of disturbing symptoms and curtails side effects and dependence, while ensuring a return visit, at which time a patient's problems might be better clarified. Psychiatrists seemed to be involved in a public health practice designed to cope with widely prevalent community mental health problems. While many patients returned for follow-up visits and continued outpatient care, many did not. Indeed, psychiatrists seemed to feel that after they concluded treatment, patients would continue to be followed by local popular practitioners and faith healers.

Many healers, not just psychiatrists, seemed relatively unconcerned about the wide prevalence of the 'acute fires' occasioned by psychiatric condition. They saw the community as peppered with acute mental health problems, all connected to several systems of mental health care and strict medical care, and which were likely to continue to be handled in a pluralistic, public way following contact with a psychiatrist. Few case histories or descriptions of psychiatrists' interactions with patients included subtle details of the life circumstances, personal experience, or social ramifications of afflicted persons; apparently this aspect of psychiatric care was simply impossible to pursue, given how the institution was structured in this region.[1017] Thus the epidemic, public health model of psychiatric practice appears to preclude attending to the social, cultural, and psychological aspects of patients' problems. However, in seeking to give a general picture of how psychiatry functions as a system of mental health practice in contemporary India, Nunley may have been forced to concentrate on generic features while disregarding more personal aspects of doctor-patient relations, such as those provided by

[1017] There was more extended anamnesis and attention to the personal details that make up the content of psychiatric condition when patients were seen in private consultation.

Kakar in his study of indigenous traditions of mental health care.[1018] Kakar made it his task to interview and observe healers and their interactions with victims of psychopathology. His emphasis was precisely the insights and wisdom of a diverse number of local healers who were steeped in the knowledge of the culture, psychologically intuitive, long ago conditioned to the exigencies of epidemic care – and who were frequently knowledgeable of their client's problems.

Actual patients (individual victims) apparently played a comparatively small role in how psychiatry was practiced in this region of India. This may be true for the country as a whole, and wherever psychiatry has spread. Except for rare occasions, family members always accompany the patient when visiting the hospital clinic, sit in and often dominate history taking in outpatient settings, and, as noted, live with and attend the patient during hospitalization.

> The ones who control the records, compliance, and other aspects of Indian psychiatry are not the patients, but the patients' families.[1019]

Family members define what a psychiatric condition consists of, who needed treatment, and who should be consulted. One or more members of the family dictated the content and flow of doctor–patient relations when patients were finally seen by a psychiatrist. A family member also decided about admission to hospital and the appropriateness of discharge. The family controlled the administration of treatment and the patient's compliance with the medical regimen. This was true for both inpatient and outpatient psychiatry, and it appeared to be true for both general medicine and alternative, non-Western and popular forms of medical care, including that of faith healers. This has wide-ranging implications as suggested in earlier discussions: A 'social medicine', an erasing of the boundaries of personal suffering and a visible openness to things regarded as painful and private in the West, is a feature of mental and general health practice that probably has roots deep in the historic and prehistoric past of India.

The central role of the family in how psychiatric condition is configured, played out, and dealt with in India is hardly surprising, given the strategic role of the family in regulating and controlling social life in

---

[1018] Kakar 1982.

[1019] Nunley 1992: 324.

villages, towns, and cities. Indian culture does not promote an atomistic view of society, with persons seen as embodiments of individualism and autonomy. Instead there is a family-oriented, sociocentric perspective in which social responsibility and obligation are foremost. It seems logical that psychiatric condition should be seen as a family affair – even an affair of one's caste and religion, Indian cultural anthropologists contend, although this may be waning – and that psychiatrists may conceive of their patients as 'client families', shaping their decisions and recommendations in a way that reinforces traditional authority relations within the family. Given the open, group-connected character of personal identity, the social and moral emphasis of India's cultural psychology, and its emphasis on *dharma*, or obligation, not only for family members, but for groups defined by lineage, religion, occupation, and caste, this is understandable. Indeed, this is consistent with earlier generalizations about how psychiatric condition was configured and played out in ancient and medieval India.

AGING AND DEMENTIA IN INDIA

Social relationships and old age

In contemporary psychiatry the elderly are vulnerable to many distinct psychiatric conditions as well as to poor general health. How these inevitabilities were played out in traditional communities of the subcontinent constitute an important chapter in the social history of psychiatric conditions there. However, this was given scant attention in earlier chapters because of absence of empirical information.

In general, absence of formal welfare institutions means that in traditional societies tensions and conflicts can be expected to be pronounced when individuals live comparatively long lives, are unable to contribute to their own sustenance, and come to depend on others for care and support, particularly family members. With respect to India, themes given attention to in earlier chapters, for example, emphasis on moral obligation as exemplified in Dharmaśāstras, the high value placed on sons and on their relationship with mothers and their duty to care for parents in general, and conflicts across generations particularly between mothers-in-law and daughters-in-law, can be expected to create social dilemmas and problems with respect to the care of aging populations.

Key features of the cultural psychology of India are implicated in how Indians perceive and experience old age. As in so many other areas of social life, aging is viewed in light of traditional notions of family duty, moral obligation, authority, and responsibility for decision making. As indicated earlier, at least for the higher castes ('the twice-born'), an individual's life follows idealized stages during each of which appropriate forms of behaviour are expected. Four phases describe essential characteristics of how an individual's identity and life career is conceptualized. This begins during early youth when instruction in the Vedas takes place, followed by that of householder, ascetic retreats to forests, and ending with life as a renunciant. This social plan encompasses proper conduct between the sexes and within the family, especially behaviour by sons toward fathers and daughters-in-law toward mothers-in-law; the expectations of widows; how to cope with loss of energy, loss of will, and fatigue; and whatever constitutes normal psychological behaviour. Such an ideal life career obviously does not allow for pathology of body or mind. Yet one can surmise that all of these identities and routines can be warped by psychiatric conditions such the dementia associated with aging. To study behaviour of aging peoples in India provides an opportunity to examine conflicts between modernity and tradition in various social spaces of India.

Stages of life as exemplified in Dharmaśāstras indicate that a preoccupation with social responsibilities among family members had a high priority. The ideal stages of life culminate in withdrawal, forest dwelling, and renunciation but it should be obvious that options such as these are possible in only contexts in which health and resources permit. Given the inevitability of decline and poor health that come with old age, such alternatives are likely to be closed. Whether traditional attitudes toward the aged were upheld in practice and, more pointedly, how exactly the old and infirm were cared for in traditional times, is simply not known.[1020] Social structures, demographic patterns, mortality figures, and duration of life span might not have created problems and the hold of traditional values could have been strong. On the other hand, modernity causes social dislocation, shrinks extended families, heightens inequalities, objectifies and rationalizes social relationships and roles, and tends to create emphasis on individual responsibility.

[1020] L. Cohen 1992.

That these emphases will clash with traditional values goes without saying.

Vatuk encountered what one may suppose are remnants of traditional attitudes and values towards the age in an urbanized village in New Delhi.[1021] Her focus was on how adult residents and the aging members of the population conceptualized the prospects of dependency and need for care and of becoming 'a burden on others'. She indicates the salience of the notion 'that children owe their parents a tremendous debt' for their care throughout the life cycle.

> The concept of long-term inter-generational reciprocity is communicated to children at an early age, in a very direct and explicit manner ... [suggesting] that the care lavished upon the child has been motivated largely by the desire to ensure the parent's own security and wellbeing in old age.[1022]

What she encountered was a high level of concern and anxiety among the aging members of the village about the consequences of physical incapacitation and dependence. That village life has a public dimension and hence all residents were witnesses to the helplessness, pain, misery, and associated ordeals of infirmity no doubt underscored the realities of old age. Discrepancies between cultural ideals and real conduct were all too evident. Vatuk describes the constructs, general beliefs, and values that villagers have about the ideal and the contemporary that describes inevitable happenings as people lose control of their vital functions. Preparing for old age was an important preoccupation among the aging population and attitudes towards death emphasized the importance of dying early while command of faculties and ability to care for self and vital functions were present. Praying for death, in other words, was an appropriate activity 'even for those in good health and comfortable circumstances'.[1023] Disposition of property served as a fulcrum that parents could use to insure their wellbeing, and adopting or co-opting villagers or distant family for future care taking roles was not uncommon. Interestingly, in making sense of cautionary tales of the unfortunate spectacles played out on the stage of village life residents emphasized the prior behaviour of the person. The karmic debts in-

---

[1021] Vatuk 1990.

[1022] Vatuk 1990: 66.

[1023] Vatuk 1990: 83.

curred in this life in relation to others including family and not debts inherited from previous lives commanded attention of residents.

Lamb provides a detailed account of social relations among Bengalis of a rural community in West Bengal that complements the material reported by Vatuk.[1024] Her study elaborates on Indian conceptions and construction of personhood by detailing how residents of the village relate to one another emotionally. The sheer physical aspect of emotional exchanges are noteworthy – various kinds of bodily gestures, feeding, touching, and stroking and, in the case of sick persons and the elderly, cleaning the body. How bodies come into contact, communicate closeness and bonding or distance and fear of contamination, is an idiom of social relationships among kin and between members of different castes. Individuals monitor their relations and communicate their feelings toward one another through physical contact. Lamb writes that individuals appeared to sometimes build and avoid crossing boundaries between themselves. In other ways, they sought to become parts of one another by sharing and exchanging bodily substances, food, possessions, words, feelings of affection and even places of residence. These kinds of relations were described by the villagers as *māyā*, the 'net' of bodily-emotional 'ties', 'pulls', or 'connections' that comprised the worlds in which they lived.[1025]

Lamb also focuses on family members' ties with one another that included obligations and responsibilities. Each phase of life is associated with favours owed and debts paid in the human exchange of physical substances, moral conduct, responsibility and obligation, and finally love. Parents feed, clothe, love, comfort, heal, and clean the bodies of their children. The explicit understanding is that as parents grow old their children will provide for them, ideally as they have cared for their children. Lamb focuses on the practices and discourses surrounding old age, its various phases, how relationships change with age, the expectations, entitlements, and actual exchanges across age grades, connecting them with constructed notions of personhood and emotion. The pains and sufferings of growing old are explicit concerns, as is physical incapacity. Older people contemplate old age in light of what children owe their parents, fearing infirmity, particularly urinary and faecal incontinence, which are common concerns. The elderly rely on their children's

[1024] Lamb 1993.

[1025] Lamb 1993.

obligations as a way of confronting their fears of loss of control, suffering, and death.

Attention has already been given to the use of physical metaphors in Vedic texts to express mental and emotional experience. Formulations of health and disease in Ayurveda medicine are also couched in a conception of physical processes. It is interesting that among the residents of the village studied by Vatuk and Lamb physical attributes are central not only to conceptions of human psychology and bodily health and resiliency but also of old age. What exactly residents feared and desired in the scenario of debility and dependence was framed in concrete terms that drew on physical actions. For example, bodies are said to grow 'cold' with age, and as people age they cut back on 'hot' activities. These include not only sexuality and reproduction, but also cooking (mixing things in the fire), mingling in crowds, talking vociferously (in a 'heated' exchange), expressing anger or passion, and even experiencing intense mental activity. At the same time, many reported that as the body grows older and people become increasingly 'cold', their minds or heads (*mata*) remain 'hot', especially with anger (*rāg*). They speak of hot minds, hot temperaments, hot anger, and excessive hot chatter.

Relationships and activities that are believed to affect the temperature and constitution of the body, then, are modified as people mature to facilitate the process of aging. Another dimension of the old body concerned the question of bodily decay. Older residents spoke of their bodies as changing, becoming cool and dry, for example, but also 'weak' (*durbal*), no longer able to 'move' or 'work' (*ar cale na*). They emphasized changes in the colour of their hair (*cul peke geche*), teeth (*dant bhengehe*), and tightness of their skin wrinkled (*gayer camra jar jar hae geche*). Physical decay of this type was conceptualized as inherent in the process of growing old and having lived a long life. A common term for the body, *śarīr*, meant 'that which decays'.[1026]

The physical aspects of aging are complemented with a moral vocabulary. Parents and maturity are important in the life cycle of families. The obligations of sons toward their fathers and mothers are viewed as reciprocity for what parents did for them when they were young. Social bonds prevailed throughout life and extended after death as well. Elderly parents were cared for by their juniors and the latter re-shaped relations with their parents through ritual nourishment after the parents

[1026] Lamb 1993.

had died. These repay debts owed for parental care during infancy and childhood. A moral obligation to repay vast incurred debts was the main reason given for why adult children cared for their aged parents and nurtured them after death.[1027]

There is a darker side to the expectations linked to advancing age in India as detailed by Vatuk and Lamb. Many informants, especially the very old, dreaded the body's dilapidation, mental infirmity, and physical dependence that awaited them. On the other hand, traditional notions of responsibility, love, obligation, and duty as propounded in traditional codes of conduct seemed to sustain most residents:

> Many people ... do indeed wonder and worry whether their children will in fact feed them rice in old age; others live in such poverty that they are unable to support aged family members even if they wish to; and still others are left barren with no children even to hope to depend on. Nonetheless, I found most Bengalis still tend to think of and define parent–child relations as long-term reciprocal ones. The notion that one may depend on a child in late life is thus not one to be avoided or despised by any means, but rather expected and valued as a rightful and due reciprocation of gifts and effort expended earlier in life. And the majority of old people in Mangaldihi while I was there were indeed cared for by sons and their wives in households crowded with cooking fires and descendants.[1028]

Aging and dementia

Material just reviewed provides a realistic picture of what aging means and how it is culturally understood and socially shaped and enacted in traditional India. Vatuk and Lamb described what individuals expected, how they coped, and how they managed to preserve continuity across generations as old age supervened. Cohen examines changing attitudes and conceptions about this same phase of life, now framed in terms of constructs of gerontology, pathology such as senility, dementia, Alzheimer's disease, and madness/psychosis in several communities in contemporary India.[1029] He analyzes how a category of biomedical psychiatry, ontologically demarcated and epistemically explained in terms of chronological age, gerontological facts about physiology, and scores

---

[1027] Lamb 1993: 102.

[1028] Lamb 1993: 112.

[1029] L. Cohen 1998.

on a mental status examination inventory, plays out in many parts of India. Compared to the 'naturalistic' behavioural and social architecture of dementia and aging in the US, and given the social and cultural life conditions of many aged persons in India as described by Vatuk and Lamb, one can well imagine the kinds of problems and conflicts that would accompany 'real' dementias among the elderly in settings where social supports were less resilient and more under the sway of modern ideas.

Cohen's analysis, however, is hardly an epidemiological study of senility or dementia. Rather, he provides a critical analysis of how knowledge of medicine and psychology exported to India – as per colonialism and psychiatric imperialism – is in the process of being assimilated and propounded by lay, professional, and administrators concerned to 'bring India up to date' with Western developments. His study involves a cultural exegesis about the play or relationship that knowledge of the body had in relation to age and social station in contemporary India. He reviews how ideas of modern gerontology and geriatric psychiatry clash with, are exploited by, and wreak havoc on, and get insinuated into traditional idioms of health and age-related problems posed by the aged population. While Cohen's study is firmly in the traditions of cultural exegesis and symbolic anthropology, his material nonetheless provides a slant on psychiatric aspects of aging in India.

While Vatuk and Lamb concentrate on one village and deal with general cultural themes and normative patterns (beliefs, values, orientations, apprehensions, ideals), Cohen covers all varieties of the tragic drama of old age and dementia in modern India, describing the clash of values between old and new, between what has always been expected and what is stipulated by the new discourse of contemporary psychiatry. He describes the dilemmas of aging in a language that mixes emic (intracultural), local concepts, with the new etic (external and analytically imposed) idioms of gerontology and psychiatry. Cohen presents vignettes that highlight what happens when valued traditions confront uncomfortable realities – instead of receiving support, love, and respect, the elderly may find themselves abandoned, neglected, fearful, and angry.

Cohen dramatizes the plight of the elderly, many suffering from dementia and related maladies of gerontology, which are caught between two frames of thinking and feeling. His informants expect favours and respect based on old concepts of responsibility and obligation, such as those described by Vatuk and Lamb and covered in earlier chapters. However, juxtaposed against this older, traditional framework that has long been a basis for comfort, confidence, and moral integrity one sees the new idiom of contemporary psychiatry. The latter codifies and thereby explains 'scientifically' how incapacity, dementia, or simple advanced age affect individuals and their families, in many ways reducing their significance to physical deficiencies and problems. In other words, in India one finds (at least) two discourses about old age and its infirmities.

Ironically, in some respects, Cohen's impressions were similar to those of Nunley when studying inpatient psychiatric treatment in Uttar Pradesh. Cohen's informants used the science of gerontology and modern psychiatry as though they authorized a new weapon with which they could combat the 'epidemic' of dementia and infirmities of old age and seem to use a 'gunshot' approach. Indeed, medicines and pharmaceutical preparations recommended by the new credo are used as potential magic bullets to cure or alleviate the myriad of problems and maladies of aging now reified and materialized in the biomedical idiom. As in Nunley's community, in those covered by Cohen, older traditions are being overlaid by and come into conflict with new ones, alternately generating hope and despair as problems (hospitalized psychopathologies as compared to failing, demented minds and bodies) have been removed from the old, comforting discourses and traditions. These constructs and values had managed to rationalize and thereby at least spiritually, morally, and psychologically contain medical problems of aging in a framework of traditional meaning. Meanwhile, the effectiveness of the new biomedical doctrine, while alluring, seems very shallow indeed. Again, as in the case of Nunley's descriptions, new vocabularies seem to have emerged and to have claimed sponsorship of a means of coping with myriad new problems now made more visible by the erosion of traditional values and world-view brought by the same new religion of modernity. The latter, it is hoped, will be able to cope with psychiatric conditions and related social, psychological, and biological problems but the mentalities and social structures for this are shallow and do not resonate with traditional thought worlds and habit patterns.

A previous chapter reviewed studies of dementia in traditional Indian communities conducted under the auspices of a comprehensive, internationalist collaboration. Emphasis was given to how cultural considerations had been carefully factored out of research procedures. In the India studied by Cohen, old age and dementia and associated psychiatric conditions are not treated as local epidemiological 'facts'. He implies that old age and dementia in India should be understood in light of cultural themes discussed at length in previous studies and many additional factors that illustrate the clash between tradition and modernity, between 'medical' and non-medical traditions. An elderly individual may be labelled as suffering from dementia, or Alzheimer's disease, or 'madness', but the fact of diagnosis, however well it meets internationalist criteria and indicators of psychiatric disturbance, carries little social significance. Rather, what comforts the afflicted and their families are adequate family resources, the employment status of relatives, the family's status in the community and in society at large, the perseverance of family members, and reliance on traditional spiritual values in the face of political and economic exploitation. These goals are difficult to achieve, given the lack of resources, burden of modern pressures and competing values on the family, in which traditional concepts of responsibility and obligation are floundering and failing.

For Cohen, dementia, Alzheimer's disease, or more simply the infirmities of old age in contemporary India are best construed as culturally embedded objects that are caught in the maelstrom of competing claims about knowledge played out in a society undergoing social and cultural change. Such objects are pasted together by conflicting ideas and values. He conceptualizes 'maladies' of the aged as psychological and existential dilemmas created by the clash of medical traditions as compared to measures derived from a mental status examination or from internationalist diagnostic criteria. As we have seen, roughly analogous human problems are seen in patients treated in psychiatric hospitals in Uttar Pradesh.[1030] Nunley's observations were limited to phase of hospitalization, of course, and have a much more limited compass. Yet some of the same issues described by Nunley apply in the local, popular, community settings described by Cohen. However, in Nunley's case the conflicts are more concentrated in that they bring into direct opposition the tradition-bound positions of patients and family members who cling to old conceptions of health and medical problems and those of psychiatrists who are intent on spreading the new, secular, and reductionist logic of biomedicine.

[1030] Nunley 1992.

CONCLUDING COMMENT

The encroachment and imposition of modern psychiatric practice described by Nunley and Cohen illustrate some of the conflicts between traditional and modern perspectives about conditions of psychiatric interest in India. One can discern the local, indigenous traditions that, with obvious variations of emphasis and tone due to borrowings and reactive accommodations to outsiders over the centuries, nonetheless mirror perspectives and social practices that go deep into the past. Time-honoured values about health and social conduct, and for handling psychiatric condition in particular, correspond roughly to what Nunley and Cohen describe as lying beneath the veneer of modern psychiatric labels and practices. Traditional institutions and their practitioners, who include experts on sacred topics about human conduct, diviners and priests, non-allopathic physicians, other folk medical practitioners, and 'faith healers', have managed over the millennia to culturally domesticate indigenous forms of sickness, social maladaptation, and conditions of psychiatric interest.

Because traditional conceptions of such problems have emphasized physical, somatic factors as well as personal experience and conduct, they have culturally prepared the soil for the reductive bias of modern psychiatry. This has facilitated the seeming conversion of afflicted persons and their families to the new religion about mental health. While psychiatrists also compete with practitioners of the traditional 'system of mental health' and medical care, they also depend on them, since patients are first seen by them and then (usually in the case of serious, recalcitrant syndromes) referred to psychiatric clinics. Like Kakar, both Nunley and Cohen acknowledge that the traditional system seems more integrally connected to the community and family, for purveyors of ancient wisdom and healing appear to involve themselves in the lives of patients and families in a concrete way.

Modern psychiatry also plays a role in how this other alternative mental health system and its practitioners function: it gets referrals from them, can dispense new magic bullets that can aid healing and can provide new vocabularies for describing human problems of disease, psychiatric condition, and general infirmities of old age. That all practitioners, new and old, do commerce with and acknowledge the authority of the family unit is another point of correspondence. Nunley points out that since the family determines which type of practitioner is consulted, whether treatments are followed, and if and when client families return for follow-up visits, psychiatrists are forced to structure interactions in a way that supports traditional values. This applies also to how modern psychiatry formulates its consumer market with respect to infirmities of old age, as described by Cohen.

On the other hand, psychiatrists also stand apart from the traditional system of medical and mental health care. They strongly espouse a Western-centred scientism about mental illness and old age, are motivated by an almost deterministic neurobiological approach to diagnosis and treatment, endorse an epidemic, public health conception of their work, and strive to maintain a biomedical emphasis not only to distinguish themselves from the ways of traditional practitioners but to earn the respect of their colleagues in other branches of medicine. It is these underlying features of the discourse of modern psychiatry that renders it so invasive and potentially pernicious in the new market of psychopathology that it is mining.

Chapter 12

Tensions Surrounding the Application of Modern Psychiatry

CONTESTATION BETWEEN RIVAL TRADITIONS OF MEDICINE AND HUMAN WELFARE

The arrival of modern clinical neuroscience psychiatry and its rise to a position of influence in contemporary India has brought into sharp relief contrasting approaches to the resolution of the problems of mental health. Its approach to diagnosis and practice gained ascendancy and command over a territory replete with indigenous landmarks of meaning and action relevant to the psychiatric enterprise. This required that complex mental phenomena and associated symbolic behaviour of traditional Indian derivation be reduced and fitted into tight abstract categories. Representation of the new, modern psychiatric disorders involve a finite number of sharply divided compartments of abstract, impersonal categories of signs and symptoms, virtually devoid of social meaning and cultural significance in the society at large. The result is that discrepant systems of knowledge and practice for interpreting problems of mental health operate side by side.

Contemporary clinical neuroscience psychiatry is isolating and objectifying, whereas the traditional system is inclusive and existentially resonant. Chemical imbalances and functionally altered brain networks leave the self out of the picture of mental illness, whereas morally laden religious constructs and beliefs and theosophical dimensions of Indian cultural psychology tie the self to an anthropology of mental health that encompasses cosmology and cosmogony.[1031] A recent and relatively impersonal protocol about behaviour breakdowns is in competition with and seeks to supplant time-honoured traditions about problems of

[1031] Biardeau 1989.

mental health that have existed in India and that for millennia have been managed in intellectually encompassing and emotionally satisfying ways.

The traditional cultural representation of conditions of psychiatric interest involves a complex amalgam of feelings, orientations and behaviours that are morally and religiously toned, and social activities replete with traditional significance to groups of society in different ways. The complexity of such groups – for example, differences in gender, family, occupation, lineage, caste, religion and living circumstances – translates into diverse idioms for understanding and shaping psychiatric conditions. While commonalities in thought worlds and behavioural habits exist across many groupings, variation nevertheless is significant. The system of mental health practices of India is geared to this variation of indigenous understandings and social practices. Ayurveda is an important medical component of this indigenous psychiatry but not the only one, since it exists in a pluralistic matrix of local, folk, popular and sectarian religion and associated medical and indigenous practices involved in the management of mental health. Indigenous medicine is simply one of various institutions that address human problems involving emotional and behavioural disaffection.

Modern diagnostic categories are designed to exclude concerns that have wide social significance in the lives of individuals, not to say families, who are members of different castes, religions, villages, and towns. Criteria for diagnosis and treatment are relatively abstract, socially sanitized, and culturally de-contextualized signs and symptoms that are regarded as universal features of how behaviour breaks down. In reaching a diagnosis, Indian biomedical psychiatrists concentrate on such indicators as level of motivation and energy, logical attributes of reasoning and their plausibility, intensity and degree of control over emotions, and equally concrete, depersonalized attributes of attention, orientation, and cognition mechanically conceived. Diagnostic practices are geared to expedient modes of treatment. Several potentially relevant diagnoses dictate which of several psychoactive agents should be prescribed and whether electroconvulsive therapy is indicated.

A culturally content-less system of cubicles that define psychiatric disorders in very formal and formulaic terms is being used to enclose a complex, protean, and inchoate plethora of culturally meaningful psychological, social and general sickness problems that have always connoted moral and spiritual implications about the self. The psychiatric diagnostic system is being used like a net cast into an ocean of human emotional and behaviour problems with the intention of collecting, identifying and naming material specimens that can then be handled in equally impersonal, formal, objective ways by means of specific psychopharmacological agents and formulaic psychiatric practices of psychotherapy. In short, two domains of knowledge, one traditional, the other modern, are brought to bear on a complex array of behavioural problems with little attempt to make them compatible and mutually understandable to the subjects who require mental health care. Few seem to appreciate the full implications of the fact that the two approaches reflect entirely different social histories and cultural mentalities. To point to this clash of traditions is not to criticize India's social planners, policy makers, or psychiatrists. Rather, it is to underscore (1) the conceit of modern clinical neuroscience psychiatry and attendant dilemmas and quandaries inherent in its evolution; and (2) its spread and impact in societies and civilizations like India's that are culturally far removed from those where modern psychiatry initially evolved and in which the basic phenomena of concern have a rich, diverse and alternative cultural history.

The contemporary contest over how to heal psychiatric conditions in India dramatizes the latest phase of the cultural evolution of psychiatric phenomena worldwide. The contest and its implications can be formulated in terms of the differences in the philosophy and ethics of medicine, and it is particularly highlighted by the history of Indian civilization. Earlier chapters made it abundantly clear that in India there is a considerable overlap between medicine, social welfare, religion, moral educative precepts, and legal administration. Excluding outright instances of crime, healing and rehabilitation covered a broad terrain of human problems. Even the quintessentially naturalistic, medical tradition is profoundly comprehensive, while nonetheless featuring an academic, rational view of disease and medical care, thereby legitimately earning the title of a major turning point in the history of world medicine.

Even India's naturalistic indigenous psychiatry incorporates all aspects of an individual's personal, social and spiritual life. It is anchored securely in and re-enforces the cultural psychology of India. As discussed earlier, central medical facts of diagnosis and treatment bring into play aspects of Ayurveda: hygiene, dietetics, social activities and habits, sexual behaviour, ethical beliefs and actions, the spiritual and supernatural realm, moral outlooks, and emotional dispositions. Moreover, and here it shares its rationale and epistemology with all other great traditions of medicine (China, the Mediterranean basin), Ayurveda focuses on unique attributes of the individual. In other words, an ayurvedic physician takes to heart an individual's biography and life circumstances in reaching diagnosis and prescribing treatment. The large perimeter of human concerns that is contained within Ayurveda theory and practice as per conditions of psychiatric interest underscores the range of other allegedly non-medical institutions and traditions of India whose function has been and continues to be the promotion of human welfare. As indicated earlier, a broadly conceived healing rationale, with the medical Buddha's pronouncement as, perhaps, an exemplar, underpins the academic, scientific medical traditions of traditional India as well as other social institutions and traditions. Their rationale and purpose is to help individuals remain connected, functional, and responsive to occupational, moral, legal, and spiritual requirements amidst the vagaries of human suffering of all types. Efforts of establishment psychiatrists and social planners to develop social and community psychiatry, as alluded to in Chapter 11, and taken up in detail below, are examples motivated to bridge the gap between the old and the new in relation to mental health and social welfare.

Against the broad sweep of human concerns over health and well-being exemplified in traditional Indian culture, the medical narrowness of contemporary biomedical psychiatry stands out sharply. The latter reduces the myriad concerns that are entailed in the complex amalgam of psychiatric condition to more or less reified entities. The logic of diagnosis and treatment in modern psychiatry, as in biomedicine more generally, makes of disorders concrete realities that have an existence independent of the individual. Not only are their defining properties disconnected from human concerns and problems broadly conceived, but, in addition, they are conceptualized as though they were foreign to the individual. The person is held to catch, develop, or be attacked by a pernicious entity that has its own separate reality. This rationale obviously excludes the manifold concerns and features of personal identity and social functioning that render a psychiatric condition a human problem associated with distress and suffering. Protocols and laboratory procedures aim to validate that a disorder exists in the patient, whereupon drugs and electroconvulsive therapy are employed to neutralize, banish, or exterminate the disorder. The socially and culturally unique person is left out of the equation of diagnosis and treatment. In short, in the contest between approaches to psychiatric condition during this latest phase of cultural history in the subcontinent, one witnesses a profound clash of traditions about human welfare.

THE 'OLD' INDIGENOUS PSYCHIATRY IN THE 'NEW' CLINICAL NEUROSCIENCE REGIME

The spread and incorporation of clinical neuroscience psychiatry in India, however intellectually seductive and politically, economically empowered it might be, cannot simply erase its rivals for hegemonic control over the market trading in the control of mental health problems. Traditional ideas, beliefs, and attitudes about health and wellbeing are simply too deeply ingrained in the history, social interpretations of ordinary circumstances, and cultural psychology of India to simply go away. What the 'old' indigenous psychiatry taught and practiced lives on in contemporary India. Some of the traditional beliefs and practices have not only retained their autonomy and authenticity, rejuvenated with modernist attires. They have fought back and continue to control their cultural space in India and have managed to exert their own muscle internationally as a force to be reckoned with in quest for better mental and physical health.[1032] Indeed, what has been termed here the traditional indigenous psychiatry of India is alive and well in today's India, indeed, its health is good worldwide.

It cannot be doubted that in the India of today one will find outside the confines of modern establishment psychiatry, which derives from Western doctrines, a veritable industry of indigenous psychiatry, still deeply steeped in ancient ways of thought and practice about psychiatric phenomena. It would include modern-styled gurus, yogins, shamanistic and related folk practitioners, wise men and a plethora of popular religious sects and cults that address among many other things problems involving emotional and behavioural disaffection, much like their counterparts did centuries and indeed millennia ago. In present context, this indigenous psychiatry can be construed as alternative and complementary to clinical neuroscience psychiatry, which is official and

[1032] Alter 2004; De Michelis 2004; Fields 2001; Langford 2002; Feuerstein 1998.

state supported and bears the imprimatur of science. There is an irony here: looking at the expanse of social life in the Indian subcontinent during pre-modern era, one can safely assert that the complex amalgam of ideas and practices that constituted indigenous psychiatry was hardly alternative. It was preponderant. Indeed, somewhat astride the indigenous nexus stood ayurvedic or medical psychiatry, perhaps pre-modern India's establishment psychiatry although, as repeatedly emphasized in earlier chapters, ayurvedic tenets and practices were deeply rooted in traditional philosophical, spiritual, and moral tenets and not just strictly medical in nature: it was not just organic but also metaphysical.

What is of concern in this section of the chapter is the extent to which traditional indigenous conceptions are represented in modern psychiatry's clinics, hospitals, and private practice. In tracing the history of mental illness in India, and in seeking to understand the cultural evolution of psychiatric phenomena more generally, an important question involves the degree to which traditional, indigenous ideas and beliefs about mental illness are made use of in official psychiatric practice. One seeks to determine whether and if so where in the fabric of contemporary clinical neuroscience psychiatry one finds the resonance of traditional thought patterns and feelings inherent in disturbances of emotion and behaviour that have a long history in the subcontinent. In other words, in the language of comparative medical studies of today, is the heterodox or alternative system of indigenous psychiatry, really complementary, when viewed from within the orthodox establishment nexus? (Indeed, one could even ask: Is not clinical neuroscience psychiatry really the alternative or complementary system considered in relation to Ayurveda psychiatry?)

It needs to be appreciated that when viewed from a general anthropological, naturalistic, and metacultural frame of reference, the constitution and biopsychosocial resonance of conditions of psychiatric interest has been carried forward from traditional times up until the present. Cultural psychologies and the disturbance that they shape do not just pass away or dissolve: they continue to resonate perhaps in subdued terms, perhaps slowly altered, and *perhaps purposely concealed* by victims as new generations become acquainted with, copy, and seek to internalize Western conceits about self, experience, behaviour, social reality, and what is now represented in cacophonous moral overtones in the modern conception of 'mental illness'.

In addition to the requisite allegedly culture-free (sometimes termed pancultural) diagnostic indicators of clinical neuroscience psychiatry one should expect to find in individuals diagnosed with bona fide psychiatric disorders echoes of the effects of traditional cultural psychological structures. As discussed in previous chapters, disturbances that affect thought, emotional experience and regulation, moral disposition and morale, sense of embodiment, and social behaviour come together and are packaged in a traditional idiom that has been carried in thought worlds and habit patterns of Indian peoples through history. All of the preceding resounds with traditional indigenous conceptions, perceptions, and attitudes emblematic of the 'older' traditional conditions of psychiatric interest and can be presumed to remain embedded within or under the secular and impersonal veneer of clinical neuroscience psychiatry and its disorders. The latter are simply later versions of the same conditions of psychiatric interest that remain resonant in traditional idioms of behaviour and which can be accessed by careful anamnesis that probe cultural models of illness. Problems of acculturative and social stress and disarticulation that come with modernity are naturally layered on top of conflicts inherent in traditional culture patterns and the effects of both blend the old cultural psychology with the emerging one. Ideally, the aim of a truly authentic Indian psychiatry (just like one for China and East Asia, for example) should involve accessing, responding adaptively to, and integrating the sciences and insights of traditional thought with those of the modern era.

One place to look for traditional constituents is in the new social and community psychiatry. Basically this is the part of modern psychiatry, well established across nation states, that seeks to connect with communities outside the clinic and hospital. Its *raison d'etre* is prevention of psychiatric disorders. Once psychiatric disorders are recognized, appreciation of community factors can enhance compliance and effective implementation of treatment programs because this emphasis of modern psychiatry acknowledges that psychiatric disorders are socially, culturally embedded. The story of community mental health in India has a long history. Leaving aside the obvious irony that the indigenous psychiatry of India constitutes a community-oriented mental health system that is millennia old, a need to relate the modernist antiseptic preoccupation with medical categories to the social, cultural realities of contemporary Indian communities was an early concern of individuals seeking to improve mental health.

The beginnings of the community mental health movement in India is said to have started in the 1950s. It involved the efforts of Dr Vidya Sagar who at that time linked the treatment of the mentally ill patients in the Amristar Mental Hospital with programs that included their families. Open case conferences were conducted every evening with families and patients designed to acquaint them with mental illness and methods of treatment. The need to bridge the modern and the indigenous psychiatry was salient.

> In these sessions, Dr Vidya Sagar drew freely upon his knowledge of classical Hindu texts, the very style of his address resembling that of a Hindu holy man ... This experiment helped to kick-start a major movement to involve family members in treatment of the mentally ill.[1033]

Indeed, the latter focus remains a cornerstone of contemporary psychiatric care the world over.

Kapur traces the various steps of the community mental health movement in India and sees it as geared to de-institutionalization, that is, efforts to facilitate early treatment, reduce confinement, and return the mentally ill to their families and communities. He includes in this picture the establishment of psychiatric units in general hospitals ('general hospital psychiatry'). This step is generally regarded as crucial to making psychiatry a self-respecting medical discipline and linking it with comparable treatment programs of other specialties. It was community psychiatry in the sense that it placed clinical neuroscience in hospitals and clinics already situated in local communities and not in asylums far away and inaccessible to families. In 1975 actions by the director and minister of health of India gave the National Institute of Mental Health and Neurosciences (NIMHANS) a mandate and authority to launch a number of experimental efforts to improve sensitivity to community, better construed as socio-cultural factors. These included programs involving primary health centre and rural mental health programs designed to educate workers to recognize severe mental illnesses, education of general medical practitioners, school mental health emphases on recognition of mental health problems, home-based follow-up of psychiatric patients, and psychiatric camps that were instrumental in involving village leaders of regions far away from hospitals in thera-

---

[1033] Kapur 2004: 93.

peutic processes and reduction of psychiatric stigma. Many other efforts designed to promote the community mental health movement in India are described.[1034] An overriding goal has been to ensure the availability and accessibility of minimum mental health care for all who need it within a reasonable period of time. The goals of early and subsequent efforts have not all been met for a number of reasons.[1035]

An urgent necessity in the plan to connect with social background of patients and address as much as possible problems of mental health in community settings has been to measure the scope of the problem posed by mental illness in India. This involved carrying out surveys of untreated mental illness in urban and rural areas. Indeed, the focus of social and community psychiatry in India cannot be separated from the growth of psychiatric epidemiology there. Early on, surveys involving prevalence of mental illness in India brought to light the hold of indigenous psychiatry in the continent.

> As late as the 1970s, when the author carried out a survey of mental disorders in a south Karnataka district, which boasted of two medical colleges and above average infrastructure for delivery of modern medicine, 75 per cent of those suffering from severe mental illness were still being taken for treatment to the traditional folk-healers. The same study showed that there were 26 traditional healers for a population of 10,000, which is a fair therapist–patient ratio by any standard.[1036]

It is not clear whether establishment psychiatry has made efforts to incorporate indigenous practitioners towards its goal of better connecting modern programs of treatment with community resources. While community psychiatry depends on sensitivity to personal, social, and cultural characteristics of patients, its aim is to facilitate understanding, acceptance, and incorporation of the new clinical neuroscience conception in the psychology of modern India. It cannot be said to exemplify a culturally sensitive vision of psychiatric phenomena, such as an Indian ontology and epistemology of psychiatric condition, but rather to promote, consolidate and make salient the modern credo.

An important and very early landmark in the attempt to provide a comprehensive vision of psychiatric conditions in India involves the

---

[1034] Kapur 1979, 2004.

[1035] Kapur 1979, 2004.

[1036] Kapur 2004: 92.

coming of age of clinical psychology. This is traced to the pioneering efforts of Dr Girindrasekar Bose (1886–1953), a medical practitioner interested in the treatment of mental illness.

> Bose felt the need to increase his knowledge of human behaviour and chose to join the postgraduate programme in psychology begun at Calcutta University in 1915. In 1921 he was the first candidate to obtain a doctorate in psychology ... in 1938, he headed the Department of Applied Psychology at Calcutta University, when a separate department was created.[1037]

Further considerations regarding the role of clinical psychology practice in the program of a socially and culturally responsive modern mental health program are taken up later.

The greater relevance of psychiatric nurses and especially psychiatric social workers to the clinical neuroscience enterprise gained momentum from the establishment of general hospital psychiatry that Kapur sees as so important. Psychiatric nurses and social workers provide additional examples of personnel allied to the contemporary clinical neuroscience program of psychiatry in India who can be expected to show sensitivity to and make room for social, cultural, and personal problems and needs of patients as traditionally formulated by them.[1038] Psychiatric nurses and social workers, like psychologists and trained general medical personnel, are placed in positions in psychiatric clinics and hospitals, where they attempt to integrate the requirements of clinical neuroscience psychiatry practice with lay understandings, misconceptions, and compliance problems. How well psychiatric social workers and nurses along with clinical psychologists manage to package modern dicta about mental illness in terms of traditional conceptions regarding emotional and behavioural problems is not clear.

Selling clinical neuroscience psychiatry is easier for serious disorders since effects of psychotropic agents are often dramatic and it is largely such disorders that one finds in hospital settings where nurses and social workers often function as the key mediators between clinical deliberations of psychiatrists involving diagnosis and treatment planning and the aches and pains of patients and families who shoulder the burden of emotional and behavioural breakdowns. However, while

---

[1037] Prabhu and Shankar 2004: 124.

[1038] Reddemma and Nagarajaiah 2004; Parthasarathy and Ranganathan 2004.

pharmacological treatments often produce marked improvements, they all too often cause debilitating side effects that are of concern of patients and their families. Personnel of the psychiatric establishment, including clinical psychologists and especially nurses and social workers, are caught in an intellectual, emotional cross-fire. On the one hand, as members of the therapeutic team they seek to promote acceptance and compliance of a clinical regimen, worked out in dispassionate dialogues with psychiatrists conducted away from patients and families, that is relatively easy tc follow and that promises relief and betterment in the short run. On the other hand, most of their time is spent in contact with their clients who directly see and feel the effects of treatment.

For a number of reasons, and compared to psychiatrists, the hearts and minds of psychiatric nurses and social workers and clinical psychologists are likely to identify poignantly with the wrenching psychological, cultural, moral, and spiritual dimensions of mental illness that their clients exemplify and display. For the latter, a mental illness is constituted of stuff very different from the stuff of clinical neuroscience. A nurse, social worker, and to some extent a clinical psychologist, is more likely to hear requests for advice from families who wish to resort to indigenous psychiatric measures. Furthermore, the cost–benefit realities of modern treatments should also be communicated to their clients. Long-term effects of medications involve not only a sapping of energy and a dulling of thought and sensibility, but outright damage to physiological functions (increased vulnerability to diabetes, heart disease). How well and at what personal costs nurses, social workers, and clinical psychologists negotiate traffic between the moral combat zone between clinical neuroscience and indigenous psychiatry constitutes a topic of great interest.

Rehabilitation services represent another arm of clinical neuroscience psychiatry that is immersed deeply in the territory of orientations, dispositions, attitudes, and behaviours that exemplify the indigenous construction of mental health and illness. Such services cannot easily be separated from the treatment, data gathering, and educative functions and services provided by clinical psychologists and psychiatric social workers and nurses. The mission of psychiatric rehabilitation is to address highly specific yet essential humanistic – read in here physical/ behavioural as well as moral-psychological – burdens associated with mental illness. Its target is not only patients but families of patients as well. Rehabilitation services range from activities of daily living, such as self-care and personal hygiene, on, through skills in social communication and occupational functioning, and ultimately involve, or should involve, moral re-integration of the patient within his or her own family and in the community. The aim is to enable patient and family to function at their optimal capacity.

Psychiatric rehabilitation in India divides into two periods. The first, for approximately 25 years following Independence, was centred in Government hospitals and aimed to keep long-term patients occupied with work or other social activity. The second phase, starting during the early 1970s, involved attempts to reintegrate patients with their families and in the community. This phase involves hospital-based services and community-based services.[1039] Hospital-based services have not met optimal goals largely because of difficulty in recruiting clinical psychologists and psychiatric social workers. On the other hand, community-based rehabilitation services are said to have fared well. In view of the pervasive influence of indigenous mental health ideas and practices on the cultural psychology of Indian patients, this is hardly surprising:

> Community-based rehabilitation (CBR), by definition, targets settings resonant with traditional conceptions and where social and community bonds are quite strong and deep rooted. The challenge of CBR, and its success, depends on whether people with disabilities, their families, and concerned governmental agencies pertaining to health, education, welfare and social service can work together to make use of the resources in the community.[1040]

Severe psychiatric disorders, especially those that are chronic, impose a heavy burden that all societies have to cope with. In traditional India, like in other pre-modern societies, it was undoubtedly the family that shouldered this. In modern era, this is still the case and represents a burden that rehabilitation services seek to meliorate. Serious disorders in young adults hinder their life chances and leads parents to conceal their manifestations. If they are successful in marrying them off, their symptoms and signs cause hardship in their new families producing rejection or annulment and resentment between families.[1041] The burden again falls on the family of the victim, which is forced to reach psycho-

---

[1039] Murali and Rao 2004.

[1040] Murali and Rao 2004: 154.

[1041] Thara and Srinivasan 2000; Thara, Kamath, and Kumar 2003.

logical, physical, and some form of accommodation to the signs and symptoms and distribution of tasks and efforts left undone or unfinished by the victim and which are required to keep the family unit functional. Family size and resources and indigenous views about the metaphysical implications of severe mental illness, how the individual victim is to be perceived and related to, in an existential sense, are critical factors that enable families to handle the burden of severe mental illness.

One function of any medical care system is not simply treating and reversing disorders, but of preserving the victim's moral integrity and self-respect and of meaningfully maintaining the victim integrating and appropriating his or her efforts into the social fabric as much as this is possible.[1042] Modernization in India, as elsewhere, breaks apart and undermines a family's social, moral, and economic structures and resources that are needed to accomplish this. It places a high premium on employment and self-sufficiency, but job markets even for healthy family members are often non-existent, especially among the non-educated and disadvantaged.[1043] However, not only poverty, marginality, and unemployment prove defeating, but the new ethos of modernity and secularization itself can prove defeating: it can shatter intellectual and philosophical idioms that earlier had enabled families to make sense of social problems posed by severe mental illness and thereby meet deeply felt foundational moral responsibilities tied to *dharma*. Traditional ways of meeting needs of patients and of coping with conflicts involving responsibility are often derailed.

The difficulties that this combination of factors poses to effective psychiatric rehabilitation in India are well attested. Finding jobs for their clients is very difficult, especially when resources for vocational training are wanting. Patients often perceive low social support from family and less than encouraging support for independence, and express need for family members to be educated so that caregivers can have better understanding of their plight in the family and show more positive attitudes about their condition. Such behaviours are hardly surprising in view of the burdens including stigma that primary caregivers for patients of severe mental illness report.[1044] Patients with severe and chronic mental illness report feeling unwanted. Most patients in a hospital that was

---

1042 Fabrega 1976a.

1043 Murali and Rao 2004.

1044 Thara and Srinivasan 2000.

studied did not need hospitalization, yet three quarters of them received no visits from family or friends.

> This is a sentiment shared, even today, by many clinicians especially those working in government hospital settings. However, studies indicate that this neglect is not due to negative attitude towards the patient, but because of financial difficulties, fear, and stigma. In the absence of viable alternatives, families that are both financially and socially marginalized may be left with no choice but to abandon their mentally ill relative.[1045]

Yet it remains true that the family in India initiates treatment and ensures compliance with regimen and provides considerable emotional support to patients.

An important and potentially influential territory located in the crossroads between traditional compared to contemporary psychiatric theory and practice involves mental health non-governmental organizations termed MHNGOs.[1046] Such organizations proved of great value in the effort to develop government-financed and establishment psychiatry based community-centred rehabilitation services discussed earlier. MHNGOs involve efforts of individuals seeking to coordinate educative and practical needs dictated by orthodox clinical neuroscience ('establishment') psychiatry and those based on socially and culturally resonant needs of victims of mental illness. Such organizations often bring a missionary zeal to their efforts to educate families about modern conceptions and promote acceptance of treatment regimen dictated by those conceptions. They include a focus on rehabilitation of the mentally retarded and those victimized by mental illness.

> These MHNGOs were started as a means to fulfil the need for a broader, holistic approach to the management of severe mental disorders ... activities ranging from family counseling vocational rehabilitation, which were rarely provided in psychiatric out-patient clinics, were given greater attention. Another area of [concern over] mental health ... was substance abuse.[1047]

MHNGOs involving suicide prevention are said to have mushroomed in India in relation to the alarm caused by reports of high sui-

[1045] Murali and Rao 2004: 155.

[1046] Patel and Varghese 2004.

[1047] Patel and Varghese 2004.

cide among young people. Scepticism and cynicism directed at the medical community, lack of cooperation, and indifference of government officials are among the factors that are used to explain the rise of MHNGOs. Many of the latter receive minimal if any government funding support and most rely on general public and donor agencies for financial resources. Many of the MHNGOs actually charge fees for services.

This brings into focus private sector psychiatry, and psychology, for that matter, an almost entirely post-Independence development. It represents an arena of mental health care strategically placed so as to potentially interact with and draw on traditional ideas and practices. A privately licensed psychiatrist in the India of today is by definition a modern disciple of clinical neuroscience psychiatry. He or she – actually only around 10 per cent of today's practicing psychiatrists are female – is comparatively young, recently graduated and trained expert in modern clinical neurosciences, psychopharmacology, and modalities of psychotherapy.[1048] However, a licensed practicing psychiatrist is also in the business of making a living directly off his clients who pay his fees. This is the case since he is usually not receiving fixed remuneration from a governmental or private corporation – 70 per cent of private psychiatrists are in full-time practice, the rest in part-time private practice. By definition, a private psychiatrist or clinical psychologist provides a greater modicum of confidential care to his clients. A private practitioner is usually situated in the community where he practices. Privacy breeds more direct, personal involvement with clients, compared to the exigencies of meeting standardized protocols of care and public clinic and hospital structures of rules, practices, and the like, which may very well be directed at treating patients at some geographic remove. Fee for services are paid by clients who can afford them, and the latter tend to be educated and middle class, a substantial proportion of the clientele of private psychiatrists. Taken together, one can propose that these and related considerations mean that private psychiatrists are more likely to know and participate in the personal lives of their clients and tailor the delivery of services so as to better mesh with the expectations, attitudes, ideological orientations, and emotional needs of their clients.[1049]

[1048] Kala 2004.

[1049] The activities of psychoanalysts like Kakar and Roland, discussed in detail in previous chapters, who are not psychiatrists, provide a window into the conduct likely to be displayed

Thus it comes as no surprise to find out that private sector psychiatry in India has experienced a 'phenomenal growth' and that an inspection of its structures of practice will reveal significant involvement in community and related institutions where traditional, indigenous formulations of mental health are not only still regnant but dominant.[1050] The private psychiatric sector was non-existent in the 1950s. It received an enormous boost from the general hospital psychiatry movement that placed psychiatry in the market place of hospital inpatient and outpatient care on a par with other physicians serving to rationalize its domain in the intellectual imagination of the public. Most private psychiatrists are found in cities although not necessarily large metros or state capitals, only 7 per cent, however, work in small towns.

> Private psychiatric services in India have the most outreach, are the most decentralized and are almost at the doorstep of the patient. In fact, most acute and fresh cases are seen in the private sector.[1051]

Moreover, close to 80 per cent of private psychiatrists appear to be engaged in some form of mental health education of the community where they live as per giving lectures and the like. In larger cities, many private psychiatrists handle problems of mental health in collaboration with non-governmental organizations and many consult with schools, police and prison administrators, and personnel involved in crisis intervention programs. There can be little doubt that all of these and related activities aim to place in good light the tenets of modern clinical neuroscience for private consumers, undoubtedly dressed up in constructs that make sense with respect to tenets of traditional, indigenous psychiatry.

> These facts reflect not only a public acceptance of mental health professionals but also the community's need to know about psychological problems, and a healthy reciprocation from the profession. At another level, it indicates integration of the city psychiatrist in the community where he resides.[1052]

---

by private, licensed psychiatrists and clinical psychologists in relation to their clients: both of these individuals drew deeply from the wellspring of indigenous ideas and practices of their clients so as to modify standard professional dicta, making treatments more palatable yet still scientifically relevant and financially remunerative.

[1050] Kala 2004.

[1051] Kala 2004: 162.

[1052] Kala 2004: 162.

Despite these rather sanguine generalizations, the impact that private psychiatry actually has in the subcontinent today can certainly be questioned. All 1890 full-time and part-time private psychiatrists who were listed in the directory of the Indian Psychiatric Society were polled and furnished information discussed above. The actual number of psychiatrists working in the private sector is unclear, but one may presume that their number represents a small percentage of the Indian population of close to 1 billion. Moreover, how well private psychiatrists are able to conceptually translate their clinical neuroscience language with traditional idioms of patients is unclear as is also how well they integrate their practical activities with their expectations. Good skills in communication and practice across these two assumptive worlds would seem to represent a basic requirement for effectively handling the plethora of mental health ailments and needs of peoples who, conditioned by their cultural psychology, expect big answers to big questions as well as comprehensible treatments for relief of their predicaments. Individuals like Vidya Sagar, Kakar and Roland are exemplary of what private psychiatry can offer, but they are also exceptional. Like all other efforts of clinical neuroscience psychiatry to weave itself into the social fabric of today's India, one must presume that the private sector, if only because of its small size, fails to bridge the gap to satisfactorily integrate with ideas and practices of indigenous psychiatry. The latter is alternative, but certainly not complementary, to clinical neuroscience psychiatry. In fact one can argue the reverse is the case, viewed general context: clinical neuroscience psychiatry functions as an alternative and complementary system to the indigenous psychiatry.

An interesting contemporary snapshot of indigenous conceptions and practices regarding the reality of mental illness in today's India is provided looking at so-called 'common mental disorders'. As much as 10 per cent of the population is said to suffer from problems related to anxiety, depression, and somatic symptoms of psychiatric relevance. These afflictions are viewed as responses to the strain of modern life and are more pronounced in females, the poor, members of lower castes, migrants from the countryside to cities with their attendant dislocation and dilution of old social values all of which are regarded as influential in producing common mental disorders including problems of substance abuse. How such disorders are handled today brings into focus the dilemma of clinical neuroscience psychiatry reductionism and the vitality of millennia old indigenous psychiatric practices:

> Modern psychiatry has very little to offer for these conditions except an increasing use of minor tranquillisers, which has become a curse in its own right. Fortunately, attempts are being made in India to use psycho-social methods to attend to this major need. We have programmes in which lay volunteers after a short period of training are able to counsel such patients. There is a rise in growth therapies. Many industrial organizations provide personality enhancement programmes for their employees. The elites are willing to pay large sums to learn exotic techniques like Reiki, transactional analysis and past-life therapies. According to some estimates, more than 5,000–6,000 people in Bangalore enter such programmes every year and this must be true for other big cities also ... It is in this context that the role of folk-healing, spiritual and religious counselling, and ancient techniques like Yoga and medication [presumably meditation] acquire significance. Many people with emotional problems go to folk-healers and spiritual teachers. It is easy for a modern psychiatrist to decry these institutions as unscientific but what do they have to offer instead? ... What one requires when assessing the impact of religious figures ... is to first look at the contented smiles on the faces of thousands of devotees who attend his prayer meetings every day and then to interview a few to find out how he has changed their lives. Is going to spiritual healers worse than doling out expensive tranquillisers under the pressure of various drug companies?[1053]

It is unclear how important and effective culturally sensitive community mental health emphases, along with similar ones seeking to better link the modern with the indigenous, play out in the contemporary scenario of clinical neuroscience psychiatry. In general, these and related efforts are natural concomitants of the problematization of mental illness in modern India discussed earlier. Such emphases and efforts exemplify attempts to militate against the corrosive reductionism, insensitivity, and impersonality of the clinical neuroscience representation of emotional and behavioural disaffections. In real social life and in the context of existential burdens of the imagination and spirit, psychiatric conditions have constituted one of the reasons for being of the culture and civilization of India considered here narrowly as an evolved system of meaning and practices for promoting mental health. In a basic sense, community psychiatry and its network of institutions within the establishment function so as to enhance the delivery and acceptance of foreign ideas and practices about psychiatric phenomena that have been imported and imposed on indigenous populations. These centres of in-

[1053] Kapur 2004: 97–98.

fluence and the movement they embody require clients and disseminators of the goods proffered by clinical neuroscience psychiatry. Such agents ultimately seek to bring profits and personal satisfactions to the patrons of the now global world capitalist drift of clinical neuroscience in the post-modern era. This hegemonic behemoth requires clients who can transform mindless antiseptic directives and imperatives of clinical neuroscience psychiatry into understandable, emotionally palatable, and more effectively complied with and hence economically profitable programs of therapy.

A BRIEF EXCURSUS: TWO SNAPSHOTS OF MODERN PSYCHIATRY IN INDIA

Not long after Independence, in the early 1950s, Hoch, who was at the time a European-trained psychiatrist and psychoanalyst, began to live and practice in India and was deeply immersed in its traditional culture.[1054] She read about its philosophy, religion, and popular literature. She also acquired some proficiency in local languages and was able to communicate with clients. In 1972 she published an article about the potential role that psychotherapy might play in helping India modernize.[1055] She described the obstacles that stood in the way of effective delivery of modern mental health services and these involved material obstacles including lack of sufficient and adequate facilities, not enough professionally trained personnel, and financially poor circumstances of native peoples that militated against their turn to and use of modern psychotherapeutic care and at the same time meet its costs. One can use Hoch as a participant-observer of the Indian mental health scene during this time period and use her observations as though she were a principal informant of that culture.

Her article provides a snapshot of how an apparently well-meaning, orientalist therapist saw the terrain of mental health need at that point in history and attempted to improve it as best she could. Given the ethos of the time, Hoch naturally construed individual psychotherapy as a modality for emancipation of the self that if and when successful in a set of individuals could spread and function as an aid to development of

[1054] Hoch 1993.

[1055] Hoch 1972.

the society as a whole. The psychotherapy she described was insight-oriented and designed to educate a client about the self, constraints on a free vision of social reality that might serve to problematize circumstances for an individual, the nature of psychological conflicts and impediments in reaching these goals, and how best to meet needs of patients for a flourishing life in the modern world. It is the obstacles that Hoch perceived in the patient's level of emancipation that bears examination.

Most of the patients she saw in the capital of Kashmir were illiterate or at least poorly educated, peasants that had migrated into cities. Among them she encountered some showed a 'remarkable degree of maturity and practical wisdom'.

> More often, however, illiteracy is associated with a lack of individual awareness and a state of being. It is as if the dim, precarious flame of consciousness were able to illuminate only just the immediate 'here and now', and even this only in the form of objective perception, not in a self-reflecting manner, as a conscious experience, as an assimilation of something that is recognized as one's own.[1056]

Confronting the patient with a need to formulate aspects of self and social situation produced the retort: 'We? We people never think'. If Hoch persisted in her efforts to force insight, patients often broke down and developed 'hysterical loss of consciousness' and related signs and symptoms. She saw such anxiety, hypochondria, and hysterical maladies as defences

> against the very necessity of venturing one step further into a wider, brighter sphere of consciousness. The psychiatric illness appears as expression of a crisis, in which lethargy of habits, clinging to the powerful protection of the anonymous crowd or to the traditional structure of family and society come into conflict with inner progressive tendencies that aim at individual development.[1057]

Hoch made similar observations about the way clients formulated self, experience, and body:

> I would feel that it is not justified to label the somewhat strangely expressed body sensation of an illiterate peasant as a symptom of

[1056] Hoch 1972: 229–230.
[1057] Hoch 1972: 230.

> 'depersonalisation'. One would rather have to speak of 'impersonalization', as he has not lost a once-present identification with his body, the feeling of being at home within his somatic sphere; on the contrary, he is only just about to take conscious possession of his physical frame.[1058]

Hoch reported frustration in trying to persuade local personnel and fellow Indian practitioners to frame ideas about psychiatric care and psychotherapy in a form that clients might better understand and be enabled to use. The following addresses the gaping chasm that appeared to be taking place between traditional 'indigenous' sector psychiatric thinking and the idiom of the invading modernist credo:

> I, therefore, find that, with my own knowledge about the cultural and social background, with my intuitive appreciation for subtle shadings of meanings in Indian languages and the possibility of drawing on traditional parables and metaphors from the patients' own life spheres for illustrating an explanation, I am not only ahead of my Indian students, but also of many of my colleagues. Knowledge of this type, however, occasionally runs the risk of being looked down upon as reactionary or backward, as, after all, it is much more modern and scientific to characterize the phenomena observed in the patient with current technical terms or to label them neatly according to a generally-accepted descriptive or psychodynamic classification.[1059]

One may now turn the clock forward and look at a complementary snapshot of modern psychiatry in India. One can examine how an experienced, humanitarian, enlightened, and highly respected and placed modern exponent of modern psychiatry sees the contemporary scene. S. P. Agarwal is the editor of the remarkable *Mental Health: An Indian Perspective, 1946–2003*.[1060] This compendium comprehensively summarizes the impressive path taken by modern clinical neuroscience psychiatry in the subcontinent since Independence illustrating also the efforts to interweave the modern and the traditional. It is a remarkable document filled with compelling descriptions of the successes that all facets of modern psychiatry has had since Independence. It also discusses in a critical way the unmet needs and limitations in reaching goals. The best of scientific and academic psychiatry appears represented in Agarwal's edited volume.

[1058] Hoch 1972: 230.

[1059] Hoch 1972: 231.

[1060] S. P. Agarwal *et al.* 2004.

One may take a look at what Agarwal has to say about modern psychiatry in India today in the way of a plea to private sector psychiatry for a need for an ethical approach. One may presume that it is not unlikely that Agarwal's perception of private sector psychiatry is overly negative and that his (implied) perception of academic, state-sponsored psychiatry on the sanguine side. Be that as it may.

> For centuries people have gone to the city of Kashi seeking spiritual solace. In an increasingly tension-ridden world, the search for mental peace goes on, but perhaps on a different plane. Vārāṇasī is no longer the favoured destination. The benzodiazepines and alprazolam provide convenient pharmacological short cuts to oblivion, providing temporary escape from the anxieties of everyday living. The adverse long-term consequences of these instant solutions arouse little concern among users and prescribers alike. Aggressive attractively packaged marketing gimmicks employed by a profit-driven pharmaceutical industry, further fuel this pernicious quest, which carries within itself the seeds of eventual destruction. Occasional warnings ... highlighting the danger of the commercialization of medical practise, pass largely unheeded.
>
> Commercialization also threatens to distort the growth of psychotherapy and other counselling modalities. The bandwagon effect has drawn a large number of inadequately trained opportunists who style themselves as counsellors or therapists with the sole aim of cashing in on the need for quick-fix solutions. At the other end of the spectrum, are the modern day gurus who seek to promote the quest for spiritual peace as a marketable commodity, complete with best-selling do-it-yourself manuals, guaranteed to improve the disciple's quality of life. It is an index of the age of insecurity we live in that these self proclaimed gurus often command huge followings, despite their all too obvious feet of clay.[1061]

This quotation reflects some disappointment, if not demoralization and resentment, about what clinical neuroscience psychiatry has managed to evolve and how it is being deployed. It decries the injudicious application of its wares. It contains a more negative, less open and less optimistic conception of what the indigenous sector of mental health practices is capable of providing when compared with the quote from Kapur presented earlier. Nevertheless, it is no less chiding of the perversities resulting from a rash, simplistic, and impudent resort to the alleged magical bullets of clinical neuroscience psychiatry. Both quotes are

[1061] S. P. Agarwal 2004: 293.

indictments of the perniciousness of an unbridled application of clinical neuroscience psychiatry.

While Hoch's observations provide an early orientalist's account of how the traditional indigenous wisdom about mental health and illness may need to be transformed and lifted up and brought into juxtaposition with culturally contextualized modern liberating ideas about human nature and the self, those of Kapur and Agarwal provide contemporary and hard-nosed accounts of experienced experts about some of the ugly realities of the clinical neuroscience colonization of Indian indigenous psychiatry, something that Hoch had warned over 30 years ago.

EFFORTS DIRECTED AT CONSTRUCTING AN AUTHENTIC MODERN INDIAN PSYCHIATRY

The appropriateness of a Western model of psychotherapy as discussed by Hoch has been a relatively long-standing concern of Indian psychiatrists. This was argued by Neki in his article on the *guru–celā* relationship.[1062] Similarities and differences in these two types of relationships are discussed, including not only their dynamics and goals, but philosophies. Neki emphasized that psychotherapy as construed in the West is more impersonal and a distinctive product of an expressive culture that values independence, individual freedom and self-expression. Dependency is de-valued in this relationship. The model of an Indian dyadic relationship from which a client or disciple and guru work through is much more personal and dependency is fostered and valued. Disciple is on a spiritual quest: he or she seeks and is provided with advice, clarification, mental cleansing of illusions, self-discipline, and self-realization in a cosmic, temporally extended framework. The guru conceptualizes his or her disciple in light of succession of existences. This includes his own relationship with the disciple likewise which is thought to extend both before and after the present life. While there are similarities in the two relationships, the culturally-conditioned expectancies create sharp differences.

[1062] Neki 1973, 1975.

> The Western psychotherapist – with such weaponry as free-association, dream interpretation, and working through - is a product of an overly expressive culture; while the guru – which is meditational, contemplative, and other 'mind-quieting' procedures is an evolute of suppressive culture.[1063]

While the non-directive Western psychotherapist does not give advice and waits for insight to sprout from within the patient, the guru prefers being directive and pedagogically instructive via his prestige and power of suggestion, usually rallying scriptural authority. To Neki, the cultural bases, duration, and goals of a guru-relationship sharply set it apart from that of psychotherapist and patient or client in the West.

Neki's exhortations are examples of a trend that runs counter to the wholesale importation and application of biomedical psychiatry and studies that exemplify this perspective seek to evolve a viable model of psychotherapy that is consistent with Indian values and cultural assumptions (which, as emphasized earlier, should be a cornerstone of a truly integrated and responsive modern psychiatry in India). For example, Vahia adopted techniques from Patañjali's *aṣṭāṅgayoga* to devise a rationalistic psychotherapy that creates a relaxed, detached attitude that enables patients, with help from the therapist, to focus constructively on identified problems of living.[1064] This therapy, based on concepts prevalent in India, was used on patients suffering from 'psychoneurotic and psychosomatic disorders'. Jaipal discusses the applicability of Western models of psychotherapy to India, concluding that Western psychology and psychotherapy are problematic for several reasons.[1065] Western approaches, she argues, stress the 'micro' context of self-examination, as compared to the more 'macro', social interactive mode that is consistent with Indian cultural psychology; they reflect the closed, bounded personality structure of the West, which is so different from the more open, permeable boundaries of the Hindu concept of personality; an impersonal, open exploration of self with a stranger, a neutral therapist, is inapplicable in a culture in which rank, age, gender, and social relations are based on shared values, shared communities, and shared assumptions about everyday happenings; and people in India tend to anticipate social advocacy and action as part of the therapeutic package, which is

---

[1063] Neki 1973: 764.

[1064] Vahia 1969.

[1065] Jaipal 1997.

antithetical to most models of psychotherapy in the West. Jaipal reviews the work of Paranjpe, Balodhi, Sinha, and Misra, all of whom formulate what kind of approach to psychotherapeutic helping is more appropriate to the cultural psychology of India. It is difficult to determine the extent to which more authentically Indian models of healing and psychotherapy have actually 'taken hold' in Indian clinical neuroscience psychiatry. Besides psychotropic drugs, today's clinical neuroscience psychiatry emphasizes many types of Western therapies that Indian psychiatrists continue to urge need to be framed in a culturally sensitive idiom.[1066]

Balodhi argues that the roots of a workable approach to mental illness are to be found in ancient India.[1067] He points to philosophical traditions involving the study of logic and language that he believes provide a way of understanding and measuring the thought disorder found in schizophrenia. His basic position is that ancient India's system of logic, as expounded in Nyāyaśāstra, can be used to understand schizophrenic speech. He reviews the basic tenets of the system designed to analyze sentences, not only from a linguistic point of view, but also from a logical perspective. He describes the five fallacies outlined by Gautama, who is credited with having compiled the Nyāya system: discrepancy, contradiction, ambiguity, futility, and mistiming.[1068] Balodhi essentially reviews the appropriateness of relying on these ancient canons of logic and exhorts his colleagues to use the theory to develop an appropriate instrument, akin to a mental status examination, to better understand schizophrenia in Indian terms. He seems to urge Indian psychiatrists to turn to ancient sources of Hindu knowledge to develop methods for studying contemporary problems. Implied in this exhortation is the view that ancient India was an integrated and complete society, able to handle its social and psychological problems quite well – so well, in fact, that its characteristics should be heeded by contemporary mental health workers.

Another example of efforts that are consistent with a move to an authentic native approach to treating psychiatric condition involves actually testing the usefulness of procedures and drugs belonging to the native indigenous medical tradition. For example, Vasudevan and col-

---

[1066] Paranjpe 1988; Balodhi 1991; Sinha 1993; Misra and Gergen 1993.

[1067] Balodhi 1986a, 1986b; see also Gautama 1999.

[1068] Gautama 1999.

leagues used Yoga meditation procedures in treating tension headache and found them effective in relieving pain.[1069] Sharma and co-workers used Vipassana meditation on similar patients and also demonstrated relief.[1070] The ayurvedic herbal preparation termed *mentat* was used to test memory span, fluctuations of attention, and aspects of autonomic nervous system and muscle functioning in university students. Results showed significant increases in memory span and galvanic skin conductance and significant decrease in fluctuation of attention and myographic potential that indicated 'multipoint effects of the herbal formulation'.[1071]

Gelderloos and co-workers compared the influence of a Maharishi ayurvedic herbal preparation with placebo on age-related visual discrimination tasks in 48 male practitioners of Transcendental Meditation who were over the age of 35.[1072] The experimental group had improved significantly more than the control group after three to six weeks of treatment. The researchers concluded that the preparation 'may enhance attentional capacity or alertness, and thus reverse some of the detrimental cognitive effects of aging'.

Ramu and colleagues report on attempts to compare the treatment of acute schizophrenics using ayurvedic and contemporary methods.[1073] They review in detail the forms of treatment prescribed for psychosis (*unmāda*) and the efforts of others to use indigenous treatments. The researchers conducted a controlled study of 30 patients, aged 16 to 45, who suffered with symptoms of acute psychosis, diagnosed as schizophrenia. Patients were placed in two groups that were rater-blind. One group was treated with chlorpromazine, an older but still representative of conventional antipsychotics used in biomedical psychiatry; the other group received a range of methods intrinsic to Ayurveda.[1074] The study:

> was intended to examine the combined effects of the general line of ayurvedic treatment comprising of *śodhana* (cleaning) and *śamana*

[1069] Vasudevan *et al.* 1994.

[1070] M. P. Sharma *et al.* 1990.

[1071] A. Agarwal, Dubey, and Dubey 1990; see also Dixit, Agrawal, and Dubey 1993.

[1072] Gelderloos *et al.* 1990.

[1073] Ramu *et al.* 1992.

[1074] Given the small sample and the availability of different types of ayurvedic treatments that were used, it was not possible to have identical treatment protocols in the 'experimental' group.

(palliative) measures and *sattvavajayacikitsā* (psycho-behavioural therapy).[1075]

In keeping with the pragmatic, empirical method associated with Ayurveda, if symptoms did not subside by 50 per cent by the fifteenth day of the experimental period, there was a shift in ayurvedic strategy. A number of evaluation procedures were used to assess efficacy of treatment. Both forms of treatment produced significant improvement, but the chlorpromazine- and ayurvedic-treated groups did not differ statistically. The procedural methods followed in this study suggest several potential difficulties, some of which were acknowledged by the researchers, but others cannot be determined from the report. For instance, how were groups selected? Did both groups receive some form of behavioural treatment, and if so were they comparable? Did researchers approach patients of both groups with the same degree of interest and enthusiasm regarding treatment? How pure were the ayurvedic medicines, and were they truly rooted in ayurvedic knowledge? Despite its limitations, the study by Ramu *et al.* reflects a rationale for a methodology that could be used to assess the applicability of ayurvedic treatment to psychiatry. In effect, it attempts to compare ancient, traditional approaches to treatment associated with Ayurveda with newer methods linked to biomedical psychiatry.

That an ancient tradition of medicine germane to people espousing the ancient Hindu world image and culture is being used to treat contemporary Hindus raises an important theoretical question regarding the cultural history of psychiatric phenomena and the comparative study of medical systems. Ramu and co-workers apparently approached their study with the following assumptions: (1) schizophrenia, or some analogous form of psychiatric condition, existed in ancient India; (2) the naturalistic approach to its diagnosis and treatment that evolved in ancient India (Ayurveda) was a relatively complete system and seems to have coped with conditions like schizophrenia – probably a human universal – reasonably well; (3) Ayurveda treatments, evolved for Indian patients suffering from Indian varieties of psychiatric condition, should apply to contemporary Indian victims of such conditions, whose forms of mental pathology are either universal or at least indigenous to Hindu people; (4) the efficacy of ayurvedic methods of treatment have the cul-

---

[1075] Ramu *et al.* 1992: 43.

tural and medical validity of millennia and for this reason should be honoured and tested in a reasonable way with contemporary scientific methods.

Many of these assumptions may be based on false premises. For example, some believe that disorders like schizophrenia may not have existed during the ancient millennia when Ayurveda evolved. No one variety of *unmāda,* Ayurveda's 'madness or insanity', or psychosis, may correspond to schizophrenia of today. Even if Ayurveda's disease *unmāda* 'is' or embraces schizophrenia, viewed neuro-biologically, and even though it may be equated with contemporary schizophrenia diagnostically, it may still not be the same as contemporary schizophrenia, given the social, ecological and cultural changes that have transpired over the centuries. Finally, it is not clear whether the exact medicaments or procedures of traditional ayurvedic practices are recoverable. Even if they were, it is unclear whether they would be relevant as per evaluative criteria based on culture and public health standards of modernity that are far different from that of earlier historical eras.

Exclusive reliance on the placebo-controlled paradigm of comparison raises additional questions. In this paradigm medical efficacy is broken down into two components: one determined by strict, measurable influences linked to chemistry, anatomy, and pharmacology, and a so-called placebo response. The latter, a non-specific effect ascribed to expectation, is no doubt a human universal. All persons inherit a central nervous system that when properly engaged and activated by means of culturally, psychologically meaningful influences, such as those presented by respected healers, bring about changes in autonomic nervous system, hormonal, and general physiological functions that can change the course of sickness. Instead of a *placebo response,* this should be called a *natural healing response* and regarded as a variable that is potentially useful in all therapies. While its benefits usually average around 30 per cent, it can go as high as 70 per cent. Putting aside the purely measurable effects linked to the pharmacology and physiology of ayurvedic treatments, an interesting question is whether these treatments can activate and entrain natural healing responses in environments that are culturally different from those that prevailed when the Ayurveda tradition enjoyed more exclusive power over the imagination of Indian subjects. It needs to be emphasized, however, that Ayurveda healing encompasses far more than just a placebo response. All great traditions of medicine include procedures and medicaments that pass contemporary scientific standards and that also challenge its premises.[1076]

These are the kinds of issues brought into focus when one compares and tests systems of medical practice between cultures widely separated by time, place, and level of modernization.[1077] Studies are now needed to better document not only the efficacy of ayurvedic pharmacological treatment, but also other aspects of Ayurveda, such as its spiritual, moral, ethical, and psychological impact. Modern psychotherapy is a secular approach grounded in notions of individualistic personhood. Compared to secular methods of psychotherapy such as cognitive, insight-oriented, and interactive approaches, Ayurveda apparently relied on entirely different assumptions about personhood, social responsibility, duty, community values, and moral-spiritual traditions. These themes need further evaluation to establish the validity of Ayurveda for treating Indian patients. If ayurvedic physiological and psychological therapies were tested in an appropriate manner, for example, with respect to culturally defined varieties of psychiatric condition, the validity of indigenous medical psychiatry of India might be further enhanced.

Comment

Building an authentic modern Indian psychiatry that is fully resonant with its indigenous traditions of mental health is a risky and difficult task. Much can be said in favour of the reductive logic that is used in modern biological psychiatry. The science of mental state examination and clinical psychiatry, even though influenced greatly by specific cultural and philosophical assumptions, in this case largely derived from German phenomenology, evolved by concentrating on phenomena tied to the brain and physiology. This required peeling away aspects of personal experience and behaviour tied to social circumstances, values, motivations, and existential traditions.[1078] Researchers look for universal indicators or markers of disorders to yield an alleged common language for psychiatry, with its associated goal of a truly international diagnostic system.[1079] This idiom works well when its narrow categories are

---

[1076] Fabrega 2002b.

[1077] See Ramu *et al.* 1992.

[1078] Berrios 1984.

[1079] Sartorius *et al.* 1993; see also Fabrega 1994, 1995.

searched for and applied to the Indian landscape of psychiatric phenomena as native researchers have shown. However, it can exclude much of the tumult of despair and disappointment that is recorded by Nunley and Cohen, feared but optimistically coped with by means of the methods described by Lamb, and by the obvious benefits that come with Ayurveda psychiatry.

The reductive, impersonal, and allegedly universal language of modern psychiatry is based on a secular, rationalist, and individualist psychology. Its logic is consistent with the liberal ideals spawned in the Enlightenment and promoted by worldwide industrial capitalism. Moreover, psychiatry and its disorders are now considered to be embodiments of real, scientific, ontological, and epistemologically grounded entities (i.e. reïfications), and there is obvious justification for applauding the successes of this version of medicine, including psychiatry. Consequently, not raising biomedical psychiatry to a dominant position may prove too big and risky an obstacle to the development of an authentic Indian psychiatry. Since a representative indigenous psychiatry should ideally be based on valid indigenous disorders, these might prove difficult to operationalize and even then be poorly handled by biomedical treatment. An authentic non-Western system of psychiatry might then find itself without magic bullets with which to slay its culturally specific maladies or disorders.

CAN PSYCHIATRY IN INDIA PRESERVE THE VISION OF ITS CULTURAL TRADITION?

The complex array of problems encompassing emotional and behavioural disaffections that across human history have been inherent in any society or civilization has been reconfigured by modern psychiatry. They now go by the name of psychiatric diseases or disorders, *scientific and clinical objects* that have been created in modern and postmodern society as a consequence of advances in neuroscience and clinical studies. What modern psychiatry addresses certainly involves a hard-to-demarcate core of brain- and body-based physiological disruptions. This is indisputable. However, material reviewed earlier makes clear that psychiatric conditions comprise far more than this neurological substratum. The materialization of disturbances of internal mechanisms of control yields an amalgam of behaviour and bodily signs and symptoms. This amalgam attains social significance only in a context of cultural symbols and meanings that communicate alterations of experience and behaviour that throw individuals off course and can cause suffering and distress. In this whole process, psychiatric condition and the person showing it create a scenario that is only interpretable within a social context. Modern psychiatry tends to reduce, if not eliminate, personal, social, and cultural dimensions of psychiatric conditions, trading these for objective, reliably measured markers or indicators.

The social mandate and associated culture pattern that sponsors biomedical, including psychiatric, science is part of a political and economic world-view that has spread across the globe in modern times. It involves a hegemonic capitalist order that has come to play a dominant role in improving health, maintaining social stability, administering criminal justice, and providing social welfare. The ideology inherent in the culture pattern that fosters modern psychiatry is also supported by purely economic considerations – for example, reimbursement schemes for medical care, sponsorship of medical enterprises by international pharmaceutical cartels, and myriad other activities of the capitalist market economy that sponsor research and promote scientism, which in turn brings profits. Stated baldly, biomedical science including neuropsychiatry has acquired a social momentum based on politico-economic power and this has led to its spread and colonization of worldwide native traditions of medicine. Of course, the reasons for the hegemony of Western science and its associated cultural conventions and traditions are complex and cannot be ascribed exclusively to the power of science and/or to private politico-economic interests. The state itself has also come to sponsor scientific medicine and psychiatry in ways that seek to undo the inequality of power between colonizer and colonized in contestation over hegemony.[1080]

In the prevailing internationalist doctrine about psychiatric condition, diagnostic criteria are often held to 'carve nature at its joints', *nature* here meaning properties of thought or mentation, emotion, and patterns of visceral somatic behaviour that reflect how the nervous system shapes behaviour and bodily function and experience and, by extension, how behavioural breakdowns are structured. Descriptions of conditions such as anxiety, depression, schizophrenia, and somatoform conditions

---

[1080] Prakash 1999.

are formulated in the modern perspective as though they were natural objects or categories. The assumption is that any perturbation of the universal brain and mind, materially structured in the same common way for all members of Homo sapiens regardless of culture, will be manifested in a particular type of psychiatric disorder, seen as a universal, neurobiologically specific malfunction of the brain. Scientists seek an international common language to allow shared diagnoses and communication among biomedically trained clinicians, regardless of where they practice. The hope is that psychiatric disorders might eventually be defined, diagnosed, and treated with data and measurements pertaining to aspects of central nervous system functioning. Hence the biomedical perspective insists on a hard description of disorder that delineates clinically significant and persistent symptoms and signs that meet scientific criteria of measurement. It asserts that disorders are ontologically different from ordinary worries, sufferings, and miseries. Modern biomedical psychiatry has availed itself of the power and seductiveness inherent in the language of science as a cultural force in India.

As earlier discussions have emphasized, clinical research and practice by psychiatrists in India deal with contemporary scientific formulations of psychiatric conditions. They may take account of social life and culture, but their concern is to understand how biomedically specified disorders are played out there. Imbued with the power of science, such clinicians and researchers are primarily intent on determining how best to use their science in the Indian setting. Indian psychiatrists whose works have been examined are, literally speaking, experts steeped in biomedical psychiatry who share the assumptions of internationalist, Western scientific brand of psychiatry and whose research is geared to applying it in the subcontinent. However, a review of the social history of psychiatric phenomena in India reveals a broader picture: as patterns of distress, emotions that spell danger or dread, as interference or inefficiency in the conduct of everyday activities, as failure to meet expected goals and obligations, and sometimes as frank behavioural breakdowns and dilapidations, all of this constructed in the cultural idiom of Indian culture psychology. Of course, psychiatric conditions may not always manifest and be relevant from standpoint of complex ideas of philosophical psychology and morality (karmic debts, breaking of caste prescriptions, impulses and ideas that fail to meet expectations of *dharma*). They are often obscured by the quotidian preoccupations of everyday life. However, even though everyday conflicts and concerns may permeate the distress and breakdown of a psychiatric condition, why and how these undermine wellbeing is culturally resonant. The modern biomedical psychiatrist, nevertheless, finds it necessary, when examining a patient, to dust away and look through cultural shadows so as to discount encumbrances and bring out into the biomedical light what lies beneath: the indicators and criteria that point to and make up the sharp outlines of universal entities, or pan-cultural psychiatric disorders (delusions, sleep disturbance, problems in thinking, hallucinatory experiences, emotional breakdown). This gaze in the name of science is one that not only leaves out or minimizes native, traditional interpretations, but can at times seem to deny and denigrate the relevance and implications of the true wisdom of an authentic Indian approach to psychiatric phenomena.

For thousands of years, the subcontinent of India has had a rich tradition in its interpretation of the human condition. The Hindu tradition that fuses philosophy, psychology, religion, and moral precepts involving duty and obligation has enabled Indian societies not only to persist and maintain their integrity but to also surmount and constructively assimilate crises of poverty, public health, and politico-economic hardship and exploitation. But for an elitist core of politicians and scientists, who have fully internalized the ethos of the modern age and largely applied it objectively and impersonally, the bulk of the population of India still lives emboldened by the fullness and integrity of conceptions about morality, responsibility, and sanctity. It seems misplaced, insensitive, inappropriate, and also highly simplistic to now attempt to indiscriminately impose a model of psychiatric condition and a regimen of treatment on persons distressed and burdened by emotional and behavioural disorders, to which are attached not only foreign and suppressive tenets, but also structures of control, regimentation, and economic efficiency.

This discussion leaves open a number of questions. Does this latest phase of the cultural history of psychiatric phenomena in India necessarily and inexorably entail a defeat of ancient wisdom and morality of an indigenous system of mental health therapies? Is it adequate and defensible, in a humanistic sense, to impose in a traditional society like India a secular, individualistic model of behaviour and mental afflictions in order to control of disorders that have evolved in another region of humanity wherein special cultural and politico-economic contingencies prevailed? Is it possible for societies like India to constructively blend the benefits of scientific knowledge and technologies of application developed in another part of the world with its ancient values and traditions? Can India demonstrate to itself and the world that it can minister to the needs of victims of psychiatric condition in a way that respects not only their interpretation of their circumstances and miseries but also the traditional ontology and understanding of suffering? Human culture, experience, and history teach that it is not disorders, diseases, or syndromes that configure and play out psychiatric conditions in human societies, but rather composites of disappointments, frustrations, failures to cope, and inefficiencies to blend one's personal needs with those of others and of society. In India, this state of affairs is still visible and alive with energy and special integrity, a result of its rich cultural heritage and tradition. It remains to be seen whether or not a culturally valid and useful interpretation of psychiatric phenomena can be developed in India that successfully integrates the products of the scientific method with the insights of its cultural tradition.

A SOCIALLY RESPONSIVE PSYCHIATRY IN INDIA

Indian biomedical psychiatrists have contributed in a significant way to clarification of important theoretical and empirical problems involving contemporary psychiatry. The greater attention now paid to problems of mental illness and the formal recognition of needs and priorities in this area of public health imply that general principles of emotional and behavioural wellbeing, including the benefits of biomedical psychiatry, have become an integral and official part of medical policy in India.[1081] It is important, however, not to lose sight of the insights of traditional Indian conceptions and approaches to psychiatric phenomena. Indeed, one can propose that the social and cultural history of such Indian psychiatry provides a much-needed remedy for some of the deficiencies and weaknesses of contemporary biomedical psychiatry.

Biomedicine is an integral part of contemporary, modern Western culture and a quintessential product of a non-spiritual world-view. Its claims to expertise are based on a philosophy about the material reality of the outside world and of the human body that is termed scientific

---

[1081] S. P. Agarwal 2004.

objectivism and realism. Western culture stipulates a *secular credo* in medicine. This evolved during a slow process that is generally held to have started in ancient Greco-Roman societies, continued on through the Christian-medieval and the early modern European periods, and culminating during the modern era. Evolution of the biomedical approach to disease and healing has involved a progressive sharpening of a scientific image of medicine. The long view of this process involves the discarding of earlier cultural, existential, humanistic, and ultimately religious/spiritual approaches to disease ending with the secular credo.

Modern concepts of psychiatric condition and the practice of psychiatry share a similar history and its associated secular philosophy. The process has resulted in a historically unique conceptualization and approach to sickness and healing that is dualistic, drawing distinctions between body and mind. In reality, the sufferings and agonies of both physical and mental illnesses undermine and disable a person's sense of self and the whole social and cultural standing and bring into play basic existential considerations that raise spiritual and religious questions. Yet, the secular credo of biomedicine formulates these changes as falling outside the periphery of medical theory and practice.

General social criticisms of contemporary medicine regarding the impersonality, objectivity, and exclusive focus on disease and healing, at the expense of the person and his or her wellbeing, considered in a broad cultural framework, apply to all of medicine as for psychiatry. This *general clash* of values between science and secularism contra spirituality and culture (another type of dualism), a function of modern medicine's shedding of its older, broader healing mandate, provide the context for the basic theme that is pursued in this chapter.

An appreciation of the cultural history of psychiatric phenomena in India cannot but lead one to examine biases inherent in and question characteristics of modern biomedical psychiatry. We have seen that India embodies a distinctive system of mental health theory and practice that was an outgrowth of and deeply connected to its special cultural blend of *dharma*, religion, spirituality, philosophical psychology, as well as bodily physiology and medicine. Social practices and institutions pertaining to social responsibility, moral obligation, spiritual fulfilment, and medical healing constituted a system of knowledge and belief that served to shape and condition personal experience and normative behaviour. On the one hand, this system authorized and validated distinctive personal and communitarian values. On the other hand, it also provided a rationale for regulation, control, educative moral therapies, and outright medical treatment in the event psychological anomalies of feeling and thought and social conflicts occasioned the special mix of distress, sickness, and behavioural breakdowns that add up to psychiatric condition.

In contrast to this Indian psychiatry, the modern credo of biomedical psychiatry stipulates a reductive, secular approach that is also eliminative in that it excludes broader considerations that are encompassed by culture and spirituality. Objective, impersonal, and technical dimensions of cognition, feeling, behaviour, and bodily experience are singled out as appropriate, *biological markers* of psychiatric condition, conceptualized now as psychiatric disorders. Such a biomedical formulation leaves out hallmarks of Indian psychiatry; namely, concerns involving values, morality, responsibility, spirituality and religion, and the whole existential matrix of meaning associated with human suffering as reflected in altered personal experience, behaviour, and bodily function. The stark contrast between the two systems of knowledge and practice pertaining to psychiatric phenomena compels one to take notice, seek explanations about, and examine implications surrounding the difference. To examine the cultural evolution of psychiatry in India is to bring into focus questions about the very foundations and presuppositions of how a social system or institution we label psychiatry is configured and enacted in relation to society and culture.

It may well be the case that not much should be expected of psychiatry per se in efforts to control and alleviate the suffering of mental illness. Perhaps psychiatric practice should be formulated as a technical clinical neuroscience discipline and practice: it evolved a system of constructs, conventions about disorders, and approaches to treatment based on biomedical sciences that have established medical validity. After all, contemporary psychiatry in fully developed pluralistic Western societies is hardly immune to the criticism of overlooking social and cultural dimensions of patients showing psychiatric disorders.[1082] Cultural psychiatry in modern Western societies exists as an area of research focus. Its rationale and goal is to sensitize general psychiatrists and physicians to the subtleties of diagnosis and practice; in other words, to the diverse ways in which cultural beliefs and orientations are insinuated and becloud psychiatric conditions; and that require sensitive appreciation in

---

[1082] Mezzich *et al.* 1996.

order to make mental health care meaningful and effective. This line of thinking suggests that India's limitations in integration of modern and traditional perspectives on psychiatric phenomena are simply examples, perhaps more striking, of problems inherent in the evolution of modern psychiatry. India's dilemmas reviewed earlier are little different from dilemmas encountered in general medicine worldwide wherein, again, the impersonal, secular credo of biomedicine encounters remnants of traditional orientations and meanings. The task for a responsive Indian psychiatry in this view of the matter is to build around the practices of psychiatric clinicians a cadre of non-medical mental health workers who are able to provide meaningful linkages between the new and old ways of perceiving and coping with universal disturbances.

WHAT THE CULTURAL EVOLUTION OF PSYCHIATRY IN INDIA TEACHES

The causes of psychiatric conditions and the ways in which they are understood and dealt with in societies that have carried forward the civilization of India up to contemporary times chronicle one representation of social and cultural evolution of psychiatry. A similar evolutionary pathway could be described for China and, indeed, for any culture and civilization. While distinctive, the pathways merge with the advent and spread to dominance of biomedical psychiatry within respective traditional societies during the contemporary period. Factors affecting demography, the ecology of disease, level of public health, patterns of politico-economic exploitation, and the inevitable play of human social conflicts create conditions that in vulnerable individuals lead to varieties of psychiatric condition and their sufferings. All societies show this dialectic and manifest the associated social problems and institutions created to handle them in socially constructed ways. Contingencies of history, political economy, and culture determine how the complex amalgam of psychiatric phenomena is symbolically represented and dealt with in contingent, practical terms.

Developments in the subcontinent that have been discussed illustrate the important role that a society's many social ecological conditions and cultural traditions play in producing and shaping psychiatric phenomena. In a general sense, similar contingencies prevailed in Western societies during earlier historical periods. In India, however, one encounters a different civilization, culture, and set of traditions. What has been formulated as India's cultural psychology plays a pivotal, intermediary role in its *formulation and construction* of health and problems of sickness, including psychiatric condition. On the one hand, the cultural psychology *creates Indian varieties* of such conditions; that is, it provides a social idiom, vocabulary, set of cognitive models, and patterns of emotional expression in terms of which the psychiatric conditions acquire a social identity and meaning. On the other hand, the cultural psychology is represented in a corresponding way in the set of social practices, traditions, and institutions in terms of which varieties of human suffering and behavioural breakdowns can be repaired by means of idioms and procedures, the rationale of which is integral to that psychology.

An Indian pattern of psychiatry began to take shape in Vedic times and rose to prominence in the early historical period. This psychiatry addressed distinctive cultural varieties of psychiatric condition and provided for ways of ameliorating their effects. It was embedded in religious tenets about the meaning of existence, in patterns and standards regarding personal experience and moral behaviour, and in the various systems of philosophical, spiritual, and medical healing that comprised its intellectual traditions.

During the early medieval era, possibly in relation to conflicts involving spread and incorporation of the 'great' tradition of Indian culture into once isolated villages and inter-village networks where 'little' traditions predominated, peoples experienced considerable crises of order and organization. Such a process, described as Sanskritization, contributed to new religious beliefs and patterns of devotion and mystical longing. The indigenous system of beliefs involving mental health and practice broadened and deepened and as a result Indian psychiatry expanded its reach. Its system of knowledge and educative, rehabilitative procedures of healing maintained their salience and spread to incorporate patterns of longing and devotion of the expanded movement of Bhakti revivalism. This system of ideas and meanings was concentrated in homes and intimate, private settings, to be sure. More importantly, the culture and social institutions surrounding the interpretation and handling of psychiatric condition was located in more public, shared settings of healing. This would have included, for example, temples, monasteries, places of cultic sanctity, assemblies or meetings of village leaders, private establishments of diviners, shamans, indigenous practitioners of different brands of medicine and healing, and homes, compounds, clinics and hospitals operated by the more academic, learned physicians of Ayurveda. Together, these healers perpetuated basic tenets of the cultural psychology that made sense of psychiatric condition and provided new ways for healing it.

In the centres of administration, commerce, and politico-economic influence, learned traditions were preserved, continued to be refined, and were elaborated. There, the academic Ayurveda, its offspring of Siddha medicine, related academic philosophical systems and traditions pertaining to human psychology, social conduct, and bodily control continued to be refined, grew, and evolved. As knowledge and practices about psychiatric phenomena grew and diversified, psychiatric condition considered as an Indian prototype or exemplar was itself evolving. Understandings and practices that came into prominence spread and diffused into distant centres of administration and power, towns and eventually in villages where it was incorporated in the minds of healers and their clients, the consumers of the knowledge and expertise that constituted newer representations of psychiatric phenomena. To the academic, indigenous stream of knowledge about diagnosis and practice one has to add that produced by insightful practitioners who could combine units of information pertaining to diagnosis and healing in creative ways, invent new units of information, and avail themselves of new interpretations that came with the diffusion of knowledge from other centres of civilization.

One must assume that a new phase of the cultural history of psychiatric phenomena in the subcontinent of India took place during the medieval era proper and in association with Muslim influences. Before partition, these were most fully realized in regions and sectors where intermarriage, conversion, and patterns of mutual accommodation and assimilation between traditions took place in a prominent way. In such communities, sharp conflicts and tensions affecting the configuration, enactment, and handling of psychiatric condition were created by the clash between, on the one hand, Hindu representations of psychiatric phenomena and, on the other hand, Unani principles of medicine. The latter included generalizations about disease derived from Prophetic Medicine, moral principles of conduct articulated in the sayings of the Prophet and interpretations made of these by legal scholars. Islamic culture of medicine included general religiously inspired tenets about human psychology, their effects on personal experience and behaviour, and practices of devotion, spirituality, and mystical longing linked to Sufism. After partition and mass resettlement, there still remain communities in which one finds strong Muslim influences along with remaining Hindu conceptions. These exist largely in mere contiguity, if not actual social isolation, although no doubt there exist patterns of complex syncretism in many communities of India.[1083]

Detailed studies about this chapter of Hindu/Muslim interchange in the story of the cultural evolution of psychiatric phenomena in India are not available. Despite the differences in culture and traditions and the clearly documented history of tension, hostility, and resentment one can assume that for the most part the main tenets of Hindu civilization and culture have maintained their integrity and insularity. For the medieval, early modern era, only the general contact between physicians of the two traditions of academic medicine has been given attention. Putting aside mass conversions to Islam, in the literature available, there is little mention of the actual residues of Muslim influence in the corpus of knowledge and systems of practice that bear on general medicine and almost nothing about beliefs, attitudes, and practices related to mental illness. Since much of Unani medicine emphasizes a predominantly secular, humoral approach to sickness and healing that is formally like but different in content from Ayurveda, and since there exist striking differences in the character and thrust of religion and spirituality in Islam compared to Hinduism, one can assume that the cultural history of psychiatric phenomena in India during the 12 centuries of intermittent Hindu–Muslim jostling and tensions has involved some diffusion and mutual influence and borrowings.[1084] However, Ayurveda and related Hindu mental health institutions have retained their identity and vitality. In short, the systems of meaning and practices surrounding psychiatric phenomena in the subcontinent that were set in motion during the Vedic age and early historical period have retained their organization and meaning. During the medieval period and later in centres of predominant Hindu culture and up until the modern era when a system of biomedicine was imposed in the subcontinent under the aegis of colonialism and has influenced developments to the present, traditional conceptions and approaches to psychiatric phenomena continue to be influential.

[1083] Ahmad 1964b.

[1084] Ahmad 1964a, 1964b.

It would then appear that the major collision and resulting deflection in the flow of the cultural history of psychiatry in the subcontinent was brought about by the exportation and promulgation of biomedical psychiatry. Beginning in the 1970s, modern Western psychiatry deepened its mantle of medicalization with respect to diagnosis and treatment. As indicated elsewhere, swings between organic, neurological as compared to psychological, social, and moral emphases have constituted a historical pattern in the evolution of modern psychiatry.[1085] At the present time, a neurobiological and neuro-pharmacological reductionism holds centre stage in societies and this phase of the cultural evolution of psychiatric phenomena is very much orchestrated in the homophonic tune of world capitalism.

During decades preceding 1970, psychoanalysis and existentialism as part of this, along with social, community, and cultural emphases, were influential in how psychiatry was patterned and practiced in Western societies. These developments with respect to psychiatry appear to have had a comparatively smaller influence in the Indian psychiatry of the subcontinent. Psychoanalysis has had a distinguished career in India beginning in the 1950s but its influence was predominantly intellectual and confined to urban centres and among cosmopolitan, elite, intelligentsia. Its impact on the psychiatric phenomena in the society at large was smaller. Only since then and in comparatively recent times has a modern definition of psychiatric condition as disease or disorder become prevalent in India. Along with this came the establishment of a profession of medical psychiatry, an official, state-sponsored policy involving family/community principles of prevention, research, and medical treatment in hospitals and clinics.

Previous chapters discussed the contrast and clash between biomedical psychiatry and indigenous Indian traditions. This collision has given rise to valiant, and committed efforts to diagnose and treat the newly diagnosed, modern varieties of psychiatric condition. Does the future of the cultural evolution of psychiatry in Indian civilization promise a further imposition of the biomedical ideology and its associated procedures and technologies with eventual spread and rise to prominence of an exclusivist, secular credo? Will the spread of biomedical psychiatry as a feature of the language of science and modernity continue to be influential or will a nationalist strain of re-affirmation of

[1085] Fabrega 2000b.

Hindu traditions manage to assimilate and appropriate the best of what biomedical psychiatry has to offer and also retain the wisdom of its deeply rooted conceptions and practices involving psychiatric phenomena? These are questions but prompt one to take stock of what the modern discipline and profession of psychiatry are all about.

SUMMARY COMMENT

The science and practice of contemporary biomedical, internationalist psychiatry can be viewed as a powerful, effective disinfectant. When applied to a new social fabric this psychiatry appears to neutralize and cleanse many of the varieties of psychiatric disorders and diseases that it has identified. It can also be viewed as a disinfectant so powerful that it manages to bleach the fabric of its essential colouration, destroying natural defences and established practices of healing, in the process eradicating some old problems but also creating new ones that it is unable to reverse.

A study of the cultural history of psychiatric phenomena in India brings to light precisely this irony and conundrum. The importation and colonization of biomedical reductionism has produced beneficial effects in terms of its own science and practice. However, while effective it has also caused strains and tensions. One can point to features of the rationale and mode of operation of biomedical psychiatry that contrast and conflict with an indigenous Indian psychiatry in ways that are inimical to and potentially destructive of its cultural integrity. Rhetorically, one can suggest that international biomedical psychiatry embodies and perpetuates seven cultural and spiritual 'sins' that are in need of absolution. These sins are evident in the subcontinent of India, a setting whose history and culture particularly predisposes it to the associated insults and ills. These are: (1) failure to appreciate the *biological and cultural* roots of psychiatric condition and of the implications that this has about its symbolic character; (2) advocacy of a secular, reductionist credo of diagnosis and practice that neglects the evolved wisdom of Ayurveda as well as empirical findings in cultural psychiatry pertaining to the integrated character of psychiatric condition; (3) reliance on a philosophy and nosology of diagnosis that negates the importance of human cultural psychology and the importance of the character of a person's social, existential reality in affecting the character of psychiatric condition; (4) disregard of the social, moral mandate that gave rise to the discipline and profession of psychiatry which was to help disadvantaged, exploited, and marginalized social groups whose plight requires addressing more broadly based concerns about meaning, culture, and spirituality as well as the realities of political and economic exploitation; (5) a neglect and devaluing of the essential cultural and religious/spiritual meanings that are integral to the experience and diagnosis of psychiatric condition in India and that are in special need of re-affirmation in the contemporary world; (6) undue reliance on a system of pharmaceutical treatment the rationale of which minimizes if not excludes the role of social practices based on indigenous cultural psychology; and (7) the endorsement of forms of psychotherapy that bypass the importance of cultural, religious, and spiritual concerns in favour of objective, economistic, pre-formulated, behavioural rubrics.

India presents one with an interesting slant on the cultural evolution of psychiatric phenomena. Biomedical developments provide a seductive appeal to social planners, scientists, practitioners and especially the lay population: new and foreign tenets of great theoretical appeal and economic momentum that promise the normalization of behaviour, fuller realization of the potentials of personal biography, rectification of deviance, and relief of human suffering. The appeal of biomedical psychiatry almost cannot and should not be resisted in India, nor in other nations to which it spreads. However, India provides a conjunction of features of a civilization the culture of which is not duplicated anywhere in the world: a rich tradition of welfare and spirituality regarding problems of mental health, a preserved medical tradition of great ancestry that has a proven track record of understanding and coping with those problems, and a democratic and comparatively open society that has embraced the science and humanism of the West.

The unfolding of the features that distinguish societies of the subcontinent logically entail that biomedical psychiatry cannot fail to politically and economically colonize India successfully. In the West, the premises of biomedical psychiatry have deep roots and have evolved naturally and slowly, with its many intrusions and disruptions worked out and incorporated into the institutions where psychiatric conditions are emplaced in the social fabric. It is possible to evaluate the strengths and limitations of modern psychiatry relatively easily in societies where its culture and history spanned movements that created the science and profession of psychiatry in the first place.[1086] Its premises constitute and are deeply entrenched in the Western culture. In attempting to conquer India, however, biomedical psychiatry enters into a terrain where the soil has not been suitably prepared and the benefits of its products cannot be easily anticipated. Moreover, the secular, antiseptic idiom of psychiatry not only clashes with local cultural traditions about mental health and human welfare but also runs the risk of undermining and destroying their credibility. How this clash between antithetical and potentially irreconcilable approaches to the preservation and promotion of psychological and spiritual health is to be resolved poses serious questions and requires careful and thoughtful study. The goal, as discussed earlier, is success in integrating the two perspectives into creative social and scientific policies.

[1086] Fabrega 2000a.

Bibliography

1. REFERRED SOURCES

Adityanjee, G. S. Raju and S. K. Khandelwal 1989. Current status of multiple personality disorder in India. *American Journal of Psychiatry* 146: 1607–1610.

Agarwal, A. K. 1998. The forgotten millions. *Indian Journal of Psychiatry* 40: 103–119.

Agarwal, Aruna, M. L. Dubey, and G. P. Dubey 1990. Effects of mentat on memory span, attention, galvanic skin resistance (GSR) and muscle action potential (EMG) among normal adults. *Pharmacopsychoecologia* 3: 39–42.

Agarwal, S. P. 2004. Contemporary issues-II: private sector psychiatry: the need for an ethical approach. In: S. P. Agarwal *et al.* (eds.), *Mental Health: An Indian Perspective, 1946–2003*: 293–295. New Delhi: Elsevier for the Directorate General of Health Services, Ministry of Health and Family Welfare. (Freely available at mohfw.nic.in/Mental%20Health.pdf).

Agarwal, S. P., D. S. Goel, R. L. Ichhpujani, R. N. Salhan, and S. Shrivastava (eds.) 2004. *Mental Health: An Indian Perspective, 1946–2003*. New Delhi: Elsevier for the Directorate General of Health Services, Ministry of Health and Family Welfare.

Ahmad, Aziz 1964a. Introductory: the Muslim impact. In: Aziz Ahmad, *Studies in Islamic Culture in the Indian Environment*: 73–100. Oxford: Clarendon Press.

—— 1964b. *Studies in Islamic Culture in the Indian Environment*. Oxford: Clarendon Press.

Alexander, P. J. and J. S. Das 1997. Limited utility of ICD-10 and DSM-IV classification of dissociative and conversion disorders in India. *Acta Psychiatrica Scandinavica* 95: 177–192.

Alter, Joseph S. 2004. *Yoga in Modern India: The body between science and philosophy*. Princeton, NJ: Princeton University Press.

Arnold, David 1988. Introduction: disease, medicine and empire. In: David Arnold (ed.), *Imperial Medicine and Indigenous Societies*: 1–26. Manchester: Manchester University Press.

Arnold, David 1993. *Colonizing the Body: State medicine and epidemic disease in nineteenth-century India*. Berkeley: University of California Press.

Arora A, A. Avasthi, and P. Kulhara 1997. Subsyndromes of chronic schizophrenia: a phenomenological study. *Acta psychiatrica Scandinavica* 96: 225–229.

Assayag, Jackie 1999. But, they do move ... Religion, Illness and Therapeutics in Southern India. In Marine Carrin (ed.), *Managing Distress: Possession and Therapeutic Cults in South Asia*: 30–50. New Delhi: Manohar Publishers.

Aṣṭāṅgasaṃgraha 1999. *Aṣṭāṅgasaṃgraha: The compendium of eight branches of Ayurveda*. Trans. by a board of scholars. 3 vols. Delhi: Sri Satguru Publishers.

Atran, S. and A. Norenzayan 2005. Religion's evolutionary landscape: counterintuition, commitment, compassion, communion. *Behavioral and Brain Sciences* 27: 713–730; discussion 730–770.

Avalos, H. 1995. *Illness and Health Care in the Ancient Near East: The role of the temple in Greece, Mesopotamia and Israel*. Atlanta, GA: Scholars Press.

—— 1999. *Health Care and the Rise of Christianity*. Peabody, MA: Hendrikson Publishers.

Babb, L. 1983. Destiny and responsibility: karma in popular Hinduism. In: Charles F. Keyes and E. Valentine Daniel (eds.), *Karma: An anthropological inquiry*: 163–181. Berkeley, CA: University of California Press.

Bagadia, V. N., K. S. Ayyar, P. D. Lakdawala, S. M. Sheth, V. N. Acharya, and P. V. Pradhan 1986. Psychiatric morbidity among patients attending medical outpatient department. *Indian Journal of Psychiatry* 28: 139–144.

Bagchi, A. K. 1997. *Medicine in Medieval India: Eleventh to eighteenth Century*. Delhi: Konark Publishers.

Bala, Poonam 1982. The Ayurvedic and Unani systems of medicine in medieval India. *Studies in History of Medicine* 6: 282–289.

—— 1984a. Ayurveda and the British Raj: Factors influencing state policy in British India. *Studies in History of Medicine* 8: 13–19.

—— 1984b. Indigenous medicine and the state in India. *Ancient Science of Life* 5: 1–4.

—— 1991. *Imperialism and Medicine in Bengal: A Sociohistorical perspective*. New Delhi: Sage Publications.

Balodhi, J. P. 1986a. Logical structure of a sentence as a tool for the assessment of thought disorder (Ancient Indian View). *Indian Journal of Psychiatry* 28: 253–257.

—— 1986b. Perspective of Rajayoga in its application to mental health. *NIMHANS Journal* 4: 133–138.

Balodhi, J. P. 1987. Constituting the outlines of a philosophy of Ayurveda: mainly on mental health import. *Indian Journal of Psychiatry* 29: 127–131.

—— 1989. In pursuit of Indian Shastric sources for community mental health. *NIMHANS Journal* 7: 49–54.

—— 1991. Holistic approach in psychiatry: Indian view. *NIMHANS Journal* 9: 101–104.

Balodhi, J. P. and J. Roy Chowdhary 1986. Psychiatric concepts in Atharvaveda: a review. *Indian Journal of Psychiatry* 28: 63–68.

Balodhi, J. P. and M. S. Keshavan 1986. Bhagavadgita and psychotherapy. *NIMHANS Journal* 4: 139–143.

Banerji, B. 1981. Historical and sociocultural foundations of health services systems. In: G. R. Gupta (ed.), *The Social and Cultural Context of Medicine in India*: 1–29. New York, NY: Vikas Publishing House.

Banerji, D. 1985. *Health and Family Planning Services in India: An epidemiological, socio-cultural and political analysis and a perspective.* Delhi: Lok Paksh.

Barth, Fredrik 1990. The Guru and the conjurer: transactions in knowledge and the shaping of vulture in Southeast Asia and Melanesia. *Man* (NS) 25: 640–653.

Basalla, G. 1967. The spread of Western science: a three-stage model describes the introduction of modern science into any non-European nation. *Science* 156: 611–622.

Basham, Arthur Llewellyn 1954. *The Wonder that Was India: A survey of the culture of the Indian subcontinent before the coming of the Muslims.* London: Sidgwick & Jackson; New York, NY: Grove Press.

Beaglehole, Robert and Ruth Bonita 1997. *Public Health at the Crossroads: Achievements and prospects.* Cambridge: Cambridge University Press.

Beals, Alan R. 1962. *Gopalpur: A South Indian village.* New York, NY: Holt, Rinehart and Winston.

Beidelman, Thomas Owen 1959. *A Comparative Analysis of the Jajmani System.* Locust Valley, NY: J. J. Augustin Inc. for the Association for Asian Studies.

Bell, C. 1989. Religion and Chinese culture: toward an assessment of "popular religion". *History of Religions* 29: 35–57.

Berrios, German E. 1984. Descriptive psychopathology: conceptual and historical aspects. *Psychological Medicine* 14: 303–313.

Berrios, German E. and Roy Porter (eds.) 1995. *A History of Clinical Psychiatry: The origin and history of psychiatric disorders.* London: Athlone.

Berry, J. W., Y. H. Poortinga, M. H. Segall, and P. R. Dasen 1992. *Cross-cultural Psychology: Research and applications*. New York, NY: Cambridge University Press.

Bharati, A. [Agehananda Bharati, Swami] 1985. The self in Hindu thought and action. In: Anthony J. Marsella, George DeVos, and Francis L. K. Hsu (eds.), *Culture and Self: Asian and Western perspectives*: 185–230. New York, NY: Tavistock Publications.

Bhatia, M. S. and S. C. Malik 1991. Dhat syndrome: A useful diagnostic entity in Indian culture. *British Journal of Psychiatry* 159: 691–705.

Bhattacharyya, Deborah P. 1986. *Pāgalāmi: Ethnopsychiatric knowledge in Bengal*. (Foreign and Comparative Studies/South Asian Series, No. 11.) Syracuse, NY: Maxwell School of Citizenship and Public Affairs, Syracuse University.

Bheḷasaṃhitā 2000. *Bheḷasaṃhitā*. Text with English Translation, Commentary and Critical Notes. Trans. by K. H. Krishnamurthy, ed. by P. V. Sharma. Varanasi: Chaukhambha visvabharati.

Bhugra, Dinesh 1992. Psychopathology in ancient Indian texts: a review. *History of Psychiatry* 3: 167–186.

—— 1996. Hinduism and Ayurveda: implications for managing mental health. In: Dinesh Bhugra (ed.), *Psychiatry and Religion: Context, consensus and controversies*: 97–110. London: Routledge.

—— 2001. The colonized psyche: British influence on Indian psychiatry. In: Dinesh Bhugra and Roland Littlewood (eds.), *Colonialism and Psychiatry*: 46–76. New Delhi: Oxford University Press.

Bhugra, Dinesh and P. De Silva 1995. Sexual dysfunction and sex therapy: a historical perspective. *International Review of Psychiatry* 7: 159–166.

Biardeau, Madeleine 1989. *Hinduism: The anthropology of civilization*. Trans. by Richard Nice. New York, NY: Oxford University Press.

Bird-David, Nurit 1990. The giving environment: another perspective on the economic system of gatherer-hunters. *Current Anthropology* 31: 189–196.

—— 1992a. Beyond "The Hunting and Gathering Mode of Subsistence": culture-sensitive observations on the Nayaka and other modern hunter-gatherers. *Man* (NS) 27: 19–44.

—— 1992b (with Allen Abramson, Jon Altman, M. G. Bicchieri, Ernest S. Burch, Jr., Carol R. Ember, Kirk M. Endicott, Roy Richard Grinker, Steve Gudeman, Mitsuo Ichikawa, Tim Ingold, and George W. Wenzel). Beyond "The Original Affluent Society": a culturalist reformulation [and Comments and Reply]. *Current Anthropology* 33: 25–47.

Bird-David, Nurit 1994. Sociality and immediacy: or, past and present conversations on bands. *Man* (NS) 29: 583–603.

—— 1996. Puja or sharing with the gods?: on ritualized possession among Nayaka of South India. *Eastern Anthropologist* 49: 259–276.

—— 1999 (with Eduardo Viveiros de Castro, Alf Hornborg, Tim Ingold, Brian Morris, Gisli Palsson, Laura M. Rival, and Alan R. Sandstrom). "Animism" revisited: personhood, environment, and relational epistemology [and Comments and Reply]. *Cultural Anthropology* 40 (Suppl.): S67–S91.

—— 2004. Illness-images and joined beings: A critical/Nayaka perspective on intercorporeality. *Social Anthropology* 12: 325–339.

Birnbaum, Raoul 1979. *The Healing Buddha*. Boulder, CO: Shambhala.

Blair, Chauncey J. 1961. *Heat in the Rig Veda and Atharva Veda*. Doctoral dissertation, University of Pennsylvania (1957). New Haven, CT: American Oriental Society.

Boehm, Christopher 1999. *Hierarchy in the Forest: The evolution of egalitarian behavior*. Cambridge, MA: Harvard University Press.

Boltz, Judith M. 1985. *Taoist Rites of Exorcism*. Doctoral dissertation, University of California, Berkeley.

Bottero, Alain 1991. Consumption by semen loss in India and elsewhere. *Culture, Medicine and Psychiatry* 15: 303–320.

Boyer, Pascal 1994. *The Naturalness of Religious Ideas: A cognitive theory of religion*. Berkeley, CA: University of California Press.

Brockington, J. L. 1987. The Puranas – priestly or popular? *Hasyana Sahitya Akademi* [*Journal of Indological Studies*] 2: 122–134.

—— 1996. *The Sacred Thread: Hinduism in Its Continuity and Diversity*. 2nd edition. Edinburgh: Edinburgh University Press.

Brown, Donald E.1991. *Human Universals*. Philadelphia, PA: Temple University Press; New York: McGraw-Hill.

Brown, W. Norman 1966. *Man in the Universe: Some continuities in Indian thought*. Berkeley, CA: University of California Press.

Buitenen, J. A. B., van (ed. and trans.) 1981. *The Bhagavadgītā in the Mahābhārata: A bilingual edition*. Chicago, IL: University of Chicago Press.

Carakasaṃhitā 1996. *Caraka Saṃhitā*. Trans by A. C. Kaviratna and P. Sharma, 5 vols. 2nd revised edition, vols I–IV. Delhi: Sri Satguru Publications.

Carlson, L. E., M. Speca, K. D. Patel, and E. Goodey 2003. Mindfulness-based stress reduction in relation to quality of life, mood, symptoms of stress, immune parameters in breast and prostate cancer outpatients. *Psychosomatic Medicine* 65: 571–581.

Carstairs, G. M. and R. L. Kapur 1976. *The Great Universe of Kota: Stress, change, and mental disorder in an Indian village*. Berkeley, CA: University of California Press; London: Hogarth Press Ltd.

Castel, Robert 1988. *The Regulation of Madness: The origins of incarceration in France*. Trans. by W. D. Halls: Berkeley, CA: University of California Press; Cambridge: Polity Press.

Chakravorti, Haripada 1996. *Criminal Justice in Ancient India*. Delhi: Sharada Publishing House.

Chakravorty, Ranes C. 1993. Diseases of antiquity in South Asia. In: K. F. Kiple (ed.), *The Cambridge World History of Human Disease*: 408–413. Cambridge: Cambridge University Press.

Chandra, L. 1984. Introduction. in: Clifford, Terry, *Tibetan Buddhist Medicine and Psychiatry: The diamond healing*: xv–xxx. York Beach, ME: Samuel Welser, Inc.

Chandra V., M. Ganguli, R. Pandav, J. Johnston, S. Belle, and S. T. DeKosky 1998a. Prevalence of Alzheimer's disease and other dementias in rural India: The Indo–US study. *Neurology* 51: 1000–1008.

Chandra, V., S. T. DeKosky, R. Pandav, J. Johnston, S. H. Belle, G. Ratcliff, and M. Ganguli 1998b. Neurological factors associated with cognitive impairment in a rural elderly population in India: The Indo–US Cross-National Dementia Epidemiology Study. *Journal of Geriatric Psychiatry and Neurology* 11: 11–17.

Charney, Dennis S. 2004. Psychobiological mechanisms of resilience and vulnerability: implications for successful adaptation to extreme stress. *American Journal of Psychiatry* 161: 195–216.

Chattopadhyaya, Brajadulal 1994. *The Making of Early Medieval India*. Delhi: Oxford University Press.

Chattopadhyaya, Debiprasad 1977. *Science and Society in Ancient India*. Calcutta: Research India Publications.

Chowdhury, A. N., D. Sanyal, S. K. Dutta, S. Banerjee, R. De, K. Bhattacharya, S. Palit, P. Bhattacharya, R. K. Mondal, and M. G. Weiss 2000. Stigma and mental illness: pilot study of laypersons and health care providers with the EMIC in rural West Bengal, India. *International Journal of Medicine* 7: 257–260.

Clifford, Terry 1984. *Tibetan Buddhist Medicine and Psychiatry: The diamond healing*. York Beach, ME: Samuel Welser, Inc.

Cohen, Lawrence 1992. *No Aging in India*. Doctoral dissertation, Department of Anthropology, Harvard University; Ann Arbor, MI: UMI Dissertation Information Service.

—— 1998. *No Aging in India: Alzheimer's, the bad family, and other modern things*. Berkeley, CA: University of California Press.

Cohen, Mark Nathan 1989. *Health and the Rise of Civilization*. New Haven, CT: Yale University Press.

—— 1998. Were early agriculturalists less healthy than food collectors? In: C. R. Ember, M. Ember, and P. N. Peregrine (eds.), *Research Frontiers in Anthropology*, Vol. 1: *Archaeology*: 75–90. Upper Saddle River, NJ: Prentice Hall.

Cohen, Mark Nathan and G. J. Armelagos (eds.) 1984. *Paleopathology and the Origins of Agriculture*. New York, NY: Academic Press.

Cohn, Bernard S. 1955. The changing status of a depressed caste. In: McKim Marriott (ed.), *Village India: Studies in the Little Community*: 53–77. Chicago, IL: University of Chicago Press.

—— 1965. Anthropological notes on disputes and law in India. *American Anthropologist* (NS) 67: 82–122.

—— 1987. Some notes on law and change in North India. In: B. S. Cohn (ed), *An Anthropologist among the Historians and Other Essays*: 554–574. Delhi: Oxford University Press.

Conrad, Lawrence I. 1993. Arab-Islamic medicine. In: W. F. Bynum and R. Porter (eds.), *Companion Encyclopaedia of the History of Medicine*, vol. 1: 676–727. London: Routledge.

—— 1995. The Arab-Islamic medical tradition. L. I. Conrad, M. Neve, V. Nutton, R. Porter, and A. Wear (eds.), *The Western Medical Tradition: 800 BC To AD 1800*: 93–138. Cambridge: Cambridge University Press.

Conrad, Peter and Joseph W. Schneider (eds.) 1980. *Deviance and Medicalization: From badness to sickness*. St. Louis, MO: Mosby.

Coreil, J. 1997. Health behavior in developing countries. In: David S. Gochman (ed.), *Handbook of Health Behavior Research III: Demography, development, and diversity*: 179–199. New York, NY: Plenum Press.

Csordas, T. J. 1994. *Embodiment and Experience: The existential ground of culture and self*. Cambridge: Cambridge University Press.

Daniel, E. Valentine 1984. *Fluid Signs: Being a person the Tamil way*. Berkeley, CA: University of California Press.

Dasgupta, Surendranath 1922. *A History of Indian Philosophy*. 5 vols. Cambridge: Cambridge University Press. (Reprint: Delhi: Motilal Banarsidass, 1975).

Davidson, R. J., J. Kabat-Zinn, J. Schmacher, M. Rosenkranz, D. Muller, S. F. Santorelli, F. Urbanowski, A. Harringtron, K. Bonus, and J. F. Sheridan 2003. Alterations in brain and immune function produced by mindfulness meditation. *Psychosomatic Medicine* 65: 564–570.

Davis, Kingsley 1951. *The Population of India and Pakistan*. Princeton NJ: Princeton University Press.

De Michelis, Elizabeth 2004. *A History of Modern Yoga: Patanjali and Western esotericism*. London: Continuum.

Demiéville, Paul 1985. *Buddhism and Healing Demiéville's article "Byo" from Hobogirin*. Trans. by Mark Tatz. Boston, MA: University Press of America.

Derasari, S. and V. D. Shah 1988. Comparison of symptomatology of depression between India and USA. *Indian Journal of Psychiatry* 30: 129–134.

De Sousa, Alan and D. A. De Sousa (eds.) 1984. *Psychiatry in India*. Bombay: Bhalani Book Depot.

Devereux, G. 1956. Normal and abnormal. In: J. Casagrande and T. Gladwin (eds.), *Some Uses of Anthropology, Theoretical and Applied*: 23–48. Washington, DC: Anthropological Society of Washington.

Diamond, Jared M. 1997. *Guns, Germs and Steel: The fates of human societies*. New York, NY: W. W. Norton.

Dixit, S.P., U. Agrawal, G. Dubey 1993. Executive fatigue and its management with "mentat". *Pharmacopsychoecologia* 6: 7–9.

Dols, Michael Walters (trans.) 1984. *Medieval Islamic Medicine: Ibn Ridwan's treatise 'On the prevention of bodily ills in Egypt'*. Arabic text ed. by Adil S. Gamal. Berkeley, CA: University of California Press.

—— 1985. Insanity in Byzantine and Islamic medicine. In: John Scarborough (ed.),*Symposium on Byzantine Medicine* (Dumbarton Papers, no. 38): 135–148. Baltimore, MD: Dumbarton Oaks Publishing Service.

—— 1992. *Majnun: The madmen in medieval Islamic Society*. Oxford: Clarendon Press.

Doniger, Wendy and Brian K. Smith (trans.) 1991. *The Laws of Manu*. New York, NY: Penguin Books.

Dörner, Klaus 1981. *Madmen and the Bourgeoisie: A social history of insanity and psychiatry*. Trans. by Joachim Neugroschel and Jean Steinberg. Oxford: Basil Blackwell.

Dube, K. C. 1970. A study of prevalence and biosocial variables in mental illness in a rural and an urban community in Uttar Pradesh, India. *Acta Psychiatrica Scandinavica* 46: 327–359.

—— 1978. Nosology and therapy of mental illness in Ayurveda. *Comparative Medicine East and West* 6: 209–228.

Dumont, Louis 1970. *Homo hierarchicus: The caste system and its implications*. complete revised English edition. Trans. by Mark Sainsbury, Louis Dumont, and Basia Gulati. London: Paladin. (Reprint: Delhi: Oxford University Press, 1998).

Dyson, Tim 1989. Indian historical demography: developments and prospects. T. Dyson (ed.), *India's Historical Demography: Studies in Fam-*

ine, Disease and Society (Collected Papers on South Asia, No. 8): 1–15. London: Curzon Press; Riverdale: The Riverdale Company.

Eaton, S. Boyd and Stanley B. Eaton III 1996. Gatherers and human health. In: R. B. Lee and R. Daly (eds.), *The Cambridge Encyclopedia of Hunters and Gatherers*: 449–455. Cambridge: Cambridge University Press.

Edgerton, R. B. 1992. *Sick Societies: Challenging the myth of primitive harmony*. New York, NY: Free Press.

Edwards, J. W. 1983. Semen anxiety in South Indian cultures: cultural and transcultural significance. *Medical Anthropology* 7: 51–67.

Eliade, Mircea 1969. *Yoga: Immortality and Freedom*. Trans. from the French by Willard R. Trask. 2nd edition. Princeton, NJ: Princeton University Press. (1st edition: 1958). Original published in French as *Le yoga. Immortalité et liberté* by Librairie Payot, Paris 1954).

—— 1964. *Shamanism: Archaic techniques of ecstasy*. Trans. from the French by Willard R. Trask. Princeton, NJ: Princeton University Press; New York, NY: Pantheon Books.

Epstein, Mark and Lobsang Rapgay 1989. Mind, disease, and health in Tibetan medicine. In: A.A. Sheikh and K. S. Sheikh (eds.), *Healing East & West: Ancient Wisdom and Modern Psychology*: 124–145. New York, NY: John Wiley & Sons. (Also published as *Eastern and Western Approaches to Healing*, New York, NY: Wiley, 1989).

Erikson, Erik H. 1950. *Childhood and Society*. New York: W. W. Norton; London: Imago.

Erndl, Kathleen M. 2000. A trance healing session with Mataji. In: David Gordon White (ed.), *Tantra in Practice*: 97–118. Princeton, NJ: Princeton University Press.

Ernst, Waltraud 1987. The establishment of "native lunatic asylums" in early nineteenth-century British India. In: G. Jan Meulenbeld and Dominik Wujastyk (eds.), *Studies on Indian Medical History*: Papers presented at the International Workshop on the Study of Indian Medicine held at the Wellcome Institute for the History of Medicine, 2–4 September, 1985: 169–204. Groningen: Egbert Forsten. (Reprint: Delhi: Motilal Banarsidass, 2001).

—— 1988. The European insane in British India, 1800–58: A case study in psychiatry and colonial rule. In: David Arnold (ed.), *Imperial Medicine and Indigenous Societies*: 27–44. Manchester: Manchester University Press.

—— 2002. Plural medicine, tradition and modernity: Historical and contemporary perspectives: view from below and from above. In: W. Ernst (ed.), *Plural Medicine, Tradition and modernity, 1800–2000*: 1–18. New York, NY: Routledge.

Fabrega, Horacio, Jr. 1974. *Disease and Social Behavior: An Interdisciplinary Perspective.* Cambridge, MA: Massachusetts Institute of Technology Press.

—— 1975. The need for an ethnomedical science. *Science* 189: 969–975.

—— 1976a. The function of medical care systems. *Perspectives of Biology and Medicine* 20: 108–119.

—— 1976b. The biological significance of taxonomies of disease. *Journal of Theoretical Biology* 63: 191–216.

—— 1989a. Cultural relativism and psychiatric illness. *Journal of Nervous and Mental Disease* 177: 415–425.

—— 1989b. The self and schizophrenia: a cultural perspective. *Schizophrenia Bulletin* 15: 277–290.

—— 1989c. An ethnomedical perspective of Anglo-American psychiatry. *American Journal of Psychiatry* 146: 588–596.

—— 1992a. The role of culture in a theory of psychiatric illness. *Social Science and Medicine* 35.1: 91–103.

—— 1992b. Culture and the psychosomatic tradition. *Psychosomatic Medicine* 54.5: 561–566.

—— 1993. A cultural analysis of human behavioral breakdowns: an approach to the ontology and epistemology of psychiatric phenomena. *Culture, Medicine and Psychiatry* 17: 99–132.

—— 1994. International systems of diagnosis in psychiatry. *Journal of Nervous and Mental Disease* 182: 256–263.

—— 1995. Cultural challenges to the psychiatric enterprise. *Comprehensive Psychiatry* 36: 377–383.

—— 1997. *Evolution of Sickness and Healing*. Berkeley, CA: University of California Press.

—— 2000. Culture, spirituality and psychiatry. *Current Opinion in Psychiatry* 13: 525–530.

—— 2002a. *Origins of Psychopathology: Phylogenetic and cultural aspects of mental illness*. New Brunswick, NJ: Rutgers University Press.

—— 2002b. Culture, spirituality and psychiatry. *Current Opinion in Psychiatry* 13: 525–530.

—— 2005a. Commentary: Biological evolution of cognition and culture: Off Arbib's mirror neuron system stage? *Behavioral and Brain Sciences* 28.2: 131–132.

—— 2005b. Consciousness and emotion are minimized. Commentary on *Religion's Evolutionary Landscape: Counterintuition, Commitment, Compassion, and Communion*, by A. Atran and A. Norenzayan. *Behavioral Brain Sciences* 27.6: 736–737.

Fabrega, Horacio, Jr. 2005c. Dynamic systems modeling and psychiatric conditions. *Behavioral and Brain Sciences* 28.2: 199–201.

—— 2006a. Why psychiatric conditions are special. *Perspectives in Biology and Medicine* 49: 586–692.

—— 2006b. Making sense of behavioral irregularities in chimpanzees. *Neuroscience and Biobehavioral Reviews* 30: 1260–1273.

—— 2007. How psychiatric conditions were made. *Psychiatry: Interpersonal and Biological Processes* 70: 130–153.

Feuerstein, Georg 1998. *The Yoga Tradition: Its history, literature, philosophy and practice*. Prescott, AZ: Hohm Press. (Reprint: New Delhi: Bhavana Books, 2002).

—— 2006. *Holy Madness: Spirituality, crazy-wise teachers, and Enlightenment*. Prescott, AZ: Hohm Press.

Fields, Gregory P. 2001. *Religious Therapeutics: Body and health in Yoga, Ayurveda, and Tantra*. Albany, NY: State University of New York Press. (Reprint: Delhi: Motilal Banarsidass, 2002).

Filliozat, Jean 1964. *The Classical Doctrine of Indian Medicine: Its origins and its Greek parallels*. Trans from the original in French by Dev Raj Chanana. Delhi: Munshiram Manoharlal.

Flood, Gavin 1996. *An Introduction to Hinduism*. Cambridge: Cambridge University Press.

—— (ed.) 2003. *The Blackwell Companion to Hinduism*. Oxford: Blackwell Publishing.

Foucault, Michael 1965. *Madness and Civilization: A history of insanity in the Age of Reason*. Trans from the French by Richard Howard. New York, NY: Pantheon Books.

Freed, Stanley A. and Ruth S. Freed 1964. Spirit possession as illness in a North Indian village. *Ethnology* 3: 152–171.

Fried, Morton H. 1967. *The Evolution of Political Society: An essay in political anthropology*. New York, NY: Random House.

Fuller, Christopher J. 1992. *The Camphor Flame: Popular Hinduism and society in India*. Princeton, NJ: Princeton University Press.

Furedi, Frank 2004. *Therapy Culture: Cultivating vulnerability in an uncertain age*. London: Routledge.

Gandhi, Raj S. 1981. An interactionist approach to the sociology of illness and medicine and its relevance to the Indian situation. In: Giri Raj Gupta (ed.), *The Social and Cultural Context of Medicine in* India: 55–75. New Delhi: Vikas Publishing House Pvt Ltd.

Ganguli M, G. Ratcliff, V. Chandra, S. Sharma, J. Gilby, R. Pandav, S. Belle, C. Ryan, C. Baker, E. Seaberg, and S. Dekosky 1995. A Hindi version of the MMSE: the development of a cognitive screening instrument for a largely illiterate rural elderly population in India. *International Journal of Geriatric Psychiatry* 10: 367–377.

Ganguli M., V. Chandra, J. E. Gilby, G. Ratcliff, S. D. Sharma, R. Pandav, E. C. Seaberg, and S. Belle 1996. Cognitive test performance in a community-based nondemented elderly sample in rural India: the Indo–US Cross-National Dementia Epidemiology Study. *International Psychogeriatrics* 8: 507–524.

Ganguli M., S. Dube, J. M. Johnston, R. Pandav, V. Chandra, and H. H. Dodge 1999. Depressive symptoms, cognitive impairment and functional impairment in a rural elderly population in India: a Hindi version of the geriatric depression scale (GDS-H). *International Journal of Geriatric Psychiatry* 14: 807–820.

Gardner, Peter M. 1982. Ascribed austerity: A tribal path to purity. *Man* (NS) 17: 462–469.

Gardner, Peter M. 1991a. Pragmatic meanings of possession in Paliyan Shamanism. *Anthropos* 86: 367–384.

Gardner, Peter M. 1991b. Foragers' pursuit of individual autonomy. *Current Anthropology* 32: 543–572.

Gautama, Shiv 1999. Mental health in ancient India and its relevance to modern psychiatry. *Indian Journal of Psychiatry* 41: 5–18.

Gelderloos P., H. H. Ahlstrom, D. W. Orme-Johnson, D. K. Robinson, R. K. Wallace, and J. L. Glaser 1990. Influence of a Maharishi Ayur-vedic herbal preparation on age-related visual discrimination. *International Journal of Psychosomatics* 37: 25–29.

Gellner, Ernest 1988. *Plow, Sword and Book: The structure of human history.* Chicago, IL: University of Chicago Press; London: Collins Harvill.

Ghurye, Govind Sadashiv 1952. *Caste and Class in India.* New York, NY: Philosophical Library 1952. (1st edition: *Caste and Race in India,* London: K. Paul, Trench, Trubner & co., 1932).

Goody, J. 1977. *Domestication of the Savage Mind.* Cambridge: Cambridge University Press.

—— 1986. *The Logic of Writing and the Organization of Society.* Cambridge: Cambridge University Press.

—— 1987. *The Interface between the Written and the Oral.* Cambridge: Cambridge University Press.

Gopinath, P. S. and S. K. Chaturvedi 1992. Distressing behavior of schizophrenics at home. *Acta psychiatrica Scandinavica* 86: 185–188.

Gough, E. Kathleen 1955. The social structure of a Tanjore village. In: McKim Marriott (ed.), *Village India: Studies in the Little Community*: 36–52. Chicago, IL: University of Chicago Press.

Grmek, Mirko D. 1989. *Diseases in the Ancient World*. Baltimore, MD: Johns Hopkins University Press.

Guha, Sumit 1999. *Environment and Ethnicity in India*. New York, NY: Cambridge University Press.

Gupta, Satya Pal 1976. *Psychopathology in Indian Medicine: Ayurveda with special reference to its philosophical sources*. Delhi: Chaukhamba Sanskrit Pratishthan. (Reprint: Aligarh: Ajaya, 1977).

Gururaj, G. and M. K. Isaac 2004. Psychiatric epidemiology in India: Moving beyond numbers. In: S. P. Agarwal, D. S. Goel, R. L. Ichhpujani, R. N. Salhan, and S. Shrivastava (eds.), *Mental Health: An Indian perspective, 1946–2003*: 37–61. New Delhi: Elsevier for the Directorate General of Health Services, Ministry of Health and Family Welfare. (Freely available at mohfw.nic.in/Mental%20Health.pdf).

Halbfass, Wilhelm 1988. *India and Europe: An essay in understanding*. Albany, NY: State University of New York Press.

—— 1991. *Tradition and Reflection: Experiments in Indian thought*. Albany, NY: State University of New York Press.

Haldipur, C. V. 1984. Madness in ancient India: concept of insanity in *Charaka Samhita* (1st century AD). *Comprehensive Psychiatry* 25: 335–344.

—— 1985. The meanings of psychotherapy. *Psychological Medicine* 15: 727–732.

—— 1989. Psychiatric nosology and taxonomy in ancient India. *Acta Psychiatrica Scandinavica* 80: 148–150.

Hartranft, Chip (ed.) 2003. *The Yoga-Sutra of Patnajali: A new translation*, with commentary. Boston, MA: Shambhala.

Hausman, Gary J. 1996. *Siddhars, Alchemy and the Abyss of Tradition: "Traditional" Tamil Medical Knowledge in "Modern Practice" (INDIA)*. Doctoral dissertation, University of Michigan. Ann Arbor, MI: UMI Dissertation Services.

Hilgard, Ernest Ropiequet 1986. *Divided Consciousness: Multiple controls in human thought and action*. Revised edition. New York, NY: Wiley. (1st edition: 1977).

Hoch, Erna M. 1961a. Contents of depressive ideas in Indian patients. *Indian Journal of Psychiatry* 3: 28–36.

—— 1961b. Contents of depressive ideas in Indian patients. *Indian Journal of Psychiatry* 3: 120–129.

—— 1972. Psychotherapy as aid for development. *Psychotherapy and Psychosomatics* 20: 226–240.

—— 1993. *Sources and Resources: A Western Psychiatrist's Search for Meaning in the Ancient Indian Scriptures*. Delhi: Book Faith India.

Hoffman, J. W., H. Benson, P. A. Arns, G. L. Stainbrook, G. L. Landsberg, J. B. Young, and A. Gill 1982. Reduced sympathetic nervous system responsivity associated with the relaxation response. *Science* 215: 190–192.

Hymavathi, Polavarapu 1993. *History of Ayurveda in Andhradesa (A.D. 14th – c. 17th c.)*. Warangal: Bhargava Publishers.

Inden, Ronald B. 2000. *Imagining India*. Bloomington, IN: Indiana University Press.

Ingold, Tim. 1987. *The Appropriation of Nature: Essays on human ecology and social relations*. Iowa City: University Of Iowa Press.

—— 1993. Tools and hunter-gatherers. In: A. Berthelet and J. Chavaillon (eds.), *The Use of Tools by Human and Non-human Primates*: 281–295. Oxford: Clarendon Press.

—— 1995. Hunting and gathering as ways of perceiving the environment. In: Roy Ellen and Katsuyoshi Fukui (eds.), *Redefining Nature: Ecology, Culture and Domestication*: 117–156. Oxford: Berg Publishers.

—— 1999. On the social relations of the hunter-gatherer band. In: R. B. Lee and R. Daly (eds.), *The Cambridge Encyclopedia of Hunters and Gatherers*: 399–410. Cambridge: Cambridge University Press.

—— 2000. *The Perception of the Environment: Essays in livelihood, dwelling, and skill*. London: Routledge.

Israili, A. H. 1980. Education of Unani medicine during Mughal period. *Studies in History of Medicine*: 177–182.

Ivanow, W. 1923. A witch case in medieval India. *Journal of the Asiatic Society of Bengal* 19: 43–50.

Jaggi, O. P. 1977. *Medicine in Medieval India*. Delhi: Atma Ram & Sons.

Jaipal, R. 1997. The holistic Indian world view and conceptions of mental health and individuality. Paper presented at HYAS Conference. New York, NY: Culture, Therapy and Healing, November 1997.

Jamison, S. W. and M. Witzel 2003. Vedic Hinduism. In: Arvind Sharma (ed.), *The Study of Hinduism*: 65–113. Columbia, SC: University of South Carolina Press; London: Eurospan. (pdf of long version, written in 1992 at www.people.fas.harvard.edu/~witzel/mwbib.htm).

Jeffery, Roger 1988. *The Politics of Health in India*. Berkeley, CA; London: University of California Press.

Jha, Dwijendra Narayan 1998. *Ancient India: In Historical Outline*. Revised edition. New Delhi: Manohar Publishers & Distributors.

Johnson, Allen W. and Timothy Earle 2000. *The Evolution of Human Societies: From foraging group to agrarian state*. 2nd edition. Stanford, CA: Stanford University Press.

Johnson, Mark 1987. *The Body in the Mind: The bodily basis of meaning, imagination and reason*. Chicago, IL: University of Chicago Press.

Jolly, Julius 1977. *Indian Medicine*. Trans from German by C. G. Kashikar. 2nd revised edition. New Delhi: Munshiram Manoharlal Publishers.

Joshi, V. N. and John Money 1995. Dhat syndrome and dream in transcultural sexology. *Journal of Psychology and Human Sexuality* 7: 95–99.

Justice, Christopher 1997. *Dying the Good Death: The pilgrimage to die in India's Holy City*. Albany, NY: State University of New York Press.

Kakar, D. N. 1988. *Primary Health Care and Traditional Medical Practitioners*. New Delhi: Sterling Publishers Pvt. Ltd.

Kakar, Sudhir 1968. The human life cycle: The traditional Hindu view and the psychology of Erik Erikson. *Philosophy East and West* 28: 127–136.

—— 1981. *The Inner World: A Psychoanalytic Study of Childhood and Society in India*. 2nd edition. Delhi: Oxford University Press.

—— 1982. *Shamans, Mystics and Doctors: A psychological inquiry into India and its healing traditions*. Boston, MA: Beacon Press.

Kala, A. K. 2004. Private sector psychiatry: phenomenal growth and persistent myths. In: S. P. Agarwal, D. S. Goel, R. L. Ichhpujani, R. N. Salhan, and S. Shrivastava (eds.), *Mental Health: An Indian perspective, 1946–2003*: 161–165. New Delhi: Elsevier for the Directorate General of Health Services, Ministry of Health and Family Welfare. (Freely available at mohfw.nic.in/Mental%20Health.pdf).

Kala, A. K. and R. Kala 1981. Psychotic jealousy: a phenomenological study. *Indian Journal of Psychiatry* 23: 237–241.

Kane, Pandurang Vaman 1968–72. *History of Dharmasastra: Ancient and mediaeval religious and civil law in India*. 2nd edition. Poona: Bhandarkar Oriental Research Institute.

—— 1990. *History of Dharmasastra*, vol. 2. 3rd edition. Poona: Bhandarkar Oriental Research Institute.

Kapur, R. L. 1979. The role of traditional healers in mental health care in rural India. *Social Science and Medicine* 13B: 27–31.

—— 2004. The story of community mental health in India. In: S. P. Agarwal, D. S. Goel, R. L. Ichhpujani, R. N. Salhan, and S. Shrivastava (eds.), *Mental Health: An Indian perspective, 1946–2003*: 92–100. New Delhi: Elsevier for the Directorate General of Health Services, Ministry of Health and Family Welfare. (Freely available at mohfw.nic.in/Mental%20Health.pdf).

Kapur, R. L., Malavika Kapur, and G. M. Carstairs 1974. Indian Psychiatric Survey Schedule (IPSS). *Social Psychiatry* 9: 71–76.

Kennedy, Kenneth A. R. 1990. Reconstruction of trauma, disease and lifeways of prehistoric peoples of South Asia from the skeletal record.

In: Maurizio Taddei (ed.), *South Asian Archaeology*, Proceedings of the Ninth International Conference of the Association of South Asian Archaeologists in Western Europe, Venice, 1987, Vol. 1: 61–77. Rome: Istituto Italiano per il Medio ed Estremo Oriente.

—— 1995. Have Aryans been identified in the prehistoric skeletal record from South Asia? Biological anthropology and concepts of ancient races. In: G. Erdosy (ed.), *The Indo-Aryans of Ancient South Asia: Language, material culture and* ethnicity: 32–66. Berlin: Walter de Gruyter.

—— 2000. *God-Apes and Fossil Men: Paleo-anthropology in South Asia.* Ann Arbor, MI: University of Michigan Press.

Kenoyer, Jonathan Mark 1997. Early city-states in South Asia: comparing the Harappan phase and early historic period. In: Deborah L. Nichols and Thomas H. Charlton (eds.), *The Archaeology of City-States: Cross-Cultural Approaches*: 51–70. Washington, DC: Smithsonian Institute Press.

—— 1998. Birth of a civilization: how a disparate collection of regional settlements evolved into one of the world's first great societies. *Archaeology* 51: 54–64.

Keyes, Charles F. and E. Valentine Daniel (eds.) 1983. *Karma: An anthropological inquiry.* Berkeley, CA: University of California Press.

Kinsley, David 1974. "Through the Looking Glass": divine madness in the Hindu religious tradition. *History of Religions* 13: 270–305.

Kiple, K. F. (ed.) 1993. *The Cambridge World History of Human Disease.* Cambridge: Cambridge University Press.

Kirmayer, L. J. 1984. Culture, affect and somatization, I. *Transcultural Psychiatric Research Review* 23: 159–188.

Kittrie, Nicholas Nehemiah 1971. *The Right to be Different: Deviance and enforced therapy.* Baltimore, MD: Johns Hopkins Press.

Kleinman, Arthur 1980. *Patients and Healers in the Context of Culture: An exploration of the borderland between anthropology, medicine, and psychiatry.* Los Angeles, CA: University of California Press.

—— 1988. *Rethinking Psychiatry: From cultural category to personal experience.* New York, NY: Free Press.

Kleinman, Arthur and Byron Good (eds.) 1985. *Culture and Depression: Studies in the anthropology and cross-cultural psychiatry of affect and disorder.* Berkeley, CA: University of California Press.

Kochhar, Rajesh 2000. *The Vedic People: Their history and geography.* New Delhi: Orient Longman Private Ltd.; London: Sangam.

Kroeber, Alfred Louis 1963. *An Anthropologist Looks at History.* Edited by Theodora Kroeber. Berkeley, CA: University of California Press.

Kulaichev, Alexy P. and Dina M. Ramendic 1989. Śrīyantra – The ancient instrument to control the psychophysiological state of man. *Indian Journal of History of Science* 24: 137–149.

Kulhara, Parmanand 1994. Outcome of schizophrenia: some transcultural observations with particular reference to developing countries. *European Archives of Psychiatry and Clinical Neuroscience* 244: 227–235.

Kulhara, Parmanand and G. Prasad Rao 1985. Obsessive compulsive neurosis in north-west India: a phenomenological study. *India Journal of Psychiatry* 27: 243–248.

Kulhara, Parmanand, K. Chandiramani, S. K. Mattoo, and A. Awasthi 1986a. A phenomenological study of delusions in schizophrenia. *Indian Journal of Psychiatry* 28: 281–286.

Kulhara, Parmanand, S. K. Mattoo, K. Chandiramani, S. Bhave, and A. Awasthi 1986b. Diagnostic systems for schizophrenia: a cross-sectional study of concordance from India. *Acta Psychiatrica Scandinavica* 74: 55–61.

Kulhara P, A. Avasthi, R. Chadda, K. Chandiramani, S. K. Mattoo, S. K. Kota, and S. Joseph 1989. Negative and depressive symptoms in schizophrenia. *British Journal of Psychiatry* 154: 207–211.

Kulke, Hermann and Dietmar Rothermund 1986. *A History of India*. 2nd edition. London: Croom Helm. (Reprint: New York, NY: Routledge, 1990).

Kutumbiah, P. 1969. *Ancient Indian Medicine*. Revised edition. Hyderabad: Orient Longman.

Lahiri, Tarapada 1986. Preface. In: T. Lahiri, *Crime and Punishment in Ancient India*. New Delhi: Radiant Publishers.

Lakoff, George 1987. *Women, Fire, and Dangerous Things: What categories reveal about the mind*. Chicago, IL: University of Chicago Press.

Lal Gaur, B. 1992. Agadatantra and bhūtovidyā. In: Priya Vrat Sharma (ed.), *History of Medicine in India: (from antiquity to 1000 A.D)*: 363–372. New Delhi: Indian National Science Academy.

Lamb, Sarah 1993. Growing in the Net of Maya: Persons, gender and life processes in a Bengali society. Unpublished PhD dissertation; Division of Social Sciences, Department of Anthropology, University of Chicago.

Langford, Jean M. 2002. *Fluent Bodies: Ayurvedic remedies for postcolonial imbalance*. Durham, NC: Duke University Press.

Larson, Gerald James 1987. Ayurveda and the Hindu philosophical systems. *Philosophy East and West* 37: 245–259.

—— 1993. Ayurveda and the Hindu philosophical systems. In: Thomas P. Kasulis (ed., with Roger T. Ames and Wimal Dissanayake), *Self as*

Body in Asian Theory and Practice: 103–122. Albany, NY: State University of New York Press.

Lazar, S. W., Catherine E. Kerr, Rachel H. Wasserman, Jeremy R. Gray, Douglas N. Greve, Michael T. Treadway, Metta McGarvey, Brian T. Quinn, Jeffery A. Dusek, Herbert Benson, Scott L. Rauch, Christopher I. Moore, and Bruce Fischl 2005. Meditation experience is associated with increased cortical thickness. *NeuroReport* 16: 1893–1897.

Leff, J., N. N. Wig, A. Ghosh, H. Bedi, D. K. Menon, L. Kuipers, A. Korten, G. Ernberg, R. Day, and N. Sartorius 1987. Expressed emotion and schizophrenia in north India, III. Influence of relatives' expressed emotion on the course of schizophrenia in Chandigarh. *British Journal of Psychiatry* 151: 166–173.

Leslie, Charles 1974. The modernization of Asian medical systems. In: John J. Poggie Jr. and Robert N. Lynch (eds.), *Rethinking Modernization: Anthropological perspectives*: 69–107. Westport, CT: Greenwood Press.

—— (ed.) 1976. *Asian Medical Systems: A comparative study*. Berkeley, CA: University of California Press.

Leslie, Charles and Allan Young (eds.) 1992. *Paths to Asian Medical Knowledge*. Berkeley, CA: University of California Press.

LeVine, R. A. 1973. *Culture, Behavior and Personality*. Chicago, IL: Aldine.

—— 1990. Enculturation: a biosocial perspective on the development of the self. In: D. Cicchetti and M. Beeghly (eds.), *The Self in Transition: Infancy to Childhood*: 99–117. Chicago, IL: University of Chicago Press.

LeVine, Robert. A. and Karin Norman 2001. The infant's acquisition of culture: early attachment re-examined in anthropological perspective. In: Carmell C. Moore and Holly F. Mathews (eds.), *The Psychology Of Cultural Experience*: 83–104. Cambridge: Cambridge University Press.

Liebeskind, Claudia 2002. Arguing science: Unani *tibb*, hakims and biomedicine in India, 1900–50. In: Waltraud Ernst (ed.), *Plural Medicine, Tradition and Modernity, 1800–2000*: 58–75. New York, NY: Routledge.

Lilienfeld, A. M. 1982. The Fielding H. Garrison Lecture: *Ceteris paribus*: the evolution of the clinical trial. *Bulletin of the History of Medicine* 56: 1–18.

Lindberg, David C. 1992. *The Beginnings of Western Science: The European scientific tradition in philosophical, religious, and institutional context, 600 BC to AD 1450*. Chicago, IL: University of Chicago Press.

Lingat, Robert 1973. *The Classical Law of India*. trans. from the French with additions by J. Duncan M. Derrett. Berkeley, CA: University of California Press.

Linrothe, Rob (ed.) 2006. *Holy Madness: Portraits of Tantric Siddhas*. New York, NY: Rubin Museum of Art; Chicago, IL: Serindia.

Lloyd, G. E. R. 1979. *Magic, Reason and Experience: Studies in the origins and development of Greek science*. Cambridge: Cambridge University Press.

Lukacs, John R. 1990. On hunter-gatherers and their neighbors in prehistoric India: contact and pathology. *Current Anthropology* 31: 183–186.

—— 1992. Dental paleopathology and agricultural intensification in South Asia: New evidence from Bronze Age Harappa. *American Journal of Physical Anthropology* 87: 133–150.

—— 1996. Sex differences in dental caries rates with the origin of agriculture in South Asia. *Current Anthropology* 37: 147–153.

Lutz, Catherine A. 1988. *Unnatural Emotions: Everyday sentiments on a Micronesian atoll and their challenge to Western theory*. Chicago, IL: University of Chicago Press.

Lynch, Owen M. (ed.) 1990a. *Divine Passions: The social construction of emotion in India*. Delhi: Oxford University Press; Berkeley, CA: University of California Press.

—— 1990b. The Mastram: emotion and person among Mathura's Chaubes. In: Owen M. Lynch (ed.), *Divine Passions: The social construction of emotion in India*: 91–115. Berkeley, CA: University of California Press.

McDaniel, June 1989. *The Madness of Saints: Ecstatic religion in Bengal*. Chicago, IL: University of Chicago Press.

McDowell, T. W. 1897. The insane of India and their treatment. *Journal of Mental Science* 43: 683–703.

McEwen, Bruce S. 1998. Protective damaging effects of stress mediators. *New England Journal of Medicine* 338: 171–179.

McKeown, Thomas 1988. *The Origins of Human Disease*. Oxford; New York, NY: Basil Blackwell.

McNeill, William Hardy 1977. *Plagues and People*. Garden City, NY: Anchor Press; Oxford: Blackwell.

—— 1992. *The Global Condition: Conquerors, catastrophes, and community*. Princeton, NJ: Princeton University Press.

Madan, Triloki Nath 1987. *Non-renunciation: Themes and interpretations of Hindu culture*. New Delhi: Oxford University Press.

Mandelbaum, David G. 1955. The world and the world view of the Kota. In: by McKim Marriott (ed.), *Village India: Studies in the Little Community*: 223–254. Chicago, IL: University of Chicago Press.

—— 1966. Transcendental and pragmatic aspects of religion. *American Anthropologist* 68: 1174–1191.

Mandelbaum, David G. 1970. *Society in India*, vol. 1: *Continuity and Change*; vol. 2: *Change and Continuity*. Berkeley; Los Angeles, CA: University of California Press.

—— 1988. *Women's Seclusion and Men's Honor: Sex roles in north India, Bangladesh, and Pakistan*. Tuscon AZ: University of Arizona Press.

Markovitz, Claude (ed.) 2002. *A History of Modern India: 1480–1950*. Trans. from French by Nisha George and Maggy Hendry. London: Anthem.

Marriott, McKim (ed.) 1955a. *Village India: Studies in the Little Community*. Chicago, IL: University of Chicago Press.

—— 1955b. Little communities in an indigenous civilization. In: McKim Marriott (ed.), *Village India: Studies in the Little Community*: 171–222. Chicago, IL: University of Chicago Press.

—— 1976. Interpreting Indian society: a monistic alternative to Dumont's dualism. *Journal of Asian Studies* 36: 189–195.

—— 1990. Constructing an Indian ethnosociology. In: McKim Marriott (ed.), *India through Hindu Categories: Workshop on ethnosociology: Annual conference on South Asia: Selected papers*. Contributions to Indian Sociology Occasional Studies 5: 1–40. New Delhi: Sage Publications.

Marriott, McKim and Ronald B. Inden 1977. Towards an ethnosociology of South Asian caste systems. In: Kenneth David (ed.), *The New Wind: Changing identities*: 227–238. The Hague: Mouton.

Marsella, Anthony J., George DeVos, and Francis L. K. Hsu (eds.) 1985. *Culture and Self: Asian and Western perspectives*. New York, NY: Tavistock.

Meadow, Richard H. 1996. The origins and spread of agriculture and pastoralism in northwestern South Asia. In: David R. Harris (ed.), *Origins and Spread of Agriculture and Pastoralism in Eurasia*: 390–412. London: UCL Press.

Mehta, J. P. 1995. The health scenario in India. In: Upendra Baxi and Bhikhu Parekh (eds.), *Crisis and Change in Contemporary India*: 280–294. New Delhi: Sage (In association with the Book Review Literary Trust).

Mehta, P. J. A. and J. A. Verghese 1985. An epidemiological study of psychiatric patients disorders in Tamil Nadu. *Indian Journal of Psychiatry* 27: 153–158.

Menon, Usha and Richard A. Shweder 1994. Kali's tongue: cultural psychology and the power of shame in Orissa and India. In: Shinobu Kitayama and Hazel Rose Markus (eds.), *Emotion and Culture: Empirical Studies of Mutual Influence*: 241–284. Washington, DC: American Psychological Association.

Menon, Usha and Richard A. Shweder 1998. The return of the "White Man's Burden": the moral discourse of anthropology and the domestic life of Hindu women. In Richard A. Shweder (ed.), *Welcome to Middle Age! (And Other Cultural Fictions)*: 139–188. Chicago, IL: University of Chicago Press.

Meulenbeld, Gerrit Jan 1987. Reflections on the basic concepts of Indian pharmacology. In: G. Jan Meulenbeld and Dominik Wujastyk (eds.), *Studies on Indian Medical History:* Papers presented at the International Workshop on the Study of Indian Medicine held at the Wellcome Institute for the History of Medicine, 2–4 September, 1985: 1–17. Groningen: Egbert Forsten. (Reprint: Delhi: Motilal Banarsidass, 2001).

—— 1997. Aspects of Indian psychiatry. In: Yosio Kawakita, Shizu Sakai and Yasuo Otsuka (eds.), *History of Psychiatric Diagnoses,* Proceedings of the 16th International Symposium on the Comparative History of Medicine – East and West, September 1–8, 1991, Susono-shi, Shizuoka, Japan: 183–237. Tokyo: Ishiyaku Euro-America Publishers.

—— 1999–2002. *A History of Indian Medical Literature*. 5 vols. Groningen: Egbert Forsten.

Mezzich, Juan E. 1996. Arthur Kleinman, Horacio Fabrega, Jr., and Delores L. Parron (eds.), *Culture and Psychiatric Diagnosis: A DSM-IV perspective*. Washington, DC: American Psychiatric Press.

Michaels, Axel 2004. *Hinduism: Past and present*. Trans. by Barbara Harshav. Princeton, NJ: Princeton University Press.

Miller, J. G. 1997. Cultural conceptions of duty: implications for motivation and morality. In: Donald Munro, John F. Schumaker, and Stuart C. Carr, (eds.), *Motivation and Culture*: 178–193. New York, NY: Routledge.

Misra, G. and K. J. Gergen 1993. On the place of culture in psychological science. *International Journal of Psychology* 28: 225–243.

Mlecko, Joel D. 1982. The guru in Hindu tradition. *Numen* 29: 33–61.

Money, John, Venkat N. Joshi, and K. Swayam Prakasam 1992. *Kama Sutra*: Women's sexology versus semen conservation theory in Sanskrit teachings. In: M. Kessler, S. E. Goldstein, J. Joffe, and G. W. Alhee (eds.), *The Future of Prevention*: 214–224. Newbury Park, CA: Sage.

Moore, Carmella C. and Holly F. Mathews (eds.) 2001. *The Psychology of Cultural Experience*. Cambridge: Cambridge University Press.

Moore, Erin P. 1985. *Conflict and Compromise: Justice in an Indian village*, (University of California, Berkeley, Center for South and Southeast Asia Studies Monograph no. 26.) Lanham, MD: University Press of America.

—— 1998. *Gender, Law and Resistance in India*. Tucson, AZ: University of Arizona Press.

Morris, Brian 1976. Whither the savage mind? Notes on the natural taxonomies of a hunting and gathering people. *Man* (NS) 11: 542–556.

—— 1981. Hill gods and ecstatic cults: notes on the religion of a hunting and gathering people. *Man in India* 61: 203–236.

Mujeeb, Mohammad 1967. *The Indian Muslims*. London: George Allen and Unwin.

Mumford, D. B. 1996. The "Dhat syndrome": a culturally determined symptom of depression? *Acta Psychiatrica Scandinavica* 94: 163–167.

Murali, T. and Kiran Rao 2004. Psychiatric rehabilitation in India: issues and challenges. In: S. P. Agarwal, D. S. Goel, R. L. Ichhpujani, R. N. Salhan, and S. Shrivastava (eds.), *Mental Health: An Indian perspective, 1946–2003*: 152–160. New Delhi: Elsevier for the Directorate General of Health Services, Ministry of Health and Family Welfare. (Freely available at mohfw.nic.in/Mental%20Health.pdf).

Murthy, R. Srinivasa 1998. Emerging aspects of psychiatry in India. *Indian Journal of Psychiatry* 40: 307–310.

—— 2004. The National Mental Health Programme: progress and problems. In: S. P. Agarwal, D. S. Goel, R. L. Ichhpujani, R. N. Salhan, and S. Shrivastava (eds.), *Mental Health: An Indian perspective, 1946–2003*: 75–91. New Delhi: Elsevier for the Directorate General of Health Services, Ministry of Health and Family Welfare. (Freely available at mohfw.nic.in/Mental%20Health.pdf).

Nandi, D. N., S. P. Mukherjee, G. C. Boral, G. Banerjee, A. Ghosh, S. Sarkar, and S. Ajmany 1980. Socio-economic status and mental morbidity in certain tribes and castes in India – a cross-cultural study. *British Journal of Psychiatry* 136: 73–85.

Nandi, D. N., G. Banerjee, S. P. Mukherjee, S. Sarkar, G. C. Boral, A. Mukherjee, and D. C. Mishra 1986. A study of psychiatric morbidity of a rural community at an interval of ten years. *Indian Journal of Psychiatry* 38: 179–184.

Nandi, P. S., G. Banerjee, S. P. Mukherjee, S. Nandi, and D. N. Nandi 1997. A study of psychiatric morbidity of the elderly population of a rural community in West Bengal. *Indian Journal of Psychiatry* 39: 122–129.

Nandy, Ashis 1980. *At the Edge of Psychology: Essays in politics and culture*. Delhi: Oxford University Press.

—— 1983. *The Intimate Enemy: Loss and recovery of self under colonialism*. Delhi: Oxford University Press.

—— 1995. The politics of application and social relevance in contemporary psychology. In: Upendra Baxi and Bhikhu C. Parekh (eds.), *Crisis and Change in Contemporary India*: 266–279. New Delhi: Sage Publications.

Narayana Reddy, G. N. 1992. Mental health planning and policy development at national level. In: R. Srinivasa Murthy and B. J. Burns (eds.), *Community Mental Health: Proceedings of the Indo-US Symposium* (National Institute of Mental Health and Neurosciences publication no. 29): 17–39. Bangalore: NIMHANS.

Nath, Vijay 2001. *Puranas and Acculturation: A historico-anthropological perspective.* New Delhi: Munshiram Manoharlal Publishers.

Neki, J. S. 1973. Guru-Chela relationship: The possibility of a therapeutic paradigm. *American Journal of Orthopsychiatry* 43: 755–766.

—— 1975. *Sahaja:* An Indian ideal of mental health. *Psychiatry* 38: 1–10.

Nisbett, Richard E. 2003. *The Geography of Thought.* New York, NY: Free Press.

Nisbett, Richard E., K. Peng, I. Choi, and A. Norenzayan 2001. Culture and systems of thought: holistic versus analytic cognition. *Psychological Review* 108: 291–310.

Nunley, Michael R. 1992. *The Mind Doctor's* Dharma*: On the social construction of hospital psychiatry in eastern Uttar Pradesh, India.* Doctoral dissertation, University of California, San Francisco. Ann Arbor, MI: UMI Dissertation Information Service.

Obeyesekere, Gananath 1970. Ayurveda and mental illness. *Comparative Studies in Society and History* 12: 282–296.

—— 1977. The theory and practice of psychological medicine in the Ayurvedic tradition. *Culture, Medicine and Psychiatry* 1: 155–181.

—— 1982. Science and psychological medicine in the Ayurvedic tradition. In: Anthony J. Marsella and Geoffrey M. White (eds.), *Cultural Conceptions of Mental Health and Therapy*: 235–248. Dordrecht: D. Reidel.

O'Flaherty, Wendy Doniger (ed.) 1980. *Karma and Rebirth in Classical Indian Tradition.* Berkeley, CA: University of California Press.

—— 1984. *Dreams, Illusion and other Realities.* Chicago, IL: University of Chicago Press.

Opler, Morris E. 1958. Spirit possession in a rural area of North India. In: William A. Lessa and Evon Z. Vogt (eds.), *Reader in Comparative Religion*: 553–566. Evanston, IL: Row Peterson.

Padmavathi, R., S. Rajkumar, N. Kumar, A. Manoharan, and S. Kamath 1987. Prevalence of schizophrenia in an urban community in Madras. *Indian Journal of Psychiatry* 31: 233–239.

Pakaslahti, Antti 1998. Family-centered treatment of mental health problems at the Balaji temple in Rajasthan. In: Asko Parpola and Sirpa Tenhunen (eds.), *Changing Patterns of Family and Kinship in South Asia*: Proceedings of an international symposium on the occasion of the 50th anniversary of India's independence held at the University of Helsinki, 6 May 1998 (Studia Orientalia, 84): 129–166. Helsinki: Finnish Oriental Society.

Paranjpe, Anand C. 1988. A personality theory according to Vedānta. In: Robert W. Rieber, David Y. F. Ho, and Anand C. Paranjpe (eds.), *Asian Contributions to Psychology*: 185–214. New York, NY: Praeger.

Paris, Joel 1992. Dhat: The semen loss anxiety syndrome. *Transcultural Psychiatric Research Review* 29: 109–118.

Parpola, Asko and Sirpa Tenhunen (eds.) 1998. *Changing Patterns of Family and Kinship in South Asia*: Proceedings of an international symposium on the occasion of the 50th anniversary of India's independence held at the University of Helsinki, 6 May 1998. (Studia Orientalia, 84.) Helsinki: Finnish Oriental Society.

Parthasarathy, R. and M. Ranganathan 2004. Psychiatric social work: past, present and future. In: S. P. Agarwal, D. S. Goel, R. L. Ichhpujani, R. N. Salhan, and S. Shrivastava (eds.), *Mental Health: An Indian perspective, 1946–2003*: 138–144. New Delhi: Elsevier for the Directorate General of Health Services, Ministry of Health and Family Welfare. (Freely available at mohfw.nic.in/Mental%20Health.pdf).

Patel, Vikram and Mathew Varghese 2004. NGOs and mental health: search for synergy. In: S. P. Agarwal, D. S. Goel, R. L. Ichhpujani, R. N. Salhan, and S. Shrivastava (eds.), *Mental Health: An Indian perspective, 1946–2003*: 145–151. New Delhi: Elsevier for the Directorate General of Health Services, Ministry of Health and Family Welfare. (Freely available at mohfw.nic.in/Mental%20Health.pdf).

Patterson, T. J. S. 1987. The relationship of Indian and European practitioners of medicine from the sixteenth century. In: G. Jan Meulenbeld and Dominik Wujastyk (eds.), *Studies on Indian Medical History:* Papers presented at the International Workshop on the Study of Indian Medicine held at the Wellcome Institute for the History of Medicine, 2–4 September, 1985: 119–129. Groningen: Egbert Forsten. (Reprint: Delhi: Motilal Banarsidass, 2001).

Pfleiderer, Bearix 1981. Mira Datar Dargah: The psychiatry of a Muslim shrine. In: Imtiaz Ahmad (ed.), *Rituals and Religion among Muslims of India*: 195–233. Delhi: Manohar.

Porter, Roy 1987. Mind-Forg'd Manacles: A history of madness in England from the Restoration to the Regency. London: Athlone Press.

Prabhu, C. G. and Rashmi Shankar 2004. Clinical psychology: coming of age. In: S. P. Agarwal, D. S. Goel, R. L. Ichhpujani, R. N. Salhan, and S. Shrivastava (eds.), *Mental Health: An Indian perspective, 1946–2003*: 123–131. New Delhi: Elsevier for the Directorate General of Health Services, Ministry of Health and Family Welfare. (Freely available at mohfw.nic.in/Mental%20Health.pdf).

Prakash, Gyan 1999. *Another Reason: Science and the imagination of modern India.* Princeton, NJ: Princeton University Press.

Prakesh, Indira Jai and Vinod N. Murthy 1981. Psychiatric morbidity and the menopause. *Indian Journal of Psychiatry* 23: 242–246.

Quigley, D. 2003. On the relationship between caste and Hinduism. In: Gavin Flood (ed.), *An Introduction to Hinduism*: 495–508. London: Blackwell Publishing.

Raguram, R., S. Jadhav and M. Weiss 1994. Historical perspectives on Dhat syndrome. *NIMHANS Journal* 12: 117–124.

Raguram, R., M. G. Weiss, S. M. Channabasavanna, and G. M. Devins 1996. Stigma, depression, and somatization in South India. *American Journal of Psychiatry* 153: 1043–1049.

Raguram, R., M. G. Weiss, H Keval, and S. M. Channabasavanna 2001. Cultural dimensions of clinical depression in Bangalore, India. *Anthropology & Medicine* 8: 31–46.

Raguram, R., T. M. Raghu, P. Vounatsou, and M. G. Weiss 2004. Schizophrenia and the cultural epidemiology of stigma in Bangalore, India. *Journal of Nervous and Mental Disease* 192: 734–744.

Raj, L., P. Kulhara, and A. Avasthi 1991. Social burden of positive and negative schizophrenia. *International Journal of Social Psychiatry* 37: 242–250.

Rajkumar, S. 1995. Epidemiology and cause of schizophrenia in India in decade of the brain. In: Stephen H. Koslow, R. Srinivasa Murthy, and George V. Coelho (eds.), *Decade of the Brain*, Proceedings of the Indo–US Scientific Symposium on Mental Health and Neurosciences in the Decade of the Brain, held 7–13 Feb. 1993 in Bangalore, India: 95–100. Rockville, MD: US Department of Health and Human Services, National Institute of Mental Health.

Rama Rao, B. 1975. Medical allusions in some inscriptions of Andhra Pradesh. *Bulletin of the History of Medicine* 5: 198–206.

—— 1992. The great trio. In: P. V. Sharma (ed.), *History of Medicine in India: From antiquity to 1000 A.D.*: 205–221. New Delhi: Indian National Science Academy for the Indian National Commission for History of Science.

Ramachandra Rao, S. K. 1985. *Encyclopedia of Indian Medicine*, Vol. I: *Historical Perspectives*. Bombay: Ramdas Bhatkal, Tardeo.

Ramanathan, A. 1982. Reality of auditory hallucinations in schizophrenia. *Indian Journal of Psychiatry* 24: 55–60.

Ramu, M. G., B. S. Venkataram, and N. Janakiramaiah 1988. Manovikaras with special reference to *udvega* (anxiety) and *vishada* (depression). *NIMHANS Journal* 6: 41–46.

Ramu, M. G., B. S. Venkataram, Hemalata Mukundan, M. R. Shankara, S. Leelavathy, and N. Janakiramaiah 1992. A controlled study of Ayurvedic treatment in the acutely ill patients with Schizophrenia (*Unmada*): rational and results. *NIMHANS Journal* 10: 1–16.

Rappaport, Roy A. 1979. *Ecology, Meaning, and Religion*. Berkeley, CA: North Atlantic Books.

—— 1999. *Ritual and Religion in the Making of Humanity*. Cambridge: Cambridge University Press.

Raz, Amir and Jason Buhle 2006. Typologies of attentional networks. *Nature Reviews Neuroscience* 7: 367–379.

Raz, Amir, Jin Fan, and Michael I. Posner 2005. Hypnotic suggestion reduces conflict in the human brain. *Proceedings of the National Academy of Sciences* 102: 9978–9983.

Reat, N. Ross 1990. *The Origins of Indian Psychology*. Berkeley, CA: Asian Humanities Press.

Reddemma, K. and Nagarajaiah 2004. Psychiatric nursing: The perpetual Cinderella. In: S. P. Agarwal, D. S. Goel, R. L. Ichhpujani, R. N. Salhan, and S. Shrivastava (eds.), *Mental Health: An Indian perspective, 1946–2003*: 132–137. New Delhi: Elsevier for the Directorate General of Health Services, Ministry of Health and Family Welfare. (Freely available at mohfw.nic.in/Mental%20Health.pdf).

Reddy, R. V. N. V. N. Lakshmi, and R. R. Venkata Raju 2000. Traditional phytotherapy for epilepsy, fits and hysteria by Yanadis of Cuddapah District, A.P. *Ancient Science of Life* 19.3–4: 92–95.

Redfield, Robert 1941. *The Folk Culture of Yucatan*. Chicago, IL: University of Chicago Press.

—— 1953. *The Primitive World and Its Transformations*. Ithaca, NY: Cornell University Press.

—— 1955. *The Little Community: Viewpoints for the study of the human whole*. Chicago, IL: University of Chicago Press.

—— 1956. *Peasant Society and Culture: An anthropological approach to civilization*. Chicago, IL: University of Chicago Press.

Renfrew, Colin and Paul Bahn 1996. *Archaeology: Theories, methods and practice*. 2nd edition. London: Thames & Hudson.

Renou, L. 1968. *Religions of Ancient India*. Revised edition. New York, NY: Schocken Books. (1st English edition: *Religions of India*. London: Athlone Press, 1953).

Richerson, Peter J. and Robert Boyd 2005. *Not By Genes Alone: How culture transformed human evolution*. Chicago, IL: University of Chicago Press.

Robins, Lee N. and Darrel A. Regier (eds.) 1991. *Psychiatric Disorders in America: The epidemiologic catchment area study*. New York, NY: Collier Macmillan; Toronto: Free Press.

Rocher, L. 2003. The *Dharmasastras*. In: Gavin Flood (ed.), *The Blackwell Companion to Hinduism*: 102–115. Oxford: Blackwell Publishing.

Roland, Alan 1988. *In Search of Self in India and Japan: Toward a cross-cultural psychology*. Princeton, NJ: Princeton University Press.

—— 1994. Selves in motion: An Indian-Japanese comparison. In: Roger T. Ames (ed., with Wimal Dissanayake and Thomas P. Kasulis), *Self as Person in Asian Theory and Practice*: 359–378. Albany, NY: State University of New York Press.

Roşu, Arion 1981. Medicine and psychology in ancient India. *Curare* 4: 205–210.

Roy, Mira 1986. Ayurveda. In: Priyadaranjan Ray and S. N. Sen (eds.), *The Cultural Heritage of India*, vol. 6: *Science and Technology*: 152–176. 2nd edition. Calcutta: Ramakrishna Mission Institute of Culture.

Runciman, W. G. 1987. On the tendency of human societies to fix varieties. *Proceedings of the British Academy* 72: 148–165.

—— 1989. Evolution in sociology. In: A. Grafen (ed.), *Evolution and its Influence*: 19–33. Oxford: Oxford Clarendon Press.

—— 1998. The selectionist paradigm and its implications for sociology. *Sociology* 32: 163–188.

—— 2001. From nature to culture, from culture to society. In: W. G. Runciman (ed.), *The Origin of Human Social Institutions*: 237–254. Oxford: Oxford University Press.

Sahlins, Marshall David 1972. *Stone Age Economics*. New York, NY: Aldine de Gruyter.

Said, M. 1993. Diseases of the pre-modern period in South Asia. In: K. F. Kiple (ed.), *The Cambridge World History of Human Disease*: 413–417. Cambridge: Cambridge University Press.

Sanderson, Stephen K. 1990. *Social Evolutionism: A critical history*. Cambridge, MA: Blackwell.

—— 1995a. *Macrosociology: An Introduction to human societies*. 3rd edition. New York, NY: Harper and Collins.

—— 1995b. *Social Transformation: A general theory of historical development*. London: Blackwell.

Sarada Menon, M. 2004. Mental health in independent India: The early years. In: S. P. Agarwal, D. S. Goel, R. L. Ichhpujani, R. N. Salhan, and S. Shrivastava (eds.), *Mental Health: An Indian perspective, 1946–2003*: 30–36. New Delhi: Elsevier for the Directorate General of

Health Services, Ministry of Health and Family Welfare. (Freely available at mohfw.nic.in/Mental%20Health.pdf).

Sartorius, N., C. T. Kaelber, J. E. Cooper, M. T. Roper, D. S. Rae, W. Gulbinat, T. B. Ustun, and D. A. Regier 1993. Progress toward achieving a common language in psychiatry. Results from the field trial of the clinical guidelines accompanying the WHO classification of mental and behavioral disorders in ICD-10. *Archives of General Psychiatry* 50: 115–124.

Satija, D. C., D. Singh, S. S. Nathawat, and V. Sharma 1981. A psychiatric study of patients attending Mehandipur Balaji temple. *Indian Journal of Psychiatry* 23: 247–250.

Scull, Andrew T. 1984. *Decarceration: Community treatment and the deviant: A radical view.* 2nd edition. Cambridge: Polity Press.

—— 1989. *Social Order/Mental Disorder: Anglo-American psychiatry in historical perspective.* Berkeley, CA: University of California Press.

—— 1993. *The Most Solitary of Afflictions: Madness and society in Britain, 1700–1900.* New Haven, CT: Yale University Press.

Sen, Biswajit 1987. Psychiatric phenomena in primary health care: their extent and nature. *Indian Journal of Psychiatry* 29: 33–40.

Sen-Gupta, Nares Chandra 1953. Introductory. In: N. C. Sen-Gupta (ed.), *Evolution of Ancient Indian Law*: 1–10. Calcutta: S. Sen-Gupta Trust.

Service, Elman R. 1975. *Origins of the State and Civilization: The Process of Cultural Evolution.* New York, NY: W. W. Norton.

Sethi, B. B., S. C. Gupta, and R. Kumar 1967. Three hundred Indian families: a psychiatric study. *Indian Journal of Psychiatry* 9: 280–294.

Sethi, B. B., S. C. Gupta, R. K. Mahendru, and P. Kumari 1974. Mental health and the urban life: a study of 850 families. *British Journal of Psychiatry* 124: 243–246.

Shaffer, J. G. and D. A. Lichtenstein 1995. The concepts of "cultural tradition" and "palaeoethnicity" in South Asian archaeology. In G. Erdosy (ed.), *The Indo-Aryans of Ancient South Asia: Language, Material Culture and Ethnicity*: 126–154. Berlin: Walter de Gruyter.

Shah, L. P. 1999. Forensic psychiatry in India: current status and future development. *Indian Journal of Psychiatry* 41: 179–185.

Sharma, M. P., V. Kumaraiah, H. Mishra, and J. P. Balodhi. Therapeutic effects of Vipassana meditation in tension headache. *Journal of Personality and Clinical Studies* 6: 201–206.

Sharma, P. S. V. N., D. Muralidhar, and P. S. Gopinath 1985. Neuro-psychiatric morbidity in a beggar's colony. *Indian Journal of Psychiatry* 27: 303–310.

Sharma, Priya Vrat 1972. *Indian Medicine in the Classical Age*. (Chowkhamba Sanskrit studies, 85.) Varanasi: Chowkhamba Sanskrit Series Office.

—— 1992a. Vedic medicine. In: P. V. Sharma (ed.), *History of Medicine in India: From antiquity to 1000 A.D.*: 12–36. New Delhi: Indian National Science Academy for the Indian National Commission for History of Science.

—— 1992b. Siddha medicine. In: P. V. Sharma (ed.), *History of Medicine in India: From antiquity to 1000 A.D.*: 445–452. New Delhi: Indian National Science Academy for the Indian National Commission for History of Science.

Sharma, Ram Sharan 1983. *Material Culture and Social Formations in Ancient India*. New Delhi: Macmillan.

—— 1991. *Aspects of Political Ideas and Institutions in Ancient India*. 3rd revised edition. Delhi: Motilal Banarsidass Publishers.

—— 1995. *Perspectives in Social and Economic History of Early India*. 2nd revised edition. New Delhi: Munshiram Manoharlal Publishers.

—— 1996. *The State and Varna Formation in the Mid-Ganga Plains: An ethnoarchaeological view*. New Delhi: Manohar Publishers.

Sharma, S. D. 2004. Mental health: the pre-independence scenario. In: S. P. Agarwal, D. S. Goel, R. L. Ichhpujani, R. N. Salhan, and S. Shrivastava (eds.), *Mental Health: An Indian perspective, 1946–2003*: 25–29. New Delhi: Elsevier for the Directorate General of Health Services, Ministry of Health and Family Welfare. (Freely available at mohfw .nic.in/Mental%20Health.pdf).

Shaw, W. S. 1932. The Alienist Department of India. *Journal of Mental Science* 78: 331–341.

Shukla, K. P. and C. P. Mishra 1991. Traditional healers in health care. In: T. M. Dak (ed.), *Sociology of Health in India*: 106–122. New Delhi: Rawat Publishers.

Shweder, Richard A. 1991. *Thinking Through Cultures: Expeditions in cultural psychology*. Cambridge, MA: Harvard University Press.

—— 1993. The cultural psychology of the emotions. In: Michael Lewis and Jeannette M. Haviland (eds.), *Handbook of Emotions*: 417–431. New York, NY: Guilford Press.

Shweder, Richard A. and Robert A. LeVine 1984. *Culture Theory: Essays on mind, self, and emotion*. Cambridge: Cambridge University Press.

Shweder, Richard A., M. Mahapatra, and J. G. Miller 1990. Culture and moral development. In: James W. Stigler, Richard A. Shweder and Gilbert Herdt (eds.), *Cultural Psychology: Essays on comparative human development*: 130–204. Cambridge: Cambridge University Press.

Shweder, Richard A., N. C. Much, M. Mahapatra, and L. Park 1997. The "big three" of morality (autonomy, community, divinity) and the "big three" explanations of suffering. In: A. M. Brandt and P. Rozin (eds.), *Morality and Health*: 119–169. New York, NY: Routledge.

Siddiqi, T. 1981. Unani medicine in India, 1524 to 1605 AD. *Indian Journal of History of Science* 16: 22–25.

Siegel, Bernard J. and Alan R. Beals 1960. Pervasive factionalism. *American Anthropologist* (NS) 62: 394–417.

Singer, Milton (ed.) 1959. *Traditional India: Structure and change*. Austin, TX: University of Texas Press.

—— 1972. *When a Great Tradition Modernizes: An anthropological approach to Indian civilization*. New York, NY: Praeger; London: Pall Mall.

Singer, Milton and B. S. Cohn (eds.) 1968. *Structure and Change in Indian Society*. Chicago, IL: Aldine Pub. Co. for Wenner-Gren Foundation for Anthropological Research, Inc.

Singh, G. 1985. Dhat syndrome revisited. *Indian Journal of Psychiatry* 27: 119–122.

Sinha, Durganand 1993. Indigenization of psychology in India and its relevance. In: Uichol Kim and John W. Berry (eds.), *Indigenous Psychologies: Research and experience in cultural context*: 30–43. Newbury Park, CA: Sage Publications.

Sivananda, Sarasuti 1974. *Mind: Its Mysteries and Control*. Shivanandanagar: Divine Life Society.

Smith, Donald Eugene 1963. *India as a Secular State*. Princeton, NJ: Princeton University Press.

Smith, Frederick M. 2006. *The Self Possessed: Deity and spirit possession in South Asian literature and civilization*. New York, NY: Columbia University Press.

Somasundaram, O. 1984. History of psychiatry in India. In: Alan De Sousa and D. A. De Sousa (eds.), *Psychiatry in India*: 13–20. Bombay: Bhalani Books.

Somasundaram, O., T. Jayaramakrishnan, and M. Sureshkumar 1986. Psychiatry in Siddha (Tamil) system of medicine. *Indian Journal of Psychological Medicine* 9: 38–45.

Spiro, Melford E. 1986. Cultural relativism and the future of anthropology. *Cultural Anthropology* 1: 259–286.

Srinivas, Mysore Narasimhachar 1952. *Religion and Society among the Coorgs of South India*. Oxford: Clarendon Press.

—— 1955. The social system of a Mysore village. McKimMarriott (ed.), *Village India: Studies in the Little Community*: 1–35. Chicago, IL: University of Chicago Press.

Srinivas, Mysore Narasimhachar 1962. *Caste in Modern India*. Bombay: Asia Publishing House.

—— 1966. *Social Change in Modern India*. Berkeley, CA: University of California Press; Cambridge: Cambridge University Press.

—— 1976. *The Remembered Village*. Oxford: Oxford University Press; Berkeley, CA: University of California Press.

Staal, J. Frits 1963. Sanskrit and Sanskritization. *Journal of Asian Studies* 22: 261–275.

Stein, Burton 1998. *A History of India*. Oxford: Blackwell Publishers.

Sternbach, L. 1965. Legal positions of physicians in Ancient India. In: L. Sternbach (ed.). *Juridical Studies in Ancient Indian Law*: 280–320. Delhi: Motilal Banarsidass.

Strickmann, Michel 2002. *Chinese Magical Medicine*. Ed. by Bernard Faure. Stanford, CA: Stanford University Press.

—— n.d. Magical medicine: Therapeutic rituals in East Asian tradition. Unpublished manuscript.

Sudsuang, R., V. Chentanez, and K. Veluvan 1991. Effect of Buddhist meditation on serum cortisol and total protein levels, blood pressure, pulse rate, lung volume and reaction time. *Physiology and Behavior* 50: 543–548.

Sumathipala, A., S. H. Siribaddana, and D. Bhugra 2004. Culture-bound syndromes: the story of *dhat* syndrome. *British Journal of Psychiatry* 184: 200–209.

Suśrutasaṃhitā 1998–99. *The Sushruta Samhita*. Trans. by K. K. Bhishagratna. 3 vols. Varanasi: Chowkhamba, Sanskrit Series Office.

Susser E, V. K. Varma, S. Malhotra, S. Conover, and X. F. Amador 1995. Delineation of acute and transient psychotic disorders in a developing country setting. *British Journal of Psychiatry* 167: 216–219.

Swedlund, Alan C. and George J. Armelagos (eds.) 1990. *Disease in Populations in Transition: Anthropological and epidemiological perspectives*. New York, NY: Bergin and Garvey.

Teja, J. S., B. S. Khanna, and T. B. Subrahmanyam 1970. "Possession states" in Indian patients. *Indian Journal of Psychiatry* 1: 71–87.

Thakar, V. J. 1992. Basic concepts of Ayurveda. In: Priya Vrat Sharma (ed.), *History of medicine in India: (from antiquity to 1000 A.D.)*: 375–390. New Delhi: Indian National Science Academy.

Thapar, Romila 1984. *From Lineage to State: Social formations in the mid-first millennium BC in the Ganga Valley*. Delhi: Oxford University Press.

—— 1997. *Asoka and the Decline of the Mauryas*. 2nd edition. Delhi: Oxford University Press.

Thapar, Romila 2002. *Early India: From the origins to AD 1300*. Berkeley, CA: University of California Press; London: Allen Lane.

Thara, R. and T. N. Srinivasan 2000. How stigmatizing is schizophrenia in India? *International Journal of Social Psychiatry* 46: 135–141.

Thara, R., S. Kamath, and S. Kumar 2003. Women with schizophrenia and broken marriages – doubly disadvantaged? Patient perspective. *International Journal of Social Psychiatry* 49: 225–232.

Thara, R., M. Henrietta, A. Joseph, S. Rajkumar, and W. W. Eaton 1994. Ten-year course of schizophrenia: the Madras longitudinal study. *Acta Psychiatrica Scandinavica* 90: 329–336.

Tomasello, Michael 1999. *The Cultural Origins of Human Cognition*. Cambridge, MA: Harvard University Press.

Ullmann, Manfred 1978. *Islamic Surveys*, vol. 2: *Islamic Medicine*. Edinburgh: Edinburgh University Press.

Vahia, N. S. 1969. A therapy based upon some concepts prevalent in India. *Indian Journal of Psychiatry* 11: 7–14.

Vahia, N. S., S. L. Vinekar, and D. R. Doongaji 1966. Some ancient Indian concepts in the treatment of psychiatric disorders. *British Journal of Psychiatry* 112: 1089–1096.

Varma, L. P., D. K. Srivastava, and R. N. Sahay 1970. Possession syndrome. *Indian Journal of Psychiatry* 12: 58–70.

Vasudevan, A., V. Kumariah, H. Mishra, and J. P. Balodhi 1994. Yogic meditation in tension headache. *NIMHANS Journal* 12: 69–73.

Vatuk, S. 1990. "To be a burden to others": Dependency anxiety among the elderly in India. In: O. M. Lynch (ed.), *Divine Passions: The social construction of emotion in India*: 64–88. Berkeley, CA: University of California Press.

Venkataramaiah, V. M. Mallikarjunaiah, C. R. Chandrasekhar, C. K. Vasudeva Rao, and G. N. Narayana Reddy 1981. Possession syndrome: An epidemiological study in West Karnataka. *Indian Journal of Psychiatry* 23: 213–218.

Venkataswamy Reddy, M. and C. R. Chandrashekar 1998. Prevalence of mental and behavioral disorders in India: a meta-analysis. *Indian Journal of Psychiatry* 40: 149–157.

Venkoba Rao, A. 1966. Dreams: Some gleanings from Upanishads. *Indian Journal of History of Medicine* 11: 13–18.

—— 1975. History of psychiatry – India. In: John G. Howells (ed.), *World History of Psychiatry*: 624–649. New York, NY: Bruner/Maesel; London: Baillière Tindall.

—— 1978. Psychiatric thought in ancient India. *Indian Journal of Psychiatry* 20: 102–111.

Venkoba Rao, A. 1984. Bhagavad Gita and psychiatry. In: Alan De Sousa and D. A. De Sousa (eds.), *Psychiatry in India*: 53–69. Bombay: Bhalani Book Depot.

Verghese, Abraham and Ahmed Beig 1974. Neuroses in Vellore town – An epidemiological study. *Indian Journal of Psychiatry* 16: 1–7.

Verghese A., J. K. John, S. Rajkumar, J. Richard, B. B. Sethi, and J. K. Trivedi 1989. Factors associated with the course and outcome of schizophrenia in India. Results of a two-year multi-centre follow-up study. *British Journal of Psychiatry* 154: 499–503.

Verma, Vinod 1995. *Ayurveda: A Way of Life*. York Beach, ME: Samuel Weiser.

Wadley, Susan Snow 1975. *Shakti: Power in the conceptual structure of Karimpur Religion*. Chicago, IL: Dept. of Anthropology, University of Chicago.

Waxler, N. E. 1974. The domain called "madness" in the peasant villages of Ceylon. Unpublished manuscript.

—— 1979. Is outcome for schizophrenia better in non-industrial societies? The case of Sri Lanka. *Journal of Nervous and Mental Disease* 167: 144–158.

Weiss, Mitchell G. 1975. Psychopathology in classical India. Unpublished manuscript.

—— 1977. *Critical Study of Unmada in the Early Sanskrit Medical Literature: An analysis of Ayurvedic psychiatry with reference to present-day diagnostic concepts*. Doctoral dissertation, University of Pennsylvania. Ann Arbor, MI: UMI Dissertation Information Service.

—— 1980. *Caraka Samhita*: on the doctrine of karma. In: Wendy Doniger O'Flaherty (ed.), *Karma and Rebirth in Classical Indian Traditions*: 90–115. Berkeley, CA: University of California Press.

Weiss, Mitchell G. and Jayashree Ramakrishna 2006. Health-related stigma: rethinking concepts and interventions. (Abridged version of background paper presented by Mitchell Weiss at the Research Workshop on Health-Related Stigma and Discrimination, Royal Tropical Institute (KIT), Amsterdam, 29 November – 2 December 2004). *Psychology, Health and Medicine* 11: 277–287.

Weiss, Mitchell G., R. Raguram, and S. M. Channabasavanna 1996. Cultural dimensions of psychiatric diagnosis: A comparison of DSM-III-R and illness explanatory models in South India. *British Journal of Psychiatry* 166: 353–359. (Erratum in *British Journal of Psychiatry* 167: 119).

Weiss, Mitchell G., S. Jadher, R. Raquram, P. Vounatsou, and R. Littlewood 2001. Psychiatric stigma across cultures: Local validation in Bangalore and India. *Anthropology and Medicine* 8: 71–87.

Weiss, Mitchell G., S. D. Sharma, R. K. Gaur, J. S. Sharma, A. Desai, and D. R. Doongaji 1986. Traditional concepts of mental disorder among Indian psychiatric patients: preliminary report of work in progress. *Social Science and Medicine* 23: 379–386.

Weiss, Mitchell G., A. Desai, S. Jadhav, L. Gupta, S. M. Channabasavanna, D. R. Doongaji, and P. B. Behere 1988. Humoral concepts of mental illness in India. *Social Science and Medicine* 27: 471–477.

Weiss, Mitchell G., D. R. Doongaji, S. Siddhartha, D. Wypij, S. Pathare, M. Bhatawdekar, A. Bhave, A. Sheth, and R. Fernandes 1992. The Explanatory Model Interview Catalogue (EMIC): contribution to cross-cultural research methods from a study of leprosy and mental health. *British Journal of Psychiatry* 160: 819–830.

Wen, J.-K. and C.-L. Wang 1981. *Shen-K'uei* syndrome: a culture-specific sexual neurosis in Taiwan. In: A. Kleinman and T. Lin (eds.), *Normal and Abnormal Behavior in Chinese Culture*: 357–369. Dordrecht: D. Reidel.

Wezler, Albrecht 1984. On the quadruple division of the Yogaśāstra, the Caturvyohatva of the Cikitsaśāstra and the "Four Noble Truths" of the Buddha. *Indologica Taurinensia* 12: 289–337.

Whicher, Ian 1998. *The Integrity of the Yoga Darśana: A reconsideration of classical yoga*. Albany, NY: State University of New York Press.

White, David Gordon 1996. *The Alchemical Body: Siddha traditions in medieval India*. Chicago, IL: University of Chicago Press.

—— 2000. Introduction: Tantra in practice: mapping a tradition. In: D. G. White (ed.), *Tantra in Practice*: 3–38. Princeton, NJ: Princeton University Press.

Whitney, William Dwight (trans.) 1905. *Atharva-Veda-Saṁhitā*, Rev. and ed. by Charles Rockwell Lanman. 2 vols. (Harvard Oriental Series, 7–8.) Cambridge MA: Harvard University. (Reprint: Delhi: Motilal Banarsidass Publishers, 1996).

Wig N. N., D. K. Menon, H. Bedi, A. Ghosh, L. Kuipers, J. Leff, A. Korten, R. Day, N. Sartorius, and G. Ernberg 1987a. Expressed emotion and schizophrenia in north India, I. Cross-cultural transfer of ratings of relatives' expressed emotion. *British Journal of Psychiatry* 151: 156–160.

Wig N. N., D. K. Menon, H. Bedi, J. Leff, L. Kuipers, A. Ghosh, R. Day, A. Korten, G. Ernberg, and N. Sartorius 1987b. Expressed emotion and schizophrenia in north India, II. Distribution of expressed emotion components among relatives of schizophrenic patients in Aarhus and Chandigarh. *British Journal of Psychiatry* 151: 160–165. [Erratum in *British Journal of Psychiatry* 151 (1987): 870].

Wing, John Kenneth, J. E. Cooper, and N. Sartorius, *Measurement and Classification of Psychiatric Symptoms*. London: Cambridge University Press.

Winternitz, Moriz 1967. *A History of Indian Literature*. vol. 3.1. Delhi: Motilal Banarsidass.

—— 1981. *A History of Indian Literature*. vol. 1. Delhi: Motilal Banarsidass.

Witzel, Michael E. J. 1979. *On Magical Thought in the Veda*. Leiden: Universitaire Pers.

—— 1997. The development of the Vedic canon and its schools. In: Michael E. J. Witzel (ed.), *Inside the Texts. Beyond the Texts: New approaches to the study of the Vedas* (Harvard Oriental Series, Opera Minora, vol. 2): 257–345. Cambridge, MA: Department of Sanskrit and Indian Studies, Harvard University.

—— 2003. Vedas and Upanishads. In: Gavin Flood (ed.), *The Blackwell Companion to Hinduism*: 68–101. Oxford: Blackwell Publishing.

Wujastyk, Dominik 1998. *The Roots of Ayurveda: Selections from Sanskrit medical writings*. New Delhi: Penguin Books India.

—— 2003. The science of medicine. In: Gavin Flood (ed.), *The Blackwell Companion to Hinduism*: 393–409. Oxford: Blackwell Publishing.

Zaehner, Robert Charles 1962. *Hinduism*. Oxford: Oxford University Press.

Zimmermann, Francis 1987. *The Jungle and the Aroma of Meats: An ecological theme in Hindu medicine*. Berkeley, CA: University of California Press. (Reprint: Delhi: Motilal Banarsidass, 1999).

Zysk, Kenneth G. 1985. Towards the notion of health in the Vedic phase of Indian medicine. *Zeitschrift der Deutschen Morgenländischen Gesellschaft* 135: 312–318.

—— 1986. The evolution of anatomical knowledge in ancient India, with special reference to cross-cultural influences. *Journal of the American Oriental Society* 106: 687–705.

—— 1989. *Mantra* in *Ayurveda:* A study of the use of magico-religious speech in ancient Indian medicine. In: Harvey P. Alper (ed.), *Mantra*: 123–143. Albany, NY: State University of New York Press.

—— 1991. *Ascetism and Healing in Ancient India: Medicine in the Buddhist monastery*. New York, NY: Oxford University Press.

—— 1992. Reflections on an Indo-European healing tradition. In: Perspectives on Indo-European Language, Culture and Religion: Studies in honor of Edgar C. Polomé, vol. 2 (Journal of Indo-European Studies, Monograph no. 9): 321–336. McLean, VA: Institute for the Study of Man.

—— 1993. *Religious Medicine: The history and evolution of Indian medicine*. New Brunswick, NJ: Transaction Publishers.

Zysk, Kenneth G. 1999. Mythology and the brahmanization of Indian medicine: transforming heterodoxy into orthodoxy. In: Folke Josephson (ed.), *Categorisation and Interpretation:* Indological and comparative studies from an international Indological meeting at the Department of Comparative Philology, Göteborg University: a volume dedicated to the memory of Gösta Liebert: 125–145. Göteborg: Meijerbergs institut för Svensk etymologisk forskning, Göteborgs universitet.

2. ADDITIONAL READINGS (not referred to in footnotes)

Ackernecht, E. H. 1946. Natural diseases and rational treatment in primitive medicine. *Bulletin of the History of Medicine* 19: 467–497.

Alter, Joseph S. 1999. Heaps of health, metaphysical fitness: Ayurveda and the ontology of good health in medical anthropology. *Current Anthropology* 40 (Suppl.): S43–S66.

Appadurai, Arjun 1981. *Worship and Conflict under Colonial Rule: A South Indian case.* Cambridge: Cambridge University Press.

Arnold, Edwin (trans.) 1885. *The Song Celestial, or, Bhagavad-Gītā.* Boston: Roberts Bros. (Reprint: Mineola, NY: Dover Press, 1993).

Auboyer, Jeannine 1961. *Daily Life in Ancient India: From approximately 200 BC to AD 700.* London: Weidenfeld and Nicolson. (Reprint: New Delhi: Munsiram Manoharlah Publishers Pvt Ltd, 1994).

Bagadia, V. N., K. S. Ayyar, P. D. Lakdawala, U. Susainathan, and P. V. Pradhan 1985. Value of the general health questionnaire in detecting psychiatric morbidity in a general hospital. *Indian Journal of Psychiatry* 27: 293–296.

Bharati, A. [Agehananda Bharati, Swami] 1978. *Great Tradition and Little Traditions: Indological investigations in cultural anthropology.* Varanasi: Chowkhamba Sanskrit Series Office.

Bhugra, Dinesh and Roland Littlewood (eds.) 2001. *Colonialism and Psychiatry.* New Delhi: Oxford University Press.

Bhugra, Dinesh, Ranjith Gopinath, and Rahul Bhintade 2004. Mental health of Indians in the UK. In: S. P. Agarwal, D. S. Goel, R. L. Ichhpujani, R. N. Salhan, and S. Shrivastava (eds.), *Mental Health: An Indian perspective, 1946–2003*: 249–255. New Delhi: Elsevier for the Directorate General of Health Services, Ministry of Health and Family Welfare.

Boyden, Stephen V. (ed.) 1970. *The Impact of Civilization on the Biology of Man.* Toronto: University of Toronto Press.

—— 1987. *Western Civilization in Biological Perspective: Patterns in biohistory.* Oxford: Clarendon Press.

Brown, Peter J. 1998. *Understanding and Applying Medical Anthropology.* Mountain View, CA: Mayfield Publishing Company.

Bynum, W. F. and R. Porter (eds.) 1993. *Companion Encyclopedia of the History of Medicine,* vol. 1. London: Routledge.

Cawte, John 1974. *Medicine is the Law: Studies in psychiatric anthropology of Australian tribal societies.* Honolulu: University of Hawaii Press.

Chakraborty, Ajita and Gouranga Banerji 1975. Ritual, a culture specific neurosis, and obsessional states in Bengali culture. *Indian Journal of Psychiatry* 17: 211–216.

Cipolla, Carlo M. 1976. *Public Health and the Medical Profession in the Renaissance.* Cambridge: Cambridge University Press.

Donald, Merlin 1991. *Origins of the Modern Mind: Three stages in the evolution of culture and cognition.* Cambridge, MA: Harvard University Press.

Dunbar, Robin I. M., Chris Knight, Camilla Power (eds.) 1999. *The Evolution of Culture.* New Brunswick, NJ: Rutgers University Press; Edinburgh: Edinburgh University Press.

Eisenberg, D. M., R. B. Davis, S. L. Ettner, S. Appel, S. Wilkey, M. Van Rompay, and R. C. Kessler 1998. Trends in alternative medicine use in the US, 1990–97: results of a follow-up national survey. *Journal of the American Medical Association* 280: 1569–1575.

Eisenberg, D. M., R. C. Kessler, C. Foster, F. E. Norlock, D. R. Calkins, and T. L. Delbanco 1993. Unconventional medicine in the United States. Prevalence, costs, and patterns of use. *New England Journal of Medicine* 328: 246–252.

Fabrega, Horacio, Jr. 1971. The study of medical problems in pre-literate settings. *Yale Journal of Biology and Medicine* 43: 385–407.

—— 1991. The culture and history of psychiatric stigma in early modern and modern western societies: a review of literature. *Comprehensive Psychiatry* 32: 97–119.

—— 2006. Evils of medical psychologisation. *Psychiatry: Interpersonal and Biological Processes* 69: 167–182.

Fabrega, Horacio, Jr. and D. Silver 1973. *Illness and Shamanistic in Zinacantan Standard.* Stanford, CA: University of California Press.

Geertz, Clifford 1973. *The Interpretation of Cultures: Selected essays.* New York, NY: Basic Books.

Hallowell, A. I. 1960. Self, society, and culture in phylogenetic. In: S. Tax (ed.), *The Evolution of Man: Mind, culture, and society,* Vol. 2: *Evolution after Darwin*: 309–372. Chicago, IL: University of Chicago Press.

Heesterman, Jan C. 1985. *The Inner Conflict of Tradition: Essays in Indian ritual, kingship, and society.* Chicago, IL; London: Oxford University Press.

Jablensky, A. 1988. Methodological issues in psychiatric classification. *British Journal of Psychiatry* 152: 15–20.

Lewis, Gilbert 1975. *Knowledge of Illness in a Sepik Society: A study of the Gnau, New Guinea*. London: Athlone Press.

Lukacs, John R. and V. D. Mista 1995. The people of Lekhahia: a biocultural portrait of Mesolithic Hunter-Foragers on north India. In: Raymond Allchin and Bridget Allchin (eds.), *South Asian Archaeology*, vol. 2: 873–889. Cambridge: Cambridge University Press.

Lukacs, John R. and S. R. Walimbe 1998. Physiological stress in prehistoric India: new data on localized enamel hypoplasia linked to climate and culture change. *Journal of Archaeological Science* 25: 571–585.

Malhotra, Kailash C. 1990. Changing patterns of disease in India with special reference to childhood mortality. In: A. C. Swedlund and G. J. Armelagos (eds.), *Disease in Populations in Transition: Anthropological and epidemiological perspectives*: 313–331. New York, NY: Bergin and Garvey.

Manson, S. M., J. H. Shore, and J. D. Bloom 1985. The depressive experience in the American Indian communities: A challenge for psychiatric theory and diagnosis. In: Arthur Kleinman and Byron Good (eds.), *Culture and Depression: Studies in the anthropology and cross-cultural psychiatry of affect and disorder*: 331–368. Berkeley, CA: University of California Press.

Matchett, F. 2003. The *Purāṇas*. In: Gavin Flood (ed.), *The Blackwell Companion to Hinduism*: 129–143. Oxford: Blackwell Publishing.

Menon I. A. and H. I. Haberman 1970. The medical students' oath of ancient India. *Medical History* 14: 295–299.

Mezzich, Juan E., Yutaka Honda, and Marianne C. Kastrup (eds.) 1994. *Psychiatric Diagnosis: A world perspective*. New York, NY: Springer Verlag.

Nash, June 1967. The logic of behavior: curing in a Mayan Indian town. *Human Organization* 26: 132–140.

Noble, William and Iain Davidson 1996. *Human Evolution, Language and Mind: A psychological and archaeological inquiry*. Cambridge: Cambridge University Press.

Nunley, Michael 1996. Why psychiatrists in India prescribe so many drugs. *Culture, Medicine and Psychiatry* 20: 165–197.

—— 1998. The involvement of families in Indian psychiatry. *Culture, Medicine and Psychiatry* 22: 317–353.

Pandey, Gyanendra 1997. *Traditional Medicine in South-East Asia and Indian Medical Science*. Delhi: Sri Satguru.

Pandurangi, A. K. and R. L. Kapur 1980. Reactive psychosis: a prospective study. *Acta Psychiatrica Scandinavica* 61: 89–95.

Pfeiffer, John E. 1982. *The Creative Explosion. An inquiry into the origins of art and religion.* New York, NY: Harper & Row.

Prince R. and F. Tcheng-Laroche 1987. Culture bound syndromes and international disease classifications. *Culture, Medicine, and Psychiatry* 11: 3–52.

Raguram, R. and Weiss, M. 1997. *Explanatory Model Interview Catalogue (EMIC) Interview for Study of Outpatient Psychiatry Problems and Stigma in Bangalore, India.* Bangalore: NIMHANS; Basel: Swiss Tropical Institute.

Raguram, R., A. Venkateswaran, J. Ramakrishna, and M. G. Weiss 2002. Traditional community resources for mental health: a report of temple healing from India. *British Medical Journal* 325: 38–40.

Reddy, D. V. S. 1941. Medical relief in medieval South India: centres of medical aid and types of medical institutions. *Bulletin of the History of Medicine* 9: 385–400.

Richards, John F. 1993. *The New Cambridge History of India,* vol. 1, no. 5: *The Mughal Empire.* Cambridge: Cambridge University Press.

Robert, A. H., D. G. Kewman, L. Mercier, and M. Hovell 1993. The power of non-specific effects in healing: Implications for psychosocial and biological treatments. *Clinical Psychology Review* 13: 375–391.

Saberwal, Satish 1996. *Roots of Crisis: Interpreting contemporary Indian society.* New Delhi: Sage Publications.

Sachs L. 1989. Misunderstanding as therapy: doctors, patients and medicines in a rural clinic in Sri Lanka. *Culture, Medicine and Psychiatry* 13: 335–349.

Sangar, Satya Prakash 1998. *Crime and Punishment in Mughal India.* New Delhi: Reliance Publishing House.

Sharma, M. P. 1995. A note on Samskara. *Journal of Indian Psychology* 13: 51–53.

Shweder, Richard A. 1985. Menstrual pollution, soul loss, and the comparative study of emotions. In: Arthur Kleinman and Byron Good (eds.), *Culture and Depression: Studies in the anthropology and cross-cultural psychiatry of affect and disorder*: 182–215. Berkeley, CA: University of California Press.

—— 1990. Introduction. In: James W. Stigler, Richard A. Shweder, and Gilbert Herdt (eds.), *Cultural Psychology: Essays on comparative human development*: 1–46. Cambridge: Cambridge University Press.

Somasundaram, O. 1987. Indian Lunacy Act, 1912: The historical background. *Indian Journal of Psychiatry* 29: 3–14.

Temkin, O. 1963. The scientific approach to disease: specific entity and individual sickness. In: Alistair Cameron Crombie (ed.), *Scientific Change: Historical studies in the intellectual, social and technical conditions for scientific discovery and technical invention, from antiquity to the present.* Symposium on the History of Science, University of Oxford, 9–15 July 1961: 629–647. London: Heinemann.

Trawick, Margaret 1989. *Notes on Love in a Tamil Family.* Berkeley, CA: University of California Press.

Weiss, Mitchell G. 1983. The treatment of insane patients in India in the lunatic asylums of the nineteenth century. *Journal of Psychiatry* 25: 312–316.

Witzel, Michael E. J. 1996. How to enter the Vedic mind? Strategies in translating a Brahmana text. In: Enrica Garzilli (ed.), *Translating, Translations, Translators: From India to the West*: 163–176. Cambridge, MA: Department of Sanskrit and Indian Studies, Harvard University.

Young, Allan 1976. Some implications of medical beliefs and practices for social anthropology. *American Anthropologist* 78: 5–24.

Zysk, Kenneth G. 1982. Studies in traditional Indian medicine in the Pali canon: Jivaka and Ayurveda. *Journal of the International Association of Buddhist Studies* 5: 70–86.

—— 1993. The science of respiration and the doctrine of the bodily winds in ancient India. *Journal of the American Oriental Society* 113: 198–213.

Index